Religion & Classical Warfare

Religion & Classical Warfare

The Roman Empire

Edited by
Matthew Dillon and
Christopher Matthew

Pen & Sword
MILITARY

First published in Great Britain in 2022 by
Pen & Sword Military
An imprint of
Pen & Sword Books Ltd
Yorkshire – Philadelphia

Copyright © Matthew Dillon and Christopher Matthew 2022

ISBN 978 1 47383 430 9

The right of Matthew Dillon and Christopher Matthew to be identified as Authors of this work has been asserted by them in accordance with the Copyright, Designs and Patents Act 1988.

A CIP catalogue record for this book is
available from the British Library.

All rights reserved. No part of this book may be reproduced or transmitted in any form or by any means, electronic or mechanical including photocopying, recording or by any information storage and retrieval system, without permission from the Publisher in writing.

Typeset by Mac Style
Printed and bound in the UK by CPI Group (UK) Ltd,
Croydon, CR0 4YY.

Pen & Sword Books Limited incorporates the imprints of Atlas, Archaeology, Aviation, Discovery, Family History, Fiction, History, Maritime, Military, Military Classics, Politics, Select, Transport, True Crime, Air World, Frontline Publishing, Leo Cooper, Remember When, Seaforth Publishing, The Praetorian Press, Wharncliffe Local History, Wharncliffe Transport, Wharncliffe True Crime and White Owl.

For a complete list of Pen & Sword titles please contact

PEN & SWORD BOOKS LIMITED
47 Church Street, Barnsley, South Yorkshire, S70 2AS, England
E-mail: enquiries@pen-and-sword.co.uk
Website: www.pen-and-sword.co.uk

Or

PEN AND SWORD BOOKS
1950 Lawrence Rd, Havertown, PA 19083, USA
E-mail: Uspen-and-sword@casematepublishers.com
Website: www.penandswordbooks.com

Cover illustration: The river god Danuvius (Danube) looks on benignly as Roman soldiers invade Dacia using the bridge Trajan had constructed over the god's waters. Trajan's Column, Rome.

Spine illustration: A bronze statuette of the god Jupiter Dolichenus dressed as a Roman Army officer, from his temple at Mauer an der Url (Austria). First half of the third century AD; height: 32cm. Courtesy Kunsthistorisches Museum Wien, Antikensammlung, Inventory M1.

Contents

Abbreviations		viii
Notes on Contributors		xxiv
List of Figures		xxvi
Preface		xxix
Chapter 1	Introduction: New Perspectives on Religion and Warfare in the Roman Empire (Matthew Dillon)	1
Chapter 2	The Roman Military Oath: the *Sacramentum Militiae* (Tristan S. Taylor)	19
Chapter 3	The Gods on Campaign in the Roman Empire (Matthew Dillon)	43
Chapter 4	*Heros invictus* and *pacator orbis*: Hercules as a War God for Roman Emperors (Megan Daniels)	94
Chapter 5	Roman Military Medicine: The Nexus of Religion and Techne (Georgia L. Irby)	127
Chapter 6	The Soldier and Death. Funerary Practices of Soldiers under the Principate (Yann Le Bohec)	159
Chapter 7	The Role of the Rising Sirius in Ancient Apocalyptic Tradition Concerning the Terrorist Background of the 'Neronian Fire' on 19 July AD 64 (Gerhard Baudy)	186
Chapter 8	The Cult of Mithras and the Roman Imperial Army (Oliver Stoll)	227
Chapter 9	Constantine and Christianity in the Roman Imperial Army (Christopher W. Malone)	250
Chapter 10	'Anointed with your Blood and Holy Oil': Byzantines, Crusaders and Warrior Saints in the Eastern Mediterranean (324–1099) (Lynda Garland)	290
Index		346

Abbreviations

Editorial abbreviations

c.	circa (about or approximately, used for dates)
ed., eds	edited by
ed. pr.	*editio princeps* (the first edition of an inscription, papyrus or manuscript)
F, FF	Fragment, Fragments
flor.	*floruit*: flourished; active during
no., nos	number, numbers
praef.	preface
sv, svv	*sub vide*, see under
trans.	translated by

Abbreviations of Ancient Sources

Adamnan	(*c.* AD 624–704) *De locis sanctis* (On the Holy Places)
Ael.	Aelian (*c.* AD 165/170–230/235)
Hist.	*Varia historia* (Hercher, R. (ed.), *De natura animalium, Varia historia, epistolae, fragmenta*, Leipzig, 1864–66)
Nat. An.	*De natura animalium* (On the Nature of Animals)
Ael. *Tact.*	Aelian the Tactician (second century AD) (Köchly, H. & Rustow, M. (eds), *De libris tacticis*, Leipzig, 1885)
Akropolites	George Akropolites (AD 1217–1282) *History*
Amb.	St Ambrose of Milan (AD *c.* 340–397)
Ep.	*Epistles*
Fide	*De fide* (Concerning Faith)
Amm. Marc.	Ammianus Marcellinus (*c.* AD 330–400) *Res gestae* (History)
Anna Komnene	(AD 1083–*c.*1154) *Alexiad*
Anth. Pal.	*Anthologia Palatina* (Palatine Anthology / Greek Anthology), compiled *c.* AD 940
Apoll. *Argon.*	Apollonios of Rhodes (third century BC) *The Argonautika* (schol.: Wendel, K. (ed.), *Scholia in Apollonium Rhodium vetera*, Berlin, 1935)
Apollod. *Bibl.*	Apollodorus (first or second century AD) *Bibliotheke* (The Library of Mythology)
App.	Appian (*c.* AD 95–165)
Civ.	*Civil War*
Hisp.	*Spanish War*
Iber.	*Iberian War*

It.	*Italian War*
Lib.	*Punic War*
Mith.	*Mithridatic War*
Sam.	*Samnite History*
Aratus *Phaen.*	Aratus (*c.* 315–240 BC) *Phainomena* (Phenomena) (schol.: Martin, J. (ed.), *Scholia in Aratum vetera*, Stuttgart, 1974)
Archil.	Archilochus (*c.*680–630 BC) (West, M.L. (ed.), *Iambi et elegi Graeci ante Alexandrum cantata*, vols 1–2, Oxford, 1971–72)
Arist.	Aristotle (384–322 BC)
Hist. An.	*Historia animalium* (History of Animals)
Pol.	*Politics*
[Arist.]	Pseudo–Aristotle
Mir. Ausc.	(late fourth–third century BC?) *De mirabilibus auscultationibus* (On Marvellous Things Heard)
Aristid. *Or.*	Aristides (AD 117–*c.* 181) *Orations*
Arnob. *Adv. Nat.*	Arnobius (late third–early fourth century AD) *Adversus nationes* (Against the Nations; sometimes translated as Against the Heathens)
Arr. *Anab.*	Arrian (second century AD) *Anabasis* (Journey of Alexander the Great)
Ascensio Isaiae	(late first–early third century AD) *The Ascension of Isaiah*
Athanasius *Ep.*	(*c.* AD 296–373) *Epistles*
Athen. *Deip.*	Athenaeus (*c.* AD 200) *Deipnosophistae* (Wise Men at Dinner)
Aug. *Res Gest.*	Augustus (63 BC–AD 14) *Res gestae divi Augusti* (The Achievements of the Deified Augustus)
August.	St Augustine (AD 354–430)
Civ.	*De civitate dei contra paganos* (City of God Against the Pagans)
Enn. in Ps.	*Enarrationes in Psalmos* (Expositions on the Psalms)
Ep.	*Epistles*
Faust.	*Against Faustus*
Aur. Vict. *Caes.*	Aurelius Victor (*c.* AD 320–390) *De Caesaribus* (On the Caesars)
	See also Ps.-Aur. Vict.
Avesta: Yasna	(fifth–sixth century AD?) (Panaino, A. (ed.), *Tištrya*. Part I: *The Avestan Hymn to Sirius*. Part II: *The Iranian Myth of the Star Sirius*, Rome, 1990–95)
Basil *Ep.*	St Basil (AD 330–379) *Epistles*
Caes.	Julius Caesar (100–44 BC)
Afr.	*De bello Africo* (The War in Africa)
Civ.	*De bello civili* (Civil War)
Gall.	*De bello Gallico* (The War in Gaul)
Calendarium Gemini	Geminus (first century BC) *Calendar* (Manitius, C. (ed.), *Gemini elementa astronomiae*, Leipzig, 1898)

Callim. *Aet.*	Callimachus (*c*. 320–245 BC] *Aetia* (Causes) (Pfeiffer, R. (ed.), *Callimachus*, vols 1–2, Oxford, 1949–53)
Calp. *Ecl.*	Calpurnius Siculus (*c*. AD 50) *Eclogues* (Korzeniewski, D. (ed.), *Hirtengedichte aus neronischer Zeit. Titus Calpurnius Siculus und die Einsiedler Gedichte*, Darmstadt, 1971)
Cat.	Catullus (*c*. 84–54 BC) *Poems*
Cato	Cato the Elder (234–149 BC)
Agr.	*De agri cultura* (On Agriculture), *c*. 160 BC
Mil.	*De re militari* (Concerning Military Matters) (Jordan, H., (ed.), *M. Catonis Praeter librum de re rustica quae extant*, Leipzig, 1860)
Celsus *Med.*	(reign of Tiberius, AD 14–37) *De medicina*
Cens. *Die Nat.*	(third century AD) *De die natali*
Charisius *Gramm.*	(fourth century AD) *Ars grammatica* (Barwick, C. (ed.), *Flavii Sosipatri Charisii artis grammaticae libri V*, Leipzig, 1964)
Choniates *Hist.*	Niketas Choniates (*c*. AD 1155–1217) *Chronike diegesis* (History)
Chron. Pasch.	*Chronicon Paschale* (AD 284–627)
Cic.	Cicero (106–43 BC)
Att.	*Letters to Atticus*, 65–43 BC
Caecin.	*Pro Caecina*, 69 BC
Catil.	*Against Catiline*, 63 BC
Deiot.	*Pro rege Deiotaro ad C. Caesarem oratio*, 45 BC
Div.	*De divinatione* (On Divination), 44 BC
Dom.	*De domo sua* (On His House), 57 BC
Fam.	*Ad familiares* (Letters to His Friends), 62–43 BC
Fin.	*De finibus bonorum et malorum* (On the Ends of Good and Evil), 44 BC
Font.	*Pro Fonteio*, 69 BC
Har. Resp.	*De haruspicum responsis* (On the Response of the Haruspices), 57 BC
Leg.	*De legibus* (On the Laws), 52–43? BC
Leg. Agr.	*De lege agraria* (On the Agrarian Law), 63 BC
Leg. Man.	*De lege Manilia* (*De imperio Gnaei Pompei*: On the Command of Gnaeus Pompey), 66 BC
Marcell.	*Pro Marcello*, 46 BC
Nat. Deor.	*De natura deorum* (On the Nature of the Gods), 45 BC
Off.	*De officiis* (On Duties), 44 BC
Orat.	*De oratore* (On Oratory), 55 BC
Phil.	*Philippicae* (Philippics), 44–43 BC
Pis.	*In Pisonem* (Against Piso), 55 BC
Prov.	*De provinciis consularibus* (Concerning the Consular Provinces), 56 BC
Rep.	*De re publica* (On the Republic), 51 BC

Sull.	*Pro Sulla* (In Defence of Sulla), 62 BC
Tusc.	*Tusculanae disputationes* (Tusculan Disputations), 45 BC
Verr.	*In Verrem* (Against Verres), 70 BC
Claud.	Claudian (*c.* AD 370–404)
Carm. Min.	*Carmina minora* (Shorter Poems)
VI Cons. Hon.	*VI Consulatu Honorii Augusti* (On the Sixth Consulship of the Emperor Honorius)
Clem. Al. *Protr.*	Clement of Alexandria (*c.* AD 150–215) *Protreptikos* (Exhortation to the Greeks)
Cod. Just.	*Codex Justinianus* (Lawcode of Justinian)
Const. Porph.	Constantine Porphyrogennetos (AD 905–959)
Cer.	*De ceremoniis* (On Ceremonies)
DAI	*De administrando imperio* (On the Administration of the Empire)
Corippus	Flavius Cresconius Corippus (sixth century AD) *Iohannis* (Tale of John)
Curt.	Curtius Rufus (died AD 53) *Historiae Alexandri Magni* (History of Alexander the Great)
C. Th.	*Codex Theodosianus* (Lawcode of Theodosius)
Cypr. *Ep.*	Cyprian (*c.* AD 200–258) *Epistles*
Dio	Cassius Dio (*c.* AD 155–235) *Roman History* (753 BC–AD 229)
Dio Chrys. *Or.*	Dio Chrysostom (*c.* AD 40–112) *Orations*
Diod.	Diodorus Siculus (first century BC) *Bibliotheca historica* (World History)
Diog. Laert.	Diogenes Laertius (third century AD) *Eminent Philosophers*
Dion. Hal. *Rom. Ant.*	Dionysius of Halicarnassus (60–*c.* 7 BC) *Roman Antiquities*
Dioscorides	(first century BC) *De materia medica* (On Medical Matters)
Enn.	Ennius (239–169 BC)
Ann.	*Annals* (Skutsch, O. (ed.), *The Annals of Q. Ennius*, Oxford, 1985)
Hec. Lyt.	*Hectoris lytra* (Ransom of Hector) (*ROL*: see below)
Ephraim Syrus	(*c.* AD 306–373) *Hymni contra Iulianum* (Hymns Against the Emperor Julian)
Epict. *Disc.*	Epictetus (*c.* AD 50–130) *Discourses*
Eur. *Alc.*	Euripides (480s–407/06 BC) *Alcestis* (438 BC)
Euseb.	Eusebius of Caesarea (*c.* AD 260–339)
Chron.	*Chronicle*
Hist. Eccl.	*Historia ecclesiastica* (Ecclesiastical History)
Laus Const.	*Laus Constantini* (In Praise of Constantine; or Tricennalian Oration)
Vit. Const.	*Vita Constantini* (Life of Constantine)
Eutr.	Eutropius (*c.* AD 350–400) *Breviarium historiae Romanae* (Summary of Roman History)
Evagrius	Evagrius Scholasticus (*c.* AD 537–after 594) *Historia ecclesiastica* (Ecclesiastical History)

Festus	Festus (late second century AD) *De verborum significatu* (On the Meaning of Words) (L: Lindsay, W.M. (ed.), *Sexti Pompei Festi De verborum significatu quae supersunt cum Pauli epitome*, Stuttgart, 1913)
Flor. *Epit.*	Florus (*c*. AD 74–130) *Epitome of Roman History*
Front. *Strat.*	Frontinus (died AD 103/04) *Stratagems*
Fulcher *Hist.*	Fulcher of Chartres (*c*. AD 1058–1127) *Historia Hierosolymitana* (History of Jerusalem)
Gai.	Gaius (*c*. AD 140–180) *Institutes*
Galen	Galen (AD 129–216) (K: Kühn, C.G., *Claudii Galeni opera omnia*, Leipzig, 1821–33) See *CMG* (below)
Gell. *Noct. Att.*	Aulus Gellius (*c*. AD 130–180) *Noctes Atticae* (Attic Nights)
Gennadius	Gennadius II Scholarius (Patriarch of Constantinople: *c*. AD 1400–1473) *Dialogus Christiani cum Iudaeo* (Dialogue of a Christian with a Jew) (Jahn, A. (ed.), *Anecdota Graeca theologica*, Bern, 1893)
Geoponica	*Agricultural Matters* (tenth century AD) (Beckh, H. (ed.), *Geoponica sive Cassiani Bassi Scholastici, De re rustica eclogae*, Leipzig, 1895)
Germ. *Aratus*	Germanicus (15 BC–AD 19) *Claudi Caesaris Arati Phaenomena* (Germanicus' Translation of the *Phaenomena* of Aratus)
Greg. Naz. *Or.*	(*c*. AD 329–390) *Orations*
Gregory of Nyssa	(*c*. AD 335–395) *Homily on the Forty Martyrs*
Gregory of Tours	(*c*. AD 538–594)
Hist. *Franc.*	*History of the Franks*
Hdn	Herodian of Antioch (*c*. AD 170–240) *History of the Roman Empire from the Death of Marcus Aurelius* (AD 180–238)
Hdt.	Herodotus (second half of the fifth century BC) *Histories*
Heracl. *Quaest. Hom.*	Heraclitus (*c*.500 BC) *Quaestiones Homericae* (Homeric Questions)
Herakl. Pont.	Herakleides Pontikos (Wehrli, F. (ed.), *Die Schule des Aristoteles. Texte und Kommentar*, vol. 7, Basel, 1969)
Hes. *Theog.*	Hesiod (writing around 700 BC) *Theogony* See also Ps.-Hes.
Hippocr.	Hippocrates (the writings date to the late fifth–mid-fourth century BC] (Jones, W.H.S. (ed.), *Hippocrates*, London, 1923; Littré, E. (ed.), *Oeuvres complètes d'Hippocrate*, Paris, 1839–61)
Epid.	*Epidemics*
Reg.	*On Regimen in Acute Diseases*
Hippol. *Ref.*	Hippolytus (*c*. AD 170–236) *Refutation of Heresies*
Hom.	Homer (eighth century BC)
Il.	*Iliad*
Od.	*Odyssey*

Hor.	Horace (65–8 BC)
Epist.	*Epistles*, 1: 21 BC; 2: 11 BC
Epod.	*Epodes*, 30 BC
Od.	*Odes*, 23 BC
Sat.	*Satires*, 35–30 BC
Hyg. *Astr.*	Hyginus (first century AD) *Astronomica*
Isid. *Etym.*	Isidore (AD 560–636) *Etymologies*
Isoc. *Philip.*	Isocrates (436–338 BC) *Philippus*
Jer.	St Jerome (Hieronymus) (AD 347–420)
Ep.	*Epistles*
Vir. Ill.	*De viris illustribus* (Lives of Illustrious Men)
Johanan b.Zakkai	(Jewish sage, first century AD) (Goldschmidt, L. (ed.), *Der Babylonische Talmud*, Berlin, 1897–1912; trans. Gittin, V., *The Babylonian Talmud*, vol. 6, Berlin, 1932)
John of Nikiu	*Chronicle* (late seventh century AD)
Joseph.	Josephus (AD 37–*c.* 100)
Jud. Ant.	*Jewish Antiquities*
Bell. Jud.	*Bellum Judaicum* (Jewish Wars)
C. Ap.	*Contra Apion* (Against Apion)
Julian	Julian (Emperor) (AD 331–363)
Ep.	*Epistulae* (Letters)
Ep. Ath.	*Epistula ad SPQ Atheniarum* (Letter to the Senate and People of Athens)
Julius Exuperantius	*History* (fourth or fifth century AD)
Just.	Justin (second century AD) *Epitome of the Philippic History of Pompeius Trogus*
Justinian *Novellae*	Justinian I (Emperor) (*c.* AD 482–565) *Novellae Constitutiones* (Novels/New Constitutions) See also *Cod. Just.*
Juv. *Sat.*	Juvenal *Satires* (*c.* AD 65–127)
Kekaumenos	(*c.* AD 1020–1080) *Strategikon* (Precepts)
Lactant.	(*c.* AD 250–325)
Div. Inst.	*Divine Institutes*
Mort. Pers.	*On the Deaths of the Persecutors*
Leo Deac.	Leo the Deacon (*c.* AD 950–995) *History*
Liban. *Or.*	Libanius (AD 314–393) *Orations*
Livy	Livy (59 BC–AD 17) *History of Rome*
Per.	*Periochae* (Summaries of the Books)
Luc.	Lucan (AD 38–65) *Pharsalia* (On the Civil War)
Lucian *Menippus*	(*c.* AD 125–180) *Menippus* (The Descent into Hades)
Lucill.	Gaius Lucillius (180–102 BC) (Marx, F. (ed.), *C. Lucili carminum reliquiae*, vols 1–2, Leipzig, 1904–05)
Lucr.	Lucretius (first century BC) *De rerum natura* (On the Nature of Things)

xiv Religion & Classical Warfare

Lycophron	(third century BC) (Scheer, E. (ed.), *Lycophronis Alexandra. Scholia*, vol. 2, Berlin, 1908)
Lyd. *Mens.*	John the Lydian (sixth century AD), *De mensibus* (Concerning the Months)
Macrob. *Sat.*	Macrobius (fifth century AD) *Saturnalia*
Malalas	John Malalas (*c.* AD 491–578) *Chronicle*
Manil. *Astr.*	Manilius (first century AD) *Astronomica*
Maximus of Turin	(*c.* AD 380–465) *Sermons*
Mart. *Ep.*	Martial (*c.* AD 38–104) *Epigrams*
Mart. *Cap.*	Martianus Capella (*flor.* AD 425) *De septem disciplinis* (On the Seven Disciplines)
Maurice *Strategikon*	(attributed to the Byzantine emperor Maurice: AD 539–602)
Min. Fel.	Minucius Felix (late second or early third century AD) *Octavius*
Naev. *Inc.*	Gnaeus Naevius (*c.* 270–200 BC) *Incertis fragmenta* (*ROL*: see below)
Nechepso & Petosiris	(second–first century BC) (Ries, E. (ed.), *Nechepsonis et Petosiridis fragmenta magica*, Leipzig, 1891)
Nep. *Att.*	Nepos (100–24 BC) *Life of Atticus*
Nigidius Figulus	Nigidius Figulus (98–*c.* 45 BC) *Sphaera graecanica* (Swoboda, A. (ed.), *P. Nigidii Figuli operum reliquiae*, Amsterdam, 1889)
Nikander *Ther.*	(second century BC) *Theriaka* (On Venomous Beasts)
Nonn. *Dion.*	Nonnos (*flor.* AD 450–470) *Dionysiaca*
Not. *Dig.*	*Notitia dignitatum* (List of Offices) (*c.* AD 395–420)
Obsequens	Julius Obsequens *Liber de prodigiis* (Book of Prodigies; fourth-century AD epitomator of the prodigies recorded in Livy for 249–11 BC)
Olympiodorus	(sixth century AD) (Stüve, W. (ed.), *Olympiodori in Aristotelis meteora commentaria*, Berlin, 1900)
Onasander *Strat.*	(first century AD) *Strategikos* (On Generalship)
Optat.	St Optatus of Milevis (St Optate) (fourth century AD)
Oracula Sibyllina	*Sibylline Oracles* (compiled sixth century AD) (Kurfeß, A. & Gauger, J.-D. (eds), *Sibyllinische Weissagungen. Griechisch-deutsch*, Darmstadt, 1998)
Oration to the Saints	Constantine I (Emperor) (*c.* AD 272–337) *Oratio ad sanctos* (Oration to the Saints)
Oribasius *Coll. Med.*	(*c.* AD 320–400) *Medical Collections*
Origen *Cels.*	(*c.* AD 184–253] *Contra Celsum* (Against Celsus)
Oros.	Paulus Orosius (AD 375–after 418) *Historiae adversus paganos* (History Against the Pagans)
Ovid	(43 BC–AD 17)
Am.	*Amores*
Fasti	*Festivals of the Roman Calendar* (January–June)
Her.	*Heroides*
Metam.	*Metamorphoses*
Trist.	*Tristia*

Pac. *Teuc.*	Pacuvius (220–130 BC) *Teucer* (*ROL*: see below)
Palladius	(late fourth or early fifth century AD) *Opus agriculturae* (On Farming)
Pan. Lat.	*Panegyrici latini* (The Latin Panegyrics) (AD 289–389; multiple authors)
Passio sancti Pauli	*Passio sancti Pauli apostoli* (fourth–fifth century AD) (Lipsius, R.A. (ed.), *Acta apostolorum Apocrypha* I, Leipzig, 1891)
Paul of Aegina	(AD 620–690) *Medical Compendium*
Paul the Deacon	(eighth century AD) *Historia romana* (Roman History) See Festus
Paulinus of Nola *Ep.*	(AD 354–431) *Epistles*
Paus.	Pausanias (wrote *c.* AD 150) *Description of Greece*
Petron.	Petronius (died AD 66) *Satyricon*
Philo	Philo Judaeus (*c.* 15 BC–AD 50) *Embassy to Gaius (Caligula)*
Philostorgios	(AD 368–*c.* 439)
Hist. Eccl.	*Historia ecclesiastica* (Ecclesiastical History)
Philostr. *Apoll.*	Philostratos (died AD 244–249) *Life of Apollonios of Tyre*
Phlegon *Mir.*	Phlegon of Tralles (reign of Hadrian AD 117–138) *Mirabilia* (Curiosities)
Plaut.	Plautus (254–184 BC)
Asin.	*Asinaria*
Amph.	*Amphitryon*
Bacch.	*Bacchides*
Capt.	*Captivi*
Cas.	*Casina*
Epid.	*Epidicus*
Mil.	*Miles Gloriosus*
Mostell.	*Mostellaria*
Stich.	*Stichus*
Truc.	*Truculentus*
Pliny *Nat. Hist.*	Pliny the Elder (AD 23/24–79) *Natural History*
Pliny	Pliny the Younger (AD 61–117)
Ep.	*Epistles*
Pan.	*Panegyricus*
Plut.	Plutarch (second century AD)
Aem.	*Aemilius Paulus*
Alex.	*Alexander*
Ant.	*Mark Antony*
Caes.	*Julius Caesar*
Cam.	*Furius Camillus*
Cat.	*Cato*
Comp. Dem. Ant.	*Comparison of Demetrius and Antony*
Cor.	*Coriolanus*
Crass.	*Marcus Licinius Crassus*

Fab.	Fabius Maximus
Gal.	Galba
Luc.	Lucullus
Mar.	C. Marius
Marc.	M. Claudius Marcellus
Mor.	Moralia
Nic.	Nicias
Num.	Numa
Pomp.	Cn. Pompey (Magnus)
Pyrrh.	Pyrrhus
Rom.	Romulus
Rom. Quest.	Roman Questions (Moralia)
Sull.	L. Cornelius Sulla
Them.	Themistocles
Thes.	Theseus
Tib. Gr.	Tiberius Gracchus
Polyb.	Polybius (c.200–118 BC) Histories
Porph. Nymph.	Porphyry (AD 234–c. 305) De antro nympharum (On the Cave of the Nymphs)
Procop.	Procopius (c. AD 507–after 555)
Pers.	Persian War
Vand.	Vandalic War
Prop. El.	Propertius (c. 50–15 BC) Elegies
Prosper of Aquitaine	(c. AD 390–455) De vocatione omnium gentium (Concerning the Calling of All Peoples)
Epitome chronikon	(Epitome of Chronicles)
Prudent. Symm.	Prudentius (AD 348–c. 405) Libri contra Symmachum (Books Against Symmachus)
Ps.-Aur. Vict.	Pseudo-Aurelius Victor (date unknown)
Orig. Gent. Rom.	De origo gentis romanae (The Origin of the Roman People) See also Vir. Ill.
Ps.-Herakl. Ep.	Pseudo-Herakleitos Epistulae (Westermann, A. (ed.), Heracliti, Epistolae quae feruntur, Leipzig, 1857)
Ps.-Hes.	Pseudo-Hesiod (sixth century BC ?) Scutum (The Shield of Hercules)
Ps.-Hyg. Mun. Cas.	Pseudo-Hyginus (late first–early second century AD) De munitionibus castrorum (On the Fortifications of Camps)
Ps.-Sen. Oct.	Pseudo-Seneca (early second century AD) Octavia
Ps.-Skyl.	Pseudo-Skylitzes (eleventh century AD?) Orbis descriptio (Description of the World)
Psellos Chron.	Michael Psellos (AD 1018–after 1081) Chronographia (History)
Quint. Inst.	Quintilian (c. AD 35–100) Institutio oratoria (Institutes of Oratory), AD c. 95

Rhetorius	(fifth–sixth century AD) (Cumont, F. & Boll, F. *et al.* (eds), *Catalogus codicum astrologorum graecorum*, Brussels, 1898–1953)
Robert of Clari	(died after AD 1216) *La conquête de Constantinople* (Conquest of Constantinople)
Rufinus *Hist. Eccl.*	(*c.* AD 344–411) *Historia ecclesiastica* (Ecclesiastical History)
Rufus	Rufus of Ephesus (*c.* AD 100) *Medical Questions*
Russian Primary Chronicle	(*c.* AD 1113)
Sall.	Sallust (86–35 BC)
Cat.	*The Conspiracy of Catiline*
Hist.	*Histories*
Jug.	*Jugurthine War*
Scribonius Largus	(*c.* AD 1–after 47) *De compositione medicamentorum liber* (On the Composition of Medicines)
Sen.	Seneca the Younger (1 BC–AD 65)
Ben.	*De beneficiis* (On Benefactions)
Clem.	*De clementia* (On Clemency)
Constant.	*De constantia sapientis* (On the Constancy of the Sage)
Ep.	*Epistles*
Nat. Quaest.	*Naturales quaestiones* (Questions of Natural Philosophy) See too Ps.-Sen. *Oct.*
Serv.	Servius (late fourth–early fifth century AD) *Commentary on Virgil*
Aen.	*Aeneid*
Ecl.	*Eclogues*
Georg.	*Georgics*
SHA	*Scriptores historiae Augustae* (late fourth century AD)
Alex. Sev.	*Alexander Severus*
Aurel.	*Aurelian*
Comm.	*Commodus*
Hadr.	*Hadrian*
Marc.	*Marcus Aurelius*
Sil. Ital. *Pun.*	Silus Italicus (AD 25–101) *Punica*
Skylitzes	John Skylitzes (second half of the eleventh century) *Synopsis historiarum* (Synopsis of History)
Socrates *Hist. Eccl.*	(*c.* AD 380–439) *Historia ecclesiastica* (Ecclesiastical History)
Solin. *Coll. Mem.*	Solinus (early third century BC) *Collectanea rerum memorabilium* (Collections of Curiosities)
Sozom.	Sozomen (AD 400–*c.* 450) *Historia ecclesiastica* (Ecclesiastical History)
Stat.	Statius (AD 45–96)
Sil.	*Silvae*
Theb.	*Thebaid*

Strabo	Strabo (born *c.* 64 BC, writing in Augustus' reign) *Geography*
Suet.	Suetonius (*c.* AD 69–122) *Lives of the Twelve Caesars*
Aug.	*Augustus*
Caes.	*Julius Caesar*
Calig.	*Caligula*
Claud.	*Claudius*
Dom.	*Domitian*
Galb.	*Galba*
Ner.	*Nero*
Oth.	*Otho*
Tib.	*Tiberius*
Vesp.	*Vespasian*
Vitell.	*Vitellius*
Suida	(end of the tenth century AD) (Adler, A. (ed.), *Suidae lexicon*, vols 1–5, Leipzig, 1928–38)
Sulpicius Severus	(*c.* AD 363–425) *Vita Martini* (Life of St Martin)
Symm. *Rel.*	Symmachus (*c.* AD 345–402) *Relationes* (Letters to Emperors)
Tac.	Tacitus (AD 56–120)
Agr.	*Agricola*
Ann.	*Annals*
Germ.	*Germania*
Hist.	*Histories*
Tert.	Tertullian (*c.* AD 155–240)
Anim.	*De anima* (On the Soul)
Apol.	*Apologeticus* (Apology)
Cor. Mil.	*De corona militis* (On the Military Crown)
Idol.	*De idolatria* (On Idolatry)
Nat.	*Ad nationes* (To the Nations)
Scap.	*Ad scapulam* (To Scapula)
Spect.	*De spectaculis* (Concerning the Spectacles)
Theocritus	Theocritus (*c.* 300–260 BC) *Idylls*
Theodore Synkellos	(first half of the seventh century) *Homily on the Siege of Constantinople in 626*
Theodoret	(*c.* AD 393–466)
Ep.	*Epistles*
Hist. Eccl.	*Historia ecclesiastica* (Ecclesiastical History)
Theoph.	Theophrastos (372–288 BC)
Caus. Plan.	*De causis plantarum* (On the Causes of Plants)
Char.	*Characters*
Hist. Plant.	*Historia plantarum* (Enquiry into Plants)
Theophylact	Theophylact Simocatta (seventh century AD) *Historiae* (Histories)
Tib. *El.*	Tibullus (55–19 BC) *Elegies*
Tyr.	Tyrtaeus (*c.* 640 BC)

Ulpian	(*c.* AD 170–230) *Domitii Ulpiani fragmenta*
Val. Flacc.	Valerius Flaccus (first century AD) *Argonautica*
Val. Max.	Valerius Maximus (writing in the reign of Tiberius: AD 14–37) *Facta et dicta memorabilia* (Memorable Deeds and Words)
Varro	M. Terentius Varro (116–27 BC)
Ant. Hum. Div.	*Antiquitates rerum humanarum et divinarum* (Antiquities of Human and Divine Matters) (Cardauns, B. (ed.), *M. Terentius Varro: Antiquitates rerum humanarum et divinarum*, vols 1–2, Wiesbaden, 1976)
Ling. Lat.	*De lingua latina* (On the Latin Language)
Rust.	*Rerum rusticarum* (On Rural Matters)
Vita Pop. Rom.	*De vita populi romani* (On the Life of the Roman People) (Riposati, B. (ed.), *M. Terenti Varronis de vita populi romani*, Milan, 1939)
Veg. *Mil.*	P. Flavius Vegetius Renatus (late fourth century AD) *Epitoma rei militaris* (Epitome of Military Matters)
Vell. Pat.	Velleius Paterculus (19 BC–AD 31) *Historia romana* (Roman History)
Vir. Ill.	Pseudo-Aurelius Victor *De viris illustribus urbis Romae* (On the Famous Men of the City of Rome) (Pichlmayr, F. (ed.), *De viris illustribus urbis Romae*, Leipzig, 1911)
Virg.	Virgil (70–19 BC)
Aen.	*Aeneid*
Ecl.	*Eclogues*
Georg.	*Georgics*
Vita Alexandri	*Life of Alexander (the Great)* (van Thiel, H. (ed.), *Leben und Taten Alexanders von Makedonien. Der griechische Alexanderroman nach der Handschrift L*, Darmstadt, 1974)
Vitr. *Arch.*	Vitruvius (first century BC) *De architectura*
William of Tyre	(AD *c.* 1130–1186) *History of Deeds Done Beyond the Sea*
Xanth. *Hist. Eccl.*	Nikephoros Kallistos Xanthopoulos (*c.* AD 1256–1335) *Historia ecclesiastica*
Xen.	Xenophon (430–*c.* 355 BC)
Hell.	*Hellenica*
Mem.	*Memorabilia*
Zon.	Zonaras (AD 1074–1130) *Epitome historiae* (Historical Epitome)
Zos.	Zosimus (*c.* AD 500) *Historia nova* (New History)

Abbreviations of Modern Works, including Editions of Inscriptions

AB	*Analecta Bollandiana*
AC	*L'Antiquité classique*
AE	*L'Année épigraphique*
Aevum	*Aevum: rassegna di scienze storiche, linguistiche e filologiche*
AJA	*American Journal of Archaeology*

AJAH	*American Journal of Ancient History*
AJPh	*American Journal of Philology*
AncSoc	*Ancient Society*
ANRW	*Aufstieg und Niedergang der Römischen Welt*
ArchClass	*Archeologia classica*
BABesch	*Bulletin antieke beschaving: Annual Papers on Classical Archaeology*
BAR	*British Archaeological Reports*
BCTH	*Bulletin archéologique du Comité des travaux historique*
BHG	Halkin, F. (ed.), *Bibliotheca hagiographica graeca*, 3rd edn, Brussels, 1957
BICS	*Bulletin of the Institute of Classical Studies of the University of London*
BM	British Museum
BMC	Mattingly, H., *Coins of the Roman Empire in the British Museum (BMC)*, London, 1923
BN	*Biblische Notizen*
BS	*Byzantinoslavica*
BSA	*Annual of the British School at Athens*
Byz	*Byzantion*
BZ	*Byzantinische Zeitschrift*
CCID	Hörig, M. & Schwertheim, E., *Corpus cultus Iovis Dolicheni*, Leiden, 1987
CGL	*Corpus grammaticorum latinorum*
ChHist	*Church History*
CIL	*Corpus inscriptionum latinarum*, Berlin, 1893–1986
CIMRM	Vermaseren, M.J. (ed.), *Corpus inscriptionum et monumentorum religionis Mithriacae*, vols 1–2, Den Haag, 1956–60
ClAnt	*Classical Antiquity*
CMG	*Corpus medicorum graecorum*
CNG	*Classical Numismatic Group*
CPh	*Classical Philology*
CQ	*Classical Quarterly*
Crawford *RRC*	Crawford, M.H., *Roman Republican Coinage*, Cambridge, 1974
CrSt	*Cristianesimo nella Storia: Ricerche Storiche, Esegetiche, Teologiche*
CSIR	*Corpus signorum imperii romani*, Oxford, 1982–present
CW	*The Classical World*
DHA	*Dialogues d'histoire ancienne*
DialArch	*Dialoghi di archeologia*
DOP	*Dumbarton Oaks Papers*
Emerita	*Emerita: revista de linguística y filologia clásica*
EO	*Echos d'Orient*

FGrH	Jacoby, F., *Die Fragmente der Griechischen Historiker*, Berlin, 1923–58; Fornara, C.W., vol. iiic fasc. 1–, Leiden, 1994
FHG	Müller, K. (ed.), *Fragmenta historicorum graecorum*, vols i–iv, Paris, 1841-73.
G&R	*Greece and Rome*
GRF	Funaioli, G. (ed.), *Grammaticae romanae fragmenta*, Stuttgart, 1969
Helios	*Helios. A Journal Devoted to Critical and Methodological Studies of Classical Culture, Literature and Society*
Hermes	*Hermes: Zeitschrift für klassische Philologie*
Historia	*Historia: Zeitschrift für alte Geschichte*
HSCPh	*Harvard Studies in Classical Philology*
HThR	*Harvard Theological Review*
ICUR	Rossi, J.B. de (ed.), *Inscriptiones Christianae urbis Romae*, Rome, 1857–88
IDR	*Inscriptiones Daciae Romanae*
IG ii^2	*Inscriptiones Graecae*, vol. ii, 2nd edn, Berlin, 1913–40
IG iv^2 1	*Inscriptiones Graecae*, vol. iv, part 1, 2nd edn, Berlin, 1929
ILAf	Wilmanns, G. et al. (eds), *Inscriptiones latinae Africae*, Berlin, 1881–1916
ILCV	Diehl, E. (ed.), *Inscriptiones latinae Christianae veteres*, Berlin, 1961
ILLRP	Degrassi, A. (ed.), *Inscriptiones latinae liberae rei publicae*, vols 1–2, Florence, 1957–63
ILS	Dessau, H. (ed.), *Inscriptiones Latinae Selectae*, vols 1–5, Berlin, 1892–1916
ILTun	Merlin, A. (ed.), *Inscriptiones latines de la Tunisie*, Paris, 1944
InscrIt xiii	Degrassi, A. (ed.), *Inscriptiones Italiae xiii: Fasti et elogia*, vols 1–2, Rome, 1937
JAAR	*Journal of the American Academy of Religion*
JAH	*Journal of Ancient History*
JBL	*Journal of Biblical Literature*
JDAI	*Jahrbuch des Deutschen Archäologischen Instituts*
JECS	*Journal of Early Christian Studies*
JMH	*Journal of Medieval History*
JRA	*Journal of Roman Archaeology*
JRMES	*Journal of Roman Military Equipment Studies*
JRS	*Journal of Roman Studies*
KAI	*Kanaanäische und aramäische Inschriften*
Klio	*Klio. Beiträge zur alten Geschichte*
Latomus	*Latomus: Revue d'études latines*
LIMC	*Lexicon iconographicum mythologiae classicae*
LSJ^9	Liddell, H.G., Scott, R., Jones, H.S. et al., *A Greek-English Lexicon*, 9th edn with a Revised Supplement, Oxford, 1996
MAAR	*Memoirs of the American Academy in Rome*

MDAI(A)	Mitteilungen des Deutschen Archäologischen Instituts, Athenische Abteilung
MDAI(R)	Mitteilungen des Deutschen Archäologischen Instituts, Römische Abteilung
MEFRA	Mélanges d'archéologie et d'histoire de l'École française de Rome. Antiquité
Mnemosyne	Mnemosyne: bibliotheca classica Batava
NC	Numismatic Chronicle
Nikephoros	Nikephoros: Zeitschrift für Sport und Kultur im Altertum
NTS	New Testament Studies
Numen	Numen. International Review for the History of Religions
OJA	Oxford Journal of Archaeology
OLD	Glare, P.G.W., *Oxford Latin Dictionary*, 2nd edn, vols 1–2, Oxford, 2012
Ollodagos	Ollodagos: Actes de la société belge d'études celtiques
Pallas	Pallas. Revue d'études antiques
PP	Parola del Passato
P. Bodmer	Bodmer Papyri
P. Dura	Dura Papyri
P. Oxy.	Oxyrhynchus Papyri
PBSR	Papers of the British School at Rome
PEG i	Bernabé, A., *Poetarum epicorum Graecorum testimonia et fragmenta*, Pars i, Leipzig, 1987
PG	*Patrologia Graeca* (Migne, J.-P. (ed.), vols 1–161, Paris, 1857–66)
Philologus	Philologus: Zeitschrift für Antike Literatur und ihre Rezeption
Phoenix	Phoenix: Journal of the Classical Association of Canada / Revue de la société canadienne des études classiques
PL	*Patrologia Latina* (Migne, J.-P. (ed.), vols 1–221, Paris, 1841–65)
PLRE	Martindale, J.R. (ed.), *The Prosopography of the Later Roman Empire*, vol. 2, Cambridge, 1980
Powell *CA*	Powell, J.U. (ed.), *Collectanea Alexandrina: reliquiae minores poetarum graecorum aetatis ptolemaicae, 323–146 A.C.*, Oxford, 1925
PSI	Papiri della Società Italiana
RA	Revue Archéologique
RAC	Rivista di Archeologia Cristiana
RE	Pauly Realencyclopädie der classischen Altertumswissenschaft, Stuttgart, 1890–1978
REB	Revue des études byzantines
REJ	Revue des études juives
REL	Revue des études latines
RevPhil	Revue de philologie, de littérature et d'histoire anciennes
RHR	Revue de l'histoire des religions

RIB	*Roman Inscriptions of Britain*
RIC	Mattingly, H. *et al.* (eds), *The Roman Imperial Coinage*, vols 1–10, London, 1923–94
RIU	*Die römischen Inschriften Ungarns*
RhM	*Rheinisches Museum für Philologie*
ROL	Warmington, E.H. (ed. & trans.), *Remains of Old Latin*, vols 1–4, London, 1935–40
RPAA	*Rendiconti della Pontificia Accademia Romana di Archeologia, Serie III*
RPC	Burnett, A. *et al.*, *Roman Provincial Coinage*, vols 1–2, London, 1992
RRC	Crawford, M.H., *Roman Republican Coinage*, vols 1–2, Cambridge, 1974
RVW	Engels, D. (ed.), *Das römische Vorzeichenwesen (753-27 v. Chr.): Quellen, Terminologie, Kommentar, historische Entwicklung*, Stuttgart, 2007
Saeculum	*Saeculum: Jahrbuch für Universalgeschichte*
Scheer	Scheer, E. (ed.), *Lycophronis Alexandra. Scholia*, vol. 2, Berlin, 1908
SE	*Studi etruschi*
Steinby *LTUR*	Steinby, E.M. (ed.), *Lexicon topographicum urbis Romae*, vols 1–6, Rome, 1993–2000
StudPat	*Studia Patristica*
Sydenham *CRR*	Sydenham, E.A., *The Coinage of the Roman Republic*, London, 1952
TAPhA	*Transactions and Proceedings of the American Philological Association*
TAPhS	*Transactions of the American Philosophical Society*
ThesCRA	*Thesaurus cultus et rituum antiquorum*
ThlL	*Thesaurus lingua latina*
VChr	*Vigiliae christianae*
WS	*Wiener Studien: Zeitschrift für Klassische Philologie, Patristik und Lateinische Tradition*
YCS	*Yale Classical Studies*
ZAC	*Zeitschrift für Antikes Christentum*
ZNW	*Zeitschrift für die neutestamentliche Wissenschaft*
ZRGG	*Zeitschrift für Religions- und Geistesgeschichte*

Notes on Contributors

Gerhard Baudy
Gerhard Baudy, born in 1950 in Zweibrücken, Germany, studied Classical Philology and German studies in Saarbrücken and Tübingen, where in 1977 he completed his dissertation concerning ancient Greek attitudes to death. Between 1977 and 1989 he was Assistant Professor at the University of Kiel, until his habilitation with a thesis concerning agricultural myths in ancient Greek literature. From 1994–2015 he was Professor for Greek Studies at the University of Konstanz. His publications concern mainly the religions of the eastern Mediterranean area.

Yann le Bohec
Yann le Bohec, born in Carthage (Tunisia) in 1943, is an Emeritus Professor at Sorbonne University. He has especially studied Roman Gaul, Roman Africa and the Roman Army. He has written some thirty books and more than 200 articles. Among his publications, particular mention must be made of his seminal monograph, *The Imperial Roman Army* (London, 1994). He was also General Editor of *The Encyclopedia of the Roman Army* (Wiley-Blackwell, 2015, in three volumes). His latest book is in French, *La vie quotidienne des soldats romains* (*31 avant J.-C.-235 après J.-C.*) (Paris, 2020).

Megan Daniels
Megan Daniels is Assistant Professor of Greek Material Culture at the University of British Columbia. Her interests focus on cultural interactions in the eastern Mediterranean in the Late Bronze and Iron Ages. She is currently completing a monograph on the shared ideologies of divine kingship between the Aegean and western Asia through the figure of the Queen of Heaven. Further interests include interdisciplinary approaches to ancient migration and the intersections of religion and economy in the ancient Mediterranean. She publishes mainly on religious syncretism in the contexts of economic and political expansion in the Mediterranean, and is also currently preparing publications on pottery from sites in Greece and Tunisia.

Matthew Dillon
Matthew Dillon, the Professor of Classics and Ancient History at the University of New England, Armidale, studied as an undergraduate and postgraduate at the University of Queensland. He has published on Greek and Roman history, with a special focus on ancient Greek religion. His most recent monograph is *Omens and Oracles: Divination in Ancient Greece. Prophecy for the Future, Guidance for the Present, Knowledge of the Past* (Routledge, 2017). He has wide teaching interests, reflected in two source-books and two textbooks on ancient Greece and Republican Rome.

Lynda Garland

Lynda Garland was Professor of Ancient and Medieval History at the University of New England, Australia. She is now an Honorary Research Professor in the School of Historical and Philosophical Inquiry at the University of Queensland. Her main research interests are in the areas of Byzantine studies, the Crusades and ancient history. With Matthew Dillon, she is the author of two source-books and two textbooks on ancient Greece and Republican Rome.

Georgia L. Irby

Georgia L. Irby, Professor of Classical Studies at William and Mary, works on the history of Greek and Roman science. She received her PhD in Classical Philology from the University of Colorado at Boulder. She is the author of *Military Religion in Roman Britain* (E.J. Brill, 1999) and editor of *A Companion to Science, Technology and Medicine in Ancient Greece and Rome*, in two volumes (Wiley-Blackwell, 2016). Her current book project, *Water in the Greco-Roman World* (two volumes: vol. 1: *Conceptions of the Watery World*; vol. 2: *Using and Conquering the Watery World*), is forthcoming from Bloomsbury.

Christopher W. Malone

Christopher W. Malone is currently an Honorary Associate at the University of Sydney. His research interests include intersections of religion and warfare, the depiction of imperial ideals in Rome and Byzantium, and the administration of the late Roman Empire. He has published on late antique history and the iconography of imperial violence, and is currently working on a book about identities in late imperial administration.

Oliver Stoll

Oliver Stoll studied Classical Archaeology, Ancient History and Prehistory at the Universities of Mainz and Freiburg. In 1992 he graduated in Classical Archaeology (Mainz), and in 2001 graduated with the postdoctoral lecture qualification in Ancient History (Mainz). After several academic positions as research assistant and research fellow at the Universities of Stuttgart-Hohenheim, Mainz and Bamberg, he became Fellow (Scholarship) of the Römisch-Germanisches Zentralmuseum in Mainz (RGZM). Since 2007 he has been the Chair for Ancient History at the University of Passau. His research interests are the military history of antiquity, economic and social history, the history of religions in Imperial Rome, ancient slavery and provincial archaeology.

Tristan S. Taylor

Tristan S. Taylor is a lecturer in Classics and Ancient History at the University of New England, and a University Associate in the College of Arts, Law and Education at the University of Tasmania. He researches in comparative genocide studies and the ancient world, usurpation in the Roman Empire and Roman law.

List of Figures

1.1 Augustus' monumental temple of Mars Ultor, the Augustan Forum.
1.2 Solidus (gold). Valentinian I and the goddess Victory.
2.1 Gold half-stater. Obverse: laureate, Janiform head of Dioscuri. Reverse: oath-taking scene.
2.2 Silver denarius. Obverse: draped bust of Mars; legend in exergue: *VITELIÚ* (Italy, in Oscan). Reverse: oath-taking scene.
3.1 Jupiter Tonans (Jupiter of the Thunderbolt) in the heavens hurling a thunderbolt.
3.2 Trajan receiving an embassy of Dacians.
3.3 A bronze statuette of Jupiter Dolichenus.
3.4 The Bridgeness Slab.
3.5 Silver sestertius depicting Nero's closure of the doors of the temple of Janus.
3.6 The river god Danuvius (Danube), and Roman standards.
3.7 The rain miracle on the column of Marcus Aurelius.
3.8 Marcus Aurelius in triumphal procession in Rome.
3.9 Marcus Aurelius making a thanksgiving sacrifice to the gods.
3.10 The *Gemma Augustea* depicting gods with the divine Augustus.
3.11 Silver denarius. Minerva as war goddess puts the finishing touches to a *tropaeum*.
3.12 Gold coin (aureus). Drusus' victory arch with stone tropaea.
3.13 The winged goddess Victoria prepares to inscribe a shield.
3.14 Augustus' monumental *tropaeum* at La Turbie in France.
3.15 A modern reconstruction of Trajan's *tropaeum* monument at Adamklissi.
4.1 'Master of Lions' figurine.
4.2 The Alexander Sarcophagus showing Alexander in lion-skin cap.
4.3 Hercules and Minerva terracotta statues.
4.4 Bronze equestrian statue of Domitian.
4.5 Bronze quadrans showing Hercules in the lion skin.
4.6 Silver denarius reverse showing Hercules on a pedestal with club and lion skin.
4.7 Silver denarius showing on the obverse laureate bust of Hadrian and Hercules sitting on arms and armour, with club on the reverse.
4.8 Marble bust of Commodus as Hercules.
4.9 Bronze sestertius showing radiate bust of emperor on obverse and Hercules standing holding lion skin and olive branch.
4.10 Silver-copper alloy antoninianus, showing radiate bust of Maximian on obverse and Hercules standing with club, bow and lion skin on reverse.

List of Figures   xxvii

5.1   Battlefield triage.
5.2   Bivalve rectal speculum.
5.3   Iapyx tends Aeneas' arrow wound.
5.4   Dioclean cyathiscus.
5.5   Achilles tends to Patroclus' wounds.
5.6   Remains of the legionary *valetudinarium*.
5.7   Aesculapius and Hygieia.
5.8   Apollo Grannus at Baden.
5.9   Bone fist and phallic pendants.
5.10 Pierced dog's canine.
6.1   The necropoleis of Lambèse.
6.2   The mausoleum of Igel.
6.3   The types of funerary monuments found in Africa.
6.4   The funerary monument of Marcus Licinius.
6.5   The funerary monument of Marcus Attius.
6.6   The funerary monument of Lucius Aurelius.
6.7   The funerary monument of Publius Clodius.
6.8   The funerary monument of the *aquilifer* Cnaeus Musius.
6.9   The funerary monument of Marcus Caelius.
6.10 Common motifs in funerary inscriptions.
8.1   Mithras-relief, red sandstone, second century AD.
8.2   Distribution map of Mithraea throughout the Roman provinces.
8.3   Red sandstone Mithras altar, second–third century AD.
8.4   The third–fourth century AD Mithraeum under the Basilica St Clemente.
9.1   Ticinum Medallion (obverse), showing Constantine wearing the *chi-rho*.
9.2   *SPES PVBLICA* ('Public Hope') issue, showing the *labarum* piercing a serpent.
9.3   *GLORIA EXERCITVS* ('Glory of the Army'), showing soldiers flanking the *labarum*.
9.4   *FEL TEMP REPARATIO* ('Re-establishment of Fortunate Times'). Constantius II on galley with phoenix, Victory and *labarum*.
9.5   Magnentius adopts the *chi-rho*.
9.6   *RESTITVTOR REI PVBLICAE* ('Restorer of the State'). Reverse: Valentinian I with *labarum*.
9.7   *VICTORIA AVGGG* ('Victory of the Augusti'). Obverse: Anastasius I. Reverse shows Victory holding a reversed variation of the old *labarum*.
9.8   Gilt silver plate showing Constantius II in triumph.
9.9   Mosaic of Justinian from San Vitale, Ravenna.
10.1 The martyrdom of St Blaise of Sebaste (Armenia).
10.2 A sixth-century icon from the Monastery of St Catherine, Mount Sinai, depicting Saints Theodore (left) and George.
10.3 A replica of a miniature of Basil II in triumphal garb as a Roman general.
10.4 An icon from the Church of St Merkourios, Old Cairo, depicting St Merkourios killing Julian the Apostate.

10.5   A seventh-century mosaic from the Church of St Demetrios in Thessaloniki, depicting St George.
10.6   An engraved agate seal ring (intaglio) depicting St Theodore Teron slaying a many-headed dragon.
10.7   An ivory icon of St Demetrios with spear and shield.
10.8   A gold and enamel pendant reliquary, 37mm in diameter, with the enamelled half-figure of St George carrying a sword.
10.9   Parliamentary Recruiting Committee Poster No. 108, Spottiswoode and Co Ltd, 1915. St George is shown in full plate armour on horseback.

Preface

The editors of this work hope that readers will find *Religion and Classical Warfare: The Roman Empire* of significant assistance in reaching an understanding of the relationship which the ancient Romans of the Empire believed they had with their gods in their military organization and in their waging of war. This collection of essays is the third of a three-part series, and was preceded by *Religion and Classical Warfare: Ancient Greece* and *Religion and Classical Warfare: The Roman Republic*. This volume on the Roman Empire stands alone in its own right, but readers might also like to consult the previous two. This work and its predecessors would not have been possible without the Pen & Sword editor Philip Sidnell, whom the editors would like to thank most sincerely for encouraging this three-volume project: both his support and patience have been most appreciated.

The editors have aimed to make the volume as accessible as possible to a wide readership. Many of the ancient authors cited by the contributors are little-known and obscure, even to scholars. The abbreviations list should make clear the various ancient authors, coins, statues and reliefs, and inscriptions being referred to, discussed and interpreted in this volume. Many of the ancient authors are familiar ones, but details are given of editions where the texts of these authors, some unfortunately still not translated into English, can be consulted.

This volume has a judicious blend of a select group of international scholars, from seasoned veterans of academia with numerous publications in their fields of expertise, to newly established younger scholars starting to make an intellectual impact in ancient world studies. German, French and English-speaking academics have contributed to make this volume possible. These contributions combine to provide detailed information and an extensive, original treatment of the crucial nexus between Roman religious activity and the ritual practices of the Roman military in peace and armed conflict. These chapters taken together present a society in which military activity, the gods and rituals were inseparable, and in which the state, its commanders and soldiers believed that without the assistance of the gods, their military endeavours would fail, and the Roman Empire collapse.

Chapter 1

Introduction: New Perspectives on Religion and Warfare in the Roman Empire

Matthew Dillon

Although Rome possessed an empire by the end of the third century BC, the period known as the Roman Empire technically begins when Octavian was transformed into Augustus in 27 BC by a series of senatorial decrees regularizing his constitutional position. He became the first *princeps* of the many who would reign over the Roman Empire, which endured for several hundred years. As rulers, the emperors believed that they required the unqualified support of the gods in order both to maintain Rome's rule (its imperium) and to wage war successfully. Rome's religious traditions in the imperial period with regard to its military forces were largely carried over from the Republic. There were, however, both minor and major shifts in emphasis, and some marked features of Rome's religious military practices in the Republic faded away, while more emphasis came to be given to others. Roman gods still received their sacrifices before battle and a share of the booty once a successful campaign was concluded, but supplications to win their favour were very much a ritual of the past, and few new temples (albeit important ones) were now built to celebrate military successes and thank the gods' role in these. Much more emphasis was placed on permanent military monuments for commemorative purposes: the *tropaea* (victory trophies) and the stone arches celebrating triumphs.

Jupiter and Mars were still the main Roman military deities. But some gods, such as Mars Ultor, received greater emphasis, while 'new' gods such as Mithras and Jupiter Dolichenus also emerged as a focus of attention. In the fourth century, the old gods were displaced by a newcomer, the Christian god: yet many traditional features of military religion did not change, or were simply modified rather than abandoned. The emperor and his family, and previous emperors and their families, became objects of veneration during the Roman Empire, and the rituals of the army incorporated rites for them. Soldiers 'speak' in increasing numbers in the imperial period through their inscribed offerings to the gods and dedications of cult objects. An eclectic mix of Roman, indigenous and 'Eastern' deities (Mithras, Jupiter Dolichenus and Christ) were worshipped. Yet the veneration of any god had the same purposes: the safety of the soldier and victory for the state in battle.

Existing Scholarship on Religion and Roman Warfare in the Roman Empire

This volume aims to make a significant contribution to a topic that has received little examination in English language scholarship. While there are now numerous works on the Roman military establishment, few deal in any significant degree with the religious activities and beliefs of those who served in Rome's armed forces. Some previous scholarship, however, needs to be noted, to indicate how this field of study currently stands.

For the religion of the Roman armies, Jörg Rüpke's study on the religious 'construction' of war in the Roman Republic and Empire remains a standard guide.[1] Some of the topics which it covers are also dealt with in this volume, but purely for the imperial period, such as the military *sacramentum* (oath), the fetiales, omens, the military calendar of Dura-Europos and the *spolia opima*. This current volume, moreover, places these aspects of imperial military religion within an overall consideration of the ways in which the Romans venerated the gods and the rituals which they practised to achieve maximum efficacy in their military endeavours.

Chapter-length studies in the English language include the still invaluable contribution of John Helgeland,[2] who divided military religion in the Empire into two broad categories: 'official' and 'unofficial' religion. His 'official' category refers to the army cultic observances as organized by the state, with the 'unofficial' being the private religious life of the army, in terms of their worship of the traditional Roman gods, as well as the indigenous gods of soldiers, who took the deities of their homeland with them to wherever they served. Helgeland's conclusion that there was a Roman Army 'religious system' would probably now not be accepted, with the emphasis in modern scholarship being to stress the heterogeneity of belief within the army, with the official rituals providing a ritual homogeneity helping to create a single Roman Army familiar across the length and breadth of the Empire.

More recently, Oliver Stoll has written an excellent discussion in an edited collection of essays on the Roman Army, with much important information and analysis.[3] Its title, 'The Religions of the Army', with religion in the plural, points to the multiple cults venerated by soldiers in the Roman Army, and has a strong emphasis on the imperial period. Krzysztof Ulanowski's edited volume on warfare and religion in the ancient world has three chapters of relevance to this current volume:[4] one on the *Ara Pacis Augustae*, another on the legitimization of warfare under Antoninus Pius and a third, short chapter of particular relevance, on the Army's experience of official, state religion.[5]

One publication, arising from a conference, particularly addresses religion in the Roman Army, in the period which its editors describe as the 'High Empire'. This contains a mixture of English, French and German-language chapters, and especially worthy of note are the chapters on soldiers' religion in Roman Britain; the role the gods were believed to play in Roman battle; the traditional Roman gods in the military calendar from Dura-Europos; and soldiers and the cult of Mithras. The volume as a whole looks at broad themes as well as soldiers' religion in particular parts of the Empire.[6] In particular, Wheeler's long chapter in this conference proceedings on the gods in warfare in the imperial period focuses on literary and inscriptional evidence, and is recommended reading.[7] Another, recent, conference publication has English and French chapters on religion and war in the ancient world, with a chapter in French by Yann Le Bohec on religion and warfare in ancient Rome.[8]

Also worthy of mention is Stoll's monumental study in German on the religion of the Army in the Roman East, in which he examines military religion in this region in terms of how integrated it was with Roman religion as such, and what local tendencies existed, with an emphasis on the Army and its relationship with 'civilian', or non-military, cults.[9] In another area of the Empire in the imperial period, Georgia Irby has studied the military religion of Britain in detail.[10] Her book has a particular focus on the material evidence, making an exhaustive study of the wealth of inscriptions from this Roman province in order to examine key aspects such as the importance of traditional Roman religion and indigenous ritual practices amongst the military stationed in the province.

The Lived Religious Experience of the Roman Military

Such volumes and book chapters are invaluable and of course represent important contributions to the topic. Religion and military practice were intertwined to such an extent that no Roman military activity was in fact possible without corresponding religious activity, and the chapters in this volume will demonstrate this clearly and profoundly. This current volume emphasizes the 'lived experience' of religion amongst the soldiers – as well as the generals and emperors – of the Roman imperial period. Contributors focus on individuals' experiences as revealed in their inscriptions and their dedications of altars and other cult objects. Many individual commanders and soldiers are met in the chapters that follow, and their experiences as military personnel of a rich and varied religious life in the Roman Army constitute an important lens through which Roman beliefs and practices pertaining to war can be understood. Emperors' conceptualization of their own particular and individual relationship with the gods, as they went off to campaign and into battle, becomes clear through the literary and material record. Chapters in this volume will indicate the rich and diverse religious life which soldiers and their leaders experienced: not just in the official religion of the Roman state that was prescribed, but through their individual and personal devotions.

Sworn by all members of the Roman Army, the Roman military oath – the *sacramentum militiae* – remained a persistent feature from the archaic Republic to late antiquity. Tristan Taylor, in his chapter 'The Roman Military Oath: the *Sacramentum Militiae*', explores how understanding the nature and content of the oath, and its evolution, is complicated by the fact that a full text of the oath does not survive, nor any direct evidence of the subjective view of soldiers concerning the nature of the obligation created by the oath. This chapter surveys what is known of the oath from archaic Rome to the late Empire, including its content, development and effect. The origins of the military oath and its early form remain obscure, but at the outbreak of the Second Punic War (in 218 BC) it comprised a compulsory *sacramentum* (oath) to assemble at the consul's orders until permitted to depart, and a voluntary oath (*ius iurandum*) not to flee or leave the ranks. During the course of the war, the latter became compulsory. This oath also marked a 'transition' from citizen (*Quiris*) to soldier (*miles*), that had to be renewed each time someone served in the Army, a transition that absolved soldiers of pollution from the act of killing in war. As other social, economic and political factors caused soldiers to become ever more focused on their particular commanders, so the oath – always with a personal element – became an important part of the bond of loyalty between soldier and commander. As the Principate (Empire) followed the Republic, the oath became another performative act in the bond of loyalty between the soldier and the *princeps* (the emperor). In this period, not only was the oath administered on enrolment in the Roman Army, but it was also renewed annually. When civil conflict occurred in the Empire, the oath played a similar role as in the Republic. That is, it could occasionally act as a restraint on revolt; but despite it sometimes failing, it was still considered an important bond between soldier and commander, and the oath continued to be thought important right through into the Christian period.

Joining up and taking the military oath was but the commencement of an array of religious activities which those serving in the Roman Army entered into upon enlistment. In 'The Roman Gods on Campaign in the Empire', Matthew Dillon explores two aspects of military religious activity: the ritual practices of the Roman Army at peace, and those engaged in when it was at war. Roman soldiers went into battle with the gods on their side, with Jupiter carried into battle at the front of a legion in the form of his sacred eagle, one for each of Rome's legions, a symbol of Roman dominion wherever its soldiers marched. Jupiter was also the god who sent omens of victory, often a flight of living eagles. Other gods also supported Rome's military endeavours: Mars had been prominent in the Republic, and, from Augustus onward, this god in his guise as Mars Ultor (Mars the Avenger) becomes a divinity of considerable potency. The cult of Jupiter Dolichenus provided soldiers with the opportunity to venerate a deity dressed as a Roman soldier and girded for battle. The goddess Victory and her 'trademark' *tropaea* (assemblages of arms and armour captured from the enemy) dominate coins, reliefs and architecture: she was the only martial deity whose iconography made a seamless transition from pagan to Christian Rome.

Roman beliefs in their various war-gods were expressed through a variety of state and personal rituals, and manifested themselves in art and monumental architecture. In Rome itself, the monumental temple of Mars Ultor and the engraved stone columns of Trajan and Marcus Aurelius, as well as arches commemorating imperial victory celebrations – the triumphs – gave state acknowledgement of the vital contribution which Rome believed its gods made to its worldwide dominion. Throughout the provinces, numerous triumphal arches etched the Roman gods' dominance in war onto the urban landscape. Wherever the legionary eagles camped or marched, the gods were with Rome's armies and soldiers. Soldiers expressed their individual piety in inscriptions, venerating Jupiter Optimus Maximus, the main god of victory, but also numerous other Roman gods and their own indigenous deities if they were from places other than Italy.

While Jupiter Optimus Maximus and Mars Ultor were crucial to military activities, other gods were also important for the Roman conduct of war. Megan Daniels, in '*Heros invictus* and *pacator orbis*: Hercules as a War God for Roman Emperors', explores the long-term, multifaceted engagement of the god Hercules as a warrior and conqueror by Roman leaders from the Republic through to the late Empire, utilizing a variety of interrelating media from literature to numismatic iconography. This chapter orientates this engagement within a much broader context of the employment of Hercules by rulers across the Near Eastern and Mediterranean worlds over the first millennium BC as a triumphant hero whose peregrinating feats around the Mediterranean won him not only immortal fame, but immortality itself. Hercules thus became the pre-eminent ancestor and exemplum, who legitimized royal bloodlines, provided charters for conquest and connected peoples across the Mediterranean and Near East in a widespread symbolic language of power, legitimacy and rulership. Yet he was also an equivocal figure, who migrated between venerable warrior ancestor, maddened brute and exotic effete, making him an important counterpoint for ancient authors on the more ambivalent aspects of empire and conquest.

Roman imperial engagement with Hercules thus entangled Roman leaders in a much older cross-cultural symbolic language. Yet Hercules – alongside his Mediterranean and Near Eastern counterparts – proved to be a very malleable deity when it came to serving the needs of empire and diverse imperial subjects. This malleability is charted in this chapter first through Hercules' Mediterranean and Near Eastern past, including the emergence of his characteristic bellicose and leonine iconography in the Archaic and Classical periods, and his increasing focus as a triumphant hero in the later Classical and Hellenistic periods, via the royal ideologies of Alexander and his successors and the rulers of the western Mediterranean. It then focuses on the surge of Roman interest in Hercules in the Middle and Late Republic, as Rome rose to hegemony in the eastern and western Mediterranean. By the time Augustus channelled Rome into a new system of imperial rule, Hercules had long provided rulers with a divine mandate towards conquest and expansion, yet this necessitated more than simply military force: the warrior Hercules was also the great civilizer and pacifier. For Hercules, war was not an end: it was a means to the true greatness of empire, namely lasting peace and prosperity.

War is violent: wounds and death are a necessary consequence. Two chapters explore the themes of sickness, wounds and death. Georgia Irby, in 'Roman Military Medicine: The Nexus of Religion and *Techne*' ('skill'), examines how the imperial Roman Army employed a multifaceted approach to maintaining health and treating disease and wounds. She examines how physicians and camp commanders relied on advances in medical science together with superstition, folk traditions, religion – both local and imperial – and even politics. This chapter explores Roman approaches to medicine, especially with regard to wound treatment, the evidence for a professional Roman imperial medical corps and the synergy of 'rational' and alternative/'divine' methods of healing. Roman theoretical initiatives, literary accounts of battle wounds and the evidence for surgical and pharmaceutical treatments are investigated.

Epigraphical and archaeological evidence is then interrogated to tease out the extent to which a professional medical corps was attached to Roman Army hospitals. Epigraphical, literary and archaeological data is examined to determine the variety of ways in which Roman imperial soldiers sought medical treatment along the frontiers. Military physicians and imperial soldiers availed themselves of many approaches to their health, including magical chants, apotropaic amulets, curative waters, incubation and prayer. Although (Greek) humoral theory was largely rejected by the Romans in favour of mechanistic (rational, empirical) models of the human body, alternative medicine was embraced in conjunction with state-sponsored 'rational' medicine. Neither 'rational' nor 'divine' healing was pursued in isolation, and military medicine was seen as a partnership between the individual and external environmental factors, including divine favour and the health/success of the state and its leaders.

For those who were not healed or cured of their battle wounds, there was an honourable death; but many soldiers of course died peacefully as well, having survived their period of military service. Yann Le Bohec, in 'The Soldier and Death. Funerary Practices of Soldiers under the Principate', examines the burial practices of the Roman Army. When soldiers died in times of peace, away from battlefields, they were buried with the usual Roman funerary traditions. Because soldiers had no private cemeteries, especially not in the sense of a modern military cemetery, they were buried among civilians: according to Roman law, individual tombs were individual properties. But actual military cemeteries developed organically, as soldiers were buried one by one at the gates of military fortifications. Deceased soldiers were usually cremated and the ashes placed in funeral urns. Above the urns, monuments could be set up: *stelae* (steles: first to second centuries), altars (second to third centuries) and *cupulae* (third century); *cupulae* are half-columns on a stone slab. For soldiers killed en masse in action, it is surprising that Roman officers paid them little attention; they generally received no special monuments and were buried together in communal graves.

Funerary monuments were engraved with inscriptions and sometimes sculptures. Such inscriptions usually mentioned, after the name of the man, his rank and unit; sometimes it added other information, such as his length of service. In stone funerary reliefs, the deceased could be portrayed in civilian clothes (the toga) or in military dress, with cavalrymen depicted as killing a prostrate enemy. Alternatively, the deceased could be shown making a sacrifice on an altar, or with his family or at a meal. The sculptors followed Roman or, more rarely, local traditions. For soldiers who were commemorated with monuments after death in battle, or having died peacefully, such monuments and associated reliefs memorialized their life and occupation.

In his chapter 'The Role of the Rising Sirius in Ancient Apocalyptic Tradition Concerning the Terrorist Background of the "Neronian Fire" on 19 July AD 64', Gerhard Baudy examines the conflicts between East and West, which in antiquity had a symbolic dimension: political dominance was legitimized by the brightest star in heaven, Sirius (the Dog Star). The observation of its heliacal rising at the end of the agricultural year after the cereal harvest in July had a multivalent prophetic function in the eastern Mediterranean. Because the star was seen as the ruler of the world, it directed the universal fate of humanity in the coming year, deciding not only if there would be rain or drought, food or hunger, health or disease, peace or war, but also if there would be a political change by the coming of a new ruler. Already in the *Iliad*, the destructive splendour of the rising Sirius functioned as a prophetic sign of victory in the different battles between Greeks and Trojans. Later, Alexander the Great, who understood himself to be a new Achilles, followed this mythical paradigm. As the victor over eastern enemies, he usurped the splendour of the rising Sirius, a kingly symbol in both Iranian and Egyptian tradition. Hellenistic monarchs used the same paradigm in their struggle against Rome, the 'new Troy': the city of Rome should be destroyed in the fire of Sirius. A fictive dating of Rome's conflagration to 19 July 390 BC can be seen as a defensive response to anti-Roman propaganda, because on this date Sirius rose, according to the traditional Egyptocentric astronomy. This must have provoked oriental minorities living in the city, whose homelands were occupied by the Romans and deprived of their autonomy. This explains the occurrence of the conflagration of Rome in AD 64 precisely on the same calendar date of 19 July, and this chapter examines Christian involvement in this conflagration.

Three chapters are concerned with the religion of soldiers in the later part of the Roman Empire, and deal with Mithras; Constantine and Christianity; and the cult of the Christian warrior saints. Mithraism has long been considered by scholars as a military religion, and the army was once considered to be the vehicle of the so-called 'oriental' religions like the cults of Mithras (and Jupiter Dolichenus), but Oliver Stoll, in 'The Cult of Mithras and the Roman Imperial Army', definitively argues that the Mithraic cult was far from being a 'religion for soldiers'. Mithraism's chronological and spatial expansion, temples and sanctuaries, the belief and ritual of the Mithraic mysteries, hierarchy of the cult, rivalry with Christianity and its decline are also examined. There are, in fact, sections of the Roman frontier (for example, Upper Germania and Hadrian's Wall) where temple compounds form an integral part of the sacral topography of the civilian settlements surrounding the military forts. On the other hand, entire sectors of the *limites* (such as Lower Germania and Egypt) yield virtually no military evidence for the Mithras cult, and there is plenty of substantiation for the cult existing away from the frontiers. Examination of the adherents – and also a closer look at the social strata of the followers – of this so-called 'soldier religion' show that less than 20 per cent of Mithras worshippers were military men. Soldiers did not play a prominent role in constituting the small Mithraic 'congregations'. Rather, a Mithraic organization at a local level was a cultic community characterized by joint ritual practice by male civilians and military personnel – Mithraism was a 'personal' cult, and not worshipped only by soldiers.

In late antiquity, the emperor Constantine irrevocably changed the religious milieu of the Roman Army. In 'Constantine and Christianity in the Roman Imperial Army', Chris Malone discusses the introduction of Christianity into the Roman Army, with particular interest in the role of the emperor Constantine the Great. Religious change is one of the central phenomena of late antiquity, not only for the Roman Empire as a whole, but in the Roman military. Part of the enduring legacy of Constantine was the process of the Christianization of the imperial army. Having come to Christianity in an essentially military context, according to the story of his famous battlefield vision, Constantine understood his new God as one who would win him battles and safeguard the Empire. As such, he took steps to incorporate some Christian elements into the Roman Army, to make room for a religious group that had often seen itself as incompatible with military service.

As well as religious changes in the Army, the objections and debates concerning military service within Christian thought are explored – serving in the legions had raised questions of divided loyalties, violence and most importantly idolatry, but the emperor Constantine's apparent conversion and church-friendly acts forced some changes in perspective. In time, the old army rites, banners and symbols were replaced by new Christian ones, and ultimately even the military oath, once a major problem in the view of patristic authors, would be sworn before the Christian Trinity. At the start of the fifth century, the Army already appeared very Christianized, although the full 'conversion' of the military would take some two centuries to take full effect. Nonetheless, Constantine's measures produced noticeable effects relatively quickly – the reign of Julian, his attempts to rid the army of Christian influences, and what can be perceived as the reaction of the soldiery themselves to contemporary religious changes, serve as a kind of test case for Constantine's impact on Roman Army religion.

To conclude the volume, Lynda Garland, in '"Anointed with your Blood and Holy Oil": Byzantines, Crusaders and Warrior Saints in the Eastern Mediterranean (324–1099)', discusses the role that warrior saints were thought to have played in victories won by Byzantines against enemies of the Empire and by crusaders in Asia Minor and Syria against the Seljuqs and Fatimids. Warrior saints, the '*martyroi hoi stratelatoi*' (military martyrs), including the six major figures called the '*état-major*' (officer corps) by Delehaye – Saints Theodore Teron (the Recruit), Theodore Stratelates (the General), George, Prokopios, Merkourios and Demetrios – were not so-called because they had served in the military (though some of them had), but because they were martyrs who had willingly died for their faith, mostly in the persecution of Diocletian. Hence they were soldiers of Christ ('*milites Christi*'), fighting under the standard of the Cross. While, increasingly, they came to be associated with interventions in battle, for some saints this is a later development, and it is only in the tenth century that the warrior saints come to be seen as a coherent, homogenous corps. At this point, a new iconography developed, showing them fighting on horseback against demons and dragons (Theodore Teron was the original dragon-slayer, though from the seventh century he and George together are shown attacking serpents). Prior to this, many of their miracles were concerned with healing or with saving people from captivity, and they were generally depicted in court dress, rather than in armour, and infrequently acted in concert. The saints' early exploits primarily consisted of individual interventions, such as the assassinations of the pagan emperor Julian by St Merkourios and the Arian (heretic) emperor Valens by Saints Sergios and Theodore Teron, with these interventions being communicated through dreams.

Saints also defended the cities of which they were patron, a role St Demetrios had assumed for Thessaloniki from the earliest times, often by a personal appearance on the city walls or on the field of battle, although saints could also confuse the enemy by a vision of non-existent defenders, as Sergios did at the siege of Resafa, when he forced Khusrau I to withdraw. When they come to the aid of a Byzantine army, warrior saints generally routed the enemy single-handedly, like Theodore Stratelates, who helped John I Tzimiskes defeat the Rus at Dorystolon in 971, or Demetrios, who drove off the Bulgars from Thessaloniki in 1041. In contrast, the First Crusade, which adopted many Eastern warrior saints in its travels through Asia Minor, expanded this tradition by envisaging a number of saints working together and leading a 'heavenly host' in battle: at Antioch in 1098, according to the earliest source, the *Gesta Francorum*, Saints George, Merkourios and Demetrios led 'an innumerable host of men on white horses' when they drove off the Turks. Crusaders' visions of the intervention of warrior saints took place in the context of exhaustion, starvation and battle fatigue, and the visions were encouraged and publicized by the crusade leadership. Similarly, modern armies have experienced apparitions of supernatural entities, such as saints, lending assistance at a crucial stage of a battle or in a retreat (even though the vision of St George and the 'angels of Mons' in 1914 was a fabrication), and warrior saints – St George in particular – were still seen as valuable recruitment icons as late as the First World War.

These contributions by both seasoned veterans of academia and emerging international scholars provide a solid foundation for any study of the religion of the Romans in military contexts in the imperial age. While the range of topics covered is not exhaustive, those chosen are treated definitively and comprehensively. From these chapters, the Romans of the Empire emerge as particularly concerned with the role the gods could and did play in both military endeavours and in peacetime. Roman and non-Roman gods of the Empire were crucial to the imperial period in its first three centuries, while from the fourth century AD, the Christian God increasingly became the imperial and military deity.

Military Religion: Differences between the Roman Republic and the Empire

A distinctive contrast between the Republic and the Empire in terms of concepts and practices concerning the role of the Roman gods in warfare revolves naturally around the chief distinctive difference between these two periods: the existence of a sole ruler, the *princeps*. The emperor became the focus for several military rituals and ceremonies; for example, the military oath (*sacramentum*), sworn by soldiers in the Republic (see Figures 2.1, 2.2), was sworn in the Empire to the person of the emperor.[11] Under the principate, religious systems for the military across the Empire were organized in a uniform fashion, as can be seen in the more extensive cult of the legionary standards and the Empire-wide religious military calendar.[12] Emperors such as Trajan and Marcus Aurelius presided over traditional rituals such as the sacrificial purification of the Army in the suovetaurilia ceremony: only they did so as the emperor, whereas in the Republic it was the responsibility of the officials known as censors.

Moreover, the position of the emperor allowed for and facilitated a particular centralization of focus on the gods, through aspects such as state-sponsored iconography (coinage, reliefs and statuary), architecture and religious rituals. Emperors stressed their military relationship with the gods through coins, displaying martial deities such as Victory (see below), Jupiter and Mars Ultor on their monetary issues. Imperial military achievements were equated with those of Hercules, with whom emperors identified themselves (see Figures 4.5–4.7). Coinage was now issued for imperial purposes, not so that Roman money-makers could recall the military victories of their illustrious ancestors, as was the case in the Republic. Coins boasted of contemporary imperial victory, showing the gods who supported the emperors, their triumphal arches and the Victory goddess with *tropaea*.

In a material, physical sense, there was also a very marked change architecturally in the expression of Roman warfare and religion in the imperial period. While wars had always been waged in the name of the Roman state during the Roman Republic, generals had conducted those wars and had benefitted quite substantially in the acquisition of honours and prestige, as well as financially (considerably so in some cases). Generals in the field might vow to build and pay for a temple to a particular god in return for victory: they would sell their share of war booty and from this money construct the promised temple. In this way, many temples had been built at Rome in the period of the Middle and Late Republic. In the imperial period, generals no longer had the proceeds from the sale of war booty: all this now went into the imperial coffers. From these proceeds, emperors constructed monumental architecture thanking the gods – and glorifying themselves. For example, Augustus in his forum at Rome constructed the immense temple to Mars Ultor, which ushered in a period of military pre-eminence for this god (see Figure 1.1). A marked architectural change appears with the two columns of Trajan and Marcus Aurelius (see Figures 3.1, 3.2, 3.6, 3.7, 5.1), with the former depicting several significant religious themes, the latter fewer, although both give iconographic attestation to the presence of the gods: in each of them, the river-god Danube supports the Roman crossing of his river by benignly looking on (see Figure 3.6), while Jupiter Tonans makes an appearance for Trajan and an unknown rain god for Marcus Aurelius (see Figures 3.1, 3.7).

Another distinction was the growth and spectacular expansion of what can be called epigraphic and dedicatory habits amongst the soldiery throughout the entire Empire. 'Voices' of soldiers, as individuals or groups, are heard to a degree never encountered in the Republic: their dedications, vows and sacrifices are inscribed on stone as stelae and altars. Inscriptions speak to the historian of a soldier's individual beliefs, hopes and fears (see Figures 6.4–6.9).[13] Soldiers and their commanders trusted not only in Rome's traditional gods and rituals, but in the gods of their own ethnic backgrounds, if these were of non-Italian origin. In addition, many soldiers also worshipped 'new gods' such as Mithras and Jupiter Dolichenus, and, from the second century AD on, Christ. Emperors adopted Christianity in the fourth century and went to war with its emblems (see Figures 9.1–9.8), while retaining the pagan symbolism of the goddess of Victory, now incorporated with the Christian symbol of the chi-rho (see Figures 9.6–7). Soon, emperors went to war with the assistance they

Introduction: New Perspectives on Religion and Warfare in the Roman Empire 11

Figure 1.1: Augustus' monumental temple of Mars Ultor, the Augustan Forum. (*Courtesy of Wikimedia*)

believed of military saints (see Figures 10.1–2, 10.4, 10.6–10.8). Hercules receives special attention as a war god in the imperial period, and is even invoked by soldiers serving there as the saviour of Britain.[14] The cult of the healing god Aesculapius also spread to the remotest corners of the Empire and served the soldiers' need for a healing deity (see Figure 5.7, cf. 5.8).[15]

Individual war-gods (especially Jupiter and Mars Ultor) in the fourth century AD start to give place to Christ, whose imagery now appears on imperial military paraphernalia, both on legionary and other military standards and on coinage.[16] Such deities of war disappear and are replaced by Christ, while at some point after Constantine's vision at the Milvian Bridge, a new standard came into use, the *labarum*, which consisted of the chi-rho symbol fixed to the tip of a long lance, with a flag bearing the imperial medallion hung on a crosspiece (see Figure 9.2). In addition, the Mother of God and warrior saints are said to have appeared on the walls of besieged cities and battlefields, securing victories for the armies of Rome.[17]

Differences in emphasis in religious rituals and practices become apparent in the imperial period, as well as a change in focus. Several key religious rituals of the Republic as performed in times of military crisis were no longer invoked: possibly because these had faded away in the last century of the Roman Republic and its interminable civil wars. The ritual feasting of the gods in the lectisternium ritual disappears from view, while the 'sacred spring' (*ver sacrum*), in which the gods would be promised a set share of the produce – animal and plant – of the season of spring in times of military crisis, was no longer important. Supplicating the gods for victory, the *supplicatio*, no longer occurs, with the *supplicatio* taking on a new meaning, with incense and wine offerings to divinized members of the imperial families. The *evocatio* ritual, in which the Romans called out the gods of enemy cities, enticing them to come to Rome with the promise of better worship and a temple, is not heard of after 75 BC.[18] Moreover, when Titus captured Jerusalem, he did not call out the Jewish god to Rome, and certainly did not promise to build for him a temple at Rome as in the Republican *evocatio* ritual, but rather sacked his sanctuary when he captured the city.[19]

Other rituals which were prominent in the Republic are no longer in evidence. When Rome was threatened by Hamilcar in 211 BC, the city's matrons hastened to its temples to supplicate the gods.[20] They flocked there too of their own accord when news of Octavian's victory at Actium in 31 BC reached Rome.[21] Yet when Varus was defeated and lost three legions in the Teutoburg Forest, and Rome was afraid the Germans would march south, Augustus did not command Roman matrons to go to the temples and pray, nor did they do so. But he did make a *votum* (a vow or promise) of great games (ludi) to Jupiter Optimus Maximus, and the source for this information, Suetonius, notes that such vows had been made in the crisis of the wars against the Cimbri and the Marsi (in the Republic).[22]

Many Republican ritual practices in the context of warfare fell by the wayside, and when they were occasionally revisited it underscores the uniqueness of the action in imperial times, as in the reign of Domitian when Vestal Virgins were punished, a reasonably frequent practice at Rome in times of military crisis during the Republic. In 114 BC, when the Cimbri threatened Italy, the Roman state resorted as it sometimes did to the ritual burial alive in Rome of two Greeks and two Gauls, a rite which did not occur at all in the imperial age. As noted above, games were vowed to Jupiter in this crisis. In the same year (114 BC), three Vestal Virgins were tried and one found guilty of breaking her vow of chastity (the crime of *incestum*), and hence bringing upon Rome the wrath of the gods, reflected in the contemporary military crisis. There was a public outcry that the other two Vestals involved should not have been acquitted. A new trial was held in 113 BC (the Cimbri were still a threat) and they too were convicted; the Sibylline Books were also consulted.[23]

The next occasion on which Vestals were found guilty of *incestum* was in the reign of Domitian. Sometime in AD 81–83, he (as Pontifex Maximus) found two Vestals guilty of *incestum* but allowed them to choose their own death. In about AD 91, he found the senior (oldest) Vestal (the *virgo maxima*), Cornelia, guilty of *incestum* and sentenced her to the traditional death by entombment. Her alleged lovers were publicly beaten to death with rods. At her trial (this was in fact the second time she had been tried for this offence), Cornelia protested at her treatment, and Pliny the Younger, who was alive at the time, records her words: 'Caesar considers me guilty of *incestum*, yet he has conquered and celebrated military triumphs while I have performed the sacred rites.'[24] This connection between the chastity of the Vestals and the safety of the state and military successes was a concept reaching back far into the Republic.[25] For the rest of the imperial period, the Vestals were never again charged with *incestum* or linked with any military failures of the Empire. Domitian had undertaken an antique revival after some two centuries, anxious to prove his own piety and moral rigour, and desiring to be seen as active in maintaining Rome's relationship with the gods, the *pax deorum* (the 'peace with the gods').

The Altar of Victory and the Demise of Roman Paganism

Jupiter had promised the Romans an 'empire without end', rather akin to the British Empire on which the sun would never set.[26] The altar of Victory (the goddess Victoria, personifying success in war) and the statue of the goddess Victory in the Senate House at Rome came in the fourth century AD to symbolize state paganism as opposed to the triumph of Christianity.[27] A temple to Victory had been erected in Rome in 294 BC on the Palatine Hill, not because of a military victory, but prior to a major campaign. L. Postumius Megillus had this temple constructed from fines levied when he was an aedile (annual official in charge of public buildings, civic administration and festivals), and then dedicated it as consul just before setting off on campaign against the Samnites (who were defeated). Victory's cult at Rome dates essentially from the time of the temple. She frequently appears on coins of the Republic and Empire in association with military victories, and in iconography on triumphal arches of the emperors and their sons, relatives and heirs.[28]

In 29 BC, to commemorate his victory at Actium and the defeat of Antony and Cleopatra, Octavian placed a statue of the goddess Victory in the Roman Senate House (*curia Julia*), a building which Augustus had completed in that year in the Roman forum.[29] As Dio states, this was to indicate that he believed that it was from this goddess that he had gained the empire.[30] Dio adds that Augustus decorated the statue with war booty from 31 BC, emphasizing the role which the goddess had played in this military success. One of the inscribed *fasti* (calendars) indicates that Augustus dedicated the altar of Victory in the Senate, at the entrance to the Senate House, in front of a statue of the goddess.[31] Coins indicate that there was also a prominent statue of Victory on the peak of the roof.[32]

Prudentius (for whom see below) provides the only literary description of the statue: the goddess was of gilded bronze, with 'flashing' wings, barefoot and with a belted flowing robe.[33] This description, some 400 years after Octavian dedicated the statue, appears to be accurate when compared to the images of a goddess on Augustus' coinage. For example, a gold quinarius of Augustus dating to 18–17 BC has on the reverse a Victory on a globe (not mentioned in Prudentius' description), which is almost certainly the statue of Victory in the Senate House.[34] This coin adds the detail that in her left hand she carries a long staff with a flag atop: this is the *vexillum* (standard) of the Roman Army. There are in fact many images of Victory in one guise or another on Augustus' coinage.

This altar and statue then became an important focal point of senatorial allegiance, with the senators burning incense and pouring a libation before the statue when they entered the Senate House, and making prayers each year for the security of the Empire, as well as swearing allegiance to a new emperor.[35] Altar and statue resided there for some 350 years, the altar (but not the statue) being removed by the Christian emperor Constantius II (reigned AD 337–361) in AD 357.[36] His attitude was ambivalent, however: in his tour of Rome, he expressed admiration for its buildings, gave money for state (pagan) cults and admired temple architecture.[37] The altar was soon after restored to its position in the Senate House, and this was probably carried out by the apostate emperor Julian (AD 361–363), who unsuccessfully attempted to reintroduce paganism as the official religion of the Empire, for the altar needed removing again a few decades later,[38] by Gratian (AD 367–383) as emperor in AD 382.[39]

An appeal by pagan senators – with a counter appeal by Christian senators – against the decision was unsuccessful, with both the Pope Damasus[40] and (St) Ambrose (Bishop of Milan) involved: the latter claimed there were more Christian senators than pagan. If so, the pagan senators were nevertheless vocal and clearly thought that their appeal might have some chance of success. Quintus Aurelius Symmachus, senator and prefect of Rome, spearheaded the pagan attempt. In all, there would be six appeals by pagan senators to Roman emperors of both the East and West over the next twelve years for the restoration of the Altar of Victory: in AD 382, 384, 390, 391 and 392 (in which year there were two requests).[41] The late fifth- to early sixth-century pagan historian Zosimus has Theodosius visiting Rome sometime between September 394 and January 395 and attempting unsuccessfully to turn the Roman Senate away from paganism, implying that many senators at this time were non-Christian. According to Zosimus, not a single (pagan) senator was convinced and they told Theodosius that 'they had lived according to their observances for almost 1,200 years, during which their city had never been conquered, and if they changed them for others, they could not foresee what might ensue'.[42]

Despite being unsuccessful, the pagan senators decided to try again. Symmachus wrote in AD 384 (his *Relationes* 3) to the emperor Valentinian II attempting to have the altar brought back to the Senate House (the altar clearly had not been destroyed), emphasizing the role of the altar in senatorial tradition and Roman history.[43] The emperor is asked who is in such a state of friendship with barbarians as not to require the altar of Victory? Symmachus attempted to see Valentinian in person but was unsuccessful.[44] Ambrose, as Bishop of Milan, where the imperial court was residing, made two responses, one short immediate response and one longer, to Valentinian concerning Symmachus' written request: Ambrose criticized the Altar of Victory and many other points of Roman traditional religion. The emperor agreed, and the altar was not reinstated.[45]

Victory herself as a symbol of triumph in war aroused no opposition from Christian emperors, and this presumably explains why her statue was not removed from the Senate House in AD 357 or later. Valentinian II, for example, who refused two requests for the altar of Victory to be returned to the Senate House, issued coins – in the same way as other Christian emperors before and after him – depicting the goddess Victory: it was a standard motif. Valentinian I, for example, is shown on a gold solidus standing in military garb with one foot on a kneeling enemy, looking right at a winged Victory on a globe in his left hand who is extending a victory wreath towards him with her right hand. There is a chi-rho on the military standard (in this period known as a *labarum*) which he holds; the legend is *SALUS REPVBLICAE* 'Safety of the Republic' (see Figures 1.2, 9.7).

In AD 390, the pagan senators, aware of a disagreement between the then emperor Theodosius I and Ambrose, sent another request for the altar's reinstatement, but Ambrose spoke to the emperor and the request was refused: Ambrose was no doubt pleased to relate that the attempt was unsuccessful.[46] Another request to Valentinian II in AD 391 also failed.[47] In AD 392, the pagans in the Senate sent two embassies to

Figure 1.2: Solidus (gold); Valentinian I and the goddess Victory. Obverse: bust of Valentian I, with pearl diadem. Reverse: Valentinian I with Victory on a globe, in his left hand, with a *labarum* with the chi-rho symbol for Christ, and a kneeling captive. Legend: *SALVS REIP* (Safety of the Republic). January, AD 365. (*Courtesy of the Classical Numismatic Group*)

the Western emperor Eugenius, who temporized by making some concessions – but not the restoration of the altar (to which Ambrose had again objected).[48] Eugenius was defeated in battle by Theodosius in AD 394 and no more is heard of the altar. Prudentius the Christian poet (AD 348 – after 405), in writing his long poem in two books against Symmachus in AD 402, when the issue was basically a dead letter, was clearly trying to emphasize the demise of pagan symbols and paganism itself.[49]

In all of this, the sources – Symmachus himself and Ambrose – focus on the altar and do not mention the statue of Victory itself, which was still there in AD 404. In that year, Claudian, a pagan, in his panegyrical poem praising the sixth consulship in AD 404 of the (of course Christian) Western emperor Honorius (AD 393–423), son of Theodosius I, could refer to the statue in the Senate House as Rome's protector (*tutela*) and as a companion of Rome's armies. In his poem, the statue speaks and promises that just as Honorius protects her, she will protect him, and that her statue will stand in the Senate House for all time (wishful thinking no doubt on Claudian's part).[50] But Theodosius II a few years later entirely put an end to the debate, by prohibiting pagan statues in AD 408.[51] After Claudian's panegyric of AD 404, however, the statue of Victory is not heard of again.

Christians for the Roman Empire

Ambrose should not be thought of as an opponent of the Roman Empire: far from it. The altar of Victory was pagan and had to be prevented from being returned to the Senate House, but he saw the Christian God as very much acting in the interests of the Roman Empire: Christian Rome would continue to uphold the *pax Romana* of Augustus. Ambrose writes to the emperors of Rome knowing that they rule the Roman Empire: what was important was that they should do so in the name of the

Christian God.[52] Elsewhere, in his commentary on Psalm 45, he sees God granting imperium to Rome, to rule over all peoples.[53] Shortly after Ambrose, Augustine protested in Book Two of his *City of God* against those who saw the sack of Rome by the Goths in AD 410 as a sign of the displeasure of Rome's gods at their abandonment for the Christian God, and in Book Four he argued that it was God who had given Rome its empire – not the gods of the *pagani*:[54] Christian authors saw Christ as the author of the Roman Empire.

Prudentius, who penned his attack on Symmachus in two books of poetry, summed up the Christian position: Christ was the saviour of the race of Romulus, and granted Rome (as a pagan city) its triumphs until it was time for him to rule the city.[55] Rome was now devoted to Christ, and governed by Him: Rome's rule would extend forever.[56] Prudentius appropriates for Christ the promise which Jupiter made to the Romans, that they would have imperium *sine fine*, empire without end.[57] For Christ, Prudentius writes, makes the very same promise:[58]

'No bounds indeed did Christ set, no limits of time did he lay down.
Unending sway [imperium *sine fine*] he taught, so that the valour of Rome
Should never grow old, nor the glory she had won know age.'

'denique nec metas statuit nec tempora ponit:
imperium sine fine docet, ne Romula virtus
iam sit anus, norit ne gloria parta senectam.'

Notes

1. Rüpke (1990); the title can be translated as *Domi Militiae. The Religious Construction of War in Rome*.
2. Helgeland (1978). Note the bibliographic survey of Birley, 1978 (in the same volume of *ANRW* as Helgeland, 1978), covering the main scholarship and themes in Roman Army and religion studies from 1895–1977.
3. Stoll (2007). See his chapter in this volume.
4. Ulanowski (2016).
5. *Ibid.*
6. Wolff & Le Bohec (eds) (2009).
7. Wheeler (2009).
8. Le Bohec (2016); see his chapter in this volume.
9. The title can be translated as: *Between Integration and Demarcation: The Religion of the Roman Army in the Middle East. Studies on the Relationship Between the Army and Civilian Population in Roman Syria and the Neighbouring Areas*.
10. Irby-Massie (1999).
11. See Taylor, in this volume.
12. See Malone and Dillon, in this volume.
13. See Bohec, in this volume.
14. See Daniels, in this volume.
15. See Irby, in this volume.
16. See the chapters by Dillon, Malone and Stoll, in this volume.
17. See Garland, in this volume.
18. For *lectisternium*, sacred spring, *supplicatio* and *evocatio* in the Republic, see Dillon (2020).
19. Joseph. *Bell. Jud.* 6.8 (403–07).
20. Livy 26.9.7–9.

21. Virg. *Aen.* 8.718.
22. Suet. *Aug.* 23.2.
23. Plut. *Rom. Quest.* 83.
24. Suet. *Dom.* 8.4 (cf. 11, for allowing those convicted of crimes to choose the manner of their death); Pliny *Ep.* 4.11.4–8 (7: '*Me Caesar incestam putat, qua sacra faciente vicit triumphavit!*'); Dio 67.3.3–4.
25. See esp. Parker (2004), pp.586–88.
26. Virg. *Aen.* 1.278–83.
27. The most important – and contemporary – sources are Ambrose's *Epistles* 17, 28, 57; and Symmachus *Relationes* 3. The main modern scholarship is still Sheridan (1966) and Pohlsander (1969); cf. Evenepoel (1998); Cameron (2011), pp.33–40. See now also Chenault (2015), for Damasus (see below) in AD 384. For Symm. *Rel.* 3, see esp. Evenepoel (1998–99), pp.284–89.
28. Temple: Livy 10.33.9; *InscrIt* xiii.489; Platner-Ashby (1929), p.570; Richardson (1992), p.243, fig. 53, 420. On triumphal arches: see Dillon, in this volume.
29. The Senate House (*curia Julia*) was dedicated in 29 BC: Aug. *Res Gest.* 19; Plin. *Nat. Hist.* 35.10.27; Dio 51.22.1; Platner-Ashby (1929): Richardson (1992), pp.103–04.
30. Dio 51.22.1–2. See also for the statue there: Suet. *Aug.* 100.2; Hdn 5.5.7.
31. *ILS* 8744. But cf. Platner-Ashby (1929), p.570 in the entry on this altar; see too Richardson (1992), pp.420–21.
32. Richardson (1992), p.102.
33. Prudent. *Symm.* 2.27–38; at 2.33–34 (cf. 31–32) he states that no legion has ever seen a winged girl (*puella*) (i.e., Victory) go before it, directing its spears.
34. *RIC* 1 Augustus 122. This Victory statue is very similar to a stone statuette of Victory in the Naples Archaeological Museum, as noted by Pohlsander (1969), pl.1.
35. Hdn 5.5.7 (cf. 7.11.3); cf. Suet. *Aug.* 35.3; Sheridan (1966) p.187; Pohlsander (1969), p.593.
36. Symm. *Rel.* 3.5. Note Symmachus' praise for the altar at 3.6.
37. AD 357: admires Rome's architecture: Amm. Marc. 16.10.1, 13–15; money, and admired temples: Symm. *Rel.* 3.8, cf. 3.7. See esp. Edbrooke (1976) (p.58 for the altar); Sheridan (1966), p.187; Pohlsander (1969), p.593; Cameron (2011), p.33.
38. Julian: Sheridan (1966), p.187; Pohlsander (1969), p.594; Evenepoel (1998–99), p.284; Cameron (2011), p.33.
39. Amb. *Ep.* 18.32; Symm. *Rel.* 3.4–6. See Sheridan (1966), p.187; Pohlsander (1969), p.594; Cameron (2011), p.34.
40. See esp. Amb. *Ep.* 17.10 (cf. 17.17). For Pope Damasus, see esp. Chenault (2015), pp.47–58.
41. Amb. *Ep.* 17.10. Symm. *Rel.* 3 does not mention Gratian by name; see Sheridan (1966), p.187. For the numbers of Christians in the Senate: Amb. *Ep.* 17.9–10, with Sheridan (1966), pp.188–92 (agreeing with Ambrose that Christian senators outnumbered pagans).
42. Zos. 4.59.
43. This letter is Symm. *Rel.* 3. For Symmachus, see esp. Sheridan (1966), p.194; also Cameron (2011), pp.37–38; Chenault (2015), p.46.
44. Symm. *Rel.* 3.4.
45. Amb. *Ep.* 17–18. For these epistles, see esp. Sheridan (1966), p.196; on *Ep.* 17, Evenepoel (1998–99), pp.289–94; on *Ep.* 18, Evenepoel (1998–99), pp.294–303.
46. Amb. *Ep.* 57.4 (cf. 57.1 on Symmachus again); Sheridan (1966), p.205; Pohlsander (1969), p.595.
47. Amb. *Ep.* 57.5 (Ambrose did not need to intervene this time); Sheridan (1966), p.205; Pohlsander (1969), 595.
48. See Amb. *Ep.* 57, esp. 57.1; Sheridan (1966), pp.205–06; Pohlsander (1969), p.596.
49. Prud. *Symm.* 1.622; with Prudentius should be mentioned Paulinus of Milan's favourable biography of Ambrose, written in AD 422, with his praise for Ambrose's handling of Symm. *Rel.* 3: *Vita Ambrosii* 26 [8].
50. Claud. *VI Cons. Hon.* [xviii] 636–41.
51. *C.Th.* 16.10.19.

52. For example, Amb. *Ep.* 57.
53. Amb. *Enarrationes in xii. Psalmos Davidicos xlv* (*PL* 14.1143), verse 10 (21, 934).
54. Esp. August. *Civ.* 4.7–8
55. Prudent. *Symm.* 1.70, 1.287–90.
56. Prudent. *Symm.* 1.587–90.
57. Virg. *Aen.* 1.278–83.
58. Prudent. *Symm.* 1.541–43.

Bibliography

Birley, E., 'The Religion of the Roman Army: 1895-1977', *ANRW* 2.16.2 (1978), pp.1506–41.

Cameron, A., *The Last Pagans of Rome* (Oxford, 2011).

Castriota, D., *The Ara Pacis Augustae and the Imagery of Abundance in Later Greek and Early Roman Imperial Art* (Princeton, 1995).

Chenault, R.R., 'Beyond Pagans and Christians: Politics and Intra-Christian Conflict in the Controversy over the Altar of Victory', in Salzman, M.R., Sághy, M. & Testa, R.L. (eds), *Pagans and Christians in Late Antique Rome. Conflict, Competition, and Coexistence in the Fourth Century* (New York, 2015), pp.46–63.

Dillon, M.P.J., 'Introduction: New Perspectives on Religion and Warfare in the Roman Republic: 509–27 BC', in Dillon, M.P.J. & Matthew, C. (eds), *Religion and Classical Warfare: The Roman Republic* (Barnsley, 2020), pp.1–16.

Edbrooke, R.O., 'The Visit of Constantius II to Rome in 357 and its Effect on the Pagan Roman Senatorial Aristocracy', *AJPh* 97.1 (1976), pp.40–61.

Evenepoel, W., 'Ambrose vs. Symmachus: Christians and Pagans in AD 384', *AncSoc* 29 (1998–99), pp.283–306.

Helgeland, J., 'Roman Army Religion', *ANRW* 2.16.2 (Berlin, 1978), pp.1470–1505.

Irby-Massie, G.L., *Military Religion in Roman Britain* (Leiden, 1999).

Le Bohec, Y., 'La religion et la guerre au temps de Rome', in Baechler J. (ed.), *Guerre et religion* (Paris, 2016), pp.61–69.

Parker, H.N., 'Why Were the Vestals Virgins? Or the Chastity of Women and the Safety of the Roman State', *AJPh* 125.4 (2004), pp.563–601.

Platner, S.B. & Ashby, T., *A Topographical Dictionary of Ancient Rome* (London, 1929).

Pohlsander, H.A., 'Victory: the Story of a Statue', *Historia* 5 (1969), pp.588–97.

Richardson, L., *A New Topographical Dictionary of Ancient Rome* (Baltimore, 1992).

Rüpke, J., *Domi Militiae. Die religiöse Konstruktion des Krieges in Rom* (Stuttgart, 1990).

Sheridan, J.J., 'The Altar of Victory – Paganism's Last Battle', *AC* 35.1 (1966), pp.186–206.

Silberberg-Peirce S., 'The Many Faces of the Pax Augusta: Images of War and Peace in Rome and Gallia Narbonensis', *Art History* 9.3 (1986), pp.306–24.

Stoll, O., *Zwischen Integration und Abgrenzung: Die Religion des Römischen Heeres im nahen Osten. Studien zum Verhältnis von Armee und Zivilbevölkerung im römischen Syrien und den Nachbargebieten* (St Katharinen, 2001).

Stoll, O., 'The Religions of the Army', in Erdkamp, P. (ed.), *A Companion to the Roman Army* (Chichester, 2007), pp.451–76.

Townend, G.B., 'Tacitus, Suetonius and the Temple of Janus', *Hermes* 108.2 (1980), pp.233–42.

Ulanowski, K. (ed.), *The Religious Aspects of War in the Ancient Near East, Greece, and Rome* (Leiden, 2016).

Wheeler, E.L., 'Shock and Awe: Battles of the Gods in Roman Imperial Warfare', in Wolff, C. & Le Bohec, Y. (eds), *L'armée romaine et la religion sous le Haut-Empire romain* (Lyon, 2009), pp.225–67.

Wolff, C. & Le Bohec, Y. (eds), *L'armée romaine et la religion sous le Haut-Empire romain* (Lyon, 2009).

Chapter 2

The Roman Military Oath: the *Sacramentum Militiae*

Tristan S. Taylor[1]

Roman military success has since antiquity often been seen as a product of a distinctive Roman military discipline (*disciplina militaris*). Conversely, military failure was frequently conceptualized as a breakdown of such discipline.[2] This *disciplina* consisted of more than the physical element of drilling, or the mental component of fear of the harsh punishments that have often attracted the attention of moderns, particularly the brutal – but rare – ritual of decimation, whereby every tenth man in a cohort would be clubbed or stoned to death by their comrades.[3] The Roman military oath – or *sacramentum militiae* – sworn on enlistment, and at various points in time thereafter, also played an important role as a mental component of this famous discipline.[4] Of course, the use of oaths as a binding element, ensuring compliance with an obligation or undertaking through fear of some divine retribution, was widespread in Roman culture specifically, and Mediterranean culture more broadly.[5] Oaths were used in manifold settings, from judicial proceedings to political conspiracies (such as the failed one of Catiline in 63 BC).[6] Bearing this wide spread in mind, we will here focus primarily on military oaths of loyalty.[7]

This military oath was hardly static – evolving to fit changing social, political and military circumstances as the basis for the Roman Army shifted from the clan-based war bands of archaic Rome, through the ad hoc citizen military forces of the Republic to the standing army of the Empire and beyond.[8] The persistence of this oath is curious, as the history of Rome is marked by notable periods of civil war and apparent disregard for this oath.

A Question of Evidence

A further preliminary is to acknowledge that, in our examination of the history and role of the Roman military oath, we must deal with several evidentiary problems. In relation to the origin of the oath, and its original form, we are faced with the problem that bedevils much study of Roman history before Polybius in the second century BC. To put it simply, we have only the barest fragments from this earlier period. All of our crucial surviving accounts for this era, such as that found in Livy, were written in the first centuries BC or AD, or later. This historiography had a strong tendency to imagine the issues of the past in terms of present concerns. Further, the annalistic work of Livy is, at least in part, based on an annalistic tradition that is now lost but that, at some point, had become greatly inflated by more elaborate narrative than would have existed in the available record.[9] Here, the approach used by ancient historians was somewhat different to that which a modern historian might adopt. Namely, they elaborated upon bare records of facts with narrative strongly influenced by the historian's rhetorical training. Such narrative would provide a detailed recording of what a historian thought might plausibly happen at a given event, such as the sacking of a city or declaration of a revolt, rather than what actually happened.[10] As we move through the centuries, our record does not always improve. Significant gaps appear in reliable sources due to the imperfect survival of texts and, for the third century AD – when military discipline was at a significantly low ebb – we have little in the way of reliable historical narrative.[11]

A second complication is not unrelated to this problem of gaps in our narrative sources. We possess no complete text of the military oath, only summaries. We do have texts of a related oath – taken by civilians during the imperial period; however, not only do these texts vary in content, but we do not know for certain how such oaths relate to the military oath (see further below).[12]

Finally, as all too often with the ancient world, it is nearly impossible to retrieve the voices or understand directly the mindset of the majority of those who took the oath. We have no subjective account from a soldier about what taking the oath meant to him, or what the common soldier might have thought were the implications of breaking such an oath. What we do possess are accounts recorded by historians, who were generally members of the social elite and removed from the immediate experience of most soldiers, which give us some sense of the importance that they believed the soldiers attributed to the oath.

The Republican Period: the Origins

As noted above, the evidence for archaic Rome and the early Republic prior to Polybius is very obscure, and the history of the early Roman Army is no less opaque. Such as it is, the evidence suggests an evolution from an archaic army consisting often of war bands based on the Roman *gens* or clan, with strong social, familial and religious ties between soldier and leader, to a citizen army in the fourth century BC that served under elected magistrates.[13] The existence of an oath, both as a means of initiation and of ensuring loyalty (see further below), cannot be excluded from these archaic, clan-based war bands. As the Roman Army evolved, however, it came to serve an additional important purpose. By the fifth century, Rome's military forces consisted of a mix of clan-based soldiers, loyal through ties of kinship to Rome's most senior military commander – an aristocratic *praetor* (likely unelected) – and plebeian soldiers, who were not from the elite families or clans and lacked strong connections to them, and thus motivated more by the needs of the state than loyalty to a particular *gens* or clan. In this context, Armstrong has argued that the *sacramentum* played an important role in ensuring the loyalty of this plebeian element in the absence of the kinds of ties that ensured clan loyalty.[14]

Can the *sacramentum*'s origins be traced back further? No direct evidence is available prior to the Republic. It has been argued that the bloody Samnite ritual described by Livy as used to initiate their *legio linteata*, or 'linen legion', discussed below, provides an archaic form of the oath from which the Roman ritual derived.[15] However, the passage is quite problematic: it could equally be the case that Livy – or more likely his source – has fleshed out his narrative on the one hand by retrospectively projecting aspects of the Roman ritual onto the Samnites, and on the other by including fanciful and macabre elements, such as the gory details provided of a supposedly secret ritual, like the decapitation of those who refused to take the oath.[16]

While the origins of the Roman military oath are lost, and its earliest forms uncertain, some idea is gained of what happened prior to 216 BC when the first-century BC historian Livy writes of an important change introduced in that year. The passage is worth quoting in full:

> 'When the levy had been completed, the consuls delayed a few days until soldiers came from the allies and Latins. Then the soldiers were compelled to swear an oath [*ius iurandum*] by the military tribunes, which had never happened before. For until that day there had been nothing except the oath [*sacramentum*] to come together by order of the consuls, and not to go away except under order. In addition, when they had assembled in their decuries or centuries, by their own will they swore amongst themselves – the cavalry in their decuries and infantry in their centuries – not to leave in flight or fear, nor to leave their rank except to acquire or seek a weapon, to strike an enemy or to save a citizen. That voluntary compact among themselves and a formal process of swearing an oath were transferred to the tribunes.'[17]

Taken at face value, this passage tells us that prior to 216 BC, there were two oaths:

- An oath, or *sacramentum*, to come together when ordered by the consuls, and not to depart without orders.[18] This oath was probably administered by the military tribunes.[19]
- A voluntary oath (*ius iurandum*) by the soldiers amongst themselves not to flee through fear, and only to leave their ranks in limited circumstances: to acquire a weapon, to strike the enemy, or save a citizen's life.

The change in 216 BC altered the second oath from a voluntary one to an obligatory one, and from one sworn by the soldiers to each other to one administered by the military tribunes. It does not appear that the second oath initially became incorporated into the *sacramentum*,[20] although subsequent narratives do not distinguish these two oaths into distinct stages. Polybius, writing in the mid- to late second century BC, tells us that the oath was taken by one person selected for each unit as 'most suitable',[21] and the subsequent soldiers merely stated that they swore as the first person had done, perhaps using the formula '*idem in me*' ('likewise for me').[22]

The origin of these two forms of oath are uncertain. How old are they? Do they go back to the archaic Roman Army? The evidence does not allow us to ascertain with any certainty. It may nonetheless be ventured that the voluntary pre-216 BC *ius iurandum* here is suggestive of the citizen-based community army, rather than the archaic *gens*-based army. It seems more apt for forging a sense of community within an army consisting of people of diverse kinship loyalties, than where clear kinship bonds already existed.

Sacramentum Versus *Ius Iurandum*

In his discussion of the change in 216 BC, Livy uses two Latin terms – *ius iurandum* and *sacramentum* – both of which are used for oaths. It has been argued that there is a distinction between the two terms, in particular that a *sacramentum* included something called a *sacratio* – where a person consigned themselves to the wrath of the gods should they break the oath. On violation of the oath, the person would become *sacer* – forfeit to the gods – and could be killed with impunity.[23] This archaic idea can be found in Rome's first law code, the XII Tables, formulated in the mid-fifth century BC, in relation to matters of good faith – thus to become *sacer* is a penalty for a patron who defrauds a client:[24] 'If a patron shall have committed fraud towards a client, he is to be *sacer*.'[25]

This archaic formality had become, by the time we have written sources, rationalized as discipline (*disciplina*). That is, rather than regarded as the purview solely of divine vengeance, breaches of oaths were treated as a matter of military discipline, enforceable in the secular realm. This is reflected in the fact that the threshold for the application of the death penalty to soldiers was, theoretically, lower than that for other citizens, with numerous breaches of discipline involving execution.[26] In other words, the former concept of *sacratio* was now given effect as the capital penalty. Sources other than Livy use the two terms (*sacramentum* and *ius iurandum* and related words – such as the verb *iuro*, to swear, and their Greek equivalents) in varying ways,[27] such that no clear distinction emerges between the two concepts Livy separates here.[28]

The Change in 216 BC

Why the change from a voluntary oath to the formal, obligatory one in 216 BC? The answer may well lie in the contemporary historical context: the turmoil that followed Hannibal's invasion and crushing initial successes over the Romans, and subsequent divisions within the elite as to what to do in the face of this threat. In particular, there was a division between those who favoured immediate and decisive combat, based on traditional Roman martial values and ideals of *uirtus*, and those who preferred a strategy of exhaustion against their Carthaginian opponent.[29] The soldiers themselves were divided, with the majority seeming to favour direct confrontation. This in turn led to near mutinies in response to the dictator Fabius Maximus' – the delayer's – strategy of avoiding direct combat, despite Hannibal's ravaging of Roman lands and towns.[30] More immediately, the oath also followed the disastrous destruction of a Roman army in a Hannibalic ambush at Lake Trasimene. In the face of such a crisis, it would not be surprising if the consuls and tribunes believed that a more consistent version of the oath, reliant on more than the voluntary will of the soldiers, was required to reinforce their commitment to the consuls in charge, whoever the consuls might be and whatever strategy they might adopt.[31] As Rüpke has argued, and as we shall see further below, there is a tendency for oaths to occur in moments of crisis, where they are seen as a means of providing mutual encouragement among those taking the oath.[32] Such oaths are additional to the traditional military oath, but exemplify the importance reposed in oaths in such critical times. Thus, in the wake of the disaster at Cannae, young Scipio Africanus thwarted the flight of the *equites* by swearing an oath accompanied by a *sacratio* to Jupiter:[33]

> 'He said "I solemnly swear that I will neither desert the republic of the Roman people nor will I suffer any other Roman citizen to desert. If I have knowingly spoken false, then may Jupiter Optimus Maximus destroy my household, family and property with most foul destruction."'[34]

Occasion and Content in the Republic

In regular times, the *sacramentum* was initially sworn at the point of recruitment.[35] We also know that it was sworn when commanders changed, such as when a commander had died or was replaced on a long campaign.[36] In irregular times, such as the series of crises that beset the Republic in its last century, the oath (or variations of it) could also be sworn in more diverse circumstances. These will be discussed further below.

Exactly to which gods the Romans swore, and the exact content of the oath, are all matters that are not clear – including what changes may have occurred over time. We can identify a number of general commitments, and it is clear that Livy, in his discussion of the content of the oath and its change from a voluntary to compulsory basis, does not give us all of it. Thus, Polybius also informs us that the soldiers swore to obey their commanders, and execute their orders as far as they were able.[37] Dionysius of Halicarnassus, although writing later than Polybius in the first century BC, gives similar information in his version of the content of the Republican oath: to follow the consuls in wars; not to desert the standards – nor their commanders;[38] and not to act contrary to the laws.[39] Servius, writing in the fourth century AD, further adds that soldiers swore that they would act 'on behalf of the state' (*pro re publica*).[40] As Servius includes elements of both Republican and imperial oaths in his description – such as a strict term limit for the army – it is uncertain when (or even if) this latter aspect was incorporated.

Visual depictions of oath-taking are found on some Republican coins, although these differ in their representation from literary descriptions of the taking of the *sacramentum*, and are thought perhaps to refer to the formation of treaties rather than to the military oath.[41] For example, a gold coin from 225–212 BC, around the period of the Second Punic War, depicts two soldiers facing each other, one in armour and beardless, the other bearded and without armour, with a kneeling figure holding a pig – each of the standing figures is touching the pig with his sword as the oath is sworn (see Figure 2.1).[42] No mention is made of the presence or sacrifice of a pig, nor touching it with a sword, in our literary descriptions, and this coin is thought to

Figure 2.1: Gold half-stater. Obverse: laureate, Janiform head of the Dioscuri. Reverse: oath-taking scene. Two soldiers, one in armour and the other without, each holding a spear in his left hand and touching a pig, held by a kneeling figure between them, with their swords; legend in exergue: *ROMA*; 225–212 BC. (*Courtesy of Classical Numismatic Group*)

perhaps be a call to loyalty to Rome's allies in the Second Punic War. A near identical type appears on the reverse of a later silver coin of 137 BC, which perhaps refers to supporting a controversial treaty with the Spanish town of Numantia in the same year.[43] Later coins minted by Rome's opponents, the Marsic Confederation, during the Social War of 91–89 BC between Rome and its Italian allies depict either a similar scene,[44] or an oath taken more en masse, with two, three or four soldiers on either side of the figure bearing the pig (see Figure 2.2).[45]

Figure 2.2: Silver denarius. Obverse: draped bust of Mars; legend in exergue: *VITELIÚ* ('Italy', in Oscan). Reverse: oath-taking scene. Four soldiers, two on each side, touch a pig held by a kneeling figure between them with their swords. Legend in exergue: *C. PAAPII. C.* (in Oscan); 90–88 BC. (*Courtesy of Classical Numismatic Group*)

An 'Initiation' or 'Transition' or a Bond of Loyalty[47]

Ancient Roman warfare was steeped in religion – from the fetial rite and taking of auspices prior to a campaign, to the offering of thanks to the gods at its successful conclusion.[48] The Roman military oath was also part of this phenomenon. Beyond the aspect of an oath with which we are perhaps most familiar – a sacred affirmation of loyalty – the Roman military oath also marked an important point of transition: from citizen – a *civis* or *Quiris* – to soldier, or *miles*.[49] The symbolic importance of this distinction is well illustrated by an anecdote attached to Caesar, who reportedly was able to regain the loyalty of his soldiers merely by addressing them as *Quirites* (citizens) as opposed to *milites* (soldiers), suggesting they had lost the privileged and distinct status of being a soldier.[50] This is particularly true of the oath taken at the point of a citizen soldier's enrolment in the legions. However, when the oath was sworn again subsequent to this point of enrolment, such as when there was a change of a commander or simply an annual renewal of the oath under the Empire (see below), the emphasis was instead on loyalty, in particular to the commander – later emperor – reflected in the fact that the oath had to be taken again when the commander changed.[51]

The transition from *civis* to *miles* had important secular aspects. Soldiers were in a somewhat anomalous position, in some respects legally privileged – thus soldiers were exempt from strict requirements on will-making – but in other respects disadvantaged: for example, they were liable to corporal punishment and even summary execution in a way that citizens were not and, between the time of Augustus and Septimius Severus, they could not marry.[52]

The transition also had an important religious consequence. In particular, it exempted the soldier from the pollution associated with killing.[53] This emerges clearly in an anecdote preserved in the work of the first-century BC orator Cicero about the famous second-century BC politician Cato the Elder. Cato's son had been discharged from service while fighting against the Macedonian king Perseus in 168 BC. Cato's son wished to continue serving in the army, but his father advised him to renew his military oath or *sacramentum*, as Cato thought 'it was not right [or *ius*] for a person who was not a *miles* to fight the enemy' (*negat enim ius esse, qui miles non sit, cum hoste pugnare*).[54] In a similar manner, Servius, the late fourth-century AD commentator on Virgil, states that the *sacramentum* was the distinguishing mark of 'legitimate military service' (*legitima militia*), as opposed to other types of military action.[55]

Was this transition between *Quiris* and *miles* the equivalent of an 'initiation', such as that involved in antiquity in joining a mystery religion like the Eleusinian Mysteries?[56] Key to this question is the murky connection with an ancient Samnite ritual described at length by Livy in his history. Prior to a crucial battle with Rome in 293 BC, the Samnites are said to have recruited a special legion by a process known as a *lex sacrata*, where one man in turn chooses another man to join the army, which was then followed by a particularly gruesome ritual – alleged to be an ancient rite (*ritu ... uetusto*) – where each individual swore an oath cursing himself and his family if he did not follow his commander into battle, fled or did not kill another who was in flight. Those who refused the oath were themselves killed and left beheaded before the altar amongst the sacrificial victims as a warning to others.[57] Livy deliberately associates this ritual with initiation into mystery religions, making an analogy between the soldiers and initiation.[58] Livy further uses similar language to describe this initiation and that of the infamous Bacchanalian conspiracy, involving an actual mystery religion, which he elsewhere describes in detail.[59] In particular, Livy attributes a speech to the Roman consul stating that young men who had been initiates of the Bacchic religion could not be soldiers.[60] On the basis of this description, it has been argued that the military oath of the Romans can be traced back to a Samnite – or even Indo-European – origin, and that the Roman *sacramentum* also had a similar initiatory aspect.[61] However, the Livian narrative presents a number of difficulties, such as how secret recruiting could possibly have worked in this context, and its historicity is highly dubious.[62] There is, further, an important distinction here between soldiers' oaths and mystery religion initiations in antiquity, that is, the *sacramentum* lasted no longer than the soldier's period of military service; once released from service, the oath had no lasting impact – hence the need for Cato's son to take the oath again.[63] Rüpke has thus rejected the concept of the *sacramentum* as a '*rite de passage*'.[64] Thus, we might perhaps best see the oath as transitional, without being 'initiatory'. We can see a similar transitional oath in the famous pledge of gladiators 'to be burned, bound, beaten and to die by the sword' that sacralised the takers and marked their transition to a gladiator, although like the oath of a soldier, this was not necessarily a life-long transition.[65]

Religious Conviction

The Greek historian Polybius, writing in the second century BC to explain the dominance of the Romans to his fellow Greeks, was of the opinion that the Romans' success was at least partially explicable on the basis of their superiority in terms of the nature of their religious convictions. For Polybius, such religious conviction helped to maintain cohesion in the state, particularly among the masses – whom Polybius, in typical ancient elitist fashion, regards as 'fickle, full of lawless desires, unreasoned passion and violent anger'[66] – and permeated Roman public and private life.[67] Polybius gives an example of the strength of 'superstition' amongst the Romans compared to among the Greeks:

> 'Members of the [Greek] government, if they are entrusted with no more than a talent, though they have ten copyists and as many seals and twice as many witnesses, cannot keep their faith; whereas among the Romans those who as magistrates and legates are dealing with large sums of money maintain correct conduct just because they have pledged their faith by oath.'[68]

Thus in government, so in the Roman Army – the oath was seen as a means of maintaining discipline. Violation of the oath was regarded as *nefas*, a concept that carried with it connotations of religious violation.[69] The persistence of this religious conviction, and also Roman self-identity as a most pious people, perhaps helps explain – in part – why the military oath was to enjoy such a long life, even after numerous civil wars and rebellions that might otherwise be thought to have discredited its efficacy.

Additional Oaths

In addition to this main oath taken upon enlistment, oaths were used at other times to bind soldiers to various duties. Thus, when construction of a camp was completed, all in the camp – including slaves – were made to swear to the tribunes that they would steal nothing from the camp or 10 miles around it, and bring anything found, with some limited exceptions, to the tribunes or other officers.[70] After enlistment, troops would also swear to appear at a certain location and day to rendezvous with the commander, unless a certain exemption applied.[71] Soldiers also vowed not to leave behind the standards.[72]

The Military Oath at the Fall of the Republic

Dionysius of Halicarnassus observed that the military oath was one that 'the Romans uphold above all others'.[73] Nonetheless, it proved frangible in times of stress. The civil wars in the final century of the first millennium BC saw the paradox – to be repeated throughout Roman history from this point – of the breaking of oaths by soldiers, yet at the exact same time a repeated emphasis on the oath as an important performative demonstration of loyalty: that is, the very person who encouraged the breaking of the *sacramentum* demanded a new oath immediately upon the act of rebellion as a symbol of the changed bond of loyalty. Thus, as the *sacramentum* initially played a role in forging loyalty to a commander in the absence of *gens*-based ties, so oaths continued to play an important role in buttressing support for a commander as other changes to Roman military service increased the bond between soldier and general – a bond that would ultimately be exploited to lead Roman to fight Roman.

The various changes that occurred in relation to military service over the course of the Republic, particularly in the wake of Marius' reforms to the military, are quite well known: increasing length of campaigns and service under one commander, the inclusion in the Roman Army of those for whom the army was the main hope of social advancement, and the reliance of soldiers on their commander – rather than the state – to secure for them benefits at the end of service, such as retirement money and land.[74] In addition, commanders also relied on the impact of an oath in attempting to secure the loyalty of their soldiers for civil war or other ventures that could, ostensibly, be cast as against the state. As before, we do not have specific evidence of the oath's terms in the wake of Marius' reforms.[75] The fact that the commander, as far as our evidence allows us to see, had always been a central focus of the *sacramentum*, made it readily malleable to use in favour of the personal ambitions of that commander.

The complex events of the civil strife of the 80s BC between Marius and Sulla provide some good evidence of this manipulation of oaths for personal advancement. Whether the oaths of allegiance sworn at these particular moments of crisis mirrored the *sacramentum*, or were particular to the circumstances, is not always clear in the sources. Nonetheless, on some occasions, at least, it seems likely that the oaths were peculiar to the needs of the specific situation, rather than a general oath.

We cannot hope to recover the full kaleidoscope of personal subjective experiences, or decisions, of the soldiers who made new oaths, or broke with old ones, in these times of crisis and civil war. Instead, we have to rely on generalizations and assumptions made usually by historians, and often long after events. Appian's analysis of the civil war in 41 BC is illustrative of ancient thinking on the causes of the breakdown of military discipline in this period:

> 'The cause was that the generals, for the most part, as is usually the case in civil wars, were not regularly chosen; that their armies were not drawn from the enrolment according to the custom of the fathers, nor for the benefit of their country; that they did not serve the public so much as they did the individuals who brought them together; and that they served these not by the force of law, but by reason of private promises; not against the common enemy, but against private foes; not against foreigners, but against fellow-citizens, their equals in rank. All these things impaired military discipline, and the soldiers thought that they were not so much serving in the army as lending assistance, by their own favour and judgment, to leaders who needed them for their own personal ends. Desertion, which had formerly been unpardonable, was now actually rewarded with gifts, and whole armies resorted to it, including some illustrious men, who did not consider it desertion to change to a like cause, for all parties were alike, since neither of them could be distinguished as battling against the common enemy of the Roman people. The common pretence of the generals that they were all striving for the good of the country made desertion easy in the thought that one could serve his country in any party. Understanding these facts the generals tolerated this behaviour, for they knew that their authority over their armies depended on donatives rather than on law.'[76]

Nonetheless, even in this period of indiscipline, the good of the state was held forth as a pretext for civil war, and this was true throughout the conflict in the late Republic. Thus it cannot be assumed that venality or mercenary motivations were the only driving force for soldiers breaking their oaths.[77] Certainly, those Romans writing about the period could envisage that the oath mattered to both leaders and soldiers,[78] and that the soldiers would need to be persuaded either as to reasons to break their oaths, or as to why they might be convinced that they were no longer bound by them. Caesar addresses this issue explicitly when he attributes a speech to his general, C. Scribonius Curio, as he addresses soldiers that had previously served under the Pompeian general L. Domitius:

> 'They say that they were abandoned and betrayed by you, and refer to your former oath [*sacramentum*]. But did you abandon Lucius Domitius, or did Domitius abandon you? Was it not the case that he forsook men who were prepared to endure the worst? Did he not seek safety for himself in flight without your knowledge? After you were betrayed by him, were you not saved by Caesar's favour? How could he have used the oath to hold you, given that, after having thrown away the insignia of office and relinquished command, as a private citizen and prisoner of war he has himself come into the power of another? The result is a strange sort of obligation: you are to neglect the oath that currently binds you and respect one that has been invalidated by the general's surrender and loss of citizen status.'[79]

Here, Caesar both imagines that allegations of oath breaking will have resonance with the soldiers, and attributes a speech to Curio that is designed to address these concerns by emphasizing the delegitimizing of L. Domitius through his loss of command.

One of the first examples of this strategic use of the oath is the consul Cinna, elected after the Roman proconsul Sulla had marched on Rome in 88 BC to prevent the transfer of command of an expedition to the East to Sulla's rival Marius.[80] Cinna was driven from Rome by his consular colleague, Octavius, after proposing to reintroduce controversial legislation. Cinna went to the town of Nola, where Sulla had left an army besieging the city. Cinna won this army over, either through persuasion or with the promise of rewards (or both), and the tribunes had the army swear the oath of loyalty to him.[81] Subsequently, Fimbria, who had murdered a consul and taken his army, attempted to use an oath to secure the support of this army in the face of Sulla's approach.[82]

An important turning point in this regard is located by some scholars in Sulla's rebellion commencing in 84 BC.[83] The first-century AD biographer Plutarch, who had access to Sulla's memoirs,[84] tells us that Sulla bound the army to himself by an oath to follow him as he was about to lead his army back to Italy against Rome:

> 'When Sulla was about to transport his soldiers, and was in fear lest, when they had reached Italy, they should disperse to their several cities, in the first place, they took an oath of their own accord to stand by him, and to do no damage to Italy without his orders; and then, seeing that he needed much money, they made a free-will offering and contribution, each man according to his abundance.'[85]

In some respects, these oaths of the 80s BC are an evolution of the tradition. As we have seen, the taking of an oath in a time of crisis has a long history. Further, the oath had always possessed, as far as our evidence allows us to see, a strong personal element between soldier and commander – in fact, it is unclear when a reference to the state was included in the oath. Such a reference only appears in late sources from the fourth century AD, and may only have been included in the imperial period when the distinction between state and emperor, to whom the oath was given, had broken down.[86]

The two-edged nature of the oath is shown by instances where reference to it could restore order. Thus, during the civil war between Caesar and Pompey, Curio was able to restore order by reminding soldiers of their oath.[87] However, the continual undermining of discipline that persisted through the civil conflicts at the end of the Republic had deleterious effects on discipline and loyalty as a whole, including regard for the *sacramentum*. Hence, when mutiny broke out among Octavian's soldiers in Sicily after he had lured away those of Lepidus through promises of bonuses, and a disregard for their own oaths to Lepidus, Octavian found that reminding soldiers of their oaths – and harsh discipline – did little to restore order.[88]

Nevertheless, the persistence in demanding the oath must have reflected a belief that it could play some role in securing the loyalty of the soldiers, even as its repeated use diminished its reputation.[89] Thus, oaths were not only used when commanders changed, but were explicitly exacted – in addition to the oath already sworn – when a crisis was suspected. Thus, in the civil war between Pompey and Caesar in 49 BC, the

Pompeian general in Spain, Petreius, suspected desertion and exacted an additional oath from the troops not to desert the army and its leaders nor to adopt any course of action that had not been agreed to by all.[90] Caesar goes so far as to assert the effectiveness of this oath – increasing the resolve of the soldiers on account of the new sanction (*religio*) of the oath.[91] These oaths, while overlapping with the core of the traditional *sacramentum* – such as the obligation not to desert – appear also to have incorporated elements particular to the situation at hand.[92]

Not only did the competitors for dominance in the Roman world after Caesar bind the soldiers with oaths, they also made use of oaths on the civilian population.[93] Thus, in 44 BC, with conflict looming between Antony and Octavian, Caesar's heir had suborned two of Antony's legions through a bribe. Antony, on the verge of marching to Gaul to confront Decimus Brutus, who had refused to surrender his command, was swearing in soldiers to himself at Tibur – both those present and a large group of veterans – when a group of senators, *equites* and other influential men arrived and voluntarily took an oath not to fail in friendship and faith to Antony (οὐκ ἐκλείψειν τὴν ἐς Ἀντώνιον εὔνοιάν τε καὶ πίστιν). It is uncertain what to make of this formulation: the idea of εὔνοια or 'good will' seems out of place in the *sacramentum*, given what we otherwise understand of its content focused on discipline regardless of the soldiers' disposition towards the commander.[94]

Perhaps more famously, in the lead-up to Octavian's decisive battle with Antony and Cleopatra at Actium in 32 BC, Italy – along with the Gallic and Spanish provinces, Africa, Sicily and Sardinia – swore an oath of allegiance to Octavian and called on him to take command in the civil war.[95] The formulation of this oath is unknown and unknowable on the present evidence.[96] It does seem, however, that the unusual order of events (usually the appointment of commander preceded the oath) links the oath with an attempt to legitimize Octavian's command now that his power to command – that had been granted to him as a triumvir, along with Antony and Lepidus – had expired following Caesar's assassination.[97] Such oaths of loyalty by civilians continue as a feature of the principate, as discussed below, and some from the imperial period have survived intact, as opposed to the text of the soldier's oath.

The Coming of the Principate

Octavian's victory in the civil conflict with Antony and his subsequent establishment of the system of government we today call the 'principate' were based to a large extent on his domination based on military power.[98] Utilizing – and expanding upon – Republican precedents, Octavian secured a near monopoly of military power in 27 BC when he was granted a *provincia* – or command – that comprised the provinces in the Roman Empire that contained the vast majority of Rome's legions. These he commanded through legates, rather than in person. As a consequence of this delegated command, the soldiers swore their oath not to their immediate commander, but to Octavian – now Augustus – as their supreme commander.[99] As before, the oath could summon soldiers back to obedience. Thus, soldiers on the frontiers in Pannonia, restive in the wake of Augustus' death and Tiberius' accession in AD 14, lost their enthusiasm for rebellion out of concern for the impact of breaking their oath.[100]

Occasion for Taking the Oath

Both the occasion for taking the oath, and its content, underwent some change during the imperial period. During the Republic, as noted above, the *sacramentum* was taken on two occasions: when recruits joined the Army and when its commander changed. These two occasions for swearing the oath remained in the Empire, although modified to reflect the position of the emperor as the commander of the Roman Army. In addition, the oath became the subject of annual ceremonial renewal in the Empire.[101] Thus, we find evidence of new recruits swearing an oath on joining the Army right through to late antiquity.[102] However, Augustus' creation of a standing army with fixed terms of service required a change to the oath taken on enlistment.[103] Whereas, formally, the oath only lasted for the length of a campaign, now it was for the period of service, or *stipendium militiae*.[104] As a change of commander in the Republic had required a renewal of the oath, so too in the Empire with a change of emperor, now supreme commander of all the armies.[105]

Although the oath was taken for the duration of service, nonetheless in the Empire it became the subject of renewal on at least two occasions, although it is unclear when each of these dates was instituted as a regular date for renewing the oath.[106] By the AD 60s, it had become usual to renew the oath on the first day of January.[107] However, by the reign of Trajan, it appears that the oath was renewed on 3 January, the day on which annual vows (*vota*) were taken for the health of the reigning emperor and that the Roman Empire might be eternal.[108] In addition, by the time of Trajan, the oath was also renewed on the anniversary of the emperor's accession to power – referred to as his *dies imperii* ('day of power').[109] The importance of this additional occasion is easy to discern: it was a deliberate expression of the bond between the emperor and the soldiers who simultaneously reinforced this connection. The correspondence between Pliny and Trajan, where Trajan explicitly acknowledges his pleasure at the oath-taking of the soldiers and citizenry, shows that the emperors themselves took a keen interest in the fact that these oaths were taken.[110]

It is easy to see why the imperial period saw the institution of such annual symbolic expressions of loyalty to create and reinforce the bond between emperor and soldier. In the Republic, the soldiers could expect to see the leader to whom they took the *sacramentum* on a fairly regular basis, even in a large army that would at times be divided among subordinate commanders, such as Caesar's army in his campaigns in Gaul. However, in the early principate, it was relatively rare for an emperor to lead an army, and even if he did, he would almost never see his entire army. Even when it became more common for emperors to command from the Severan period onwards, they would be unlikely to see the entirety of their armies. This greatly enhanced the importance of the creation of symbolic bonds of loyalty between emperor and soldier, such as the annual renewal of the *sacramentum*.[111]

There also appears to have been a change from the Republic in the manner in which the oath was sworn, at least in relation to the annual renewal of the oath. Thus, in the tumult that attended the 1 January renewal of the oath for Galba, the soldiers appear in their ranks to take the oath but 'only a few in the front rows repeated it [the oath], the rest remained silent, waiting on the courage of his neighbour'.[112] This suggests that the soldiers took the oath en masse, rather than individually.[113]

It seems highly likely that the presence of the Roman military standards (*signa militaria*) at the occasion of swearing the oath helped, or was intended to help strengthen the binding effect of the oath. The hand symbol found on Roman standards has been interpreted as representing the raised hand of the soldier during the oath-taking ceremony, and its presence served as a constant reminder of this oath. Indeed, this type of standard is often depicted on coins along with legends celebrating the army's loyalty.[114]

Content of the Oath

We are no better informed as to the content of the imperial oath than in the Republic, although what evidence there is suggests some continuity. Thus, Servius, writing in the fourth century AD, informs us that the oath included an obligation to obey and an obligation not to desert. The stoic Epictetus, writing around the turn of the second century AD, also informs us that the oath included an obligation to protect the safety of the emperor above all others.[115] This later obligation is not mentioned in relation to the earlier Republican oaths and suggests that the military *sacramentum* had absorbed an element found in civilian oaths to the emperor (see below).[116]

Did the oath involve a reference to the state, or the *senatus populusque Romanus*, in addition to the emperor? Here the evidence is unclear. Two late sources, the commentator Servius and military writer Vegetius, both of the fourth century AD, indicate that the oath did include such a reference. However, when describing the beginnings of a revolt against Galba, Tacitus states that the soldiers of Legion IV did not take an oath to Galba, but rather to the 'now forgotten names' of the Senate and People of Rome.[117] On the one hand, this could be taken to indicate that the oath did not usually include these words. However, on the other hand, this Tacitean remark may be more figurative than literal: that is, it is not that such terms were not regularly invoked in the oath, but that either the actions of the armies in the period covered by his *Histories* showed scant regard for the Roman state or the soldiers' omission of Galba highlighted the presence of the *res publica* in the oath.[118]

In the imperial period, as in the Republic, there appear to have been supplementary oaths sworn by the soldiers in addition to the *sacramentum* upon recruitment and the annual renewal of the oath. Thus, we know that the cohort at Dura-Europos swore an oath daily that they would 'do what has been ordered and will be ready for all orders'.[119]

Soldier Oaths Versus Civilian Oaths[120]

A further change between the Republic and principate was the institutionalization of a civilian oath of loyalty to the *princeps*, or emperor. Such an oath had, as we have seen, its roots in the civil conflict at the end of the Republic. While no complete text of a military oath has been preserved, several versions of the civilian oath survive in inscriptions when members of provincial communities wished to both preserve, and advertise, their demonstrations of loyalty through public commemoration.[121]

The texts of these oaths vary, but include at times a military orientation and also an obligation to place the welfare of the emperor ahead of oneself and one's own – a parallel with the idea contained in Epictetus' description of the military oath. Further, Pliny informs us that the annual renewals of oaths of loyalty could occur at the same ceremony for soldier and provincial alike.[122] Similarly, there is evidence that civilians and soldiers may have taken oaths at the same time at the accession of an emperor.[123]

What should we make of this overlap? It has been argued that the military *sacramentum* was sworn by soldiers at the time of enlistment, and perhaps change of commander, but, at the annual renewals, soldier and civilian alike swore the same oath.[124] However, there is no firm evidence to support this hypothesis. Further, there are some arguments to suggest why this might not have been the case. For example, when Tacitus describes the mutinous legions' decision to give their *sacramentum* to the Senate and People, rather than to the emperor, this action seems more apt for the regular military oath than the personalized oath of allegiance taken by the People. Further, the distinctive aspects of the military oath would appear to be as worthy of repetition as the obligations contained in the civilian oath of allegiance.[125] Crucially, while an obligation not to desert the commander seems to have been a central clause of the *sacramentum*, such an obligation is not included in the surviving texts of the civilian oath.[126] It does seem likely, however, that the content of both the civilian and military oaths may well have changed depending on circumstances. Thus, Suetonius states that Caligula caused his sisters to be included in 'all oaths' (*omnia sacramenta*).[127]

Effectiveness of the Oath?

As with the Republican period, we lack any direct evidence of the subjective experience of soldiers of the obligations stemming from the oath. Thus, while on the one hand we have texts like the first-century AD philosopher Seneca the Younger's claim in his epistles that the soldier's primary bond was *religio* and it was considered *nefas* – or a breach of divine law – to desert the army,[128] we also have plentiful evidence of soldiers breaching their *sacramenta* in times of civil war.

We do have some evidence that religious scruples were still of some influence on the soldiers. Thus, a mutiny at the accession of the second emperor, Tiberius, in AD 14 was quelled when soldiers became suspicious that an eclipse was an omen of the failure of their revolt.[129] In AD 42, the legate of the province of Dalmatia, Furius Camillus Scribonianus, attempted to suborn the legions to revolt against the emperor Claudius. The second-century AD biographer Suetonius records that the revolt was short lived, as the soldiers refused to follow Scribonianus after an ill omen: they were unable to remove the standards from the ground.[130]

More directly related to the oath are examples of soldiers demonstrating some scruples in relation to it in moments where revolt was in the air, such as the civil war of the period AD 68–69, when there were four different claimants for the imperial purple. Thus, in an example already discussed, soldiers contemplating revolt from Galba chose to change the object of their oath from the emperor himself to the

Senate and People of Rome.[131] Similarly, soldiers who had previously sided with Vitellius either murmured or passed over Vespasian's name in silence when called upon to make an oath to him following the significant victory of Vespasian's army at Cremona.[132] In the same way, the call to take the oath is seen as a critical time when legions loyal to Vitellius refused to take an oath to Vespasian.[133]

It is not only in their interpretation of the motivations of soldiers that historians refer to the oath. Such references also appear in speeches that the historians construct for their historical protagonists, which, however loose a connection they bore to whatever was actually said, should at least have appeared as plausible to the historian's audience. In this context, the third-century historian Herodian imagines Pupienus (Maximus) would have laid great emphasis on the military oath in addressing the former troops of Maximinus Thrax after their overthrow of this emperor – he even has Pupienus refer to the oath as the 'holy secret' (σεμνὸν μυστήριον) of the Roman Empire:

> 'In place of war you are at peace with the gods in whose name you took your oaths, and you are now being true to your military vow, which is the sacred secret [σεμνὸν μυστήριον] of the Roman empire.'[134]

Why did the oath appear as a restraint in some instances, but not others? It is difficult to come to general conclusions. The ancient sources themselves often explain periods of anarchy in very similar terms to those in which Appian explained the breakdown of military discipline in the Republic, such as a lack of discipline and the soldiers' greed, of which Plutarch provides an eloquent summary:

> 'Many dire events, and particularly those which befell the Romans after the death of Nero … show plainly that an Empire has nothing more fearful to show than a military force given over to untrained and unreasoning impulses … the Roman empire was prey to convulsions and disasters like those caused by the Titans of mythology, being torn into so many fragments, and again in many places collapsing upon itself, not so much through the ambition of those who were proclaimed Emperors, as through the greed and licence of the soldiers, which drove out one commander with another as nail drives out nail.'[135]

While the free-flow of bribes and other promises from aspiring claimants to the purple certainly suggest material motives as a driving force in determining whom soldiers supported, the extensive efforts of such claimants to contest the legitimacy of other claimants to the throne on various grounds relating to their suitability highlights that – as in the Republican civil wars – more than just material concerns were involved. The legitimacy of an emperor in part depended on his charismatic authority.[136] As the oath focused on the individual, should that individual – such as a Nero – appear to lose his legitimacy, the oath itself could appear to lose its validity.

A Period of Turmoil: AD 235–285

Although the period following AD 235 was one of much greater political turmoil, with many more usurpations than had happened previously – particularly from AD 235–

285, when there were over fifty aspirants to the imperial purple in almost as many years – nonetheless the *sacramentum* continues to be envisaged by authors writing about this period as an important component of securing the bond between emperor and soldier. Thus, upon hearing of Maximinus Thrax's revolt against him, Severus Alexander is said to have thought it was rash of the recruits to violate their oaths, and Herodian has Pupienus invoke the *sacramentum* following the defeat of Maximinus.[137]

Why soldiers were ever-more willing in this period to break their oaths is complex, and worthy of more discussion than we might provide here.[138] Nonetheless, we might identify three key factors. Firstly, the weakness of the Roman imperial succession system: whenever the dynastic system collapsed (as it did repeatedly in the third century), the absence of a clear succession system rendered the legitimacy of competing claimants more questionable. Secondly, increased external pressure from invasion, combined with the focus on the emperor as protector of the Empire, led to the support of successful local commanders as 'emperor' – such as for the pretender Postumus in the so-called Gallic empire in the AD 260s, when the more distant emperor had failed to provide protection. Lastly, the increased conflict from civil and external wars helped precipitate an economic crisis that, with rampant inflation, made soldiers even more susceptible to bribes in support of a new contestant for the purple.[139] In essence, while the *sacramentum* might strengthen an army's fidelity, loyalty largely depended on the army's attitude to the emperor,[140] which could be affected by their material and circumstantial needs – such as whether the emperor had proved an adequate leader.

The Later Empire

Although the fourth century AD was more stable than the preceding one, nonetheless this era saw more than ten usurpers – including two very successful ones who went on to reign (Constantine and Julian).[141] Vegetius, writing most likely in the late fourth century AD, makes it clear that the *sacramentum* continued to be sworn, only adopting a Christian focus:[142]

> 'The soldiers are marked with tattoos in the skin which will last and swear an oath when they are enlisted on the rolls. That is why they are called the sacraments of military service. They swear by God, Christ and the Holy Spirit, and by the majesty of the Emperor which second to God is to be loved and worshipped by the human race. For since the emperor has received the name of the "August", faithful devotion shall be given, unceasing homage paid him as if to a present and corporeal deity. For it is God whom a private citizen or a soldier serves, when he faithfully loves him who reigns by God's authority. The soldiers swear that they will strenuously do all that the Emperor may command, will never desert the service, nor refuse to die for the Roman state.'[143]

The Christian component of the oath represents a late development, probably of the reign of Theodosius or his children, and even then it was probably not universal.[144]

Despite the ongoing turmoil, oaths in the fourth century are seen as playing a role in securing the loyalty of the soldiers in the usurpations of Julian and Procopius, and in Constantius II's efforts to recall to loyalty the soldiers who had joined the usurpation of Vetranio in AD 360.[145] Nonetheless, usurpations continued, the oath being only one aspect of the bond between emperor and soldier.[146]

There are two descriptions of oath-taking by the soldiers during usurpations in the fourth century. Procopius, a usurper posing as a successor after feigning that the reigning emperor Valens was dead, has troops swear 'allegiance to Procopius with dire penalties for disloyalty, promising to stand by him and protect him with their lives', which broadly corresponds to Vegetius' descriptions of the oath, with the addition of references to penalties.[147] The most detailed description of the ceremony involved is of the soldiers swearing allegiance to the future emperor Julian as he commenced his usurpation against Constantius in AD 361:

> 'All had been bidden to take the usual [*sollemniter*] oath of allegiance in Julian's name; aiming their swords at their throats, they swore in set terms under pain of dire execrations that they would endure all hazards for him, to the extent of pouring out their life-blood, if necessity required; their officers and all the emperor's closest advisers followed their example, and pledged loyalty with like ceremony.'[148]

Although Ammianus describes this as 'customary' (*sollemniter*), the extent to which we might generalize from it is complicated by the fact that this is an oath taken at the commencement of a usurpation. As in the civil war context of the late Republic, and at earlier points in the Empire, such a context can produce modifications to the usual form – thus, while Vegetius refers to the state in his description of the oath, the loyalty described here is intensely focused on Julian himself. The process of the soldiers holding a sword at their own throats – not earlier or elsewhere attested for the *sacramentum* – is most likely a reflection of the changed recruiting patterns of the Roman Army. The majority of Julian's troops would have consisted of people from a non-Romanized background, and this custom is elsewhere attested for Quadi.[149] Importantly, one officer – the praetorian prefect Nibridius – refused to swear the oath due to his loyalty to Constantius, demonstrating further the seriousness with which swearing the oath was still taken.[150]

Christian Attitudes to the Oath

By the time Vegetius is writing, in the late fourth or early fifth century AD, the *sacramentum* had become Christian, or at least could be sworn in Christian terms. Earlier Christian texts occasionally use the military oath as a foil to contrast the civil *militia* with the *militia Christi*. Such texts are quite polemical and unreliable: Christians served in the Roman Army beyond Diocletian's purge in the early fourth century AD, so most did not openly struggle with the obligation imposed by the oath.[151] Nonetheless, despite their exaggerations, the fact that the Christian sources are able to deploy the oath in the rhetorical way that they do suggests that the *sacramentum* was generally conceptualized more broadly as having some significance. Thus the centurion Marcellus in the late third century AD renounces his military oath, saying that he cannot serve under his oath, only for Jesus Christ.[152] Tertullian, writing in the late second and early third centuries AD, also discusses the incompatibility of the *sacramentum* with service to Christ.[153]

Cult of the *Genii Sacramenti*

Beyond the rituals involved in the initial swearing of the *sacramentum* and the annual renewals of the oath, it appears that there also existed a cult specifically dedicated to the *genius* – or tutelary deity – of the *sacramentum* (the *Genius sacramenti*).[154] What this cult involved and when it evolved are unclear, although it is clear that it was one of many cults of *genii* particular to the military that contributed to the morale and cohesiveness of the soldiers as a group, such as cults of the *genius* of the standards (*Genius signorum*) or particular military groups (for example, the *Genius cohortis*).[155]

Conclusion

The origins and terms of the Roman military oath may be obscure, but its longevity is clear. The persistence of the oath seems on the one hand curious given the frequency with which it was broken, particularly in times of crisis – such as the collapse of the Republic, the succession wars in the imperial period of AD 69–70 and 193–197, and the so-called third-century crisis of AD 235–285. Nevertheless, this persistence is testament to the important role that it was conceived as playing, both as marking a transition from citizen to soldier and, particularly in the Empire, as symbolizing the ongoing loyalty between the soldier and an often distant emperor.

Notes

1. This author gratefully acknowledges his appointment as a University Associate of the University of Tasmania in the School of History and Classics within the College of Arts, Law and Education, which facilitated completion of this paper. The assistance of Dr Mark Hebblewhite and Prof. Matthew Dillon is also gratefully acknowledged. Infelicities and errors are of course the author's own.
2. See, for example, Hebblewhite (2016b), pp.128–32.
3. For a summary of punishments, see Watson (1969), pp.117–26; for decimation, see Watson (1969), pp.119–20; Polyb. 6.38. For physical and mental elements of discipline, see Brice (2011), pp.36–39.
4. Brice (2011), p.37.
5. For the use of the oath in archaic and classical Greek culture, see the helpful website maintained by Nottingham University: <https://www.nottingham.ac.uk/~brzoaths/database/>.
6. On the use of *sacramentum* in civil law, see Gai. 4.14–16; Rüpke (1990), pp.80–81; Ando (2011), pp.46–63.
7. On oaths to emperors more broadly, see Hermann (1968).
8. Brice (2011), p.37.
9. The annalistic historians take the year as their organizing principle, as do Livy and Tacitus in their historical works.
10. Two key foundational works highlighting these issues and the literary approach to be taken to them (sometimes referred to as 'New Historiography') are Wiseman (1979) and Woodman (1988); but see Lendon (2009).

11. See, for example, Potter (1990), pp.356–69.
12. The matter of the civilian oath is dealt with at length by Hermann (1968).
13. This evolution has been discussed by Armstrong (2016).
14. Armstrong (2016), p.273 n.241.
15. Tondo (1963), pp.70, 108–12.
16. Salmon (1967), p.185.
17. Livy 22.38.1–5. Virtually identical information is given in Front. *Strat.* 4.1.4, which probably depends on the Livian passage: Momigliano (1967), p.253.
18. See also Livy 3.20.3–6, 8.34.7–10 for references to this oath.
19. Front. *Strat.* 4.1.4.
20. Rüpke (1990), pp.77–79.
21. What made a man 'most suitable' (ἐπιτηδειότατος) is not specified, but it may have involved someone with a name of good omen – as was the case in selecting the first person to be levied: Cic. *Div.* 1.45; Poma (2015), p.705.
22. Polyb. 6.21.1–3. The phrase '*idem in me*' is found in Paul the Deacon's eighth-century AD abbreviation of the second-century AD lexical epitomizer Festus: Paul. *Fest.* 250L: '*praeiurationes facere dicuntur hi, qui ante alios conceptis verbis iurant; post quos in eadem verba iurantes tantum modo dicunt: idem in me*': 'Those are said to make *praeiurationes* who swear before others using set words, after whom in the same words the others swearing merely say "likewise for me".'
23. Brand (1968), p.91 and n.33.
24. Patron-client relationships were an important part of Roman social relations: see, for example, Garnsey & Saller (2015), pp.177–79.
25. *XII Tables* 8.10. See Crawford (1996), pp.689–90.
26. Rüpke (1990), p.80.
27. For example: ὅρκος (oath), ὀμνύω/ὀμνῦμι (swear); Hebblewhite (2016b), p.175 n.113.
28. See Hebblewhite (2016a), p.120 n.1; Rüpke (1990), pp.76–77.
29. On the Second Punic War, see, for example, Hoyos (2013). *Virtus* is a difficult term to translate, but its semantic range includes valour and steadfastness, especially as displayed in war: see *OLD 'uirtus'* 1.
30. For example, Livy 22.14.15.
31. See also Hinard (1993), pp.257–58.
32. Rüpke (1990), pp.78–79. While Rüpke is correct that the oath passage serves multiple purposes in Livy's narrative, this does not itself provide grounds for rejecting Livy's dating to this year of a change to a more formal method of taking the oath.
33. Brand (1968), p.95.
34. Livy 22.53.10–11.
35. For example, Polyb. 6.21.3; Livy 22.38.1–5. See also Caes. *Gall.* 6.1.2 for the oath sworn at a levy (*dilectus*): Harmand (1967), p.301.
36. Brice (2011), p.38.
37. Polyb. 6.21.3.
38. Brand (1968), p.92.
39. Dion. Hal. *Rom. Ant.* 10.18.2, 11.43.2; Watson (1969), p.49.
40. Serv. *Aen* 8.1.
41. See, for example, Crawford (1973), pp.4–6; Crawford (1974), pp.266, 715.
42. Found in Ghey, Leins & Crawford (2010), nos 28.1.2, 28.2.1; interpretation: Crawford (1974), p.715.
43. Found in Ghey, Leins & Crawford (2010), no. 234.1.4; interpretation: Crawford (1973), pp.4–6; Crawford (1974), p.266.
44. Sydenham (1952), no. 640a.
45. Sydenham (1952), for example, no. 637 (four soldiers in total); 619a (six soldiers in total); 619, 626, 629 (eight soldiers in total).
46. Ghey, Leins & Crawford (2010), no. 28.2.1.

47. Brand (1968), pp.90–91.
48. For a summary of many of these, see Vendrand-Voyer (1983), pp.27–35; Rich (2013).
49. Dyck (1996), p.145; Nicolet (1980), pp.102–03.
50. Suet. *Caes.* 70; Chrissanthos (2013), p.321.
51. Brice (2011), p.38.
52. See, for example, Hebblewhite (2016b), pp.120–28.
53. Tondo (1963), p.25; Tondo (1968), p.381.
54. Cic. *Off.* 1.36–37. The fact that this story is told twice in a row – in longer form at 1.36 and then more succinctly at 1.37 – indicates a textual problem here. It is thought that the first version (which explicitly mentions the *sacramentum*) is an interpolation: Dyck (1996), pp.143–45.
55. Serv. *Aen.* 2.157, 7.614 and 8.1. On some difficulties with these passages, see Rüpke (1990), pp.70–75.
56. On the Eleusinian mysteries, see, for example, Larson (2016), pp.268–76.
57. Livy 10.38.11.
58. Livy 10.38.2.
59. The suppression of the Bacchanalia is dealt with in Livy 39.8–19; commentary: Briscoe (2008), pp.230–94. See Tondo (1963), pp.87–94, 110; Tondo (1968), p.384; Oakley (2005), pp.400, 404–05.
60. Livy 39.15.3; Rüpke (1990), p.84.
61. Tondo (1963), pp.108–12; Tondo (1968), p.389.
62. On which, see Salmon (1967), pp.183–86; Oakley (2005), pp.396–97; Rüpke (1990), pp.81–82.
63. Rükpe (1990), p.88.
64. Rüpke (1990), pp.90–91.
65. Terms of oath: Petron. 117.5–6; Sen. *Ep.* 37.1, 71.23; Kyle (1998), p.87; Barton (1994), p.52.
66. Polyb. 6.56.11 (trans. Paton); see also Livy 1.19.4 on Numa's alleged use of religion as a means of controlling the masses.
67. Polyb. 6.56.6–14.
68. Polyb. 6.56.13–14 (trans. Paton).
69. Brand (1968), p.91; see, for example, Sen. *Ep.* 95.35; Campbell (1984), p.29.
70. Polyb. 6.33.1; Gell. *Noct. Att.* 16.4.2.
71. Polyb. 6.26.2; Gell. *Noct. Att.* 16.4.3–4.
72. Ando (2000), pp.260–61.
73. Dion. Hal. *Rom. Ant.* 11.43.2.
74. See, for example, Crawford (1992), pp.123–27.
75. Hermann (1968), pp.61–62.
76. App. *Civ.* 5.17 (trans. White): see Brunt (1962), p.76.
77. Brunt (1962), p.76.
78. Campbell (1984), p.23.
79. Caes. *Civ.* 2.32.8–10 (trans. Damon): see Campbell (1984), p.21.
80. A succinct narrative of these events can be found in the classic Scullard (1982), pp.68–72.
81. Vell. Pat. 2.20.4 (promise of rewards); App. *Civ.* 1.8.66 (persuasion). Appian specifically refers to this oath as ὁ ὅρκος ὁ στρατιωτικός: the 'military oath'.
82. App. *Mith.* 9.59.
83. For example, Campbell (1984), p.20; Phang (2008), p.119; Hebblewhite (2016a), p.122.
84. For example, Plut. *Sull.* 23.3.
85. Plut. *Sull.* 27.3 (trans. Perrin).
86. Rüpke (1990), p.89; our only references for it are Serv. *Aen.* 2.157, 8.1; Veg. *Mil.* 2.5 (clearly a late imperial context).
87. Caes. *Civ.* 2.32–33; Brice (2011), p.38.
88. Vell. Pat. 2.81.2; App. *Civ.* 5.128; Dio 49.13.2–14.1; Brice (2011), pp.48–49.
89. Brunt (1962), p.77.
90. Caes. *Civ.* 1.76: see Campbell (1984), pp.20–21. See also, earlier, when Fimbria attempted to have the army swear loyalty in the face of the advancing Sulla during the Mithridatic war

(App. *Mith.* 9.59); and when Pompey's officers, then soldiers, swore not to desert him before Dyrrachium in the civil war with Caesar (Caes. *Civ.* 3.13.3): see Hermann (1968), pp.62–63.
91. Caes. *Civ.* 1.76.5: *nova religio iuris iurandi*; see Campbell (1984), p.23.
92. Hermann (1968), p.63.
93. For example, in 49 BC, M. Terrentius Varro compelled the province Hispania Ulterior to swear allegiance to himself and Pompey (Caes. *Civ.* 2.18.15): see Hermann (1968), p.82.
94. Appian's formulation is vague, and the possibility suggested by Hermann (1968), p.4, that they simply said '*idem in me*' (likewise for me) as the soldiers had done, cannot be certain.
95. Aug. *Res Gest.* 25.1; see Hermann (1968), pp.78–89. Suetonius (*Aug.* 17.2) states that one town with historic loyalty to Antony was excused from swearing with the rest of Italy on behalf of Octavian's 'party' or 'faction' (*pro partibus suis*).
96. Hermann (1968), p.88.
97. Hermann (1968), pp.85–86.
98. On the basis for Augustus' power, and the importance of the military, see Crook (1996).
99. Stäcker (2003), p.293; Hebblewhite (2016a), p.121.
100. Tac. *Ann.* 1.28; Dio 57.4; Brice (2011), p.38.
101. Stäcker (2003), pp.295–96; Hebblewhite (2016a), pp.124–25.
102. Plin. *Ep.* 10.29; Veg. *Mil.* 2.5.
103. On the Augustan military reforms, see, for example, Raaflaub (2015).
104. Serv. *Aen.* 2.157; Isid. *Etym.* 9.3.53: see Campbell (1984), p.23.
105. For example, Dio 57.3.2; Tac. *Ann.* 1.7, 1.37 (Tiberius), *Hist.* 1.36 (Otho); Hdn 2.2.10 (Pertinax): see Campbell (1984), pp.25–27; Hebblewhite (2016a), p.125.
106. Hebblewhite (2016a), p.125.
107. Tac. *Hist.* 1.55.
108. Plin. *Ep.* 10.100–01; *P. Dura* 54.2–6: see Hebblewhite (2016a), p.125; Ando (2000), pp.359–61.
109. Plin. *Ep.* 10.52: see Hebblewhite (2016a), p.125; Campbell (1984), p.27.
110. Stäcker (2003), p.296.
111. Campbell (1984), p.28.
112. Tac. *Hist.* 1.55: *et raris primorum ordinum vocibus, ceteri silentio proximi cuiusque audaciam expectantes*.
113. Stäcker (2003), p.297.
114. Hebblewhite (2016b), pp.165–66.
115. Epict. *Disc.* 1.14.15.
116. Hermann (1968), pp.113–14.
117. Tac. *Hist.* 1.55: *senatus populique Romani oblitterata iam nomina sacramento advocabant*.
118. Stäcker (2003), p.297.
119. *P. Dura* 47: see Hebblewhite (2016a), p.126.
120. On the civilian oath, see Hermann (1968).
121. These are helpfully collected in Hermann (1968), pp.122–26.
122. Plin. *Ep.* 10.52, 10.100: Strächer (2003), pp.298–300.
123. Hdn 2.2.10 (Pertinax's accession): see Campbell (1984), p.27.
124. The argument of von Premerstein, summarized in Stäcker (2003), p.300.
125. Stäcker (2003), pp.300–01; Hermann (1968), p.120.
126. Hermann (1968), p.88. The original Greek and Latin texts of many of these oaths can be found in Hermann's appendix, pp.122–26.
127. Suet. *Calig.* 15.3: see Hebblewhite (2016a), p.124.
128. Sen. *Ep.* 95.35: 'In such a manner, the primary bond of a soldier is religious awe [*religio*] and love of the standard, and the sin [*nefas*] of desertion, then next easily other obligations may be given to him, and trusts exacted once the oath has been given': *Quemadmodum primum militiae vinculum est religio et signorum amor et deserendi nefas, tunc deinde facile cetera exiguntur mandanturque iusiurandum adactis*.
129. Tac. *Ann.* 1.28.
130. Suet. *Claud.* 13.2. Note that Dio focuses instead on the soldiers' belief that Scribonianus' programme would lead them to strife: Dio 60.15.3; see Campbell (1984), p.30; Stäcker (2003), pp.302–03.

131. Tac. *Hist.* 1.55: see Stäcker (2003), pp.304–05.
132. Tac. *Hist.* 4.21: see Campbell (1984), p.31.
133. Tac. *Hist.* 4.21: see Campbell (1984), p.31.
134. Hdn 8.7.4 (trans. Whittaker): see Campbell (1984), p.30.
135. Plut. *Gal.* 1.3–4 (trans. Perrin): see Hebblewhite (2016b), pp.128–31.
136. See Ando (2011), p.293, for the impacts of charismatic authority in a civil war context.
137. Hdn 6.9.2 (Severus Alexander); 8.7.4 (Pupienus).
138. See further on this period Potter (1990); Potter (2014); Hebblewhite (2016a); Hebblewhite (2016b).
139. See Taylor (2010), esp. pp.378–90.
140. Hebblewhite (2016a), pp.141–42.
141. There can thus be counted in this century Constantine, Maxentius, Magnentius, Decentius, Vetranio, Calocaerus, Procopius, Marcellus, Julian, Magnus Maximus and Eugenius.
142. Hebblewhite (2016a), p.132.
143. Veg. *Mil.* 2.5 (trans. Milner).
144. Liban. *Or.* 30.53 suggests that oaths were still taken 'by the gods' by some high officers in Theodosius' reign: Hebblewhite (2016a), pp.132–33.
145. Julian: Amm. Marc. 21.5.10; Procopius: Amm. Marc. 26.7.9; Constantius II: Zos. 2.44.1–2: Hebblewhite (2016a), pp.134–35.
146. Hebblewhite (2016a), 141–42.
147. Amm. Marc. 26.7.9 (trans. Rolfe): see Hebblewhite (2016a), p.131.
148. Amm. Marc. 21.5.10 (trans. Rolfe, adapted).
149. See Amm. Marc. 17.12.16, where the tribespeople beg for a sword to be held at their throat as part of a pledge of loyalty: Hebblewhite (2016a), pp.139–40.
150. Hebblewhite (2016a), p.140.
151. Phang (2008), pp.119–20.
152. *Acta S. Marcelli, Rec. M.* 2.19–21, as quoted in Hebblewhite (2016a), pp.128–29.
153. Tert. *Idol.* 19.2, *Cor. Mil.* 11.1: see Hebblewhite (2016a), p.137.
154. Attested in *AE* 1953, p.10; see Stäcker (2003), pp.305–06; Hebblewhite (2016a), p.127.
155. See further Stoll (2011), p.462.

Bibliography

Ando, C., *Imperial Ideology and Provincial Loyalty in the Roman Empire* (Los Angeles, 2000).
Ando, C., *Law, Language and Empire in the Roman Tradition* (Philadelphia, 2011).
Armstrong, J., *War and Society in Early Rome: From Warlords to Generals* (Cambridge, 2016).
Barton, C.A., 'Savage Miracles: The Redemption of Lost Honor in Ancient Rome and the Sacrament of the Gladiator and Martyr', *Representations* 45 (1994), pp.41–71.
Brand, C.E., *Roman Military Law* (Austin, 1968).
Brice, L.L., 'Disciplining Octavian: A Case Study of Roman Military Culture, 44–30 BCE', in Lee, W.E. (ed.), *Warfare and Culture in World History* (New York, 2011), pp.35–59.
Briscoe, J., *A Commentary on Livy, Books 38–40* (Oxford, 2008).
Brunt, P.A., 'The Army and the Land in the Roman Revolution', *JRS* 52 (1962), pp.69–86.
Campbell, J.B., *The Emperor and the Roman Army 31 BC–AD 235* (Oxford, 1984).
Chrissanthos, S.G., 'Keeping Military Discipline', in Campbell, B. & Tritle, L.A. (eds), *The Oxford Handbook of Warfare in the Classical World* (Oxford, 2013), pp.312–29.
Crawford, M., '*Foedus* and *sponsio*', *PBSR* 41 (1973), pp.1–8.
Crawford, M., *Roman Republican Coinage*, vols 1–2 (Cambridge, 1974).
Crawford, M., *The Roman Republic* (London, 1992).
Crawford, M. (ed.), *Roman Statutes*, vols 1–2 (London, 1996).
Crook, J.A., 'Augustus: Power, Authority, Achievement', in Bowman, A.K., Champlin, E. & Lintott, A. (eds), *Cambridge Ancient History Vol. X: the Augustan Empire 44 BC–AD 70* (Cambridge, 1996), pp.113–46.
Dyck, A.R., *A Commentary on Cicero, De Officiis* (Ann Arbor, 1996).

Garnsey, P. & Saller, R., *The Roman Empire: Economy, Society and Culture* (Oakland, 2015).

Ghey, E. & Leins, I. (eds), with Crawford, M.H., *A Catalogue of the Roman Republican Coins in the British Museum, with Descriptions and Chronology Based on M.H. Crawford*, Roman Republican Coinage (1974) (London, 2010).

Harmand, J., *L'armeé et le soldat à Rome 105–57 BC* (Paris, 1967).

Hebblewhite, M., '*Sacramentum militiae*: Empty Words in An Age of Chaos', in Armstrong, J. (ed.), *Circum Mare: Themes in Ancient Warfare* (Leiden, 2016a), pp.120–42.

Hebblewhite, M., *The Emperor and the Army in the Later Roman Empire, 235–395* (London, 2016b).

Hermann, P., *Der römische Kaisereid: Untersuchungen zu seiner Herkunft und Entwicklung* (Göttingen, 1968).

Hinard, F., '*Sacramentum*', *Athenaeum* 81 (1993), pp.251–63.

Hoyos, D., 'The Second Punic War', in Campbell, B. & Tritle, L.A. (eds), *The Oxford Handbook of Warfare in the Classical World* (Oxford, 2013), pp.688–707.

Kyle, D.G., *Spectacles of Death in Ancient Rome* (London, 1998).

Larson, J., *Understanding Greek Religion* (London, 2016).

Le Bohec, Y. (ed.), *The Encyclopedia of the Roman Army* (Malden MA, 2015).

Lendon, J.E., 'Historians Without History: Against Roman Historiography', in Feldherr, A. (ed.), *The Cambridge Companion to the Roman Historians* (Cambridge, 2009), pp.41–61.

Milner, N.P. (trans.), *Vegetius: Epitome of Military Science* (Liverpool, 1993).

Momigliano, A., 'Review of Salvatore Tondo, *Il 'Sacramentum Militiae' nell'ambiente cultrale Romano-Italico*, 1963', *JRS* 57 (1967), pp.253–54.

Nicolet, C., *The World of the Roman Citizen*, trans. Falla, P.S. (London, 1980).

Oakley, S.P., *A Commentary on Livy Books VI–X: Vol. IV: Book 10* (Oxford, 2005).

Phang, S.E., *Roman Military Service: Ideologies of Discipline in the Late Republic and Early Principate* (Cambridge, 2008).

Poma, G., 'Oath: Republic', in Le Bohec, Y. (ed.), *The Encyclopedia of the Roman Army*, vol. 2 (Malden MA, 2015), p.705.

Potter, D.S., *Prophecy and History in the Crisis of the Roman Empire: A Historical Commentary on the Thirteenth Sibylline Oracle* (Oxford, 1990).

Potter, D.S., *The Roman Empire at Bay AD 180–395*, 2nd edn (London, 2014).

Raaflaub, K.A., 'The Political Significance of Augustus' Military Reforms', in Edmondson, J. (ed.), *Augustus* (Edinburgh, 2015), pp.203–28.

Rich, J., 'Roman Rituals of War', in Campbell, B. & Tritle, L.A. (eds), *The Oxford Handbook of Warfare in the Classical World* (Oxford, 2013), pp.542–68.

Rüpke, J., *Domi militiae: die religiöse Konstruktion dese Krieges in Rom* (Stuttgart, 1990).

Salmon, E.T., *Samnium and the Samnites* (Cambridge, 1967).

Scullard, H.H., *From the Gracchi to Nero*, 5th edn (London, 1982).

Stäcker, J., *Princeps und Miles: Studien zum Bildungs- und Nahverhältnis von Kaiser und Soldat im 1. und 2. Jahrhundert n. Chr.* (Hildesheim, 2003).

Stoll, O., 'The Religions of the Armies', in Erdkamp, P. (ed.), *A Companion to the Roman Army* (Malden, 2011), pp.451–76.

Sydenham, E., *The Coinage of the Roman Republic* (London, 1952).

Taylor, T., *Usurpation in the Roman Empire 68–305 CE*, PhD thesis (New Haven, 2010).

Tondo S., 'Il "Sacramentum Militiae" nell'ambiente culturale Romano-Italico', *Studia et Documenta Historiae et Iuris* 29 (1963), pp.1–131.

Tondo S., 'Sul sacramentum militiae', *Studia et Documenta Historiae et Iuris* 34 (1968), pp.376–96.

Vendrand-Voyer, J., *Normes civiques et métier militaire à Rome sous le principat* (Clermont-Ferrand, 1983).

Watson, G.R., *The Roman Soldier* (London, 1969).

Wiseman, T.P., *Clio's Cosmetics: Three Studies in Greco-Roman Literature* (Leicester, 1979).

Woodman, A.J., *Rhetoric in Classical Historiography: Four Studies* (London, 1988).

Chapter 3

The Gods on Campaign in the Roman Empire

Matthew Dillon

Romans went to war with the gods on their side, or, in the case of Jupiter, literally with this god at the front – carried into battle in the vanguard of each legion in the form of his sacred eagle. Mounted on a pole, the eagle, one for each of Rome's legions, was a symbol of Jupiter and of Roman dominion wherever the legions marched. Jupiter was also the god who sent omens of victory, often a flight of living eagles. Other gods supported Rome's military endeavours: Mars had been prominent in the Republic, but from Augustus on, Mars in his guise as Mars Ultor (Mars the Avenger) becomes a divinity of considerable potency. The goddess Victory and her 'trademarks', the *tropaea* – assemblages of arms and armour captured from the enemy – dominate coins, reliefs and architecture: and she was the only martial deity whose iconography made a seamless transition from pagan to Christian Rome. Roman beliefs in their various war-gods were expressed through a variety of state and personal rituals, and manifested themselves in art and monumental architecture. Soldiers expressed their individual piety in inscriptions on both reliefs and altars, venerating Jupiter Optimus Maximus, the main god of victory, but also numerous other Roman gods, and their own indigenous deities if the soldiers were from places other than Italy.

New cults sprang up in the imperial period: the *genius* (embodiment) of the emperor and deified emperors became part of the formal worship of the soldiery, and the cult of the legionary eagle and standards became quite sophisticated. The worship of Jupiter Dolichenus provided soldiers with the opportunity to venerate a deity who looked the part, dressed as a Roman soldier and girded for battle. In the imperial centre itself, Rome, the monumental temple of Mars Ultor and the columns of Trajan and Marcus Aurelius, as well as marble arches commemorating imperial victory celebrations – the triumphs – gave state acknowledgement to the contribution the Romans believed their gods made to their worldwide dominion and success in battle. Throughout the provinces, monumental *tropaea* and numerous triumphal arches etched the Roman gods' dominance in war onto the urban landscape. Wherever the legionary eagles camped or marched, the gods were with Rome's army and soldiers. Nowhere is this clearer than in the iconographic narrative of Trajan's Column, where in one encounter with the Dacians, Jupiter Tonans (Jupiter of the Thunderbolt) can be seen casting a thunderbolt – his traditional weapon – at the Dacian enemy and striking them dead (see Figure 3.1).

Figure 3.1: Jupiter Tonans (Jupiter of the Thunderbolt) in the heavens hurling a thunderbolt at the Dacians; Trajan's Column (panel 24, scenes 59–62; Jupiter is at the top centre), Rome. (*Courtesy of Wikimedia*)

The Gods of the Roman Soldier

In the Roman Empire, the range of religious cults available to its inhabitants was extensive. Similarly, a Roman soldier, whether serving near the Thames or the Euphrates, had numerous cultic activities in which he could engage. Firstly, there was the 'compulsory' army religion prescribed by the state, as evidenced by the military calendar of religious observances at Dura-Europos, regulating the days for certain cult activities and their type. Jupiter Optimus Maximus as the traditional Roman military god received many dedications from soldiers, as well as in a new guise from the early second century AD, as Jupiter Dolichenus. There were also cults that grew up around the legionary eagle and the standards carried by units in the Roman Army; in addition, there were deities of the camp and the parade ground. Soldiers brought the indigenous gods of their homeland to wherever they were stationed. A wide range of religious experience for soldiers was the result, and few days would have gone by without some form of religious observance by an individual soldier or the military units (centuries, cohorts and legions) to which he belonged.

The Military Calendar of Dura-Europos

The *feriale Duranum* is the third-century AD religio-military calendar of Dura-Europos in the Roman province of Mesopotamia.[1] This calendar, written in Latin on papyrus, covers the months of January to September in its surviving state; 1 January is missing, and it breaks off after the entry for 23 September. This calendar is assumed to have been a copy of that circulated to the legions and auxiliary formations and their constituent parts throughout the Empire. Discovered in Dura-Europos in the excavations of 1931–32 in the Temple of Artemis Azzanathkona (the latter an important goddess of Syria), which served as a document archive for the auxiliary cohort stationed in the town, the Cohors XX Palmyrenorum (the cohort of Palmyrenes serving at Dura-Europos). Dating to the reign of Severus Alexander (AD 224–235), the calendar prescribed that sacrifices were to be made for his welfare (*salus*) annually on 3 January.

This calendar was definitely for military rather than civilian application, as the emphasis is on military worship, including ceremonies attendant upon the discharge of soldiers and the veneration of the army standards (*signa*). Such military calendars presumably had a long history, probably going back to Augustus or even before.[2] Yet with each new dynasty and reign they received modification: as the *feriale Duranum* indicates, it is 'up-to-date' with days for the veneration of the reigning emperor and his family. Various festivals and other celebrations listed in the calendar worked to create an official religion for the army, which provided cohesion in the military throughout the Empire. Various days are listed in the calendar, giving the type of ritual to be celebrated on that particular day (sacrifice or *supplicatio*: a bloodless offering of wine and incense), and if a sacrifice, what type of animal was to be sacrificed and to which god.

There are three types of religious activities: military rituals, festivals for the gods and cult observances for the imperial family. Firstly, as noted, on 3 January the cohort was to sacrifice for the safety of the emperor Marcus Aurelius Severus Alexander Augustus and for the everlasting empire of the Roman people. (Before this, there would have been an entry for 1 January specifying rites to welcome the New Year.) The *votorum nuncupatio* ('a public pronouncement of vows') was held on 3 January, when *vota* ('vows'; singular, *votum*) were made for the welfare of the reigning emperor and his family, a practice begun in 30 BC (with Octavian, soon to be Augustus) and celebrated by all communities, not just the military, throughout the Empire. While the names of the deities to be sacrificed to on this day are largely restored in the *feriale Duranum*, it appears that Jupiter Optimus Maximus, Jupiter Victor, Juno, Minerva, Mars Pater (Father), Mars Victor and Victory received worship.

Two specific military events are celebrated in the calendar. On 7 February, soldiers who had completed their period of military service were discharged (the *honesta missio*): this was celebrated with a sacrifice to Jupiter Optimus Maximus of an ox, with cows to Juno, Minerva and Salus ('Safety' or 'Welfare'), and to Mars Pater a bull, with the male deities receiving male and the female deities female sacrificial victims. On 9 May, the other exclusively military festival was celebrated, the *rosaliae signorum* ('the flower festivals of the standards'), with a *supplicatio* (involving incense and wine): the standards (including the *aquilae*, or eagles) were decorated with flowers and venerated.

In addition, the calendar indicates that there were six days on which Roman festivals were to be celebrated by the Roman Army. For Mars Pater and Mars Victor, on 1 March, a bull was sacrificed for his birthday, and again on 12 May, when his circus games (*circenses Martiales*) were celebrated at Rome and elsewhere. The Quinquatria festival at Rome, on 19 March, was to be celebrated by the army with four days of *supplicationes* (19–22 March). This was a festival particularly associated with the Roman Army, with a *lustratio* (purification) of the army occurring on 19 March. It

Figure 3.2. Trajan receiving an embassy of Dacians. A legionary eagle and two *signa* (standards) are placed prominently in front of the podium (centre) on which Trajan stands, as symbols of Roman dominance and military might; the eagle and *signa* were venerated by Roman soldiers. Two *signa* can also be seen to the left. Trajan's Column (panel 27, scene 68), Rome. (*Courtesy of Alamy*)

was celebrated in honour of Minerva, whom Ovid in his *Fasti* entry for this festival describes as a 'war goddess'.[3] Tertullian, in referring to soldiers wearing wreaths of olive in honour of Minerva, whom he refers to as the 'goddess of arms', is probably referring to this festival.[4] On the *dies natalis urbis Romae*, 21 April, the birthday of the 'Eternal City of Rome', Roma received a sacrificial cow in celebration. At the *circenses Salutares*, on 5 August, circus games were held at Rome to honour Salus, and the army sacrificed a cow. Vesta Mater's festival of the Vestalia, 9 June, was celebrated with a *supplicatio*. At his festival of the Neptunalia, 23 July, Neptune received a *supplicatio* and an *immolatio* (this term refers to a sacrifice after the sprinkling of the beast with the sacred spelt, a coarse flour). The entries for 24 September through to the end of the year are missing, but there must have been several other Roman festivals which were celebrated in these months by the cohort at Dura-Europos. Amongst them was surely the Augustalia, celebrated for the divine Augustus (who was venerated on the date of his birthday), the Armilustrium (the purification of the army at the end of the campaigning season), and the Saturnalia festival, celebrated wherever the Romans were present, in December.[5] For example, from his province of Cilicia in December 51 BC, Cicero wrote to his friend Atticus that 'the Saturnalia was a very merry time for men as well as officers'.[6]

All in all, the deities worshipped by the legions, and in this case by the cohort of the Palmyrenes, were the standard, traditional Roman gods. These were the gods venerated in a uniform pattern by all the legions across the Empire on their respective festival days: Juno, Jupiter Optimus Maximus, Jupiter Victor, Mars (Pater, Ultor and Victor), Minerva, Neptune, Roma, Salus, Vesta and Victory; some other gods may have been venerated in the missing section, 24 September–1 January. None of these are local gods, and there is no deviation from the traditional Roman pantheon. Soldiers were, however, free to worship their local gods. Another deity venerated in the calendar was 'Parthian Victory' for the Parthian victories of Severus, but with a sacrifice to the deified Trajan on the same day (28 January), doubtless because of his Parthian victories.

Imperial Cult at Dura-Europos

Many days were set aside in the Dura-Europos calendar for venerating deified members of the imperial family and the reigning emperor: the days when Severus Alexander, the reigning emperor, and other emperors, became emperor (the *dies imperii*), imperial birthdays (*dies natales*, for example, Augustus, Antoninus Pius, Claudius, Julius Caesar, Matidia – see below – and Trajan). Deified emperors received sacrifices (given here in the order of their reigns): Augustus, the first *princeps*, of course, on his birthday (as well as his adoptive father, the deified Julius Caesar); then Claudius, Nerva, Trajan, Hadrian, Lucius Verus, Marcus Aurelius, Antoninus Pius, Pertinax, Caracalla and Septimius Severus. The Severi, of course, were particularly venerated, including the *genius* of Lucius Seius Caesar, the emperor's father-in-law, as well as the *genius* of the emperor himself. The birthday of Germanicus (15 BC–AD 19) was celebrated with a *supplicatio* ritual on 24 May – nearly two-and-a-half centuries after the event. He was an important military figure and clearly considered worthy of soldiers' veneration, even though he had not been deified.

Deified women also received ritual observances: Trajan's elder sister Ulpia Marciana and his niece Matidia;[7] Faustina, wife of Marcus Aurelius; Julia Maesa, Severus' maternal grandmother, and her daughter Julia Mamea, mother of Alexander Severus, who was the 'deified empress'. Of note is that there was a deity, Juno Mamaea Augusta, the Juno of Mamaea Augusta, Severus' mother. These women received either sacrifices or *supplicationes*.

In the sanctuary now known as the 'Temple of the Palmyrene Gods', in the northwest of the town of Dura-Europos, there is a small third-century AD fresco on the north wall of the temple *pronaos* (vestibule), including text in Greek and Latin as part of the fresco. The Latin identifies the central figure, who is burning incense on an incense stand (thymeterion), as one Julius Terentius, tribune, known from other evidence at Dura as belonging to the Cohors XX Palmyrenorum. Next to Terentius is an army vexillarius, holding a *vexillum* (see below: a 'flag' on a pole or spear) on which something, now obscure, was painted. Behind and around Terentius, his soldiers raise their right hand in adoration towards three male figures, each on a podium and each with a *nimbus* ('halo') around their heads: clearly deities of some kind, but these are not identified with inscriptions. All three are dressed as Roman soldiers, with spears; one also has a shield. These are obviously divinized Roman emperors being venerated by the cohort. A large flower in the bottom left of the fresco, not far from the *signum* (standard), might be a reference to the *rosaliae signorum* veneration of the standard on 9 May.

There is also a priest present (named in Greek); and in the bottom left of the fresco two figures wearing a mural crown (like a city wall), and identified in Greek as the Tyche of Dura and Tyche of Palmyra: the tutelary (protector) deities of these two places. The three deities, each with a *nimbus*, may be Palmyrene deities, or more probably are Roman emperors being venerated, given their military dress.[8] The fresco shows the soldiers joined with their military tribune in making an incense offering (a *supplicatio*) and venerating deities; since the soldiers are doing so in their capacity as soldiers in their military unit, the desired outcome of this act of worship would have been benefits for the cohort, such as protection in battle. In addition, an incense burner from Dura-Europos has bilingual inscriptions – in Greek and Palmyrene – dedicated to the Tyche of Dura depicting an eagle flying with a palm branch (a symbol of victory) and a military standard.

Less of a religious calendar for worshipping the gods of the Roman pantheon, the *feriale Duranum* is in fact an imperial calendar for venerating deified emperors and some of the deified women associated with them. Of the 41 entries preserved in the *feriale Duranum*, 21 – half – are for divinized members of imperial dynasties.[9] Thus the calendar focuses on the veneration of the emperor and his predecessors, and only a handful of festivals – which were deemed mandatory for the military – are listed. 'Exotic', 'foreign' and indigenous gods are not accorded any notice. Yet soldiers worshipped their own particular local divinities, and the evidence from throughout the Empire attests to a thriving number of cults separate from that of the official religious calendar.

Jupiter Dolichenus: The Soldier's God

One such deity outside the official military pantheon was the 'new' god, Jupiter Dolichenus, always shown dressed as a Roman Army officer, who emerged as a deity in the Roman Empire sometime in the early second century AD and continued to be worshipped until the mid-third century.[10] This cult was particularly prominent among the soldiery, especially in Britain and along the Danube and Rhine frontiers (as well as in Africa, Gaul and Spain).[11] Dolichenus, the god's epithet, derived from the town of Doliche in Commagene (a Roman province since AD 72), where he had a major sanctuary: how he arrived in the Roman Empire and came to have a fairly extensive cult, and why it took the form it did, are indeterminable questions also pertaining to the cult of Mithras. His origins seem to lie in the second millennium BC, when Hittite and Syrian storm gods are shown with the double axe, as is Jupiter Dolichenus.[12] In the Roman Empire, he was referred to as Jove Dolichenus,[13] or Jove Optimus Maximus Dolichenus,[14] being assimilated to Jupiter in the latter's capacity as a martial deity and patron (and guarantor) of the Roman Empire; he also took over Jupiter's consort, Juno Regina (Queen Juno).

His iconography (sculpture and metal plaques: see below) depicts a military deity. A particularly fine example of a dedication, of a statue of the god standing on a sacrificial bull, comes from the site of one of his major temples at Mauer an der Url (Austria), where several important cult finds were excavated (see Figure 3.3). The inscription on the pedestal states that it was dedicated to 'I(ove) O(ptimus) M(aximus) D(olichenus) by the (army) veteran Mar<r>ius Ursinus', in fulfilment of a vow. The god wears typical Roman legionary officer's clothing and equipment: the moulded breastplate, slashed leather skirt, tunic, military cloak and eagle-headed sword. As with Jupiter, his attributes included the thunderbolt (held in his left hand), an important part of the synchronization of this god with the Roman deity, as well as a double-headed axe (in his right hand: damaged in this dedication), which was quite unknown for Jupiter and was of Near-Eastern origin. He is of solid build and wears the so-called Phrygian cap, which in Roman short-hand terminology stood for 'eastern' or 'non-Roman'. He is standing on a bull in this dedication, as he frequently is in the cult's iconography. Redolent of power and strength, the bull itself is worthy of the god. There is a decorative band around his waist, indicating that he has been prepared for sacrifice to the god. This is a particularly fine piece of work and will have been an expensive dedication, and perhaps also commemorates the sacrifice of this bull to the god.

Figure 3.3: A bronze statuette of Jupiter Dolichenus from his temple at Mauer an der Url, dedicated by a veteran soldier in fulfilment of a vow. First half of the third century AD; height: 32cm. (*Courtesy of Kunsthistorisches Museum Wien, Antikensammlung, Inventory M1*)

Triangular bronze plaques were a major feature of his cultic paraphernalia, and were designed with cylindrical grommets to attach them to poles. These generally had four (but sometimes fewer) registers, and most have been excavated from temples in military areas.[15] There is often an eagle (another attribute of Jupiter's) in the upper register. An example from Mauer an der Url, dating to the first half of the third century AD, is 54cm high with four registers, and includes a depiction of Juno Regina, also standing on a bull, holding a double-headed axe and lightning bolt, hence mirroring her consort. This example also includes, in the lower register, two military standards with the usual decorations, one standard each flanking Jupiter Dolichenus and Juno Regina.[16] Between the deities on their bulls hovers the winged goddess Victoria standing on a globe, extending a wreath to Jupiter Dolichenus; Sol, Luna and the Dioscuri (Castor and Pollux) also appear on these plaques with the god. An inscription on the base of the plaque indicates that it was dedicated by the decurion (a cavalry officer in charge of ten men), Postumius Celer.

Jupiter Dolichenus' cult was found mainly on the western borders of the Empire where there were concentrations of military personnel, especially along the Danube and Rhine rivers, and in Britain; there were two temples in Rome (on the Aventine Hill and Esquiline Hill),[17] and he had a major shrine at Dura-Europos.[18] Modern scholars refer to these temples as *Dolichena* (singular, *Dolichenum*), but the cult followers simply used the word *templum* (plural, *templa*). Temples of the cult are found, for example, at the military sites of Brigetio (modern Szony in Hungary), Carnuntum (Austria), Mauer an der Url (Austria), Saalburg (Germany), Vetoniana (Germany), Vetus Salina (Hungary), Vindolanda (Britain) and Virunum (Austria). The Roman camp at Vindolanda was almost at the furthest extent of the Empire from Commagene.[19] Most of these temples were modest in size, and the seating areas within, as excavated, catered for small numbers of devotees, as with the Mithraea. Part of the cult's attraction was no doubt that of belonging to a select group: for example, the seating reconstruction for the Dolichenum at Brigetio suggests twelve worshippers.[20]

The (probably) first epigraphic attestation of Jupiter Dolichenus in the Empire in a specific cult context is from the city of Carnuntum (which began as a military camp) on the Danube, the capital of Pannonia Superior, from the reign of Hadrian, and the current temple (or its predecessor) may well date from this period;[21] a legion was stationed there. From his temple here, too, come several outstanding representations of the god, in stone and metal, which are housed in the Carnuntum Museum (Austria). While there were a number of non-military worshippers, it is the military who are the most conspicuous in terms of dedications. Many altars were dedicated by army officers to this god, with a number of these known from Britain. One of these was dedicated to Iove Optimus Maximus Dolichenus (here Dolichenus shares Jove's, that is Jupiter's, stock epithets, in payment of a vow). As usual, what the vow specifically requested is unspecified:[22]

> 'To Jupiter Dolichenus, Best and Greatest, for the safety [*salus*] of the detachments of Legion I Victrix, and of the army of both Germanies under the charge of Marcus Lollius Venator, centurion of Legion II Augusta. They paid their vow willingly and deservedly.'

After the end of the Severan dynasty, Maximinus Thrax as emperor in the West (AD 235–238) pillaged temples for financial reasons.[23] Many shrines to Jupiter Dolichenus were destroyed at this time, judging from the archaeological evidence, and the cult declined significantly. Twelve of the god's temples were destroyed in the provinces of Germania Superior, Moesia Superior, Noricum, Pannonia (both Upper and Lower) and Raetia. Caches of cult material have been found buried at these sites, presumably where worshippers deposited them to avoid their being looted.[24] For example, the hoard of eighty-eight cult objects (including Figure 3.3) from Mauer an der Url dates to the time of the sanctuary's destruction.[25] Archaeological evidence is conclusive that these cult centres were destroyed in about AD 235. These were in the provinces over which Maximinus Thrax had authority, and the temple contents fell victim to his financial needs. In addition, in AD 253, the Persian King Shapur I destroyed the home temple of Jupiter Dolichenus, at Doliche in Commagene, which must have been a major blow to his worshippers in the Roman Army. The cult had been decidedly popular with soldiers in the second century, being particularly prominent under the Severan dynasty.[26] Closely assimilated with Jupiter, who was also a military deity, the appeal of Jupiter as Dolichenus will have been his blatantly military characteristics, as he is always shown in military dress with his weapons, ready to come to the aid of his worshippers.

The Religion of the Military Camp

An inscription on an altar discovered at Auchendavy fort in southern Scotland reads:[27]

'To Mars, Minerva, the Goddesses of the Campestres, Hercules, Epona, and Victory, Marcus Cocceius Firmus, centurion of Legion II Augusta.'

This is not the only altar set up by the centurion M. Cocceius Firmus, of Legion II Augusta. There are several points of interest: firstly, the deity Epona, who was an indigenous Celtic goddess of horses, and who became popular with the cavalry serving in the Roman Army (as in this example).[28] Mars, Minerva, Hercules and Victory were all associated with military activity, while the Campestres, the deities of 'the parade ground', had a more specialized function. Numerous inscriptions – some 32[29] – in Roman Britain attest to their significance and importance for the Roman Army there. These Campestres were venerated by cavalry units: in AD 238, for example, a unit of Spanish cavalry at Condercum (Benwell) set up an inscription recording that they had restored a temple to the Campestres and to the *genius* of the First Cavalry Regiment of Asturian Spaniards, from the foundations up.[30]

Campestres, goddesses of the cavalry parade ground, were worshipped elsewhere in the Western empire, with inscriptions both of dedications and vows; several examples other than those from Britain are known.[31] This is a substantial epigraphic record. These deities probably originated with the Celtic (Gallic) cavalry units serving in the Empire, but took a Latin name.[32] Campestres are sometimes associated in dedications with the Matres, a triad of goddesses from Germany, venerated by the equites singulares (mounted imperial bodyguard), who were recruited largely from the Rhine.[33]

The Imperial Cult of the Legionary Eagles and Standards

Vegetius, writing in the fourth century AD, viewed the Roman soldiers' celebration of festivals, religious rites and military parades as key factors in strengthening discipline.[34] There was even a cult of '*Discipulina*' (Discipline), who received veneration from soldiers.[35] An altar at Chesters (Cilurnum) in Britain provides the earliest epigraphic reference to this, being dedicated to 'The Discipulina of the Emperor Hadrian Augustus, [dedicated by] the Cavalry Regiment called Augusta'.[36] Such altars could also be dedicated to the *Discipulina* of two emperors reigning jointly (their *Discipulinae*). Two such altars were found beneath the *aedes principiorum* (for which see below) of a military camp.[37]

Each legion possessed one eagle (the *aquila*) as its standard (*signum*). This was life-size, originally of silver and then gold, shown resting on Jupiter's thunderbolts, held aloft on a long spear (see Figures 3.2, 3.6), and this was carried into battle and in ceremonies by an individual known as an aquilifer ('eagle-bearer'; see Figure 6.8).[38] Eagles were Jupiter's emissaries, which he sent to convey messages via omens (see below), and symbolized the god himself: the legion took Jupiter before it into battle when it carried the eagle. Vegetius indicates that the eagle preceded the first cohort of the legion, and was the symbol par excellence of the legion. A legion also went into battle with an imaginifer carrying the images (*imagines*) of the emperors on a standard known as a *signum* (Vegetius states that the eagle was the chief *signum*).[39] A legion's birthday, commemorating the day on which it was formed, was the *natalis (dies) aquilae* – the birthday of the eagle – and was celebrated as a festival. Moreover, the cult of the legionary eagles as a whole was celebrated from 19–23 March, when festivities were held in their honour. Josephus, the Jewish author who wrote about the Roman sack of Jerusalem, observed that as the Romans under Vespasian's command marched into Galilee, the eagle went before each legion, for the Romans considered it to symbolize dominion, a sign that they would be victorious over all those against whom they marched.[40]

In 210 BC, the soldiers and sailors of P. Cornelius Scipio (Africanus) were said by Livy to have been so willing to perjure themselves that they were prepared to swear falsely by the *signa*, by the eagles and by their military oath. Clearly, these should have been inviolable, and Livy writing under Augustus obviously thought that his contemporary readers would agree.[41] Tacitus could write of the *numina* ('spirits') of the legionary eagles,[42] and in relating one historical incident refers to the standards and legionary eagle being housed together in a legionary headquarters.[43] Dionysius of Halicarnassus could in fact compare the eagle standards to divine statues.[44]

Each of the cohorts (and possibly each century) of an imperial legion had its own *signum*, carried on a spear, with each *signum* carried by a signifer. This spear was decorated with a wreath at the top, within which was often a hand (palm outwards), or the hand might simply be on top of the lance, not encircled by a wreath; there were several circular ornaments down the length of the spear, with tasselling underneath these towards the end.[45]

Another standard, the *vexillum* (plural, *vexilla*), a banner of square cloth also held on a long spear, attached by a short horizontal pole, was carried by a vexillarius.[46] It is unclear which units within a legion had a *vexillum*: possibly the centuries or the cohorts. Auxiliary units also possessed standards: the foot soldiers a *signum* and the cavalry a *vexillum*. The legionary eagle and standards appear several times on Trajan's Column, in particular when the Roman army crosses over the Danube on the platoon bridge (see Figure 3.6), and as Trajan receives a Dacian embassy (see Figure 3.2), while to the left of that two *signa* are visible (see Figure 3.2). One scene on the column shows soldiers with two standards and a *vexillum* (see Figure 5.1); and a *vexillum* is depicted being carried by the goddess Victory on a coin of Augustus (see Figure 1.2), and on the Bridgeness Slab (see Figure 3.4).[47] To carry the eagle, to be an aquilifer, was an honour, and the funerary monument of the aquilifer Gnaeus Musius as erected by his brother ensured that he was commemorated in this role (see Figure 6.8).

Not only was the eagle in the imperial period especially venerated by its legion, but so too were the *signa* of the cohorts of the legions:[48] Tertullian criticized Roman army camp religion as consisting entirely of worship of the *signa*. In this, he is subsuming the *aquilae* under the category of *signa* (as does Vegetius). He argues that the Romans set the standards of the legion above the very gods themselves, even Jupiter. He mocked the pagans by noting that the *vexilla* and *signa* were in fact in the shape of the (Christian) cross (because the spear bar holding the parts of the *signa* formed a cross: a long cross with a short bar).[49] In the Christianized army, the *signum* was surmounted by the chi-rho symbol, and the chi-rho appeared on the *vexillum* (see Figures 9.2-9.4).

Signa were housed in a special room in the building which served as the headquarters of an army camp; this room is sometimes termed by historians as the *sacellum* (sanctuary), but it could be referred to as the Capitolium, as in an inscription at Aalen, and often as the *aedes principiorum* (the shrine of the standards at headquarters), in the vicinity of which, in Roman Britain, altars have been excavated.[50] Catiline, in keeping a legionary eagle in his own home, placed it in a room which Cicero refers to as a *sacrarium* (a place where sacred objects are housed).[51] On the Bridgeness Slab (see Figure 3.4), the *suovetaurilia* of Legion II Augusta takes place before a small shrine, and depicts a *signum* within: this is the shrine within which the *signum* was housed.

One of the 'distance' slabs from the Antonine Wall in Britain (giving the length of the wall as completed by a particular legion), from Hutcheson Hill, depicts in its middle register an eagle standard held by an aquilifer who leans forward slightly, bent at the hips, looking downward and averting his gaze from a draped standing female figure who has in her left hand a patera (shallow bowl), tilted downwards (denoting that she has just poured a libation from it), while she has her right arm raised and her fingers level with the beak of the eagle on the standard. She is perhaps the goddess Britannia, in this way congratulating Legion XX for its role in conquering the area. Her fingers hold a small circular object – apparently a miniature wreath – up to the beak of the bird, a legionary eagle. Each of the two registers, left and right, depict a naked, bound captive who looks towards the central scene.[52]

In 53 BC, Crassus the triumvir suffered a crushing defeat at the hands of the Parthians at Carrhae in Mesopotamia, losing his own life, thousands of soldiers and several legionary eagles. This spectacular disaster had been foretold by several omens, one of which was that the first eagle to be raised as the army set out turned around of its own volition, and that when the sacrifice for the purification (*lustratio*) of the army was being made, Crassus dropped the entrails of the sacrificial victim when the diviner handed them to him.[53] There was an earlier 'precedent' for this, the disastrous battle for the Romans when Hannibal trounced them at Cannae in 216 BC, which was also portended by several omens, including the signifer of the first hastati formation (as the Roman Army was then organized) being unable to remove the *signum* from the ground, despite several soldiers coming to his assistance.[54] No such ill-omens from *aquilae* and *signa* are, perhaps surprisingly, recorded to have preceded the disaster in the Teutoburg Forest (AD 9) at the forest itself – but Augustus at Rome felt that there had been several omens of disaster when he looked back on events shortly afterwards (see below). Nearly 300 years later, entrails could still be ominous: when Diocletian sacrificed continuously for good omens at Antioch in AD 299, he failed to achieve these; his diviners blamed the Christians who were present, who had made the sign of the cross. According to Lactantius and Arnobius, this was one of the reasons why Diocletian was persuaded by Galerius to persecute the Christians.[55]

In addition to the eagles being *numina*, according to Tacitus, and worshipped according to Tertullian, cults of the *genii* (singular, *genius*) of various aspects of the Roman military establishment were prominent in the imperial period. '*Genius*' refers to the embodiment of some object, place or person. A living emperor was not worshipped, but his *genius* was venerated, especially in the Roman Army. Moreover, from the legion down, nearly every unit of the Roman Army had a *genius* which received worship. The first known dedication by an army unit to their *genius* is that by Legion XI in Germany. There are numerous known dedications to the *genius* of a century by members of such a unit, as well as (though fewer) to the *genius* of a legion.[56] A temple to the Campestres and the '*Genius* of the First Cavalry Regiment of Asturian Spaniards' has been noted above.[57] Such cultic activities, particularly at the level of the century, served no doubt to unite its members, creating an *esprit de corps*, in the same way as did any sacrificial practices undertaken by soldiers as a group.

The Bridgeness Slab: Sacrifice by Legion II Augusta

Eighteen distance slabs survive from the length of the Antonine Wall in Britain, placed on the southern side; these record the length of the wall completed by a particular legion or part thereof.[58] Legion II Augusta commemorated their work in building 4,652 paces of this wall by commissioning and erecting a sandstone slab in AD 142–143 (Figure 3.4): it is called the Bridgeness Slab after its find-spot (Bridgeness, West Lothian, in 1868).[59] Despite Roman themes, it was nevertheless executed by a Celtic artist. On the left, a cavalryman holds his spear aloft in battle, while underneath him, to the left, a Celtic warrior is prostrate under his shield while trampled by the horse. Next to him, a warrior has been impaled by a spear in his back, while on the right, a soldier is overcome by psychological terror and cowers, his left hand in his mouth, biting his fingers, with the sword he has thrown down below him. A fourth figure, in the middle of the horizon of the scene, has been decapitated, with his head to the right. In the middle of the slab is the inscription:

> 'For the Emperor, Caesar Titus Aelius Hadrianus Antoninus Augustus Pius, Father of his Country, Legion II Augusta completed [the wall] for a length of 4,652 paces.'

The Gods on Campaign in the Roman Empire 55

Figure 3.4: The Bridgeness Slab, commemorating Legion II Augusta's building of a section of the Antonine Wall; AD 142–143; width 2.743 metres; height 0.864 metres. National Museum Scotland (Hunterian Collection) X.FV 27. (Courtesy of Alamy)

On the far right, a religious rite, a *suovetaurilia*, is taking place, almost certainly to mark the completion of the construction by the soldiers.[60] A *suovetaurilia* was the sacrifice of three male domestic animals; these could be a piglet, lamb and calf, which was known as the *suovetaurilia minora* (or *suovetaurilia lactentia*; from *lac*, milk), but in military contexts three adult male victims – a boar, sheep and bull – were sacrificed: the *suovetaurilia maiora*. This was often performed as a *lustrum*, a purification, of the Roman Army.[61] Cato the Elder describes a *suovetaurilia* in a non-military context as a purification involving leading the three victims around the border of a farm and invoking Mars, as well as Janus and Jupiter, and then conducting the sacrifice.[62] Examples of the ritual are found on Trajan's Column (see below).

In this scene on the Bridgeness Slab, the figure at the altar with a shallow bowl (patera) from which he has just poured a libation of wine onto a tall, narrow (typically Roman) altar, and behind whom the legionary flag, the *vexillum* (clearly marked 'Leg[io] II Aug[usta])', is displayed, is the commander of this legion. His officers cluster around him. Crouched at the altar is the *victimarius*, who is responsible for dispatching the three sacrificial victims to the gods. A double-flute player is present, playing with cheeks distended. Bracketing the scene is a very small shrine, an *aedes* or *aedicula*.

Other distance slabs, but not all, from the Antonine Wall have a religious theme. For example, a slab of Legion VI has its inscription panel held aloft by two winged Victory figures, who stand on globes (marking Roman dominion over the world).[63] On their left stands Mars as god of war (presumably Mars Victor or Mars Ultor), and on their right a female figure, Virtus Augusta, who in her left hand holds a sheathed sword and in her right hand the legion's *vexillum* which identifies her, reading as it does '*Virtus Augusta*' ('Augustan virtus'; manliness or courage). Another slab of interest shows a semi-recumbent, winged goddess Victory, her left arm resting on a globe of the world, holding in the crook of her arm a large palm tree, the ancient symbol of victory.[64] Her pose here is typical of that for river gods in Greco-Roman art, as the site is near to the River Clyde; moreover, waves are lapping around her knees. With the conquest of this area of Scotland complete, Victory is resting from her labours.

Many other gods were worshipped by soldiers. Not all of these of course would have been for military reasons. Yet the predominance of inscriptions set up by soldiers or their military units relates to military deities and invokes their assistance. Through public display of their piety by means of inscribed altars and dedications, soldiers called the gods' attention to their piety and to their needs. There was a very real sense of genuine piety and trust in the gods – both those mandated by the state as requiring worship and other more personal deities.

Omens of victory and defeat sent by the gods

For the Roman Republic, Livy provides a wealth of omens which accompanied Roman military activity, as well as a number experienced by the Romans in non-military contexts. For example, prior to the catastrophic military defeat at Cannae by Hannibal, the gods gave several signs to the Romans of their impending defeat. Unfortunately, Julius Obsequens did not continue his *Liber de prodigiis* (*Book of Prodigies*) into the imperial period: he was the fourth-century AD epitomator of the prodigies recorded in Livy for 249–11 BC. For the imperial period, there is no continuous narrative such as Livy's or a record such as Obsequens' compilation.[65] But Tacitus for the first and second centuries AD provides evidence that, in the early imperial period, the connection in Roman religious thought between warfare and divination was still in place. For example, he reports that three bad omens attended Paetus' campaign against the Parthians which ended in disaster in the reign of Nero. Yet Paetus, much like Clodius Pulcher who threw the sacred chickens overboard when they failed to give a favourable omen, did not heed the signs sent by the gods: Tacitus specifically notes that Paetus rejected them.[66] Suetonius, too, in about the same period, was extremely interested in recording omens in military contexts (see below), and reports an omen in which Tiberius trusted when on campaign – one which had always reassured his forebears as well: if, on the night before battle, the lamp he was working by went out without any reason, this was a propitious sign for the coming battle.[67]

Germanicus and Victory Omens

When in AD 15 Germanicus, Augustus' grandson and Tiberius' adopted heir, led an attack against the Germans – in particular the Cherusci tribe – Tacitus records without any incredulity the omens which occurred. Germanicus had a dream before the battle that his toga was bespattered with the blood of a sacrificial victim, at which his grandmother Augusta (Livia) handed him a clean toga to replace it. He was encouraged by this omen, as well as by favourable auspices. These auspices would have come from an actual sacrifice which he performed prior to battle, which was propitious. When examined by the professional soothsayers – haruspices – who travelled with the army – the entrails of the victim were favourable. Tacitus follows this with a rousing speech from Germanicus, in which he pointed out to his troops how they could in fact defeat the Germans.[68]

As they engaged the enemy, Tacitus reports that a 'most splendid omen' (*pulcherrimum augurium*) was seen by Germanicus: eight eagles flew in front of the Roman army towards and into the nearby woods, where the Germans awaited. He duly shouted encouragement to his soldiers that they should advance into battle and 'follow the Roman birds', the true *numina* ('spirits') of the legions (*propria legionum numina*).[69] Of no concern to the modern historian is the veracity or otherwise of the incident: what matters is that the Romans believed that the gods could send a sign, an *augurium* (an augury), to encourage them before battle, and that this sign portended success. These eagles, the *numina* of the legions as Germanicus terms them, were interpreted as having been sent by Jupiter, for they were his particular messenger. Success in fact followed this god's support, with the Germans thoroughly routed and their dead strewn across a 10-mile area. The Roman soldiers constructed a mound and piled up the captured arms as if erecting a victory trophy (*tropaeum*). A dream, the auspices of the sacrifice and the augury of the eagles had all vouchsafed the support of the gods, especially that of Jupiter.[70]

After the disaster in the Teutoburg Forest in AD 9 when Varus lost his life, as well as the three legions' eagles, with thousands of soldiers slain in battle, Dio notes that Augustus recollected what he realized had been a series of bad omens both before and after the battle. As Dio lists them, they comprise a compendium of the unpropitious, including lightning striking the temple of Mars (Ultor) in Rome, comets and a statue of Victory which faced towards the enemy in the province of Germania turning and facing Italy.[71] Suetonius notes that in the aftermath of the disaster, Augustus vowed 'great games' to Jove (Jupiter) Optimus Maximus for an improvement in the state of the Republic, as had been done, Suetonius notes, during the Cimbric and Marsic wars. As in the past, the vow was quite conditional: when the state recovered, Jupiter would be honoured and thanked with the games. Augustus followed, as in many instances in his reign, an historical religious precedent.[72]

Dreams such as Germanicus' were not unusual, with the most famous martial dream in the Republic being that of Sulla in 88 BC, in which he dreamt of Luna Lucifera (light-bearer) or the Cappadocian war goddess Ma-Bellona handing him a thunderbolt with which to smite his enemies.[73] In AD 15, Aulus Caecina, the legate of Lower Germania, on the eve of battle against the Germans, dreamt according to Tacitus of Publius Quinctilius Varus, who had recently lost three legions and their eagles – as well as the accompanying auxiliary force – in the Teutoburg forest disaster. In an 'ominous dream' (*dira quies*), Varus appeared to him covered in blood, rising out of the swamps, calling to him. As Varus' hand stretched out to him, Caecina thrust it away. This presaged a good ending: while the campaign started badly for the Romans, they were victorious, and the dream had predicted the outcome.[74]

Omens in the Year of the Four Emperors (AD 69)

There were several bird omens in connection with the battles fought amongst the contenders for the throne in the 'Year of the Four Emperors', AD 69. Moreover, there were numerous omens and prophecies related to the four claimants to the principate: Galba, Otho, Vitellius and Vespasian, with the last, as the successful contender, attracting positive omens, while the others experienced unpropitious signs in their attempts at power (except initially for Galba). Tacitus describes AD 69 – with its four claimants to the throne, numerous battles and the loss of tens of thousands of lives, including 50,000 when Rome fell to Vespasian's forces – as preceded by several omens of forthcoming disaster, and numerous prodigies (*prodigia*) were recorded, including Caesar's statue in the forum turning east (towards Vespasian).[75]

Galba succeeded Nero as the first of the four emperors in mid-AD 68. He was encouraged by several portents, collected by Suetonius, which Galba must have circulated amongst his troops and followers. A young girl of 'honest background' prophesied that there would one day be a Roman emperor from Spain (Galba was governor in that province). This prediction was confirmed by the priest of Jupiter at Clunia, who, following instructions in a dream, found the girl's very prediction recorded in the inner shrine of the temple – and it too had been spoken by a girl, some 200 years earlier. The combination of prophecy, dream and antique context was a formidable combination. To this was added the discovery of what could be termed a sacred relic: while a town was being fortified as Galba's headquarters, an ancient ring was uncovered, with a precious stone engraved with a Victory goddess and a trophy of arms (see below for a discussion of the Roman *tropaeum*). Even further, a ship full of weapons arrived in Spain from Alexandria – with no captain, sailor or passenger aboard. This last removed 'all doubt in anyone's mind that the war was just and pious, to be undertaken with the gods' approval'. All of these omens came true and Galba became emperor: but only from June 68 to January 69, when he was assassinated by Otho's soldiers.[76]

After Otho murdered and succeeded Galba, he was challenged by Vitellius. Prior to the battle between their forces at Bedriacum (in northern Italy) in April AD 69, Vitellius divided his forces into two, one led by Fabius Valens, which was to proceed against Otho, and another by himself. An eagle went before Valens' forces, flying just before the army on its journey, and was of course seen, as Tacitus notes, as 'no doubtful omen of great and successful achievements', which indeed it was, with Valens defeating Otho's forces at Bedriacum.[77] Otho committed suicide after the battle, his death also presaged by a bird omen, although Tacitus seems apologetic about reporting it:[78]

> 'While, however, I must consider that it is far from the seriousness of the work which I am writing to collect here fabulous accounts, to entertain my readers with fiction, I must not, however, malign the veracity of the reports [of the omens] which have been circulated.'

Galba appeared in a dream to Otho, his murderer, which so frightened him that he fell violently out of bed. On the next day, while Otho was taking the auspices a great storm arose, which was taken as a bad omen. Later, Otho fell over while sacrificing, presaging that he had undertaken a task he could not fulfill.[79]

Suetonius also notes the propitious omen of an eagle sent to Valens (Vitellius' general), but not to the force led by Vitellius. Moreover, Suetonius records, equestrian statues of Vitellius as emperor which were being erected all collapsed with broken legs, the laurel crown he was wearing as emperor fell into a stream, and, at Vienna, sitting on a judiciary tribunal, a rooster perched on his shoulders and then his head. Suetonius notes that 'the outcome corresponded with these omens'. He does not need to indicate to his readers what the omens meant: the imperial statues collapsing heralded the collapse of Vitellius' power, while his imperial wreath falling off meant the loss of the imperial status it represented. The omen of the rooster had an interesting fulfilment and had to be explained: Vitellius was killed at Rome, when Vespasian and his soldiers conquered the city, by one Antonius Primus, who 'when he was young, had the surname Becco, which means, "the beak of a rooster"'.[80]

Suetonius, in his life of Vespasian, adds another bird omen, that two eagles fought on the battlefield at Bedriacum in April AD 69 before the forces clashed. One defeated the other, but then a third eagle flew in from the east (or as Suetonius puts it, from the direction of the rising sun), signifying that while the eagle Vitellius had defeated the eagle Otho, the forces of the eagle Vespasian, from the east, were going to win against Vitellius' forces in a second battle at Bedriacum (neither Vespasian nor Vitellius were present at this second engagement there, which took place in October).[81]

Many centuries later, Dio Cassius reported other omens preceding Vitellius' death in the battle in the city of Rome in AD 69. However, these might be ones invented since Suetonius wrote his biography, or Suetonius might have chosen only a few examples out of a larger number of omens which were reputed to have occurred. 'Baleful omens', Dio commences, took place: a comet was sighted, the moon appeared to have two eclipses – on the fourth and then the seventh day of the month – and two suns were seen simultaneously, the one in the west being pale (i.e., Vitellius), and that in the east strong and iridescent (i.e., Vespasian). On the Capitol in Rome, many large footprints were seen, as if spirits (*daimones*) had descended from the hill. The soldiers on duty at the temple of Jupiter that night said that the temple doors had crashed open, without human agency, with a great noise, and some of the guards had fainted with terror.[82] When Vespasian's troops were in the city and Vitellius knew he was defeated, he recollected that at a sacrifice over which he had presided, vultures had swept upon his sacrificial offerings, scattering them and almost knocking him over as he addressed his troops.[83]

Vespasian's Omens Predicting his Ascent to the Imperial Estate

Vespasian (AD 69–79), ultimately the successful claimant to the throne in AD 69, established the relatively short-lived Flavian dynasty to which his sons Titus (AD 79–81) and Domitian (AD 81–96) succeeded. Just as Otho and Vitellius met their ends as predicted by omens, Vespasian also received prophetic intimations – except his were favourable, and for these Tacitus is the main source. When Vespasian was contemplating seizing power, one of his supporters, Mucianus, encouraged him in a speech which the historian reports. After this, others with him remembered prophecies spoken by seers, as well as relevant movements of the stars, while Tacitus remarks that Vespasian now recollected omens from his own past and recalled one concerning a cypress tree on his estate when he was a young man: the tree had fallen over, but on the next day was upright again and fully rejuvenated. The haruspices interpreted this as signifying that he would reach the highest of positions.[84]

A similar omen of an overthrown and rejuvenated tree had occurred, Pliny remarks, in the wars against the Cimbri and at the Battle of Philippi (42 BC, when Antony and Octavian defeated Brutus and Cassius). He also reports a tree at Cumae that sank into the ground prior to the civil war between Pompey and Caesar, with only a few branches left still above ground. The Sibylline Books were consulted, and the oracle was that great loss of life would occur, and the closer to Rome, the greater the loss.[85]

After Mucianus' speech, Vespasian went to the sanctuary of the aniconic god Carmelus in Judaea, where he sacrificed. The officiating priest, Vespasian's freedman Basilides (see below), examined the sacrificial entrails several times and informed Vespasian that in whatever he attempted he would succeed. This oracle, in particular, was one which Vespasian's supporters discussed in his presence – 'nothing indeed was more often on men's lips'.[86] Interestingly, Tacitus notes that 'as for the hidden decrees of fate, the omens and the oracles that singled Vespasian and his sons out for imperial power, we only believed in them after his successes'.[87]

Suetonius, too, records several omens signifying that Vespasian would defeat Vitellius and become emperor. As Vespasian was a successful *princeps*, and deified on his death, the divinatory narrative is quite extensive. These omens, of course, were not simply to demonstrate that events had been preordained by the gods, but were a means to legitimize the imperial power which had been placed in his hands: the gods had brought the prophecies to fruition, indicating their approval of his victory over Vitellius, and his assumption of the imperial toga. Suetonius' veritable catalogue of omens and predictions were divine validations of Vespasian: a statue of the deified Julius Caesar in the Roman forum turned to the east, while others involved mud in Vespasian's toga, a severed human hand brought to him by a stray dog, a runaway plough ox, a cypress tree (as in Tacitus), a tooth, and a prophecy from the god Carmelus. Josephus (the historian), when he was put in chains by the Romans under Vespasian in Judaea, said he would be released by Vespasian when the latter became emperor; and a prophetic dream was sent to Nero. Last in this compendium of Vespasianic imperial omens, Vespasian went alone to consult Serapis in his temple in Alexandria to inquire how long his rule would last if he seized imperial power. There he had a vision of his freedman Basilides – even though he had gone into the temple alone and Basilides was so crippled with rheumatism that he could not walk. The name Basilides comes from the Greek word for king, *basileus*, and clearly Suetonius intends his audience to realize that this had been an omen. In his account, Tacitus specifically states that Vespasian recognized that the vision of Basilides was an omen because of the fortuitous circumstance of his name, and because Basilides at the time was some 80 miles away.[88] Basilides, therefore, was a key player in providing divinatory, and hence divine, support to Vespasian's claim to the imperial purple.[89]

Tacitus also describes the prodigies (*prodigia*) which attended the fall of Jerusalem to Titus in AD 70: these were meant to indicate after the event that the city was preordained by the gods to be destroyed. Tacitus observed that the Jewish people, imbued with an 'obnoxious superstition', did not undertake sacrifices and vows (as Romans would) to expatiate the omens of their destruction: heavenly hosts battling in the skies with gleaming armour, the Temple irradiated by light from the clouds, and the doors of its inner shrine suddenly opening of their own accord, with a non-mortal voice crying out that the gods (plural) were leaving the Temple (clearly a Roman invented this omen), with a noise as if of departure. Next he relates a prophecy in the ancient writings of the Jewish priests that at this time the East would become powerful, and rulers coming from Judaea would gain universal empire: these prophecies, continues Tacitus, applied to Vespasian and Titus.[90]

Omens, prodigies and any sort of unusual phenomena were signs from the gods, to be heeded and respected. They particularly occurred in times of military conflict, crisis and disaster. Omens conveyed by eagles were sent by Jupiter; others were not usually ascribed to any divine agent but viewed as being sent by 'the gods' generically. Vespasian's assumption of the imperial throne was given added legitimacy by the various signs which occurred in AD 69. Throughout imperial history, omens continued to play a role, generally recollected or invented after the event, in indicating the gods' interest in the outcome of conflict and their support for the Romans, or in the civil wars of AD 69, their preferred imperial candidate.

The Sacred Topography of Roman Imperial Warfare

In the Republic, numerous temples had been vowed on the battlefield by Roman generals requesting divine aid, but temple construction in return for divine assistance was not a marked feature of the imperial period. That fewer were dedicated was probably due to the fact that many of the gods already had temples due to the Senate and the religious devotion of successful generals. Moreover, it was now the emperor alone who dedicated temples, rather than military commanders, and perhaps the most notable temple constructed was that by Augustus for Mars Ultor. In the imperial period, the doors of the temple of Janus were rarely closed (closure signifying that the Empire was conducting no wars), but Augustus boasted that this had occurred three times during his principate, and Nero later considered that a closure during his own reign was worth commemorating on coins. Trajan's monumental stone column in Rome, as well as its imitation by Marcus Aurelius, bears witness to the belief that the gods intervened directly in battles when circumstances required, and gods are depicted in their columnar reliefs. A marked feature of the imperial period was the erection of stone arches, not only in Rome but throughout the Empire, to commemorate military triumphs, and many of these reflect the divine assistance which victorious emperors believed they had received from the gods in battle. Art and architecture depict many *tropaea* of arms and armour taken from the enemy. The term *tropaea* also became attached to large permanent monumental structures, such as those of Augustus and Trajan which celebrated victories over Rome's enemies.

The Gods Sanction the Declaration of War by the Roman State

In 32 BC, Octavian carried out the fetial rite, the *ius fetiale*, which the Romans employed in declaring war against their enemies: in his case, against Cleopatra (as a foreign power, being Queen of Egypt). Dio is the authority for the ritual followed:

Octavian and others, dressed in their military cloaks, went to the temple of the war goddess Bellona in Rome, and Octavian in his capacity as a fetial priest (a *fetialis*, plural *fetiales*) performed the rites to declare war.[91] In his *Res Gestae*, Augustus lists being a fetial as amongst the various religious offices which he held (he was a member of all the priestly colleges). Dio does not describe the rites involved, although Book One of Livy does so in connection with Roman conflicts with the Latins, and various other sources mention the ritual, which may have been one of the traditions revived by Augustus after a considerable lapse of time.[92]

The priestly collegium (college) of the fetials at Rome had twenty members, of whom two were involved in any declaration of war: one called a *verbenarius* (whose role was limited to carrying certain herbs employed in the ritual) and the other the *pater patratus* (the 'ratifying father'), responsible for carrying out the main ritual actions. His role was to dip a spear with a shaft of cornel wood in blood (from a sacrifice), either with its wooden tip sharpened in a fire or with an iron tip, and to throw it into enemy territory. This indicated that war had been declared, but was also part of a process whereby the Romans ensured that the gods would know that the war was a just war (*iustum bellum*) and that they could therefore rely on divine assistance. The *pater patratus* called Jupiter to witness that Rome had been wronged, and then in making the declaration of war called upon Jupiter, Janus Quirinus (Janus of the Roman People) and the celestial deities, and those of the earth and the underworld, to witness the act. In this way, the Romans ensured that they called upon their gods to witness that they had acted appropriately and justly.

When Rome's wars extended beyond Latium and into territory with which it did not have borders, as in the case of Cleopatra, the traditional practice was followed at the temple of Bellona of casting the spear into symbolic enemy territory, which action served as a declaration of war.[93] Ovid notes that a small pillar stood in the temple grounds from which the spear was thrown.[94] Marcus Aurelius, also according to Dio, performed the rite in AD 178 when going to war against the Scythians. Here he mentioned Aurelius hurling a bloody spear, kept in Bellona's temple, adding that he heard of this from men who were present at the time.[95]

This rite is not heard of again after AD 178. Although this does not mean it was not practised, the likelihood is that it was not, as Dio was clearly interested in reporting it on these two occasions as a historical curiosity. Octavian was interested in reviving old, lapsed rituals, which explains his action: moreover, he wanted to declare the war on Cleopatra (and so Antony) in the name of the Roman people, as in the formula for the declaration of war which Livy quotes,[96] to stress that this was not a civil war, but a war against a foreigner. As the declaration took place within the grounds of the temple of the goddess Bellona, the sacral nature of going to war was emphasized.

The *Spolia Opima*

A portion of the sale of the booty acquired in war (the *manubiae*) was dedicated to the gods, and this was often used by generals in the Republic to pay for the construction of the temples they had vowed. Yet the ultimate spoils of battle were the *spolia opima*, 'highest spoils', the armour and weaponry taken from an enemy commander killed in battle in single combat. While Livy, on the authority of a conversation with Octavian himself in 29 BC, indicated that it had to be a Roman commander with consular imperium (see below) who slew the enemy commander, the antiquarian Varro indicated that any Roman soldier who slew an enemy commander could dedicate the *spolia opima*: but this never eventuated.[97]

Jupiter Feretrius received the *spolia opima* in his temple on the Capitoline Hill.[98] Such a dedication was a great honour to the dedicant, as in Roman history there were only three cases of *spolia opima* dedicated to the god: Romulus, who defeated Acron of Caeci; A. Cornelius Cossus, who in 428 BC killed Lar Tolumnius, king of the Etruscan city of Veii (see below); and C. Claudius Marcellus, who in 225 BC killed Viridomarus, the king of the Insubrians. One of Marcellus' descendants minted coins depicting Marcellus carrying into the temple a *tropaeum* (see below) of Viridomarus' armour and weapons.[99] Propertius in his elegy on the temple devoted several lines to each of these three dedicants (also see below).[100] The issue of *spolia opima* occurs only twice more in the annals of Roman history. Dio reports that amongst the various honours voted to Caesar after returning from Spain in 45 BC was that of dedicating *spolia opima* in the temple of Jupiter Feretrius – even though he had not actually slain an enemy commander in the field of war.[101] Presumably this honour was to reflect his numerous military achievements and the commanders he had defeated (but not killed in battle). Battlefield encounters between Roman generals and their enemy counterpart were largely a thing of the past, but Caesar could be accorded this honour, which only three Romans – one of them his ancestor Romulus – had achieved.

One commander under Octavian in 29 BC did have a claim to be able to dedicate *spolia opima* to Jupiter Feretrius. Marcus Licinius Crassus, grandson of the Crassus who was Caesar's and Pompey's triumviral colleague (and who had lost the eagles to the Parthians), as proconsul of Macedonia killed in battle Deldo, king of the Bastarnae, a tribe from across the Danube. Dio notes that he would have dedicated the armour in Jupiter Feretrius' temple if he had been supreme commander.[102]

Dio is here clearly relying on Livy's history, which does not mention Crassus but provides an interesting account of the second commander who won the *spolia*. Livy indicates that he had previously written that A. Cornelius Cossus, who in 428 BC had killed the commander of the enemy, was a military tribune and had dedicated the *spolia opima*.[103] But Octavian informed Livy that he had himself seen in the temple of Jupiter, on the linen breastplate dedicated by Cossus, that he had in fact been consul (that is possessed consular imperium) when he killed his enemy. Livy therefore inserted this new information into his history, revising it upon Octavian's information. Clearly the contemporary situation is being referenced: Crassus was not allowed to dedicate the *spolia opima* because he had proconsular not consular imperium. Cossus had been a consul – Crassus was not. This might seem a quibble, but it was one that allowed Octavian, as he was in 29 BC, not to diminish his glory in having restored the temple,[104] in which only three dedications had taken place, all from much earlier in Roman history.[105]

Propertius wrote a forty-eight line elegy on the temple, probably about ten years' after Crassus missed out on the award, specifically referring to the three dedicants, and his elegy, intended for an imperial audience, reflected the Augustan reality that there were only three commanders who had earned the *spolia*: 'three sets of armour from three leaders'.[106] Nero Claudius Drusus, Tiberius' younger brother, aspired to achieve *spolia opima*, even going so far, Suetonius writes, as to pursue German commanders on the battlefield in an attempt to kill one and so have the distinction of dedicating their armour.[107] He did not succeed.[108] The rectangular temple itself was a small one (there was no need for much interior space), and the longest sides of the temple were a mere 15ft.[109] Augustus restored it, and ensured M. Licinius Crassus did not undermine his prestige for having done so. In the period of the Empire, no *spolia opima* were dedicated to Jupiter Feretrius.

Other Booty for the Gods

Rome's gods would always receive their share of any booty from war, especially particularly valuable items. It was the custom in the Republic that the general commanding a victorious army would undertake to make dedications to the gods: several of the temples in Rome had been built in the Republic by generals making use of the funds from the spoils of their campaign or campaigns. Augustus continued this pious tradition of thanking the gods for the victories of the Roman Senate and People. In his *Res Gestae*, he placed particular emphasis on the religious activities he had undertaken with the spoils from his wars: the temple of Mars Ultor (Mars the Avenger) and Augustus' forum were built from these. In addition, he writes:[110]

> 'From the spoils of war [*manubiae*], I consecrated gifts in the Capitoline temple, in the temple of the divine Julius, in the temple of Apollo, in the temple of Vesta, and in the temple of Mars Ultor, which cost me in the vicinity of some 100,000,000 sesterces.'

When Vespasian dedicated the Temple of Peace at Rome in AD 75 to celebrate the destruction of Jerusalem and the conquest of Judaea, he deposited there many of the spoils from the Temple in Jerusalem, including solid gold vessels and musical instruments, and also collected there artworks from around the known world.[111] Many of the spoils of war from Jerusalem depicted on Titus' arch – items such as the menorah, the sacred seven-branched lamp-holder from the Temple – were dedicated to this god, Peace, in thanksgiving for the conquest of the city and the Jewish people.

Aulus Gellius in the second century AD discusses the meaning of the term *manubiae*.[112] In a scene in his *Attic Nights*, his friend Favorinus, when walking through Trajan's forum, asked his companions what they thought the meaning was of the phrase '*ex manubiis*' ('from the *manubiae*'), prompted when Favorinus gazed at the roofs of the colonnades where there were gilded statues of horses and military standards (*signa*), underneath which was written '*ex manubiis*'.[113] He points out that the *manubiae* were not the actual spoils of war, but the financial proceeds from the sale of these spoils, and that Trajan's horses and military standards on his colonnades were paid for from this.

The *Ara Pacis Augustae*: Altar of Augustan Peace

Complementing Augustus' temple of Mars Ultor, the *Ara Pacis Augustae*, Augustus' 'Altar of Peace', stood on the Campus Martius (Field of Mars). This was voted by the Roman Senate on his return from Spain and Gaul on 4 July 13 BC, and was dedicated on 30 January 9 BC. By senatorial decree, each year the magistrates, priests and Vestal Virgins were to perform a sacrifice to Pax Augusta, 'Augustan Peace'.[114] The altar resides within a 6-metre-high engraved marble wall, forming a rectangle about 11 by 12 metres: the altar inside is reached by steps, but is too small for actual animal sacrifice, which must have taken place outside. Augustus and his family are shown in the well-known processional scene on the southern and northern walls, presumably processing to the altar complex.[115] Coins of Nero depict the altar, but after Augustus' reign there is no literary mention of it. Nero must have been advertising a connection with Augustus' altar (and that *princeps*) and periods of peace in their reigns, just as he advertised that he also was responsible for the closing of the doors of the temple of Janus.[116]

Augustus' Temple of Mars Ultor

Octavian had vowed to build a temple to Mars Ultor (Mars the Avenger) to avenge his father, Julius Caesar, before the battle at Philippi between the triumvirs and the senatorial forces in 42 BC.[117] Forty years later (2 BC), Mars received the fulfilment of this promise (see Figure 1.1). 'Ultor' in Octavian's vow refers to 'revenge' against his adopted father Caesar's assassins, who were defeated at Philippi; the temple was also to house the eagles recovered from the Parthians. Mars' temple was the main feature of Augustus' forum (*forum Augusti*), so much so that it was sometimes referred to as the forum of Mars (*forum Martis*). Even in its current ruined state, the temple is an impressive, imposing structure, signifying the importance of this god in Augustus' military and imperial ideology. As Augustus notes, it was built from the *manubiae* of his successful campaigns.[118]

With eight white marble Corinthian columns (hence the temple is referred to as octostyle) 18 metres in height on three sides, and raised – as was usual with most Roman temples – on a podium, the frontage measures some 20 metres. A bronze winged Victory stood on both front corners of the temple roof; within was a large statue of the god himself. Coins minted in Spain and Ephesus, depicting legionary eagles returned to Rome in 20 BC in a round temple (tholus) and inscribed 'Mars Ultor', apparently have no reference to an actual temple at Rome: the standards were dedicated in Augustus' temple in his forum when it was completed. Housing the recovered eagles was clearly a primary function of the temple.[119]

Augustus also states that in this year of the dedication he gave games for Mars (*ludi Martiales*) for the first time, and the Senate decreed that henceforth each year the consuls would organize these with Augustus. The consuls were involved, not only because they were Rome's chief magistrates, but because of their military responsibilities.[120] Mars' temple also became the focal point for various activities related to the military, as Dio describes.[121] Those making the transition from boyhood to enrolment amongst those of military age were to visit the temple frequently, while those setting out to their military commands were to depart Rome from the temple, presumably after worshipping in it and invoking Mars' assistance. (Suetonius notes that Augustus decided that the Senate was to meet in this temple when deliberating on whether to declare war.)[122] The Senate also met there to vote on whether a victorious general should be awarded a triumph. Once a general had celebrated his triumph (in the imperial age, only someone connected with the imperial family could do so), they were to dedicate to Mars the triumphal paraphernalia of sceptre and crown in the temple, and bronze statues of them were to be erected in Augustus' forum. Other sources indicate that Augustus set up here statues of all the generals throughout Roman history who had held triumphs (the *triumphatores*).[123]

Dio also reports that the cavalry commanders were to celebrate a festival (panegyris) annually in front of the steps. Furthermore, any military standards recovered from an enemy were to be housed in the temple. Dio's extensive summary of activities now to be associated with the temple through Augustus' initiative exponentially increased the prominence of Mars Ultor: it was very much an Augustan cult, and as such was emphasized by many of his successors, notably Trajan. Mars Ultor appears on the coins of those who rebelled against Nero in AD 68: Vindex in Gaul and Galba in Spain. The god is depicted naked, helmeted and advancing with shield and spear, both raised, with a sword at his side. Such a numismatic choice of this god by the two rebels seems unusual: it is hard to see how they were taking vengeance on Nero. Augustus' own relationship with Mars Ultor was, however, well-known, and these two were presumably seeking to make a connection with the founder of the principate.[124]

Trajan dedicated his column in his new forum on 12 May AD 113, mirroring Augustus' dedication of the temple of Mars Ultor on the same day about a century earlier: 12 May 2 BC.[125] In addition, it has been argued that the dedication of the column was to coincide with the beginning of Trajan's Parthian campaign for that year, AD 113.[126] Mars Ultor also appears on the coinage of the emperor Septimius Severus (reigned AD 193–211); in AD 193, Severus defeated several contenders for the throne after Pertinax's death. His coins date to the time of his campaigns against the Parthians, presumably explaining his invocation of Mars Ultor,[127] who appears on his coins in full battle dress, unlike the heroic but armed nude of the AD 68 issues. Alexander Severus also portrayed Mars Ultor, similarly fully armed and in the same pose as on one of Severus' coins, presumably in imitation of him.[128]

The Temple of Janus Closed under Nero

When the Roman state declared war in the Republic, the doors of the temple of Janus – Janus Geminus (Twin) or Janus Quirinus (of the Roman people) – would be opened, to be closed again when peace was secured. In the imperial period, the same held true. Janus was a double-headed deity, whose temple was located close to the Roman forum and as such in a conspicuous place near the heart of the city's political life. Ovid refers to Janus as 'hiding' in his temple during times of peace, with the temple doors closed, so that peace could not escape from it.[129] Varro, who describes many of Rome's rites and practices, states that the practice of opening the doors in times of war was instituted by Numa, Rome's second king (to whom the Romans ascribed the introduction of many religious practices);[130] while the ascription to Numa might well be legendary, the practice was clearly an ancient Roman tradition. Rome's wars were so extensive during the Republic that this temple's door were rarely closed from the third century BC on.

Augustus took due credit in his *Res Gestae* for closing the temple, specifically noting that it was an ancestral custom that the doors were shut when the Roman people had been victorious on land and sea throughout the Empire: that is, when all conflict had ended. He boasts that the temple before he became *princeps* had only been closed twice, but that while he was *princeps* the Senate had authorized the closure on three occasions, indicating Augustus' pursuit of peace throughout the Empire and on its borders. In Book One of Virgil's *Aeneid*, set many centuries prior to the first *princeps*, Jupiter issues a prophecy to Venus, Aeneas' mother, that Augustus (referred to obliquely, not by name) will close 'the gates of war' (that is, Janus' temple).[131] The first closure occurred as part of the celebration of the victory over Mark Antony and Cleopatra VII in 29 BC after the Battle of Actium (31 BC); the second in 25 BC at the conclusion of the war against the Cantabrians; the third occasion is unknown.

Nero's coinage takes up this theme in connection with the peace made in his reign with the Parthians, and the closing of the temple doors in AD 65. Clearly he was seeking to draw a direct comparison with his great-great-grandfather Augustus. Issued in several denominations, silver coins depict Nero on the obverse with his various imperial titles. On the reverse, the closed doors of the temple of Janus can clearly be seen, with a garland hung across the entrance arch to symbolize peace. The lattice window, a prominent feature, also appears, placed up high in the wall: this barred window symbolized that Peace was safely locked within so that she could not escape. 'Peace having been obtained for the Roman People on land and sea, the doors of Janus have been shut; coin issued under the authority of the Senate' (PACE PR TERRA MA[RI]Q PARTA IANVM CLVSIT, SC) reads the legend (see Figure 3.5).[132] His doors were not closed for long, however, with the rebellion in Judaea causing their opening again soon after in AD 66.

The Christian historian Orosius (AD 375–after 418) records that Vespasian and Titus, after their triumph in AD 71 for the suppression of the Jewish revolt and the sack of Jerusalem, closed the gates of Janus' temple.[133] Vespasian's dedication of the temple of Peace (see above), which he commenced building in AD 71 after the Jewish War and dedicated in AD 75,[134] may have been intended to complement this closure. Peace's temple, known to the Romans as one of Rome's largest and most magnificent buildings, was destroyed by fire towards the end of the reign of Commodus, but was rebuilt, probably by Septimius Severus.[135] As with Nero, the Flavian emperors were eager to mirror the Augustan achievement, which was especially important for them as the new dynasty replacing the Julio-Claudians. After this, specific occasions when the temple of Janus was closed are not known. Ammianus Marcellinus mentions that the temple doors were open when Constantius visited Rome in AD 357.[136]

Figure 3.5: Silver sestertius depicting Nero's closure of the doors of the temple of Janus. Obverse: bust of Nero (reigned AD 54–68). Reverse: the closed doors of the temple. Minted AD 65. (*Courtesy of Classical Numismatic Group*)

The Gods of Trajan's Column: Jupiter Tonans

Augustus had vowed in 26 BC and consecrated in 22 BC a temple on the Capitoline Hill in Rome to Jupiter Tonans, 'Jupiter of the Thunderbolt', because of a narrow escape he had from lightning when campaigning against the Cantabrians in Spain. Of solid marble, the temple quickly became popular with worshippers.[137] Jupiter Tonans appears on Trajan's Column, which was voted by the Senate and the People of Rome, and constructed as part of the impressive Forum of Trajan; it was probably dedicated in AD 113.[138] Trajan's Column consists of specific panels, each with a number of scenes, representing the events of his First (AD 101–102) and Second (AD 105–106) Dacian Wars. His column is 30 metres high, with the pedestal it stands on 5 metres tall. Consisting of twenty hollow drums of Carrara marble, each some 4 metres in diameter, one upon the other, 155 scenes are engraved in a spiralling fashion from bottom to top. In this way, the spiral frieze has a length of some 190 metres; the scenes are about 1 metre high. Trajan appears fifty-nine times. A bronze statue of him stood at the top; it went missing in the medieval period, and in 1587 a statue of St Peter was placed on top and remains there.

In a dramatic battle encounter between the Romans and Dacians, Jupiter Tonans is depicted in the heavens (panel 24, scene 61).[139] He energetically raises his right arm to hurl a thunderbolt (once metal, but now lost) at the Dacians who are attacking the Roman forces. His intervention means that the outcome is clear and the Dacians will be defeated.

Two other gods are portrayed on the column. On the pedestal on which it stands, winged Victories on one side hold the dedicatory inscription, and there are piles of arms and armour on all four sides. At the very base of the column itself, in the scenes depicting the commencement of the campaign, the river god Danuvius (the modern River Danube) watches passively as the Roman army crosses his river into Dacia on a pontoon of boats: his enigmatic gaze and the smooth unruffled waves of his waters indicate his consent to the crossing and his support for Trajan's invasion (Figure 3.6).[140] The placidity of the river towards the Romans is in stark contrast to the turbulence when the cavalry allies of the Dacians are crossing to come to their aid, and some riders are shown tossed from their horses into the waves (panel 31). Trajan clearly viewed the support of the god as crucial, and he features on the reverse of several coins of this emperor's reign.[141] Marcus Aurelius also portrays the god Danuvius on his column as present at the start of his campaign (for which see below). As on Trajan's Column, the god looks on benignly as the Romans cross his river, in this case holding his right hand over the water to calm it. In much the same way, about a century earlier, Ovid had referred to the River Rhine as giving Germanicus its waters 'as his slaves'.[142]

Trajan, at the outset of the campaign in Dacia, is shown pouring a libation onto a lit altar outside his tent in the Roman camp (panel 8).[143] He is dressed in his capacity as Pontifex Maximus, the high priest of Rome, and to the right are three animals – a bull, sheep and pig, all decorated – being led by a soldier as part of the traditional *suovetaurilia* ritual. Musicians are present, as at all sacrifices, to drown out any outside noise and sounds of ill-omen. The bare-chested figure to Trajan's left is the *victimarius* (plural, *victimarii*), whose role is to dispatch the victims: his clenched right hand would have closed around a metal axe, now missing. This *suovetaurilia* is presumably a *lustratio exercitus*, a purification of the army before battle.[144]

Figure 3.6: The river god Danuvius (Danube) and Roman standards. Danuvius looks on benignly as Roman soldiers invade Dacia using the bridge Trajan had constructed over the god's waters; note the eagle and standards (right) which the soldiers carry as they lead the army across. Trajan's Column (panel 3, scenes 11–15), Rome. (*Courtesy of Alamy*)

Another *suovetaurilia* scene occurs later in which Trajan, in his priestly robes, holds his hand over an altar, perhaps placing incense on it; the three sacrificial animals are depicted, together with *victimarii* and their axes (panel 53).[145] Later, Trajan presides in ordinary clothing over a sacrifice of a bull at a harbour town (panel 87). A few scenes later, at a particularly magnificent sacrifice of several bulls, each held by a *victimarius*, Trajan, in non-military clothing, pours a libation at one of six wreathed altars (panel 91). These were no doubt thanksgiving sacrifices for victory.

War, however, broke out again soon after, and Trajan is again shown sacrificing at his bridge over the Danube (panel 99). As the campaign proper commences, he is greeted by his soldiers (panel 102); as Pontifex Maximus, he conducts a *suovetaurilia* to purify the army, the *lustratio* (panel 103); and then he addresses his troops (panel 104: the *adlocutio*, delivered before battle). This is the last of the several religious scenes on the column. Trajan brings the war to a successful conclusion and Dacia becomes a Roman province. The female deity Dacia appears on Trajan's arch at Beneventum (for which see below), kneeling before Trajan, who appears to be extending his arms (they are broken off) to lift her up. Two local (Dacian) river gods are also depicted.

While the deities Danuvius and Victoria appear on Aurelius' Column in imitation of Trajan, Aurelius is not shown, unlike Trajan, as an assiduous sacrificer. Like Trajan, however, he commences his campaign with the traditional *suovetaurilia*, shown early in the sequence of scenes on the column, in a badly damaged relief (scene 6). Aurelius is in a toga with several *victimarii*, with the usual bull, boar and ram, each with an attendant, as well as musicians.[146] In one scene, far into the visual narrative of the campaign, Aurelius is depicted sacrificing, in military dress, pouring a libation onto a flaming altar, with no sacrificial victims present (scene 76). His attendants have their mouths open, clearly making a prayer in unison. While the whole scene might be simply a random afterthought, showing Aurelius sacrificing, it might reflect a libation and prayers for a specific occasion at this point in the campaign.

The Rain Miracle on the Column of Marcus Aurelius

Aurelius' Column in Rome, constructed in the period AD 176–193, and voted by the Senate and the People, shows 116 scenes of his successful campaign against the Marcomanni in Germania (AD 169–175).[147] Only a few scenes on the column itself relate to religion and warfare:[148] that of the goddess Victory and the *tropaea*, the *suovetaurilia*, and the libation and prayer (see discussion above). This might have been balanced by the scenes on the column's four-sided pedestal: the sides each carried reliefs of sacrifices and Victories, but these, already damaged, were destroyed in 1590 as part of a restoration of the monument.[149] *Tropaea* were also shown on Marcus Aurelius' triumphal arch in what is now Tripoli in Libya.

Other religious episodes are iconographically expressed on Aurelius' Column: a *lustratio exercitus* (scene 6); Aurelius offering a sacrifice at a river crossing (scene 13); and another sacrifice at a river (scene 30). Aurelius, having triumphed over Rome's enemies, also celebrated a triumph in Rome in AD 177, and commemorated this with the traditional Roman triumphal arch, constructed from AD 177–180 to celebrate, as with his column, the defeat of the Marcomanni (and the Quadi and Sarmatians). The arch is now destroyed. Eight panels from this arch were reused in Constantine's triumphal arch, and three more panels depicting Aurelius, now in the Capitoline Museum, clearly also come from Aurelius' arch. Incorporated into the south side of Constantine's triumphal arch, on the right-hand side of the attic, a relief shows Aurelius making the traditional *suovetaurilia* sacrifice, with the pig, sheep and bull clearly visible, as part of the *lustratio* ritual. A young boy (the *camillus*) holds an incense box; Aurelius is pouring a libation from a patera bowl, now missing, unless the intention of the artist is to show him placing incense into the flames on the altar. A decorative ribbon around the adult pig is clearly visible, and a legionary standard with eagle is held high.[150] Setting out against the Marcomanni, Aurelius publicly invoked the gods.

Two religious episodes in particular were recorded on the column, one of which attracted the attention of both ancient pagan and Christian authors. Firstly, the scene on the column which is called the lightning miracle (scene 11):[151] at the siege of a Roman fort, the enemy siege tower and the enemy themselves are blasted by a visible bolt of lightning. The tower is in flames and the enemy are struck down, with one of the enemy, who has fallen forward and who has in vain attempted to protect himself by holding his shield above his head, shown alight.[152] A hand-grip is clearly visible on the thunderbolt, which is therefore a fashioned weapon, wielded by some supernatural agent, who is not depicted – presumably Jupiter was responsible. This scene recalls that involving Jupiter Tonans coming to the aid of Trajan (see above).[153] The author of the life of Marcus Aurelius in the *Scriptores Historia Augusta* writes that the emperor had summoned the lightning from heaven through his prayers,[154] and it is possible that the author has taken his details from the column itself.

Quite independent of any connection with Trajan's Column is the second episode. When Marcus Aurelius and his army were in the territory of the Quadi in AD 174, and the Roman troops were suffering from the extremes of thirst, divine intervention caused it to rain. A panel on the column (scene 16), depicting what is now known as the rain miracle (Aurelius is not present), illustrates the event:[155] a male god with long sleeves, similar to wings, representing rain clouds, is depicted above the Roman soldiers and enemy. A sudden downpour of rain of such strength is occurring that some of the Roman soldiers are shown holding their shields above their heads to protect themselves from the deluge, while some of the enemy have been killed by its impact (see Figure 3.7).[156] According to Dio's description of the incident (see below), the enemy were blasted with lightning and killed (but no lightning occurs in this scene, so Dio or his epitomator is wrong on this detail and has compressed the previous thunderbolt miracle into his account of the torrential rain).[157] A soldier in the top corner (scene 16) looking up at the sky is raising his right hand in a gesture which could be interpreted as prayer (he is not visible in Figure 3.7).[158] Alternatively, he could simply be drawing attention to the coming rain (he is facing away from the rain, but that is an effect of the diachronic sequence – he is part of the scene before the rain has started falling).[159]

Figure 3.7: The rain miracle on the column of Marcus Aurelius. A rain god sends a deluge to relieve the Romans of their thirst and to destroy the encircling enemy. Column of Marcus Aurelius (scene 16), Rome. (*Courtesy of Alamy*)

Most detailed of the literary descriptions of the miracle is that by Cassius Dio, but this is known only from the summary made of Dio's history by the eleventh-century AD Christian author Xiphilinos, who paraphrased Dio's account – and then criticized it in detail.[160] According to Dio, the Roman army was suffering from thirst, being hemmed in by the Quadi so that they could not break out and obtain water, when a deity took the situation in hand. Dio records that an Egyptian magician (*magos*) with Aurelius caused it to rain by invoking the gods, and especially Hermes (who for the Romans was Mercury), god of the air (*aerios*). Earlier than Dio, the Christian author Tertullian, in his *Apology* (about AD 195) – written only two decades after the incident – and his *ad Scapulam* (AD 211–13), wrote briefly that the Christian soldiers in Aurelius' army prayed for rain and their God sent it.[161]

Xiphilinos, in his précis and criticism of Dio's account, agreed with both Tertullian and Eusebius in his *Church History*:[162] the Christian soldiers in a particular division of the army were responsible for the rain. Eusebius recounts that in Aurelius' army there was a legion known as the Melitene, which included Christian soldiers, who in their dire need for water kneeled on the ground and supplicated the Christian God for rain. He cites an earlier Christian author, Apollinaris, that the emperor therefore named this legion the 'Thundering Legion'.[163] Tertullian,[164] as well as Eusebius, also mentions letters of Aurelius in which the emperor acknowledged that the army had in fact been saved by the Christians, but clearly any such letter (Xiphilinos mentions one letter) was a forgery. Christian authors were eager to have it believed that the pagan emperor Aurelius acknowledged that the Christians saved an entire Roman army and brought about the defeat of the enemy.[165]

Xiphilinos adds a few further details, including the fact that the prefect of the army informed the emperor that there were Christians in the army, who through their prayers were able to accomplish anything. Aurelius therefore asked the Christian soldiers to pray to their God, who immediately heard the prayers and sent the rain (and a thunderbolt to kill the enemy). This account gives Aurelius an active agency in events, in which he seeks the help of the Christians and asks – not orders – them to have their deity intercede for him. Some enterprising Christian also penned an oracle, which made its way into the Sibylline Oracle collection, that in answer to Aurelius' prayer, the Christian God sent rain out of its proper season of the year.[166]

That rain fell for the Romans just as they were suffering severely from lack of water, and were penned in by an enemy who were prepared to wait for them to die of thirst, seems indisputable, and is recorded on the column. Very early on – within twenty years it was being referred to in Christian writings – a narrative existed amongst the Christians that it was Christian soldiers who prayed and made it rain so that Aurelius could defeat the barbarians threatening the Empire. Christians were serving in the Roman Army at this date (though there would certainly not have been an entire legion specifically made up of Christians), and probably they did pray for rain when on the point of death. No pagan source mentions Aurelius or the pagans praying, only that the rain was conjured up by an Egyptian magician with the army. Pagan and Christian practices were already side by side by the last quarter of the second century AD, and in this case something of a contest for the credit of the miracle occurred.

Triumphal Processions and the Gods

There are three relief panels from Aurelius' arch now in the Capitoline Museum in Rome: one, a scene of imperial clemency, is known as the 'Clementia', the second is of an imperial triumph and the third depicts Aurelius sacrificing outside the temple of the Capitoline triad in Rome.[167] The triumph scene has Aurelius in his triumphal chariot, drawn as usual by four horses and advancing towards the Porta Triumphalis, the Triumphal Gate (see Figure 3.8).[168] A winged Victory hovers above him, with

Figure 3.8: Marcus Aurelius in triumphal procession in Rome, relief in the Capitoline Museum (Inv. Scu 808). (*Courtesy of Alamy*)

three figures portrayed on the upper register of the chariot. On the left is Neptune with his trident: this is Neptune as Neptunus Redux, 'Neptune who brings about return', who has protected the emperor on his nautical return from the East.[169] On the right is the war goddess Minerva, and in the centre, a seated figure, with one bare breast, represents the goddess Roma of the Amazon type (i.e., the warrioress Roma). In the lower register, on the chariot and slightly obscured by the horses, are winged Victories. The relief of the procession deliberately includes one temple, the identity of which is uncertain; it is presumably one of the many temples along the triumphal route, and the temple of Jupiter Tonans, Jupiter Custos or Saturn have all been suggested.[170]

Thanksgiving Sacrifice after the Triumph

One of the panels in the Capitoline Museum depicts Aurelius presiding over a sacrifice outside the temple of Jupiter Optimus Maximus on the Capitoline: its three doors, leading into the chambers of Minerva, Jupiter and Juno, are clearly visible. A large bull stands next to the *victimarius*, who has his axe ready to dispatch it.[171]

Figure 3.9: Marcus Aurelius making a thanksgiving sacrifice to the gods for his victory over the Marcomanni and others. Relief from his triumphal arch, Capitoline Museum Inv. Scu 807. (*Courtesy of Alamy*)

Aurelius holds a patera over the altar to pour a libation onto it. Jupiter's priest, the *flamen Dialis*, is present to the immediate right of Aurelius, conspicuous by his spiked hat (his spike is shown on the column behind him). Aurelius, with his head covered (*capite velato*) for the sacrifice, is officiating as Pontifex Maximus.

A thanksgiving to the Capitoline triad for victory is also shown as part of the triumph celebrated by Tiberius on a silver skyphos (cup) from the Boscoreale treasure. On one side of the cup, Tiberius processes in his triumphal chariot, on the other a *victimarius* is about to bring his axe down upon the head of a bull, in front of a wreathed temple of Capitoline Jupiter.[172] This triumph was that of either 7 BC or AD 12.[173] Tiberius and Aurelius through their sacrificial acts outside the temple of Jupiter Optimus Maximus, Rome's greatest god, thanked him for their military victories. Trajan and Aurelius, war-leaders and heads of state, displayed their piety through libations, incense burning and the sacrifice of the *suovetaurilia* which purified their armies in the *lustratio* rite, invoking the gods of the Roman state to bring victory to the Roman Army: without divine support, there could be no success. After a triumphal ceremony, an arch was erected to commemorate their victory and, as can be seen in Aurelius' case, the reliefs expressed the emperor's thanks to the gods for their assistance.

The Victory Trophy: *Tropaeum*

The ancient Greeks had invented the *tropaion*, or battle-trophy, which was erected on the site of the engagement by the side which had been victorious on the field of battle. A *tropaion* consisted of a set of the armour and weapons taken from the enemy, affixed vertically to a wooden pole, log or branch. Rome adopted the practice, and the trophy was known in Latin as the *tropaeum* (plural, *tropaea*). One is shown being erected in the lower register of the early first-century AD so-called *Gemma Augustea* ('Augustan gem'), an engraved piece of double layered (white and black) Arabian onyx (see Figure 3.10). The figures on it are carved in low relief raised only a few millimetres: the width of the gem is 230mm and the height is 190mm. It is probably by the famed Greek sculptor Dioskourides. The gem has been copied in modern times. It has two registers, the upper one depicting Augustus and the lower one the *tropaeum* scene.

In the upper register, left, a male – possibly Tiberius – descends from a triumphal chariot with a winged Victory (there are clearly four horses, indicating a triumphal chariot, with one of the horses no longer in its traces: compare the position of the outside horse in Figure 3.8). Next to him stands a young Germanicus – although the latter was not deified, he was still receiving veneration from soldiers in the third century AD in the religious calendar from Dura-Europos (see above). Then there is a seated goddess with helmet and spear; her sword sheath is also visible. She is resting her feet on a breastplate and shield, with a helmet placed on the breastplate: she is probably the military aspect of the goddess Roma (and her resemblance to Augustus' wife Livia will have been deliberate). Enthroned sitting next to her, naked from the waist up and hence signifying his apotheosis as a Roman god, is the deified Augustus holding a sceptre representing his authority, and a *lituus*, the main ritual implement of the Roman augurs, with the eagle of Jupiter, looking up at him, under his throne. Augustus' zodiac sign, Capricorn, is shown between Roma and himself. He is being crowned with a wreath by a goddess. This is possibly Oikoumene, goddess of the world, and she is shown as usual with a turreted crown. The wreath itself is the *corona civica*, made of oak leaves and awarded to those who had saved the lives of Roman citizens in battle; Augustus had been awarded this (as had Julius Caesar previously) in 27 BC by the Senate.[174]

Oikoumene and the male god next to her look directly at the wreath, drawing the viewer's attention to it. This male divinity has been identified as Oceanus, who with Oikoumene represents the realms of the world over which the gods had given Augustus and the Romans suzerainty. Leaning casually against Augustus' throne is a goddess with well-endowed breasts who holds a cornucopia (horn of plenty); she might well be Tellus Italiae, the personification of Mother Italy, and the two children with her (one carrying a sheaf of grain) are personifications of Italia's fecundity.

In the lower register, four soldiers are shown raising a heavy log vertically, on top of which is attached a set of arms and armour; next to it (left) is Tiberius' zodiac sign,

Figure 3.10: The *Gemma Augustea* depicting gods with the divine Augustus, in the upper register. Mars assists in raising the *tropaeum* (left), while Diana and Mercury show mercy to captives (right), in the lower register. Double-layered Arabian onyx; AD *c*.20s–30s. Kunsthistorisches Museum, Vienna, inv. IXa 79. (*Photo courtesy of Alamy*)

the scorpion. Several captives are shown, in a generic 'barbarian' style. If Tiberius in the upper scene is descending from a triumphal chariot, these captives could refer to his triumph in 7 BC or AD 12. If this does not represent a triumph (which is unlikely), then perhaps this is his entrance (*adventus*) into Rome in AD 9 after his successful campaigns against the Illyrians. One of the four soldiers is shown in helmet and military uniform and cape: given the other divine figures in the lower register (as in the upper), this is probably the god Mars (perhaps as Mars Ultor, Augustus' favourite manifestation of Mars; see above). Diana, generally a goddess of hunting, is shown with two spears with their points to the ground (indicating a cessation of hostilities), and the god Mercury (wearing his traveller's hat, with his left hand on his sword sheath to indicate he has housed his sword). Both are showing mercy to the vanquished: the *pax Romana* has been established.[175] The cameo stresses the first emperor's relationship with the gods, his victories, the *pax Romana* over which he presided and of course Rome's military successes under the auspices of the gods.

Tropaea also frequently appeared on coins in the aftermath of a military victory. Coins, for example, from the reign of Domitian (AD 81–96) show the emperor on the obverse, wearing a laurel wreath of victory, and on the reverse the goddess Minerva, armed with shield and spear and wearing a helmet, who has her right hand on a victory *tropaeum* (see Figure 3.11). Such coins were intended to advertise Domitian's military victories – an important consideration given the brilliant military successes of his father and brother. This particular example is from Judaea, where it might have had particular resonances due to Vespasian and Titus' victories there, but such coins were also issued elsewhere in Domitian's reign. He did have a predilection for Minerva apart from her military aspect, but the coins indicate that he considered that her assistance was intrinsic to his military victories;[176] she also appears as a fully armed goddess on many of his coins.[177]

In addition to setting up a *tropaeum* on the field of battle when victorious, using the arms and armour of the defeated enemy, *tropaea* were rendered in stone and used

Figure 3.11: Silver denarius. Minerva as war goddess puts the finishing touches to a *tropaeum* (reverse). Obverse: wreathed bust of Domitian. Reign of Domitian, AD 81–96. (*Courtesy of Classical Numismatic Group*)

in the imperial period to decorate the arches which commemorated the victory of a Roman general awarded a triumph (from 29 BC he had to be the emperor or a member of the imperial family to so triumph, or if a general, the emperor celebrated the triumph in his own name). Upon his death, Drusus (brother of Tiberius) was voted a triumphal arch with *tropaea* on the Via Appia by the Senate.[178] His son Claudius also had a victory arch erected for his conquests in Britain. Coins of his reign show this, with the legend '*de Brittanis*' ('for Britain'), surmounted by a cavalryman with a *tropaeum* of arms, each with two shields, on either side of him.[179] This victory arch was dedicated at Rome in AD 51 or 52 – there was also one at Gesoriacum (Boulogne), from where Claudius had embarked for Britain. There are scant remains of this arch: the dedicatory inscription survives, but there is no mention of divine assistance,[180] unlike Trajan's later reference to Mars Ultor at Adamklissi. Other coins of Claudius' reign show a triumphal arch, also with a cavalryman and two-shielded *tropaea* on the reverse, and with the legend of his father Drusus' titles and his bust on their obverse; some, but not all of them, have '*de Germanis*' ('for Germany') on the arch. This was Drusus' triumphal arch, erected posthumously (see Figure 3.12; the obverse is not given). Claudius through his coinage was displaying both his own and his father's arch, and the similar statuary crowning the attic was intended to draw favourable comparisons with his father.[181] Nothing is known about the *tropaea* of Germanicus which were erected near the temple of Fides in Rome.[182]

After the successful conclusion of his first Dacian campaign (scene 78), Trajan's Column shows double-shielded *tropaea* (as on Drusus' arch) with a helmet and Dacian clothing on the traditional branch, with a pile of captured weapons below (see Figure 3.13). In between the *tropaea*, the winged goddess Victoria (victory) prepares to inscribe a shield, to make clear that Trajan is dedicating this armour to the gods, or perhaps is writing 'Dacia conquered'. An *aureus* depicts Trajan in the guise of a heroic nude Greek athlete with a spear in his left hand standing next to a *tropaeum* and apparently putting the final touches to it. There is a Dacian at his knees, extending his right arm upwards to ask Trajan for mercy.[183] Another divine correspondence between Trajan's and Marcus Aurelius' columns is that the goddess Victoria also appears on Aurelius', who once again is drawing a parallel not merely to the columns, but to the campaigns of his illustrious military predecessor. Aurelius reads from a scroll to his assembled soldiers, perhaps announcing military decorations for some of them, while a winged Victoria commences writing on a large shield. To

Figure 3.12: Gold coin (*aureus*). Drusus' victory arch with stone *tropaea*, with the legend '*de Germanis*', 'for Germany', with a *tropaeum* from his campaigns on either side of an equestrian statue of Drusus. (*Courtesy of the Trustees of the British Museum, BM 1864,1128.243*)

Figure 3.13: The winged goddess Victoria prepares to inscribe a shield, with a double-shielded *tropaeum* of Dacian clothing and weapons on either side of her. Trajan's Column (panel 78, scenes 204-06), Rome. (*Courtesy of Wikimedia*)

her left and right stand typical *tropaea*, with captured enemy clothing, shields (two shields per 'arm', as on Trajan's Column) and weapons (scene 78).[184]

Winged Victories each carrying a *tropaeum* appear in the spandrels (the space between the curve of an arch and the next horizontal feature) of the arch of the emperor Septimius Severus (reigned AD 193–211) in the Roman forum: the Victories each carry a long branch with the tunic and head-gear of a defeated enemy.[185] Similarly, on the marble arch of Trajan at Beneventum in southern Italy, dated to the mid 110s AD, marking his extension of the Via Appia,[186] the faces of the piers of each long side (east and west) of the single arch show carved winged Victories (in the second, narrow registers), who in this case are making sacrificial offerings of bulls. What has not been noted previously about these is that they are cutting the beasts' throats: this is the sphagia ceremony which is depicted in Greek art, the sacrifice that occurred just before battle was joined, and which Victories (Nikai in the Greek) were thought to perform, for success in battle.[187]

There are the usual winged Victories in the spandrels of the Beneventum arch, but not carrying *tropaea*. Above the register of Victories making sacrifices, on the left side (south pier, west face), Mars is portrayed in the garb of a Roman officer, his shield on his left arm. He appears with Trajan and children, accompanied by three goddesses, around one of whose shoulders he rests an arm. This is a reference to Trajan's *alimenta* scheme, which provided subsidies for the support of children in Italy, and the goddesses presumably represent deities of prosperity. Mars is present, perhaps as Mars Pater, Father Mars.[188] (There was a nearby temple of Mars.) Clearly, however, the association between Trajan and Mars will have been largely due to Trajan's Dacian conquests.

A panel on the arch also shows the Capitoline triad (Jupiter, Juno and Minerva), with four other deities (who are unidentifiable). Jupiter carries his sceptre and in his right hand he is holding out his thunderbolt. He is facing towards and into another relief which depicts Trajan taking his leave for the Dacian campaign, and Jupiter is presumably indicating to Trajan that the divine thunderbolts will come to his assistance (as indeed they did).[189] In the interior of the span of the arch, that is in the vault, a winged Victory crowns a standing Trajan.[190] On the west side, in the middle of a scene in a panel on the south pier, a bearded figure who is naked to the waist holds a thunderbolt. This is, of course, none other than Jupiter, with Trajan to his left and a Dacian chief to his right making his surrender: Jupiter's presence seals the sacredness of the occasion, which would have involved the exchange of sacred oaths.[191]

Mainly found throughout Roman Germany (and in Belgica, Belgium), with a few other examples elsewhere, are the remains of several so-called 'Jupiter columns'. Most date to AD 150–260 and were set up both by civilians, and by Roman and auxiliary soldiers, both serving and discharged. Many such columns were about 4–5 metres high (though a few are as high as 12 metres), fairly slender, not necessarily decorated and surmounted with a statue of Jupiter (sometimes on a horse, in which case he is shown trampling a Giant) carrying his thunderbolts (as in the example in Strasbourg's Musée Archéologique).[192] The most famous example comes from Mainz, where it was excavated, with the pieces now in the museum there. It would have stood about 10 metres high, plus the statue of Jupiter on top. An inscription indicates it was set up by the local community, was about 10 metres high and dates to the reign of Nero, with the inscription indicating that it was dedicated for the health (*salus*) of the emperor. It has a *tropaeum* on an upright branch, presumably referring to a military victory of Nero's reign. There is a completely modern reconstruction of the Mainz column at the Roman fort at Saalburg (near Bad Homburg), which stands 12.5 metres high.

The Monumental *Tropaea* of Augustus

As in Greece, however, there was, in the Roman imperial period, a second form of the *tropaeum*, which comprised a permanent monument to victory on the field of battle or nearby.[193] In the imperial period, the first of these was that of Octavian to commemorate his victory at Actium in 31 BC. He established a city, Nicopolis ('Victory City'), near Actium in 29–27 BC, and restored the existing temple of Apollo there, establishing a four-yearly festival (the Actia) with contests, with Apollo of Actium as the presiding deity. He dedicated ten ships captured in the battle to Apollo, and these were housed in boatsheds near Apollo's existing sanctuary.[194]

Suetonius notes that Octavian also decorated the area where his camp had been at Actium with 'naval spoils', and consecrated the area to Neptune and Mars, gods who, with Apollo, had fought for Octavian.[195] Dio also notes that the structure erected on his campsite was dedicated to Apollo.[196] Germanicus visited the city and saw the spoils dedicated by Augustus:[197] the ruins are still standing of a permanent marble *tropaeum* which had been decorated with the bronze rostra (ramming beaks) of thirty-six ships,[198] with the monument measuring some 62 by 50 metres. According to the dedicatory inscription, Octavian consecrated to Neptune and Mars the camp from which he set out to fight the enemy, and decorated the monument with the spoils of battle.[199] Its wording 'peace having been obtained on land and sea' (*pace parta terra marique*) must refer to the closing of the temple of Janus at Rome in the aftermath of the battle. This *tropaeum* was a permanent reminder of Octavian's gratitude to the gods whom he saw as having enabled his victory, from which he emerged as master of the Roman world.

A permanent *tropaeum* was erected by Augustus in c.25–20 BC at modern St Bernard-de-Commagne, ancient Lugdunum Convenarum, in southern France in the central Pyrenees. His monument survives as three rectangular bases on which sculptural groups were placed. These remains include a marble statue of the emperor, on whose breastplate a double-shielded *tropaeum* was carved with two bound captives at its base, as well as statues of a Victory and the usual captives, and a marble tree trunk with the traces of a *tropaeum*. This monument probably celebrated Augustus' victories in the region against several tribal groups in Gaul and Spain.[200] At another triumphal arch at modern Orange (ancient Arausio) in France, possibly dating to the reign of Tiberius to commemorate the quelling of a local revolt, the artist or artists took a different approach, with the bays above the lateral arches, instead of having *tropaea*, depicting an assorted medley of weapons and armour captured from the enemy. Some of the shields are inscribed with the names of Gallic chieftains, to indicate their subjugation. A similar approach was taken in the lower attic, in which naval *spolia* (such as ship rams) are piled up.[201]

A particularly spectacular monumental *tropaeum* is that of Augustus at La Turbie in France, the Tropaeum Augusti (or in modern parlance, the Trophée des Alpes). Constructed in 6 BC to commemorate Roman victories over forty-six tribes in the alpine region nearby (see Figure 3.14), it is located on the border of what was the

Figure 3.14: Augustus' monumental *tropaeum* at La Turbie in France. (*Courtesy of Wikimedia*)

province of Gallia (Gaul) Narbonensis with Italy.²⁰² Pliny recorded the dedicatory inscription, to the effect that the Senate and People of Rome constructed it for Augustus (as it was under his imperium and auspices that the conquests took place). A circular structure on a square base, the rotunda had twenty-four columns, its current height being 35 metres; the whole was surmounted by a colossal statue of Augustus, and hence the structure may have reached a total of 50 metres high. There is a carved *tropaeum* on the west face with two captives underneath.²⁰³

The Monumental Tropaeum Traiani at Adamklissi

Trajan's *tropaeum* at Adamklissi, also circular, was almost certainly architecturally modelled on Augustus' at La Turbie, in order to stress a continuum between the achievements of Augustus and Trajan. Trajan constructed a large, permanent *tropaeum* in AD 107–108, now referred to as the Tropaeum Traiani, for his defeat of the Dacians and Sarmatians in AD 101–102, at what is now Adamklissi in modern Romania, then the Roman province of Moesia Inferior (see Figure 3.15).²⁰⁴ According to an inscription on the monument, it was dedicated to Mars Ultor (Mars the Avenger).²⁰⁵ A circular structure some 30 metres in diameter and probably about 18 metres in height (or even 38 metres, depending on the reconstruction), it was decorated with fifty-four carved metopes (a sculptural relief carved on a stone slab) around the uppermost part, each metope being separated from its neighbour by a triglyph (a stone slab with three carved vertical bars), depicting Romans fighting these tribesmen. None of the surviving scenes – although six are missing – is religious in nature: perhaps one of the lost scenes was the essential *suovetaurilia* sacrifice made in the field prior to a campaign.²⁰⁶

Situated around the actual top of the drum in crenellation form were twenty-six metopes portraying enemy captives. The structure itself may have been surmounted by a traditional *tropaeum* of captured armour on a wooden support several metres high.²⁰⁷ On a monumental altar (12 metres square and 6 metres high) separate from the *tropaeum* were listed the names of about 3,800 Roman and auxiliary soldiers; a few fragments of names on the altar survive. This altar probably dates to Domitian's reign and commemorates the dead from his campaign in the region.²⁰⁸

Trajan's *tropaeum* is unique in terms of a Roman monument commemorating Roman soldiers, celebrating the fact that Mars Ultor had given him victory against these tribesmen. Trajan dedicated Adamklissi to Mars Ultor, possibly in vengeance against the Dacians for the eagle lost under Domitian, which Trajan recovered.²⁰⁹ When Trajan had engaged the Dacians near Tapae and defeated them, he gave honours to the fallen Roman soldiers, ordering that an altar be erected to them and that funeral rites for them be held there annually.²¹⁰ Presumably there would have been annual commemoration services at Adamklissi as well.

Not all of the *tropaea* erected were of such a permanent character as Adamklissi: Florus writes that Drusus constructed a tumulus, an earthen mound, as a *tropaeum* in 9 BC after a victory over the Marcomanni, decorating it with the spoils and insignia of the defeated.²¹¹ Similarly, Germanicus constructed a less permanent

Figure 3.15: A modern reconstruction of Trajan's *tropaeum* monument at Adamklissi. (*Courtesy of Alamy*)

trophy in AD 15, although Tacitus refers to it as a monument. He piled up the arms captured from (the many thousands of) the enemy slain, and had an inscription erected that having conquered the '*nationes* [peoples] between the Rhine and Elbe rivers', he dedicated these arms to Mars, Jove (Jupiter) and Augustus. These three were Rome's war god Mars, its supreme god Jupiter and the deified Augustus (Germanicus' grandfather), the latter now seen as worthy of receiving the spoils of war and presumably, as with the other two deities, viewed as having lent his divine support to Germanicus.[212] Upon the death from natural causes of Drusus, Tiberius' son, in AD 23 he was honoured by the army with the erection of a tumulus around which, on a set day each year, the soldiers would make a ceremonial run (the *decursio*), and the cities in Gaul (hence it appears the tumulus was in that country) would observe the day with prayers; the Senate voted him a marble arch, with *tropaea*, to be erected on the Appian Way.[213]

Tropaea as stone monuments, as piles of weapons or in the form of the traditional attaching of a suit of captured armour from the enemy onto a wooden fixture, were a necessary material expression of Roman victory in the Empire. Architecture in the form of temples, altars, arches and columns, and media such as coinage, the *Gemma Augusta* and carved reliefs, celebrated Rome's relationship with the gods believed to support the Empire in its wars and conquests. These visible, tangible expressions of Roman thanksgiving to their gods were seen as necessary to ensure that the gods knew that their assistance was appreciated. Above all, it was Jupiter Optimus Maximus and Mars Ultor who were thought to be the primary war-gods.

Conclusion

The religion of the Roman Army in the Empire was diverse and manifold. There was compulsory worship directed by the current regime with its military religious calendar, though this is not to suggest that the soldiers did not enter into these ceremonies willingly and enthusiastically. Various cults were associated with the legionary eagles and standards, and with the camp itself. Soldiers venerated the traditional Roman gods, but nothing prevented their attachment to their own indigenous gods or from becoming involved with 'Eastern' cults such as those of Mithras and Jupiter Dolichenus. Soldiers articulated their devotion through the erection of inscribed altars and other forms of dedication. Individual soldiers, generals, emperors and the very state believed without qualification that the gods decided the outcome of battles. Numerous incidents, especially in the first-century AD civil wars, indicate that the Romans believed the gods did take sides in military conflicts, and that they encouraged a commander such as Vespasian to engage in war to secure the imperial throne, sending him positive omens and unpropitious ones to the eventual losers.

At the state level, the support of the gods was sought through rituals such as the declaration of war, with the fetial priests in the temple grounds of the war goddess Bellona carrying out ancient ceremonies. *Suovetaurilia* sacrifices proclaimed the commencement of war. Demonstrable large-scale indications to the gods of the state's devotion to them and thanks to them for their assistance came in the form of the temple of Mars Ultor and many reliefs on triumphal arches, not to mention the columns of Trajan and Marcus Aurelius, representing the gods within actual battle contexts. Emperors are shown taking part in sacrifices and in the company of the gods, or near their temples, and Trajan was careful to indicate on his column that he had regularly sacrificed to the gods while on campaign in Dacia. Coins displayed the original *tropaea* of battlefields, and invoked, together with triumphal arches, the goddess Victory, the personification of battle, glory and military success.

Rome's military success depended on the gods, and the individual and state devotion to war gods and cults of many varieties indicates that this belief was strong, personalized and also institutionalized. The religious life of an individual soldier, his century, cohort and legion, was a busy and regular one. As a state, the Romans equipped themselves with augury, temples, regular sacrifices and thanksgivings, preparing for ordinary and extraordinary military commitments and exigencies. The gods received worship on a regular basis, and of course during the extraordinary crisis of war. Whether the legions were at peace or at war, Jupiter as his legionary eagle went with them, providing his support. And when Jupiter gave way to Christ, in Roman belief the divine was still with their armies, delivering them victories over their enemies.

Notes

1. *P. Dura* 54; editions: Fink *et al.* (1940); translations: Fink (1971), pp.422–29, no. 117 (with Latin text); Helgeland (1978), pp.1481–88; (with Latin text); translation: Hekster & Zair (2008), pp.127–29, no. 26 (somewhat patchy). See Irby-Massie (1999), pp.14–17. For the calendar, see Nock (1952), esp. pp.187–88; Gilliam (1954); Fishwick (1988); Pollard (2001), pp.142–44; Stoll (2007), p.453; Hekster & Zair (2008), pp.54, 66.

2. Fink *et al.* (1940), pp.28–29; Nock (1952), pp.194–95; Gilliam (1954), pp.183–84; Birley (1978), p.1510; Helgeland (1978), pp.1487–88; Fisher (1988), esp. pp.349–50.
3. Ovid *Fasti* 3.814.
4. Tert. *Coron.* 12.2. See, for the Quinquatria, Fink *et al.* (1940), pp.94–97.
5. Cf. Fishwick (1988), pp.359–60.
6. Cic. *Att.* 5.20.5.
7. Gilliam (1954), p.187.
8. For a sound overview and discussion of the fresco, see Kaizer (2006), outlining previous scholarship and convincingly arguing that these are three Palymyrene deities. Many scholars consider the triad to be Palymyrene, but an imperial group makes more sense.
9. Fink *et al.* (1940), pp.181–90.
10. For the cult of Jupiter Dolichenus, the standard treatment is Speidel (1978); see also Nash-Williams (1952); Tóth (1973); Walsh (2016); Walsh (2020).
11. See the catalogue of cult material in these locations in *CCID*.
12. See Nash-Williams (1952), pp.72–73; cf. Speidel (1978), pp.1–2.
13. For example, *AE* 1940, 71.
14. For example, *AE* 1940, 72, 73. See *RIB* 3253, discussed below.
15. For the plaques, see Turcan (1996), pp.163–64.
16. Kunsthistorisches Museum Wien, Antikensammlung Inv. M5.
17. Platner-Ashby (1929), p.292; Richardson (1992), p.218; Turcan (1998), p.127.
18. For the geographical locations of the cult, see Nash-Williams (1952), pp.73–74; Turcan (1996), pp.167–68; in Britain and Pannonia: Walsh (2020). For Jupiter Dolichenus and the army in Britain, see Irby-Massie (1999), pp.67–91.
19. For the sites, see Ratimorská & Minaroviech (2009), pp.1, 5; Walsh (2020), pp.277, 279–80; note esp. Collar (2011). For Vindolanda, see esp. Birley & Birley (2012).
20. Ratimorská & Minaroviech (2009), p.11, fig. 28.
21. *CCID*, no. 217.
22. *RIB* 3253, AD 217 (*AE* 1967, 259). Legion II Augusta also erected an altar to the 'Discipline of the Augusti': *RIB* 1127.
23. Hdn 7.3.5; see esp. the discussion of this passage by Tóth (1973), pp.112–13, 116.
24. See, in particular, the discussion of Tóth (1973), pp.109–11, who lists these provinces and the sites themselves, with a detailed analysis of the destructions. Cf. Walsh (2016), discussing temple building and restorations in Noricum and Pannonia.
25. Tóth (1973), pp.109–11.
26. Spiedel (1978), pp.74–75; Walsh (2020), pp.287–88.
27. *RIB* 2177 (*CIL* 7.114; *ILS* 4831c); Hunterian Museum F.27; Keppie (1998), pp.104–05, no. 36, pl. xiii.
28. For Epona, see Linduff (1979); for the cult in Britain, see Irby-Massie (1999), pp.154–55.
29. Birley (1976), pp.108–10.
30. *RIB* 1334 (see same for the date; *CIL* 7.510).
31. Irby-Massie (1996), pp.298–300.
32. For the Campestres, see esp. Irby-Massie (1996); for the cult in Britain: Irby-Massie (1999), pp.152–53.
33. See Irby-Massie (1996), p.293.
34. Veg. *Mil.* 3.4.3, cf. 1.1.2; see Stoll (2007), p.453. For the cult of the standards, see Irby-Massie (1999), pp.38–45.
35. Birley (1978), pp.1514–15; Le Bohec (1994), p.107; Stoll (2007), p.453.
36. *RIB* 3298 (*AE* 1979, 388).
37. *RIB* 990, 1127. See Birley (1978), p.1514, for other Discipulina inscriptions from Roman Britain (*RIB* 1128, 1723, 1978, 2092).
38. For the term aquilifer and signifer (carrier of the standards, the *signa*), note Tac. *Ann.* 1.48; Veg. *Mil.* 2.6, 2.13. For the imaginifer: Veg. *Mil.* 2.7.
39. Veg. *Mil.* 2.6, 2.7, 2.8, 2.13.

40. Joseph. *Bell. Jud.* 3.6.2.
41. Livy 26.48.12: *signa militaria et aquilas sacramentique.*
42. Tac. *Ann.* 2.17.7; see Helgeland (1978), pp.1476–78.
43. Tac. *Ann.* 1.39 (the *vexillum* was kept in Germanicus' *domus*, literally house: his quarters); cf. Pliny *Nat. Hist.* 10.16.
44. Dion. Hal. *Rom. Ant.* 6.45.2.
45. For the hand as part of the *signa*, and for this as an iconographic reference to the swearing of the soldier's *sacramentum* (oath), see Taylor in this volume.
46. Veg. *Mil.* 2.13.1.
47. Also in other scenes, usually but not always involving military activity: scenes 24, 28, 52, 55–56, 66, (perhaps 67), 68, 82, 103, 104, 112, 121–22, 127–28, 136, 154, 193–94, 197–98, 203, 208, 226, 230–31, 258–59, 269–70, 275–76, 279, 284, 301, 335, 339, 347 and 365; note the cavalry *vexilla* at scenes 20–21.
48. For the religious rites for legionary eagles and signa, see esp. Stoll (2007), pp.457–58; cf. Wheeler (2009), pp.31–35.
49. Tert. *Apol.* 16.8; he repeats the claim at Tert. *Nat.* 1.12.15–16.
50. *AE* 1989, 581; cf. Hdn 4.4.5. The *aedes principiorum* appears in inscriptions from Roman Britain. The term was first found in *RIB* 3027, published in 1961.
51. Cic. *Catil.* 1.24, 2.13.
52. *RIB* 3507 (*CSIR* 1.4, 53–4, no. 149, pl. 37), cf. 2198. Keppie & Arnold (1984), no. 149; Le Bohec (1994), pl. 5, fig. 7; Keppie (1998), p.66, fig. 28, 81–82, no. 9, pl. 5; Durham & Fulford (2013), pp.90–91, fig. 7.
53. Plut. *Crass.* 19.3–6; Dio 40.17.3–18.2; Val. Max. 1.6.11.
54. Cic. *Div.* 1.35.77; Livy 22.3.11; Val. Max. 1.6.6.
55. Lactant. *Mort. Pers.* 10 (cf. 11–17); Arnob. *Adv. Nat.* 1.46.9.
56. Speidel & Dimitrova-Milceva (1978), p.1545, discussing *AE* 1926, 69. See their list of military units with *genii* at p.1544, structures associated with the army (e.g., the *castra*, camps, with their *Genius castrorum*) at p.1549 and *passim* for a discussion of military *genii*. See also, for the military *genii* in Britain, Irby-Massie (1999), pp.45–47.
57. *RIB* 1334.
58. Sixteen of these eighteen can be seen in The Hunterian Collection, University of Glasgow, National Museums of Scotland. A map at Keppie (1998), p.3 fig. 2 shows their location along the Antonine Wall.
59. The Bridgeness Slab: *RIB* 2139 (*CIL* 7.1088); The Hunterian Collection X.FV 27. See MacDonald (1900), p.53, no. 5; Phillips (1972–74), with pl. 9; Keppie (1998), p.61, fig. 25, p.63, fig. 26; Henig (2004), pp.228–29, fig. 12.6; Stoll (2007), p.454, fig. 25.1. The *aedicula* on the right is matched by one framing the cavalryman, but with an arched roof.
60. Actually, while there is clearly a ram and perhaps a bull, the third animal cannot be a sow – it is clearly a dog; even allowing for some clumsiness on the part of the Celtic artist, there is nothing porcine about this canine. He might have misunderstood his instructions to carve a pig.
61. E.g., Livy 1.44.2.
62. Cato *Agr.* 141; see also Varr. *Rust.* 2.1.10, cf. *Ling. Lat.* 6.86–87; Val. Max. 4.1.10; Fest. 154L.
63. *RIB* 2200 (*CIL* 7.1135); MacDonald (1900), p.54 no. 3; Keppie & Arnold (1984), pp.54–55, no. 150, pl. 37; Keppie (1998), pp.83–84, no. 11; Irby-Massie (1999),p. 243, no. 109. Virtus Augusta appears in many inscriptions, particularly referring to imperial victories: e.g., *RIB* 844, 1995.
64. *RIB* 2208 (*CIL* 7.1141; *CSIR* 156); MacDonald (1900), p.56, no. 1; Keppie & Arnold (1984), p.57, no. 156, pl. 38; Keppie (1998), p.23, fig. 12, p.65, fig. 27, p.88, no. 16; Keppie (2014), p.353, fig. 3.
65. See, for Roman prodigy lists, Rasmussen (2003), pp.224–25.
66. Tac. *Ann.* 15.7.1–18.
67. Suet. *Tib.* 19.
68. Tac. *Ann.* 2.14.1.

69. Tac. *Ann.* 2.17.2; victory: 2.17–18.
70. Trophy: Tac. *Ann.* 2.18. For this dream and eagles, see Allen (1961), pp.558–59, in the context of other dreams in military situations. For omens in Livy, Suetonius and Tacitus, see Krauss (1930).
71. Dio 56.24.1–5.
72. Suet. *Aug.* 23.2.
73. Plut. *Sull.* 9.4.
74. Dream: Tac. *Ann.* 1.65.1; the campaign: 1.65–68. Note too the dream of Otho (see above): Suet. *Oth.* 7.2.
75. Tac. *Hist.* 1.86.
76. Suet. *Galb.* 9.2, 10.4.
77. Tac. *Hist.* 1.62.2–3; see esp. Morgan (1993), pp.321–24; cf. Helgeland (1978), p.1474.
78. Tac. *Hist.* 2.50.2; Dio 63.10.3; see esp. Morgan (1993), pp.321–24.
79. Suet. *Oth.* 7.2. Galba experienced an omen too: Suet. *Galb.* 4.2, which he misinterpreted.
80. Suet. *Vitell.* 9, also at 18; there was a previous bad omen for Vitellius at *Vitell.* 8.2.
81. Suet. *Vesp.* 5.7.
82. Dio 64.8.1–2.
83. Dio 65.16.1.
84. Tac. *Hist.* 2.76–78. For the cypress tree as an omen, see also Suet. *Vesp.* 5.4, cf. 5.2 (below), *Dom.* 15.2; Dio 66.1.
85. Pliny *Nat. Hist.* 17.243; see also 16.132–33.
86. Tac. *Hist.* 2.78 is discussed esp. by Morgan (1996); see also McCulloch (1980), pp.239–42. See also Suet. *Vesp.* 5.2, 5.4, 5.7, 7.3, discussed below. For Basilides and his role in these omens, see Scott (1934).
87. Tac. *Hist.* 1.10.3.
88. Suet. *Vesp.* 5.4–7, 7.1; Tac. *Hist.* 1.86.1, 4.82. See also, for similar omens pertaining to Vespasian, Dio 59.12.3, 66.1.2–4; Oros. 7.9.3. Suetonius' details of Vespasian's visit to the god Carmelus are significantly different from those in Tacitus.
89. Tac. *Hist.* 5.13.2; Suet. *Vesp.* 5.4; Oros. 7.9.1–2.
90. Tac. *Hist.* 5.13.1–2; Suet. *Vesp.* 5.4.
91. Dio 50.4.4–5. For her temple, see Platner-Ashby (1929), pp.82–83; Richardson (1992), pp.57–58; and for Bellona as a war-goddess, Serrati (2020), pp.21–22, 30–36 (with fig. 2.2).
92. The main description is at Livy 1.32.6–14, esp. 13; see Serrati (2020), pp.19–22 for a detailed discussion; Dillon & Garland (2021), pp.94–95.
93. Wiedemann (1986), p.482 argues that until Octavian's performance of the rite, no source had mentioned spear-throwing; cf. however, Serrati (2020), pp.20–22.
94. Ovid *Fasti* 6.205–08. See also Serv. *Aen.* 9.52, discussing the fetial rite, the role of the *pater patratus*, and the spear and the pillar; as well as the Latin lexicographer Festus 30L; and the fifth–sixth-century AD author Placidus, at 14. On the column, see Platner-Ashby (1929), p.131.
95. Dio 72.33.3.
96. Livy 1.32.13, cf. 7, 11.
97. Varro as cited by Festus 204.4–6L, discussed by Harrison (1989), p.410.
98. For the temple of Jupiter Feretrius, see Platner-Ashby (1929), pp.293–94, with ancient sources; Richardson (1992), p.219.
99. See Dillon (2020), pp.84–85, and, for the coin, fig. 3.4.
100. Prop. *El.* 4.10.5–34; for Propertius, see further below.
101. Dio 44.4.3. See Harrison (1989), pp.408–09, who defends Dio's account from scholars – for example, Syme (1959), p.80 n.85 – who doubt this honour, recorded as it is only by Dio.
102. Dio 51.24.4.
103. Livy 4.19.1; *spolia opima*, 4.20.2.
104. Nep. *Att.* 2.30; Aug. *Res Gest.* 19; Livy 4.20.7. It was one of the eighty-two temples which he stated that he had restored at Rome: Aug. *Res Gest.* 20.

105. Livy 4.20.7–11; with esp. Syme (1959), pp.43–45; also Harrison (1989), pp.409–11; Garani (2007), pp.101–02. Livy does not mention Crassus' case but is clearly alluding to it. Livy 4.32.4 repeats the information that Cossus as military tribune (as at 4.19.1) dedicated the spoils: clearly he forgot to revise this later reference. See Dillon & Garland (2021), pp.671–72.
106. Prop. *El.* 4.10.2; Harrison (1989), 411; Garani (2007), esp. pp.101–02.
107. Suet. *Claud.* 1.4.
108. For Drusus and his quest for *spolia omina*, see Rich (1999).
109. See Dion. Hal. *Rom. Ant.* 2.34; cf. Livy 1.33.8.
110. Aug. *Res Gest.* 21.2. Cf. Suet. *Aug.* 30.2.
111. Joseph. *Bell. Jud.* 7.5.7. Individual (non-Jewish) artworks in the Temple of Peace: Paus. 9.6.3; Pliny *Nat. Hist.* 12.94, 34.84, 35.102–03, 35.109, 36.27, 36.58.
112. Gell. *Att. Noct.* 13.25 (485).
113. Gell. *Att. Noct.* 13.25.1–2 (485); also 13.25.2–29.
114. Aug. *Res Gest.* 12; *InscrIt* xiii.176; Ovid *Fasti* 1.709–22; for the altar: Richardson (1992), pp.287–89. For an exhaustive study of the artistic features of the altar, see Castriota (1995), with numerous plates including reconstructions.
115. Richardson (1992), p.288.
116. Richardson (1992), p.287, refers to coins of Nero.
117. Ovid *Trist.* 2.549–52, *Fasti* 5.577; Suet. *Aug.* 29.2.
118. Aug. *Res Gest.* 21; see for the temple, dedicated on 12 May 2 BC, Suet. *Aug.* 29.2, 56.2; Ovid *Fasti* 5.545–98; Vell. Pat. 2.100.2; Dio 55.10.1–8, 60.5.3; Macrob. *Sat.* 2.4.9; *InscrIt* xiii.490. See Platner-Ashby (1929), pp.220–23; Richardson (1992), pp.160–62.
119. Two temples: Platner-Ashby (1929), p.330; but see Simpson (1993) (esp. on Dio 54.8.3) correctly arguing that there was only one temple of Mars Ultor in Rome, in Augustus' forum; Richardson (1992), pp.245–46, considers there was only one temple. For the coins, see Beckmann (2016), pp.132–34, with figs 5–9; Matthew (2020), p.146, fig. 5.
120. Aug. *Res Gest.* 22. Dio 55.10.6–9 describes the *ludi* of 2 BC; cf. Dio 60.5.3 for a celebration under Claudius.
121. Dio 55.10.2–4; a similar, smaller list is given at Suet. *Aug.* 29.2, and note *Calig.* 44.2.
122. Suet. *Aug.* 29.2.
123. Suet. *Aug.* 31.1; Ovid *Fasti* 5.563–566; Pliny *Nat. Hist.* 22.13; Gell. *Noct. Att.* 9.11.10; Dio 55.10.3; *SHA Alex. Sev.* 28.6 – references from Platner-Ashby (1929), p.221.
124. See Beckmann (2016), pp.136–37, with figs 10–11.
125. Simpson (1977), p.94 n.31; with Beckmann (2016), p.124.
126. Beckmann (2016), pp.124, 126.
127. As suggested by Beckmann (2016), pp.140–41, with figs 12–13.
128. *RIC* 4.2, Alexander Severus, no. 636. See Manders (2004), p.128, fig. 1.
129. Ovid *Fasti* 1.277–82. For the temple of Janus, see Platner-Ashby (1929), pp.278–80; Richardson (1992), pp.206–07; and, for the closing of its doors: Silberberg-Peirce (1986), pp.306–08; DeBrohun (2007), pp.257–60; Dillon (2020), pp.7–8.
130. Varro *Ling. Lat.* 5.156, 5.165 (see also Livy 1.19; Plin. *Nat. Hist.* 34.33).
131. Aug. *Res Gest.* 13; Suet. *Aug.* 22.1; Dio 51.20.4. Jupiter's prophecy: Virg. *Aen.* 1.291–96.
132. *RIC* 1.326 (R2).
133. Oros. 9.9; not mentioned by Suetonius; with esp. Townend (1980), p.238.
134. Suet. *Vesp.* 9.1; Platner-Ashby (1929), pp.386–88, with references; Richardson (1992), pp.286–89.
135. Hdn 1.14.2–3; cf. Amm. Marc. 16.10.14; Richardson (1992), p.286.
136. Amm. Marc. 16.10.1. See below for his visit to Rome.
137. Aug. *Res Gest.* 19.5; Suet. *Aug.* 29.3, 91.2; Ovid *Fasti* 2.69; Mart. *Ep.* 5.16.5, 7.60.1–2; Pliny *Nat. Hist.* 34.78–79, 36.50; Dio 54.4.2–4; *CIL* 12 pp.244, 248; *CIL* 6.432 (*ILS* 3046), 6.2241, 6.2295, 6.32323, line 31; *InscrIt* xiii.504. See Platner-Ashby (1929), pp.305–06; Richardson (1992), pp.226–27. The hexastyle (six-columned) temple with a statue of the god within is shown on a silver denarius of 19 BC (*CNG* 90).

138. *CIL* 6.960; with Dio 68.16.3; see for the column, Platner-Ashby (1929), pp.238–39; Richardson (1992), pp.176–77.
139. *LIMC* 5 Iuppiter 342.
140. On the Roman cult of the Danube, and the god's appearance on the two columns, see esp. Kovács (2017), pp.47–50.
141. Kovács (2017) draws attention to the coins at *BMC* 3.84–85, 395–99.
142. Ovid *Fasti* 1.285–86. Cf. Stat. *Silv.* 4.3.81–82: a river god cedes his banks to Domitian.
143. There are three *suovetaurilia* scenes shown on Trajan's Column (scenes 8, 53 and 103).
144. Ryberg (1955), pp.109–13, pl. 36–38; *ThesCRA* iv.68, no.28.
145. Ryberg (1967), pl. 28, fig. 28.
146. See Petersen (1896), p.54, for this description of the damaged relief.
147. Aur. Vict. *Caes.* 16.15; cf. *CIL* 6.1585.
148. For the column itself, there are many studies: see, for a recent overview, Beckmann (2012); Kovács (2008), p.155–68.
149. For the column, see Platner-Ashby (1929), 132–33; Richardson (1992), pp.95–96.
150. Ryberg (1967), pp.37–43, pl. 27, fig. 27, pls 29–31, fig. 29–31, esp. pl. 31, fig. 31; *ThesCRA* iv.86, no. 93. For the eagle and standards: Ryberg (1967), pp.39–40.
151. Kovács (2008), p.178, figs 3–4; Beckmann (2012), p.258, fig. 15.6.
152. See the description of this scene in Petersen (1896), pp.56–57 (scene 11). Petersen gives plates and German commentary on all the scenes of Marcus Aurelius' column and remains an indispensible resource. He does not mention any altar or sacrifice.
153. It has been suggested that scene 11 depicts Aurelius sacrificing to request divine assistance – Kovács (2017), p.52 – but there is no altar, and Petersen's interpretation that Aurelius is addressing the Germans across the river is correct – Petersen (1896), pp.55–56.
154. *SHA Marc.* 24.4; see Beckmann (2012), p.259.
155. Kovács (2008), pp.179–80, figs 5–8; Beckmann (2012), p.258, fig. 15.5.
156. For the rain miracle, see the exhaustive study of Kovács (2008), esp. pp.137–53, also Kovács (2017), pp.50–56. Note also Israelowich (2008).
157. But cf. Kovács (2017), p.52, who thinks Dio is nevertheless correct (but clearly this is a miracle of rain alone).
158. *LIMC* 5 Iuppiter Tonans 343.
159. See Petersen (1896), pp.58–59, with plates.
160. Kovács (2008), p.30.
161. Tert. *Apol.* 5.25, *Scap.* 4; Eusebius refers to the passage in Tert. *Apol.* at Eus. *Hist. Eccl.* 5.5.5. Dates: Kovács (2008), p.24. The key passages of Tertullian, Dio, Xiphilinos, Eusebius and others are given in the Latin and Greek and translated into English by Kovács (2008), pp.23–93, with discussion. See also for the sources, Israelowich (2008), pp.85–91.
162. Eusebius *Hist. Eccl.* 5.5.
163. Eusebius *Hist. Eccl.* 5.5.4.
164. Tert. *Apol.* 5.25.
165. Euseb. *Hist. Eccl.* 5.5.1–7. For his account, see esp. Sage (1987).
166. *Sibylline Oracle* xii.194–200; text and translation at Kovács (2008), pp.38–39.
167. Ryberg (1967), pp.15–20, figs 9–13.
168. On this gate, see Platner-Ashby (1929), pp.418–19.
169. Ryberg (1967), p.16, citing coins of Aurelius showing Neptune.
170. Ryberg (1967), pp.19–20.
171. *LIMC* 5 Iuppiter 359 – Ryberg (1955), pp.157–58, pl. 56.86; Ryberg (1967), pp.21–27, esp. 22–23, pls 15–16, figs 14b–14c.
172. Boscoreale skyphos: height 10cm, diameter 12.5cm; Musée du Louvre, inv. no. BJ2367.
173. See esp. Ryberg (1957), pp.20–22, 141–43, figs 13, 77.
174. Aug. *Res Gest.* 34; cf. Suet. *Caes.* 2.
175. See Jeppesen (1994) for a different interpretation of the identity of the figures; for the usual interpretation, see Fischer (2016), pp.41–44, 42 fig. 3.1. In particular, Jeppesen views the

deities in the right lower register as Bendis and Neoptolemus rather than Diana and Mercury, as the former represent Thrace and Greece, and the campaign being celebrated as that against the Illyrians north of those regions.

176. *RPC* 2.2305. For his devotion to the goddess, see Suet. *Dom.* 4.4, 15.3 (Minerva appears in a dream to Domitian and tells him that she can no longer protect him as Jupiter has disarmed her: his assassination followed shortly after.) This coin was also minted in Pamphylia, where in a variation she carries thunderbolts in her left hand: *RPC* 2.1524a.
177. E.g., *RPC* 2.38, 2.1532a.
178. Suet. *Claud.* 1.3 (specifically mentioning the *tropaea* on the arch); Dio 55.2.3.
179. See the reconstruction of the arch at Barrett (1991), p.18, fig. 5 showing the *tropaea*.
180. *CIL* 6.920a; *ILS* 216.
181. Coins: Barrett (1991), p.2, figs 1 (Claudius' arch) & 2 (Drusus' arch). For Claudius' arch, see Dio 60.22.1.
182. Richardson (1992), p.402.
183. E.g., BM 1896,0608.22 (*RIC* 2.70); AD 101–102.
184. The figure is from Cichorius (1896–1900), pl. 57 (scene 58). Cichorius' publication of the column and its scenes is still invaluable.
185. Jones (2000), p.56, fig. 11.
186. The discussion of Merrill (1901) is still very useful; for the reliefs, see the figures at Torelli (1997).
187. *LIMC* 5 Iuppiter 364a; Torelli (1997), p.146, fig. 1, p.147, fig. 2, p.151, fig. 7, p.152, fig. 8, p.157, fig. 18, p.158, fig. 20.
188. Torelli (1997), p.146, fig. 1, p.153, fig. 10.
189. *LIMC* 5 Iuppiter 364b. The suggestion is that of Merrill (1901), p.49; for the scene, see Torelli (1997), p.161, fig. 24.
190. Torelli (1997), p.163, fig. 26.
191. *LIMC* 5 Iuppiter 364a; Torelli (1997), p.151, fig. 7, p.152, fig. 9.
192. See for an introduction to the Jupiter columns, Woolf (2001), esp. pp.118–19.
193. For Greek *tropaia*, see Stroszeck (2004); Schmitz (2020); for Greek and Roman trophies (*tropaia* and *tropaea* respectively), see *ThesCRA* iv.357–359; for the Roman monumental permanent *tropaeum*, esp. Picard (1957).
194. Strabo 7.7.6.
195. *Tropaeum*: Suet. *Aug.* 18.2. For the *tropaeum* at Actium, with plans and photographs, see esp. Murray & Petsas (1989); see also the invaluable archaeological report of Zachos (2003). The gods fought for Octavian: Virg. *Aen.* 8.698–706 gives the list of gods on his side, namely Neptune, Venus, Minerva, Mars, Bellona (a Roman war goddess) and Apollo (of Actium).
196. Dio 51.1.3.
197. Tac. *Ann.* 2.53.
198. See esp. Murray & Petsas (1989), pp.55–56, cf. 103–07.
199. For the Latin text of the inscription (the letters are each 1ft high) and discussion, see Murray & Petsas (1989), pp.76–77, trans. at p.86; see also Zachos (2003), p.76.
200. See Picard (1957), pp.257–74; *ThesCRA* iv.358–59, fig. 9; Schenck-David (2003).
201. See Rodríguez (2020), p.406, figs 2–3.
202. Pliny *Nat. Hist.* 3.20.136; the actual inscription: *CIL* 5.7817 (*AE* 1973, 323).
203. See, for the Tropaeum Augusti, Schenck-David (2003); *ThesCRA* iv.358 no. 10; Picard (1957), pp.291–301; Hope (2003), p.81, pl. 1; Stroszeck (2004), pp.306–07, fig. 7; Rodríguez (2020), pp.11–12, fig. 10. Schenck-David (2003) has several photos of the remains of the sculptural elements, and a reconstruction (p.31, figs 3–4).
204. See, for the Tropaeum Traiani, Picard (1957), pp.391–406; *ThesCRA* iv.359 no. 12. The fundamental study is that of Florescu (1960); and there is also a solid discussion by Richmond (1967), as well as by Turner (2013). Also useful are Rossi (1997); Stroszeck (2004), p.306; cf. Hope (2003), pp.91–92.
205. *CIL* 3.14214 (*ILS* 9107; *AE* 1980, 794).

206. As Richmond (1967), p.37 suggests.
207. See esp. the reconstruction at Richmond (1967), pl. 12a.
208. For the altar, see Turner (2013), pp.279–86 (esp. 285–86, 288, suggesting probably correctly, that the altar may in fact be a monument from the reign of Domitian). For the inscribed names: Turner (2013), pp.286–300.
209. Eagle recovered: Dio 68.9.3.
210. Dio 68.8.
211. Flor. *Epit.* 2.30.23.
212. Tac. *Ann.* 2.22 (with 2.21; this episode occurred after another battle immediately subsequent to that involving the eight eagles: see above). See Richmond (1967), p.32 on the deities involved: he supports amending the Latin to read Mars Ultor and Augustus (deleting Jove), but this is not necessary; cf. Hope (2003), p.81. Note too Germanicus' burying of the remains of Varus' three legions, and Germanicus' recovery of the standards: Tac. *Ann.* 1.62; Suet. *Calig.* 3.1–3; Dio 57.18.1.
213. Suet. *Claud.* 1.3–4. Cf. Suet. *Caes.* 84.4; Dio 56.42. A *decursio* by cavalry and infantry is shown on the pedestal of the column of Antoninus Pius in Rome.

Bibliography

Allen, W., 'Epic and Etiquette in Tacitus' "Annals"', *Studies in Philology* 58.4 (1961), pp.557–72.
Ando, C., 'Interpretatio Romana', *CPh* 100.1 (2005), pp.41–51.
Barrett, A.A., 'Claudius' British Victory Arch in Rome', *Britannia* 22 (1991), pp.1–19.
Beckmann, M., 'The Column of Marcus Aurelius', in van Ackeren, M. (ed.), *A Companion to Marcus Aurelius* (Chichester, 2012), pp.251–63.
Beckmann, M., 'Trajan's Column and Mars Ultor', *JRS* 106 (2016), pp.124–46.
Birley, E., 'An Inscription from Cramond, and the Matres Campestres', *Glasgow Archaeological Journal* 4.4 (1976), pp.108–10.
Birley, E., 'The Religion of the Roman Army: 1895–1977', *ANRW* 2.16.2 (1978) pp.1506–41.
Birley, A. & Birley, A., 'A New Dolichenum, Inside the Third-Century Fort at Vindolanda', in Blömer, M. & Winter, E. (eds), *Iuppiter Dolichenus. Vom Lokalkult zur Reichsreligion* (Tübingen, 2012), pp.231–57.
Cichorius, C., *Die Reliefs der Traianssäule*, vols 1–3 (Berlin, 1896–1900).
Collar, A., 'Military Networks and the Cult of Jupiter Dolichenus', *Asia Minor Studien* 64 (2011), pp.217–46.
CCID: Hörig, M. & Schwertheim, E., *Corpus Cultus Iovis Dolicheni (CCID)* (Leiden, 1987).
Dillon, M.P.J., 'Introduction: New Perspectives on Religion and Warfare in the Roman Republic: 509–27 BC', in Dillon, M.P.J. & Matthew, C. (eds), *Religion and Classical Warfare: The Roman Republic* (Barnsley, 2020), pp.1–16.
Dillon, M. & Garland, L., *The Ancient Romans. History and Society from the Early Republic to the Death of Augustus* (Oxford, 2021).
Durham, E. & Fulford, M., 'Symbols of Power: The Silchester Bronze Eagle and Eagles in Roman Britain', *Archaeological Journal* 170.1 (2013), pp.78–105.
Fink, R.O., *Roman Military Records on Papyrus* (Cape Western Reserve University, 1971).
Fink, R.O., Hoey, A.S. & Snyder, W.F., *The Feriale Duranum* (Yale, 1940).
Fischer, C.J., 'A Woman's Weapon: Private Propaganda in the Imperial Cameos of the Early Roman Empire', in Fischer, J.C. (ed.), *More Than Mere Playthings: The Minor Arts of Italy* (Newcastle, 2016), pp.39–54.
Fishwick, D., 'Dated Inscriptions and the "Feriale Duranum"', *Syria* 65.3–4 (1988), pp.349–61.
Florescu, F.B., *Monumentul de la Adamklissi, Tropaeum Traiani* (Bucharest, 1961).
Garani, M., 'Propertius' Temple of Jupiter Feretrius and the Spolia Opima (4.10): A Poem Not to be Read?', *AC* 76 (2007), pp.99–117.
Gilliam, J.F., 'The Roman Military Feriale', *HThR* 47.3 (1954), pp.183–96.
Harrison, S.J., 'Augustus, the Poets, and the Spolia Opima', *CQ* 39.2 (1989), pp.408–14.

Hekster, O. & Zair, N., *Rome and its Empire, AD 193–284* (Edinburgh, 2008).
Helgeland, J., 'Roman Army Religion', *ANRW* 2.16.2 (1978), pp.1470–1505.
Henig, M., 'Roman Religion and Roman Culture in Roman Britain', in Todd, M. (ed.), *A Companion to Roman Britain* (Oxford, 2004), pp.220–41.
Hope, V.M., 'Trophies and Tombstones: Commemorating the Roman Soldier', *World Archaeology* 35.1 (2003), pp.79–97.
Irby-Massie, G.L. 'The Roman Army and the Cult of the Campestres', *ZPE* 113 (1996), pp.293–300.
Irby-Massie, G.L., *Military Religion in Roman Britain* (Leiden, 1999).
Israelowich, I., 'The Rain Miracle of Marcus Aurelius: (Re-)construction of Consensus', *G&R* 55.1 (2008), pp.83–102.
Jeppesen, K.K., 'The Identity of the Missing Togatus and other Clues to the Interpretation of the Gemma Augustea', *OJA* 13.3 (1994), pp.335–55.
Jones, M.W., 'Genesis and Mimesis: The Design of the Arch of Constantine in Rome', *Journal of the Society of Architectural Historians* 59.1 (2000), pp.50–77.
Kaizer, T., 'A Note on the Fresco of Iulius Terentius from Dura-Europos', in (no ed.) *Altertum und Mittelmeerraum: die antike Welt diesseits und jenseits der Levante* (Stuttgart, 2006), pp.151–59.
Keppie, L.J.F., *Roman Stones in the Hunterian Museum* (London, 1998).
Keppie, L.J.F., 'The Hunterian Collection and its Museum', *Journal of the History of Collections* 26.3 (2014), pp.355–62.
Keppie, L.J.F. & Arnold, B.J., *Scotland* (Oxford, 1984).
Kovács, P., *Marcus Aurelius' Rain Miracle and the Marcomannic Wars* (Leiden, 2008).
Kovács, P., 'Deities in Trajan's and Marcus Aurelius' Column', *Acta Archaeologica Academiae Scientiarum Hungaricae* 68.1 (2017), pp.47–58.
Krauss, F.B., *An Interpretation of the Omens, Portents, and Prodigies Recorded by Livy, Tacitus, and Suetonius* (Philadelphia, 1930).
Le Bohec, Y., *The Imperial Roman Army*, trans. Bate, R. (London, 1994).
Linduff, K.M., 'Epona: A Celt among the Romans', *Latomus* 38.4 (1979), pp.817–37.
MacDonald, J., 'The Inscriptions of the Distance-Slabs of the Vallum or Wall of Antoninus Pius', *Transactions of the Glasgow Archaeological Society* 4.1 (1900), pp.49–64.
McCulloch, H.Y., 'Literary Augury at the End of "Annals" XIII', *Phoenix* 34.3 (1980), pp.237–42.
Manders, E., 'Religion and Coinage: Heliogabalus and Alexander Severus. Two Extremes?', *Talanta* 36 (37) (2004), pp.123–38.
Matthew, C., 'The Cult of the Eagles in the Roman Republic', in Dillon, M. & Matthew, C. (eds), *Religion and Classical Warfare: The Republic* (Barnsley, 2020), pp.129–54.
Merrill, E.T., 'Some Observations on the Arch of Trajan at Beneventum', *TAPhA* 32 (1901), pp.43–63.
Morgan, M.G., 'Two Omens in Tacitus' *Histories* (2.50.2 and 1.62.2–3)', *RhM* 136.3-4 (1993), pp.321–29.
Morgan, M.G., 'Vespasian and the Omens in Tacitus "Histories" 2.78', *Phoenix* 50.1 (1996), pp.41–55.
Murray, W. & Petsas, P., 'Octavian's Campsite Memorial for the Actian War', *TAPhS* 79.4 (1989), pp.1–172.
Nash-Williams, V.E., 'Iuppiter Dolichenus', *G&R* 21 (1952), pp.72–77.
Nock, A.D., 'The Roman Army and the Roman Religious Year', *HThR* 45.4 (1952), pp.187–252.
Nock, A.D., *Essays on Religion and the Ancient World*, vol. 2 (Oxford, 1972), pp.736–90.
Petersen, E., *Die Marcus-säule auf Piazza Colonna in Rom* (Munich, 1896).
Phillips, E.J., 'The Roman Distance Slab from Bridgeness', *Proceedings of the Society of Antiquaries of Scotland* 105 (1972–74), pp.176–82.
Picard, G.C., *Les trophées romains: contribution à l'histoire de la religion et de l'art triomphal de Rome* (Paris, 1957).
Platner, S.B. & Ashby, T., *A Topographical Dictionary of Ancient Rome* (London, 1929).
Pollard, N., *Soldiers, Cities, and Civilians in Roman Syria* (Michigan, 2001).
Rasmussen, S.W., *Public Portents in Republican Rome* (Rome, 2003).

Ratimorská, P. & Minaroviech, J., 'Roman Sanctuary of Jupiter Dolichenus in Brigetio and its Hypothetical Reconstruction', *Anodos. Studies of the Ancient World* 9 (2009), pp.1–14.
Rich, J.W., 'Drusus and the Spolia Opima', *CQ* 49.2 (1999), pp.544–55.
Richmond, I.A., 'Adamklissi', *PBSR* 35 (1967), pp.29–39.
Rodríguez, G., 'Before and After Rome: The Incised Contours Technique in the Art of Gallia Narbonensis', *Theoretical Roman Archaeology Journal* 3.1 (2020), pp.1–17.
Rossi, L., 'A Synoptic Outlook of Adamklissi Metopes and Trajan's Column Frieze: Factual and Fanciful Topics Revisited', *Athenaeum* 85 (1997), pp.471–86.
Rüpke, J., *Domi Militiae. Die religiöse Konstruktion des Krieges in Rom* (Stuttgart, 1990).
Ryberg, I.S., *The Rites of the State Religion in Roman Art* (Rome, 1955).
Ryberg, I.S., *Panel Reliefs of Marcus Aurelius* (New York, 1967).
Sage, M.M., 'Eusebius and the Rain Miracle: Some Observations', *Historia* 36.1 (1987), pp.96–113.
Schenck-David, J.L., 'Le trophée augustéen de Saint-Bertrand-de-Comminges ou les tribulations antiques et modernes d'un monument triomphal dans les Pyrénées centrales', *La revue du Louvre et des musées de France* 1 (2003), pp.29–36.
Schmitz, M., 'Thanking the Gods and Declaring Victory: Trophies and Dedications in Classical Greek Warfare', in Dillon, M., Matthew, C. & Schmitz, M. (eds), *Religion and Classical Warfare: Archaic and Classical Greece* (Barnsley, 2020), pp.325–61.
Scott, K., 'The Rôle of Basilides in the Events of A.D. 69', *JRS* 24 (1934), pp.138–40.
Serrati, J., 'Religion and Roman Warfare in the Middle Republic', in Dillon, M. & Matthew, C. (eds), *Religion and Classical Warfare: The Republic* (Barnsley, 2020), pp.17–52.
Silberberg-Peirce S., 'The Many Faces of the Pax Augusta: Images of War and Peace in Rome and Gallia Narbonensis', *Art History* 9.3 (1986), pp.306–24.
Simpson, C.J., 'The Date of Dedication of the Temple of Mars Ultor', *JRS* 67 (1977), pp.91–94.
Simpson, C.J., 'A Shrine of Mars Ultor Re-Visited', *Revue belge de philologie et d'histoire* 71.1 (1993), pp.116–22.
Speidel, M., *The Religion of Jupiter Dolichenus in the Roman Army* (Leiden, 1978).
Speidel, M. & Dimitrova-Milceva, A., 'The Cult of the Genii in the Roman Army and a New Imperial Deity', *ANRW* 2.16.2 (1978), pp.1541–55.
Stoll, O., 'The Religions of the Army', in Erdkamp, P. (ed.), *A Companion to the Roman Army* (Chichester, 2007), pp.451–76.
Stroszeck, J., 'Greek Trophy Monuments', in Bouvrie, S. des (ed.), *Myth and Symbol ii: Symbolic Phenomena in Ancient Greek Culture* (Bergen, 2004).
Syme, R., 'Livy and Augustus', *HSCPh* 64 (1959), pp.27–87.
Torelli, M., '"Ex his castra, ex his tribus replebuntur": The Marble Panegyric on the Arch of Trajan at Beneventum', *Studies in the History of Art* 49 (1997), pp.144–77.
Tóth, I., 'Destruction of the Sanctuaries of Iuppiter Dolichenus at the Rhine and in the Danube Region (235–238)', *Acta Archaeologica Academiae Scientiarum Hungaricae* 25 (1973), pp.109–16.
Turcan, R., *The Cults of the Roman Empire* (Malden MA, 1996).
Turcan, R., *The Gods of Ancient Rome*, trans. Nevill, A. (Edinburgh, 1998).
Turner, B., 'War Losses and World View: Re-viewing the Roman Funerary Altar at Adamclisi', *AJPh* 134.2 (2013), pp.276–305.
Walsh, D., 'The Fate of Temples in Noricum and Pannonia', *AJA* 120.2 (2016), pp.221–38.
Walsh, D., 'Military Communities and Temple Patronage: A Case Study of Britain and Pannonia', *AJA* 124.2 (2020), pp.275–99.
Wheeler, E.L., 'Shock And Awe: Battles of the Gods in Roman Imperial Warfare', in Wolff, C. & Le Bohec, Y. (eds), *L'armée romaine et la religion sous le Haut-Empire romain* (Lyon-Paris, 2009), pp.225–67.
Wiedemann, T., 'The Fetiales: A Reconsideration', *CQ* 36.2 (1986), pp.478–90.
Woolf, G., 'Representation as Cult: the Case of the Jupiter Columns', in Spickermann, W. *et al.* (eds), *Religion in den germanischen Provinzen Roms* (Tübingen, 2001), pp.117–34.
Zachos, K.L., 'The Tropaeum of the Sea-Battle of Actium at Nikopolis: Interim Report', *JRA* 16 (2003), pp.65–92.

Chapter 4

Heros invictus and *pacator orbis*: Hercules as a War God for Roman Emperors

Megan Daniels

'People of Rome! Caesar, who was reported but now to have sought a crown of bay at the cost of his life, comes home, victorious like Hercules from the Spanish shore.'[1]

Introduction

To study how the Roman emperors engaged with the imagery and symbolism of Hercules in matters of war requires engaging with the palimpsest of meanings associated with this god and his corresponding cultural manifestations over the long term. Throughout the first millennium BC, Hercules emerged amongst the varied cultural groups around the Mediterranean as a multifaceted deity representative of many themes pertinent to empire. As a mortal who obtained immortality and who wandered to the limits of the known world siring royal houses and conquering monstrous forces, he epitomized the ideals of *imperium* and *virtus*, and it is little wonder why dynasts from the Roman worlds adopted Herculean symbolism in their self-representations. Yet he was also an equivocal figure, who migrated between venerable warrior ancestor, maddened brute and exotic effete, making him an important counterpoint for ancient authors on the more ambivalent aspects of empire and conquest.

The clearest way to summarize Hercules' military appeal to Roman emperors is his long history of mythical and dynastic prominence around the Mediterranean world, a history which went back to the Iron Age, and likely earlier. Hercules was a model for Rome's rulers because he was a symbol of social power with a long history, recognized across numerous cultural groups who were incorporated into the Empire. His characteristic imagery, which included the lion-skin cap and club, was a widely shared symbolic language that could be employed in various cultural contexts, while the mythical tropes surrounding this god provided fodder for more erudite musings on the workings of power.

The Roman imperial engagement with Hercules thus involved a symbolic language that was much older than the Empire itself, but timelessly suitable and malleable to the purposes of empire. While this language was associated with bellicose endeavours like hunting and warfare, Hercules' persona encompassed much more than brute force, channelling martial prowess into the grander civilizing missions of imperial rule. This lofty messaging can be read through the interrelation of a number of media – literary, numismatic, epigraphic and iconographic – that formed a dynamic and fluid 'symbolic system' of communication across the Empire, both official and unofficial.² The first part of this chapter provides an overview of the warlike symbolism of Hercules from the Iron Age to the Republic, followed by case studies into the Roman imperial employment of Hercules as a war god.

The Mediterranean Backdrop

Hercules' bellicose character is seen in relation to the 'Master of Lions' imagery that emerges on Cyprus at open-air sanctuaries around the Mesaoria plain in the early sixth century BC and takes the form of limestone figurines depicting a male in smiting pose (see Figure 4.1). There may be earlier iconographies of the Greek Heracles, but all instances are conjectural: Hermary cites the Cypriot plate dating to the tenth century BC from Palaepaphos showing two hunters attacking a two-headed serpent as possible evidence for early versions of the Heracles myth. Cypro-Phoenician-style silver cups from Kourion in Cyprus and Praeneste in Italy from the eighth and seventh centuries BC showing the same narrative scene of a hunter departing from a city, killing a deer in the mountains, making a sacrifice and attacking a monster with the help of a goddess may also suggest an early dissemination of the myth of Heracles across the Mediterranean.³

In the 'Master of Lions' imagery, his raised right arm holds a club and his left hand grasps a lion by the tail, hind legs or neck. He wears a short belted chiton and lion skin draped over the head and shoulder, with the front legs knotted at the chest.⁴ The hunter in lion skin calls to mind the classic iconography of Heracles that appears in Greece and Italy in vase painting,⁵ while the smiting pose derives from Mesopotamian and Egyptian divine imagery, as does the general theme of hunting.⁶ There is some rightful scholarly hesitation to accept this Cypriot imagery wholesale as Heracles or Melqart,⁷ and it is perhaps most apt to see both the Master of Lions imagery and Heracles/Melqart as figures who evoked a venerable symbolic language of the king/hero/god who conquers chaotic forces like the lion and also assumes a leonine persona in the establishment of worldly order.⁸ Mario Attilio Levi argued that there were no common origins before the Hellenistic-Roman era between

Figure 4.1: 'Master of Lions' figurine (c.530–520 BC) from Cyprus, heavily restored. (© *The Metropolitan Museum of Art*, 74.51.2455; public domain)

Heracles, Melqart and Hercules;[9] this may be so as far as actual origins go, but interrelations between all of these figures were made well before the Hellenistic period in the context of the rampant cultural and commercial interactions within the Mediterranean.

With the expansion of numerous groups in the Archaic and Classical periods, for instance, the mythical and iconographic tropes of Heracles and Melqart played a clear role in dynastic and territorial claims.[10] Bilingual inscriptions on twin *cippi* from Malta dating to the second century BC make the conflation of Heracles and Melqart as founder gods clear. In the Phoenician inscription, Melqart is invoked as *b'l ṣr* ('Lord of Tyre'); Heracles is called *archēgetēs* ('Founder') in the Greek version.[11] Engraved bronze razors from the necropolis of Saint Monica at Carthage, which date to the third century BC, combine Hellenizing imagery of Melqart (e.g., a standing male in lion skin holding a club) and more traditional Punic imagery (e.g., a bearded male in long skirt and pointed cap holding a fenestrated axe).[12] In many ways, 'Founder' did not just denote a leader of colonists, but also, in Bonnet's words, a process '*d'appropriation culturelle du cosmos et d'espaces habitables par les communautés, tyriennes et diasporiques*' ('of cultural appropriation of the cosmos and habitable spaces by communities, Tyrians and diasporas').[13] This appropriation extended to Heracles: the prince Dorieus of Sparta, from the line of Heracles, was advised to plant a colony, Heraclea, in western Sicily, 'since Heracles himself had acquired it'.[14] The mythical geographies of Heracles–Melqart reflected colonial endeavours, particularly in the western Mediterranean at Phoenician foundations such as Lixus and Gades. At Gades, mythical tradition had Heracles kill Geryon and affix two pillars into the earth, the 'Pillars of Hercules'.[15]

As U. Huttner notes, '*der militärische Bereich ursprünglich nur am Rande zu seinen Ressorts zählte*' ('the military aspect was originally only a small part of his portfolio').[16] Yet the employment of Heraclean imagery in the context of war and conquest comes into clearer focus with the Macedonian rulers – namely Philip and Alexander – and their successors, the *Diadochoi*, as the military duties of these kings were transferred to their patron. The Macedonian royal house claimed Heracles as its divine ancestor, and the exploits of Philip and Alexander were legitimized via recourse to their Heraclean ancestry.[17] An inscription naming Herakles Patroos was found in the royal palace at Vergina.[18] The association between Alexander and Heracles is witnessed clearly in the widely distributed tetradrachm showing Heracles in his lion skin on the obverse – possibly with Alexander's features – and a seated Zeus on the reverse.[19] Alexander besieged Tyre in 332 BC after the city refused to allow him to sacrifice to Heracles; he then honoured the god with yearly festivals.[20]

Alexander and the *Diadochoi* popularized the epithets *Aniketos* and *Kallinikos*, associated with the gods of the Macedonian dynasty, Heracles and Dionysus, both conquerors of the East, and Weinstock notes that Heracles was called *Kallinikos* and *Aniketos* much more frequently after Alexander, although he was addressed by these terms as early as the late seventh century BC.[21] The links with the earlier first-millennium symbolism and ideology surrounding Heracles are evident: the late fourth-century Alexander Sarcophagus, commissioned by King Abdalonymous of

Figure 4.2: The Alexander Sarcophagus showing Alexander in lion-skin cap fighting Persians on long side A. (*Photo by Ronald Slabke; CC BY-SA 3.0*)

Sidon,[22] for instance, hearkens back to the Master of Lions imagery by depicting Alexander atop a horse in smiting pose in lion-skin cap on long side A, with a lion-hunt scene on long side B (see Figure 4.2).

Alexander's successors continued to capitalize on the symbolic language of Heracles through widely disseminated numismatic iconographies, in particular the Seleucids in the East. For instance, Seleucus I continued to produce the Alexandrine tetradrachm showing an unbearded Heracles in the lion skin on the obverse and an enthroned Zeus holding Nike or an eagle and sceptre on the reverse. Almost every mint that produced silver coinage issued these tetradrachms: Sardis, Tarsus, Antioch-on-the-Orontes, Antigonea-on-the-Orontes, Seleucia-in-Pieria, Laodicea-by-the-Sea, Carrhae, Babylon, Seleucia-on-the-Tigris, Susa, Ecbatana and several uncertain mints,[23] while other dynasties also engaged with Heracles' imagery and mythology – the Ptolemies, Antigonids and Attalids.[24] This widespread use of Heracles continued under Seleucus' successors, albeit with certain modifications of the Heracles type: for instance, Antiochus I issued coins in the western part of the empire showing Heracles resting after his labours – possibly symbolizing the security of the kingship – while the eastern part of the empire issued coins emphasizing the military aspects of Heracles, including images of his weapons, the club and bow.[25]

The appropriation of Heracles as victorious conqueror and divine ancestor took hold in the West as well, and incorporated the persona of Melqart.[26] In Sicily, the Carthaginian and Sicilian leaders rapidly began minting coins at the end of the fourth century with the head of Heracles-Melqart in his lion-skin helmet, which alluded to the Alexander prototype and likely represented the appropriation by Siculo-Carthaginian leaders of the current dominant imagery of rulership via a widely recognized deity. Earlier Siculo-Punic coins from the fourth century depicted a bearded male head with earring and had the legend *RŠMLQRT*, 'Rosh Melqart' or 'head of Melqart', referring to either a coastal location or a Carthaginian provincial institution.²⁷ For the Carthaginians, this imagery seems to appear following their defeat of the Syracusans in 304 BC. But the tyrant of Syracuse, Agathocles, had also used the image of Heracles on his own wartime coin issues following his return from his campaigns in Africa.²⁸ A few decades later, when Pyrrhus defeated the Punic forces of Eryx in 277 BC, he offered games and sacrifices to Heracles, just as Alexander had after his capture of Tyre.²⁹

In the third century, the imagery of Heracles/Melqart appeared on coins from many of the Phoenician cities in Spain, utilized by the Barcid dynasty to legitimize their growing power in the Iberian Peninsula.³⁰ Coin issues showing a laureate Heracles/Melqart with club on the obverse and elephant on the reverse are likely quasi-portraits of the rulers, alluding to the Barcids' wartime activities.³¹ Through these issues, the Barcids drew from the religious mentalities of the Punic cities in southern Spain, but also from broader 'Heraclean' ideologies associated with conquest and dynastic legitimacy. Finally, leaders going back to the Archaic period emulated Heracles, not only as a model founder god and royal ancestor, but also as the first victor of the Olympic Games: Milo of Croton is said to have led the army of his native city against Sybaris, clad in a lion skin and wielding a club;³² Polydamus of Scotoussa supposedly killed a lion with his bare hands in deliberate imitation of Heracles' first labour.³³

It is against this broader background that we must interpret Roman rulers' employment of Hercules, as a syncretistic hero-god whose martial and royal symbolism translated across numerous cultural contexts. Indeed, the peoples of the Italian peninsula had formulated their own interactions with this peregrinating deity long before the Roman imperial period. From the excavations around the church of Sant'Omobono in the Forum Boarium in Rome in the mid-twentieth century came a two-thirds life-size terracotta statue, dating to the sixth century BC, of a god in a lion skin knotted at the chest and belted at the middle in the manner of Cypriot Master of Lions figurines, although the workmanship of the statue is reminiscent of types produced in eastern Greece (Ionia) (see Figure 4.3). He stands beside a female consort in Ionian helmet, generally interpreted as Minerva/Athena.³⁴ Although her identity is disputed, Minerva/Athena would make sense, given Athena's role as protector of Heracles during his labours, and bronze mirrors from Etruria show Hercle (Heracles) and Menrfa (Athena) together.³⁵ While important in this early period for its strategic commercial and transhumant

Figure 4.3: Hercules and Minerva terracotta statues from the archaic temple at Sant'Omobono, Rome, sixth century BC, now in the Capitoline Museum, Rome. (*Photograph by author*)

position on the fordable part of the Tiber and as a locale for trade in staples like salt,[36] the Forum Boarium would, in the late Republic and early Empire, become an epicentre for Rome's mytho-history, featuring Hercules in triumphal fashion (see below).[37] Accounts claim that Hercules and Evander founded the *Ara Maxima* after Hercules arrived at the Forum Boarium from Gades with Geryon's cattle and slew Cacus.[38]

Hercules as a War God: The Republican Period

Some have suggested that Hercules's persona in Rome, and in particular the Forum Boarium, underwent a transformation in the mid-Republican period, from a god associated with traders and commerce to a warrior deity as Roman rulers became increasingly engaged in Hellenistic martial and royal customs.[39] Conversely, Levi argues that the original deity of the *Ara Maxima* – the Great Altar to Hercules in the Forum Boarium, built by Hercules and Evander according to mythical tradition – was a supreme ruler god who only became associated with the Greek hero in Mid-Republican times.[40] The reality is clearly complex: the terracottas from Sant'Omobono mentioned above associate Hercules – in Cypro-Ionian style – with a warlike goddess, and Greek myths going back to the Archaic and Classical periods wrestled with the dual status of this god-hero. The use of a mortal-turned-god protected by a powerful goddess in Archaic Rome, atop a monumental temple, joins a number of other sites throughout Italy with this imagery,[41] and, like the Master of Lions imagery, ties into a deeper history of regal employment across the Mediterranean and Near East.[42]

Nonetheless, while Hercules was long associated with royal and martial power, his focal point as a military deity associated with the Roman triumph does emerge in the Mid- to Late Republican period, alongside Rome's expansion as an imperial power. Livy states that Roman generals were erecting statues to Hercules by 305 BC,[43] and triumphal coinage depicts the hero with increasing frequency. An increasing number of temples and monuments were built to Hercules in this period – although it is important to note that the mid-Republican period in general saw an explosion of temple building in the capital.[44] In the Campus Martius, the starting point for the triumphal procession, M. Fulvius Nobilior built the temple to Hercules Musarum (Hercules of the Muses) in the early second century.[45] Another temple, that of Hercules Custos ('Guardian'), is also mentioned in the ancient sources, but its location is unknown.[46]

In the Forum Boarium, M. Octavius Herennus built a temple to Hercules Victor in the second century BC after he escaped pirates.[47] Scipio Africanus Aemilianus, the conqueror of Carthage in 146, built a round temple to Hercules, the *aedes Aemiliana Herculis* (an over-life-size bronze statue now in the Museo del Palazzo dei Conservatori in Rome – no. 1265 – may come from this temple),[48] and rebuilt the precinct of the *Ara Maxima*. An inscription from the Caelian Hill records that Lucius Mummius, conqueror of Corinth in 146 BC, built a temple to Hercules Victor.[49] Yet it was not just Hercules who was Victor and Invictus: Scipio Africanus was referred to as *invictus*,[50] Pompey was called *invictissimus*[51] and Caesar *unus invictus*.[52]

Most importantly, the *Ara Maxima* was located on the triumphal route, as was an ancient bronze statue of Hercules in triumphal clothes that dated to the time of Evander.[53] Hercules' cult at this altar took the epithet *Invictus*, and in 312 BC, the cult was transferred from the private management of the Pinarii and Potitii to the state under Appius Claudius Caecus.[54] By the first century BC, generals customarily offered a tithe from their spoils of war to Hercules on the *Ara Maxima*, along with an extravagant public banquet. The tithe, or *decuma*, to Hercules had been customary amongst Italic traders,[55] but in the first century BC, Sulla, Crassus, Licinius, Lucullus, Pompey and Caesar were all offering this tithe and/or providing the public feast.[56] The banquet was located in the '*hieron* [shrine] of Hercules',[57] which Marzano argues signifies the *Ara Maxima*.[58] Sulla also refurbished the shrine of Hercules Custos ('Guardian') near the Circus Flaminius, while Pompey refurbished a shrine to Hercules Invictus near the Circus Maximus (see below).[59]

The connection between Roman triumphs, the dedication of war spoils to Heracles and the provision of a banquet in Heracles' precinct integrated this god's persona as divine ancestor and victorious conqueror with the lavish public spectacles of wartime spoils drawn from eastern Hellenistic traditions.[60] Marzano locates this increasing stress on Hercules and lavish banquets in Roman triumphs to the second century BC, specifically to Aemilius Paullus' celebrations following his victory at Pydna (168 BC).[61] The linking of Hercules to wartime victory was no doubt influenced by both the long-term martial persona of this deity as outlined above and Hercules' more immediate historical contexts of exploitation by Alexander the Great, the Hellenistic kings and the Punic rulers in the western Mediterranean. Q. Fabius Maximus reportedly moved the Hercules temple *ad Portam Collinam* to the Capitoline hill, the culmination of the triumphal route, during the war with Hannibal.[62] According to John Scheid, however, Hercules was not a commercial or military deity full stop, but a god of triumphal returns and civilizing qualities, particularly the Hercules of the Forum Boarium: 'Hercules connects the two major qualities stressed by myth and celebration in the Forum Boarium area, namely a victorious return from strictly male activities, and civilising the first, barbaric inhabitants of the place.'[63] Colette Jourdain-Annequin writes in a similar vein, that Hercules was '*le modèle paradigmatique de la guerre conduit, au nom de la civilisation, contre les Barbares*' ('the paradigmatic model of war conducted, in the name of civilization, against the barbarians').[64] Violence and civilization were two sides of the same coin.

This ideology extended to the expanding boundaries of Rome at the turn from Republic to Empire. Diodorus' account of Hercules' adventures in Gaul portrays the god pacifying untamed regions and protecting those who took possession of those regions.[65] His syncretism with local gods drew on – and possibly shaped – his bellicose persona. For instance, in the Batavian region, Hercules was conflated with the local hero Magusanus, as demonstrated by inscriptions and cult sites.[66] A sanctuary to Hercules Magusanus at Kessel/Lith on the south bank of the Meuse showed many kinds of weaponry deposited as votive objects, while the monumental sanctuary at Empel contained dedications by Batavian and Roman soldiers. Other sanctuaries at Xanten and Bonn also yielded dedications to Hercules by legionaries

– a statue and votive altar respectively showing Hercules with club and lion skin.[67] Tacitus, in his *Germania*, noted that the Germanic peoples invoked Hercules before heading into combat.[68] For Romans pushing into frontier areas, Hercules' bellicose and pacifying qualities alike may have furthered the syncretism between Hercules and local gods in regions that, to the Romans at least, were frontiers. In the contexts of imperial expansion, Hercules' mythical exemplum thus provided a clear framework for empire: military conquest combined with a civilizing mission.[69]

The employment of Hercules in the civil war period shaped his subsequent use by the emperors. In particular, the ambiguous nature of Hercules – as a heroic civilizer yet also subject to the extremes of human emotions such as rage and fury – offered real fodder for writers characterizing larger-than-life figures like Caesar and Pompey, who could, almost in the same breath, be extolled for their magnificent accomplishments and maligned for their megalomania, hubris and lust for power.[70] These later literary expositions were fuelled by the fact that these leaders actually likened themselves to Hercules. Like Hannibal before him (before Hannibal marched on Rome), Caesar visited the temple of Melqart in Gades. Upon seeing a statue of Alexander the Great in that temple, Caesar lamented at his own failure in similar accomplishments, and forthwith had a prescient dream symbolizing his conquest of the world.[71] In the last weeks of his life, Caesar took the name *Divus Iulius* and was given a *flamen* (a priest of official Roman cults) and state temple to himself and his *Clementia*. Ovid ridiculed this act, including Liber and Hercules in his polemic against hubristic mortals conquering not only Earth and Ocean, but also Heaven.[72] Furthermore, in the temple of Quirinus, the divinized Romulus, Cassius Dio tells us that there was a statue of Caesar inscribed with *theo aniketo* (= *deo invicto*), invoking Hercules' title Invictus.[73]

Nonetheless, many of Caesar's military accomplishments could be (and were) compared with Hercules' feats. In the *Pro Marcello*, Cicero's mention of the locations of Caesar's victories – e.g., *Oceanus* (Ocean) – map onto Hercules' accomplishments in these regions that won him immortality.[74] The link between Hercules and Gaul, discussed above, also applies to Caesar's military exploits in these regions. S.J. Harrison, interestingly, notes Cicero's comparisons between Hercules and Caesar in the *Pro Marcello* as, conversely, emphasizing the *clementia* of Caesar in controlling the destructive passions of anger and revenge upon his victorious returns from civil war. Harrison notes that Hercules' labours, from a philosophical standpoint, could actually be taken to represent the moral subjugation of passion and fury, in stark contrast to the mythical interpretations of this god-hero.[75] Hercules' persona was thus an exceptionally open palette upon which to construct one's ideas of some of Rome's most controversial characters.

Pompey, perhaps more so than Caesar, explicitly featured Hercules Invictus/Victor in his political ideology. He refurbished a temple to Hercules *ad Circum Maximum*, the *aedes* (temple) *Pompeii Magni/ aedes Herculis Pompeiani*.[76] His stone theatre was dedicated on 12 August 55 BC, the festival day of Hercules Invictus at the *Ara Maxima* (also tying in the theme of victory with the temple to Venus Victrix). These associations were likely connected to Pompey's martial activities overseas, emphasizing Hercules as a god of victorious returns: he fought against Sertorius in Spain in the 70s BC, where the cult of Hercules-Melqart was prominent. His watchword used at the Battle of Pharsalus in 48 BC was Hercules Invictus.[77] Furthermore, after returning from his campaigns in the East, his son-in-law Faustus Cornelius Sulla (son of Lucius Cornelius Sulla) struck a series of coins in 56 BC, one showing Venus on the obverse and three trophies on the reverse. Another showed the head of Hercules and the *corona aurea* received by Pompey in 63 BC,[78] uniting these deities with Pompey's self-representation as invincible commander. Of course, Pompey's portrait and adopted name (Magnus, 'The Great') also alluded to Alexander.

Mark Antony famously traced his lineage back to Hercules through his mythical ancestor, Anton, one of the sons of Hercules, and Plutarch also compared Antony's physical appearance to the god.[79] A set of aurei coins from 42 BC by Livineius Regulus shows this relationship: the obverses show heads of Antony, Lepidus and Octavian, while reverses depict their mythological ancestors: Hercules/Anton, the Vestal Aemilia and Aeneas carrying Anchises.[80] An engraved stone ring from Pompeii shows Antony with the features of Hercules, alluding to actual statues of this type.[81] Antony, like Alexander, associated himself not only with Hercules, but also Dionysus, both of whom symbolized Eastern conquests and ceremonial spectacle that formed a cornerstone of Hellenistic kingship.[82] Coins struck for Antony in 43–42 BC in Gaul show a bust of Victory on the obverse and a lion on the reverse walking to the right – possibly symbolizing Hercules Victor and also alluding to Alexander.[83] Plutarch, in his *Comparison of Antony and Demetrius*, suggested, however, that Antony preferred the effete version of Heracles, stripped of his weapons and dress by Omphale, thus mirroring Antony's relationship with Cleopatra.[84] This comparison may be an attempt – influenced by Augustan propaganda – to portray Antony as the soft, un-Roman 'failed' Hercules/Alexander.[85] Nonetheless, the problematic nature of Hercules – an unconquerable hero, yet one associated with the extremes of madness and luxury – made him an equivocal character for the Roman emperors in their triumphal self-fashioning.

Augustus and First-Century Emperors

By the end of the Republic, therefore, Hercules offered a rich mosaic of associations with war and *imperium*, centred on triumphant returns to Rome of glorious and unconquerable military commanders, yet his portrayal in myth and propaganda evoked a certain ambivalence, as did Alexander's. Weinstock notes an avoidance of the term *invictus* by Augustus (reigned 31 BC – AD 14) based on its association with Caesar and Pompey.[86] Other studies suggested an avoidance of Hercules altogether by replacing him with Mars or Apollo,[87] while the denigration of Antony-Cleopatra via Hercules-Omphale has already been noted. But the evidence once again presents a more complicated picture. Hercules and his martial endeavours emerge, on the contrary, as a crucial backdrop to Rome's imperial trajectory under Augustus via a number of interrelated media: literary/rhetorical, symbolic and iconographic.[88] Virgil, for instance, compared Augustus to Hercules in the *Aeneid* as the greater divine son and hero.[89] Aeneas' association with *labor* and persecution by Juno, not to mention his donning of the lion skin, position him as a reflection of Hercules,[90] and all three characters – Augustus, Aeneas and Hercules – can be seen to oppose, respectively, Antony, Turnus and the monster Cacus.[91]

The tale told by Evander in *Aeneid* Book 8 of Hercules and Cacus in the Forum Boarium has been singled out as a seminal episode played upon by several Augustan authors, which located Hercules and his long association with this region as a focal point for Rome's mytho-history fashioned under Augustus.[92] The fact that Augustus celebrated his triple triumph on 13 August 29 BC, the festival day of Hercules Invictus at the Porta Trigemina, has not been ignored.[93] Virgil alludes to this triple triumph in the description of Aeneas' shield, and possibly also when Hercules is portrayed as returning to Rome triumphant with the spoils from 'threefold Geryon' (*tergeminus*).[94] The ode composed by Horace, quoted at the beginning of this chapter, celebrated Augustus' triumphant return from Spain as Hercules, mirroring Hercules' own route taken to Rome from Spain following his Spanish conquests against Geryon. Virgil had Jupiter prophesize that Augustus would 'circumscribe empire with ocean',[95] which was especially fitting for his conquests in Spain. Augustus played on Herculean themes through his coinage in Spain, minting coins at Gades showing the head of Hercules with lion skin and club with *DIVI F* ('son of the divine'), and in other issues showing his portrait with *DIVI F* on the obverse and what may be the temple of Melqart on the reverse.[96]

A mythical road, the Via Herculea, also traced Hercules' route from Spain to Italy.[97] Furthermore, the allusions to the Gigantomachy in the *Aeneid*,[98] and the Amazonomachy on the temple of Apollo Sosianus,[99] associate Hercules not with Antony – who is better equated with the barbaric Giants and Amazons to be vanquished – but with Augustus. It may be that Augustus was in some way reclaiming Hercules from Antony,[100] yet it is just as possible that Augustus simply employed Hercules as victorious conqueror in an iconic mythical narrative to reflect his own divinely sanctioned triumphs.[101]

Furthermore, rather than simply reclaiming Hercules from Antony, recent interpretations have instead favoured Augustus' use of Hercules as establishing a clear link between the *princeps* and triumphant Republican predecessors activated within the 'pre-Actian monumental landscape of Rome', specifically the Forum Boarium.[102] Matthew P. Loar notes how Virgil parallels Mummius – the likely raiser of the temple to Hercules Victor *ad Portam Trigeminam* in the second century BC – and his association with the illustrious past of Roman Republican triumphs with Augustus' connection to this same past through Hercules. The figure of Hercules, by 'activating a wide matrix of Republican resonances, telescopes centuries of Republican triumphs, offering a model for Augustus that reaches back not simply to Rome's recently concluded civil wars, but to a point in history when Rome was ascendant, nearing hegemonic control over the Mediterranean'.[103] It may be that Augustus chose the 'proper Hercules' associated with military victory and imperial glory over the luxurious, effete one. The reliefs from the temple to Apollo on the Palatine depicting Hercules and Apollo struggling over the Delphic Tripod may suggest a similar nuancing: it was in losing this struggle that Hercules was punished with servitude to Omphale. In David Quint's words, 'The real modern Hercules [of *Aeneid* Book 8] prevails at Actium over the dress-up one.'[104]

Yet Hercules still remains an equivocal character. Galinsky suggests that Virgil used Hercules as a foil for Aeneas (and Augustus) because he was a personal god, and thus could help meld Aeneas into a hero for the new Rome under Augustus.[105] Yet Aeneas' and Hercules' uncontrollable – even monstrous – rage are evident in the *Aeneid*, for example the episode where Aeneas is compared to the hundred-handed giant Aegaeon as he rages across the battlefield after Pallas' death.[106] The ambivalence inherent in Virgil's grand epic has certainly been acknowledged.[107] Other Augustan authors, notably Propertius, also made it clear that experiences of empire could not be boiled down to a monolithic narrative.[108] In *Elegy* 4.9, Propertius presents us both with Hercules the masculine hero and Hercules the transvestite who, more than any other mythical figure, parodies masculine Roman ideals, and also alludes to the Omphale episode. In considering Hercules as a war god for Rome's first emperors, then, we cannot ignore these multiple aspects of his persona. Hercules was always an equivocal character: he was both hero and god, the champion of masculine power and yet readily subject to inhabiting both the detrimental extremes and the structural opposite of this ideal. Hercules – like Alexander – was all at once a focal point for emulation, for cautionary tales and for irony in the face of conquest and expansion.

Indeed, emperors could be derided for equating themselves wholesale with Hercules: Philo in his *Embassy to Gaius* attacked Caligula (AD 37–41) for overstepping the bounds of human nature to think himself a god, citing, among other grievances, the wearing of the lion skin and club to the theatre.[109] Nero (AD 54–68), never an emperor that one wanted to emulate, also attempted to directly copy Hercules by (allegedly) having a lion trained in the circus so that he might kill it with a club as Hercules did the Nemean Lion, alluding to the widely disseminated iconography of Hercules (and king) as lion-slayer.[110] Nero was supposedly hailed as Hercules upon returning from Greece as Olympic victor, and fashioned his cutting of the Isthmus of Corinth as a Herculean labour.[111] What made Caligula's and Nero's usage of Hercules as an exemplum of bellicosity so disdainful? Beyond the many other well-known grievances against both emperors, Philo's accusation against Caligula's mimicry offers some clues that help us nuance the proper usage of Hercules. He demands of Caligula whether the emperor truly lived up to the ideals of the demi-gods like the Dioscuri, Dionysus and Hercules that he supposedly imitated: 'Or did you also emulate Heracles in your unwearied labours, your tireless feats of courage? Did you fill continents and islands with legality and justice, with fertility and prosperity and a lavish supply of the other boons which peace deep-founded creates?'[112]

Hercules might be cast as triumphant conqueror, but the Hercules to emulate was the one who heralded progress and civilization alongside wartime victory, who exercised *clementia* in tandem with *imperium*. Conquest and domination legitimized by a civilizing mission is one of the clearest hallmarks of an empire's self-fashioning;[113] anything less, and we slide into the degenerate Hercules filled with uncontrollable rage or bested by luxury.

The 'proper' Hercules was evidently a concern also for the Flavians, and in particular Domitian. Nero and the subsequent emperors who revolted in the civil war of AD 68–69 possibly lent Hercules a bad flavour. Vindex, the governor of Gaul who rebelled in AD 68, is associated with anti-Neronian denarii showing Hercules and the legend Hercules Adsertor ('Hercules the Liberator').[114] By the time Vespasian (AD 69–79) took the throne, Hercules may have seemed an unfavourable character, and Vespasian was said to have laughed when some Romans suggested that his family was descended from a comrade of Hercules.[115] The Porticus of Herculaneum, however, contained a number of paintings of Hercules' labours in prominent fashion, alongside the training and education of youth. This Porticus was repaired during Vespasian's reign, and the patrons of Herculaneum replaced some of the Julio-Claudian sculptural groups with statues of Vespasian and his family. Statues of Theseus and Hercules flanked a statue of Vespasian in the central niche, highlighting the Flavians as bringers of peace to the Empire.[116]

Domitian (AD 81–96) attempted to fashion himself as a 'greater Hercules',[117] with visual identifications made between the emperor and the god-hero on coins, medallions and statues: Martial, for instance, notes that a cult statue of Hercules along the Via Latina bore the features of the emperor.[118] Domitianic literature compared the emperor to Hercules: military triumphs described in Statius' *Silvae* make him equal to the greatest of heroes,[119] and Silius Italicus' *Punica* draws equation between Hercules, Domitian and Scipio.[120] Statius' *Thebaid* plays upon several Herculean themes as well. The beginning of this epic has Domitian helping his father against Vitellius in the Battle of the Capitol in AD 69, which is styled as *bella Iovis* – an allusion to the Gigantomachy, in which Hercules was the only mortal to take part.[121] The Gigantomachy and Centauromachy, another important element in the *Thebaid*, both draw on earlier Greek themes, already put to use by previous Roman rulers, which positioned Hercules – and Domitian – as vanquisher of monstrous forces. The *Thebaid* also references similar Herculean themes in the *Aeneid*, notably the Hercules-Cacus episode through the Coroebus' encounter with Apollo's child-eating monster.[122]

With Domitian we also see the emperor's *virtus* expressed through lion hunt imagery, a motif noted in earlier renditions of Hercules (see above), but largely absent from the Julio-Claudian associations with this god-hero. The fragmentary bronze equestrian statue of Domitian from Misenum, which was originally thought to show the emperor trampling a barbarian enemy in battle, has been reinterpreted as depicting the emperor spearing a lion (see Figure 4.4).[123] Domitian's cuirass on this statue shows Hercules strangling two serpents, alluding to the emperor's superhuman strength against chaotic forces, destined for him at birth.[124] The centre of his cuirass shows a winged gorgoneion over a Hercules knot, emphasizing Domitian's link with Minerva, also Hercules' patron goddess, and Martial compares Domitian's cuirass to Minerva's *aegis* with its Gorgon head.[125]

The overall composition of the statue follows Hellenistic models, both in Domitian's dress and in the horse's rearing posture and fear, which match Hellenistic lion hunt scenes, as well as such scenes on contemporary and later sarcophagi, and Cassius Dio alludes to the possibility that Domitian kept lions for hunting at his Alban estate.[126] This imagery stems from earlier Hellenistic and Near Eastern royal imagery discussed above, and in the Roman context was associated especially with the *virtus* of the emperor.[127] It is important to note that the Alexander sarcophagus also portrayed Alexander in lion-skin cap and civilian dress on rearing horse, with his right arm raised and holding a spear, but in this case he is about to spear a falling Persian warrior. Nonetheless, the Alexander sarcophagus draws clear links between military and hunting *virtus* via Herculean symbolism, and no doubt Domitian attempted to do the same through his imagery. He also allegedly placed a statue of himself with the attributes of Hercules into the lap of Jupiter's cult statue on the Capitoline, fashioning himself as the 'greater Hercules' and son of Jupiter.[128]

Figure 4.4: Bronze equestrian statue of Domitian from Misenum (Museo Archeologico dei Campi Flegrei nel Castello di Baia no. 155743). (*Tuck, 2005: 224, Figure 2; photo by S. Tuck; used with permission*)

Second-Century Emperors

Hercules as a conduit for *virtus* through pugnacious endeavours and an exemplum for civilizing *imperium* was given increased emphasis under Trajan (AD 98–117). Pliny the Younger called Trajan '*imperator invictus*' ('unconquered emperor'), and compared him to an unwearied Hercules after completing his labours. This characterization positioned the emperor as yet another new-and-improved Hercules after Domitian, now portrayed as the cruel Eurystheus.[129] Dio Chrysostom (AD 40–120) emphasized this *virtus* in his *First Discourse on Kingship*,[130] by alluding to the tale of Hercules' choice between *Virtus* and *Voluptas*, in Dio's tale portrayed as a choice between Kingship and Tyranny. Hercules' adversity with Tyranny is akin to his struggles with monstrous forces – a likely reference to Trajan's service under Domitian.[131] Trajan's association with Hercules also played upon Trajan's birthplace, Italica in Hispania: Pliny noted how Trajan was called from Hispania to labour for a lesser king (Domitian). Once again, we see 'good' emperors like Trajan praised through Hercules not only for their excellence in war and conquest, but also (and especially) for their enlightened and pacifying rulership.

Nevertheless, under Trajan, Hercules' military roles were augmented considerably.[132] Trajan provided one of the new legions, Legion II Traiana Fortis, with the emblem of Hercules with club and lion skin. The close association between Hercules and Trajan

Figure 4.5: Bronze quadrans showing Hercules in the lion skin on the obverse, with IMP CAES TRAIAN AVG GERM and club on the reverse, from Trajan's reign (AD 98–117); minted in Rome and found in Britain (*RIC* II, Trajan, no. 699; © Derby Museum Trust; CC BY 4.0). (*Courtesy of the Portable Antiquities Scheme*)

is evident on coinage: a quadrans shows Trajan's face on the obverse and a boar, a legionary symbol, on the reverse, while another shows the same boar on the reverse, but Hercules' head on the obverse and the legend *IMP CAES TRAIAN AVG GERM*, drawing a direct association between Hercules, the emperor and the imperial legions: Hercules' relation to the boar reflects his fourth labour, capturing the Erymanthian Boar.[133] The reverse of an as coin displays Trajan's Column, a triumphal record of the emperor's Dacian campaigns, in the form of Hercules' club set on a lion-skin pedestal with the legend *SPQR OPTIMO PRINCIPI S C*.[134] Another series of quadrans displays Hercules' bust on the obverse and his club on the reverse between the legend S C.[135] While the emperor's image is absent, the legend on the obverse reads *IMP CAES TRAIAN AVG GERM* (see Figure 4.5).[136]

Hercules under Trajan was thus a signifier of the emperor's martial endeavours, particularly his Dacian campaigns. The Arval Brothers in AD 101 named, for the first time, Hercules Victor amongst the gods invoked for the emperor's safety before his first Dacian campaign.[137] The emperor departed Rome on 4 June for his second Dacian campaign, the feast day of Hercules Magnus Custos ('Great Guardian').[138] Following his successful conquests in Dacia and Persia, Trajan inaugurated the Triumphal Games for Hercules (*Ludi Herculei triumphales*). Another coin type issued following Trajan's Dacian victories (among other milestones in his reign) depicts, on the reverse, a statue of Hercules, naked except for the lion-skin cap and the rest of the skin hanging over his left arm. His right hand grasps his club, and his left hand sometimes holds an apple (see Figure 4.6).[139] Coins with this imagery tended to be high-value aurei and silver denarii. Presumably this iconography was depicting a popular cult statue to Hercules, perhaps from one of the temples in the Forum Boarium, or even the precinct of the *Ara Maxima*. If so, the persistent appearance

Figure 4.6: Silver denarius reverse showing Hercules on a pedestal with club and lion skin, with Trajan on the obverse (*c.*AD 101–102) (photo by Julie Shoemark; CC BY-SA 2.0). (*Courtesy of the Portable Antiquities Scheme*)

of this cult imagery on high-value coinage linked Trajan to earlier Augustan-era rhetoric that galvanized the illustrious history of expanding Roman hegemony through Hercules and the triumphal area of the Forum Boarium.[140]

Hadrian (AD 117–138) cultivated a relationship with Hercules that further stressed the universal and civilizing reach of Roman *imperium*. Hadrian's maternal family came from Gades, home to the famous temple of Melqart. Several Hadrianic aurei celebrate this relationship with both Gades and Hercules, showing the god-hero with club and the apples of the Hesperides (another feat that that took place at the ends of the known world), sometimes standing within the *cella* (inner area) of a temple. The details of each aureus diverge slightly, but one prominently displays the words HERC GADIT – Hercules Gaditanus – across the centre. The temple presumably is the famous one to Melqart in Gades, a longstanding source of wonder amongst Roman authors and one of the few temples allowed to receive inheritances under Trajan or Hadrian.[141] Another element on this coinage is the presence of a reclining water god, Oceanus, and, in one case the head of the water god, which resembles images of Oceanus in Rome, most notably the *Bocca della Verità* in the Forum Boarium.[142] The pairing of Hercules with Oceanus, while a far cry from wartime symbolism, nonetheless presents one of the most compelling portraits of a hero who conquered the furthest reaches of the *oikoumenē* represented by Ocean, and whose civilizing persona fit nicely with Hadrian's notability for being a widely travelled emperor. The very *pomerium* of Rome became extended to the known world, a sentiment captured in Aristides' address to Hadrian's successor, Antoninus Pius (AD 138–161).[143] These achievements were celebrated near the end of Hadrian's reign with a medallion portraying Hercules in the lion skin on the obverse and the goddess Tellus atop a globe on the reverse, with the legend TELLUS STABILIS ('The earth established').[144]

A distinctive type of Hercules, closely associated with military valour, was established under Trajan or Hadrian, the Hercules Invictus type, which depicts a youthful Hercules seated on a rock covered in his lion skin surrounded by cuirasses and shields. He holds his club downwards in his right hand and a statue of Victory in his left. This symbolism, of the victorious conqueror sitting atop enemy spoils, derives from Classical and Hellenistic prototypes.[145] Denarii issued from AD 124–128 following Hadrian's tour, for instance, show Hercules Invictus seated upon a cuirass with a round shield and helmet on the ground behind. He holds his club in one hand and usually a statue of Victory, but also a distaff, apple or two arrows (see Figure 4.7).[146] The Hadrianic hunting tondi (circular reliefs) preserved on the Arch of Constantine also follow the royal hunting themes brought back into vogue at the end of the first century AD. The tondi show Hadrian hunting bear, boar and lion; one shows a statue of Hercules Invictus, similar to imagery on Hadrianic denarii, to which Hadrian dedicates the skin of a lion killed in one of his expeditions.[147] A series of medallions struck between AD 129 and 137 show Hadrian in similar hunting scenes to those on the tondi. The inscription on the medallions reads *Virtuti Augusti*, once again drawing a clear link between military and hunting prowess and *virtus*, and positioning Hercules as a persuasive medium for exemplifying these qualities. Similar medallions were struck under Antoninus Pius, Marcus Aurelius, Lucius Verus and Commodus.[148]

Figure 4.7: Silver denarius showing on the obverse a laureate bust of Hadrian, and Hercules sitting on arms and armour with club on the reverse, from Hadrian's reign (AD 119) (*RIC* II, 149; © Leicestershire County Council; CC BY-SA 2.0). (*Courtesy of the Portable Antiquities Scheme*)

Antoninus Pius' employment of Hercules departed from the far-flung travels of the hero and focused on more traditional bellicose aspects. A coin from his fourth year shows the Hercules Invictus type seated atop a cuirass and shields holding his club and arrows,[149] and imagery of the victorious Hercules crowning himself appear in several Antonine media, from medallions to reliefs, once again deriving from Hellenistic models.[150] Hercules was also centred more on Rome than abroad, with some coin types emphasizing his feats in Italy.[151] A large bronze medallion now in the Bibliothèque Nationale in Paris, for instance, depicts Hercules standing over a deceased Cacus, stretched out before the mouth of his cave, hearkening back to Augustan ideology and the Forum Boarium. Four smaller individuals thank Hercules for his deed.[152] Finally, coins from the 150s show Antoninus' portrait on the obverse and a standing Heracles holding his club and bow and arrow on the reverse,[153] once again, possibly signalling a well-recognized statue.[154]

Lucius Verus (AD 161–169) and Marcus Aurelius (AD 161–180) seem to have downplayed an association with Hercules,[155] but Marcus Aurelius' son and successor, Commodus (AD 177–192), fully embraced this deity, possibly as a way to legitimize his role as royal heir with little military or administrative experience.[156] Emperors generally attracted criticism and disdain when they seriously blurred the distinction between themselves and Hercules, attempting to portray themselves *as* Hercules, rather than simply associated with or comparable to him.[157] Such was the case with Caligula, Nero and Domitian, and was especially the case with Commodus.[158] His assimilation to Hercules took place in several stages, with numerous coin issues over the 180s displaying Hercules on the reverse, first identifying Hercules as his *comes* (companion). In his final year, he proclaimed himself to be Hercules Romanus,[159] with coins depict Hercules with club and lion skin crowning a trophy on the reverse with the legend *HERVLI ROMANO AVG*.[160] Coins minted in AD 190–191 also contain the legend *HERC COMMODIANO* on the reverse, with images of Hercules.[161] Cities in the East honoured the emperor by depicting him as various incarnations of Hercules: an Alexandrian coin, for instance, portrayed Commodus as Hercules Invictus, seated atop armour and holding a Victory.[162]

Further emphasis on Hercules Romanus can be seen in coin medallions and aurei that represent the emperor as Hercules the primeval ploughman, who founded a 'new Rome' following the fire of AD 191. Commodus in the lion skin appears on the obverse, and Hercules driving cattle is on the reverse with the legend *HERC ROM COND* (or *CONDITORI*).[163] Commodus' excesses in portraying himself as Hercules are captured in Cassius Dio's account,[164] and include renaming all the months of the year after himself and Hercules in AD 192 (e.g., Amazonius, Invictus and Herculeus).[165] He engaged in gory gladiatorial feats dressed as Hercules, and was even known to shoot audience members in the amphitheatre in imitation of Hercules killing the Stymphalian birds.[166] He allegedly had the head of Nero's Colossus replaced with his own portrait, along with club and bronze lion.[167] Commodus thus assumed the longstanding cross-cultural symbolism of Hercules to style himself as vanquisher of chaotic forces represented by the bronze lion and the many beasts slain in the amphitheatre. Or, in E. Meyer-Zwiffelhoffer's words, '*Die Arena war das Barbarenland, in dem er symbolisch die Wiederherstellung der Ordnung inszenierte*' ('The arena was the land of barbarians, in which he [Commodus] symbolically staged the restoration of order').[168]

Figure 4.8: Marble bust of Commodus as Hercules, *c.*AD 191–192, now in the Palazzo dei Conservatori (MC1120). (*Photo by Marie-Lan Nguyen, public domain*)

Beyond Commodus' gladiatorial excesses, Hercules played an important part in provincial military endeavours. The *Augustan History of Commodus* states that Commodus changed the name of his African fleet to Commodiana Herculea.[169] An aureus depicts, on the reverse, Hercules resting his club on a tree trunk with a thunderbolt, while he places his foot on a prow and clasps hands with Africa.[170] The marble bust found on the Esquiline now in the Palazzo dei Conservatori displays a decadent Commodus as Hercules, but also hearkens back to several important military moments (see Figure 4.8). Wearing the lion skin, he holds the club over his shoulder in his right hand and the apples of the Hesperides in his left hand to signify his apotheosis following the last labour. Amazons flank a globe and double cornucopia around a pelta below the bust. The globe is covered with zodiacal signs referencing important dates in Commodus' life, signalling in particular the month of October, renamed *Herculeus* by the emperor. This month saw Commodus sharing in the Parthian triumph of Marcus Aurelius and Lucius Verus (12 October AD 166), taking the title Germanicus (15 October AD 172) and being acknowledged as emperor (22 October AD 180).[171] Evidence from the provinces suggests that soldiers and civilians alike embraced Commodus as Hercules Invictus.[172] An inscription found in 1860 in Carlisle is dedicated to Hercules Invictus Conservator, the saviour of Britain,[173] likely referencing Commodus's victory against the Caledonian rebels,[174] even if it dated prior to the period of Commodus' full assumption of Hercules' identity.[175]

Hercules as a War God in the Third Century

Emperors in the third century continued to employ Hercules as a military model. Septimius Severus (AD 193–211), who hailed from Leptis Magna in Africa, combined the imagery of Liber Pater/Dionysus/Bacchus with Hercules on coin issues,[176] and Hercules also appears on the arches of Severus in Rome and Leptis Magna. The employment of these deities, Liber Pater and Hercules alongside Severus' North African background drew from longstanding Punic antecedents, namely the Phoenician gods Shadrapa (identified with the Roman Liber Pater/Dionyus/Bacchus) and Melqart.[177] These deities received an important place in Severus' *Ludi Saeculares*, and possibly represented his two sons, Geta and Caracalla, with the emperor as Jupiter.[178] Severus built a huge temple to these two deities on the Quirinal.[179] But Hercules also was portrayed alone on denarii with bow and lion skin in AD 196–197, with the legend *HERVLI DEFENS*.[180] It was during this time that Severus' war with Albinus occurred. Severus defeated Albinus at Lugdunum in AD 197, the year this coin type reached peak representation in hoards.[181] Hercules was thus the defender of the Empire, and particularly the Western part, possibly with Liber/Dionysus as traditional defender of the East, whose imagery overtakes Hercules' after AD 197.[182] Clare Rowan argues that Hercules was an essential figure for Severus' self-adoption into the Antonine family via Commodus' explicit association with this deity. Severus portrayed himself with a lion-skin cap on a medallion from AD 202, and certain coin issues showed Severus with the lion skin around his shoulder.[183] Caracalla continued his father's tradition of striking coins with Hercules as one of the patron gods of Leptis Magna and in association with the *Ludi Saeculares*.[184]

Into the second half of the third century, Herculean imagery became a major source of *virtus* for the soldier-emperors, starting with Gordian III (AD 238–244). Hercules seemed particularly important to those ruling in the Gallic and Germanic provinces, where he was already a popular deity, via his longstanding identification with Germanic gods like Magusanus.[185] Gallienus (AD 253–260) issued coins representing Hercules with attributes like the club, apples, branch, bow and lion skin, with the legend

Figure 4.9: Bronze sestertius showing radiate bust of emperor on obverse and Hercules standing holding lion skin and olive branch with the legend *HERC PACIFERO* on the reverse; from Postumus' reign (*c.*AD 260–269), found in central Bedfordshire. (*Photo by Margaret Broomfield, Surrey County Council; CC BY-SA 2.0.*) (*Courtesy of the Portable Antiquities Scheme*)

VIRTVS AVGVSTI or *VIRT GALLIENI AVG*.[186] While many of these types came from Rome, several also came from mints at Mediolanum/Milan and Siscia, which serviced the imperial field armies and were possibly used to pay donatives to troops and advertise the emperor's *virtus* via an already popular bellicose deity.[187] Another coin, an aureus from Mediolanum, shows Gallienus himself in lion-skin cap on the obverse, with a personification of Fides on the reverse holding insignia, with the legend *FIDES MILITVM*,[188] linking the Roman Army's loyalty to the *virtus* of its heroic leader, possibly at a time when the Empire was threatened by the usurper Postumus.[189]

Both Gallienus and Postumus (AD 260–269) also portrayed themselves in Alexander's fashion: a gold aureus from *c*.AD 263, for instance, depicts a three-quarter portrait of Postumus gazing upwards in the manner of Alexander's portraits.[190] This emperor associated himself closely with Hercules, likely as a way to compete with Gallienus: a number of coins show the laureate heads of Hercules and Postumus together on the obverse, with personifications such as Victory, Felicitas, Pax, Hilaritas, Sol, Luna, Mars, Apollo, Jupiter, Aesculapius and Castor on the reverse.[191] Further coin issues with similar obverses recount a number of Hercules' labours with legends including *HERCVLI LIBVCO* (strangling Antaeus), *HERCVLI GADITANO* (slaying Geryon) and *HERCVLI INVICTO* (triumphing over an Amazon, the Cretan Bull or the Nemean Lion).[192] The association with the German warrior god, Magusanus (discussed above), is expressed in an antoninianus coin from Lugdunum,[193] suggesting a longstanding identification of these deities with one another that played important roles in Rome's diverse legions. This example, along with several other coin issues from Lugdunum with the legend *HERC/HERCVLI DEVSONIENSI*, suggests local versions of Hercules at Deutz and Mainz worshipped by soldiers.[194] Another popular legend from this mint is *HERC PACIFERO*,[195] drawing on the other major aspect of Hercules' exemplum beside his bellicose persona: that of civilizer (see Figure 4.9).[196]

Following Postumus, Probus (AD 276–282) continued to issue similar coin types in the western European provinces, possibly as a way to counter Postumus' representation of Hercules, yet also presenting a sense of continuity and emphasizing, through Hercules Romanus, a connection to Rome and *romanitas*.[197] Probus' coins with Hercules also bear legends like *COMITI PROBI AVG* and *HERCVLI ROMANO AVG* and hearken back to Commodus' early portrayals of Hercules (as *comes*, companion) and his final portrayal of Hercules, Hercules Romanus Augustus.[198] He also portrayed Hercules as *comes*, expressing an intimate relationship between himself and this deity,[199] a tradition that began with Commodus and continued into the reign of the Tetrarchy, the new system of government inaugurated by the emperor Diocletian in AD 293.[200] Interestingly, most of these coins with Hercules' imagery issued by the soldier emperors were on high-value media – issues such as medallions, aurei, antoniniani and quinarii – suggesting they were meant to appeal to a specific audience,[201] possibly upper-class officials or members of the Army. None of these rulers had undisputed claims to the throne, and powerful and effective messaging was required.

Finally, Hercules was one of the major patrons of the Tetrarchs, the new, joint rulership of the Roman Empire. Their employment of Herculean symbolism was no doubt influenced by the later soldier-emperors' stress on this deity as a conduit for *virtus*. In Erika Manders' words, the 'remarkable attention to Hercules from the Tetrarchs could be characterised as the last triumph of the Roman Hercules'.[202] Diocletian (AD 284–305) assumed the *signum* 'Iovius', while his protégé, Maximian (AD 286–305), took 'Herculius', revealing these gods as imperial patrons, yet these adjectival terms could also be attached to military units.[203] A number of the coin epithets from the Gallic provinces mentioned above were incorporated into the work of the *Panegyric of 289* (from the XII *Panegyrici Latini*), possibly written by a native of Gaul, who promoted the Herculean qualifications of Maximian. Epithets borrowed include Invictus, Pacifer and Virtus alongside allusions to Hercules' role in the Gigantomachy, all drawing from earlier imperial employments of this deity. Coin issues also associate Maximian with Hercules' iconography, with legends like *VIRTVS AVGG* (see Figure 4.10).

These Herculean allusions may have been meant to centralize loyalties around Maximian rather than provincial leaders, as well as elevate Maximian's status alongside Diocletian.[204] Roger Rees notes that legends containing these *signa*, as with the soldier-emperors, were concentrated on medallions, possibly meant for the military.[205] Olivier Hekster highlights, however, that, while legends with *signa* are lacking, there is no shortage of Jovian and Herculean imagery on coins administered by these two Tetrarchs, including images of Maximian in the lion scalp.[206] Constantius Chlorus (AD 305–306) continued this symbolism: Eumenius' *Panegyric of 298* (another panegyric from the XII *Panegyrici Latini*) described him as a descendent of Hercules, and medallions show him also wearing the lion skin.[207] Finally, Maxentius (AD 306–312) also depicted himself in the lion skin on his coins, and identified Hercules as his ally on aurei, with the legend *HERCVLI COMITI AVG N* and *HERCVLI COMITI AVGG ET CAES N* on the reverse.[208] It is perhaps no surprise that his subjugator, Constantine (AD 306–337), subsequently avoided Herculean imagery, although Herculean symbolism would continue to be employed in Christian art.[209]

Figure 4.10: Silver-copper alloy antoninianus, showing radiate bust of Maximian on obverse and Hercules standing with club, bow, and lion skin on reverse, with the legend *VIRTVS AVGG*; from the reign of Maximian (*c.*AD 294), minted in Lugdunum (*RIC* V, Diocletian, no. 453; photo by Katie Hinds, Salisbury and South Wiltshire Museum; CC BY-SA 2.0). (*Courtesy of the Portable Antiquities Scheme*)

Conclusion

The second-century AD satirist Lucian, in his 'Introduction to Heracles', describes how he and a learned Celtic man observed a painting of the Celtic god, Ogmios, who was likened to Heracles. Ogmios was depicted as an old man, but dressed similarly to Heracles, with club, quiver and lion skin. Furthermore, Ogmios was dragging a crowd of more-than-eager followers by chains attached from their ears to his tongue. The Celtic man tells a bewildered Lucian, 'In general, we consider that the real Heracles was a wise man who achieved everything by eloquence and applied persuasion as his principal force.'[210] This short introduction condenses many of the apparent contradictions of Hercules discussed above into his role as an archetype for empire. The truest sense of conquest came not from brute force but from the flowering of speech and urbanity that was the intended outcome of – and justification for – the imperial mission, and demonstrated by elites like the Hellenized Syrian and his Celtic counterpart.[211] Herfried Münkler writes, 'All empires that have lasted any length of time have chosen as their self-justifying objective a world-historical task or mission that confers cosmological or redemptive meaning on their activity.'[212]

Few characters encapsulated both the activities (warfare and domination) and the justification for those activities (peace and civilization) as effectively as Hercules. Much of his success as a symbol for the Roman emperors lay in his long history of cross-cultural employment by Mediterranean rulers in their expansionist and martial endeavours, and the expert redirecting of these long-term processes towards the Roman imperial mission by the emperors and elites through ideological means. This mission centred on successful military conquest and its cosmological propensities found expression in triumphant spectacle, activities that were clearly reflected in both the mythical personas of the peregrinating hero and his widely disseminated symbolism. Over the several centuries of Roman engagement with Hercules, this god-hero mirrored an entire spectrum of features associated with imperial expansion: force, triumph, morality and decadence, yet the true ideal behind emperors invoking Hercules as a war god lay in a hoped-for aftermath of prosperity, stability and – ultimately – immortality. Montesquieu is famous for stating, 'An empire founded by war has to maintain itself by war' – the ideals of Herculean ideology offered rulers a pathway out of this conundrum. Hercules, perhaps even more than the emperors, was the ideal behind Jupiter's prophecy for the Roman Empire in the *Aeneid*: *Aspera tum positīs mītēscent saecula bellīs.*[213]

Notes

1. Hor. *Od.* 3.14.1–4, trans. Rudd (2004).
2. Noreña (2011), pp.199–200.
3. Hermary (1992), pp.133–34.
4. Hermary (1992), pp.140–41, figs 2–4; Counts (2008), pp.7–8, 11–12; Yon (1992), p.151; Bonnet (1988), pp.412–14; Papantoniou (2012), pp.265–67. This 'Master of Lions' imagery appears on other media as well, notably metallic symposium bowls, scarabs and seals.
5. Schnapp-Gourbeillon (1998); Parisi Pressice (1998); Ulanowski (2015), p.265, n.108.
6. See Jourdain-Annequin & Bonnet (2001) on the personas of Heracles-Melqart in this imagery; cf. Counts (2008). See López Grande (2002) on the Egyptian origins for the smiting god and

later relationships to Heracles; see also Bisi (1986). Statuettes of a striding/smiting god come from near Sancti Petri at Gades, where Melqart's temple possibly stood: Celestino & López-Ruiz (2016), p.229; Aubet (2001), p.203; *LIMC* 6 Melqart no. 11.
7. Counts (2008).
8. Daniels (2021).
9. Levi (1997), p.120.
10. Malkin (2005); Malkin (2011).
11. *KAI* 47; Louvre *AO* 4818; Amadasi Guzzo (2005), pp.47–48.
12. Bonnet (1986), pp.217–21; *LIMC* 6 Melqart no. 7.
13. Bonnet (2009), p.303; Bonnet & Bricault (2016), p.29.
14. Hdt. 5.43.
15. Hes. *Theog.* 289–94; la Genière (1999); Jourdain-Annequin (1989); Jourdain-Annequin (1992); Bonnet (1988).
16. Huttner (1997a), p.265.
17. E.g., Isoc. *Philip.* 76–77, 111–14; Plut. *Alex.* 2.1; Arr. *Anab.* 3.3.2.
18. Palagia (1986), p.139 n.23.
19. Palagia (1986), pp.140–41.
20. Arr. *Anab.* 2.15.7–16.8, 24.5–6; 3.6.1; Curt. 4.2.1–9. For more bibliography on coins issued by Alexander showing Heracles, see Anagnostou-Laoutides (2016), p.16 n.24.
21. Weinstock (1957), pp.214–15; e.g., Tyr. F11.1; Archil. F324 (West). On the pairing of Hercules and Dionysus in Hellenistic and Roman royal iconography, see Marzano (2009), pp.87–88; Erickson (2018).
22. Cf. Heckel (2006).
23. Erickson (2009), pp.84–85.
24. Palagia (1986), pp.142–43; Laubscher (1997); Huttner (1997a); Stafford (2012), pp.146–50; Anagnostou-Laoutides (2016), p.16 n.25 for bibliography. See Theocritus' *Idyll* 17 on the link between Ptolemy I, Alexander and Heracles: Erickson (2018), p.254. On Ptolemy Philadelphus and Heracles: Laubscher (1997).
25. Erickson (2009), p.131; Anagnostou-Laoutides (2016), p.167.
26. Yarrow (2013).
27. Nitschke (2013); Yarrow (2013), pp.358–59.
28. Rawlings (2005), p.164, fig. 1; Yarrow (2013), p.354.
29. Plut. *Pyrrh.* 22.4–6; see Huttner (1997a), pp.153–62.
30. On Heracles/Melqart and imperial activities, see Nitschke (2013); Martí-Aguilar (2018).
31. Miles (2011); Alfaro Asins (1997); Chaves (1998).
32. Diod. 12.19.6.
33. Paus. 6.5.1–9.
34. Sommella Mura (1977); Ritter (1995), pp.21–22.
35. E.g., *BM* 1847, 1101.22; see *LIMC* 5 Hercle. But cf. Levi (1996); Levi (1997), who argues that Athena/Minerva was unknown in the region of Latium at this time: this divinity instead was the supreme goddess Diana.
36. Levi (1997).
37. Coarelli (1988); (1996), pp.15–17.
38. For Hercules' cult in Italy: Mastrocinque (1993); Ritter (1995), pp.87–100; Bradley (2005); *LIMC* 5 Hercle. Note especially the temples at Pyrgi containing bilingual inscriptions in Etruscan and Phoenician mentioning the king's worship of Astarte-Uni, and possibly Melqart: Mettinger (2001); Colonna (2002). Despite the mythical stress on the Greek origins of the Hercules' cult – e.g., Dion. Hal. *Rom. Ant.* 1.40.3; Sutton (1977); Hartmann (2017); cf. Levi (1997) – in the Forum Boarium, Phoenician origins have also been suggested but never proven: Rebuffat (1966); van Berchem (1959–60); van Berchem (1967); Coarelli (1988), pp.129–30; Levi (1997), pp.43–44; Marcos Casquero (2002); Moret (2012), p.109. Levi (1997) instead argues for a sharp distinction between the Greek hero and the supreme god Hercules of the *Ara Maxima*, who was only replaced by Jupiter in the fourth century BC and *then* associated closely with the Greek Heracles.

39. This thesis is spelled out in Bayet (1926) and suggested by Weinstock (1957), p.223; Marzano (2009); cf. Scheid (2012), pp.296–97. Hercules had other cultic associations as well, for instance healing: Bolder-Boos (2017).
40. Levi (1996); Levi (1997).
41. Lulof (2000).
42. On eastern models for Roman kingship, see Grottanelli (1987). Lulof also draws associations between Roman kings and the Athenian tyrant Peisistratus, who associated himself with Hercules and Athena.
43. Livy 9.44.16.
44. See Padilla Peralta (2020).
45. For discussion of Nobilior and the temple of Hercules Musarum, see Russell (2016), p.139 n.30.
46. Ovid *Fasti* 6.209–12.
47. Macrob. *Sat.* 3.6.11.
48. Pliny *Nat. Hist.* 35.19; see Coarelli (1988), pp.164–204; Palagia (1990). Scipio may also have dedicated a cult statue to Hercules Epitrapezios, 'At the Table' – Coarelli (1988), p.129; Ritter (1995), pp.38–40). Another major aspect of this cult was the giant skyphos of Helios used by Hercules to cross the sea, and pictured in medallions of Antoninus Pius and Caracalla – van Berchem (1967), pp.336–38, pl. 16.1 – and in an unpublished mosaic from the Aventine: Palagia (1990), p.51; Berry (2011), p.21, fig. 31. See Macrob. *Sat.* 5.21.16; Serv. *Aen.* 8.278.
49. *CIL* 6.331 (*ILS* 20); Ziolkowski (1988), pp.92–103, argues that Mummius' temple mentioned in the inscription is the round temple by the Tiber, *contra* Coarelli, who associated this temple with one built by M. Octavius Herennus. Cf. Richardson (1992), pp.185–89; Popkin (2016), pp.193–94; Loar (2017). Ziolkowski matches Mummius' temple with the temple to Hercules Victor *ad Portam Trigeminam* mentioned in ancient sources, and possibly alluded to in Virgil *Aen.* 8.201–204 – Loar (2017), p.49. Servius *Aen.* 8.363 and Macrobius *Sat.* 3.6.10 both speak of two temples to Hercules Victor: one *ad Portam Trigeminam* and the other *ad Forum Boarium*. The temple of Hercules Victor *ad Forum Boarium*, within the Servian Wall, is identified as the one built by P. Cornelius Scipio Aemilianus, the *aedes Aemiliana Herculis*: Pliny *Nat. Hist.* 35.19; see Ziolkowski (1988), p.313, again, *contra* Coarelli (1988), pp.187–92. On the architectural importance of these Republican temples to Hercules, see Popkin (2016), pp.67–71.
50. Enn. *Ann.* 5.3.5.
51. Cic. *Pis.* 15.
52. Cic. *Marcell.* 12; Weinstock (1957), pp.221–28; Koortbojian (2013), p.87.
53. Pliny *Nat. Hist.* 34.16; Serv. *Aen.* 3.407, 8.288; see Coarelli (1988), pp.364–67.
54. Livy 9.29; Virg. *Aen.* 8.280–305; Weinstock (1957), p.223; Beard *et al.* (1998), p.18, 1.6c; Levi (1997), p.65; Mueller (2002).
55. On tithes offered by traders on the *Ara Maxima*: Dion. Hal. *Rom. Ant.* 1.40.6. Epigraphic attestations of the *decuma*: *CIL* 9.4672; 9.3569; 10.5708; 14.3541 – Marzano (2009), p.86, n.37. The tithe to Hercules was also known as the *Herculana pars*, and is mentioned in Plautus: *Bacch.* 665–66, *Mostell.* 984, *Stich.* 232–33. Some tie the *decuma* to Phoenician influence, e.g., Moret (2012), p.109 n.12. Hercules appeared to act as a certain guarantor over transaction mechanisms like weights and measures: *CIL* 6.282; Van Berchem (1967), p.324; Moret (2012), p.109.
56. Plut. *Sull.* 35, *Crass.* 12.2, *Luc.* 37.4, *Pomp.* 45, *Mor.* 267e–f (*Roman Questions* 18); Pliny *Nat. Hist.* 37.12–1; Diod. 4.21.4. See Marzano (2009), p.84 and n.12 for further bibliography.
57. Athen. *Deip.* 4.153c, 5.221–22f.
58. Marzano (2009), p.90; cf. d'Arms (1998); Beard (2007), pp.257–63. Note the fragment of Posidonius of Apameia dated to 146–143 BC in Athenaeus that mentions generals providing a public feast in the sanctuary of Hercules after the triumphal procession: Marzano (2009), p.90, n.78.
59. Santangelo (2007), p.229; Beard *et al.* (1998), p.232; cf. Beard (2007), p.381, n.11.
60. Bonfante Warren (1970), pp.64–65. See Erickson (2018) for the Dionysian elements woven into the ideology of these public spectacles.

61. Marzano (2009).
62. Livy 26.10.3; Richardson (1992), p.185. Interestingly, in Varro's *Menippean Satire*, Heracles Invictus is equated with Mars: Macrob. *Sat.* 3.12.6.
63. Scheid (2002), p.297.
64. Jourdain-Annequin (1992), p.278.
65. Diod. 4.19; Roymans (2009), p.223; Favreau-Linder (2009); Lampinen (2015), pp.13–14, n.13 for bibliography. The toponym Castra Herculis, on the Peutinger Map and situated along the Lower Rhine at Arnhem-Meinerswijk, may allude to a foundation myth associated with Hercules in Gaul. Castra Herculis was possibly built in connections to Germanicus' campaign in this region in AD 14 and 16: Roymans (2009), p.224 n.28. Cf. Tac. *Germ.* 3.
66. On the etymology of Magusanus, see Toorians (2003).
67. Derks (1998), pp.112–13; Roymans (2009), p.228.
68. Tac. *Germ.* 3.1.
69. Lampinen (2015); Münkler (2007). See Dauge (1981), who encapsulated the use of Heracles to articulate the relationship between Romans and barbarians under the term and concept *héracléisme*.
70. E.g., Sen. *Ben.* 1.13.1–3, 7.3.1, *Ep.* 94.63; Fitch (1987), p.19; and see Fitch (1987) on Seneca's *Hercules Furens*.
71. Suet. *Caes.* 7.1. For Hannibal: Livy 21.21.9; App. *Iber.* 28; Sil. Ital. *Pun.* 3.14–32; see Rawson (1970).
72. Dio 44.6.3–4; Ovid *Am.* 3.8.45–48; Fitch (1987), p.20; Wardle (2009), p.106.
73. Dio 43.45.3; Wardle (2009), p.106. Koortbojian (2013), pp.87–89, argues that this title referred to Quirinus, not Caesar.
74. Cic. *Marcell.* 28, cf. Cic. *Tusc.* 1.28; Diod. 4.8.1; Harrison (2018), p.340.
75. Harrison (2018); e.g., Heracl. *Quaest. Hom.* 33.3–8; Sen. *Constant.* 2.1, *Ben.* 1.13.3; cf. Huttner (1997a), pp.282–83.
76. Vitr. *Arch.* 3.3.5; Pliny *Nat. Hist.* 34.57; Santangelo (2007), p.228. A dedication day of 12 August is listed for *Hercules Invictus ad Circum Maximum* in the Fasti Allifani (*InscrIt* 13.2.181) and the Fasti Amiternini (*InscrIt* 13.2.191). Ziolkowski locates Pompey's temple closer to the Circus Maximus, but Coarelli (1988), pp.187–92, identifies the *aedes Pompei Magni* with the Temple of Hercules Victor *in Foro Boario*.
77. App. *Civ.* 2.76.319.
78. *RRC* no. 426; Santangelo (2007), p.231.
79. Plut. *Ant.* 4.1–3; Palagia (1986), p.143; Zanker (1988), pp.44–45; Huttner (1995); Hekster (2004a), p.171.
80. *RRC* no. 494.2a.
81. Zanker (1988), pp.44–45.
82. Erikson (2018); Goyette (2010).
83. *RRC* no. 489.5. But cf. Hekster (2004a); Erickson (2018), p.261 notes, however, that an aureus (now lost) of Antony showing a lion walking to the left, holding a sword, with a star above, might mimic types struck by Alexander at Babylon.
84. Plut. *Comp. Dem. Ant.* 3; see Ovid *Her.* 9.
85. Spencer (2001), p.262; Barton (2007); Erickson (2018), p.264, but cf. Hekster (2004a).
86. Weinstock (1957), pp.231–32, n.127; although this phrase is not entirely avoided: Hercules is for example called *invicte* (unconquered) in *Aeneid* 8.293.
87. E.g., Schilling (1942).
88. See Ritter (1995), Ch.6. The dissemination of ideology in pre-industrial states has been characterized under several forms: literary and rhetorical, iconographic, symbolic and ceremonial: see Hekster (2005), p.216 n.32.
89. Virg. *Aen.* 6.801–805; Quint (2018), p.98; Secci (2013), p.224; Loar (2021); cf. Dio 56.36.4–5.
90. Virg. *Aen.* 2.721–23; Galinsky (1981), p.1006; Zarker (1972).
91. Galinsky (1966), p.22; Gransden (1976), p.107; Morgan (1998), p.176; Hekster (2004b). Gransden includes Romulus in this mythic genealogy. Cf. Quint (2018), pp.131–32 and n.33.

92. Virg. *Aen.* 184–305; Schnepf (1959); Galinsky (1966); Morgan (1998); Secci (2013), p.224; see also Marinčič (2002) on Herculean mythmaking within the *Aeneid* and *Eclogues*. See Fratantuono & Smith (2018), pp.305–08, for more bibliography and discussion on the Hercules-Cacus episode. See also Loar (2021), who highlights the varying personas taken by Cacus in particular in Augustan prose and poetry. See Livy 1.7; Ovid *Fasti* 1.554; Virg. *Aen.* 7.190; Prop. *El.* 4.9; Dion. Hal. *Rom. Ant.* 1.39–44; Ps.-Aur. Vict. *Orig. Gent. Rom.* 6.
93. Galinsky (1972), p.41; Galinsky (1981), pp.1004–05; Galinsky (1996), p.223; Ritter (1995), p.131; Morgan (1998), p.176; Mueller (2002), pp.320–21.
94. Virg. *Aen.* 8.714, 8.200–04; but cf. Hekster (2004b), who tempers this argument somewhat.
95. Virg. *Aen.* 1.286–88.
96. Daniels (2017), pp.248–49.
97. Knapp (1986); Strabo 4.1.7; Diod. 4.19; [Arist.] *Mir. Ausc.* 85; Amm. Marc. 15.10.9. On the Vicarello Goblets and their representation of the mythical journey from Gades to Rome, see Schmidt (2011).
98. Hardie (1986).
99. La Rocca (1988), pp.123–24; Ritter (1995), pp.136–37; Quint (2018), p.134.
100. Galinsky (1972), pp.131–49.
101. Hekster (2004a); Hekster (2004b); Hekster (2015).
102. Loar (2017), p.46.
103. Loar (2017), p.60.
104. Quint (2018), p.135; Hekster (2004b) suggests that the Apollo temple on the Palatine may have been dictated more by mythological and religious considerations (e.g., its location close to the cave of Cacus and its role in housing the Sibylline oracles) than a blatant statement of Augustus' and Apollo's triumph at Actium.
105. Galinsky (1981).
106. Virg. *Aen.* 10.565–70.
107. Hardie (1986), p.2; Reed (2007), p.141. This ambivalence is noted specifically for Hercules: Quint (2018), p.136.
108. Spencer (2001), p.260; Welch (2004). See also Scheid (2012) on the structural oppositions between the Hercules' cult and the cults to feminine deities in the Forum Boarium. On gendered readings of Propertius *El.* 4.9, see Fox (1988); Lindheim (1998); Janan (1998).
109. Philo *Embassy to Gaius* 75–92.
110. Suet. *Ner.* 53.
111. Dio 62.20.
112. Philo *Embassy to Gaius* 90, trans. Colson (1962).
113. Münkler (2007).
114. *RIC* 1.2 Civil Wars nos 49, 130–133; Rudich (2005), p.212.
115. Suet. *Vesp.* 286.
116. Najbjerg (2007), pp.67–69.
117. Mart. *Ep.* 9.101.
118. Mart. *Ep.* 9.64–65.
119. E.g., Statius *Silvae* 4.2.50–51; 3.155–57.
120. Hekster (2005), p.206; Rebeggianni (2018).
121. Laubscher (1997), p.162; Rebeggiani (2018); Mart. *Ep.* 9.101.
122. Ganiban (2007), pp.13–22.
123. Tuck (2005). The statue is in the Museo Archeologico dei Campi Flegrei nel Castello di Baia (no. 155743).
124. Laubscher (1997), pp.162–63; cf. Mart. *Ep.* 9.101. Tac. *Ann.* 11.11 and Suet. *Ner.* 6.4 report that Nero was protected by a snake as a child; see Laubscher (1997), p.164.
125. Mart. *Ep.* 7.1; see Soldevila *et al.* (2019), pp.399–400, for more bibliography on Domitian's relationship to Minerva.
126. Dio 67.14. Note also the Alexander Sarcophagus discussed earlier, whose lion hunt scene seems to closely parallel the Misenum statue: Tuck (2005), p.244.

127. Medallions struck between AD 129 and 137 show Hadrian in similar hunting scenes to those on the Hadrianic tondi now on the Arch of Constantine. The inscription on the medallions reads *Virtuti Augusti* (see below).
128. Mart. *Ep.* 9.101; cf. 9.64; Tuck (2005), p.232.
129. Pliny *Pan.* 8.2, 14.5.
130. Dio Chrys. *First Discourse on Kingship* 94.
131. This tale is attributed to Prodicus, and appears in Xenophon (*Mem.* 2.1.21); Silius Italicus (*Pun.* 15.18–128); and Cicero (*Off.* 1.118). See Palagia (1986), p.146; Hekster (2005), p.205; Lampinen (2015), pp.14–15; Stafford (2017).
132. Jaczynowska (1981); Hekster (2005).
133. *RIC* 2 Trajan nos 695, 702. An unpublished mosaic from the Aventine shows attributes of Hercules, including a wagon drawn by two boars: Barry (2011), p.21, fig. 31.
134. *RIC* 2 Trajan no. 581. On the relationship between Hercules' club-as-column and the later iconography on the Arch of Theodosius at Constantinople, see Lampinen (2015).
135. *RIC* 2 Trajan nos 699–702.
136. Trajan does not seem to have adopted an overt visual identification with Hercules – a Trajanic-era statue in the Palazzo Massimo alle Terme wearing a lion skin as a *paludamentum* has been taken to represent Trajan, but its identity remains in doubt: Palagia (1986), p.146.
137. *CIL* 6.530; Hekster (2005), p.207; Barry (2011), p.21.
138. Dušanić (2003).
139. See *RIC* 2 Trajan nos 37, 49–51, 689, 690.
140. Hill (1985), 82–83. See above for the over-life-size bronze statue of Hercules from the Forum Boarium, which is similar to the coin iconography, but without the lion skin.
141. Ulpian F22.6; see Mangas Mangarrés (1989).
142. See Barry (2011) on arguments concerning the placement of the Bocca della Verità on the *Ara Maxima*. A monumental bronze statue from Gades depicting either Hadrian or Trajan shows Oceanus in place of the usual gorgoneion on the cuirass (Museo Arqueologico, Cadiz, 4.584). A marble statue, likely of Trajan, from Terracina (now in the Museo Civico Pio Capponi) depicted. Oceanus on the cuirass above a Triton fighting two sea monsters: Barry (2011), p.22.
143. Aristid. *Or.* 26.62.
144. *RIC* 2.3 Hadrian no. 2897; see Barry (2011) for the interweaving of Hadrian's artistic and architectural programme at his villa at Tivoli into this imperial ideology.
145. Palagia (1990), pp.59–60; see, for instance, the Roman copy of a statue with classicizing features in the Palazzo Altemps (60.316); a silver stater from Croton showing Hercules on the obverse in the Invictus style from *c*.420 BC; and an Apulian red-figure plate from the fourth century BC also showing a seated Hercules – all in Palagia (1990). Note also the Augustan-era cameo in the Louvre showing Venus Genetrix and Hercules standing facing one another with military tropaea between them. Hercules' club is lowered onto the spoils: Ritter (1995), pp.137–38; Hekster (2004a), pp.173–74.
146. *BMC* 3380341; *RIC* 2.2 Hadrian nos 731–33, 786; Hill (1985), pl. 2.9–10.
147. Hill (1985), p.91.
148. Tuck (2005), pp.238–40.
149. *RIC* 3 no. 145, a quinarius.
150. Vermeule (1957).
151. Hekster (2005), p.208.
152. See Vermeule (1957), pl. iii.13. Another medallion, without the accompanying four figures, was issued under Marcus Aurelius; see Small (1982), p.122, n.1 for more bibliography.
153. *RIC* 3 Antoninus Pius nos 726, 922, 935.
154. Hercules appears as an archer in the *Odyssey* (12.599–608), and notably on the city gates of Thasos – *Guide* (1968), pp.185–91. Silver shekels from Tyre show Melqart with bow and arrow riding a seahorse: Nitschke (2013).
155. Hekster (2005), p.208, suggests that, unlike his predecessors, Marcus Aurelius' position was indisputable: 'Perhaps Marcus' reign was sufficiently accepted not to have to hide behind

someone else's divine example.' A number of coins minted under Lucius Verus and Marcus Aurelius reference their military victories and include imagery of Mars, Hercules and Victory, for instance *RIC* 3 M. Aurelius nos 510, 517, 519 (with obverse legend: *L. VERVS AVG ARMENIACVS*).
156. Hekster (2005), p.209.
157. Loar (2021); cf. Huttner (1997b).
158. As Palagia (1986), pp.146–47, notes, there are some suggestions that earlier second-century emperors portrayed themselves *as* Hercules – for instance, a rare bronze coin from AD 134–138 shows Hadrian with a lion skin knotted around his neck; another bronze medallion shows him wearing the lion-skin cap. A ringstone in the Cabinet des Medailles in Paris (no. 1759) may show the features of Lucius Verus. For an alternative take on Commodus' assumption of Hercules' persona, see Meyer-Zwiffelhoffer (2006).
159. Dio. 73.15; Hdn 1.14.8.
160. *RIC* 3 Commodus nos 254e, 640, 643; see Palagia (1986), p.147 and n.107 for bibliography; Meyer-Zwiffelhoffer (2006), pp.192–96. For Commodus as the infant Hercules strangling snakes in statue-form, see Laubscher (1997).
161. *RIC* 3 Commodus nos 581, 586, 591.
162. Palagia (1986), p.148, n.116.
163. *BM* R.5062; *RIC* 3 Commodus no. 247.
164. Dio 75.15–22.
165. On the possible meaning of Amazonius for Commodus-Hercules: Meyer-Zwiffelhoffer (2006), pp.197–98.
166. Dio. 73.20; Hdn 1.15; Aur. Vict. *Caes.* 17.4.
167. Dio 73.22.
168. Meyer-Zwiffelhoffer (2006), p.200.
169. *SHA Comm.* 8.5.
170. *RIC* 3 Commodus no. 259.
171. Hannah (1986), p.341.
172. Meyer-Zwiffelhoffer (2006), p.205.
173. *CIL* 7.924.
174. Dio 73.8.
175. Elsewhere the devotion by imperial soldiers to Commodus Invictus Hercules Romanus is noted – for instance, an inscription from Volubilis in Mauretania – Rostovtseff & Mattingly (1923), pp.98–99. Artefacts from a hoard from a private collection from Britain near Cambridge include a votive sceptre in the shape of a club with a figure trampling a barbarian enemy and symbols of the supreme Celtic god (often identified with Jupiter or Hercules), and an emperor's head at the very summit, which had been broken off and restored. Rostovtseff & Mattingly identified this emperor with Commodus, but A. Aföldi (1949) suggested it was more likely Antoninus Pius and, furthermore, argued that the imperial bust and club could not have belonged together.
176. E.g., *BM* R.15814, an as coin.
177. Lichtenberger (2011), pp.27–99.
178. Rantala (2017), p.145.
179. Dio 77.16.3; Stafford (2012), p.155.
180. *RIC* 4.1 Septimius Severus nos 79, 97, 111, 488.
181. Rowan (2012), p.46.
182. Rowan (2012), pp.46–47; Hekster (2015), pp.257–58. Rowan (2012), p.48, argues that Hercules was an essential figure for Severus' self-adoption into the Antonine family via Commodus' explicit association with this deity. Severus portrayed himself with a lion-skin cap on a medallion from AD 202, and certain coin issues showed Severus with the lion skin around his shoulder. Caracalla continued his father's tradition of striking coins with Hercules as one of the patron gods of Leptis Magna and in association with the *Ludi Saeculares*: Manders (2012), p.113.

183. Rowan (2012), p.48.
184. Manders (2012), p.113.
185. Moitreux (2002); Marsden (2007); Manders (2012), fig. 20; Lampinen (2015), p.15.
186. *RIC* 5 Gallienus nos 5, 6, 16, 91, 327, 328, 331, 537, 539, 595, 623, 624, 671–673, 678.
187. Marsden (2007), p.72.
188. *RIC* 5 Gallienus, no. 447.
189. Marsden (2007), p.69; Manders (2012), p.114.
190. *BM* 1864,1128.141; Marsden (2007), 66–67.
191. Several types of legends mark the reverses including: *VIRTVTI AVG* (*RIC* 5 Postumus nos 283, 333); *CONSERVATORES AVG* (*RIC* 5 Postumus nos 228, 263, 338); *COMITI AVG* (*RIC* 5 Postumus no. 261); and *FELICITAS TEMP* (*RIC* 5 Postumus nos 269, 301, 339).
192. *HERCVLI LIBVCO* (*RIC* 5 Postumus, no. 273); *HERCVLI GADITANO* (*RIC* 5 Postumus, no. 346); *HERCVLI INVICTO* (*RIC* 5 Postumus nos 23, 24, 138, 305, 348). See also *RIC* 5 Claudius Gothicus no. 50, which bears the legend *AVG INVICTO*, linking this emperor to Hercules Invictus: Manders (2012), p.86.
193. *RIC* 5 Postumus no. 68.
194. Marsden (2007), pp.72–73; Moitrieux (2002). In some cases (e.g., *RIC* 5 Postumus 134) Hercules' figure is placed within a temple holding the club and lion skin, possibly referencing his temple at Deutz.
195. *RIC* 5.2 Postumus nos 67, 135–36, 203–04.
196. On Hercules as *paciferus*: see Diod. 4.19.1-2; Amm. Marc. 15.9.3–6.
197. Manders (2012), pp.113–14.
198. Manders (2012), p.113, and n.87 for bibliography.
199. *RIC* 5.2 Probus nos 70–72.
200. See Hekster (2015), pp.156–57.
201. Manders (2012), pp.56–57, figs 7–8; pp.114–15.
202. Manders (2012), p.108; Jaczynowska (1981), p.641.
203. Aur. Vict. *Caes*. 39.18; Rees (2005).
204. Rees (2005), p.43; Bardill (2012), p.66; Lampinen (2015), p.16.
205. Rees (2005), pp.235–36.
206. Hekster (2015), pp.298–300; Palagia (1986), p.151.
207. E.g., *BM* 1928,0208.2.
208. *RIC* 6 Rome nos 171, 181; Varner (2014), p.50.
209. See Eppinger (2021).
210. Lucian *Heracles* 6, trans. Harmon (1913).
211. Favreau-Linder (2009).
212. Münkler (2007), p.84.
213. Virg. *Aen*. 1.291: 'then wars shall cease and savage ages soften', trans. Fairclough (1916).

Bibliography

Afŏldi, A., 'The Bronze Mace from Willingham Fen, Cambridgeshire', *JRS* 39.1–2 (1949), pp.19–22.
Alfaro Asins, C., 'Las emisiones feno-púnicas', in Alfaro Asins, C., Arévalo González, A. & Campo Diaz, M. (eds), *Historia monetaria de Hispania antigua* (Madrid, 1997), pp.50–115.
Álvarez Martí-Aguilar, M., 'The Network of Melqart: Tyre, Gadir, Carthage and the Founding God', in Ñaco del Hoyo, T. & López Sánchez, F. (eds), *War, Warlords, and Interstate Relations in the Ancient Mediterranean* (Leiden, 2018), pp.113–50.
Amadasi Guzzo, M.G., 'Melqart nelle iscrizioni fenicie d'Occidente', in Bernardini, P. & Zucca, R. (eds), *Il Mediterraneo di Herakles. Studi e ricerche* (Rome, 2005), pp.45–52.
Anagnostou-Laoutides, E., *In the Garden of the Gods: Models of Kingship from the Sumerians to the Seleucids* (London, 2016).
Aubet, E., *The Phoenicians and the West: Politics, Colonies and Trade*, 2nd edn, trans. M. Turton (Cambridge, 2001).

Bardill, J., *Constantine, Divine Emperor of the Christian Golden Age* (Cambridge, 2012).
Barry, F., 'The Mouth of Truth and the Forum Boarium: Oceanus, Hercules, and Hadrian', *The Art Bulletin* XCIII.1 (2011), pp.7–37.
Barton. C., 'Hercules in a Skirt, or the Feminization of Victory during the Roman Civil Wars and Early Empire', in Britt, B. & Cuffel, A. (eds), *Religion, Gender, and Culture in the Pre-Modern World* (New York, 2007), pp.63–73.
Bayet, J., *Les origins de l'Hercule romain* (Paris, 1926).
Beard, M., *The Roman Triumph* (Cambridge MA, 2007).
Beard, M., North, J. & Price, S., *Religions of Rome, Volume 2: A Sourcebook* (Cambridge, 1998).
Bisi, A.M., 'Le "Smiting God" dans les milieux phéniciens d'Occident: un réexamen de la question', in Bonnet, C., Lipiński, E. & Marchetti, P. (eds), *Religio Phoenicia* (Namur, 1986), pp.69–87.
Bolder-Boos, M., 'Der Tempel des Hercules in Ostia und die Bedeutung der republikanischen Kultstätte vor den Mauern des Castrums', *MDAI(R)* 123 (2017), pp.47–72.
Bonfante Warren, L., 'Roman Triumphs and Etruscan Kings: The Changing Face of the Triumph', *JRS* 60 (1970), pp.49–66.
Bonnet, C., 'Le cult de Melqart à Carthage. Un cas de conservatisme religieux', in Bonnet, C., Lipiński, E. & Marchetti, P. (eds), *Religio Phoenicia* (Namur, 1986), pp.209–22.
Bonnet, C., *Melqart: cultes et mythes de l'Héraclès tyrien en Méditerranée* (Leuven, 1988).
Bonnet, C., 'L'identité religieuse des Phéniciens dans la Diaspora. Le cas de Melqart, dieu ancestral des Tyriens', in Belayche, N. & Momouni, S.C. (eds), *Entre lignes de partage et territoires de passage. Les identités religieuses dans les mondes grec et romain. 'Paganismes', 'judaïsmes', 'christianismes'* (Leuven, 2009), pp.295–308.
Bonnet, C. & Bricault, L., *Quand les dieux voyagent: cultes et mythes en mouvement dans l'espace méditerranéen antique* (Genève, 2016).
Bradley, G., 'Aspects of the Cult of Hercules in Central Italy', in Rawlings, L. & Bowden, H. (eds), *Herakles and Hercules: Exploring a Graeco-Roman Divinity* (London, 2005), pp.129–52.
Celestino, S. & López-Ruiz, C., *Tartessos and the Phoenicians in Iberia* (Oxford, 2016).
Chaves, F., 'The Iberian and Early Roman Coinage of Hispania Ulterior Baetica', in Keay, S. (ed.), *The Archaeology of Early Roman Baetica* (Portsmouth, 1988), pp.145–70.
Coarelli, F., *Il Foro Boario: Dalle origini alla fine della repubblica* (Rome, 1988).
Coarelli, F., 'Hercules Invictus, Ara Maxima', in Steinby E.M. (ed.), *Lexicon Topographicum Urbis Romae*, vol. 3 (Rome, 1996), pp.15–17.
Colonna, G., 'Il santuario di Pyrgi dale origini mitistoriche agli altorilievi frontonali dei Sette e di Leucotea', *Scienze dell'Antichità* 10 (2002), pp.251–336.
Colson, F.H. (trans.), *Philo, On the Embassy to Gaius* (Cambridge MA, 1962).
Counts, D.B., 'Master of the Lion: Representation and Hybridity in Cypriote Sanctuaries', *AJA* 112.1 (2008), pp.3–27.
Crawford, M., *Roman Republican Coinage*, vol. 1 (Cambridge, 1974).
d'Arms, J.H., 'Between Public and Private: The *epulum publicum* and Caesar's *horti trans Tiberim*', in Cima, M. & La Rocca, E. (eds), *Horti Romani* (Rome, 1998), pp.33–44.
Daniels, M., 'Annexing a Shared Past: Roman Appropriations of Hercules-Melqart in the Conquest of Hispania', in Loar, M.C., MacDonald, C. & Padilla Peralta, D. (eds), *Rome, Empire of Plunder: The Dynamics of Cultural Appropriation* (Cambridge, 2017), pp.237–60.
Daniels, M. 'Heracles and Melqart', in Ogden, D. (ed.), *The Oxford Handbook to Heracles* (New York, 2021).
Dauge, Y.A., *Le barbare: recherches sur la conception romain de la barbarie et de la civilisation* (Brussels, 1981).
Derks, T., *Gods, Temples and Ritual Practices. The Transformation of Religious Ideas and Values in Roman Gaul* (Amsterdam, 1998).
Dušanić, S., 'The Imperial Propaganda of Significant Day-States: Two Notes in Military History', in *BICS Suppl. 81: Documenting the Roman Army* (Oxford, 2003), pp.89–100.
Eppinger, A., 'The Early Christian Heracles', in Ogden, D. (ed.), *The Oxford Handbook to Heracles* (New York, 2021).

Erickson, K., *The Early Seleucids, Their Gods and Their Coins*, PhD Diss. (Exeter, 2009).
Erickson, K., 'Sons of Heracles: Antony and Alexander in the Late Republic', in Moore, K.R. (ed.), *Brill's Companion to the Reception of Alexander the Great* (Leiden, 2018), pp.254–74.
Fairclough, H.R. (trans.), *Virgil, Aeneid: Books 1–6* (Cambridge MA, 1916).
Favreau-Linder, A.-M., 'Lucien et le mythe d' Ἡρακλῆς ὁ λόγος: le pouvoir civilisateur de l'éloquence', *Pallas* 81 (2009), pp.155–68.
Fitch, J.G., *Seneca's Hercules Furens* (Ithaca, 1987).
Fox, M., 'Transvestite Hercules at Rome', in Cleminson, R. & Allison, M. (eds), *In/visibility: Gender and Representation in a European Context* (Bradford, 1988), pp.1–12.
Fratantuono, L.M. & Smith, R.A., *Virgil, Aeneid 8* (Leiden, 2018).
Galinsky, K., 'The Hercules-Cacus Episode in *Aeneid* VIII', *AJPh* 87 (1966), pp.18–51.
Galinsky, K., *The Herakles Theme* (Oxford, 1972).
Galinsky, K., 'Vergil's *Romanitas* and his Adaptation of Greek Heroes', *ANRW* 2.31.2 (1981), pp.985–1010.
Galinsky, K., *Augustan Culture* (Princeton, 1996).
Ganiban, R.T., *Statius and Virgil: The Thebaid and the Reinterpretation of the Aeneid* (Cambridge, 2007).
Goyette, M., 'Ptolemy II Philadelphus and the Dionysiac Model of Political Authority', *Journal of Ancient Egyptian Interconnections* 2.1 (2010), pp.1–13.
Gransden, K.W., *Virgil: Aeneid Book VIII* (Cambridge, 1976).
Grottanelli, C., 'Servio Tullio, Fortuna e l'Oriente', *DialArch* 3 (1987), pp.71–110.
Guide de Thasos, École française d'Athènes (Paris, 1968).
Hannah, R., 'The Emperor's Stars: The Conservatori Portrait of Commodus', *AJA* 90.3 (1986), pp.337–42.
Hardie, P.R., *Virgil's Aeneid: Cosmos and Imperium* (Oxford, 1986).
Harmon, A.M. (trans.), *Lucian, Heracles* (Cambridge MA, 1913).
Harrison, S.J., '*HERCVLIS RITV*: Caesar as Hercules in Cicero's *Pro Marcello*', *CQ* 68.1 (2018), pp.338–43.
Hartmann, A., 'Between Greece and Rome: Forging a Primordial Identity for an Imperial Aristocracy', in Vanacker, W. & Zuiderhoek, A. (eds), *Imperial Identities in the Roman World* (London, 2017), pp.16–35.
Heckel, W., 'Mazaeus, Callisthenes and the Alexander Sarcophagus', *Historia* 55.4 (2006), pp.85–396.
Hekster, O.J., 'Hercules, Omphale, and Octavian's "Counter-Propaganda"', *BABesch* 79 (2004a), pp.171–78.
Hekster, O.J., 'The Constraints of Tradition: Depictions of Hercules in Augustus' Reign', in Gazdac, C., Ruscu, L. & Roman, C. (eds), *ORBIS ANTIQVVS* (Cluz-Napoca, 2004b), pp.235–41.
Hekster, O.J., 'Propagating Power: Hercules as a Model for Second-Century Emperors', in Rawlings, L. & Bowden, H. (eds), *Herakles and Hercules: Exploring a Graeco-Roman Divinity* (London, 2005), pp.205–21.
Hekster, O.J., *Emperors and Ancestors: Roman Rulers and the Constraints of Tradition* (Oxford, 2015).
Hermary, A., 'Quelques remarques sur les origines proche-orientales de l'iconographie d'Héraclès', in Bonnet C. & Jourdain-Annequin, C. (eds), *Héraclès: d'une rive à l'autre de la Méditerranée* (Brussels, 1992), pp.129–43.
Hill, P.V., 'Buildings and Monuments of Rome on the Coins of the Second Century (AD 96–192): Part 2', *NC* 145 (1985), pp.82–101.
Huttner, U., 'Marcus Antonius und Herakles', in Schubert, Ch. & Brodersen, K. (eds), *Rom und der Griechische Osten* (Wiesbaden, 1995), pp.103–12.
Huttner, U., *Die politische Rolle der Heraklesgestalt im griechischen Herrschertum* (Stuttgart, 1997a).
Huttner, U., 'Hercules und Augustus', *Chiron* 27 (1997b), pp.369–91.
Jaczynowska, M., 'Le culte de l'Hercule romain au temps de Haut-Empire', *ANRW* 2.17.2 (1981), pp.631–61.
Janan, M.W., 'Refashioning Hercules: Propertius 4.9', *Helios* 25 (1998), pp.65–77.
Jourdain-Annequin, C., *Héraclès aux portes du soir: Mythe et histoire* (Paris, 1989).
Jourdain-Annequin, C., 'Héraclès en Occident', in Bonnet, C. & Jourdain-Annequin, C. (eds), *Héraclès: d'une rive à l'autre de la Méditerranée* (Brussels, 1992), pp.263–91.

Jourdain-Annequin, C. & Bonnet, C., 'Images et fonctions d'Héraclès: les modèles orientaux et leurs interpretations', in Ribichini, S., Rocchi, M. & Xella, P. (eds), *La questione delle influenze vicino-orientali sulla religion greca* (Rome, 2001), pp.195–223.

Knapp, R.C., 'La via herculea en el occidente: mito, arqueologia, propaganda, historia', *Emerita* 54.1 (1986), pp.104–22.

Koortbojian, M., *The Divinization of Caesar and Augustus* (Cambridge, 2013).

Lampinen, A., 'A Helping Hand from the Divine. Notes on the Triumphalist Iconography of the Early Theodosians', *Acta Byzantina Fennica* 4 (2015), pp.9–38.

la Genière, J. de, 'Essai sur les véhicules de la légende d'Héraclès en Occident', in Massa-Pairault, F.-H. (ed.), *Le mythe grec dans l'Italie antique. Fonction et image* (Rome, 1999), pp.11–27.

la Rocca E., 'Der Apollo-Sosianus-Tempel', in *Kaiser Augustus und die verlorene Republik* (Mainz am Rhein, 1988), pp.121–36.

Laubscher, H.P., 'Der schlangenwürgende Herakles. Seine Bedeutung in der Herrscherikonologie', *JDAI* 112 (1997), pp.159–66.

Levi, M.A., 'L'Ercole romano', *DHA* 22.1 (1996), pp.79–94.

Levi, M.A., *Ercole e Roma* (Rome, 1997).

Lichtenberger, A., *Severus Pius Augustus: Studien zur sakralen Repräsentation und Rezeption der Herrschaft des Septimius Severus und seiner Familie (193–211 n. chr.)* (Leiden, 2011).

Lindheim, S.H., 'Hercules Cross-Dressed, Hercules Undressed: Unmasking the Construction of the Propertian *Amator* in Elegy 4.9', *AJPh* 119 (1998), pp.43–66.

Loar, M.P., 'Hercules, Mummius, and the Roman Triumph in *Aeneid* 8', *CPh* 112.1 (2017), pp.45–62.

Loar, M.P., 'Heracles, Caesar and the Roman Emperors', in Ogden, D. (ed.), *The Oxford Handbook to Heracles* (New York, 2021).

López Grande, M.J., 'Rashap en la tradición antigua de la equiparación Herakles-Melqart: Las fuentes egipcias', in Ferrer, E. (ed.), *Ex Oriente Lux: Las religiones orientales antiguas en la Península Ibérica* (Seville, 2002), pp.77–86.

Lulof, P., 'Archaic Terracottas Representing Athena and Heracles: Manifestations of Power in Central Italy', *JRA* 13 (2000), pp.207–19.

Malkin, I., 'Herakles and Melqart: Greeks and Phoenicians in the Middle Ground', in Gruen, E. (ed.), *Cultural Borrowings and Ethnic Appropriations in Antiquity* (Stuttgart, 2005), pp.238–57.

Malkin, I., *A Small Greek World: Networks in the Ancient Mediterranean* (Oxford, 2011).

Manders, E., *Coining Images of Power: Patterns in the Representation of Roman Emperors on Imperial Coinage, A.D. 193–284* (Leiden, 2012).

Mangas Mangarrés, J., 'El culto de Hércules en la Bética', in Blázquez, J.M. & Alvar J. (eds), *La romanización en Occidente* (Madrid, 1996), pp.279–98.

Marcos Casquero, M.-A., 'El exótico culto a Hércules en el Ara Máxima', *Revista de Estudios Latinos* 2 (2002), pp.65–105.

Marinčič, M., 'Roman Archaeology in Vergil's Arcadia (Vergil *Eclogue* 4; *Aeneid* 8; Livy 1.7)', in Levene, D.S. & Neils, D.P. (eds), *Clio and the Poets: Augustan Poetry and the Traditions of Ancient Historiography* (Leiden, 2002), pp.143–62.

Marsden, A.B., '"Some Sing of Alexander and Some of Hercules": Artistic Echoes of Hercules and Alexander the Great on Coins and Medallions, AD 260–269', in Gilmour, L. (ed.), *Pagans and Christians – from Antiquity to the Middle Ages* (Oxford, 2007), pp.65–74.

Marzano, A., 'Hercules and the Triumphal Feast for the Roman People', in Antela-Bernárdez, B. & Ñaco del Hoyo, T. (eds), *Transforming Historical Landscapes In the Ancient Empires*, BAR International Series 1986 (Oxford, 2009), pp.83–97.

Mastrocinque, A., 'Eracle "iperboreo" in Etruria', in Mastrocinque, A. (ed.), *Ercole in occidente* (Trento, 1993), pp.49–61.

Mettinger, T.N.D., *The Riddle of Resurrection: 'Dying and Rising Gods' in the Ancient Near East* (Stockholm, 2001).

Meyer-Zwiffelhoffer, E., 'Ein Visionär auf dem Thron? Kaiser Commodus, Hercules Romanus', *Klio* 88.1 (2006), pp.189–215.

Miles, R., 'Hannibal and Propaganda', in Hoyos, D. (ed.), *A Companion to the Punic Wars* (Cambridge, 2011), pp.260–79.

Moitrieux, G., *Hercules in Gallia. Recherches sur la personnalité et le culte d'Hercule en Gaule* (Paris, 2002).
Moret, J.-M., 'Ostia, Roma, Tibur: Hercules Victor e il Pirati', in Bocherens, C. (ed.), *Nani in festa: iconografia, religione e politica a Ostia durante il secondo triumvirato* (Bari, 2012), pp.109–25.
Morgan, L., 'Assimilation and Civil War: Hercules and Cacus (*Aen.* 8.185–267)', in Stahl, H.-P. (ed.), *Vergil's Aeneid: Augustan Epic and Political Context* (London, 1998), pp.175–98.
Mueller, H.-F., 'The Extinction of the Potitii and the Sacred History of Augustan Rome', in Levene, D.S. & Neils, D.P. (eds), *Clio and the Poets: Augustan Poetry and the Traditions of Ancient Historiography* (Leiden, 2002), pp.313–29.
Münkler, H., *Empires: The Logic of World Domination from Ancient Rome to the United States* (trans. P. Camiller) (Cambridge, 2007).
Najbjerg, T., 'From Art to Archaeology: Recontextualizing the Images from the Porticus of Herculaneum', in Coates Gardner, V.C. & Seydl, J.L. (eds), *Antiquity Recovered: The Legacy of Pompeii and Herculaneum* (Los Angeles, 2007), pp.59–72.
Nitschke, J., 'Interculturality in Image and Cult in the Hellenistic East: Tyrian Melqart Revisited', in Stavrianopoulou, E. (ed.), *Shifting Social Imaginaries in the Hellenistic Period* (Leiden, 2013), pp.253–82.
Noreña, C., *Imperial Ideals in the Roman West: Representation, Circulation, Power* (Cambridge, 2011).
Padilla Peralta, D., *Divine Institutions: Religions and Community in the Middle Roman Republic* (Princeton, 2020).
Palagia, O., 'Imitation of Herakles in Ruler Portraiture. A Survey, from Alexander to Maximus Daza', *Boreas* 9 (1986), pp.137–51.
Palagia, O., 'Two Statues of Hercules in the Forum Boarium in Rome', *OJA* 9.1 (1990), pp.51–70.
Papantoniou, G., *Religion and Social Transformations in Cyprus: From the Cypriot Basileis to the Hellenistic Strategos* (Leiden, 2012).
Parisi Pressice, C., 'Eracle e il leone: paradeigma andreias', in Bonnet, C., Jourdain-Annequin, C. & Pirenne-Delforge, V. (eds), *Le Bestiaire d'Héraclès: IIIe Rencontre héracléenne* (Liège, 1998), pp.141–50.
Popkin, M., *The Architecture of the Roman Triumph: Monuments, Memory, and Identity* (Cambridge, 2016).
Quint, D., *Virgil's Double Cross: Design and Meaning in the Aeneid* (Princeton, 2018).
Rantala, J., *The Ludi Saeculares of Septimius Severus: The Ideologies of a New Roman Empire* (London, 2017).
Rawlings, L., 'Hannibal and Hercules', in Rawlings, L. & Bowden, H. (eds), *Herakles and Hercules: Exploring a Graeco-Roman Divinity* (Swansea, 2005), pp.153–84.
Rawson, B., 'Pompey and Hercules', *Antichthon* 4 (1970), pp.30–37.
Rebeggiani, S., *The Fragility of Power: Statius, Domitian and the Politics of the Thebaid* (Oxford, 2018).
Rebuffat, R., 'Les Phéniciens à Rome', *Mélanges d'archéologie et d'histoire* 78 (1966), pp.7–48.
Reed, J.D., *Virgil's Gaze: Nation and Poetry in the Aeneid* (Princeton, 2008).
Rees, R., 'The Emperor's New Names: Diocletian Jovius and Maximian Herculius', in Rawlings, L. & Bowden, H. (eds), *Herakles and Hercules: Exploring a Graeco-Roman Divinity* (London, 2005), pp.205–21.
Richardson, L., *A New Topographical Dictionary of Ancient Rome* (Baltimore, 1992).
Ritter, S., *Hercules in der römischen Kunst. Von den Anfängen bis Augustus* (Heidelberg, 1995).
Rowan, C., *Under Divine Auspices: Divine Ideology and the Visualisation of Imperial Power in the Severan Period* (Cambridge, 2012).
Roymans, N., 'Hercules and the Construction of a Batavian Identity in the Context of the Roman Empire', in Derks, T. & Roymans, N. (eds), *Ethnic Constructs in Antiquity* (Amsterdam, 2009), pp.219–38.
Rudd, N. (trans.), *Horace, Odes and Epodes* (Cambridge MA, 2004).
Rudich, V., *Political Dissidence Under Nero: The Price of Dissimulation* (London, 2005).
Russell, A., *The Politics of Public Space in Republican Rome* (Cambridge, 2016).
Santangelo, F., 'Pompey and Religion', *Hermes* 135.2 (2007), pp.228–33.

Scheid, J., 'Aspects religieux de la municipalisation. Quelques réflexions generals', in Dondin-Payre, M. & Raepsaet-Charlier, M.-Th. (eds), *Cités, municipes, colonies. Le processus de municipalisation en Gaule et en Germanie sous le Haut Empire romain* (Paris, 1999), pp.381–423.

Scheid, J., 'The Festivals of the Forum Boarium Area: Reflections on the Construction of Complex Representations of Roman Identity', in Brandt, J.R. & Iddeng, J.W. (eds), *Greek and Roman Festivals: Content, Meaning, and Practice* (Oxford, 2012), pp.289–304.

Schilling, R., 'L'Hercule romain en face de la réforme religieuse d'Auguste', *RevPhil* 16 (1942), pp.31–57.

Schmidt, M., 'A Gadibus Romam: Myth and Reality of an Ancient Route', *BICS* 54.2 (2011), pp.71–86.

Schnapp-Gourbeillon, A., 'Les lions d'Héraklès', in Bonnet, C., Jourdain-Annequin, C. & Pirenne-Delforge, V. (eds), *Le Bestiaire d'Héraclès: IIIe Rencontre héracléenne* (Liège, 1998), pp.109–26.

Schnepf, H., 'Das Herculesabenteuer in Virgil's *Aeneid*', *Gymnasium* 66 (1959), pp.250–68.

Secci, D.A., 'Hercules, Cacus, and Evander's Myth-Making in *Aeneid* 8', *HSCPh* 107 (2013), pp.195–227.

Small, J.P., *Cacus and Marsyas in Etrusco-Roman Legend* (Princeton, 1982).

Soldevila, R.M., Castillo, A.M. & Valverde, J.F., *A Prosopography to Martial's Epigrams* (Boston, 2019).

Sommella Mura, A., 'La decorazione architettonica del tempio arcaico', *PP* 32 (1977), pp.62–128.

Spencer, D., 'Propertius, Hercules, and the Dynamics of Roman Mythic Space in *Elegy* 4.9', *Arethusa* 34.3 (2001), pp.259–84.

Spencer, D., *The Roman Alexander: Reading a Roman Myth* (Exeter, 2002).

Stafford, E., *Herakles* (London, 2012).

Stafford, E., 'Hercules' Choice: Virtue, Vice and the Hero of the Twentieth-Century Screen', in Almagor, E. & Maurice, L. (eds), *The Reception of Ancient Virtues and Vices in Modern Popular Culture: Beauty, Bravery, Blood and Glory* (Leiden, 2017), pp.140–66.

Sutton, D., 'The Greek Origins of the Cacus Myth', *CQ* 27.2 (1977), pp.391–93.

Toorians, L., 'Magusanus and the "Old Lad": A Case of Germanicised Celtic', *North-Western European Language Evolution* 42.1 (2003), pp.13–28.

Tuck, S.L., 'The Origins of Roman Imperial Hunting Imagery: Domitian and the Redefinition of *Virtus* under the Principate', *G&R* 52.2 (2005), pp.221–45.

Ulanowski, K., 'The Metaphor of the Lion in Mesopotamian and Greek Civilization', in Rollinger, R. & van Dongen, E. (eds), *Mesopotamia in the Ancient World: Impact, Continuities, Parallels* (Münster, 2015), pp.255–84.

van Berchem, D., 'Hercule Melqart à l'Ara Maxima', *RPAA* 32 (1959–60), pp.61–68.

van Berchem, D., 'Sanctuaires d'Hercule-Melqart: Contribution à l'étude de l'expansion Phénicienne en Méditerranée', *Syria* 44 (1967), pp.73–109.

Varner, E.R., 'Maxentius, Constantine, and Hadrian: Images and the Expropriation of Imperial Identity', in Birk, S., Kristensen, T.M. & Poulsen, B. (eds), *Using Images in Late Antiquity* (Oxford, 2014), pp.48–77.

Vermeule, C.C., 'Herakles Crowning Himself: New Greek Statuary Types and their Place in Hellenistic and Roman Art', *JHS* 77.2 (1957), pp.283–99.

Wardle, D., 'Caesar and Religion', in Griffin, M. (ed.), *A Companion to Julius Caesar* (Malden, 2009), pp.100–11.

Weinstock, S., 'Victor and Invictus', *HThR* 50.3 (1957), pp.211–47.

Welch, T.S., 'Masculinity and Monuments in Propertius 4.9', *AJPh* 125.1 (2004), pp.61–90.

Yarrow, L.M., 'Heracles, Coinage and the West: Three Hellenistic Case Studies', in Prag, J.R.W. & Crawley Quinn, J. (eds), *The Hellenistic West: Rethinking the Ancient Mediterranean* (Cambridge, 2013), pp.348–66.

Yon, M., 'Héraclès à Chypre', in Bonnet, C. & Jourdain-Annequin, C. (eds), *Héraclès: d'une rive à l'autre de la Méditerranée* (Brussels, 1992), pp.145–63.

Zanker, P., *The Power of Images in the Age of Augustus* (Ann Arbor, 1988).

Zarker, J.W., 'The Hercules Theme in the *Aeneid*', *Vergilius* 18 (1972), pp.34–48.

Ziolkowski, A., 'Mummius' Temple of Hercules Victor and the Round Temple on the Tiber', *Phoenix* 42.4 (1988), pp.309–33.

Chapter 5

Roman Military Medicine: The Nexus of Religion and *Techne*

Georgia L. Irby

Introduction

Health remains a universal concern, no less so for the soldier in the field, from Homer's warriors to the triage physicians who populate MASH (Mobile Army Surgical Hospital) units. The Roman medical service was, like all other aspects of imperial administration, a model of aggressive efficiency, but it always remained under the shadow of the Greek medical achievement. The approach to maintaining health and treating disease and wounds in the imperial Roman Army was multifaceted, incorporating advances in medical science together with superstition, folk traditions, religion – both local and imperial – and even politics. The centralization and interconnectivity of Roman military posts allowed for the transmission of instruments, practices and findings in medical theory.[1] Yet the ill and wounded relied as much on attending physicians as on priests of Asclepius (Latin, *Aesculapius*) and other healer deities. On the model of Asclepeia (incubation temples to Asclepius) in the Greek-east, physicians and priests were possibly on staff together at the healing sanctuaries of Mars Nodens at Lydney Park in Gloucestershire and Apollo Cunomaglus at Nettleton Shrub, Wiltshire, both in southwestern England.[2] Here we shall explore the methods of wound treatment, the evidence for a professional medical corps and the synergy of 'rational' and alternative/'divine' methods of healing.

The Art of (Military) Medicine

The dichotomy of the medical art is evident in many registers. Gods of healing can moreover bring disease (most notably Apollo), and drugs can either heal, poison or enchant. The Greek word *pharmakon* (drug, cure, poison) also gives the root for *pharmakeia* (witchcraft) and related words. In Herodotus, verbs with this stem suggest the act of enchantment: *pharmakeuo* ('to administer a drug'), for example, carries the nuance of 'enchant', and *katapharmasso* implies bewitchment with drugs.[3] The Latin analogue, *venenum* (potion, juice, drug, poison), also conveys the force of a magical charm.[4] This bolsters the lingering Roman fear of the Greek-trained doctor as unreliable, unprofessional and inept, whose potions were as likely to kill as to heal, as the epigrammatist Martial dryly contends.[5] According to tradition, Cato the Elder

(234–149 BC) forbade his son from patronizing Greek physicians because they had sworn, so Cato claimed, to kill all foreigners with their medicines.[6] Cato (and others) preferred Roman self-sufficiency: his *On Agriculture* – intended as a guide for the *pater familias* (the head of the household) in managing an estate – covered numerous practical topics, from planting to the treatment of slaves. Pliny the Elder (died AD 79) viewed his own *Natural History* in the context of *enkyklios paideia* ('ordinary / general education') which would thus encourage and enable the self-sufficiency of the *pater familias*.[7] Celsus' work (first century AD) was probably similar in scope.[8]

It is within this context – the tension between the Greek-trained physician and home-grown folk and religious cures – that medicine at Rome, even in the army, flourished. Israelowich emphasizes the Roman military preference for Greek-trained physicians who were fluent in Hellenistic medical traditions. In the epigraphical record, furthermore, many military physicians have Greek names.[9] The health of the Roman soldier was an administrative priority, as evident in criteria for recruitment, training and the paradigm for establishing temporary and permanent camps. The topic is treated at some length in Vegetius' *Epitome of Military Science*, a fourth-century AD handbook on the Roman Army. Vegetius tells us that recruits from rural areas are best because they are already inured to the physical demands of military life which, in many ways, overlap the lifestyle of a farmer: i.e., working with iron tools, digging ditches and carrying heavy burdens.[10] Stamina is paramount. Unlike their rural counterparts, urban recruits must learn to endure unpleasantly hot or dusty weather, sleep outside or in tents and adopt a frugal, rustic diet. Only after the urban trainee has acquired sufficient physical and mental vigour should he undergo training, much less deployment. Recruits who failed to meet the standards might be discharged, e.g., a certain Tryphon, rejected for poor eyesight at the recommendation of three physicians.[11]

Vegetius' account of army health stems from cultural prejudices, practical considerations and theoretical trajectories.[12] He considers daily exercise and suitable food more effective than physicians at maintaining a healthy fighting force.[13] He also advises on when to march (not in the heat of the sun or in the frost and cold) and where to make camp (in temperate places, neither marshy nor arid, with sufficient water and shade). Vegetius' assertion that the best recruits hail from temperate climates[14] evokes a long tradition of ethno–climatological prejudices that is featured in the Hippocratic corpus (especially *Airs, Water, Places*), and finds expression in Aristotle, Vitruvius, Strabo (who attributed the rise of Rome to its medial and temperate, yet varied, climate) and others.[15] In Vitruvius, we see architecture as an analogue to healthcare. He believed that all human learning was relevant to architecture, and furthermore that architecture (like medicine) must be adapted to climate and topography in order to balance the elements and guarantee harmony with nature,[16] just like a Hippocratic physician can balance a patient's humours through diet, exercise and treatment in order to harmonize the body with its environment. Roman medicine, however, largely eschewed humourism, preferring instead a pragmatic, mechanistic model of the body.

In order to avoid 'the unsalutary dangers' mentioned by Vegetius, campsites were painstakingly selected.[17] In permanent camps we find sanitation systems, continuously flushed latrines, bath houses and even permanent drill halls where

Figure 5.1: Battlefield triage. Trajan's Column, spiral 6d (Panel 40, Scenes 102-03). (*Courtesy Art Resource 27439*)

soldiers could train during inclement weather.[18] Many specializations are evident in the medical staff attached to legions: *seplasarii* who oversaw medical ointments; *marsi* to treat poisonous bites;[19] *vigiles* attending to the convalescent; administrative *librarii* who kept accounts; and *veterinarii* and *pecuarii* for livestock.[20] In addition, more highly trained *medici*, with either short contracts or permanent commissions, also specialized in delicate procedures such as surgery (*medici chiurgi*), internal medicine (*medici clinici*) or eye complaints (*medici ocularii*), which were all too common because of the smoke produced from oil lamps.[21] The bearded, trousered medic on Trajan's Column was probably attached to an auxiliary cavalry unit (see Figure 5.1).[22]

Battle Wounds and their Treatment

The descriptions of battlefield wounds are often vivid. Assailants usually aimed for exposed or particularly vulnerable areas, such as the throat/neck, chest or an unprotected thigh,[23] and armour was designed to protect vital body parts.[24] In Virgil's

Aeneid, battle scenes are particularly rich. The first casualty of Aeneas' war in Italy was a young Italian lad, Almo, whose 'wound clung beneath his throat and blocked with its blood both the path of his voice and his tender life'.[25] A Trojan ally, Phegeus, was injured when a broad lance struck at him in an unprotected area (*retectum*). Turnus then swept his sword between the 'lowest rim of the helmet and the breastplate's upper edge' (where the neck is exposed) to decapitate Phegeus.[26] Among Camilla's victims was Butes, whom she struck between the corselet and helmet, a vulnerable bare spot 'where the neck shines through'.[27] Camilla herself died from a spear point 'lodged deep in her chest, between her bones and near her ribs'.[28]

Informed largely by contemporary practices, Latin poets delighted in the gore of various types of wounds. Camilla brutally dispatched Orsilochus with her axe, striking through his armour and bone until his 'wound moistens his face with his brains'.[29] Silius Italicus gives us the consul Flaminius, impaled by a javelin while fighting against the Carthaginians at Lake Trasimene (217 BC). The missile pierced through his naked ribs, and Flaminius, who could see the protruding point, tried to dislodge it.[30] Lucan describes the gruesome effects of the bite of the seps, a poisonous serpent whose toxin was thought to cause thirst: the skin around the puncture mark shrinks to reveal the white bone until the wound seems to take over the body, while poisoned blood permeates the entire body, melting off the calves, stripping the skin from the knees and rotting the muscles of the thighs until a black discharge drips from the groin. The belly snaps and the bowels burst out; every part of the body (ligaments, lungs, chest cavity, all the vital organs) is exposed, and the limbs and head melt 'more quickly than snow on a hot day'.[31] The etymological connection of 'seps' with putrefaction informs Lucan's description of the venom as causing 'instant liquefaction'.[32] Depending upon the species and virulence of its poison, effects of envenoming serpent bites can include severe necrosis of localized soft tissue and skeletal muscle, though not on a scale as described by Lucan.[33]

The average soldier seems to have possessed some rudimentary training in first aid. Galen asserts that most soldiers knew how to staunch blood-flow from severed veins and arteries.[34] The skill probably extended to the civilian population, especially slaves on administrative staffs. Cornelius Scipio Salvito's householders attempted to staunch a self-inflicted dagger-wound that resulted in Scipio's death in North Africa in 46 BC.[35] In Lucan, Caesar staunched the wounds of his soldiers on the battlefield in Thessaly.[36] In Silius Italicus, the wounded Serranus, fighting against Hannibal, lamented that no companions survived to tend his wounds.[37] Even commanding officers tended to the wounded, including Germanicus[38] and his wife, the strong-willed Agrippina.[39] Trajan reputedly tore his own cloak into strips to provide bandages for the wounded near Tapae in battle against the Dacians in AD 101/102.[40]

Trajan's Column includes a triage scene that shows Roman and auxiliary troops tending to two wounded men whose faces grimace in pain (see Figure 5.1). In right profile, a bearded soldier wearing *lorica segmentata* struggles to stand up with the help of two legionary soldiers; the veins of his right arm are visible as he clutches the rock on which he sits. To his left, a wounded cavalryman, in left profile, also grasping his seat, rests his right hand on the back of a bearded medic who wraps the injured man's left leg. The leftward medic and his patient both wear trousers, perhaps attesting non-Roman status. Where possible, wounded troops would be removed from the field, often in wagons,[41] or at least withdrawn to the rear line to be treated either by fellow soldiers or trained *medici*.[42] Troops cared for the wounded in North Africa,[43] and healthy soldiers tended to the wounded after Otho's defeat at Bedriacum in AD 69.[44] Caesar withheld caring for his wounded in 57 BC against the Alpine Seduni and Veragri, whose large supply of fresh troops prolonged that battle,[45] as did Quintus Cicero, under attack by the Nervii in Britain in 54 BC.[46] But Caesar delayed marches for the benefit of the wounded when expedient, as after devastating setbacks at Dyrrhacium.[47] The loss of medical supplies could prove disastrous, so precautions were taken to convey these valuable stores in the middle of the column for safety and ease of access.[48]

Most battlefield wounds were caused by trauma or missiles. Celsus punctiliously explicates the treatment of missile wounds. Six centuries later, Paul of Aegina would repeat Celsus' wound therapies, thereby endorsing their efficacy.[49] Celsus considers differing projectile shapes, angles of entry, depth of penetration and proximity to large blood vessels or vital organs (which can render battlefield triage tricky and troublesome: *magno negotio*). Arrow extraction should be performed only by experienced medics with practical training and exact anatomical knowledge.[50] Rufus of Ephesus (late first century AD) advises waiting for a skilled surgeon to remove arrows.[51] The wounded soldier, nonetheless, instinctively either tries to pull out the arrow himself (as had Flaminius, Pallas and Camilla),[52] or he seeks help from a fellow soldier, as had the guardsman Verennianus, who enjoined Ammianus Marcellinus to remove the arrow lodged in his thigh at Amida in AD 359.[53]

Celsus recognizes that only (un-barbed) projectiles lodged in superficial tissue should be removed at the entry point. Such projectiles can be withdrawn by carefully enlarging the wound with a scalpel, so the tip can be safely retracted. With this method, aggravation of the soft tissue is limited, thereby reducing inflammation. Otherwise, the projectile must be forced through, a procedure that facilitates healing since medicaments can be applied at each puncture. Specialized instruments facilitated arrowhead removal, such as the *dioster* ('impellent'): a rod whose pointed end was used to extract tips with sockets or whose hollow end was used for arrows with 'tails'.[54] Regardless of which end of the arrow was to be extricated first, the surgeon must take care not to prick any blood vessels or sinews. Celsus thus recommends a blunt hook to hold delicate vessels away from the scalpel.[55]

Celsus provides instructions for removing various types of projectiles, including barbed arrows, broad-bladed weapons and lead balls.[56] In Celsus, we discern an understanding of the physics of projectiles (the greater the force/speed of the hit, the deeper the penetration) and the dangers of removing barbed arrows at the entry point, as this could result in further (perhaps even fatal) irritation. Pliny mentions the barbed reed arrows, in use in the East, whose tines cannot be removed.[57] Paul of Aegina describes particularly nasty arrowheads (with hinged barbs that unfold when extraction is attempted) and those featuring small bits of metal (of unknown shape, fitted into grooves on the tip) that remain in the wound when the tip is withdrawn.[58]

The latter type is attested as early as 69 BC during the Third Mithridatic War, when Lucullus encountered a variety of poisoned double-pointed arrowheads whose second tip remained in the wound.[59] Whether such arrowheads existed at all or were designed expressly to obstruct missile extraction remains contested.[60] Celsus, nonetheless, describes a specialized instrument 'like a Greek letter' (upsilon) with which to stretch the flesh in order to remove barbed arrows safely (like a gynecological speculum; see Figure 5.2).[61]

Intact arrows should be pushed through and drawn out at the other side. Shafts, however, were designed to break off, leaving the tip in the wound, which even an experienced surgeon might miss.[62] In such cases, Celsus recommends forceps to extract the tip. If a broken arrow must be removed at the entry point, the *medicus* should use his forceps to snip off any short, fine tangs, or he should wrap larger barbs with reeds and then withdraw the point so as not to tear any more flesh.

A fresco from Pompeii depicts an attempt to extract an arrow (see Figure 5.3).[63] The Trojan healer Iapyx tries to remove a stray missile lodged in Aeneas' thigh: Iapyx 'pulled at the dart with his forceps in vain', receiving no assistance from his patron, the healer god Apollo.[64] The fresco shows Iapyx bracing his left hand behind Aeneas' right thigh while he works at the point with his forceps (the arrow had broken off at the shaft). The scalpel is not shown. The tip is ultimately removed only through divine intervention when Aeneas' mother, Venus, suffuses the river with dittany, a therapeutic, aromatic herb from Crete, popular for extracting arrows from both humans and goats, either imbibed or applied topically.[65] When Iapyx bathes Aeneas' wound with this analgising water, the arrow-head slips out and Aeneas' strength returns. Thus in Virgil we see a distinction between 'rational' healing as overseen by the cults of Apollo and Asclepius and divine healing which can be bestowed by any god (as we shall see below).

Figure 5.2: Bivalve rectal speculum. (*Courtesy of Naples Archaeological Museum, inv. no. 78031*)

For broad blades, Celsus recommends removal at the entry point with a specialized probe, the Dioclean cyathiscus ('spoon of Diocles', attested only in Celsus; see Figure 5.4). Celsus describes the instrument and its use:

'[The cyathiscus] has iron or copper blades. At each edge of one of the blades there are hooks turned downwards. The other blade is curved, moderately angled, and perforated. The latter blade of the cyathiscus is positioned next

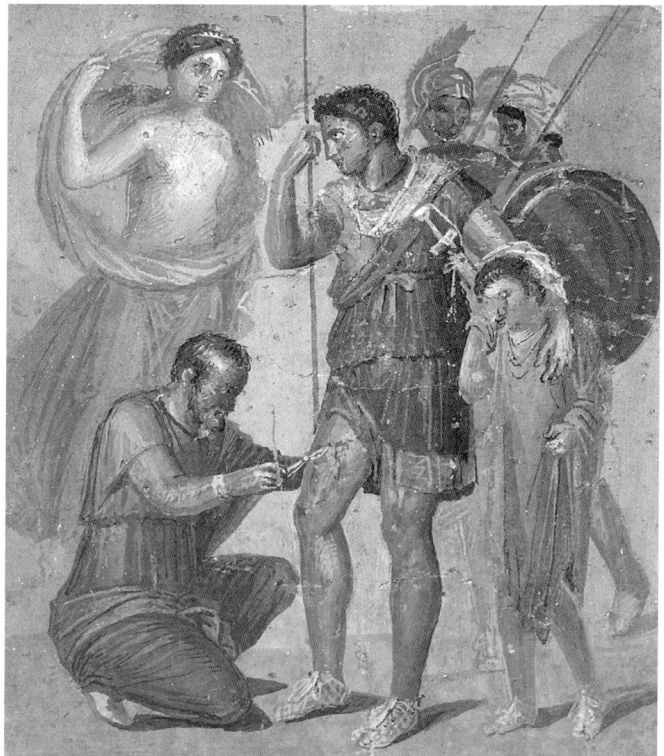

Figure 5.3: Iapyx tends Aeneas' arrow wound (Pompeii, House of Siricus, National Archeological Museum of Naples, inv. 9009). (*Courtesy Art Resource 73149*)

to the weapon and then underneath until the sword point is reached. The instrument is torqued a little bit so that the weapon catches on the aperture. When the tip is in the hollow, fingers positioned under the hooks of the first blade simultaneously extract the tool and the weapon.'[66]

Probing was often the only feasible diagnostic method for missile wounds. Probes are frequently mentioned by medical authors, and they are among the most common medical finds in both military and civilian contexts.

Extracting lead, pebble or shell ballistae lobbed by slingers has its own challenges. Ideally, an intact ball should be removed through its entry point by a forceps after the wound has been opened up. If the ballista is fixed in a bone, tooth extracting methods are applied:[67] the ball is jostled out by fingers or forceps, or a blow by 'some instrument' will (hopefully) dislodge a tenacious ball. Otherwise, the medic must resort to trepanation by boring a V-shaped hole into the bone. In the case of ballistae that have been lodged into joints, Celsus recommends stretching out the sinews at

Figure 5.4: Dioclean cyathiscus. (*Image taken from Bliquez, 2015: figure 43A*)

either end of the joint to create space within the joint, thus allowing for access to the ball, while, of course, taking care not to cause further injuries.

In addition to missile removal, the army doctor had to be proficient at treating various types of trauma, including flesh wounds, head trauma, bone injuries and complications such as haemorrhaging and inflammation, which could lead to death.[68] Instruments excavated from military sites across the Roman Empire speak to a variety of medical activities: surgical knives, scalpels, forceps, spoon scoops, hooks, needles, bone scrapers, cupping vessels, bone levers, cauterizers, male and female catheters, many types of probes (including ear probes for removing foreign objects from the ear), collyrium stamps, ointment pallets and medical boxes.[69]

Biological and chemical weapons are also known, cited by both medical and non-medical writers.[70] Scribonius Largus, who collected 271 pharmaceutical recipes at imperial request (AD 47), recommends Cassius' multi-ingredient salve for treating, in particular, wounds caused by poisoned arrows.[71] The Dacians and Dalmatians poisoned their arrow tips with *helenion* and *ninon*, otherwise obscure.[72] Silius Italicus refers to 'twice harmful missiles' dipped in 'hydra' venom in North Africa and the poisoned javelins of the Nubians.[73] As we saw above, Lucullus contended with poisoned arrows in Asia. By the late first century AD, chemical warfare seems to have been common, and Rufus advises military leadership to inquire about poisoned arrows, which in his time became increasingly virulent, killing 'even if they make a small wound'. Rufus also warns that arrows, especially poisoned ones, should be removed, but only by experts.[74] Celsus simply advises the quick extraction of the poisoned projectile and employment of the same techniques already recommended for serpent bites.[75] Paul of Aegina more helpfully prescribes the removal of discoloured, septic tissue, which 'stands out clearly' from healthy tissue.[76] Galen and Paul also knew that arrow poison was fatal only once it reached the bloodstream, probably as understood in the context of poisons used for hunting.[77] On the strength of this fact, Lucan's Cato tried to persuade his dehydrated troops to drink from a pool crawling with venomous *dipsades*.[78]

Before bandaging, the wound might be dressed with linen or wool medicated with vinegar, wine, oil or a pharmaceutical cocktail.[79] In *On Medical Matters* (*de Materia Medica*), Dioscorides of Anazarbus (first century AD) describes numerous pharmaceutical ingredients, citing wound treatment as among the particular uses of over sixty plant, animal and mineral medicinals that serve as coagulants,[80] anti-inflammatories,[81] agglutinizers[82] and cicatrizers (promoting the growth of scar tissue to heal a wound).[83] Highly esteemed for its wound-curing properties, centaury (*Centaurea centaurion* L.) is recommended for its agglutinating and astringent properties.[84] Dioscorides enthusiastically recommends amorge, the humble sediment from pressed olives: 'there is nothing like it for toothaches and for wounds when smeared with vinegar, or wine, or honey mixed with wine'.[85] Other wound remedies were made from the plastered leaves of the chaste tree – also used for sprains – the opium poppy mixed with vinegar, rosemary, gums from fruit trees and lycium for festering wounds. Devoting five books of his thirty-six-book encyclopedia to pharmaceuticals, Pliny considers hyoseris (a member of the dandelion family) 'a splendid remedy for wounds' and poterion 'a wonderful wound healer'.[86]

The professional medical corps were likely to employ more complex treatments. Scribonius Largus includes descriptions of twenty different dressings (*emplastra*) for a variety of wounds from 'fresh' (*recens*) to 'moderate' (*mediocria*), endorsing in particular Glycon's compounded 'Isis' dressing which overcomes 'all ailments' (compounded from burnt copper, verdigris, frankincense, myrrh, aloe, resin and other ingredients).[87] Two of Thrasea the Surgeon's wound recipes work 'marvellously' (*mirifice*). Among other ingredients, Thrasea's black plaster calls for wax, pitch, roasted resin, Zacynthian asphalt, white lead, verdigris, copper pyrite and alum.[88] Scribonius asserts the plaster's efficacy for dangerous wounds (*periculosa vulnera*) in 'all men', and gladiators in particular. Nowhere does Scribonius single out treatments for soldiers, despite his participation in the British invasion (Claudius' reign was largely peaceful).

Military sites might include gardens for growing medicinal herbs, as long believed by the folk who lived along Hadrian's Wall:

> 'The Roman souldiers of the marches did plant heere every where in old time for their use, certaine medicinable hearbs, for to cure wounds: whence it is that some Emperick practitioners of Chirurgery in Scotland, flock hither every yeere in the beginning of summer, to gather such Simples and wound herbes; the vertue whereof they highly commend as found by long experience, and to be of singular efficacy.'[89]

Chive (*allium schoenoprasum* Linnaeus) has been found near Walltown along the line of Hadrian's Wall.[90] At Neuss in Germany, medical staff were cultivating centaury, henbane (*Hyoscyamus* sp. Linnaeus), St John's Wort (*Hypericum perforatum* Linnaeus), plantain (*Plantago major* sp. Linnaeus), and fenugreek (*Trigonella foenum-graecum*).[91] Most *pharmaka*, however, were imported.[92] Legion II Adiutrix, stationed near Budapest, received duty-free wine 'for the account of the hospital'.[93] Horehound-flavoured wine (*Marrubium vulgare* Linnaeus) was imported to Carpow in Scotland in the early third century AD. An Egyptian papyrus also records a contract (dated to AD 138) for 'plain white blankets, six cubits by four, with finished hems', intended, perhaps, for the legionary hospital in Nicopolis.[93] Celsus had also prescribed special 'easy to digest' diets for invalids. At Neuss, such foodstuffs have been found, including lentils, peas and figs (not native to Germany but with a number of medicinal applications).[95] Radish oil was popular for bedsores and phthiriasis, and soldiers requested their own supplies of it from family and friends.[96]

Large wounds were sutured with flax or linen thread 'so that the scar might be less wide',[97] and Galen recommends taking precautions to heal the wound before the thread 'runs off' (that is, before it starts to rot).[98] To facilitate cicatrisation, the medic's arsenal included murex snail with drying and cleansing properties; cyclamen root boiled in old olive oil, vervain with honey, and burnt copper, one of the ingredients in Glycon's 'Isis' plaster.[99] Once the lesion was treated, a dressing might be applied, especially to larger injuries. We have already seen that most soldiers would have possessed this skill, and that even commanding officers (or their wives) might attend to soldiers when battles went badly and medics alone were insufficient in caring for the injured. The scene is recorded in artwork, most famously on the interior of a kylix from Vucli (c.500 BC) by the Sosias Painter, showing Achilles dressing the wound of his friend Patroclus (see Figure 5.5).[100]

An arrow, it can be assumed, has just been removed from Patroclus' upper left arm (an arrow appears almost parallel with Patroclus' bent right leg). Supporting his injured arm on his left thigh, Patroclus holds one end of the white bandage in place with his right hand while a crouching Achilles wraps the arm. It is an intimate scene fore-fronting the pathos of Patroclus' impending death. We note also that the auxiliary medic on Trajan's Column holds a bandage roll. Military bandagers (*capsaraii*) are known at Neiderbeiber, Germania Superior,[101] Carnutum,[102] Brigetio[103] and Lambaesis.[104] Soldiers were even known to bandage healthy limbs in order to feign injury and avoid fighting.[105]

Works entitled *On Bandages* are ascribed to Soranus and Galen, but the topic is addressed in most medical writers, including Celsus, who recommends cutting

Figure 5.5: Achilles tends to Patroclus' wounds; Berlin F2278. (*Courtesy of Art Resource 169160*)

bandage-linen wider than the wound.[106] Bandages were sometimes wrapped from one end (as with our auxiliary soldier on Trajan's Column) or from the middle (as was Patroclus'), depending on the degree of symmetry of the lesion – Celsus seems as concerned with aesthetics as treatment. The proper wrapping with the correct pressure facilitates healing and diminishes cicatrisation. Celsus is also concerned with the patient's comfort. He advises fewer turns of a bandage in the (hot) summer, more turns in the winter and a needle-and-thread finishing since 'a knot hurts the wound'. Fanciful names ('four-legged', 'hare with ears') suggest that wrappings could be elaborate: on Patroclus (see Figure 5.5) we see symmetrical crisscrossing wraps.[107] Salazar notes that busy field surgeons probably eschewed such elegances and may have delegated the task to assistants.[108]

The Professional Military Corps and Army Hospitals

During the Republic, military medicine was largely *ad hoc*, and no evidence suggests a formalized Republican-era medical corps, military or civilian. Scarborough laconically concludes: 'The problem of the wounded would not be too important if the Roman legion won its battles; those who were victorious in ancient warfare usually did not lose many men, whereas those who lost normally lost everything.'[109] Often included on the private staffs of provincial governors and commanders in the field were physicians, whose attentions may have extended to the ranks.[110] An off-hand remark in Cicero suggests that medics, at the very least, were common in the legions by the mid-first century BC: through their training, soldiers learned, among other things, to trust the *medicus* to treat their wounds in battle.[111] *Medicus*, however, is an ambiguous term, and may here simply refer to a soldier skilled at triage.[112] Vegetius tells us nothing more than that army doctors fell under the camp prefect's authority.[113] Nor does Caesar mention them directly, despite all his concern for the welfare of his men. Caesar's *medici* may have been soldiers who also happened to possess some medical skills.[114] But the dictator did confer citizenship on practising physicians at Rome, an economic incentive likely intended to attract skilled medical personnel to the city (citizenship included tax exemptions) and perhaps to improve conditions for soldiers in the field.[115]

Caesar's privileges to the medical corps were extended by Augustus, Vespasian and Hadrian. Whether the military medical service became professionalized remains a point of contention – the evidence is hardly conclusive.[116] On the fronts in Germany and Pannonia, Tiberius made his personal physicians and supplies available to sick and wounded officers.[117] We saw above that a fellow soldier called upon Ammianus Marcellinus to remove an arrow. Ammianus also mentions 'experts in removing arrows' and 'experts in healing' who tended to Roman troops wounded by Parthian arrows. But he does not specify if his experts are Roman Army doctors, local healers or trained laymen.[118] Nonetheless, it is the extraordinary, not the ordinary, that merits comment. Far from disproving the existence of a standing medical corps, such accounts only indicate that the medical resources to hand were insufficient in the heat of battle. Given Roman efficiency and self-reliance – soldiers are wounded in battle, and everyone falls ill at one time or another – it is reasonable to assume that a military medical service existed, regularized under Augustus when the Roman Army became a standing professional service.[119] But we cannot be certain of its precise organization or status. Members of the military medical corps were bound by the military oath but, along with other specialist ranks, they enjoyed exemption from combat and routine duties.[120] Nutton argues that the legal recognition and protection of the military *medicus* 'implies a formal organisation of the *medici* comparable with that of the administrative staff of the legion or with other specialists'.[121] Yet Galen bemoaned the poor skills and anatomical ignorance of the medics on the front during Marcus Aurelius' campaigns against the Marcomanni.[122] 'Professional', however, does not guarantee excellence, and Marcus Aurelius' medical corps may have been hastily recruited and hurriedly trained.

Nearly ninety medical personnel attached to the imperial Roman Army are attested.[123] Famously, Dioscorides wrote of his 'soldier's life', leading some to speculate that he was a practising army doctor.[124] Dioscorides does not, however, call himself a 'soldier' – he may have simply considered his occupation difficult and disciplined.[125] Scribonius Largus tells us that he travelled with Claudius' household during the British invasion in AD 43, but we do not know if he was an official army doctor or a personal physician to a high-ranking officer.[126] The historian Statilius Crito, who also wrote on pharmacy, saw action on the Danube with Trajan.[127] Advances in medical knowledge, furthermore, were made by the Roman Army medical corps. Galen recommends the headache cure of the army doctor Antigonus and the eye-salve of the *classis Britannica*'s oculist Axius.[128] The antiscorbutic properties of *radix britannica* were likely learned by Germanicus' army doctors from locals in Frisia.[129] Celsus' *barbarum* plaster for flesh wounds was also a campaign discovery. Its 'foreign' name (*barbarum*) suggests a non-Greco-Roman origin.[130] Furthermore, Celsus recognizes that those who treat the bloody wounds received by gladiators and soldiers in battle are far more knowledgeable than civilian medics regarding internal medicine.[131]

Although most practising physicians underwent little formal training (Galen is among the exceptions), evidence suggests some mechanism for medical training in military contexts. An inscription from Lambaesis in Algeria attests an organization of Roman medical military personnel that includes 'student bandagers' (*discentes capsariorum*) undergoing instruction.[132] Some trained medical doctors may have joined the army after receiving civilian training, such as Anicius Ingenuus, a *medicus ordinarius* of the first cohort of Tungrians at Housesteads in northern England who died at age 25, too young to have served long enough to attain a rank equal with centurion.[133] There were also problems with medical pretenders, and efforts were made to stem such abuse with free healthcare for soldiers in the third century AD.[134]

The military 'hospital' (*valetudinarium*; plural *valetudinaria*) has its origins with Julius Caesar, who established garrisons to accommodate soldiers who could not march with the ranks. Even earlier, attentive generals provided special accommodations for convalescing soldiers in order to ensure *esprit de corps*.[135] Before such hospitals were built on any scale, the wounded might be billeted with civilians, a practice that continued into the third century AD.[136] Whether the *valetudinarium* was a regular feature of permanent legionary camps is debated, and some of the literary evidence may have been over-interpreted.[137] Nonetheless, a description of Trajanic-era *valetudinaria* survives in Hyginus Gromaticus' *On Military Camps*. With careful attention to lighting, water supply and the setting in order to provide convalescents with maximum quiet, away from the regular bustle of camp activities, Hyginus' legionary *valetudinarium* accommodated about 200 patients.[138] *Valetudinaria* are also attested epigraphically.[139] Existing remains show a standard plan and position (see Figure 5.6).[140]

The earliest legionary hospital, at Haltern in Germany, is the single exception, resembling instead a collection of tents.[141] *Valetudinaria* usually included facilities for kitchens, wards and, perhaps, operating rooms.[142] An extant duty roster from Vindolanda provides a tantalizing glimpse into the military hospital ward: thirty-one men were cited as unfit for duty for various reasons (the ever-common eye complaints, illness and sundry injuries, not all inflicted in battle).[143] Papyri from Dura-Europos ambiguously designate men on medical leave[144] or otherwise unfit for service.[145] There are reports of food poisoning, scurvy and even prosthetic limbs.[146]

Medical and administrative duties were time-intensive and demanding, as we hear from the brothers Serenus and Marcus stationed together in Alexandria in the third century AD. In a letter to his mother, Marcus described caring for dying, wounded and battle-fatigued men, and after battle against the Anoteritae (whose precise location remains unknown) conditions remained turbulent. Marcus here seems to chronicle men suffering from post-traumatic stress disorder.[147] Serenus berated his mother who, naturally, wanted a visit from her sons, but they were simply too busy to leave their post.[148]

Figure 5.6: Remains of the legionary *valetudinarium* at Housesteads. (*Photo courtesy of Carole Raddato*)

'Alternative' and Divine Healing

Despite the efficacy of pharmaceutical and surgical cures, medicine (civilian and military) was never divorced from 'religion' or 'magic' in the ancient world.[149] Even Galen does not categorically deny the validity of 'alternative medicine'. Celsus alone seems to deny theodicy (illness as divine punishment) and divine healing.[150] Most gods had some healing associations: we have already seen Venus aid her wounded son. Minerva is attested as '*Medica*' into the third century AD,[151] and Jupiter carries the epithet 'Healing' (*Valens*) in Lambaesis in honour of the health and well-being of Septimius Severus' household.[152] Soldiers invoked an array of gods for their own health (*salus*, which consists not just in health but also prosperity and safety). We find an honorific dedication to the Augustan Mercury (a popular god with soldiers and civilians in the provinces) erected for the health of Marcus Aurelius (and the dedicator's own): thus, by expressing his allegiance to the emperor, the centurion Marcus Annius Valens linked his own health with the imperial family.[153]

Many (formulaic) entreaties were made proactively on behalf of the community. The Augustan Mars was invoked for the health of the soldiers (*pro salute militum*) and their commander.[154] Jupiter Optimus Maximus, Juno and Minerva (together comprising the Capitoline Triad which protected the city of Rome), plus the *genius* (protective spirit) of Mogontiacum (Mainz), were invoked by the praetor Marcianus Vercellis in AD 192 for the health and safety of his legion.[155] Human health was thus closely linked with geography and the favour of local deities.[156] Cassius Troianus (the *nomen* suggests an Eastern origin) fulfilled a vow to Fortune on behalf of the health of his fellow soldiers.[157] Jupiter Dolichenus, associated with Hygieia in Africa, was entreated for the health of German allies and a legionary *vexillatio* at Piercebridge in northern England,[158] for a cavalry wing in Pannonia Superior[159] and for Legion XIII Gemina (and the perpetual *imperium* of Rome!) at Apulum in Dacia.[160] The cult of Jupiter Dolichenus was especially popular under Septimius Severus and his son Caracalla.[161] Thus, human health is politicized, hinging also on the success of the reigning emperor and the strength (*imperium*) of Rome. The popular Eastern salvation deity, Mithras, was entreated on behalf of the watch commanders and armourers of two legions in Pannonia Superior, perhaps as a thank offering for initiation into the cult.[162] The popular horse goddess Epona was also invoked for human healing and protection.[163]

We can only speculate that individuals, usually ranking officers but occasionally freedmen, who invoked gods for the health (*pro salute*) of legionary legates, were on army or personal medical staffs. Names of these third-party dedicators sometimes suggest an Eastern origin. But we must not dismiss the possibility of medically trained Roman officers. The centurion Caius Iulius Africanus – a thoroughly Roman name – invoked Diana Regina and Apollo for the health of his legate Vitrasus Pollio.[164] Africanus here could have been either a medical officer or a concerned friend. The centurion Aelius Artemidorus (whose *nomen* is Greek) may also have been a personal friend of his legate, Statilius Severus. Artemidorus fulfilled a vow to Diana Regina and Apollo on behalf of the health of Statilius and his children.[165] The *tessarius* (watch commander) Aurelius Zoticus (a Greek *nomen*) and his fellow soldier

Aurelius Bello (a Celt?) invoked Silvanus, the Roman deity of the greenwood, for the health of their centurion, Julius Licinus.[166] Lucius Messius Primus, a grain supply officer in Moesia Superior, called upon Hercules for the health of his legate.[167] An unnamed freedman entreated Neptune for the health and return of his patron, a centurion of Legion III Augusta.[168] The freedman Aufidius Eutuches (Greek for 'Good Luck') fulfilled his vow to the multi-valent Sulis Minerva (below) for the health and well-being of his centurion.[169] Any of these entreaties may have been made out of friendship, respect or professional duty. The inscriptions do not betray the motivations of their dedicators.

Stones attest vows fulfilled by soldiers and officers to many deities for personal health, among them: Liber,[170] Mithras,[171] the Magna Mater[172] and Heliopolitanus, a north African deity syncretized with Jupiter and whose popularity rose with the Severan dynasty.[173] Although most of the inscriptions are formulaic, one intrigues. The veteran Caius Iulius Agelaus invoked the underworld gods Pluto and Proserpina 'for his own light' (*pro lumine suo*) and for the health (*pro salute*) of himself and his wife Meletenis.[174] Little is known of the cult of Pluto and Proserpina, whose associations included fertility and wealth, but there is a clear correlation between the dark underworld and the world of light. Those who return from the dead (Alcestis, Hercules) are often described as returning to 'light'; birth, furthermore, is an act of coming into the light.[175] The Hippocratic *On Regimen* gives expression to the dichotomy, repeating the folk belief that 'one thing increases and comes to light from Hades, while another diminishes and perishes from the light into Hades'.[176] Given the singular *lumine*, we assume that Agelaus has recovered from a near-death illness or injury.

The connection between healing and the divine remained a strong topos in Greco-Roman literature, for example the plague sent by Apollo to punish Agamemnon to Aeneas' physician, Iapyx, much esteemed by Apollo and gifted with the 'silent and inglorious' art of healing.[177] Pliny declaims that even in his own time, cures were sought from oracles.[178] Gods bestowed health or illness in response to obeisance or insult, and theodicy is widely-attested into the Roman imperial era.[179] Hippocratic (rational) medicine and the temple cult of Asclepius arose nearly simultaneously in the fifth century BC in response to the same stresses and goals: to establish medical orthodoxy over magical alternatives.[180] And Asclepius and his descendants gained divine status precisely because of their ability to heal.[181] The aims, scope and methodologies of temple and secular physicians were symbiotic. Gods were called upon to witness the Hippocratic oath; Hippocrates allegedly copied out the *iamata* (healing inscriptions) at the temple of Asclepius in Cos; and physicians were on staff at healing shrines.[182] This synergy endured into the second century AD, on evidence from Pausanias, Aristides and Philostratus, who often attest religious healing in temple contexts.[183]

Asclepius was widely worshipped at incubation shrines (Corinth, Cos, Pergamum and Epidaurus among the most famous), where the god would visit his sleeping worshippers, and his priests and physicians prescribed a variety of techniques, including exercise, diet, healing dreams and even performative rites, to treat the patient holistically.[184] Prognostication by dreams – especially those sent by Asclepius

– was an integral part of ancient medicine from the Hippocratics onward.[185] A treatise on symptomatic dream interpretation, attributed to the Hippocratic school, informed the medico-pathological approaches of later medical writers, including Rufus and Galen, who both believed that the soul could reveal humoral imbalances in the body and that the god's capacity to heal through dreams was genuine. Galen claimed that he was able to treat his own abscessed hand with instructions from the god (becoming afterwards the god's servant).[186] His fragmentary treatise on diagnosis from dreams guides readers in the use of dreams to investigate and restore humoral balance.[187] To Galen's mind, dreams could be empirically traced to the patient's habits, diet or environment.

Incubation and dream interpretation formed the core of temple healing. A full discussion of Asclepius' cult is not possible here, but about forty inscribed altars attest Asclepius in Roman military contexts. Most of the inscriptions are formulaic, but one implies that a soldier received a cure from an Asclepius-sent dream (*ex visu*). Caius Julius Frontonianus, a veteran *beneficiarius consularis* (an officer seconded to the governor's staff), supplicated Aesculapius, Hygieia and the 'other healing gods and goddesses of this place' (Apulum in Dacia) in thanksgiving for the restoration of his eyesight (*redditis sibi luminibus*).[188] No Asclepeium is known at Apulum, but Asclepius did heal through intermediaries,[189] nor are 'house-calls' entirely unfeasible. Once again, local deities are a powerful force whose favour can regulate or deny well-being.

Although there is no epigraphical proof that Roman soldiers in particular sought cures by incubation in temples of Asclepius, empirical and divine approaches are integrated in Roman military contexts. Roman military medics commissioned at least six Asclepius dedications, including the earliest epigraphic evidence of a Roman Army doctor (AD 82). Sextus Titius Alexander, a *medicus* (whose *cognomen* is Greek) attached to the Praetorian Guard at Rome, gave a gift of an inscribed altar to Asclepius and Health (Hygieia).[190] At Vinovia (Binchester) in northern England, a *medicus* fulfilled his vow to Aesculapius and Health for the well-being of his unit. The slab (late second or early third century AD) shows both gods in bas-relief (see Figure 5.7).[191] Marcus Rubrius Zosimus, a *medicus* of a cavalry cohort stationed at Obernburg-am-Main, invoked Jupiter Optimus Maximus, Apollo, Aesculapius, Health and Fortune for the health of his prefect Lucius Petronius Florentinus, whom, we assume, had fallen ill but has subsequently recovered.[192]

Figure 5.7: Aesculapius and Hygieia at Binchester: *RIB* 1028 (Heidenreich 2013: 91).

Some of these invocations were honorific, for the well-being of the sitting emperor and his family. At Aquae Flavianae in Numidia, for example, the centurion Marcus Oppius Antiochianus entreated Aesculapius and Hygieia for the health and victory of Pertinax (AD 193), an expression of Oppius' allegiance to an emperor during civil war.[193] In AD 227, the imperial bodyguard invoked the obscure Asclepius 'Zimidrenus' for Severus Alexander's health.[194] At Aquincum, the centurion Domitius Victorinus honoured the 'health of the emperor' with a neatly carved altar to Aesculapius, Hygieia, Silvanus and the gods who 'preserve' (*Conservatoribus*).[195]

Asclepius was also invoked as 'Augustan', an epithet that integrated him with the imperial house and its cult, thus politicizing the healing cult. At Apulum, for example, Olus (Aulus?) Terentius Pudens Uttedianus, legate of Legion XIII Gemina and governor of Raetia, invoked the Augustan Heaven (*Caelesti Augustae*) and Augustan Aesculapius (*Aesculapio Augusto*), together with the *genius* of Carthage and the *genius* of the Dacians. Uttedianus invoked the protective spirits of two locales: Dacia (the province where he was currently stationed) and Carthage (perhaps a former post or his home?).[196] The date of the stone is contested, but it was likely erected during a period of war or political instability.[197] Uttedianus thus adroitly linked his own health and success to both his geographical location and the emperor's well-being, as emphasized by his invocation of the *Augustan* Asclepius bolstered by the *Augustan* Heaven.

Many monuments to Asclepius were private. At Ilosva in Dacia, the cavalry prefect Caius Iulius Atianus invoked Aesculapius and Hygieia for 'restoration' (*ob restitutionem*, of his health, we presume).[198] Publius Catius Sabinus, tribune of Legion XIII Gemina in Apulum, fulfilled his vow to a pantheon that included not only Aesculapius, Health, Diana, Apollo and Hercules (gods with strong healing associations), but also the military *Lares* and *Penates* (both are protective spirits), as well as the *Lar* (protector) of the road, Neptune, Fortuna Redux, Good Will and Hope.[199] In anticipation of travel (perhaps a reassignment, soldiers rarely returned home after their tours of duty), Sabinus was taking no chances, and he sought the good will of deities with various overlapping functions, including health, safety and travel both on land and water.

In military contexts, we also see evidence of communication between gods and their patients, an essential factor of Asclepius' incubation cult. The centurion Flavius Marcianus, attached to both Legion XIII Gemina and Legion XV Apollonaris, placed an altar to the Sun, Aesculapius and Hygieia on 'their orders' (*iussu eorum*).[200] Veturius Marcianus, a veteran of Legion XIII Gemina, received a dream from the *numen* of Aesculapius, instructing him to worship Jupiter Dolichenus for the health of himself and his family.[201] Interestingly, the dream came not from the god himself but instead from his divine spirit (*numen*), which in turn recommended supplicating yet another deity. Assigned to Dacia in AD 106, the legion was not relocated until 271. Thus the dating of the stone is uncertain. Merlat suggests that Dolichenus' primacy on the dedication underscores his own healing function. Like Asclepius, Baal of Doliche (Jupiter Dolichenus) may also have overseen temple healing.[202] Asclepius' *numen* seems to suggest that Marcianus seek help from a god whose sphere of authority

(Syria) is physically closer to Dacia or whom Asclepius may deem as less busy – Asclepius' untimely absence from his own temples occasionally inconvenienced his worshippers, who staunchly criticized the god for his 'multi-locality'.[203]

Temple healing and cures by dreams were not restricted to Asclepius. Substantial deposits of small terracotta *ex-votos* representing body parts (as in the Asclepius cult) point to a robust tradition of temple healing in central Italy from the fourth century BC onwards.[204] Additional evidence comes from non-Roman traditions, both localized cults and widespread Eastern rites promulgated by Roman soldiers and merchants. In response to a vision or dream (*ex viso*), Atilius Primus, a centurion stationed at Carnuntum in Pannonia Superior, made a dedication to Jupiter Dolichenus for his health.[205] The freedman Quintus Antistius Agathopus (a Greek cognomen) erected an altar to the *genius* of the imperial house for the health of his patron, legate of Legion II Adiutrix, and his family.[206] Agathopus' entreaty is repeated four times, a magical strategy intended to increase the strength of the request.

Temple healing is also suggested in Romano-Celtic contexts. At the river Severn in Lydney Park, the syncretized Mars Nodens was honoured with an extensive temple complex that included shrines, a bath suite, courtyard house and narrow building with numerous cubicles, probably the *abaton*, where Nodens would effect cures on his sleeping worshippers.[207] Small offerings further suggest a healing cult: among these are pins of various materials,[208] objects representing the sun and water,[209] and bronze and stone dogs. Also linked with Asclepius, dogs were thought to heal wounds by licking them, and dog bones, together with other votives, were found in wells (associated with healing cults in Romano-Gaulish contexts).[210] Nodens was cultivated by soldiers stationed near Lydney Park, including a naval officer in charge of the fleet's supply depot, Titus Flavius Senilis, who may have made a pilgrimage to the site for his health.[211]

Healing cults are associated with water (springs, rivers and wells). Both cold and hot springs had long been used for their curative properties to treat many ailments.[212] In Vitruvius, we find descriptions of the medicinal properties of different types of hot springs (sulphurous, aluminous, bituminous, alkaline).[213] In Pliny, Celsus and others, we read instructions for thermo-mineral healing of various complaints: dislocations, fractures, gout, foot conditions, headaches, psoriasis, diseases of the eyes and the ears and mental illness.[214] Pliny especially recommends the sulphurous springs at Aquae Albulae, between Rome and Tivoli, for treating wounds.[215] Patients took their cures both by soaking/swimming or imbibing – thermomineral water was prescribed to relieve internal pain and bladder stones.[216] With their expansion, the Romans quickly appropriated many of the curative springs in Western Europe for medicinal and recreative use. Interestingly, under Hadrian, spas were reserved exclusively for the ill during the morning hours.[217]

Hot springs were dedicated to a variety of gods with healing associations: Apollo and Diana, Aesculapius and Hygieia, Jupiter, Vulcan, Mars, Minerva, Venus, Dionysus, Silvanus and others.[218] Pre-eminent among such deities was Hercules, who presided over thermal springs at Thermopylae, as well as spas in Italy, Sicily and Dacia.[219] Priests and physicians attended the sick at the *Fontes Sequanae*, where dwelled the water spirit who personified the River Seine, and at Bath (Aquae Sulis), where Sulis Minerva presided over a hot spring and healing sanctuary. Small finds there include *ex voto* body parts and an oculist's collyrium stamp.[220] Soldiers were sent to spas for cures and convalescence or rest and recreation.[221] The presence of the Roman Army encouraged the economic growth and prosperity of medicinal sites,[222] but locals and soldiers occasionally came into conflict over spa sites, for example at Scaptopara in Thrace (AD 238), residents complained to Gordian III that many Roman officials, including soldiers, would descend upon the hot springs and demand lodging and other services without payment.[223] In the early second century AD, Legion IX Hispania came to Aachen (Aquae Granni) to recuperate, for which convalescence its prefect and senior centurion (*primus pilus*) Latinius Macer, a native of Verona, dedicated an altar in fulfilment of his vow to Apollo (syncretized with the local patron of the springs – again human health connects with the land through its divine patron).[224] The altar shows an enthroned Apollo holding his lyre and with a quiver on his right shoulder (see Figure 5.8).

Baden (Aquae Helveticae), near the legionary headquarters for Legion VIII Augusta (Vindonissa), was the site of a military hospital and a healing spa to Mercury.[225] Water from the hot springs was piped to therapeutic basins, one of which could accommodate nearly 100 bathers.

In both civilian and military contexts, healing also straddled the supernatural.[226] Even the word *medicus*, which usually means 'healer', is used in magical contexts: Silius Italicus qualifies the snake charming Marmaridae, whose spells obviate serpent venom, as a 'medical people' (*medicum vulgus*).[227] Because of his successful medical practice, many of Galen's jealous rivals accused him of prognosticating cures by divination, dreams, astrology or sacrifices – slurs which injured Galen's delicate ego.[228] Despite his dismissal of magical cures, Galen nonetheless preserves many cures that employ 'magical' ingredients or ritual methods (such as plucking medicinals with the left hand before sunrise, or a paste of earthworms, pepper and vinegar to cure headaches).[229] Medicinal charms, chants and amulets, furthermore, were common, even in the arsenal of professional healers. In Homer, the sons of Autolycus used charms to heal Odysseus' boar wound.[230] Theophrastus handed down a chant to cure sciatica,[231] while Cato preserved one

Figure 5.8: Apollo Grannus at Baden: *AE* 1968: 323. (*http://www.wasserkalender.de/*)

for setting dislocated limbs,[232] Marcus Varro had an incantation for gout[233] and Caesar would recite a prayer for safety before travelling.[234]

Pliny asserts that there is no one who 'does not fear being cursed by dreadful invocations', and many owned amulets to shield themselves from 'all forms of harm and danger',[235] such as Sulla, who reputedly wore an amulet into battle.[236] Although Galen generally dismisses amulets as within the sphere of superstition, he prescribes green jasper amulets (both inscribed and uninscribed) for stomach ailments.[237] He explains the efficacy of peony root charms in epilepsy patients according to the tenets of the atomic theory: patients would inhale small particles from the peony root, which in turn staved off the attacks.[238] There is no shortage of amulets recovered from Roman imperial military sites, many of which were likely worn by soldiers to protect them from injury or malice. At Camulodunum (Colchester), for example, four bone fist and phallic pendants, intended to enhance the wearer's virility or potency, may have belonged to soldiers. The phallus, an obvious symbol of fertility, was also a powerful apotropaic (offering protection against evil) device, adorning gardens, walls, pottery and jewellery (see Figure 5.9).[239]

A pierced dog's canine was excavated from a grave deposit at the same site (see Figure 5.10).[240] Like the phallus, the hound's tooth may have been thought to confer strength or protection, but the dog, especially in Celtic areas, was a healing animal.

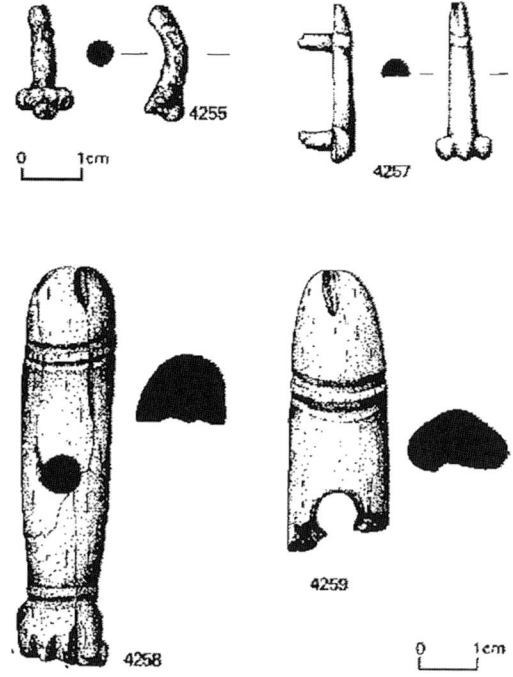

Figure 5.9: Bone fist and phallic pendants at Colchester. (*Image taken from: Crummy (1983), nos 4255, 4258, 4259*)

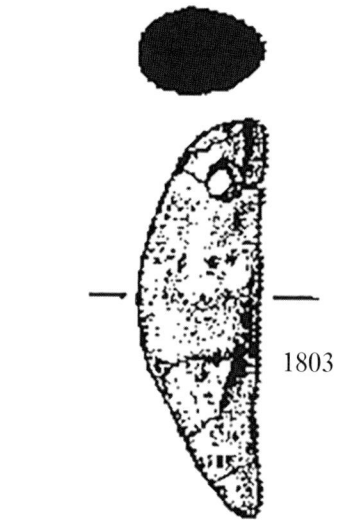

Figure 5.10: Pierced dog's canine at Colchester. (*Image taken from Crummy (1983), no. 1803*)

Conclusion

In these pages we have investigated the complex, multifaceted, synergistic and sometimes contradictory threads by which a Roman of the imperial era (soldier or civilian) might seek medical care. Although the evidence for an established, administratively regulated military medical corps seems to raise as many questions as it answers, we can be sure that some mechanism, whether formal or ad hoc, existed to ensure the health of the Roman soldier. Military physicians, many of whom were Greek by background or training, adhered to the heuristic models of treatment of illness and injury as dictated by Roman authorities. No doubt a network of military bases facilitated the swift transmission of medical practice and theory.[241] The military healthcare system was efficient, cutting-edge and (sometimes) free to enlisted soldiers. Curative drugs, bandages and foodstuffs were distributed to military bases throughout the Empire. There were criteria for selecting the most able-bodied recruits, those men who were likely to be strong and healthy enough to endure the physical demands of life on the march. There were also guidelines for ensuring health in temporary and permanent camps, principles corroborated in the archaeological record. Concern for the soldier's health is manifested in regimen and training, diet, salutary camp surroundings and state-of-the-art hospital facilities, especially at larger legionary bases.

Military physicians and imperial soldiers, nonetheless, availed themselves of many approaches to their health, including magical chants, apotropaic amulets, curative waters, incubation and prayer. Although (Greek) humoral theory was largely rejected by the Romans in favour of mechanistic (rational, empirical) models of the human body, alternative medicine was embraced in conjunction with state-sponsored 'rational' medicine. In order to maintain or restore health, local and Roman state gods were entreated for the health and well-being of units, legions and individual men. Some soldiers (including generals) hedged their bets with apotropaic amulets which were thought to avert evil and protect the wearer. The cults of healing deities flourished in many contexts well into the third century AD. Neither 'rational' nor 'divine' healing was pursued in isolation. Even during the Roman imperial era, health depended as much on the individual as on external factors, including divine favour and the health/success of the state and its leaders.

Notes

1. Israelowich (2015), pp.87–88.
2. Wedlake (1982); Irby-Massie (1999), pp.143–44.
3. Hdt. 7.114, 2.181; see also Plut. *Dion* 14.
4. Cic. *Nat. Deor.* 3.33.81; Lucr. 4.638; Virg. *Aen.* 4.514; Livy 40.24.5.
5. Especially Mart. *Ep.* 1.47, 5.9.
6. Pliny *Nat. Hist.* 29.14.
7. Pliny *Nat. Hist.* preface 14; see Naas (2002), pp.16–34; Doody (2009).
8. For more on the Roman encyclopedic tradition, see Oikonomopoulou (2016), p.973.
9. Davies (1969), p.85; Nutton (1969), p.265; Salazar (2000), p.79; Israelowich (2015), pp.87–88, 107–08. The Spartan Archagathus, the first physician on the public payroll at Rome, was a 'wound surgeon' (*vulnerarius medicus*): Pliny *Nat. Hist.* 29.13; Nutton (1981), pp.17–18. To

be sure, not all physicians, much less those attached to the Roman Army, would have been ethnically Greek. Tiberius Martius Castrensis, a *medicus* stationed in Aquincum (Budapest, Pannonia Inferior: *CIL* 13.1833) in AD 147, may have been Celtic.

10. Veg. *Mil.* 1.3.
11. *P. Oxy.* 39; Davies (1969), p.92; Davies (1970b), p.99.
12. Veg. *Mil.* 3.2. Roman legend exalts farming and country-life: from the shepherd boys who founded the city to Cincinnatus at his plough when a senatorial delegation recalled the retired statesman to service and who returned to his fields after his first dictatorship (Livy 3.26, 3.29). Only the landed were permitted to fight in the army – until the Marian reforms of the early first century BC, when the promise of land grants to retiring soldiers was a powerful recruiting incentive – Sall. *Jug.* 85; Santangelo (2016), pp.33–36; cf. Brunt (1962). Senatorial alliances were struck and broken in efforts to secure these land grants. Pompey's boon for his participation in the so-called First Triumvirate was land for his veterans, by which he assured their loyalty. See also Irby (2015), pp.257–60.
13. Although recommending moderate exercise, Galen was highly critical of excessive, competitive athletics: *Medical Collections* 6.21–36, *CMG* 6.1.1.177–87; *Protrepticus* 11 (1.29 Kühn); see König (2005), pp.280–281. In AD 128, Hadrian reviewed the troops at Lambaesis at their exercises, executed with brutal Roman efficiency. In his detailed address, Hadrian described many drills, including javelin tossing, wall building and cavalry charges. He admonished those who performed poorly and praised those whose exercises 'had the appearance of actual combat'. His speech is poorly preserved in a fragmentary monumental inscription: *CIL* 8.18042.
14. Vegetius asserts that men from cold climates have an overabundance of blood, but they lack intelligence – a condition not conducive to camp discipline. Those from warmer regions have more intelligence, but their paucity of blood renders them afraid of receiving wounds, thus making them poor soldiers – Veg. *Mil.* 1.2; see further Arist. *Pol.* 1327b; Irby (2015).
15. Arist. *Pol.* 1327b; Vitr. *Arch.* 6.1; Strabo 6.4.1.
16. Vitr. *Arch.* 6.1.2.
17. Davies (1970b), p.85; Scarborough (1981).
18. Davies (1970b), p.98.
19. This designation evokes the ancient Italic peoples' renown for curing serpent bites with their bodies, like the Psylloi of North Africa: Pliny *Nat. Hist.* 7.14; Nutton (1985); Jones-Lewis (2016), p.411; cf. Hor. *Epod.* 17.30.
20. Davies (1969); Davies (1970b), pp.86–87.
21. Hdt. 2.84, 3.1.1, on Egyptian *ocularii*; for eye salve recipes: Celsus *Med.* 6.6; Pliny *Nat. Hist.* 21.138. Celsus also provides a detailed description of cataract surgery: *Med.* 6.14. For oil lamps and eye disorders, Donahue (2016), p.613.
22. Spiral 6d; Rossi (1971), p.152; Manjo (1975), p.390.
23. Grmek (1983); Nikita, Lagia & Triantaphyllou (2016), p.466.
24. D'Amato (2016), p.804. Cf. Salazar (2000), p.20.
25. *Haesit enim sub gutture vulnus et udae vocis iter tenuemque inclusit sanguine vitam*: Virg. *Aen.* 7.532–34; cf. Luc. 3.582–91 where a naval officer suffers from a similar double-wound to both his back and chest. All translations are by the author.
26. Virg. *Aen.* 12.374–82.
27. Virg. *Aen.* 11.692–93.
28. Virg. *Aen.* 11.816–17.
29. Virg. *Aen.* 11.698.
30. Sil. Ital. *Pun.* 5.447–56.
31. Luc. 9.764–82. For the seps, Nikander *Ther.* 145–56.
32. Wick (2004), p.279; Desclos & Fontenbaugh (2011), p.203.
33. For the neurological effects of envenoming bites, Harris & Goonetilleke (2004).
34. Galen *de Atra Bile* (5.160K).
35. Caes. *Afr.* 88. Cf. Ovid *Metam.* 7.849.

36. Luc. 7.566–67.
37. Sil. Ital. *Pun.* 6.68–69.
38. Tac. *Ann.* 1.71.
39. Tac. *Ann.* 1.69.
40. Dio 68.8.2.
41. Livy 23.36.4, 23.44.5, 40.33.1; see also Tac. *Agr.* 38.1, *Germ.* 6.6.
42. Livy 30.34.11; Dion. Hal. *Rom. Ant.* 8.65.
43. Caes. *Afr.* 21; see also Caes. *Civ.* 3.75.
44. Tac. *Hist.* 2.45.
45. Caes. *Gall.* 3.4.4.
46. Caes. *Gall.* 5.40.5.
47. Caes. *Civ.* 3.75.1.
48. Onasander *Strat.* 1.13–14; Caecina lost all of his baggage including medical supplies in the marshes of the Ems in AD 15: Tac. *Ann.* 1.65.
49. Celsus *Med.* 7.5; Paul of Aegina 6.87; Davies (1970b), p.89; see also Salazar (2000), pp.47–50.
50. Galen *On Anatomical Procedures* 2.83–84 (2.394–95K).
51. Rufus *Medical Questions* 51.
52. Virg. *Aen* 10.486, 11.816.
53. Amm. Marc. 18.8.11; see also Aen. Tac. 31.16. In the chaos of battle, Ammianus fails to report if he was successful.
54. Paul of Aegina 6.88.3; Bliquez (2015), p.143.
55. On the dangers of cutting into blood vessels or sinews, Celsus *Med.* 2.10.15.
56. Salazar (2000), pp.18–20.
57. Pliny *Nat. Hist.* 16.159.
58. Paul of Aegina 6.88.2.
59. Dio 36.5.
60. Salazar (2000), p.19.
61. A bivalve speculum with open valves would indeed resemble an upper case upsilon (Y). Specula were commonly used in obstetrics and proctology, but Celsus cites this instrument only in the context of missile removal. In Celsus we have the first (extant) literary reference to the bivalve speculum. Several specula survive at Pompeii, including one quadrivalve, two trivalve and two small bivalves: Bliquez (2015), p.54.
62. Rufus 51. For a surgeon who missed part of the shaft in a man hit by a blow from a catapult, Hippocr. *Epid.* 5.95. The patient died in three days. Projectiles frequently broke on impact to prevent re-use (Amm. Marc. 31.15.11) or to complicate the extraction of the tips (Paul of Aegina 6.88.2).
63. Pompeii, House of Siricus, National Archeological Museum of Naples, inv. 9009.
64. Virg. *Aen.* 12.400–04.
65. For dittany, Theophr. *Hist. Plant.* 9.16; Pliny *Nat. Hist.* 26.142. For self-medicating goats, Cic. *Nat. Deor.* 2.126, following Arist. *Hist. An.* 9.6.1. Dioscorides (3.32) compares dittany with pennyroyal (3.31), prescribing both as abortifacients, for which purpose dittany can either be ingested or applied topically.
66. Salazar (2000), p.49; Bliquez (2015), pp.141–43. An instrument fitting this description, found in Asia Minor, has proven to be spurious, but is perhaps a copy of an authentic 'spoon of Diocles': see further Künzl (1991), pp.26–27; Krause (2009), pp.71–72.
67. See also Celsus *Med.* 7.12.1A.
68. Celsus *Med.* 5.26.21–24; Davies (1970b), p.89; Salazar (2000), pp.9–38.
69. Baker (2004), p.140, for ear probes; see appendices 4–10 for medical instrument finds. Baker lists twenty-one ear probes in her catalogue of eighty-four remains from Neuss alone.
70. Salazar (2000), pp.28–30. For a general discussion, Mayor (2003).
71. Scribonius Largus 176: also good for treating bites from rabid dogs.
72. Galen *Ad Pisonem de Theriaca* 10 (14.244–45K); Paul of Aegina 6.88.4.

73. Sil. Ital. *Pun.* 1.322, 3.272–73. That the Celts used arrow poison – (Arist.) *Mir. Ausc.* 86 – is confirmed neither in Caesar or Strabo.
74. Rufus *Medical Questions* 50–55.
75. Celsus *Med.* 5.27.
76. Paul of Aegina 6.88.4.
77. Galen (*ibid.*) and Paul of Aegina (*ibid.*). According to Pliny *Nat. Hist.* 25.61, the Gauls dipped their hunting arrows in hellebore.
78. Luc. 9.614.
79. The ingredients of many medicinals used in antiquity are chemically similar to their modern counterparts: henbane yields hyoscyamine, a tropane alkaloid, still an ingredient in medications for gastro-intestinal disorders, kidney stones and gallstones. St John's Wort remains a popular treatment for many complaints: Davies (1970a); Davies (1970b), p.91.
80. Achilles' woundwort, for example, which also closes 'bleeding wounds' and relieves inflammation: Dioscorides 4.36.
81. Especially effective, according to Dioscorides, are verdigris, 5.79.9; pine tree leaves, 1.69.2; pimpernel (*Anagallis arvensis* L.), 'good for wounds' and for removing splinters, 2.178.1. Pliny *Nat. Hist.* 23.8 specified the cooling and astringent fruit of oenanthe, the wild grapevine, both fresh and dried, as a plaster for bleeding wounds.
82. Frankincense, 1.68.2; woad (*Isatis tinctoria* L.), also an anti-inflammatory, 2.184, 185; comfrey (*Symphytum bolbosum* L.), 4.10.2; aloe (*Aloe vera* L.), 3.22.2; Pliny *Nat. Hist.* 27.18–19.
83. Murex snail, 2.4; cyclamen root (*Cyclamen graecum* Link) boiled in old olive oil, 2.164.3; vervain (*Lycopus europaeus* L.) with honey, 4.59; burnt copper, 5.76.3.
84. Pliny *Nat. Hist.* 25.67; Dioscorides 3.6; Nutton (2013), p.181, calls centaury 'a true panacea'.
85. Dioscorides 1.102. Pliny *Nat. Hist.* 12.77 recommends the exotic *enhaemon*, an Arabian 'olive', as particularly effective at closing wounds.
86. Chaste tree (*Vitex Agnus-castus* L.), Dioscorides 1.103.3; opium poppy (*Papaver somniferum* L.), Dioscorides 4.64.4; rosemary (*Rosemarinus officinalis* L.), Pliny *Nat. Hist.* 24.99, gums, *Nat. Hist.* 24.106; lycium (Dyer's buckthorn, *Rhamnus petiolaris*), *Nat. Hist.* 24.126; hyoseris (*Cichorieae Hyoseris* L.), *Nat. Hist.* 27.90; and poterion, *Nat. Hist.* 27.123. Hyoseris and poterion are not cited in Dioscorides. Poterion is known only in Pliny, perhaps tragacanth (*Astragallus gummifer* Labill.), according to LSJ^9 (sv *potērion*).
87. Scribonius Largus 201–20. Isis plaster, 206.
88. Scribonius Largus 208.
89. Camden (1806), 3.470; Davies (1970b), p.93.
90. Davies (1970b), p.93.
91. Knörzer (1970); Davies (1970b), p.91.
92. Watermann (1974), pp.167–72; Nutton (2013), pp.182–83.
93. Davies (1970b), pp.92–93.
94. Davies (1970b), p.101; Jackson (1990), p.34; Nutton (2013), p.184.
95. Celsus *Med.* 2.18.1–13; Davies (1970a), p.102; Davies (1970b), pp.91, 99. Celsus recommends figs for coughs and abscesses (*Med.* 4.10.1; 5.5, 11, 12, 14, 28). In Pliny, fig juice is an antidote to stings from scorpions and insects; its leaves function as an antidote to rabies, *Nat. Hist.* 23.117–30.
96. Pliny *Nat. Hist.* 23.94; *PSI* 683; *P. Mich.* 481 – Youtie & Winter (1951); Davies (1970a), p.104.
97. Celsus *Med.* 5.26.23B.
98. Galen *Medical Methods* 5 10.320K.
99. Dioscorides 2.4, 2.164.3, 4.59, 5.76.3.
100. Berlin F2278.
101. *CIL* 13.11979, an altar to the *genius* of the imperial house dedicated by Titus Flavius Processus, a *medicus ordinarius*, whose unit is not preserved.
102. *ILS* 9095: Legion XIV Gemina.
103. *RIU* 3.680.
104. *CIL* 8.2553.

105. Dion. Hal. *Rom. Ant.* 9.50.
106. Celsus *Med.* 26.24.
107. Galen *On Bandages* 18A.774–775K; Oribasius *Coll. Med.* 48.27.
108. Salazar (2000), pp.50–53.
109. Scarborough (1968), p.255. Plutarch omits mention of medical staff in his account of Crassus' disaster at Carrhae (*Crass.* 24–25).
110. Plut. *Mar.* 6.3, *Caes.* 34.3, *Pomp.* 2.5–6. Later, emperors would travel with private physicians.
111. Cic. *Tusc.* 2.16.38: *at vero ille exercitatus et vetus ob eamque rem fortior, medicum modo requirens a quo obligetur.*
112. See Scarborough (1968), p.256. Elsewhere in Cicero, *medicus* refers to a healing doctor: *Fam.* 16.9; Salazar (2000), p.78.
113. Veg. *Mil.* 2.10; *Dig.* 50.6.7.
114. Scarborough (1968), p.257.
115. Suet. *Caes.* 42. See Baader (1971), p.17, & André (1987), pp.86–89, for possible ulterior motives.
116. Wilmanns (1995a) contends that organized military healthcare was established during Augustus' reign.
117. Vell. Pat. 2.114.1–3; Davies (1970b), p.98; Nutton (1986), pp.37–38.
118. Am. Marc. 18.2.9, 15; see Salazar (2000), p.83.
119. Suet. *Aug.* 59; *Dig.* 27.1.6.8; Dio 53.30. See also Manjo (1975), p.390; Jackson (1993), p.83. For ranks and pay grades, Davies (1969); Davies (1970b), pp.86–87; Davies (1972).
120. Ael. *Tact.* 248 (Köchly); *Dig.* 50.6.7. On the military oath: Brand (1968), pp.91–98.
121. Nutton (1969), p.262.
122. Galen *To Postumus* 14.649–650K.
123. Davies (1969); Davies (1972). For collections of the epigraphic evidence, Briau (1866); Grummerus (1932); Heidenreich (2013), pp.275–384.
124. Dioscorides: *stratiōikon ton bion*: praef. 4; Davies (1970b), p.88; Nutton (2013), p.182.
125. Riddle (1985), p.4; Scarborough, in Beck (2005), p.xvi.
126. Scribonius Largus 163; Nutton (2013), p.175; *CIL* 3.12116 for a governor's private physician.
127. *FGrH* 2b.200; Scarborough (1981); cf. Davies (1970b), p.88.
128. Galen *de Compositione Medicamentorum* 2.13 (12.557K).
129. Pliny *Nat. Hist.* 25.20–21; Davies (1970b), p.92.
130. Celsus *Med.* 5.26.21–24; Davies (1970a), p.104.
131. Celsus *Med.* praef. 43
132. *CIL* 8.2553; Nutton (1969), p.265; Davies (1970b), p.86; Salazar (2000), p.80.
133. *CIL* 7.690 (*RIB* 1618); Callies (1968), p.24; Rossi (1987), p.282; Salazar (2000), p.81.
134. *SHA Aurel.* 7.8.
135. Caes. *Civ.* 3.78.1; see also Manjo (1975), p.382. Livy (10.35.7) tells us that, during the Samnite War (294 BC), the groans of wounded and dying soldiers demoralized the healthy soldiers.
136. In 480 BC, the consul Marcus Fabius called upon the patricians to look after troops wounded in the Etruscan wars; his own family took in the largest number and attended to them diligently (Livy 2.47.12); cf. *SHA Alex. Sev.* 47.
137. Baker (2002), p.70. E.g., *SHA Hadr.* 10.3, where Hadrian visits sick soldiers *in hospitiis* (their barracks, not necessarily military hospitals). Alexander Severus visited his sick soldiers in their tents (*per tentoria*), not in the *valetudinarium*: *SHA Alex. Sev.* 47.2. This suggests either barracks or perhaps a multi-tent MASH unit.
138. Hyginus Gromaticus (late first or early second century AD) *de munitionibus castrorum* 4. The standard bearer Domitius was able to maintain quiet for troops convalescing on the Egyptian coast by relaying signals visually, instead of audibly, thus maintaining the quiet in the vicinity of the recuperating men: *PSI* 1307 col 2.20; Davies (1970b), p.100.
139. *Valetudinarium* is specified on stones from Moesia Superior (*CIL* 3.14537 [*ILS* 9147]) and Aleppo (*AE* 1987: 952). Personnel in charge of hospitals (*optiones valetudinarii*) are also recorded at Lambaesis (*CIL* 8.2553, 2563), Bonn (*CIL* 13.8099) and in Italy (*CIL* 6.175).

140. This architectural standardization suggests an organized and centralized medical corps: Nutton (1969), pp.262–63. For a critical discussion of archaeological and artefactual remains, Baker (2002).
141. Nutton (1969), p.266; Salazar (2000), p.78. The tents for the wounded in Livy 8.36.1–8 may not reflect the accommodations made in the fourth century BC, but rather those of Livy's own day.
142. Salazar (2000), pp.81–82. For operating rooms, Schultze (1934), who took hearths in a room behind a large entrance hall as intended to sterilize instruments. Literary sources do not support the existence of dedicated operating rooms, nor was there any concept in Greco-Roman medicine of 'sterilization'. Salazar concedes the practicality of a centralized area for treating the wounded.
143. Bowman & Thomas (1991).
144. *P. Dura* 95: *aeger remansit*.
145. *P. Dura* 102: *non sanus*; Davies (1970b), p.101.
146. Food poisoning: Youtie & Winter (1951), no. 468; Jackson (1990), p.131; Davies (1970b), p.101. Scurvy: Pliny *Nat. Hist.* 25.20–21; Davies (1970b), p.105. Prosthetics: Nutton (2013), p.189; see Celsus *Med.* 7.16 on amputating limbs.
147. For post-traumatic stress disorder in antiquity, see Tritle (2000); Melchior (2011); van Lommel (2013).
148. Davies (1969), pp.93–94.
149. Edelstein & Edelstein (1998), pp.205–46.
150. Celsus *Med. proem.* 4.
151. Philippi, *CIL* 3.640; Rome, *CIL* 6.10133; Travi, *CIL* 11.1306.
152. *CIL* 8.18091. Jupiter is here cited together with Aesculapius and Silvanus Pegasianus. For Silvanus Pegasianus, see Dorcey (1992), p.64.
153. *CIL* 8.18007 (*ILS* 2625): Bescera, Numidia. For Mercury, see Caes. *Gall.* 6.17; Irby-Massie (2000). For Augustus-Augusta, see Fishwick (1987), pp.446, 448.
154. Legion II Adiutrix at Aquincum: *CIL* 3.3470 – *ILS* 2453; Heidenreich (2013), p.346.
155. Legion XXII Primigenia Pia Fidelis: *CIL* 13.6728 – Heidenreich (2013), p.155: Mogontiacum, Germania Superior. The dedication details Vercellis' distinguished military career, including his service as the *signifer* and *primus pilus*. See also *CIL* 13.11815, erected by a centurion of the same legion to the Capitoline Triad and 'all the other immortal gods' in response to a dream.
156. In ancient Near Eastern cultures, the health of the community was closely tied to the health of the land and its environment: McCall in Irby, McCall & Radini (2016), pp.296–301.
157. *CIL* 13.6471; Heidenreich (2013), p.210: Bockingen, Upper Germany.
158. *RIB* 03.3253. For Hygieia in Africa: *CIL* 3.558, 7291, 7837. For Dolichenus in general, see Speidel (1978).
159. *CCID* 235.
160. *CCID* 154.
161. Speidel (1978), p.10; Irby-Massie (1999), p.63.
162. V Macedonia and XIII Gemina Gallieni: *CIMRM* 2.1592. For Mithras, see Beck (2006).
163. *IDR* 03-05-01.71; Apulum, Dacia Alba Iulia. For Epona, see Linduff (1979); Oaks (1986).
164. *AE* 1985: 751; Municipium Montanensium, Moesia Inferior.
165. *CIL* 3.12371; Moesia Inferior.
166. *AE* 1987: 942; Apollonia, Galatia.
167. *CIL* 3.7420.
168. *AE* 2009: 1760; Africa Proconsularis.
169. *CIL* 7.40 (*RIB* 143).
170. *AE* 1993: 1304; Matrica, Pannonia Inferior: a watch commander of Legion I Adiutrix for the health of all of his friends and family.
171. *CIL* 2.2634 (*ILS* 2299; *CIMRM* 804), Asturica Augusta, Hispania Citerior; Heidenreich (2013), p.351, Aquincum, Pannonia Inferior; *CIL* 5, 811 (*CIMRM* 01.743), Aquileia; *CIL* 7.41 (*RIB* 144), Aquae Sulis (Bath).

172. *AE* 1947: 33: Brigetio, Pannonia Superior, an altar erected by Rennius Candidus, a veteran of Legion I Adiutrix, and his wife Aurelia Marcellina.
173. *CIL* 8.2627: Lambaesis, Numidia, an altar erected by Gaius Iulius Valerianus, a centurion of Legion III Augusta on behalf of his own health, his wife's, his brother Iulius Proculus, centurion of Legion V Macedonia, sister-in-law Varia Aquilina and niece Iulia Aquilina.
174. *AE* 1930: 32, Germania Inferior. *Dis Infernis / Plutoni et Proser(pinae) / C(aius) Iul(ius) Agelaus / vet(eranus) leg(ionis) I M(inerviae) P(iae) F(idelis) / pro lumine suo / pro salute sua / et Meletenis v(otum) s(olvit) l(ibens)*. In the singular (*lumine*), *lumen* refers to life, e.g., *AE* 1920, 25; *BCTH* 1953, 127 (both Africa Proconsularis, the latter with magical implications); *CIL* 2.3256; *CIL* 3.14190,1; *CIL* 06.27383.
175. Eur. *Alc.* 456; Lucian *Menippus or the Descent into Hades* 1. For Lucina, Cic. *Nat. Deor.* 1.68. See also Virg. *Aen.* 6.680, where souls are about to go to the light (*ad lumen*). 'Light' (*lux, lucis*) is the root of Lucina, the Roman goddess of childbirth.
176. Hippocr. *Reg.* 1.4.
177. Hom. *Il.* 1.34–52; Virg. *Aen.* 12.391–94.
178. Pliny *Nat. Hist.* 29.3.
179. Parker (1983), pp.234–56; Lloyd (2003), pp.12–13; Petridou (2016).
180. Gorrini (2005); Nutton (2013), p.105. On the advice of the Sibylline Books, the Asclepius cult was introduced to Rome, in response to a plague: Livy 4.25.3.
181. Edelstein & Edelstein (1998), 2.1–64.
182. Strabo 14.19, Pliny *Nat. Hist.* 29.2.2; Horstmanshoff (2004), pp.337–38.
183. Edelstein & Edelstein (1998).
184. Paus. 2.27; Hughes (2008); Melfi (2010); Petridou (2016).
185. Hippocr. *On Dreams* 6.640–42; Littré (Jones 4.422); Galen *Hygiene* 1.8.20, 1.12.15 (*CMG* 5.4.2.20, 29). See Oberhelman (1983). The atomists (Epicurus) and Methodists (e.g., Asclepiades and Soranus) were unique in rejecting dreams as diagnostic tools. Galen's medical career was launched by a vision. His father Nikon had 'vivid dreams' that compelled him to send his son to study with a physician at Pergamum: Galen *On Anatomical Procedures* 9.4 (10.609K); *On the Order of My Books* 19.59K.
186. Galen *Therapeutic Phlebotomy* 23 (11.315K). The god further forbade Galen from accompanying Marcus Aurelius to Pannonia: Galen *On His Own Books* 2.18–19 (19.18–19K).
187. Galen 6.832–35K.
188. *CIL* 3.987 (*ILS* 3847). Cf. Ovid *Metam.* 1.624, 5.248; Mart. *Ep.* 4.30.10.
189. Petridou (2016), pp.437–39.
190. *CIL* 6.20 (*ILS* 2092); Rossi (1987); Salazar (2000), p.79.
191. *RIB* 1028 – Heidenreich (2013), p.91.
192. *CIL* 13.6621 (*ILS* 2602). Consider also Titus Venusius Menenia Aper, the *medicus* of *AE* 1937, 181.
193. *CIL* 8.17726. See above on the imperial cult. See also Heidenreich (2013), p.538.
194. *CIL* 6.32543 (*ILS* 2094).
195. *AE* 2009, 1106.
196. We can only speculate on the significance of the *genius* of Carthage. Baudissin (1905), p.467, suggests that Uttedianus may have had family ties to Carthage.
197. Peaks (1907), p.192, dates the stone to 246/249 or 251/56, suggesting that an invocation of the *Genius Daciae* after 256, when the province was lost, is highly unlikely. However, Uttedianus recognized two emperors (Augg); thus a more probable date is 161–169 or 198–212. *CIL* 3.993 – *ILS* 3923; Heidenreich (2013), p.403. Another Uttedianus is known at Salernum: *CIL* 10.618. Augustan Aesculapius and Hygieia are well attested. For example, at Aquincum, Aurelius Artemidorus, a *beneficiarius legati* in charge of the prison of Legion II Piae Fidelis Severianae, fulfilled his vow to Aesculapius and Hygieia Augusta in AD 228: *CIL* 3.3412 (*ILS* 2409). For Hygieia Augusta, see also *CIL* 3.1427, dedicated by a soldier of Legion VI.
198. *CIL* 3.786 – Heidenreich (2013), p.371.
199. Heidenreich (2013), p.425.

200. *CIL* 3.242: Ancyra.
201. *CIL* 3.8044: Dacia: *I(ovi) O(ptimo) M(aximo) D(olicheno) / ex praecepto / Num(inis) Aesculapi / somno monit(us) / Veturius Marci/an(us) ve(teranus) l(egionis) XIII G(eminae) p(ro) s(alute) s(ua) suor(um)q(ue)*.
202. Merlat (1951), no. 37.
203. Petridou (2016), p.438.
204. Comella (1981); Beard, North & Price (1998), pp.1.12–13. Gods entreated *ex viso* in Roman military settings include Hercules (*CIL* 3.8082, Moesia Superior); Juno (*CIL* 3.7950, Dacia); Neptune and Diana (*CIL* 3.2970, Dalmatia); Silvanus (AE 1937, 61, Rome; *CIL* 3.1144, Dacia).
205. *CIL* 3.11129 (*CCID* 222), Pannonia Superior. For another *ex viso* dedication to Dolichenus: *CIL* 5.1870 (*CCID* 449), Concordia, Venetia et Histria.
206. *CIL* 8.18893 (*ILS* 1091), Thibilis, Numidia.
207. Grew (1981), p.357, dates the temple to the fourth century AD. Birley (1986), p.90, suggests that the temple may have been restored in response to Julian's edicts of religious tolerance (AD 361–363). Coins, dating predominantly to the third and fourth centuries, but into the fifth century as well, e.g., Honorius and Theodosius, were buried underneath a floor. This does not necessarily prove a later phase of the temple.
208. Pins were frequently offered by women after successful births. For the Lydney pins: *CSIR* 1.7.161–162.
209. Lewis (1966), pp.88–92.
210. Ross (1967), p.340. For the antibacterial properties of canine saliva: Hart & Powell (1990). Cf. Apollo Cunomaglus, 'the hound prince', who oversaw a healing shrine at Nettleton: Jenkins (1957), pp.60–76.
211. *RIB* 2.2448.3; Birley (1986), p.70.
212. Dvorjetski (2007), pp.84–85 and n.6.
213. Vitr. *Arch.* 8.4–5.
214. See, for example Celsus *Med.* 4.12 (paralysis); Pliny *Nat. Hist.* 31.3–8.
215. Pliny *Nat. Hist.* 31.6; see also Strabo 5.3.2; Mart. *Ep.* 1.12.
216. Sen. *Nat. Quaest.* 3.1.2. Pliny *Nat. Hist.* 31.59–61 warns against excessive consumption of mineral water.
217. *SHA Hadr.* 22.7–8.
218. Croon (1967), pp.230, 244; Jackson (1990), pp.5–9.
219. Thermopylae: Hdt. 7.176; Strabo 9.4.13; see also Dvorjetski (2007), pp.93–94.
220. Deyts (1985); Cunliffe (1988), pp.359–62; Allason-Jones (1989), pp.156–57. For physicians at other spas, Dvorjetski (2007), pp.109–10.
221. Davies (1970a), p.103 and n.14; Dvorjetski (2007), p.106. For Roman soldiers at Bath, see *RIB* 139, 143–44, 146, 147, 152, 156–60.
222. Goldsworthy (2003), pp.99, 142–43.
223. *CIL* 3.12336; Dvorjetski (2007), pp.106–07.
224. *AE* 1968, 323; Nesselhauf & Petrikovits (1967), pp.268–79: *L(ucius) Latinius L(uci) f(ilius) Publilia / Macer Ver(ona) p(rimus) p(ilus) leg(ionis) VIIII Hisp(anae) / praef(ectus) castr(orum) pro se et suis / Apollini / v(otum) s(olvit) l(ibens) m(erito)*.
225. Hartmann (1973), pp.45–51.
226. Gregory (2016).
227. Sil. Ital. *Pun.* 3.300; Scarborough (1968), p.256.
228. Galen *Prognostication* (12.601, 505, 615, 625K).
229. Ritual collection of medicinals: Galen *Comp. Med.* 11 (13.242K); headaches: *Remedies* 3.14.502. To the modern eye, the use of ingredients such as spider's webs (Galen *Simples* 11.22 [12.343K]) may seem supernatural, but, like many folk remedies, cobwebs have proven efficacious. Antiseptic and anti-fungal cobwebs have long been used in folk medicine to stop bleeding and heal wounds. Recently, cobweb silk has inspired research on new types of medical sutures, see Sahni *et al.* (2012).

230. Hom. *Od.* 19.457; cf. Pliny *Nat. Hist.* 28.21.
231. Athen. *Deip.* 14.18.
232. Cato *Agr.* 160.
233. Varro *Rust.* 1.2.27.
234. Pliny *Nat. Hist.* 28.21.
235. Pliny *Nat. Hist.* 28.19; Gager (1992), p.220.
236. Plut. *Sull.* 29.6.
237. For more on medical amulets: Bonner (1950), pp.51–78. Red and green jasper, engraved with lizards, proved a popular fetish against eye maladies (pp.69–71).
238. Galen *On the Powers of Simple Remedies* 10.19 and 6.3.10; Thorndike (1923), pp.172–74; Gager (1992), p.221; Bohak (2015), p.90. Galen's young epileptic patient was free of seizures as long as he wore the amulet, but would fall into a violent attack as soon as the amulet was removed.
239. See Green (1978), pp.34–35; Henig (1984), p.176; Crummy (1983), p.139 (nos 4255–4259). For the phallus as apotropaic, Johns (1982).
240. Crummy (1983), p.51 (#1803).
241. Israelowich (2015), p.87.

Bibliography

Allason-Jones, L., *Women in Roman Britain* (London, 1989).
Allason-Jones, L., 'Health Care in the Roman North', *Britannia* 30 (1990), pp.1133–46.
André, J., *Etre médicin à Rome* (Paris, 1987).
Baader, G., 'Der ärztliche Stand in der römischen Republik', *Acta Conventus XI 'Eirene'* (Warsaw, 1971), pp.7–17.
Baker, P.A., 'The Roman *Valetudinaria*: Fact or Fiction?', in Arnott, R. (ed.), *The Archaeology of Medicine* (*BAR IS* 1046) (Oxford, 2002), pp.69–79.
Baker, P.A., *Medical Care for the Roman Army on the Rhine, Danube, and British Frontiers in the First, Second, and Early Third Centuries* AD (*BAR IS* 1286) (Oxford, 2004).
Baker, P.A., *The Archaeology of Medicine in the Greco-Roman World* (Cambridge, 2013).
Baudissin, W., 'Der phönizische Gott Esmum', *Zeitschrift der Deutschen Morgenländischen Gesellschaft* (1905), pp.459–522.
Beard, M., North, J. & Price, S., *Religions of Rome*, vols 1–2 (Cambridge, 1998).
Beck, L.Y. (trans.), *Pedanius Dioscorides of Anazarbus. De materia medica*, with an introduction by Scarborough, J. (Hildesheim, 2005).
Beck, R., *The Religion of the Mithras Cult in the Roman Empire: Mysteries of the Unconquered Sun* (Oxford, 2006).
Birley, E., 'The Deities of Roman Britain', *ANRW* 2.18.1 (1986), pp.1–112.
Bliquez, L., *The Tools of Asclepius: Surgical Instruments in Greek and Roman Times* (Leiden, 2015).
Bohak, G., 'The Theoretical Foundations of the Use of Amulets in Antiquity', in Raja, R. & Rüpke, J. (eds), *A Companion to the Archaeology of Religion in the Ancient World* (Hoboken, 2015), pp.89–95.
Bonner, C., *Studies in Magical Amulets, Chiefly Graeco-Egyptian* (Ann Arbor, 1950).
Bowman, A.K. & Thomas, J.D., 'A Military Strength Report from Vindolanda', *JRS* 81 (1991), pp.62–73.
Brand, C.E., *Roman Military Law* (Austin, 1968).
Briau, R.M., *Du service de santé militaire chez les Romains* (Paris, 1866).
Brunt, P.A., 'The Army and the Land in the Roman Revolution', *JRS* 52 (1962), pp.69–86.
Byrne, E.H., 'Medicine in the Roman Army', *CJ* 5 (1910), pp.267–72.
Callies, H., 'Zur Stellung der medici im römischen Heer', *Medizinhistorisches Journal* 3 (1968), pp.18–27.
Camden, W., *Britannia*, 2nd edn, trans. Gough, R. (London, 1806).

Casarini, A., 'La medicina militare nella leggenda e nella storia', *Collana medico-militare, pubblicata dal Ministero della Guerra* XX (Rome, 1929).
Comella, A., '*Tipologia* e diffusion dei complessi votive in Italia in epoca medio-e tardo-repubblicana', *Mélanges de l'École française de Rome, Antiquité* 93 (1981), pp.717–803.
Croon, J.H., 'Hot Springs and Healing Gods', *Mnemosyne* 20 (1967), pp.225–46.
Crummy, N., *Colchester Archaeological Report 2: The Roman Small Finds from Excavations in Colchester 1971–79* (Colchester, 1983).
Cunliffe, B., *The Temple of Sulis Minerva at Bath: II: The Finds from the Sacred Spring*, Oxford University Committee for Archaeology Monograph 16 (Oxford, 1988).
D'Amato, R., 'Arms and Weapons', in Irby, G.L. (ed.), *A Companion to Science, Technology, and Medicine in Ancient Greece and Rome*, vols 1–2 (Boston, 2016), pp.801–16.
Davies, R.W., 'The Medici of the Roman Armed Forces', *Epigraphische Studien* 8 (1969), pp.83–99.
Davies, R.W., 'Some Roman Medicine', *Medical History* 14 (1970a), pp.101–06.
Davies, R.W., 'The Roman Military Medical Service', *Saalburg-Jahrbuch* 27 (1970b), pp.84–104.
Davies, R.W., 'Some More Military Medici', *Epigraphische Studien* 11 (1972), pp.1–11.
de Filippis Cappai, C., 'La pratica della medicina nell'esercito romano: una sintesi', *Minerva Medica* 81 (1990), pp.499–506.
de Filippis Cappai, C., 'Il culto di Asclepio da Epidauro a Roma: medicina del tempio e medicina scientifica', *Civiltà classica e cristiana* 12 (1991), pp.271–84.
Desclos, M.-L. & Fortenbaugh, W.W., *Strato of Lampsacus: Text, Translation and Discussion* (New Brunswick N.J., 2011)
Deyts, S., *Le Sanctuaire des Sources de la Seine* (Dijon, 1985).
Donahue, J.F., 'Culinary and Medicinal Uses of Wine and Olive Oil', in Irby, G.L. (ed.), *A Companion to Science, Technology, and Medicine in Ancient Greece and Rome*, vols 1–2 (Boston, 2016), pp.605–17.
Doody, A., 'Pliny's *Natural History*: Enkuklios Paideia and the Ancient Encyclopedia', *Journal of the History of Ideas* 70.1 (2009), pp.1–21.
Dorcey, P.F., *The Cult of Silvanus: A Study in Roman Folk Religion* (Leiden, 1992).
Dvorjetski, E., *Leisure, Pleasure and Healing: Spa Culture and Medicine in Ancient Eastern Mediterranean* (Leiden, 2007).
Edelstein, E.J. & Edelstein, L., *Asklepius: A Collection and Interpretation of the Testimonies*, 2nd edn (Baltimore, 1998).
Egger, R., 'Das Praetorium als Amtssitz und Quartier römischer Spitzenfunktionäre' (Köln, 1966).
Fishwick, D., *The Imperial Cult in the Latin West: Studies in the Ruler Cult of the Western Provinces of the Roman Empire* (Leiden, 1987).
Gager, J.G., *Curse Tablets and Binding Spells from the Ancient World* (Oxford, 1992).
Goldsworthy, A., *The Complete Roman Army* (London, 2003).
Gorrini, M.E., 'The Hippocratic Impact on Healing Cults', in van der Eijk, P. (ed.), *Hippocrates in Context* (Leiden, 2005), pp.135–56.
Green, M., *A Corpus of Small Cult Objects from the Military Areas of Roman Britain* (Oxford, 1978).
Gregory, A., 'Magic, Curses, and Healing', in Irby, G.L. (ed.), *A Companion to Science, Technology, and Medicine in Ancient Greece and Rome*, vols 1–2 (Boston, 2016), pp.418–33.
Grew, F.O., 'Roman Britain in 1980, I: Sites Explored', *Britannia* 12 (1981), pp.314–68.
Grmek, M.D., *Les maladies à l'aube de la civilization occidentale* (Paris, 1983).
Gummerus, H.G., *Der Ärztestand im Römischen Reiche nach den Inschriften* (Helsingfors, 1932).
Haberling, W., *Die altrömischen Militärärzte* (Berlin, 1910).
Harris, J.B. & Goonetilleke, A., 'Animal Poisons and the Nervous System: What the Neurologist Needs to Know', *Journal of Neurology Neurosurgery and Psychiatry* 75 (2004), pp.iii.40–iii.46.
Hart, B.L. & Powell, K.L., 'Antibacterial Properties of Saliva: Role in Maternal Periparturient Grooming and in Licking Wounds', *Physiology & Behavior* 48 (1990), pp.383–86.
Hartmann, M., 'Neue Grabungen in Baden-Aquae Helveticae 1973', *Jahresbericht der Gesellschaft Pro Vindonissa* (1973), pp.45–51.

Heidenreich, C.S., *Le glaive et l'autel. Camps et piété militaires sous le Haut-Empire romain* (Rennes, 2013).
Henig, M., *Religion in Roman Britain* (London, 1984).
Horstmanshoff, H.F.J., 'Did the God Learn Medicine? Asclepius and Temple Medicine in Aelius Aristides' Sacred Tales', in Horstmanshoff, H.F.J. & Stol, M. (eds), *Magic and Rationality in Ancient Near Eastern and Graeco-Roman Medicine* (Leiden, 2004), pp.325–41.
Hughes, J., 'Fragmentation as Metaphor in the Classical Healing Sanctuary', *Social History of Medicine* 21 (2008), pp.217–36.
Irby, G.L., 'Soldier, Ethnography, and Courage', in Futo Kennedy, R. & Jones-Lewis, M. (eds), *Routledge Handbook of Identity and the Environment in the Classical and Medieval Worlds* (London, 2015), pp.247–65.
Irby, G.L., McCall, R. & Radini, A., '"Ecology" in the Ancient Mediterranean', in Irby, G.L. (ed.), *A Companion to Science, Technology, and Medicine in Ancient Greece and Rome*, vols 1–2 (Boston, 2016), pp.296–312.
Irby-Massie, G.L., *Military Religion in Roman Britain* (Leiden, 1999).
Irby-Massie, G.L., 'Horned Gods in Britain and Greek Hero Cult', *Latomus: Studies in Latin Literature and Roman History* 10 (2000), pp.5–44.
Israelowich, I., *Patients and Healers in the High Roman Empire* (Baltimore, 2015).
Jackson, R.P.J., 'Waters and Spas in the Classical World', *Medical History Supplement* 10 (1990), pp.5–13.
Jackson, R.P.J., 'Roman Medicine: The Practitioners and their Practices', *ANRW* 2.37.1 (1993), pp.79–101.
Jenkins, F., 'The Role of the Dog in Romano-Gaulish Religion', *Latomus* 16 (1957), pp.60–76.
Johns, C., *Sex or Symbol? Erotic Images of Greece and Rome* (London, 1982).
Jones-Lewis, M., 'Pharmacy', in Irby, G.L. (ed.), *A Companion to Science, Technology, and Medicine in Ancient Greece and Rome*, vols 1–2 (Boston, 2016), pp.402–17.
King, H., *Health in Antiquity* (London, 2005).
Knörzer, K-H., *Römerzeitliche Pflanzenfunde aus Neuss* (Berlin, 1970).
König, J., *Athletics and Literature in the Roman Empire* (Cambridge, 2005).
Krause, O., *Der Artz und sein Instrumentarium in der römischen Legion* (Weinstadt, 2009).
Künzl, E., *Theodor Meyer-Steineg (1873–1936): Arzt, Historiker, Sammler* (Jena, 1991).
Lewis, M.J.T., *Temples in Roman Britain* (Cambridge, 1966).
Linduff, K., 'Epona: A Celt among the Romans', *Collection Latomus* 38 (1979), pp.817–37.
Lloyd, G.E.R., *In the Grip of Disease: Studies in the Greek Imagination* (Oxford, 2003).
Manjo, G., *The Healing Hand: Man and Wound in the Ancient World* (Harvard, 1975).
Mayor, A., *Greek Fire, Poison Arrows, and Scorpion Bombs: Biological and Chemical Warfare in the Ancient World* (London, 2003).
Melchior, A., 'Caesar in Vietnam: Did Roman Soldiers Suffer from Post Traumatic Stress Disorder?', *G&R* 58.2 (2011), pp.209–23.
Melfi, M., 'Ritual Spaces and Performances in the Asklepieia of Roman Greece', *BSA* 105 (2010), pp.317–38.
Merlat, P., *Repertoire des inscriptions et monuments figures de culte de Jupiter Dolichenus* (Paris, 1951).
Naas, V., *Le projet encyclopédique de Pline l'Ancien* (Rome, 2002).
Nesselhauf, H. & Petrikovits, H., 'Ein weihaltar fur Apollo aus Aachen-Burtscheid', *Bonner Jahrbücher* 167 (1967), pp.268–79.
Nikita, E., Lagia, A. & Triantaphyllou, S., 'Epidemiology and Pathology', in Irby, G.L. (ed.), *A Companion to Science, Technology, and Medicine in Ancient Greece and Rome*, vols 1–2 (Boston, 2016), pp.465–82.
Nutton, V., 'Medicine and the Roman Army: A Further Reconsideration', *Medical History* 13 (1969), pp.260–70.
Nutton, V., 'Continuity or Rediscovery? The City Physician in Classical Antiquity and Mediaeval Italy', in Russell, A.W. (ed.), *The Town and State Physician in Europe* (Wolfenbüttel, 1981), pp.9–46.

Nutton, V., 'The Drug Trade in Antiquity', *Journal of the Royal Society of Medicine* 78 (1985), pp.138–43.
Nutton, V., 'The Perils of Patriotism. Pliny and Roman Medicine', in French, R. & Greenaway, F. (eds), *Science in the Early Roman Empire, Pliny the Elder, his Sources, and Influence* (London, 1986), pp.30–58.
Nutton, V., *Ancient Medicine*, 2nd edn (London, 2013).
Oaks, L.S., 'The Goddess Epona: Concepts of Sovereignty in a Changing Landscape', in Henig, M. & King, A. (eds), *Pagan Gods and Shrines of the Roman Empire* (Oxford, 1986), pp.77–84.
Oberhelman, S.M., 'Galen, On Diagnosis from Dreams', *Journal of the History of Medicine and Allied Sciences* 38 (1983), pp.36–47.
Oikonomopoulou, K., 'Scientific Encyclopedias', in Irby, G.L. (ed.), *A Companion to Science, Technology, and Medicine in Ancient Greece and Rome*, vols 1–2 (Boston, 2016), pp.973–87.
Parker, R., *Miasma: Pollution and Purification in Early Greek Religion* (Oxford, 1983).
Peaks, M.B., *Administration of Noricum and Raetia* (Chicago, 1907).
Penn, R.G., *Medicine on Ancient Greek and Roman Coins* (London, 1994).
Petridou, G., 'Healing Shrines', in Irby, G.L. (ed.), *A Companion to Science, Technology, and Medicine in Ancient Greece and Rome*, vols 1–2 (Boston, 2016),: pp.434–48.
Riddle, J.M., *Dioscorides On Pharmacy and Medicine* (Austin, 1985).
Ross, A., *Pagan Celtic Britain: Studies in Iconography and Tradition* (London, 1967).
Rossi, L., *Trajan's Column and the Dacian Wars* (Cornell, 1971).
Rossi, L., 'Per Esculapio e la salute dei commilitoni: sintesi aggiornata di medicina militare romana', *Giornale italiano di cardiologia* 17 (1987), pp.281–83.
Sahni, V., Labhasetwar, D.V. & Dhinojwala, A., 'Spider Silk Inspired Functional Microthreads', *Langmuir* 28 (2012), pp.2,206–10.
Salazar, C.F., *The Treatment of War Wounds in Graeco-Roman Antiquity* (Leiden, 2000).
Santangelo, F., *Marius* (London, 2016).
Scarborough, J., 'Roman Medicine and the Legions: A Reconsideration', *Medical History* 12 (1968), pp.254–61.
Scarborough, J., 'Roman Medicine and Public Health', *Proceedings of the Fifth International Symposium on the Comparative History of Medicine East and West 1980 (Kyoto Taniguchi Foundation & Juntendo School of Medicine) (Kyoto, 1981)*, pp.33–74.
Schultze, R., 'Die römischen Legionslazarette in Vetera und anderen Legionslagern', *Bonner Jahrbücher* 139 (1934), pp.54–63.
Speidel, M., *The Religion of Jupiter Dolichenus in the Roman Army* (Leiden, 1978).
Thorndike, L., *A History of Magic and Experimental Science During the First Thirteen Centuries of Our Era* (New York, 1923).
Tritle, L.A., *From Melos to My Lai: War and Survival* (London, 2000).
van Lommel, K., 'The Recognition of Roman Soldiers' Mental Impairment', *Acta Classica* 56 (2013), pp.155–84.
Watermann, R., *Medizinisches und Hygienisches aus Germania Inferior* (Neuss, 1974).
Wedlake, W.J., *The Excavation of the Shrine of Apollo at Nettleton, Wiltshire, 1956–1971* (London, 1982).
Wick, C., *Lucan: Bellum Civile: Liber IX* (Munich, 2004).
Wilmanns J.C., 'Der Artz in der römischen Armee der frühen und hohen Kaiserzeit', *Clio medica acta Academia Internationalis Historiae Medicinae* 27 (1995a), pp.171–87.
Wilmanns J.C., *Der Sanitätsdienst im Römischen Reich: eine sozialgeschichtliche Studie zum römischen Militärsanitätswesen nebst einer Prosopographie des Sanitätspersonals* (Hildesheim, 1995b).
Youtie, H.C. & Winter, J.G., *Michigan Papyri*, vol. 8 (Ann Arbor, 1951).

Chapter 6

The Soldier and Death. Funerary Practices of Soldiers under the Principate

Yann Le Bohec
(Translated and Edited by Christopher Matthew)

The Romans of the imperial period practised several religions.[1] In one they honoured the traditional gods such as Jupiter, Juno, Minerva and Mars; in another they celebrated the emperor; still another addressed the divinities of the provinces, or the so-called Oriental gods; and finally they honoured the dead. This last type of cultic activity is often neglected in modern scholarship. Yet this religion had its own organization, with its own deities, myths, and rites. In the Roman Empire, almost the same treatment was reserved for all of the deceased, whether they were military or civilian, but specific differences are nevertheless noticeable. Firstly, unlike in the modern era, the Romans rarely erected monuments as war memorials, which became so widespread in modern Europe – especially after 1918. Some archaeologists have detected a memorializing construction of this type at Adamklissi in Dobruja, in present-day Romania.[2] On this site, Domitian had earlier erected a monument called 'The Triumph of AD 89' to commemorate the dead, which was destroyed in the time of Trajan, and which could indeed be compared to a 'monument to the dead'. An altar also exists at this site, listing the names of thousands of soldiers who lost their lives in battle in this region. In AD 109, Trajan added an enormous trophy (*tropaeum*), better known as 'the mausoleum of Adamklissi', and scholars have wanted to interpret this building as a tribute to the dead soldiers of this conflict. This was, however, actually a monument to a god; the emperor had dedicated it to Mars Ultor (Mars the Avenger) in honour of the Romans killed in the wars in Dacia.

The Pantheon of the Dead Soldier

The cult of the dead among the Romans was organized around a simple pantheon in the beginning, which became more complex thereafter. It included the souls of the dead, gods, occasionally the deities of the East and sometimes, as the centuries progressed, Christ. By tradition, the Romans honoured the souls of the dead, called *Manes* from an old Latin word which meant 'the Benevolent'; the Romans referred to them by this antiphrasis in order to appease them, because they feared them.[3] Indeed, it was believed that the *Manes* could be very vindictive and harmful if the living forgot to worship them.

Some important gods turned away from their regular occupations in order to protect the dead – at least that is what the relatives of the deceased requested them to do – mainly the Muses[4] and the Dioscuri (the two sons of Jupiter, Castor and Pollux).[5] A unique phenomenon occurring only in military contexts is attested: the ancient Romans, when they went into battle, believed that they could be inspired and protected by what could be termed 'ghosts', or 'shades': the souls of great ancestors.[6] Many generals, for example Scipio Africanus, claimed that they were 'accompanied' by 'role-models' who instructed them in *virtus* (service to the state) in both its civil and military forms (hence the meaning is derived from the word for 'courage'); they also gave them lessons in military discipline (*disciplina*). In a related manner, it is believed that Alexander the Great had a major influence on many famous conquerors: for example, Caesar and the emperors of the Severan dynasty, especially Severus Alexander. As for the private soldier, it is probable that he hoped to profit from the protective company of the souls of his family.

As is known, early Roman religion left little hope for the dead: it provided them only a mediocre 'afterlife' in the grave.[7] In consequence, when proselytizers of foreign cults promised those who would participate in such cults a more pleasant afterlife, they garnered adherents, who had eschatological (afterlife) hopes for a meaningful life after death.[8] Modern scholars have given the name *ab Oriente lux* ('the light that comes from the East') to these cults, but this is currently criticized because such cults and rites are characterized by a great diversity. Yet they did have two things in common, being called 'mystery cults' and offering a religion of 'salvation' to adherents. The faithful received an initiation, during which myths and secret rituals for the initiated were revealed to them; this allowed them to benefit from life after death. Their practice was quite compatible with the other official religions, the worship of the traditional pantheon, the imperial cult and the deities of the provinces. Three Eastern deities played a special role in this regard.

Of the 'foreign' cults which spread to Rome, neither Cybele nor Isis had much success with the military. Amongst the soldiers, it was the cult of Mithras which attracted the most followers. This god probably originated in Iran, and he was represented dressed in the fashion of his country, in trousers with a cap, and is shown in the cult's iconography energetically slaughtering a bull, whose head he holds by the nostrils; this animal symbolized the cosmic evil that the god sought to eradicate (see Figures 8.1, 8.4). Mithraism was served by a hierarchical clergy, some members of which were called *milites* (soldiers). The military played no part in the spread of Mithraism. Moreover, the extent of military participation in the cult has been exaggerated by modern scholarship. Having said that, it is difficult to calculate exactly the proportion of civilians to soldiers which practised the cult. Additionally, their places of worship, called *mithraea*, occupied very small spaces, which could normally only accommodate about twenty faithful. Scholars of the nineteenth and twentieth centuries saw this god as highly significant, to the point that he was sometimes described as a possible competitor to Christianity. Recently, R.L. Gordon has strongly qualified this idea,[9] and his conclusions are sound.

Some historians have considered that Christianity was the last of these 'Eastern religions' for three reasons: Christianity came from the East, its theology was based on a dead and resurrected God, and it promised a pleasant afterlife for the faithful who had adhered to standards of good behaviour here on Earth. Certainly, Christianity had an influence on the military, but not greatly in the first two centuries AD.[10] Christianity spread more among the armies stationed in the eastern part of the Empire than in the western, as evidenced by a centurion named Cornelius in apostolic times,[11] and Legion XII Fulminata of Cappadocia, under Marcus Aurelius,[12] up to the Theban Legion during the Tetrarchy.[13] The first undisputed historical event is reported by Tertullian;[14] it occurred in Rome, among the Praetorians, probably in AD 211. Soldiers were lined up to participate in a religious ceremony, obviously polytheistic, and there were Christians in their ranks. One of these refused to celebrate 'heathen' rites and threw his wreath (which was probably part of the ritual) on the ground. He was sentenced, probably to death. Subsequently, military martyrs are attested several more times, especially in the time of Diocletian and in Africa.[15]

The Place of the Dead Soldier

The cult of the dead had specific places, the necropoleis, for its rites. Scholars, laypeople and archaeologists, however, do not agree on the places where soldiers were buried. Some scholars argue that military cemeteries did not exist,[16] because the state did not intervene to organize or protect them. Responsibility for the burial belonged to the private domain. An individual bought a parcel of land and prepared his grave; if he neglected its care, his heir took charge of it. The authorities only intervened if there had been a dispute over the property or impious conduct towards the grave.

The views of the inhabitants of the Empire seem to have been very close to the interpretations of legal scholars in this matter. The best proof is that since the Latin language does not have a word for a necropolis, the Romans had to resort to a Greek word (κοιμητήριον, *koimeterion*). Moreover, the word νεκρόπολις (necropolis) seems to have been very little employed,[17] except in Alexandria in Egypt.[18] Latinization of *koimeterion* (as *coemeterium*) is not very common; it is late when it does occur, and its usage appears to have been limited. It seems to have had particular success in Africa, where it appears in the works of Tertullian,[19] St Cyprian,[20] Optatus (Optate) of Milevis,[21] and St Augustine.[22] It is also present in epigraphy, but particularly in Rome,[23] Ostia,[24] Velletri,[25] Florence[26] and in Cirta (Constantine) in Africa.[27] The translation *dormitorium* ('sleeping place') appears only once, in a glossary,[28] as a metaphor. In the revised edition of the dictionary of L. Quicherat, É. Chatelain mistakenly took the word *sepulcretum* as a synonym for cemetery; the Roman poet Catullus uses the term in the plural, in a context that is not confusing, to designate a person who lives from looting offerings deposited near graves.[29] It is therefore necessary to understand *sepulcretum* in the sense of an isolated burial, and not a necropolis.

Archaeologists find that graves were grouped and located outside urban centres.[30] The dead could not live with the living. These groups of funerary monuments were indeed cemeteries, especially as they were sometimes enclosed[31] and beautified by gardens.[32] Distinctions were made between the cemeteries where the remains of soldiers killed in action were deposited and those which housed men who had died a natural death.

A fact that will surprise the reader of the twenty-first century is that fallen soldiers did not receive a particularly honorific treatment – far from it.[33] After a battle, the victors tried to heal their wounded (who often died as hygiene was poor and dirty dressings caused secondary infections). The Romans collected their dead with a minimum of respect, and then buried them summarily. If the Romans were victorious, the bodies could be interred, as they would have been near their camp. One interesting inscription suggests that the remains of the soldier were brought back to his homeland (there is no evidence for a cenotaph):[34]

> 'D(iis) M(anibus). | Aur(elio) Iustino, militi | leg(ionis) II Ital(icae), (obito) in exp(editione) | Daccisca, an(nis) XXIII. | Aur(elius) Verinus, uet(eranus), et | Mes(sia) Quartina, pa | rentes, fecerunt.'
>
> 'To the spirits of the dead. Aurelius Justinus, soldier of Legion II Italica, died in the expedition to Daccisca, at the age of twenty-three. His parents, Aurelius Verinus, a veteran, and Messia Quartina, his mother, had this monument made.'

It is not known what the nature or date of this expedition to Daccisca was, although it is mentioned in another inscription.[35] Modern editors of the two epigraphic texts have thought this might relate to Dacia, but the two forms of spelling used by the inscriptions, which are very similar to each other – Daccisca and Dacisca – suggest another region, still unknown. From the time of Marcus Aurelius, Legion II Italica had been stationed in Noricum, a province that corresponds to parts of Austria, Bavaria and Slovenia. As for the relatives and friends, they merely indicated that the deceased had died in combat; the formula *desideratus in acie* ('died in battle') was also used.[36]

In the case of a defeat, on the other hand, the treatment of the dead was more expeditious. Two examples are quite well known: from Lake Trasimene and the Teutoburg Forest. After the Battle of Lake Trasimene in 216 BC, which was actually an ambush by Hannibal's Carthaginians, the bodies of the Romans killed were burned; the cremation ovens were found north of the lake at Tuoro, between Borghetto and Passignano.[37] In AD 9, the soldiers under Varus killed in the Teutoburg Forest, another ambush, were deprived of burial,[38] abandoned on the ground by the victorious Germans, who wanted to show their superiority and sought to discourage the Romans from recommencing a war of conquest. The army of the vanquished had been annihilated and their more fortunate enemies deliberately left them to rot on the ground. In Roman belief, the dead were thought to be unhappy (no one believed in a happy afterlife where they received their just deserts), and only rites, the first of which was burial, brought the deceased a little consolation. In AD 15, the soldiers of Germanicus found the bones of their unfortunate colleagues, and he had the remains, which had been scattered in heaps and without special care, buried in a tumulus.[39] This burial of the corpses of the Teutoburg legions was seen by the Romans as a means of repairing the Varian disaster.

Soldiers who died of old age or sickness in their garrison town were subject to almost the same treatment as civilians. Special necropoleis do not appear to have been reserved for them, although it seems that their presence in some cemeteries was more pronounced than in others. Possibly, however, the cemetery excavated in Am Wiegel, west of Haltern in Germany, was not open to civilians.[40] As a rule of thumb, the deceased soldiers were buried first along the roads leading from their camp or a nearby city, and then further and further away from and behind this first line of graves, which gave these clusters of burials rounded forms over time. As a result, the military was largely in the majority in burials at the exits of camps. They were in a mixed situation elsewhere, buried alongside civilians. This situation has been well studied in the case of Mainz.[41]

At Haïdra (Ammaedara) in present-day Tunisia, a camp was occupied from AD 6 until AD 75 at the latest. The military graves lined the main road that ran from the camp to the north-east, towards Carthage, the capital of the province. Lambèse provides a more interesting case (see Figure 6.1). In the second and third centuries AD, this site, located at the northern foot of the Aures in Algeria, was both the capital of Numidia – a province officially created at the end of the second century AD – and the headquarters of Legion III Augusta. The main camp has provided the largest collection of military epitaphs that is known for the Empire.[42] It was in use from about AD 115/120 until the beginning of the fourth century. There were at least three necropoleis, and possibly four, on this site. The majority of the soldiers were buried in areas which ran north from the main camp towards Cirta (Constantine). They were also buried in reasonable numbers, alongside civilians, in an area that was further east, north of the city, along the wadi Markouna.

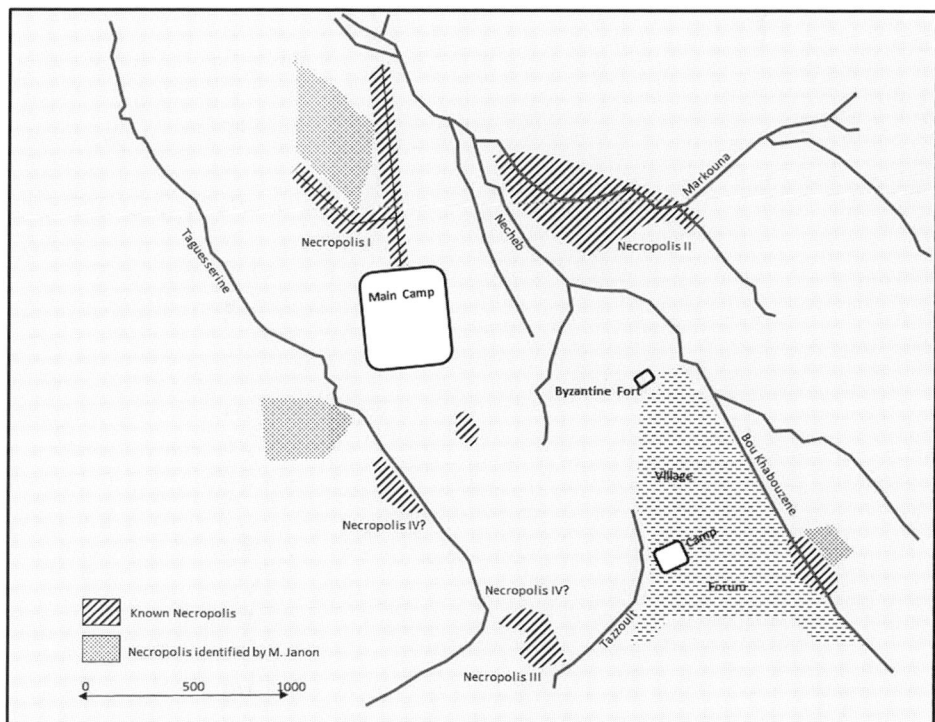

Figure 6.1: The necropoleis of Lambèse (based on Le Bohec, 1989: 108).

Monuments to Dead Soldiers

To practise the veneration of a dead man, one had, of course, to be able to locate his grave. For this purpose, and to answer a concern about locating the funerary place, it was marked by a monument. These memorials for dead soldiers were similar to those erected for civilians, but there were some significant differences.[43] Funeral rites followed a general pattern,[44] but they did change according to the date, the province and the social rank of the deceased. As a general rule, a vigil was held over the body of the deceased soldier, which was displayed to friends of the family, and then purified. The corpse was washed and anointed with ointments and perfumes. If the deceased had been a Roman citizen, he was dressed in his toga. Family members, friends and professional mourners attended the funeral procession, and the body was taken to a necropolis, where it was either buried (inhumed) or cremated, in accordance with the deceased's own traditions. For cremation, the body was burnt on a pyre, the ashes placed in an urn and deposited in the earth. The inhumed were placed in the ground, either directly or in a sarcophagus of wood or stone – those of wood were deposited in the ground like urns, and those of stone often sculpted and placed prominently. Other rites were practised after the funeral.[45] The dead were thought to exist unhappily in their tombs, and funerary rites were performed to ensure that they passed a less wretched afterlife. Monuments locating the point of burial allowed his family to locate the site and celebrate rites at the tomb, essentially consisting of food offerings.

The deceased departed for the afterlife with drink and food (these offerings will be further discussed below), and were believed to find a little life and happiness only at the time of the celebration of rites upon the grave. To provide for an easier existence in the underworld, the relatives deposited meals at the grave, along with one or more lamps, which gave the deceased a light in the darkness, and money to pay Charon, the ferryman of the souls across the River Styx in the underworld. The dead were supposed to live both in the tomb and in the underworld. This ritual seems neither logical nor consistent in the eyes of a person of the twenty-first century, but these contradictions did not disturb the ancient Romans. Small jars of vinegar allowed the dead to renew and anoint their body.

After the funeral, the soldier's relatives, on fixed dates, would meet at the grave to pour libations and hold a banquet. A part of the food was left for the deceased, and water, thanks to a pipe, went through the ground to the grave. The living made food offerings and shared a meal, bringing food (meat, fish, vegetables, fruits, honey), drinks (water, wine, milk) and flowers. These meetings were morally obligatory during celebrations that were held from 13–21 February, with the *dies parentales* ('parental days', the Parentalia festival), which ended with the *feralia* (offerings were brought to the tombs) and the *caristia* (in this case, the dead of the family were invited to their former home for a banquet). The *rosaria* (or *violaria*) were also celebrated between 18 and 21 February.[46] On 9, 11 and 13 May, the *Lemuria* rites were renewed (although, in this case, the father of the family asked the *Manes* to leave the house). Finally, the dead came out of the earth (*mundus patet*, it was said) on 24 August, 5 October and 8 November. Note, however, that these celebrations are absent from the famous military calendar of Dura-Europos: no specific rite was celebrated by or for these soldiers.

Legally, the deceased and the *Manes* (souls of the ancestors) owned the piece of land on which the grave had been dug; it could not be part of an inheritance, but remained the property of the occupant, and it was not possible to sell it or to bury a different body within it.[47] Sometimes the grave inscription specifically includes this prohibition. In addition, the inscription also gave the dimensions of the piece of land, to avoid later encroachments upon it.[48] In other cases, the inscription frequently specified the inalienability of the tomb through the widespread use of the abbreviation HMHNS or HMSLHNS:[49]

'*H*(*oc*) *m*(*onumentum*) *s*(*iue*) *l*(*ocus*) *h*(*eredem*) *n*(*on*) *s*(*equetur*).'

'This monument and its location will not be part of an inheritance.'

In case of infringement, the culprit was liable to a fine, whether or not mentioned in the inscription.[50] The heir (or the heirs) assumed responsibility for the burial,[51] as will be seen later in some inscriptions.

In theory, the Roman state and local authorities did not intervene in matters relating to graves. Heirs, however, had a legal obligation to ensure, as has been noted, that the right of property and the *locus religiosus* (sanctity of the burial place) was observed.[52] Another concern for the heir was that spoliation and alterations were forbidden, except, sometimes, if the grave was surrounded by a large piece of land. In this case, a limitation of the area could be considered. Many actions with respect to the vicinity of the grave were not permitted, and municipal magistrates were responsible for overseeing cases which involved the opening or profanation of the tomb, the burial of other people next to the deceased, the displacement of the body and the erasure of the inscription. They also had to be present during the internment of the deceased and to ensure the exclusion of intruders. Finally, if necessary, they controlled acquisition, transmission and, in rare cases, re-use.

From the point of view of architecture, the monuments can be divided into several categories. The main types were constructed in Rome,[53] where the living erected for their dead altars with garlands, columns and pilasters, facades with or without coronation, and with busts or various representations of the deceased. There were also tumuli, pyramids (such as the famous pyramid of Cestius) and exedrae ('seat-tombs'). Eisner proposed a dating of the main types between 60 and 20 BC.[54] These models were copied with some delay in Italy,[55] then, with even longer delays, in the provinces, where residents more often adapted than closely adopted. In this respect, the role of soldiers was important. Recruitment in Italy, strong during the Civil War (43–31 BC) and the beginning of the Principate (until the first third of the first century AD), favoured the diffusion in the Empire of the practices of the capital. Thus, in southern Syria, there is a mixture of respect for traditions and exogenous influences.[56] The same observation can be made for Gaul[57] and, as will be shown below, for the Germanies and for Africa.

Depending on the time and the region, the monuments were constructed in diverse and varied forms. The best known are square towers, with a pointed top (as in the mausoleum of Igel in Germany, some 30 metres high and dating to the mid-third century AD; see Figure 6.2). In any case, a chamber was fitted out to receive the urn or the body. These monuments indicated the privilege of officers, at least from the rank of centurion and above, because their construction demanded sizable financial resources. In contrast, ordinary soldiers had stelae, altars and cupolas (see Figure 6.3).[58]

In Africa, where their number is particularly apparent, the stelae were in the form of a simple flat erect stone, sometimes topped with a semi-circular or triangular pediment, rarely accompanied with parapets and often enriched with text and (or) sculptural reliefs. They were particularly widespread in the first century AD. Funerary stelae, like the monuments discussed above, allowed the living to locate the place where the deceased had been deposited, most often in an urn, after having been cremated.

A stele found in Haïdra (Ammaedara) depicts a legionary rider (see Figure 6.4; for other ranks of soldiers, see below). This stone is divided into two registers, with the inscription in the lower panel. Above, there is a crude, stylized face; the deceased is depicted wearing a tunic, and is shown with a prominent nose and with both eyes globular and quite large. He holds two horses, both very small, by the bridle. No attention has been paid by the sculptor to rendering the proportions correctly. This soldier, who had received a promotion, became a *duplicarius*, a 'double-pay man' in a cavalry unit. He had only been promoted for four months when he met his death, no doubt because

Figure 6.2: The mausoleum of Igel. (*Image taken from* Germania Romana *3.xxxiv, no. 1*)

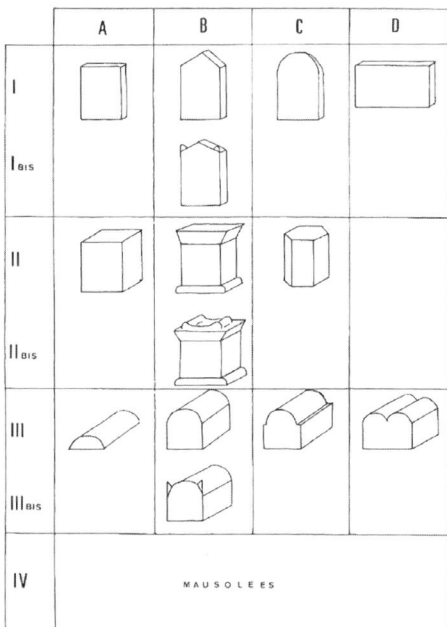

Figure 6.3: The types of funerary monuments found in Africa. (*Drawing taken from Le Bohec, 1989, p.85*)

of illness (there is no indication that he died in battle). The Pannonian Ala (wing) was in Africa, as was Legion III Augustus. The name of the second heir has been partly erased by time (see Figure 6.4):[59]

> '*M(arcus) Licinius, M(arci) f(ilius), Gal(eria tribu), Lug(uduno),* | *Fidelis, milit(auit) eq(ues) in leg(ione) III* | *Aug(usta) ann(is) XVI, fact(us) dupl(icarius) in* | *ala Pann(oniorum) mens(ibus) IIII, uix(it) ann(is) XXXII.* | *H(ic) s(itus) e(st). Q(uintus) Iulius Atticus et T(itus)* | *[…]nicius Saecularis, eq(uites)* | *[leg(ionis)] III Aug(ustae), h(eredes) eius, posuerunt.*'

> 'Marcus Licinius Fidelis, son of Marcus, enrolled in the Galeria tribe, originally from Lyon, served as a cavalryman in III Legion Augustus for sixteen years. He was sent as a double-pay man to the Pannonian wing for four months. He lived thirty-two years. He is resting here. Quintus Julius Atticus and Titus […]nicius Saecularis, cavalrymen of Legion III Augusta, his heirs, set up [this stele].'

The stelae that are catalogued chronologically below are usually dated to the second century AD and belong to members of the military who lived in Africa. These were simple blocks of stone, sometimes placed on a plinth, sometimes topped with a pediment; in rarer cases, they supported volutes. Some monuments had six faces. The urn was deposited either inside the monument, in a small prepared space, or below in the ground. Such monuments were used for rites common to all the cults of the time, especially the libations and sacrifices that preceded the funeral banquet. The officiant poured some wine on the stone and slaughtered an animal there, or burned incense, and the participants then took part in a communal meal. To represent a home, the sculptor sometimes depicted a flame, which has often been mistaken for a pine cone, a plant that has nothing to do with this context. Some current archaeologists, however, who are very cautious, do not elaborate on the nature of these sculptures and merely describe them as 'ovoid'. In addition, these small monuments were sometimes decorated with *bucranes* (emaciated cow skulls), garlands of flowers, sculptures representing Eros or Victory (triumph over death), an *urceus* (a vase or jug) or a peg. All these symbols were meant to remind those concerned that the deceased was still alive.

Figure 6.4: The funerary monument of Marcus Licinius. (*Image taken from* Le Bohec, *1989, p.102, no. 23*)

A very fine example of a funerary monument was found at Lambèse in Numidia: the upper part was damaged, as well as the lower left corner. It now bears, on the face, only an inscription. This deceased soldier was originally from Madaure, in the north-east of present-day Algeria. He did not serve long, and died when he was young (see Figure 6.5):[60]

'*D(iis) M(anibus) s(acrum)*. | *M(arcus) Att* | *ius*, *M(arci) fi(lius)*, | *Quir(ina tribu), Fes* | *tus*, *M(a)d(auris), miles* | *leg(ionis) III Aug(ustae)*, *uix(it) ann(is) XX*.'

'Consecrated to the spirits of the dead. Marcus Attius Festus, son of Marcus, enrolled in the Quirinal tribe, originally from Madaure, soldier of Legion III Augusta, lived twenty years.'

In the early third century AD, cups or boxes appeared in African and Numidian funerary iconography. They are half-cylinders placed on the edge of the monument. In more complex and infrequent cases, a half-column surmounted a rectangular base; there are also acroteria. Very rarely, the caissons were coupled. A very simple, and more classical model, was also found in Timgad. In this inscription, and others, the term *veteranus* referred to a former soldier, free from military obligation. He held the rite of *conubium* and could therefore have a legitimate wife (see Figure 6.6):[61]

Figure 6.5: The funerary monument of Marcus Attius. (*Image taken from* Le Bohec, *1989, p.90, no. 1*)

'*D(iis) M(anibus) s(acrum)*. | *L(ucius) Aurelius Felix*, | *ueteranus leg(ionis)* | *III Aug(ustae), se uiuo sibi* | *et Petronia[e S]a* | *ttullae, co[n(iugi)]* | *fecit. Vi[x(it) a(nnis) ...]*.'

'Consecrated to the spirits of the dead. Lucius Aurelius Felix, veteran of Legion III Augusta, had this monument made for himself and his wife, Petronia Satulla. He lived ... years.

Figure 6.6: The funerary monument of Lucius Aurelius. (*Image taken from* Le Bohec, *1989, p.91, no. 3*)

The image of the dead soldier

The soldier, before his death, or his heir after his death, may have wished to leave a message to the living through the iconography of his funerary marker. Historians often speak of 'self-representation', but it is also sometimes, and perhaps most often, the image that the living had of the dead.[62] Thus an iconographic evolution had taken shape. The deceased, if he lived in his grave,[63] also spent part of the year either underground in the underworld or in the heavens. The winds accompanied the deceased in his travels.[64] Symbolic garlands of flowers adorned the graves[65] and represented offerings. Bas-reliefs represented these asylums of peace on the funerary reliefs of civilians, but the military instead preferred rather to depict themselves. Whether the image came from his heirs or from himself, a dead soldier preferred to boast about what he had been (a soldier), than to turn towards what he had become (a dead person).[66] There are four major types of representations.

The dead were represented as a bust, front or profile, in a niche or in relief. They are most often dressed in a toga when they are Roman citizens, which is the normal case for legionaries. A soldier – Publius Clodius – known from his funerary stele in Bonn, Germany, is depicted frontally, under an arch. He is dressed in a toga and holds a scroll, which simply means that the deceased could read and write, or perhaps he had acquired, by initiation, religious knowledge which ensured his survival in the afterlife. Clodius does not mention his *cognomen*, nor the name of his legion. It was Legion I Germania which was garrisoned in the city of Bonn from around AD 35–70/71.[68] Originally from Liguria, this soldier was recruited aged 23. It is possible that he was a discharged veteran at the time of his death, and that he had kept, as did many of his colleagues, his title of soldier (see Figure 6.7):[67]

Figure 6.7: The funerary monument of Publius Clodius. (*Image taken from* Germania Romana *3, p.ii, no. 3*)

> '*P(ublio) Clodio, P(ublii) f(ilio), Vol(tinia tribu), Alb(intimilio), mil(iti) leg(ionis) I. (Vixit) an(nis) XLIIX, stip(endiorum) XXV. H(ic) s(itus) e(st).*'
>
> 'To Publius Clodius, son of Publius, enrolled in the Voltinia tribe, originally from Ventimiglia, a soldier of Legion I. He lived forty-eight years, and he served twenty-five years. He rests here.'

Other individuals were depicted in full on their monuments (see Figures 6.8–9) and three different types of representations were common. In one, the deceased simply faces the viewer. He is in this case dressed either in civilian clothes or as a soldier. In the latter case, it is possible to study his armament, which is particularly interesting for auxiliaries, who could be equipped with shields and armour, and who were provided with a bow, a spear or a sword. Alternatively, the dead are depicted sacrificing at an altar. In this case, they are usually in civilian clothes.

One legionary, Gaius Valerius Crispus, appears in such a representation. He is known from a stele from Wiesbaden, Germany.[69] In the depiction he stands under an arch, and is positioned face-on to the viewer. He wears a complete set of armour, a plumed helmet (the plume is often omitted in such depictions), a cuirass whose type is difficult to identify under the garment that covers it, and a tiled shield that is about 60cm high (the *umbo*, the half-ball placed in the centre of the shield, is apparent). For the offensive elements of his equipment, he wears a relatively long and very sharp sword on the right side, and holds in his hand the famous *pilum*, a thin javelin. The inscription provides further information about him; the brother referred to was perhaps a brother by blood or a brother in arms:[70]

'C(aius) Val(erius), C(aii) f(ilius), Berta, Menenia, Crispus, mil(es) leg(ionis) VIII Aug(ustae), an(nis) XL, stip(endiorum) XXI. F(rater) f(aciendum) c(urauit).'

'Gaius Valerius Crispus, son of Gaius, originally from Berta [in Macedonia], enrolled in the Menenia tribe, [rests here]. Soldier of Legion VIII Augusta. He lived forty years and he served for twenty-one years. His brother had this monument made.'

Another legionary, Quintus Luccius Faustus, was buried at Mainz amongst other military graves. The particularity of his grave lies in the fact that he was, at the moment of death, a *signifer*, bearer of the *signum* (the standard of the maniple and the cohort).[71] He too, on his stele, is on foot and he stands facing the spectator. On his left there is a little laughing head, the significance of which remains to be established. Quintus is bare headed: he is wearing armour, has a *pilum*, and his left hand carries his shield, which curves behind him. He carries, on his right side, a sword similar to that of the previous individual discussed. In the right hand he holds an upright *signum*, a long spear-shaped pole, on which are fixed six disks which are decorations for combat awarded to his unit. The inscription does not mention his rank of *signifer*, because the relief is sufficient.[72] This soldier was born in Pollenzo, Liguria. Legion XIV Gemina stayed in Mainz from AD 13–43 and from AD 71–92:[73]

'Q(uintus) Luccius, | Q(uinti) f(ilius), Pollia, | Faustus, Pol(l)e|ntia, mil(es) leg(ionis) | XIIII Gem(inae) Mar(tiae) | Vic(tricis), an(norum) XXXV, | stip(endiorum) XVII, h(ic) s(itus) e(st). | Heredes f(aciendum) c(urauerunt).'

'Quintus Luccius Faustus, son of Quintus, enrolled in the Pollia tribe, originally from Pollentia, a soldier of Legion XIV Gemina Martia Victrix, lived for thirty-five years, and served seventeen years. He is resting here. His heirs took care to make [this monument].'

A stage higher in the military hierarchy is reached with an eagle-bearer, an *aquilifer*. He is known from a stele, also found in Mainz. The soldier, the *aquilifer* Gnaeus Musius, as always shown from the front, is framed by two columns that support a pediment: he is in a temple as the dead are close to the gods, but not deified. Yet he will nevertheless join the cohort of *dii Manes*. Bare-headed, he wears a cuirass covered with nine disks, which are decorations he has won in combat. His left hand is leaning on his shield, which rests on the ground. In the right hand, he holds a shaft on the top of which is an eagle, with wings spread, standing on Jupiter's thunderbolts. This eagle standard, like the *signa*, was sacred and it was housed in the sanctuary which was in the centre of the camp. This Italian, a native of Véléia located 18km from Plaisance, died young and was probably buried by his blood brother rather than by a brother in arms (they carry the same name). (See Figure 6.8; the funerary inscription, underneath the relief, is not shown.)[74]

'*Cn(aeus) Musius, T(iti) f(ilius),* | *Gal(eria tribu), Veleias, an(nis)* | *XXXII, stip(endiorum) XV,* | *aquilif(er) leg(ionis) XIIII Gem(inae).* | *M(arcus) Musius, (centurio), frater, posuit.*'

'Gnaeus Musius, son of Titus, part of the Galeria tribe, from Veleia, lived thirty-two years and served fifteen years. He was an eagle-bearer of Legion XIV Gemina. The centurion Marcus Musius, his brother, set up [this monument].'

Figure 6.8: The funerary monument of the *aquilifer* Cnaeus Musius. (*Courtesy of Alamy*)

In another type of sculptural relief, common amongst the military, the deceased is presented reclining on a dining couch, taking part in a banquet. Before him is positioned a tripod upon which are placed food and drink. He is served by a young boy and sometimes by his wife. This theme is typically Greek, and it was an honour during the Hellenistic period and under the Roman Empire (Egypt included) to be depicted in this way.[75] From Greece, the iconography made its way to Germania, either through the agency of travellers who had taken the Danube–Rhine route, or from soldiers who served in Macedonia at the beginning of the Empire and who were then sent to other garrisons. Then it was adopted, not only by soldiers, but also by civilians. Such monuments are found in Bonn,[76] Cologne,[77] Trier,[78] Wiesbaden,[79] Karlsruhe[80] and Obernburg.[81] A civilian from Pettau, modern Ptuj in Slovenia (Poetouio in antiquity), received a monument that evokes the one that was found at Ighil Oumsed (Mauretania Caesarea, see below). A reclining figure was placed at the top, and the banquet below.[82] Legionaries from Germany, who contributed to the conquest of Britain in AD 43, brought this theme with them to that province.

Similar depictions are found on monuments in the Chester (Deva) camp of Legion XX Valeria, for soldiers[83] and civilians alike.[84] This legion left Dalmatia for Germany in AD 9 (it replaced one of the three legions destroyed in the disaster of the Teutoburg Forest). It was garrisoned in Cologne from AD 9–35 and then in Neuß from AD 35–43. It then participated in the invasion of Britain, where it remained.[85] Note that in all British cases except one,[86] the table has three feet. This iconography shows the religious feeling of the deceased, and the concept of the hereafter where he would banquet for eternity, without tiring himself.

A relief of Chester illustrates this iconographic type. The deceased is more seated than reclining, which is rather rare. He holds in his left hand a scroll which, as has been noted, may be an affirmation of some education or a religious text opening the doors into a better beyond. Near him is a small person, perhaps his wife or a servant. In front of him is positioned the small three-legged table that holds food and drink. This soldier was Thracian; he came from present-day Bulgaria. He is unlikely to have died at the age of just 40, because it is hard to imagine that he was recruited at 14. The ancients sometimes used rounded numbers in giving someone's age. Although the inscription is in somewhat rough Latin, it can be readily understood:[87]

'*D(iis) M(anibus). | C(a)ecilius Donatus, B|essus na|tione, mili|tauit ann|os XXVI, uix|it annos XXXX.*'

('To the spirits of the dead. Caecilius Donatus, from the Bessus nation, served twenty-six years, and lived forty years.')

Funeral banquet imagery for the deceased also reached Africa, and is found on a soldier's grave from Ighil Oumsed in Algeria.[88] Cavalrymen are very numerous in military representations. They were the superiors of the infantrymen: a cavalry decurion outranked a cohort centurion and was better paid.

A very interesting example of the funeral monument with a charging rider was found in Germany, from where its iconography spread to Britain and Africa. In general, the deceased is shown in the process of being about to dispatch a fallen enemy warrior. In an original pose in this particular relief, the dead cavalryman, on the point of becoming a divine hero (as he will die shortly after), is depicted in a small temple. He holds a short javelin in his hand, which he throws at his fallen enemy, and carries a large shield across his back; the harness of the horse is reproduced with precision. The defeated opponent also has a large sword, which he wears on the right side. He is lying on his back and attempts to protect himself with his large shield, on which the *umbo* can be seen. This sculpture is not accompanied by an inscribed text, which is curious, and it is possible that the letters had been painted on rather than inscribed (compare Figure 3.4).[89]

Other cavalry representations, but more rarely, depict non-violent themes. They show a 'rider on the right' (i.e., moving to the right of the viewer), advancing calmly. Such monuments were found in Karlsruhe (Germany) and Chalon-sur-Saône (Gaul),[90] as well as Ighil Oumsed (see above). When a rider had been rewarded for his merits through double pay, he also received two horses, and was thus represented between his two mounts (see Figure 6.4).

Other, more diverse subjects and objects, such as varying weapons or decorations, may also have been sculpted, without it being known why in all cases. A representation with family is rare. Indeed, the Roman dead fell into two categories. Some wanted to be totally alone in their eternal home, and these 'solitaries' represented an overwhelming majority of the population, more than 80 per cent. Others wanted to be accompanied by their wife or children. The rarest case attested, however, was one in which the whole family, including the wife, children and freedmen, benefitted from a collective burial.

Another special category is that of the cenotaphs, of which there were few in number. Most famous of these is one discovered in Germania, in Xanten (it is currently housed in the Bonn Museum, see Figure 6.9). This rectangular stele is divided into three registers. At the top is a triangular pediment. Below are three individuals, one large and two small. The relief represents a centurion who died in the disaster of Varus in AD 9; the imagery is cut-off at the height of his abdomen. The deceased wears a cuirass covered with decorations, two bracelets (*armillae*) and at least four medals. In his right hand he holds his command stick, the *vitis* ('vine stock'). He is flanked, on the left and the right,

Figure 6.9: The funerary monument of Marcus Caelius. (*Courtesy of Alamy*)

by two smaller heads, which are cut just below the level of the neck. They represent two freedmen who had followed the deceased to Germany and who died with him; below their busts, inscriptions indicate their identity.[91] *Ossa [i]nferre licebit* in the inscription has been variously interpreted – here the translation which seems to be the most acceptable is given ('May it be possible to bury his bones'):

'*M(arco) Caelio, M(arci) f(ilio), Lem(onia tribu), Bon(onia), | (centurioni) leg(ionis) XIIX, ann(is) LIII (semissis). | [Ce]cidit bello Variano. Ossa | [i]nferre licebit. P(ublius) Caelius, T(iti) f(ilius), | Lem(onia tribu), frater, fecit. || M(arcus) Caelius, | M(arci) l(ibertus), | Privatus. || M(arcus) Caelius, | M(arci) l(ibertus), | Thiaminus.*'

'To Marcus Caelius, son of Marcus, enrolled in the Lemonia tribe, originally from Bologna. Centurion of Legion XVIII, he fell in the war of Varus at the age of fifty-three and a half. May it be possible to bury his bones. Publius Caelius, son of Titus, enrolled in the Lemonia tribe, his brother, had this monument made. [Portrait of] Marcus Caelius Privatus, freedman of Marcus. [Portrait of] Marcus Caelius Thiaminus, freedman of Marcus.'

It is likely that several reliefs included painted details. On the stele of Ighil Oumsed, mentioned above, the harness of the horse is very incomplete, meaning that in its preserved state, the rider could not have led his horse. Moreover, it has no saddle or weapons, which is strange for a soldier shown in the exercise of his function. Relevant painted details on such reliefs have clearly weathered and disappeared.

| | East Africa | Africa | Lyon | Praetorians | Auxiliaries | Auxiliaries |
	Lassère	Lassère	Burnand	Clauss	Saddington	Kraft
Early first century	nominative *HSE* age dedicants	nominative *HSE* age dedicants	nominative *cognomen* and *DM* absent, then appearance	*In fronte…, in agro…*	*HSE* (except Danubian Provinces)	
Late first century	nominative *HSE* age *pius* dedicants *OTBQ* *STTL*	nominative *HSE* age dedicants *OTBQ* *STTL*	Dative or genitive *ascia* *Diis Manibus*	*Diis Manibus* *HSE* *TFI, TPI* nominative	*Diis Manibus*	*HSE*
Early second century	*Diis Manibus* *DM* nominative *HSE* age *pius* dedicants	*DM* nominative or dative, sometimes genitive *HSE* age dedicants	*praenomen* disappears *DM*	*bene merenti* *HFC* *TFI, TPI* genitive or dative	*DM* *HSE* (Danubian Provinces)	*uixit, qui uixit*
Late second century	*DM*, rarely *memoriae* nominative *HSE* age *pius* dedicants	as East Africa	No *praenomen* dative or genitive, then only dative *DM* and *memoriae*			
Early third century		*DM* and *memoriae* nominative, dative or genitive *HSE* age dedicants	Dative *DM* disappears *memoriae quieti* *aeternae*	*uixit, qui uixit, natus,* *oriundus,* *aram consecrauit*		

Figure 6.10: Common motifs in funerary inscriptions for different regions and different military functions and positions.

The word of the dead soldier

Part of the tombs bore sculptures, while another part carried engraved texts.⁹² Of course, the most detailed are those with an image accompanied by an inscription. Epigraphy greatly complements the iconography of the funerary monuments, both of which more or less developed according to the times, region and rank of the soldier. As is shown below, the different styles of inscription sometimes overlap, and it is difficult to find texts in only one style; there is nevertheless value in cross-examining the information which they provide, given that each complements the other. A difficulty arises in regard to the monuments, in that their epitaphs are almost never accurately dated. Yet some researchers have studied inscriptions which are the exceptions, because the time of writing is known; they have found that most homogeneous forms correspond to well-defined periods, and they are thus able to establish a chronology of texts taking into account their different elements.⁹³

Abbreviations

DM: *Diis Manibus*, 'To the the spirits of the dead'
HFC: *H(eres, -des) f(aciendum) c(urauit - erunt)*, 'The heir (or heirs) has (have) taken care to erect (this monument)'
HSE: *H(ic) s(itus) e(st)*, 'He rests here'.
OTBQ: *O(ssa) t(ua) b(ene) q(uiescant)*, 'May your bones find good rest'
STTL: *S(it) t(ibi) t(erra) l(euis)*, 'May the earth rest lightly [upon him]'
TFI: *T(itulum) f(ieri) i(ussit)*, 'He ordered to have the inscription engraved'
TPI: *T(itulum) p(oni) i(ussit)*, 'He ordered to have the inscription set up'

Just as a soldier's relief was intended to perpetuate the memory of the dead through the iconography of the memorial, so too the inscription through its text informed contemporaries of what was of value to him. Four main elements extolled the value of *virtus* ('virtue', 'manly excellence'). First, the soldier brought posthumous fame to the unit in which he had served, even if he was not among its most prestigious members. Secondly, it boasted of his rank, even if that had been modest. Thirdly, he did not always neglect to mention his commanding centurion. Above all, finally, the decorations he had achieved during his service are listed.

It is largely not pertinent to emphasize here certain elements common to the funerary memorials of both civilians and the military alike. Yet one feature is significant: the invocation on the graves for protection by the spirits of the dead (*dii Manibus*). In addition, during the fighting, the *Manes* were believed to accompany the soldier, who was also protected by the gods of Rome. In addition, one often finds the expressed desire, *STTL* (*S(it) t(ibi) t(erra) l(euis)*) – 'May the earth rest lightly [upon him]') – and other phrases such as *HSE* (*Hic situs est* – 'He rests here') in the funerary inscriptions.

Naturally, the soldier wanted to have his onomastics (his names) preserved after his death. His name, of course, was very important: when reading the inscription, and pronouncing the soldier's name, each passer-by gave a little life to the deceased.

In addition, for the modern historian, it helps to date the inscription, and it allows the placing of the deceased in a particular social level.⁹⁴ A free man but not a citizen (he was said to be a peregrinus), the auxiliary was entitled to only one name. As a Roman citizen, a legionary soldier bore the *tria nomina*: *praenomen-nomen-cognomen*, such as, for example, Caius Iulius Caesar. To ensure the recognition of his status as an individual, the deceased soldier was identified in an inscription only by the *praenomen* and *nomen* at the beginning of the Empire, such as Marcus Caelius and Publius Caelius in the examples given above. In such cases, the *cognomen* is omitted. From the beginning of the second century, it was the *praenomen* that tended to be omitted, and the *nomen-cognomen* couplet represented the norm.

Military elements accompanied the onomastics: the soldier wanted his rank to be remembered after his death. Some very simple texts are inspired by those engraved for civilians. Only one difference appears, the mention of the soldier's status, as can be seen in this inscription from Lambèse:⁹⁵

'*D(iis) M(anibus). | C(aio) Iulio Fortunato, armo|rum (custodi), q(ui) uix(it) an(nis) XXXVII. | Sex(tus) Pompeius Seueri|anus, uet(eranus), in suo gene|ro carissimo, s(ua) p(ecunia) f(ecit). | H(ic) s(itus) e(st). O(ssa) t(ua) b(ene) q(uiescant).*'

('To the spirits of the dead. To Caius Julius Fortunatus, weapons keeper, who lived thirty-seven years. Sextus Pompeius Severianus, a veteran, commissioned this monument at his expense for his very dear son-in-law. He is resting here. May your bones find quiet rest.')

This inscription contains only two terms connecting it to the army: the titles of weapons keeper and veteran. The place where this monument was discovered proves that the soldier served in Africa, in Legion III Augusta; the rest of the text, however, could easily have suited any civilian figure. A soldier may have also wanted the unit in which he served to be known after his death. The normal rule is that the unit is mentioned, in addition to his rank (or function) within the unit. There was a sense of pride in the name, and also a kind of patriotism and *esprit de corps*. Naming the *centuria* to which he belonged was also considered to be a means of honouring him after death, and soldiers were sometimes described with the formula 'of the x century of…'. This can be seen in an example of such a text from Rome; this soldier came from Urbinum (modern Urbino), a city in Umbria:⁹⁶

'*Sex(tus) | Vaternius, | Sex(ti) f(ilius), Ste(llatina tribu), | Certus, Vruino Mataur(ensi), | mil(es) coh(ortis) XII urb(anae), | (centuria) Metili, | milit(auit) ann(is)*'

('Sextus Vaternius Certus, son of Sextus, enrolled in the Stellatina tribe, originally from Urbino on the Mataurus, soldier of the XII urban cohort, from the century of Metilius, served … years'

With respect to rank, several epigraphic possibilities were available. The inscription may have stated that the deceased was simply a 'soldier' (*miles*): a word that covers all military connotations, from recruit to emperor (as per Trajan in the *Panegyric* of Pliny). Sailors also claimed to be *milites* and not *nautae*, that is combatants, not

The Soldier and Death. Funerary Practices of Soldiers under the Principate   177

rowers. Other soldiers were given an administrative or tactical responsibility, which meant they were exempt from other duties. They mention this exemption (*immunis*) and the duty which was assigned to them (*signifer* or *actarius*, *aquilifer* or *notarius*, or such like). Strictly military roles were also distinguished (infantry, cavalry, artillery, signaller, intelligence and trainer), as were services (logistics, engineering, workshops and priesthoods), administrative functions (many), justice and policing. Above these, there was a whole hierarchy of ranks as well, going from the centurion to the tribune, then to the legate and the emperor, the supreme commander of the armies.

For those with musical functions in the Roman Army, an example can be seen in the monument to a horn player. The stele is appropriately decorated with a sculpture of a soldier playing this instrument:[97]

'D(iis) M(anibus). M(arcus) Antonius, | M(arci) f(ilius), Ianuarius, | domo Laudicia | ex Suria, cornice(n) | ex coh(orte) VII pr(aetoria), (centuria) Apri, | uix(it) ann(is) XXXII, mil(itauit) | [ann(is) …]'

('To the spirits of the dead. Marcus Antonius Januarius, son of Marcus, from Laodicea, Syria, was a horn player in the VII Praetorian cohort, in the centuria of Aper. He lived thirty-two years, and he served … years.')

Another example is provided by a monument to a trumpet player, a *tubicen*:[98]

'D(iis) M(anibus) s(acrum). | C(aius) Iulius Victo[r], | tub(icen) leg(ionis) III Aug(ustae), u(ixit) a(nnis) XXXIII. | Auf(idia) Dona|ta, her(es), mate(r), | fecit.'

('Consecrated to the spirits of the dead. Gaius Julius Victor, trumpeter of Legion III Augusta, lived thirty-three years. Aufidia Donata, his heir, his mother, had this monument made.')

For those holding administrative positions, the records of two *frumentarii*, who are mentioned in a single inscription, serve as an example:[99]

'D(iis) M(anibus). | M(arcus) Taricius Atto, fr(umentarius) | leg(ionis) I Adiutrices (sic), Car|tinio Grato, fr(umentario) | leg(ionis) X Gem(inae), colle(gae) | b(ene) m(erenti), f(ecit).'

('To the spirits of the dead. Marcus Taricius Atto, *frumentarius* of Legion I Adiutrix, made (this monument) for Cartinius Gratus, *frumentarius* of Legion X Gemina, his colleague, who deserved it.')

Both the legions referred to in this inscription belonged to the army of Upper Pannonia. In the early days of the Roman Army, the *frumentarii* were soldiers charged with finding wheat (i.e., they were foragers). Little by little, as their mission took them away from their units, they also became scouts and couriers. Under the Principate, they were mainly employed for the exchange of letters between the provincial governors and the emperor. In Rome, they were housed in a special camp, the *castra peregrina*.

Yet it was the unit that mattered most. As an African inscription says: *Tanta legio III Augusta!* ('The great Legion III Augusta!').[100] Pride increased with the prestige of the unit. Sailors were placed at the bottom of the ladder, the auxiliaries were above them, the legionaries were positioned higher still, and the garrison of Rome – especially the *urbaniciani* (city cohorts) and praetorians – were above all these personnel. Funerary monuments have been found for many of these positions, and examples are given below.

Praetorian:[101]

'C(aius) Fabius, | C(aii) f(ilius), Ser(gia tribu), | Crispus, | Carthag(ine Noua), | specul(ator) | coh(ortis) VI pr(aetoriae), | (centuria) Flegeri, | mil(itauit) an(nis) XIII, | uix(it) an(nis) XXII. | Heres, | ex uolunt(ate), p(osuit).'

'Gaius Fabius Crispus, son of Gaius, enrolled in the Sergia tribe, originally from New Carthage, scout of the Sixth Praetorian cohort, from the centuria of Flegerus, served for thirteen years, and lived for twenty-two years. His heir had this monument erected according to his will.'

It was thought that the name Flegerus had been misread (the stone has long since disappeared), and there is an error with one of the two figures XIII and XXII: where the deceased lived XXXII years, or served III years, as recruiters never took 9-year-olds into the military. The city is New Carthage (modern Cartagena), and not Carthage, because the Sergia tribe was assigned to this Spanish city, the African being in the Arnensis. The *uoluntas* was the last will and testament.

Legionary:[102]

'D(iis) M(anibus) s(acrum). | C(aius) Valerius | Secundus, | mil(es) leg(ionis) III | Aug(ustae), u(ixit) a(nnis) XL. | Iulius Rusti|cus, | heres, fecit.'

('Consecrated to the spirits of the dead. Gaius Valerius Secundus, a soldier of Legion III Augusta, lived forty years. Julius Rusticus, his heir, had this monument made.')

It is a comrade-in-arms who buried the deceased, which does not prove the homosexuality of both, contrary to what some scholars have suggested.

Cavalryman:[103]

'Di(i)s Manibus. Flauinus, | eq(ues) alae Petr(ianae), signifer | tur(mae) Candidi, an(nis) XXV, | stip(endiorum) VII. H(ic) s(itus est).'

('To the spirits of the dead. Flavinus, a cavalryman of the Petrian Ala (wing), bearer of the *signum* (standard) in the squadron of Candidus, lived twenty-five years, and served seven years. He rests here.')

A cavalry Ala was divided into fourteen to sixteen squadrons (at least 360 men), and twenty-four when it was on campaign (with about double the number of men). Each squadron was commanded by a decurion, a junior officer. The deceased in this inscription was not a Roman citizen (note the single name), and was probably a foreigner. Note that in the following inscription, the Vangiones were a people of Germany, whose capital corresponded to the present-day Worms.

Auxiliary infantryman:[104]

> 'D(iis) M(anibus) s(acrum). Decimus Iuliu/s, Q(uinti) f(ilius), Candidus, c(o)ho(rtis) | p(rimae) Vangionum, a(nnorum) XXXX.'

> 'Consecrated to the spirits of the dead. Decimus Julius Candidus, son of Quintus, of the First cohort of Vangiones, lived forty years.'

Marine:[105]

> 'M(arcus) Epidi | us Qua | dratus, miles | ex classe | Misenens(i), | (centuria) Cn(eii) Valeri(i) | Prisci, | milit(auit) an(nis) III, | uix(it) an(nis) XXVI. | Hic situs est.'

> 'Marcus Epidius Quadratus, soldier of the fleet of Misenum, of the century of Cneius Valerius Priscus, served three years and has lived twenty-six.'

This sailor, who died young, was present as a 'soldier', and does not mention the name of the boat on which he served, but he designates the commander of his ship, who had the rank of centurion, like all the officers who fulfilled this function.

The soldier sometimes insisted that his attachment to the emperor, the supreme commander of the military, be known after his death. Indeed, from the time of Septimius Severus, units were honoured by nicknames from the imperial onomastics. These epithets were at first significant honours, but then they multiplied and became commonplace. They serve to date an inscription by reference to this or that emperor. A legion could be *seueriana* (Septimius Severus), *antoniniana* (Caracalla), *seueriana alexandriana* (Severus Alexander), and so forth. It also happened that it was honoured by an added adjective touting its merits, such as *pia* (respectful of its duties) or *fidelis* (loyal to the emperor; '*infidelis*', 'unfaithful', often being the name given to military units in civil wars). There is a very rich textual corpus of examples for such epithets, such as the funerary inscription for Julius Maximus:[106]

> '*Iulius Maxim[us]*, | *mil(es) leg(ionis) III Aug(ustae)* | *Antoni[ni]an(a)e, s(e) u(iuo), cupula(m) f(ecit) s(uo) s(umptu)*. | *An(n)oru(m) circiter* | *LIV.*'

> 'Julius Maximus, a soldier of Legion III Augusta Antoniniana Legion, had his tomb made during his lifetime and at his expense. He lived about fifty-four years.'

Here, the nickname 'Antonine' refers to Caracalla, who claimed to be a descendant of Marcus Aurelius, who belonged to the Antonine dynasty. This tomb is the type of monument described earlier, with a half-column placed on the base, characteristic of Africa in the third century.

The duration of the soldier's service could also be mentioned in three ways: *aerum*, *stipendiorum* and *militauit*. Curiously, in the first two cases, it is the number of years of wages which was mentioned by two quasi-synonyms: 'I received so many years of wages.' In the latter case, the verb is followed by the number of years of service: 'I have been a soldier for so many years.' In general, this reference was supplemented by the age at death. Entries show that soldiers were recruited between the ages of 18 and 21. They also show that the life expectancy for a legionary did not exceed 47 years on average.

Use of *aerum*:[107]

'*D(iis) M(anibus) | L(ucii) Pollenti(i) | Dextri, L(ucii) fil(ii), domo Saueria* (sic), | *mil(itis) legion(is) | I Adiutri(cis), | (centuria) Alli(i) Mar[i] | ni, anno(rum) XXIII, aerum | V. H(ic) s(itus) | e(st). Her(es), ex | testamen(to), fac(iendum) cur(auit), Q(uintus) Val(erius) Rufus.*'

'To the spirits of the dead. For Lucius Pollentius Dexter, son of Lucius, native of Savaria, soldier of Legion I Adiutrix, of the centuria of Allius Marinus. He lived twenty-three years and served five years. He is resting here. His heir, Quintus Valerius Rufus, took care to have this (monument) made under the will of the deceased.'

The soldier was from Savaria in Upper Pannonia, today Szombathely in western Hungary, and Legion I Adiutrix encamped in this province under Domitian, in Dacia in the early second century, then returned to Pannonia. As we have already noted, if a man ensures the burial of another man, that does not prove homosexuality. Epigraphists have debated whether this soldier's homeland was Carrhae in Syria or, more likely, Carreum Potentia (Chieri) in Italy.

Use of *militauit*:[108]

'*L(ucius) Mettius, M(arci) f(ilius), Poll(ia tribu), | Martialis, Carr(eo), | specul(ator), mil(itauit) an(nis) X, uix(it) an(nis) XXX.*'

'Lucius Mettius Martialis, son of Marcus, enrolled in the Pollia tribe, originally from Carreum, served as scout for ten years. He lived thirty years.'

There are still other features of the funerary inscriptions for soldiers. A soldier was most anxious that his excellence be known after his death. Simple *milites* and officers loved decorations, or *dona militaria*, and parents of the deceased never failed to mention those who had received them. Rank-and-file soldiers were awarded necklaces, bracelets (*armillae*) and so-called *phalerae* medals, always for their courage. Officers were honoured with wreaths, spears without iron (that is to say in bronze, gold or silver) and banners called *vexilla*, which were awarded to them simply for their participation in a campaign. An example of an inscription from Africa, for a cavalryman, outlines exceptional and rewarded service:[109]

'*Militauit annis XXXV. | C(aius) Titurnius Quartio, eques legionis III | Gallicae, cui imp(eratores) Aug(usti), bello Phartico* (sic), *Seleucia | (et) Babylonia, torquem et armillas donauerun[t], | uotum suum reddidit.*'

'He served thirty-five years. Gaius Titurnius Quartio, a cavalryman of Legion III Gallica, fulfilled his wish. The emperors decorated him, during the Parthian war in Seleucia and Babylon, giving him a necklace and bracelets.'

This inscription was engraved on the pediment of a shrine. Quartio had received as decorations a necklace (torque) and two bracelets (*armillae*, or 'arm bands') that were carved beside the dedication. In this case, the text and the image complement each other perfectly. Seleucia was on the right bank of the Tigris, 22 miles south of what is now Baghdad and 60 miles north of Babylon. The two emperors referred to are either Marcus Aurelius and Lucius Verus, or Septimius Severus and Caracalla. Legion III Gallica had always been part of the Syrian Roman Army; it is not known how or why this soldier ended his days in Africa (modern Tunisia).

Inscriptions may state who was responsible for the burial. Sometimes, especially at the beginning of the Principate, this task fell to a brother in arms, as was seen earlier: although two men having the same foreign name did not mean they had the same parentage; they are not brothers by blood, but by service. Some modern authors see in this kind of practice the proof that homosexuality was very widespread among legionaries, especially at this time when marriage was prohibited. Such an argument does not seem very convincing because this type of behaviour was not viewed positively within the Roman Army, despite what Veyne has suggested. In any case, soldiers were soon allowed to form relationships with women who gave them children. Although these unions were not legal, these people formed families and gave themselves family titles by courtesy: the soldier was the father of the children and the husband of the woman, who was then wife for one and mother for the others.

Finally, other people normally referred to as 'heirs' could fulfil this mission. In an inscription from Africa, which illustrates this point, it is the heir who has erected the monument:[110]

> '*M(arcus) Sempronius, | M(arci) f(ilius), Gale(ria tribu), Lugud(uno), | mil(es) leg(ionis) III Aug(ustae), (centuria) Ex(), | uix(it) an(nis) XXV, | mil(itauit) an(nis) V. | H(ic) s(itus) est. | T(itus) Baronius, (centuria) Sallu|[stii Sallu/stii, her]es, posuit.*'

> 'Marcus Sempronius, son of Marcus, of the Galeria tribe, native of Lugdunum, soldier of Legion III Augusta, in the centuria of Ex(...), lived twenty-five years and served five years. He is resting here. Titus Baronius, of the centuria of Sallustus, his heir, set up (this monument).'

Conclusion

Law and religion, archaeology and epigraphy, as well as written texts, all show how soldiers and their parents and heirs conducted the worship of the dead. As expected, the soldiers practised the same funeral rites as civilians. It can be seen, however, both in the necropoleis and in the monuments that were erected in them, that differences existed between civilian and military funerary rites, customs, and practices. Funerary monuments and stelae, by their iconography and their inscriptions, make it possible to come to a better understanding of the soldier's profession. Inscriptions clearly indicate how the military attached particular importance to their rank, their unity and their decorations. The iconography and the inscriptions of soldiers' funerary monuments from across the Empire provide evidence for standard concerns on the part of soldiers and their friends, family or heirs, that the soldiers not be forgotten. Especially, in particular, these monuments, reliefs and inscriptions reveal that soldiers and those they left behind wanted their military service to be memorialized and remembered.

Notes

1. Note the plural in the title of Beard *et al.* (1998); see also: Le Bohec (2016).
2. Stefan (2005), pp.437–38, 562–63, 703.
3. Grimal (1999), p.275.
4. Cumont (1942), pp.253–350.
5. Cumont (1942), p.64.
6. Lendon (2005).
7. Cumont (1942), pp.13–16.
8. Cumont (1949), pp.142–56, 259–74.
9. Gordon (2009), pp.379–450. See now Stohl in this volume.
10. Rankov (2015), pp.194–95.
11. *Acts* 10.
12. Le Bohec (2006), p.185.
13. Perea Yebénes (2002).
14. Tert. *Cor. Mil.* 1.1–2; Le Bohec (1992), pp.6–18.
15. A thorough investigation remains to be done.
16. From Visscher (1963).
17. *Tll* 3.1411.
18. Strabo 16.4.10.
19. Tert. *Anim.* 51.
20. Cypr. *Ep.* 80.1
21. Optat. 6.7
22. August. *Ep.* 22.6
23. *ICUR* 2.4535, 4.10404, 4.12494, 8.22408.
24. *ILCV* 2000.
25. *ILCV* 3681a.
26. *ILCV* 2171.
27. *CIL* 8.7543.
28. *CGL* 5.430.22.
29. Cat. 59.2.
30. Le Bohec (2015).
31. Toynbee (1982), pp.91–94.
32. Toynbee (1982), pp.94–100.
33. See, however, Peretz (2005).
34. *CIL* 3.5218 (3.11691), from Celeia.
35. *AE* (1909), p.144: Dacisca.
36. Reuter (2005); Perea Yébenes (2009); Bertolazzi (2015).
37. Susini (1959–60).
38. Dio, 56.22; Tac. *Ann.* 1.62.3.
39. Tac. *Ann.* 1.62; Clementoni (1990), pp.197–206.
40. Asskamp & Kühlborn (1986).
41. Witteyer (1997), pp.63–76.
42. Le Bohec (1989), pp.107–110.
43. Moretti & Tardy (2006).
44. Toynbee (1982), pp.61–64.
45. Cumont (1949), pp.29–54; Grimal (1999), p.275.
46. Grimal (1999), p.275. *Rosaria* are not to be confused with *rosalia* '*signorum*', standard celebrations, on 10 & 31 May – Groslambert (2009).
47. De Visscher (1963), pp.65–82.
48. De Visscher (1963), pp.103–06.
49. De Visscher (1963), pp.101–02.
50. De Visscher (1963), pp.112–23.

51. De Visscher (1963), pp.93–127.
52. De Visscher (1963).
53. Boschung (1987).
54. Eisner (1986).
55. Von Hesberg (2006); Sauron (2006).
56. Sartre-Fauriat (2006).
57. Sauron (2006).
58. Le Bohec (1989), pp.83–88.
59. *EA* (1969–70), p.661; Le Bohec (1989), p.102, fig. 23.
60. *CIL* 8.3043 (3.18163); Le Bohec (1989), p.90, fig. 4, no. 1.
61. *BCTH* (1946–49), p.234, no. 8; Le Bohec (1989), p.91, fig. 5, no. 3.
62. Le Bohec (1989), pp.92–93.
63. Cumont (1949), pp.55–58.
64. Cumont (1942), pp.35–77; Cumont (1949), pp.109–23, 142–84.
65. Cumont (1942); Cumont (1949).
66. Rinaldi Tufi (1988); Da Costa (1995).
67. *CIL* 13.8056; *Germania Romana*, 3.2, no. 3.
68. *CIL* 13.6898; Ritterling (1925), pp.1376–80.
69. Fischer (2012), p.163.
70. *CIL* 13.7574.
71. Von Domaszewski (1972), p.35.
72. *CIL* 13.6898.
73. Ritterling (1925), pp.1727–47; Franke, in Le Bohec & Wolff (eds) (2000), pp.191–202.
74. *CIL* 13.6901; Fischer (2012), p.231.
75. Dentzer (1982).
76. *Germania Romana* 3.10, no. 4 (civilian), and 11, 2 (*CIL* 13.8311: wing rider).
77. *Germania Romana* 3.11.3 (*CIL* 13.8283; Doppelfeld (1967), no. 140 and pl. 46: legionary veteran).
78. *Germania Romana* 3.11, no. 1 (*CIL* 13.8670: wing rider).
79. *Germania Romana* 3.11, no. 4 (*CIL* 13.7586: cohort soldier).
80. *Germania Romana* 3.10, no. 2 (civilian).
81. *Germania Romana* 3.12, no. 2 (*CIL* 13.6626).
82. *Germania Romana* 3.26, no. 2.
83. *RIB* 522 and 523.
84. *RIB* 558, 563 and 566;568: rank unknown.
85. Ritterling (1925), pp.1769–81; Keppie, in Le Bohec & Wolff (eds) (2000), pp.25–28.
86. *RIB* 522.
87. *RIB* 523.
88. Laporte (2013).
89. See Fischer (2012), p.324.
90. *CIL* 13.2613.
91. *CIL* 13.8648.
92. For the latter: Reuter (2005); Perea Yébenes (2009); Bertolazzi (2015).
93. Le Bohec (1989), p.64; updated with Burnand (1992), pp.21–27.
94. Le Bohec (2005).
95. *CIL* 13.2902.
96. *AE* (2012), p.252.
97. *CIL* 6.2627, Rome.
98. *CIL* 8.2926, Lambèse.
99. *CIL* 6.3332, Rome.
100. *CIL* 8.2756, Lambèse.
101. *CIL* 6.2607, Rome.

102. *CIL* 8.3270, and p.1741, from Lambèse.
103. *RIB* 1172, Corbridge (*Corstopitum*).
104. *RIB* 1350, Benwell (*Condercum*).
105. *CIL* 10.7592, Cagliari.
106. *BCTH* (1904), p.clxi, El-Ghara, in southern Algeria.
107. *AE* (2012), p.289, Avenches.
108. *AE* (2013), p.267, Pompeii.
109. *ILAf* 434, from Naimin-er-Rodoui, near Mateur, Tunisia.
110. *ILTun* 467, of Haïdra (*Ammaedara*).

Bibliography

Asskamp, R. & Kühlborn, J.S. 'Die Ausgrabungen im römischen Gräberfeld von Haltern', *Ausgrabungen und Funde in Westfalen-Lippe* 4 (1986), pp.129–38.
Beard, M., North, J. & Price, S. *Religions of Rome*, vols 1–2 (Cambridge, 1998).
Bertolazzi, R., 'A New Military Inscription from Numidia, *Moesiaci Milites* at *Lambaesis*, and Some Observations on the Phrase *Desideratus in Acie*', in Heckel W., Müller S. & Wrightson, G. (eds), *The Many Faces of War in the Ancient World* (Cambridge, 2015), pp.302–14.
Boschung, D., *Antike Grabaltäre aus dem Nekropolen Roms* (Bern, 1987).
Burnand, Y., 'La datation des épitaphes romaines de Lyon', *Inscriptions latines de la Gaule Lyonnaise* (1992), pp.21–27.
Clementoni G., 'Germanico e i caduti di Teutoburgo', in Sordi, M. (ed.), *Dulce et decorum est pro patria mori. La morte in combattimento nell'Antichità* (Milan, 1990), pp.197–206.
Cumont, F., *Recherches sur le symbolisme funéraire des Romains* (Paris, 1942).
Cumont, F., *Lux perpetua* (Paris, 1949).
Da Costa, V., 'The Memorialization of the Military Class: Roman Funerary Portraiture and Politics in the Eastern Roman Provinces', *AJA* 99 (1995), pp.346–47.
De Visscher, F., *Le droit des tombeaux romains* (Milan, 1963).
Dentzer, J.-M., *Le motif du banquet couché dans le Proche-Orient et le monde grec du VIIe au IVe siècle avant J.-C.* (Paris, 1982).
Doppelfeld, O. (ed.), *Römer am Rhein* (Cologne, 1967).
Eisner, M., *Zur Typologie der Grabbauten im Suburbium Roms* (Mainz, 1986).
Fischer, Th., Bockius, R. & Boschung, D. (eds), *Die Armee der Caesaren, Archäologie und Geschichte* (Regensburg, 2012).
Germania Romana, vol. 3: Tafeln, 2nd edn (Bamberg, 1930).
Gordon, R.L., 'The Roman Army and the Cult of Mithras: a Critical View', in Wolff, C. & Le Bohec, Y. (eds), *L'armée romaine et la religion sous le Haut-Empire romain* (Lyon, 2009), pp.379–450.
Grimal, P., *Dictionnaire de la mythologie grecque et romaine*, 19th edn (Paris, 1999).
Groslambert, A., 'Les dieux romains traditionnels dans le calendrier de Doura-Europos', in Wolff, C. & Le Bohec, Y. (eds), *L'armée romaine et la religion sous le Haut-Empire romain* (Lyon, 2009), pp.271–92.
Laporte, J.-P., 'Kabylie (Algérie): le retour de deux soldats maures dans leur foyer', in Bertholet, F. & Schmidt Heidenreich, C. (eds), *Entre archéologie et épigraphie. Nouvelles perspectives sur l'armée romaine* (Berne, 2013), pp.213–22.
Le Bohec, Y., *La Troisième Légion Auguste* (Paris, 1989).
Le Bohec, Y., 'Tertullien, *De corona*, I: Carthage ou Lambèse?', *Revue d'Etudes Augustiniennes et Patristiques* 38.1 (1992), pp.6–18.
Le Bohec, Y., *The Imperial Roman Army*, trans. Bate, R. (London, 1994).
Le Bohec, Y., 'Isis, Sérapis et l'armée romaine sous le Haut-Empire', in Bricault, L. (ed.), *Ier Colloque international sur les études isiaques* (Leiden, 2000), pp.129–45.

Le Bohec, Y., 'L'onomastique de l'Afrique romaine sous le Haut-Empire et les *cognomina* dits «africains»', *Pallas* 88 (2005), pp.217–39.
Le Bohec, Y., *L'armée romaine sous le Bas-Empire* (Paris, 2006).
Le Bohec, Y. (ed.), *The Encyclopedia of the Roman Army* (Malden, 2015).
Le Bohec, Y., 'Cemetery, Military', in Le Bohec, Y. (ed.), *The Encyclopedia of the Roman Army* (Malden, 2015), p.190.
Le Bohec, Y., 'La religion et la guerre au temps de Rome', in Baechler J. (ed.), *Guerre et religion* (Paris, 2016) pp.61–69.
Le Bohec, Y. & Wolff, C., *Les légions de Rome sous le Haut-Empire* (Lyon, 2000).
Lendon, J.E., *Soldiers and Ghosts* (London, 2005), (trans. 2009, *Soldats et fantômes*, Paris).
Moretti, J.-Ch. & Tardy, D. (eds), *L'architecture funéraire monumentale. La Gaule dans l'empire romain* (Paris, 2006).
Perea Yébenes, S., *La legión XII y el milagro de la lluvia en época del emperador Marco Aurelio: epigrafía de la legión XII Fulminata* (Madrid, 2002).
Perea Yébenes, S., '… in bello desideratis. Estética y percepción de la muerte del soldado romano caído en combate', in Marco F., Pina F. & Remesal J. (eds), *Formae mortis*: el tránsito de la vida a la muerte en las sociedades antiguas (Barcelona, 2009), pp.39–88.
Peretz, D., 'Military Burial and the Identification of the Roman Fallen Soldiers', *Klio* 87.1 (2005), pp.123–38.
Rankov, B., 'Christians', in Le Bohec, Y. (ed.), *The Encyclopedia of the Roman Army* (Malden, 2015), pp.194–95.
Reuter, M., 'Gefallen für Rom. Beobachtungen an den Grabinschriften im Kampf getöter römischer Soldaten', in *19e Congrès du limes* (2005), pp.255–63.
Rinaldi Tufi, S., *Militari romani sul Reno. L'iconografia degli 'Stehende Soldaten' nelle stele funerarie del I secolo d.C.*, *Archaeologica* (Rome, 1988).
Ritterling, E., '*Legio*', *RE* 12.2 (1925), pp.1211–29.
Sartre-Fauriat, A., 'Influences exogènes et traditions dans l'architecture funéraire de la Syrie du sud', in Moretti, J.-Ch. & Tardy, D. (eds), *L'architecture funéraire monumentale. La Gaule dans l'empire romain* (Paris, 2006), pp.125–39.
Sauron, G., 'Architecture publique méditerranéenne et monuments funéraires en Gaule', in Moretti, J.-Ch. & Tardy, D. (eds), *L'architecture funéraire monumentale. La Gaule dans l'empire romain* (Paris, 2006), pp.223–33.
Stefan, S., *Les guerres daciques de Domitien et de Trajan* (Rome, 2005).
Susini, G.C., 'Ricerche sulla battaglia del Trasimeno', *Annuario dell'Accademia Etrusca di Cortona* 11 (Cortona, 1959–60).
Toynbee, J.M.C., *Death and Burial in the Roman World* (London, 1982).
Von Domaszewski, A., *Aufsätze zur römischen Heeresgeschichte* (Darmstadt, 1972).
Von Hesberg, H., 'Les modèles des édifices funéraires en Italie: leur message et leur réception', in Moretti, J.-Ch. & Tardy, D. (eds), *L'architecture funéraire monumentale. La Gaule dans l'empire romain* (Paris, 2006), pp.11–39.
Witteyer, M., 'Gräberfelder der Militärbasis und Provinzhauptstadt Mogontiacum-Mainz', *Pro Vindonissa* (1997), pp.63–76.

Chapter 7

The Role of the Rising Sirius in Ancient Apocalyptic Tradition Concerning the Terrorist Background of the 'Neronian Fire' on 19 July AD 64

Gerhard Baudy
Translated and Edited by Christopher Matthew

Introduction: 'The Way'

After Jesus' death on the cross, his followers wisely avoided confessing themselves openly. This would have criminalized them. Instead of calling themselves *Christiani*, followers of an anointed king (Christ), they simply called their organization 'The Way'.[1] This revealed little to outsiders. On the other hand, the title conveyed a clear message to all those familiar with Jewish tradition: those who joined the Jesus movement saw themselves on their way to a goal that had not yet been attained, that of the God-state expected in the near future. In this new Israel, the resurrected Jesus was to occupy the post of a Davidic king. In the Gospels, however, Jesus carries not only the features of David, but also of other figures of Jewish salvation history, whose work was a necessary prerequisite for the emergence of a sovereign kingdom. These were firstly Moses, who had led the twelve tribes of Israel out of Egypt and thus redeemed them from foreign rule, and secondly his successor Joshua, under whom the Israelites crossed the River Jordan and conquered the Promised Land.[2]

Both events – exodus and conquest – were associated with the Passover. This festival was celebrated just before the exodus from Egypt and was repeated symmetrically after passing through the Jordan.[3] This myth of history ensured that every Pascha sacrifice reminded the Jews that the desert migration of their ancestors had begun and ended on this date. This gave the festival a dangerous appeal when Judea sought to regain a lost political sovereignty, animating the people to shake off foreign rule in order to bring the country into its god-desired state.[4] The Roman occupation forces feared unrest every year among those flowing into Jerusalem for the feast and, as a precaution, increased the preparedness of their troops at this time. To prevent potential uprisings was also the concern of the priestly aristocracy, who collaborated with the Romans when they imprisoned the troublemaker Jesus before a Passover feast and delivered him to the Roman governor. Jesus' name in itself indicates why he was considered politically problematic, as the Gospels follow the linguistic usage of the Septuagint, according to which Joshua, the commander of earlier Israel, was called Jesus. So Jesus could appear as someone in whose person the mythical hero of the conquest returned. As he had not only conquered the Promised Land, but distributed it among all the Israelites, his new namesake declared he would proclaim a Jubilee to liberate and reorganize a country in bondage.[5] The utopian construction of the Jobel Year saw Israel periodically restored to the ideal state it had earlier acquired through Joshua. To this end, all debts should be waived and prisoners released to recover the expropriated lands that Joshua had once assigned to their ancestors as inalienable possessions.[6]

The image of Joshua defined the figure of leading revolutionaries who wanted to redeem the country from foreign rule and reform it socially. Until the outbreak of the Jewish War of Liberation in AD 66, prophets staged their performances in such a way that they required people to see a new Moses or Joshua in themselves.[7] All these troublemakers, who appeared after Jesus of Nazareth, seem to have been inspired by his example, but because they failed the Church could of course not accept that they were members of its movement. Therefore, Jesus warns about them in the Gospels, foretelling the future coming of false prophets who would act in his name and wish to be identified with him. But in fact, they wanted to pursue his mission and to finish the way that had been interrupted before the Passover feast of AD 30.[8] Jesus was executed by the Romans because he was expected to exploit the impending Passover for a coup attempt. Nevertheless, his followers decided to remain faithful to the dead. Instead of admitting that the crucifixion of their leader had proved him a failed Messiah, they continued his Kingdom's propaganda. Instead of regarding his prophecies as falsified, they placed the predicament of suffering in his mouth, as if he had followed a divine direction and gone to his death with a seeing eye. Instead of even acknowledging that he had died, they denied that the Roman execution had been successful. For this purpose, they expressed themselves as members of the body of Christ.[9] This suggested that he lived in them collectively and could pursue his old plans in the body of the Church. This fiction was flanked by the myth that Jesus was bodily raised from the dead and then taken to heaven.[10] From there, however, he would return to establish the Kingdom of God on Earth.

To be sure, this theocracy was already present in the Church, the 'body of Christ', but in a preliminary form. Only with Jesus' *parousia* could the Kingdom of God be completed. To express this, the early Church called itself a 'Way' because it repeated the desert migration of the twelve tribes of Israel. At that time, God had preceded the Israelites on their way to the Promised Land, in the form of a pillar of fire that destroyed all the peoples who opposed them:[11] Divine Fire gave victory to the Chosen of God. Correspondingly, as the Acts of the Apostles put it, the messengers of God carried in them a fire fallen from heaven.[12] They approached an ultimate goal that was achievable only when the fire that filled them removed all resistance. For the desired restoration of the state there was only one preventing factor, namely the Roman occupying power. The burning of Rome on 19 July AD 64 can be explained against this background: it did not accidentally break out, but was started by people who, by a terrorist attack on the centre of the Roman Empire, attempted to provoke a provincial war of liberation. It can be surmised that these arsonists followed a calendar-determined apocalyptic instruction.[13]

The apocalyptic significance of 19 July

The argument here is based on the symbolic significance of this date. In Neronian Rome, the disastrous fire of that time brought back spontaneous memories of a similar event from centuries past: in 390 BC, the Gauls are said to have set fire to the city after defeating the Romans on the Allia. The day of this defeat, 18 July, was anchored in the collective memory of the Romans. The Augustan historiography dated the so-called 'Gallic fire' on the immediately following day, 19 July.[14] According to the then generally accepted Egypto-centric astronomy, the brightest star, Sirius (in Egypt called Sothis), heliacally rose on that day in the old royal city of Memphis.[15] Sirius' appearance in the hottest time of the year marked the beginning of the so-called 'Dog Days', because Sirius was the heavenly 'dog' on which the country's goddess Isis-Sothis rode, as is commonly shown in iconography.[16]

Sirius' annual rising in the morning sky repeated and anticipated the beginning and end of a 1,461-year-old 'Great Year' when periodically coinciding with the civil New Year's Day, which shifted one day every four years.[17] This day had a cosmogonic and anthropogonic significance, because at the dawn of the Dog Star, both the world and humanity originated. Sirius was considered to be their midwife, having caused souls to settle in material bodies.[18] This explains why in ancient astrology, when Sirius rises, and at the same time the sun enters the constellation of the 'lion', periodically recurring cosmic catastrophes, world conflagration and deluge set in motion the beginning of a new cycle.[19] Both are projections of an annually recurring experience: the opening of the Nile dams, which until then held back the dammed-up water, and ended a period of drought, as soon as Sirius appeared in the morning sky.[20] In mythical perspective, this was the victory of Horus, the son and secretly raised heir of the murdered Osiris over the usurper Seth (in Greek, Typhon), an 'anti-god' associated with sterility. Ritualistic expression was achieved by sacrificing animals: reddish cattle, donkeys, antelopes or hippopotamuses, all of which embodied Typhon.[21] Allegedly, people had once even been burned alive at the beginning of the Dog Days,[22] a transparent fiction based on a widespread politicization of the myth-ritual scheme. Seth was considered the god of foreign invaders who had temporarily taken Egypt into his power and plunged it into chaos. Horus, on the other hand, was the mythical representation of the reigning pharaoh, who was in charge of restraining usurpers and restoring order.[23]

In anti-Judaic versions of the Exodus myth, the ancestors of the Jews were said to worship Seth as their god.[24] They were banished from Egypt because they burned towns and villages, plundered temples, destroyed idols, burned sacred animals and maltreated the priests.[25] The shape of a donkey was attributed to their god.[26] Roman satirists made the Christians who had come out of Judaism also worshippers of a donkey-like god, and Christians were executed for arson, too, in Neronian Rome. Showcased as living torches, they represented a hostile god who had once revealed himself in a fire and had later sent his son into the world to set it on fire. Therefore, in a Roman caricature, Jesus hangs in the shape of a donkey on the cross.[27] This makes him the likeness of the Egyptian antagonist Seth, a revolutionary whose followers had acted as arsonists. As punishment for that act, the Egyptians let him be killed by fire, and later recreated this event at an annual sacrifice festival, which was held in the early Dog Days.

Every propaganda evokes a mirrored counter-propaganda. That is how it is here. The anti-Judaic literature had claimed that in the Temple of Jerusalem was the image of a donkey rider representing Moses because a donkey had carried him through the desert to Palestine.[28] The Gospels thus made the Seth-associated donkey, in an act of provocative self-stigmatization,[29] into a mount of Jesus, the new Moses. Sitting on a donkey, Jesus had gone into Jerusalem before the Passover. This raised the messianic hopes of the onlookers and made them suspect that the goal was a revolt. Modern theologians see it differently. The majority of them want to depoliticize Jesus. For them, the scene rather proves that Jesus had peaceful intentions as he had not ridden on a horse, but on a donkey which was unsuitable for war.[30] His notion of harmlessness also seems to be confirmed by the Zechariah prophecy, by which Jesus was guided, for this referred to a peaceful king carried by a donkey.[31]

Such exegesis fails, however, because of a shortened perception of the model text, which competent readers could readily supplement.[32] The peace brought by the eschatological king is preceded by a bloody war of liberation in which God himself uses entire nations as weapons:

> 'For I stretch Judah as a bow, and lay Ephraim on it as an arrow. I call your sons, Zion, to fight the sons of Javan, I make you the sword of a hero. The Lord Himself will appear above them. His arrow shoots like lightning. God the Lord blows the horn, he comes in the storms of the South. The Lord of the armies protects his own. The sling stones eat and crush. [His warriors] drink and murmur as with wine; they are full of blood like a sacrificial bowl, like the corners of an altar.'[33]

The literary template calls on an oppressed people to join a royal donkey rider and thus become the instrument of a militant god. Demonstrative riding on a donkey seems to have been part of the initiation ritual of the heir to the throne. Previously, David had put his son Solomon on a donkey.[34] David himself is said to have received donkeys for the royal family after he had fled from his other son Absalom, and – as Jesus later did – had cried and prayed on the Mount of Olives.[35] The rebel Absalom died when he passed, riding on a mule, under an oak tree and his hair was caught in its branches.[36] This Davidic dynastic founding myth bestowed a clear character value on a donkey: it characterized the rider as someone who wanted to qualify himself for a monarchical leadership role that he either did not own or had wrongly lost.

The Romans' attempt, however, to stifle insurrection in the bud by the crucifixion of the pretender failed. His devotees transformed the humiliating cross into a self-proclaiming sign, lifting Jesus to heaven, and used it on their missionary campaign in the function of a victory-promising standard. In the end, it was supposed to show that the Son of God, slain by the Romans as a Typhonic-style revolutionary, was the only legitimate king. This could inspire enemies of Rome to turn the tables, i.e., to perform a symbolic act evoking that none other than the emperor, the Antichrist, was a Typhon to be fought; especially as Nero's opponents called him a serpent or a dragon.[37] In a contemporary tragedy, Octavia implores Jupiter to fling his lightning at

Nero, whose tyranny outranks Typhon's ominous regime.[38] This may be the tradition of propaganda preceding the burning of Rome in AD 64. When Rome was on fire on 19 July, Typhon's fiery death seemed to have been repeated on the correct day of the calendar. It goes without saying that both Jewish and Christian apocalyptic notions bestialized Rome and its rulers, assigning them the role of a monster to be destroyed in a fire.[39]

The ideological instrumentalization of Sirius in ancient East–West conflicts

An analogous reversal also characterizes the star symbolism used by ancient oracle literature to express East–West conflict.[40] A star falling down from heaven on Italy will set fire to Rome, proclaimed the Sibyl. This was a polemical reaction to Roman panegyrics, which called the city the 'common star of the inhabited world'.[41] That Tyche (Fortuna) had helped the Romans would be shown by the death of Alexander the Great: like a star, he would have fallen from east to west, throwing the rays of his weapons at Italy.[42] The Romans seized this self-understanding as a right of domination in the Hellenistic East. The star of Alexander was now none other than Sirius, so his birth was fictitiously dated back to a day that corresponded in the Julian calendar, 19 or 20 July.[43] Apparently this implied reference to Sirius, the date of Alexander's birth, should prove to be the fate of the East, because Alexander identified himself with the Homeric Achilles,[44] and Achilles' armour shone before his duel with the Eastern prince Hector like the fiery Dog Star.[45] In the epic tradition, the comparison with the rising Sirius served to characterize the respective heroes as invincible opponents. Thus, the *Iliad* first lets the deputy of Achilles, Diomedes, shine in the fire of the Dog Star,[46] before he dominates on the battlefield. When Hector later gains the upper hand, Sirius temporarily changes side. Now it is the Trojan opponent whose armour blazes like the fire of the heavenly dog,[47] but only until Achilles finally intervenes in the combat and returns the Sirius-fire to the Greek camp.[48]

Alexander's campaign against the Persians gave this stellar symbolism a new relevance. Because Sirius was, in the Iranian tradition, the king of the stars,[49] it was also the celestial analogue not only of Zarathustra, but of the Persian Great King whose position Alexander the Great successfully usurped. In an Avestan text, Sirius (Tishtrya) fights in the shape of a white horse against a black horse, the demon of drought, at the time of its summer rising. After he has overcome his evil opponent, the star dives into a mythical lake, which brings its water to a boil. Rain clouds form, making the land fertile again.[50] Since then, pretenders to the throne had been trying in vain to acquire the fire of Sirius hidden in the water, but only legitimate rulers could obtain it. It gave them a regal power, the Chvarnah.[51] Since the time of Alexander the Great, it was opportune for Hellenistic monarchs to claim it. They were depicted on coins together with a star, a sign legitimizing their rule.[52]

This symbolism reached the Roman Empire via Alexander the Great. It was reflected in Augustan literature, according to which Rome had, in 396 BC, been at the end of a ten-year war against the Etruscan town of Veii. Lake Albano is said to have swelled up mysteriously at the hottest time of the year, when all other waters were dying down. An oracle was seized upon which promised the destruction of Rome, if it were not possible to drain off the water. The Romans dug channels there and thus gained control over this disastrous natural event.[53] It is obvious that the motif is due to an Egyptian tradition, the opening of the Nile dams at the early rise of Sirius.[54] The oracle text refers to the taming of the water as 'extinguishing' (*aquam extinguere*), a formulation that suggests that it is the fire of Sirius which is hidden in the flood and threatens to destroy Rome.[55] The Roman historiography here follows the epic tradition that transmits the Troy myth to Italy. Veii took over the role of the besieged city of Troy. Hence the enemy city falls in the tenth year of the war; therefore, in both wars, a seer is captured who must reveal how the besiegers can prevent the impending defeat. The kidnapping of a city goddess (Athena or Juno) is also a precondition for the imminent conquest.[56] Similarly, as the sinister fire of Sirius in the *Iliad* crosses over to his opponent Achilles at the death of Hector, so in the war against Veii the Romans pull the power of Sirius onto their side.

Why did the Romans, although alleged descendants of the Trojans, take on the role of the Greek urban conquerors, reversing the Trojan myth for their own purposes? The only reason for this could have been their wars against the Hellenistic Diadochi, who staged their struggle against the Roman Empire as a repetition of mythical precedents. Thus, the enemy of Rome, Pyrrhus, looked as the descendant of Achilles and his son of the same name, Pyrrhus-Neoptolemos.[57] Due to such typology, Achilles' victory over Hector promised not only the subsequent fall of Troy, but at the same time the ultimate destruction of Rome by a *Pyrrhus redivivus*, Pyrrhus returned. In retrospect, the Romans responded by reversing the Pyrrhos propaganda and, as part of a mythical history of the city, inventing an example that the fire of Sirius does not destroy their town but Rome's enemies.

Another reflex of anti-Roman Sirius apocalypticism is found in the Macedonian tradition. It is known only in a polemically distorted manner, a legend derived from Polybius, which Livy reports.[58] The Macedonian King Philip V intended to wage war against the Romans, for which purpose he gathered his troops in 182 BC. His army, at the foot of the Thracian Haimos mountains, marched between the two halves of a sacrificed dog. This was the usual Macedonian rite of lustration. At least in this case, however, the two-part dog seems to have held a symbolic relationship to the Dog Star because its rise took place exactly at this time.[59] After the military parade, Philip rode with his son Perseus, whom he wanted to make his heir, under great hardship to the summit of Haimos, ostensibly to spy out routes for marching against the Roman troops. On the top of the mountain they erected an altar, which was consecrated to Zeus and Helios, and made a sacrifice.

According to Livy, the futility of this endeavour,[60] and the toil of the dangerous descent, was a bad omen for the coming war, a forerunner of the Macedonian defeat. In retrospect, the winners mocked their enemies, to whom the foundation of the cult had, of course, conveyed an opposite message: prince Perseus was to be presented to the soldiers in a rite of initiation as the future conqueror of the enemy power of Rome. This explains the choice of the calendar date, for at the rise of Sirius feasts with ritual mountain ascents were organized in many places in the Eastern Mediterranean. At the top of the mountains, meteorological conditions were observed, and events were forecast for the coming year: rain or drought, good harvests or crop failures, healthy climate or disease, peace or war, victory or defeat. In addition, changes of power were prophesied at the rising of Sirius.[61]

This is what occurred on the Haimos ridge. Philip climbed the mountain with Perseus to await the rise of the Dog Star, because Sirius decided who was the coming ruler, being itself the star that ruled the world,[62] and whoever became king received his power from its shining light. For this reason, Philip then excluded his eldest son Demetrios from the succession and sent him away before he climbed alone with his younger son Perseus to the mountain peak. Demetrios had fallen out of favour because he had grown up as a hostage in Rome, and had become a friend of the Romans. Later, Philip had him murdered to ensure that he would not thwart his political plans. Perseus, on the other hand, had been known to all Macedonians as the official heir to the throne since the Sirius event, and was predestined to lead an army against Rome. For this purpose, the warriors at the foot of the Haimos had passed between the body parts of a dog. The two-part sacrificial animal apparently symbolized the heavenly 'dog'. Soldiers passing this body would feel called upon to regard themselves as Sirius-born and as such enter the service as men who were about to be blessed by the rising star. This was also ensured by the mythical elevation of the scene: on the Haimos ridge, Zeus is said to have once downed his adversary Typhon.

The mountain owes its name, 'blood mountain', to the blood of the killed dragon.[63] This suggested that the planned war should repeat a divine example. The Romans were intended to play the role of a monster to be conquered. Later, when the Romans won the victory over Perseus at Pydna and became masters of the known world, they did not neglect to taunt the Sirius propaganda of their Macedonian challengers with a legend. Before his campaign against Perseus, the general Aemilius Paullus had learned that the little dog of his daughter had just died. This dog was called Persa, which the father had immediately considered an ominous sign for the future defeat of Perseus.[64] The anecdote taunts a ruler, who – as the Romans knew – had appeared before his subjects as the incarnation of the Dog Star.

The culmination of this East–West conflict was stellar apocalypticism in Augustan times. As Caesar prepared in Rome for a campaign against the Parthians in 44 BC, a Sibylline oracle circulated in Rome announcing that only a king could defeat the Parthians.[65] It supported the request of Antonius, who in February had attempted to confer royal authority on Caesar by offering a laurel wreath around which a diadem was wound.[66] After Caesar was assassinated on the Ides of March because of his monarchical ambitions, he was deified by his supporters. The sign of his apotheosis was a star replacing the royal diadem,[67] which adorned the forehead of his statues and was widely depicted in numismatic propaganda.[68] This legitimized the leadership claims of two rivals who both wanted to assume Caesar's role. On the one hand, the star made Octavian the son of a god, who was predestined to rule as Caesar.[69] On the other hand, Mark Antony appeared as a priest of the divine Caesar[70] and intended to realize his planned Parthian campaign.[71] Later, Octavian, who had become Augustus, reclaimed this victory because he had, through a peace treaty, forced the Parthians to return captured Roman standards.[72] The historical context reveals which single value Caesar's star, the so-called *sidus Iulium*, must have had for his contemporaries:

it promised victory over Eastern enemies. As the helmet of Achilles had shone in the splendour of Sirius when he defeated the Eastern prince Hector, and Alexander the Great had conquered the Persians with his sign, Caesar's portrayed *sidus Iulium* suggested that the Parthians would not stand up to the Roman invaders.[73] In addition, it fits that the Romans sometimes referred to the Parthians as Persians.[74] Thus, they mentally retreated in their oriental campaigns to the time of Alexander the Great.

When the alliance between Antony and Octavian broke down, there was a civil war between two rivals, both utilizing the *sidus Iulium*.[75] Antony fought on the side of Cleopatra against an adversary who pretended to be somebody to whom the alleged appearance of the star in 44 BC had virtually helped to give him birth.[76] Once again, a new East–West conflict was expressed in traditional language games: Antony saw himself as an incarnation of the Egyptian god Dionysos-Osiris, while his wife, Cleopatra, represented Aphrodite-Isis.[77] As such, she was associated with not only the brightest planet, Venus, but also with the Sirius goddess Isis-Sothis. When Octavian defeated Antony and Cleopatra at Actium, it proved in the eyes of the Romans that the celestial fire was not his enemies', but rather legitimized himself monarchically. Therefore, in Vergil's state epic, Aeneas wears a shield prophetically depicting the Battle of Actium. For this, Vergil employs a stellar symbolism: above the head of Octavian shines the *sidus Iulium* (Julian star),[78] similar to the helmet in which the figure of Aeneas shines, in a fire that is compared by the poet both to a sparkling ominous comet and with the fateful fire of Sirius.[79] In Augustan propaganda, Cleopatra was a dragon killed by Octavian.[80] This implicitly assigned to Octavian the role of the dragonslayer Horus, whom the Greeks and Romans called Apollo. Just as Horus, by his victory over Typhon, had become the legitimate successor of his father Osiris, so Octavian transformed himself after Actium into Augustus, to whom now, as the sole heir of Caesar, rule had fallen not only over Egypt, but over the entire Roman Empire. Since then he was the sole bearer of *gloria Caesaris*, manifested through the *sidus Iulium*, which made him a new Caesar, the first emperor.[81]

In 46 BC, Caesar had brought Cleopatra to Rome, where she was introduced at a newly institutionalized midsummer Venus festival. In the Temple of Venus, Caesar had a statue of Cleopatra set up next to the goddess' statue.[82] During this feast, Caesar proclaimed a calendar reform, following hereby the advice of the Alexandrian astronomer Sosigenes: the new calendar correlated with a certain Egyptian model.[83] The Republican calendar was now replaced with a 365-day solar year. Because this is longer by a quarter of a day, an additional day was intercalated every four years so that the regular calendar did not shift from the solar year. This 'Julian calendar' copied the Sothis period in a small format: instead of the great year of 1,461 solar years, the four-year Roman switching cycle consisted of 1,461 calendar days.[84]

The Egyptocentric construction of the new calendar makes us understand the appointed date for the Venus Festival. According to the Roman authors, the Republican calendar was out of balance at that time. To correct this, Caesar had allegedly inserted sixty-seven additional days, so that the months fell back into their intended season.[85] If one were to trust these indications, the day of the feast of Venus, 26 September 46 BC, would have coincided with the desired date in the regular year which, according to the calendar reform, was 25 July,[86] and thus focused precisely on the day on which Sirius rose heliacally on the latitude of Rome.[87] There are reasons, however, to doubt that. After all, why was the festival since then celebrated not on 25 July, but on 20 July?[88] It seems that the Roman authors did not refer to the number of intercalated days from a tradition that was available to them, but based it on the feast day of 20 July, under an anachronistic presupposition of the Julian calendar. If one calculates back sixty-seven days from 26 September, one arrives at 20 July. If the Venus festival, however, was already celebrated by Caesar on a day that coincided with 20 July of the Julian calendar, then there can only have been one reason for it: Caesar had consulted the calendar expert Sosigenes, who came from Alexandria, the then capital of Egypt, where the rise of Sirius took place on 20 July, a day later than in a more southerly latitude such as in the old royal city of Memphis.[89]

Augustus later propagandistically transfigured this calendar day in his account of the Venus festival of 44 BC: at the *ludi victoriae Caesaris*, games organized to honour his murdered father, a miraculous star allegedly appeared in the sky, which the people regarded as the soul of Caesar, who had ascended to heaven.[90] Of course, this was the mysterious dawn of a new blessed era and the proclaiming star was no longer identified as Sirius, which had already existed in folklore and which appeared every year around the same time. The star had to be made unique for the sake of Augustus' salvation-historical rhetoric. In his memoirs, Augustus transformed the *sidus Iulium* into a comet that attracted and outshone the dog's character: while Sirius stood invisibly up in the sky during the day, the comet substituting it beamed even brighter than the sun. Only since then was the *sidus Iulium* iconographically provided with a comet's tail, although the word *sidus* never referred to comets, but always what were called fixed stars. Nor is there any contemporary testimony that proves the reality of the comet.

Nevertheless, research usually takes the Augustan fiction at face value. Many find it difficult to believe that, in his memoirs, only about twenty years later, Augustus had been able to influence the minds of the Romans, as if there were no eyewitnesses.[91] Such scepticism, however, underestimates the people's willingness to engage with imperial myths when they serve to historicize apocalyptic language games. Each ruler was expected to accept and promote legends that increased his charisma. This was the generally accepted social consensus. It would therefore have occurred to none of the contemporaries to debunk such fictions ideologically. On the other hand, a modern historian should not accept these. But this is exactly what happens through an attempt to authenticate the historicism of the Augustan comet from Chinese annals.[92] Although the annals testify to a comet for 44 BC, it appeared in another season, the Romans knew nothing about it and the Chinese tradition in turn knows of no comet in July for that year. Nonetheless, the potential identity of both celestial phenomena was attempted through the speculative computation of a cometary orbit, which influenced recent research.

Real proof of the existence of the July comet is not obtained by this method. Astronomical theories, which ignore the symbolic content of the July date, are obviously misleading. Instead, Augustus used a mythical process by reversing cause and effect: he did not place a star on the statue of Caesar because it had shown up in the sky, but he invented a miracle star to strengthen the prophetic sign of the *sidus*

Iulium on Caesar's head, unfolding a narrative through legends circulating about it. Among them was the story of a haruspex (seer) named Vulcanius, who announced that the comet indicated the end of the ninth and the beginning of the tenth era.[93]

In constructing the celestial sign, Augustus followed a Hellenistic precedent: both at the birth and during the enthronement of the Pontic king Mithridates, a comet appeared whose light outshone the sun and set the sky on fire.[94] This was considered a sign for the future length of the oriental ruler's reign, making him an alleged descendant of the kings Cyrus, Darius and Alexander the Great,[95] and a new bearer of shining monarchical power. This heavenly fire legitimized his campaign against the Roman Empire and promised him victory over a Western enemy. Augustus reversed this propaganda: the fire of Sirius, or of the comet replacing it, now vouched in return for the dominance of the West over the East.

Mithridates had followed in the footsteps of earlier challengers of Rome. He wanted to be a new Hannibal and a new Pyrrhus. To his Gallic auxiliaries, he presented the example of their ancestors, who had burned down Rome.[96] What they once had done only imperfectly, they should now complete: the final annihilation of the Roman capital. Already Hannibal, allied with Pyrrhus, used Gallic auxiliary troops in his campaign against Rome, and vigour was presumably instilled in the Gauls by reminding them of their ancestors' example. It seems likely that this 'Gallic conflagration', along with its fixation on the day of the rising Sirius, was a historiographical fiction generated in Hellenistic times, because Pyrrhus instrumentalized the Trojan myth with its Dog Star typology for propaganda purposes. Augustan historiography took this into account by dating the 'Gallic fire' on 19 July. But Rome is said to have risen from its ashes like a phoenix, being reborn by a baptism of fire. Its re-establishment allegedly took place exactly 365 years after its first foundation, the end and new beginning of a 'Great Year', which copied the solar year.[97]

This reads like an aetiological myth of the Julian calendar reform, which had indeed adapted the solar year. In addition, Camillus, who expelled the Gauls and rebuilt Rome, prefigured Augustus, who, after the end of the Civil War, was celebrated as the new founder of Rome, ordained by the *sidus Iulium*.[98] About the figure of Camillus, the rising of Sirius was entered in the fictitious city history twice: the fire of the Dog Star threatened the existence of Rome, as Camillus' army besieged Veii. But the Romans managed to avert the danger, so that they could conquer Veii and burn it down. Here, the hostile Etruscan city takes over the role of the destroyed Troy, and few years later, Rome itself, on 19 July, goes down in a fictitious fire disaster. At that time, Camillus – like the Homeric Achilles – withdrew from combat. And as Achilles' armour shone like the fire of the Dog Star when he resumed the fight against his Trojan adversary, the fire of 19 July enabled Camillus to re-establish the city after acquiring military leadership again and defeating the Gauls. Upon his succession, Augustus constructed a stellar omen, which promised a worldwide historic turn caused by him. In his eyes, the miracle star not only helped him to his own symbolic birth, but also renewed the world as a whole. The *sidus Iulium* created by him was a sign of Rome's resurrection, reversing an anti-Roman Sirius propaganda that used to foretell the city's downfall in the fire of the Dog Star.

Vergil repeatedly took up this motif in his works. In his *Eclogues*, Caesar's new star replaces the old constellations and makes the seeds fertile in their place.[99] In the *Georgics*, the beekeeper Aristaeus acts as the mythical example of Augustus: a plague has killed his bee colony; then, at the rising of Sirius, a spell is revealed to him that gives rise to a new bee colony, a narrative metaphor for Rome reborn under Augustus.[100] In the *Aeneid*, the fire of Sirius, in which Aeneas' armour glares, evokes the fact that the hero is destined to win over his opponent Turnus,[101] whose death metaphorically recounts the defeat of Antony. The *Aeneid* expands the typological series by another example. Once before, the Trojan ancestors of Rome had mastered a crisis emanating from Sirius: fleeing from their burning hometown, the Trojans land on Crete and found a new Troy there, but the embers of the rising Dog Star destroy the harvest and deprive the settlers of their livelihood. The Trojans move on and end up in Italy, where the ruined Troy would then be permanently resurrected in the guise of Rome.[102] Instead of eradicating Troy or Rome from the Earth, the Sirius fire always causes the city to regenerate itself more splendidly. Significantly, Varro, probably inspired by an epic of Ennius, had the Trojans seeking a new home following a star that led them to Italy.[103] This star was Venus, the goddess in whose honour a festival had been held by Caesar in 46 BC. The brightest fixed star and the brightest planet, Sirius and Venus, had an analogous semantic content and therefore functioned in Vergil's state epic as interchangeable bodies, which in turn fused symbiotically into a fictional comet, the *sidus Iulium*.[104]

The *sidus Iulium* outlasted the Augustan era, serving the Julian-Claudian dynasty until its end as a symbol of power. Like Caesar and Augustus, Nero was iconographically depicted with a crowning star.[105] Calpurnius Siculus updated the same pattern as part of a Nero-panegyric: in Nero's reign, a comet appeared again in the sky, which shone even brighter than the star of Caesar, signalling the return of a golden age.[106] The comet, copying the *sidus Iulium*, and at the same time surpassing it, served, of course, to intimidate the enemies of Rome and to delegitimize potential challengers of the emperor.[107] This seems, however, to have been imperfectly achieved, for on 19 July AD 64, Rome was in flames. The citizens immediately remembered the Gallic fire, which had allegedly fallen on exactly the same calendar day. The ominous coincidence led to a consultation of the Sibylline Books.[108] The new fire disaster was therefore considered a fateful preordained event. That is exactly what Nero's enemies intended. They suggested themselves, through a terrorist attack, to be the executors of a divine plan. Were these arsonists controlled by a prophecy related to the rise of Sirius?

The Neronian Fire

Most scholars do not want to accept the Christians as culprits for the fire of AD 64. If they link the fire disaster back to arson, they consider Nero to be the architect. They give credit to a historiography for which Nero was a pathological tyrant who burned down Rome, in order to make room for his planned palace, the *domus aurea*, and to rebuild the ruined metropolis all the more splendidly.[109] In his perversion, it is said, he went so far that he used the fire in the city as a backdrop for the presentation of his Troy recital.[110] What Suetonius and Cassius Dio later present as fact was a mere rumour in Tacitus' account: in order to ward off such slander, Nero would have blamed other offenders and made the Christians the scapegoats, which could easily be done, because for the Romans they were unpopular supporters of an Eastern religion.[111] According to Tacitus, they were wrongly executed. He presents his readers with the choice of considering the strange fact that Rome was hit by a devastating fire on exactly the same day as the 'Gallic fire' as either a coincidence or more likely to be the fault of the emperor.[112] His portrayal tends to suggest the latter, as his negative Nero-image ensured that the emperor was credited with the greatest crimes. For, like the senatorial-aristocratic historiography as a whole, Tacitus insists on vilifying the autocratic ruler. For that reason, he does not even consider that the Christians condemned to death by Nero were indeed the culprits, though he makes no secret of the fact that in his eyes they formed the lowest class of human beings.

The rumour that Nero reduced Rome to rubble may have been inspired by his own Trojan poetry. His lost poem *Iliupersis* portrayed the downfall of Troy, and in the epic tradition that followed Nero this event was prepared and framed by a Sirius motif. Did the emperor make use of it in a manner characteristic of epics? Does his poem combine the Trojans typologically with the 'Gallic fire' and the emblem of the Julio-Claudian dynasty, the *sidus Iulium*?[113] If so, his opponents would have had an easy time blaming him for the catastrophe of 19 July. The emperor would then have put into practice literary fantasies whose pivotal point was the early rising of the Dog Star. The fact that Nero, through the rebuilding of Rome, like Augustus in earlier times, behaved as a new Camillus seemed to confirm the truth of the rumour.[114]

Contrary to popular opinion, however, many researchers have refrained from considering Nero as an arsonist.[115] It would have been simply absurd if an emperor, who was so anxious to be loved by the people, had lit the roofs of his citizens over their heads and not even spared his own palace. In fact, Nero personally organized the firefighting and caring for the homeless. The rumours circulated by Nero's opponents had no resounding success. His affection for the people was met with affection in return. After his death, most wanted to believe he was still alive, or did not want to believe his end.[116] Therefore, pretenders to the throne who attempted to recruit troops in the eastern part of the Mediterranean could attempt to impersonate Nero several times, as if he were still alive or even risen from the dead.[117]

But if Nero was not guilty, then who was? Research still favours Tacitus' assumption of a random fire outbreak, so this question often does not arise. But if one considers the date of the fire and recognizes its symbolic apocalyptic value, the problem simply cannot be avoided. The hypothesis of a random outbreak would only be a permissible, temporary solution if there were no other explanations.

The counter-thesis is that it was, in fact, the Christians who set the fire.[118] This forces the assumption of arson and thus the question of who were the perpetrators. Anyone who considers Christians innocent would therefore need to make a more plausible counter-proposal, rather than resorting to a chance hypothesis. The first Christians arrested, according to Tacitus, confessed. In his account, other Christians were imprisoned and condemned to death, in this case not for arson, but for their hatred of humanity.[119] The Romans saw them as sympathizers of religiously motivated terrorists, viewing them as the breeding ground from which anti-Roman fantasies and religiously inspired ideas were fed. That made them accomplices. Research almost consistently refuses to accept this idea. In order to maintain their opinion that Christianity was a religion of love that had always been peaceful and remote from all violence, it is claimed either that the confessions of those initially detained were given under torture and thus worthless, or that such a confession means – contrary to the context – a pure creed.[120] But even if that were correct, why would that have been enough for the Roman judiciary to execute a confessed Christian as an arsonist? And why did Nero turn the Christians, and not the Jews among whom they had been counted, into scapegoats?

The latter presupposes that the Romans at that time knew how to make a clear distinction between admirers of a crucified Messiah, considered to be enemies of Rome, and other Jews who were loyal. This would have only been possible if the Jews had publicly distanced themselves from any enemies of Rome within their own ranks. To do this they had indeed a good motive, because an event with traumatic consequences for all Jews living in the city occurred in AD 49. They were expelled from Rome by the Emperor Claudius, because a certain Chrestus had caused riots among them. With Chrestus, no other than Christ is meant, since Tacitus also calls the Christians *Chrestiani*, followers of one Chrestus.[121] This can hardly be explained by misunderstanding, as if the meaning of the title Christ (the anointed) was not familiar to the Romans, so that they had replaced it with a word that at that time had the same phonetic value. Rather, it was a deliberate mockery: because the Christians behaved as politically harmless and wrongly pursued followers of a crucified Redeemer, the Romans mockingly called this redeemer Chrestus, the 'Decent' or 'Honest Man', and his followers *Chrestiani*.

But how could this 'Honest Man', who had been executed under Tiberius, suddenly appear under Claudius in Rome? Again, there can be no question that Suetonius or his source was subject to a misunderstanding.[122] The early Christians expected the return of their Messiah in the near future, and this made it possible for any of the charismatic claimants to take on the role of an eschatological King and Son of God. In this case, a messianic agitation against Roman rule seems to have led to the Jews having to leave the city. In Nero's time, the Jews, and with them the Christians, had returned to Rome. After the burning of Rome in AD 64, the imperial fury, unlike in AD 49, was placed solely on the latter. Why did the suspicion fall on the Christians? According to the Acts of the Apostles, the Jews who were loyal to Rome used to denounce Christians to the Roman authorities and condemn them as rebels. This is what happened in Neronian Rome. A denunciation of the Christians delivered these people to the Roman judiciary and ensured that the Jews in Rome were unscathed.[123]

In the apologetic self-portrayal of the Christians, the accusations made by the Jews against the Jesus movement were pure lies. Today's Christians are willing to believe that because it fits in with their pacifist understanding of early Christianity – although many interpreters certainly see that there was a good reason to suspect the Jesus movement as it had promised the downfall of the world in fire. The Messiah longed to be baptised in a fire falling from the sky, and was to annihilate all those who refused to recognize his leadership in a great fire.[124] Hardly anyone, however, dares to consider if Christians acted against Roman rule with real violence. Jesus' command to love one's enemies, it is believed, excluded militant actions, as had the admonition given to the Roman Christians by Paul to remain loyal to the Emperor and not to refuse him taxes.[125] Such reasoning ignores that the required peacefulness of the Christians was temporary. Paul expected the replacement of the Roman Empire by the theocracy during his own lifetime, and this eschatological change was to be brought about by a divine judicial fire.[126] In this end-time scenario, Paul attributes the role of judges to the Christians themselves.[127] Similarly, the Apocalypse of John later expects an active participation by the Christians in the downfall of Rome. They are to take revenge on the city, burning the 'Whore of Babylon' and repaying double her misdeeds.[128]

In this scripture, the returning Christ assumes the form of a white horse rider whose eyes glow like fire and out of whose mouth a sword protrudes. His name is *Logos*, 'Word',[129] because the fire prophecies heard from the mouth of Jesus were to be realized in the burning of Rome. By the same token, in the Apocalypse of John, Christian prophets spew fire that destroys their enemies.[130] In the founding myth of the Church, the Spirit of God rains down on the congregation in the form of tongues of fire.[131] The divine fire that filled them was to spread along the missionary path throughout the Roman Empire. As the followers of Jesus defined themselves as the collective body of the resurrected Christ, the fire of his missionaries could ignite torches and eventually prepare for the fall of Rome.[132]

Did partisans therefore incite a real fire in Nero's time to execute Jesus' will? Without mentioning the fire of Rome, the author of the apocryphal Pauline Acts has this in mind: Nero has Paul arrested in Rome and brought in for interrogation. Nero feels threatened by the 'soldiers of Christ' whom Paul recruits through his mission. Paul confirms that throughout the world, 'soldiers' are recruited for the cause of Christ, and recommends that the emperor should join them so that he does not perish in the fire of judgment soon to take place. Nero then gives orders to behead Paul and persecute all Christians.[133] Either the author of the Pauline Acts knew of fire prophecies that had preceded the burning of Rome, which served now as evidence of arson to the Roman authorities, or he has put the words into Paul's mouth from his letters and other New Testament writings.[134]

In the letters of Paul, Christians wear armour; they are warriors of God.[135] According to the *opinio communis*, such militant imagery was not to prepare for acts of violence, but had a purely spiritual purpose.[136] One wonders, however, if Christians actually ever believed that God would bring about the eschatological turnaround without using human help. They were expecting their Redeemer, like a nocturnal thief. If he came covertly to pick them up, they should be prepared to complete the hitherto secretly expanding Kingdom of God in the wake of Jesus on a secret day.[137] But they could only do that if the Roman Empire and its emperor were removed beforehand. The apocryphal Gospel of Thomas speaks a clearer language: 'The Kingdom of the father is like a man who wanted to kill a powerful man. He drew the sword in his house. He pushed it into the wall to see if his hand was strong enough. Then he killed the powerful.'[138]

Paul's spiritual weapons are transformed into a deadly sword in this parable. Thus, an assassin who embodies the Church conducts secret trials before he leaves home and slays the 'powerful'. This stands for the emperor and/or the Roman Empire. The metaphors of Paul are analogously interpretable. When he asks Christians to carry arms of light,[139] he quotes the Qumran war roll in which the 'sons of light' wage an eschatological war against the forces of darkness. This proves the spiritual weapons as possible placeholders for real weapons.[140]

It goes without saying that it would have been suicidal for the Christians to face armed Roman legionaries. The only course of action they were capable of was to carry out symbolic actions that would cause the peoples of the Mediterranean to raise arms against Rome. That is what happened on 19 July AD 64. Those who set the fire could then trust that the symbolic added value of this date was internationally understandable. The peoples of the Mediterranean would have been prepared for the fact that the rising of the Dog Star on this day drove the destinies of the world again on new paths. Fire breaking out in Rome attracted attention across the provinces. This is shown in an event from AD 69 when the Capitol burned. In Gaul, the Druids interpreted this as a sign that the time had come for an uprising, because now also the Capitol, which had once survived the 'Gallic fire', was destroyed. The Gallic troops were mobilized and marched against Rome to overthrow the then ruling Emperor Vitellius.[141] Therefore, if terrorists had, five years earlier, similarly chosen 19 July – the date of the 'Gallic conflagration' – to re-enact it, they could have had legitimate hope of wars of liberation by unleashing an eschatological fire. Of course, that did not happen, at least not immediately. Nevertheless, the 'Neronian fire' was not without consequences: the costs for the reconstruction of Rome were passed on to the provinces through higher tax collections, which increased their readiness to rebel. Two years later, when the governor of Judea seized money from the Jewish temple treasure, arguing that Nero needed the funds, the looting caused the cup to overflow.[142] The party of the revolutionary-minded enemies of Rome finally prevailed. The Roman occupiers of Jerusalem were massacred; this was the beginning of the Jewish-Roman War in AD 66.

An oracle originated at that time which prophesied that world domination would now return from the West to the East, in order to inspire the messianic expectations of the insurgents.[143] Later, the victorious Romans did not question the veracity of the prophecy, but used it in the opposite sense. For them, the oracle announced the world domination of the general Vespasian, whose troops had besieged and destroyed Jerusalem.[144] Vespasian had announced himself as the new emperor in the east of the Roman Empire, before he returned from there to Rome. This made it possible for him to transfer the role of a Messiah coming from the East to his own person.[145] As befits ancient propaganda wars, a miraculous star also appeared in their inventory. It was regarded, depending on the standpoint, as a sign of either victory or defeat.[146] The new Emperor Vespasian went still further. Before he celebrated his Roman triumph over the Jews in AD 71, he stayed with his son Titus on the Campus Martius in a temple of the Sirius goddess Isis-Sothis that had been erected there by Caligula.[147] Previously, he had appeared in Alexandria in the temple of the Nile god Sarapis (Osiris) as if he were his incarnation. There, he allegedly performed miracles of salvation, which certified his claim to power, and he also received a prophecy that he would be the next ruler.[148] Egypt was the first Roman province to recognize Vespasian as the new emperor. Therefore, the ruler, imitating Augustus, used Egypto-centric credentials.

As the embodiment of the Nile god Sarapis, Vespasian was able to ask the Alexandrians to 'draw from him' like from the Nile.[149] When he entered Alexandria, an unusual Nile inundation was said to have occurred at a different season than normal.[150] Since the swelling of the Nile, however, was strongly associated with Sirius' rising, the legend inevitably rose that the same star had appeared irregularly in the morning sky, as if to give the future ruler a heavenly escort upon entering the city. Thus, an imaginary star epiphany took on the function of the Augustan *sidus Iulium*, granting the new Flavian dynasty a stellar legitimacy in the tradition of the Julian-Claudian imperial family. To illustrate this to the Romans, Vespasian and Titus both spent the night in the temple of the Sirius goddess Isis-Sothis before their triumphal procession. In the tympanum of this temple, the goddess was shown riding on a dog.[151] Thus, when the two rulers emerged from the temple in the morning, Sirius seemed to float above them, bestowing upon them the star's shining light. To urge the Romans to accept Vespasian as their new emperor, the usurper hurried on his way from Egypt to Rome with 'happy messages' promising a new blessing.[152] Such 'happy messages' had already served a similar function in the time of Augustus. Spread in the eastern Mediterranean, they gave the first emperor the role of a peacekeeper and world ruler.[153]

Those who did not agree with Roman supremacy had to feel provoked by this panegyric. Even after the failure of the Jewish uprising, Christians did not give in. They opposed Vespasian's *euangelia* (good news) with a different gospel. In Mark, the 'good news' proclaimed not a new emperor, but the coming theocracy.[154] Thus, the old subversive prophecies lived on in the Flavian period. Had the spiritual resistance to Rome previously manifested itself verbally? In order to oppose the imperial ideology and to show the Romans the nullity of their claim to world domination, there was no more drastic remedy than to set their capital on fire on a day that had the same stellar connotation as the imperial propaganda. Those rulers who basked in the glow of Sirius should be shown that the star's fire brought them destruction instead. When Christians attacked with burning torches in Neronian Rome, they acted as messengers of Sirius and brought its destructive ardour down to Earth.

This would only be provable, however, if there were early Christian testimonies to a Sirius apocalypse preceding the 'Neronian fire'. Such are not known, but there are indications that such a prophecy had prepared for the arson attack. Hippolytus quotes a Christian-era exegesis that he considers heretical, indicating that within the movement of Jesus there were people who identified their heavenly Redeemer with the rising Dog Star. Christ is called here, as in the Johannine literature, *logos*. This *logos* is a dog that not only tests the plants, but also humans at its rising. Everything that is destroyed by his heavenly fire proves to be unviable and deserves death.[155] This refers to the traditional method of seed testing: seedlings of crops were placed in the sun at the rising of Sirius to test their vitality. From the speed of their withering, it became clear what part of the harvest was covered for the coming sowing and which part could be released for consumption.[156] According to the ancient linguistic convention, however, it was not the sun, but ultimately Sirius, who decided on life and death, as if the Dog Star had lit the embers of the sun at his rising.[157]

A Christian allegory has made this the model of the righteous fire announced by Jesus. As *logos*, the Son of God personifies a prophetic 'word' that has the power to fling fire upon the world. When such a fire prophecy revealed that the eschatological 'Lord's Day' was imminent, it could motivate Christians to stage Jesus' *parousia* by setting fire to Rome on 19 July. They could have chosen for their attack also 20 July, the day of the Venus festival connoted with the *sidus Iulium*, but decided rather for 19 July, because they followed the model of the 'Gallic fire'. On the same calendar day on which this was dated, Jesus was supposed to be a fiery *logos* returning to the community of his followers and making them the executing tool of his righteous fire. It is difficult to imagine that such a Sirius apocalypse would be written after the burning of Rome, because that would have confirmed that Christians actually were the arsonists. For apologetic reasons, however, the Christians endeavoured to suppress the reason for their condemnation. There is no mention of it in their literature, and the Sirius prophecy was condemned as heretical.

From the manner in which the devotees of Jesus were executed under Nero, it can be seen that the Romans were likely to resist any Christian Sirius-propaganda that was known to them. According to the *lex talionis*, some of the Christians were crucified and burned alive, others sewn into animal skins and mauled by dogs.[158] The latter punishment must have had a symbolic meaning. If arsonists had come as an incarnation of a heavenly 'dog', it was consistent to have them ripped apart by dogs. The dogs were executory manifestations of the Dog Star legitimizing Roman rule: the ritual execution was to demonstrate to the world that the Christians had tried in vain to bring the power of Sirius to their side. Therefore, the false Sirius-god of the Christians, because he wanted to trigger a revolt in the collective body of his worshippers, was not only once again put to death on the cross, but was at the same time burned alive and torn apart by dogs.

From time immemorial, potential dangers that assumedly arose from the rising of the Dog Star had been attempted to be neutralized in the city by means of ritual defensive measures. Because Sirius was supposed to cause plant diseases, the Romans sacrificed dogs to him.[159] During the imperial period they did so in the Dog Days for a peculiar reason. Because the dogs had slept when the Gauls wanted to storm the Capitol during the conquest of Rome, they were considered traitors, who collaborated with the enemies of Rome. As such, they were crucified and carried in a solemn procession through the city, but with them a goose sat in a litter on a cushion. This was in order to honour the geese, who by their chattering had awakened and saved the Romans.[160]

The Elder Pliny is the first author to testify to this Sirius festival. It could therefore have originated in this form only in the imperial era.[161] If Pliny wrote this down before the 'Neronian fire', then the execution of the Christians might have copied the crucifixion of the 'renegade dogs', because they worshipped their Redeemer as the rising Dog Star. They would then have been considered Sirius-infected rabid dogs.[162] If Pliny wrote the message after the fire, a reverse causality would be conceivable.

The ritual dog killing is not dated on 19 July, as one would expect, but on 3 August.[163] Did the bizarre ritual preserve the memory of enemies of the Romans who were executed under Nero during the Dog Days, namely on 3 August? In retrospect, the Romans wanted to ridicule an attack that copied the conquest of Rome by the Gauls, demonstratively reminding the Christians that the Roman 'head mountain', the Capitol, had miraculously survived the catastrophe. So the centre was left from which the city's body could regenerate, whereas enemies of Rome, who thought of themselves as the body of Christ and had set up a directing pseudo-Sirius as their leader, had to fail together with their divine head.

The fact that it has always been possible to connect the Christians and their Saviour with Sirius shows the nature of their appearance. They resembled wandering preachers who called themselves Cynics, 'dogs', and Jesus' parable speeches had the same character as the Cynics' diatribes.[164] The research literature therefore argues that the Christian 'migratory charismatics' were not only inspired by Cynicism,[165] but also worshipped Jesus as a 'dog'.[166] This serves the purpose of depoliticizing the movement of Jesus, because the Cynics, the 'dogs', were supposedly not political oppositionists. This is a misjudgment. Cynics were professional provocateurs. The Emperor Vespasian had banished Demetrius, who belonged to this school, from the city because of his hate speech. Although he accepted this 'muzzle', he later yelled at the emperor in an encounter. Vespasian reacted calmly and contentedly called Demetrius a contemptuous 'dog'.[167] In a famous anecdote, Diogenes, the legendary ancestor of the Cynics, expressed a stance on domination: Alexander the Great stepped in front of the beggar philosopher, who lived in a barrel, and received from him a request for the king to please step out of the sun.[168] But this same Diogenes was equated by his followers with Sirius. He had already been a 'heavenly dog' during his lifetime and had gone up to heaven after his death.[169] That can only have had the meaning of delegitimizing Alexander and his successors. As worshippers of the celestial 'dog', the Cynics claimed a monarchical rule of their own.[170] Out of the same subversive attitude, itinerant preachers in the name of the rising Sirius, in which they recognized Christ, were able to open their campaign against the Roman Empire.[171]

The affinity between the Christian enemies of the Romans and Cynics reveals details about the life of Peregrinus Proteus in the second century AD.[172] According to Lucian, he was a Church leader in the Near East. Then he quarrelled with his community and wandered around as a cynic in the Mediterranean. He then arrived in Rome, where his inflammatory speeches led the Prefect to banish him from the city. He then travelled to Olympia and made a speech there, which invited the assembled people to raise arms against the Romans. He designed the end of his life according to the model of the Heracles myth, imitating the apotheosis of the hero: he plunged into the flames of a pyre. Heracles was the divine model not only of opposing Cynics, but also of their opponents, the ancient monarchs.[173] Zeus had begotten Heracles because he wanted to make him Lord of the World,[174] which he failed to do in myth. But the kings and emperors suggested that, in their own person, Heracles had posthumously obtained glory due to their reign. Therefore, the Roman ritual of the imperial apotheosis copied the death of Heracles, which in turn could cause a Cynic to use a self-immolation to call upon his followers to see in him alone a legitimate *Hercules redivivus*. They were to follow in the footsteps of their leader, who had gone up to heaven, and to continue his anti-Roman agitation.

For the same reason, the Cynics worshipped Sirius as their school founder, since Diogenes – the new Dog Star – was already figured in the myth of Heracles, his divine prototype:[175] in the pseudo-Hesiodic *Scutum*, the hero Heracles' victory over Kyknos took place at the rising of the Dog Star.[176] Sirius' fire also scorches the bones of all his other opponents in this work.[177] The calendar date of the duel therefore had a representative significance. Heracles' first exploit, the killing of the Nemean lion, was already astrologically determined. Similarly, Sirius in the constellation of the 'dog' – like the lion's constellation, which was simultaneously rising – possessed a legitimizing function. A star in the chest of the heavenly 'lion' was called Regulus, the 'King Star'.[178] In the Greek myth, the Leo-named constellation is the lion that had been taken to heaven, after Heracles had once brought it down and whose fur he wore ever since. Therefore, monarchs could be iconographically represented as bearers of a lion's skin. In return, the Christians saw in Leo a satanic power. He was the devil who walked around like a roaring lion,[179] whom a true Messianic lion of the tribe of Judah opposed.[180] Thus they may have followed the example of the Cynics, who had reversed the dynastic intention of the Heracles myth, and had put their mission in the service of Heracles' successor, Diogenes. In Sibylline oracle literature, Nero is referred to as a lion followed by a dog.[181] This may have been a symbol of an anti-Nero agitation, as he was the common enemy of both Cynics and Christians. The model of the Cynic hero has also rubbed off on the Christian Gospels and left recognizable traces in them.[182] When, for example, the Gospel of John puts the words 'It is finished' into the mouth of the dying Jesus (19.39), it probably quotes a Herculean tragedy of Seneca published in Neronian times in which the hero decides the outcome of his life with the phrase *peractum est*.[183]

Although they were created only in the Flavian period, the Jesus biographies retain older traditions that were current during the time of the fire of AD 64. Above all, the Gospel of Matthew deserves attention. His notion of a star appearing at the time of Jesus' birth may have had only the purpose of overriding the stellar propaganda of the Romans and thus depriving all emperors, from Augustus to Vespasian, of the basis of legitimacy.[184] The star in Matthew guides the Magi, Persian priests, from the East to Bethlehem, to pay homage to the newborn Jesus as the future King.[185] How did the insertion of such a story come about? What the ancient readers understood by the star teaches us the reception history. A Matthew commentary of late antiquity quotes an apocryphal writing, the author of which was Adam's son Seth. He prophesied to a people of the Far East the future appearance of a star, and taught them how to worship it. The scripture had been handed down from generation to generation for a long time, and for just as long, each year after the wheat harvest, selected men with astrological knowledge and magicians climbed to the top of the 'victory mountain' (*mons victoralis*) to await the appearance of the star. They did this again and again in vain, until one day the star actually descended to the mountain. In it was the face of a newborn boy, but above it a sign resembling a cross. The star child ordered the magicians to travel to Judea. So they did, with the advancing star pointing the way.[186]

This miracle story is revealing to us in two respects. It informs us, first, that the ancient readers of Matthew have dated the birth of Jesus in the midsummer rather than winter. Accordingly, the Seth-Apocalypse, or at least its underlying tradition, should be older than the Constantinian version. Only since then was Jesus' birth located calendarically in the middle of winter. Second, we recognize that the Gospel of Matthew evoked an annual ritual, namely the observations of the rising of Sirius on mountain tops.[187] For this reason, magi climbed the *mons victoralis* every year after the wheat harvest.[188] With the rise of Sirius, the cereal harvest season ended everywhere in the Eastern Mediterranean. Even in Egypt, where the fields were harvested months earlier, the threshing continued for a long time. Instead of Sirius, however, a unique miracle star occurs in this story. This seems to be inspired by Augustus' dynastic founding myth, which replaced Sirius with a singular comet. Christ's birth-star should displace this. Augustus had said that he was born of the *sidus Iulium*, which was only meant metaphorically, but the Redeemer King Jesus himself was actually incarnated in the new miracle star. The sign of the cross, which rises above the head of the star child, caricatures the *sidus Iulium* hovering over the head of Caesar and his successor, an Augustan Sirius surrogate. Since Seth, the alleged author of this apocalypse, was assimilated to the Persian religious founder Zoroaster (Zarathustra),[189] the legend must be influenced by instructions for the observation of the rising Sirius, which has traditionally been attributed to him.[190] The fact that he was considered to be a Sirius-prophet is revealed in his Greek name Zoroastres, which contains the word for 'star' (*astron*).[191]

Luke's version of Jesus' nativity lacks the star motif, but he replaces it with the divine figure of an angel who reveals to shepherds that their Redeemer had just been born in the city of David. The light of the angel falling on them and shining on them infuses the shepherds with terror. Luke calls it *doxa*, 'glory',[192] evoking the stellar power and horror of ancient kings. In addition, Luke describes Jesus' birth as 'rising from the heights', which can only match the appearance of a star.[193] It seems, then, that Luke had the same Roman template in mind as Matthew, and consequently transformed the *gloria Caesaris*, which was manifested in the *sidus Iulium*, into the *doxa* given to Jesus from God. Both evangelists would have followed a common source. Whether this was a particular text or oral tradition is beyond our knowledge. But it can be assumed that a Christianized *sidus Iulium* played an important role in Nero's time in the spiritual struggle against Rome. Only then was there a precise motive for making shepherds appear as bearers of revelation. Nero's court poet Calpurnius Siculus had done the same when he imitated Vergil's *Eclogues*, and for that reason shepherds put the news of a miracle-comet, which had appeared at the emperor's accession to the throne, and outbid the splendour of *sidus Iulium*. The Gospel of Luke uses the bucolic ambience in the opposite sense of a national messianism. The herdsmen find the new-born Saviour in Bethlehem, where David once grew up as a shepherd.[194] That should mark Jesus as the new David, destined to rule Israel as a royal 'shepherd'. Thus, a legendary bandit who led a guerrilla war, conquered Jerusalem and usurped the throne of the king became a guide to a messianic career to be followed by Jesus.

The fact that Luke's Gospel and the Book of Acts only pretend that there is a relaxed relationship between Christians and Romans, and that an anti-Roman intention hides beneath the texts' surface, is most clearly seen in the dating of Jesus' birth in the year of a census ordered by Augustus.[195] Through Flavius Josephus, it is known that Judea was placed under direct Roman administration in AD 6 by such a census. This provincialization promptly triggered massive protests. Nationalists, who insisted that the land was the sole property of God, called for tax refusal and the shaking off of Roman rule.[196] Since then, rioters had repeatedly brought the country into turmoil. Thus, when Luke gave birth to the Son of God in this hour of need, he communicated to his readers a message readily understandable to them. They should see in the *lytrosis*, 'salvation', as hoped from Jesus, a release of the fetters that the Romans had laid on the enslaved people. Therefore, he made Jesus' birth the initial spark of a liberation movement that itself came about in the same year.[197]

Theological interpreters turn the meaning of the Lukan birth story on its head. They believe that the fact that Jesus' parents travelled to Bethlehem to be counted and registered shows their fidelity to the Romans. Instead, they are representatives of a national humiliation. Luke allegedly had wanted to demarcate the sacred family from Jewish resistance fighters, who then refused taxes and boycotted the census.[198] Thus, Jesus' own statement should be understood. When some Pharisees and followers of King Herod wanted to force Jesus to admit that he was a political rebel, they confronted him with the question of whether it was right to pay taxes. Then Jesus asked for a denarius, a Roman coin, on which the image of the Emperor was engraved with his name. Jesus then spoke the famous words: 'Give back to the emperor what belongs to him, and to God what belongs to God!'[199] On a cursory level, that sounds like a declaration of loyalty to the Roman occupying power, as if the Kingdom and the Empire could coexist peacefully. But behind the apparent call for tax payments hides a contrary message. As the emperor can only get back what he gave before, the case of tax would not apply. Consequently, only the imperial currency represented by the Roman coin held before Jesus can be meant. God's property, on the other hand, is the land expropriated by the Romans: whoever gives the Promised Land back to God must drive out the occupying power and its currency.[200]

Another passage, which is often used for a two-world doctrine, does not prove what it should. The Gospel of John puts the words 'My kingdom is not of this world' in Jesus' mouth when he is before Pilate.[201] But the Romans were never deceived by a spiritualized salvation concept that the Christians used to impersonate themselves as a politically benign group, knowing that the Kingdom of God for whom Jesus and his missionaries were advertising was yet to be realized on Earth. A purely heavenly kingdom, which already exists invisibly, requires no foundation and no propaganda. So Jesus' saying can only mean that the expected messianic kingdom has a heavenly model and derives its legitimacy from it. It is to come down from heaven to Earth.

Christian theologians believe that Jesus did not want his followers to bring about the dawn of the messianic end of the Earth by violent methods. Therefore, when he was arrested on the Mount of Olives, he prevented his followers from taking up arms and uttered the famous words: 'He who uses the sword will perish by the sword.'[202] In a hopeless emergency, this was an appropriate response that avoided unnecessary bloodshed. On the other hand, when theological exegetes interpret the saying of Jesus in the sense of a generally valid pacifist programme, they remove it from its narrative context. For in Luke's Gospel, in the preceding supper, Jesus commanded all his apostles to obtain swords.[203] Such militant mobilization explains why his opponents felt threatened by him and seized him in time before the Passover. The research literature acknowledges that Luke refers here to a zealot tradition that saw a freedom fighter in Jesus, yet he allegedly cited this to defuse it.[204] This would have been the reason why Jesus described two swords, which the disciples showed him, as sufficient. Of course, they could not expel the Romans with only two swords. Jesus' command to arm themselves is said to have been for future migrant missions in pairs, so that they could protect themselves against bandits.

There is no evidence, however, that missionaries carried weapons. So another interpretation is closer: at the Passover, two swords were indeed enough to commit an assassination against a Roman dignitary. Such a signal could have the hoped-for effect of inciting the people to revolt. Before the Jewish War of Liberation, 'terrorists' called *Sicarii* mingled with the assembled congregation and massacred collaborators with daggers that they hid under their robes.[205] A prominent high priest named Ananias was killed right at the beginning of the uprising.[206] Killing celebrities of his kind has always been the wish of freedom fighters. But if the militant picture of Jesus, which conveys Luke's special tradition, already existed at the time of Nero, then Christians could feel justified in performing an even more impressive symbolic action in harmony with their Redeemer.

On a symbolic date, the burning of Rome was an appeal not only to the Jews, but to all the peoples of the Mediterranean dominated by Rome, to free themselves from the Roman yoke. The Jesus of the Gospels accordingly longs for an eschatological baptism of fire and wants to set the whole Earth ablaze.[207] He did not come to bring peace, but division and the sword, as he says in the same context.[208] The martial imagery refers to the collapse of the family ties that cause Jesus' message.[209] It also, however, has a perfectly literal implication. Through Flavius Josephus, it is known that Jewish families actually split into pro-Roman and anti-Roman factions in the run-up to the Jewish revolt. The elders and the more fortunate advised themselves to submit to Roman rule, but many younger ones were ready to riot and wanted to resort to swords.[210]

Through the messianic star that leads the Magi to Bethlehem in Matthew, Jesus' role as Redeemer received an even more far-reaching explosive power that transcended the interior of the *Imperium Romanum*. For the Magi came from the Far East, where at that time not the Romans, but the Parthians, ruled, and returned to their homeland with the knowledge that world domination belonged to an Oriental king. Thus they brought to the Parthians, so to speak, the star of Caesar, who had threatened their empire, in a semantically reversed form. The Parthian Empire was now the only world power that could endanger Rome.[211] Those who rejected Roman supremacy in the Near East were therefore well advised to press for an ever-threatening invasion by the Parthians. A Parthian war in Neronian time could awaken hope for assistance in particular among the Jews seeking a war of liberation.[212] The previously mentioned oracle of the time, which expressed total Oriental expectation of the Redeemer, and that world domination would pass from the West to a king from the East, was understandable as an indirect invitation to the Parthian king to act as messianic saviour.

Since the Parthian Empire had replaced the Persian Empire and the Parthians were called Persians by the Romans, it was possible to pass the role of a Messiah to a Parthian king. As such, he would have been a new Cyrus, as Cyrus, the founder of the Achaemenid dynasty, allegedly freed the Jews from their Babylonian captivity and allowed them to rebuild Solomon's Temple. For all Jews loyal to the Persian Empire, who were content with a partial cultural sovereignty under the leadership of a high priest, Cyrus was therefore the first Messiah ever.[213] This made him a rival of a nationalist Messianism, for which only one man of David's line came into question as the future king. Both concepts are unbalanced in the Old Testament, and the New Testament texts have a similar hybrid mix. On the one hand a messianic star, which blends the stellar rule symbolism of Augustus and is experienced by the Jewish vassal king Herod as a threat to his power and position, announces a Davidic Messiah, who is recognized by the Far East as such. On the other hand, in the Apocalypse of John, the returning Christ wears a garment bearing the name 'King of Kings', the ancient royal title of the Achaemenids, which the Parthians had adopted.[214] This seems to reflect the messianic expectation of Christians who were more willing to join the Parthian king than to remain subservient to the Roman emperor. They considered the idea that the Jews could restore a politically autonomous Israel by their own accord to be an unrealistic utopia.

Indeed, the expectation of a Messiah in Parthian dress was by no means hopeless, as long as the Romans and the Parthians fought each other. In fact, Jews who came to Judea from Mesopotamia, which was under the rule of the Parthians, supported the national revolt.[215] But the hope that the Parthians themselves would campaign with the Jews against Rome did not come true. It ended in AD 63 via a peace agreement which provisionally finished the Roman–Parthian hostilities. Nevertheless, the peace always remained unstable. Even in the Flavian period, some tried to move the Parthians to intervene with stellar propaganda. This had a special punchline: with the Magi, the dominating star of the Achaemenids returned from the West to the East. In legendary traditions, the newborn Cyrus had been abandoned and nursed by a bitch.[216] The bitch was a symbolic animal of Sirius,[217] and had been stolen by Alexander and the imitating Romans from the Persians. The Gospel of Matthew causes the star to return to its former Persian territory with the Magi to promote Parthian support of a Davidic Messiah who would assist them in the common struggle against the Roman Empire.

The dispute between Romans and Parthians had brewed over control of Armenia.[218] Their King Tiridates, a brother of the then Parthian king, officially surrendered to the absent Roman emperor in Asia Minor by laying down his diadem before his portrait in AD 63.[219] Three years later, he made this symbolic gesture before Nero himself, in Rome, where he had travelled especially for this purpose with a train of Magi on a long country road. Here he laid his diadem at the feet of the emperor personally, and proved his divine honours by means of a proskynesis (prostration). Nero picked him up and put the diadem back on.[220] This was the usual ritual with which Roman emperors crowned Eastern vassal kings. Herod had previously bowed down before Augustus and received his royal crown back in the same way.[221]

The Jesus of the Gospels would have become such a marionette of Rome if he had followed the offer of the devil to give him dominion, if he worshipped him. But Jesus rejected this sovereign request, because he wanted to submit only to his divine father.[222] In this story of temptation, the devil vicariously assumes the role of the emperor;[223] the demons that Jesus fought make up his anti-God force. They deprive the souls of the people they take possession of, of their identity, so that they lose their self-control. Possession through demons acts as a narrative metaphor for the state of a foreign-dominated country in the Gospels. Jesus' exorcisms, on the other hand, promise a messianic act of liberation that will redeem his homeland from the state of national self-alienation. Therefore, the demons that Jesus forces to leave the possessed are called 'legion' in one case.[224] They are spiritual counterparts of the Roman occupying power whose expulsion is Jesus' concern.[225]

Therefore, the Christians could see an anti-Herod and anti-Tiridates in Jesus. It has long been recognized that Matthew has copied the Magi who were led by a star to Bethlehem from those Magi who accompanied Tiridates on his way to Rome.[226] The Gospel takes them back to the time of Augustus and provocatively does not let them travel to Rome but to Judea. If an imaginary comet had endowed both Augustus and Nero with heavenly legitimacy, a counter-comet now signals that a recognition of authority is due to Jesus alone. Thus, in Matthew's version of the natal story, traumatic experiences of the Augustan and Neronian times merge.[227] They present the new-born saviour as the future king, who, unlike Herod and Tiridates, will not submit to a foreign ruler.

That the divine reverence that Nero received from Tiridates and his Magi was a source of offence to opposing Christians provides a plausible explanation of why they chose AD 64 for an arson attack. At that time, the Armenian king was expected in Rome, so that he actually carried out the official submission before Nero, which he had symbolically done the year before, and thus sealed the agreed peace between the Romans and Parthians. This finally happened in AD 66. For Oriental enemies of Rome, who had hoped that a Parthian invasion would liberate their homeland from their Roman oppressors, the reason must have been enough to protest. They could not do anything more impressive than to set the capital of the *Imperium Romanum* on fire on 19 July, before the arrival of Tiridates.[228] On this day, the Redeemer was to return to Earth and destroy his enemies. For the arsonists, Christ was incarnated in the judging fire of the Dog Star. This could later give Matthew the idea of having a miracle star appear at the time of Jesus' birth, which eclipsed the comets with which Augustus and Nero had attested themselves monarchically. For, as seen, there is much to suggest that all these fictional comets were substitutes for the rising Sirius.

Conclusion

With Nero's death, the Julio-Claudian dynasty perished. But he lived on in a ghostly way in a series of coups, with people posing as Nero and agitating in the Eastern Mediterranean against the Flavian emperors. Paradoxically, their motives were the same as those which directed anti-Neronian Christians in AD 64: they wanted to persuade the Parthians to assist their attempt to expel the Romans from their country. As early as AD 69, a false Nero almost set the Parthians in motion.[229] A pseudo-Nero from the province of Asia recruited a growing number of followers in AD 80, took them to the Euphrates and found refuge with the Parthian King Artabanos, who made preparations to return him to Rome.[230] As late as AD 88/89, the Parthians supported a false Nero and reluctantly delivered him to the Romans.[231] For the Christians of the Flavian period, it was of course impossible to join such Neronian pretenders. They expressed their opposition in a different way: the star, whose message the Magi had brought into Parthian dominion, implicitly called for the Eastern enemies of Rome to take sides in favour of a Davidic Messiah. In this way, the Gospel of Matthew conserved revolutionary expectations of earlier generations. Such also seems to be behind the fire of Rome on 19 July AD 64. For Jesus' church, Nero was the Antichrist who merely parodied the true end-time king. To him, whom imperial propaganda praised as a luminous, benevolent star,[232] the Christians answered with a Redeemer in the guise of Sirius, whom no imperial power could withstand.

Notes

1. Acts 9.2, 18.25, and other references. Christians were first called *Christiani* in Antioch (Acts 11.26). Once they adopted this name, they risked political persecution. See Vittinghoff (1984).
2. Then there are Elijah and his disciple Elisha, who in turn have a mythical parallel in Moses and Joshua.
3. Ex 12; Jos 5.
4. To this and to the following, add Baudy (2006a), pp.25–49.
5. Lk 4.16–30. See Strobel (1972).
6. Lev 25.8.31. Joshua's land distribution: Jos 13–21.
7. For a comprehensive overview, see Hengel (2011); cf. also, e.g., Baumbach (1973); Horsley (1985); Horsley (1987); Horsley (2003); Krieger (1998); Baudy (2006b), pp.35–49; Aslan (2013), pp.33–107.
8. However, very few researchers believe that Jesus pursued political goals. Reimarus, who had first assumed this (1778; posthumously 1972), found only a few supporters. Exceptions include Eisler (1929–30), Brandon (1967) and Aslan (2013). Theißen (2004) considers Jesus and the early Christians to be anti-Roman, but sees them as pacifists. Bammel (1984) criticized the zealotic interpretation of Jesus from a traditional point of view.
9. Rom 12.4–6, 1 Cor 19.10, 12.12–16, Col 1.18, Eph 4.15f. See Baudy (2005b) for sources and bibliography.
10. On the political function of the resurrection myth, see Baudy (2005a). Theißen regards Jesus as belonging to the prophets who appeared unarmed and therefore represented a quietistic version of apocalypticism: e.g., Theißen (1997), p.396; Theißen (2003), p.503. That is a misjudgement, for all the prophets produced a threatening situation for the Romans, which could turn into violence at any time. Therefore, the Romans sent the military against them.
11. Num 9.15f., 10.34f.
12. On the destructive dimension of this spirit fire, cf. Baudy (2012); Baudy (2015).
13. I first represented this thesis in 1991; see the other works of Baudy in the bibliography below.
14. Livy 5.39.2ff, with 6.1.11. Neronian fire: Tac. *Ann.* 14.41.
15. Sources in Baudy (1991), p.47f., n.27.
16. Merkelbach (1995), p.110f.
17. Cens. *Die Nat.* 18.10; Gemin. *Astron.* 8.16–24.

18. Porph. *Nymph.* 24; see Solin. *Coll. Mem.* 32.12f.
19. Antiochus according to Rhetorius (Cumont & Boll, vol. 1, p.163); Lyd. *Mens.* 3.16: Psellos *de omnifaria doctrina* 125 (*PG* 122, col. 761); Gennadius *Dialogus Christiani cum Iudaeo* (Jahn (1893), p.38, 18ff.). See Baudy (1991), p.49 n.52. This tradition replaces the usual dating of the world conflagration in the summer solstice and the deluge in the winter solstice within the cosmic year: Berossos *FGrH* 680 F 21.
20. Merkelbach (1963), pp.14–28.
21. Sacrifice of reddish cattle: Diod. 1.88.3; Plut. *Is.* 31 (*Mor.* 363a); sacrifice of reddish donkeys: Plut. *Is.* 30f. (*Mor.* 362e, 363c). For Egyptian sources testifying to analogous victims, see Yoyotte (1980–81).
22. Manetho *FGrH* 609 F22. A sacrifice of typhonic humans is also asserted by Diod. 1.88.3, and Plut. *Is.* 72 (*Mor.* 380c).
23. Later historical updates of the myth are listed by Merkelbach (1963), pp.23–27.
24. Manetho in Jos. *C. Ap.* 1.26. There are good reasons to believe that the Hellenistic Exodus narratives are in the tradition of an older anti-Judaic original to which biblical tradition responded polemically: so Assmann (1998), pp.47–72.
25. Jos. *C. Ap.* 1.26 (249).
26. Mnaseas of Patara, in Jos. *C. Ap.* 2.9 (114); Damakritos *FGrH* F1; Apion in Jos. *C. Ap.* 2.7 (80). According to Tac. *Hist.* 5.3, the Israelites were led on their desert migration by a donkey herd to water and thus saved from dehydration.
27. Illustration in Guyot & Klein (1994), p.232. Christians as donkey worshippers: Tert. *Apol.* 1.14.1; Min. Fel. 28.7.
28. Poseidonios *FGrH* 87 F109.
29. This technique also includes the soteriological revaluation of the death of the cross: see Ebertz (1987).
30. E.g., Ham (2005), pp.23–30. On the other hand, Patsch (1971) argued for a political interpretation, but without considering Jesus a revolutionary prone to violence, such as Eisler and Brandon did.
31. Mt 21.1–11.
32. Mt 21.5 quotes only Sach 9.9. The cutting of the context favoured a pacifist misinterpretation.
33. Sach 9.13–15.
34. 1 Kings 1.33.
35. 2 Sam 16.2.
36. 2 Sam 18.9.
37. *Oracula Sibyllina* 5.29; Plut. *Mor.* 567e–f; Philostr. *Apoll.* 4.48.
38. Ps. Sen. *Oct.* 227–51. Commenting: Williams (1994), pp.188–91. On the other hand, Nero had himself celebrated as an Apollonian dragon slayer (*Carmina Einsiedlensia* 1.34). That this panegyric was meant ironically and aimed at imperial criticism, see Korzeniewski (1974), p.923, is I think unreasonable.
39. In Jewish apocalyptic already in the first century BC, Pompey was depicted as a dragon: Pseudo-Solomon *Odes* 2.25–29. After the destruction of Jerusalem, Rome was similarly bestialized (4 Esr 11f.). In *Oracula Sibyllina* 8.88 and Apoc 12.3, the fire-red dragon reflects the model of the also red Typhon (Plut. *Is.* 22), likewise the whore Babylon, dressed in purple and riding on a scarlet seven-headed animal (Apoc 17.3–5). See Busch (1996), p.61. Similar to Typhon, in the Apocalypse of John the two animals (Apoc 13) representing the red dragon, which meant the Roman Empire, are thrown alive into a lake of fire (19.20). Nero as a dragon-like Antichrist (Beliar) appears also in *Ascensio Isaiae* 4.1–14.
40. The following section is intended to supplement the basic work of Fuchs (1938), with a stellar component. In the vast research literature on ancient apocalypticism, Sirius to my knowledge remains unnoticed.
41. Ps.-Skyl. 233.
42. Plut. *Mor.* 326a. This refers to the imitation of Alexander by Roman generals: see Michel (1967); Kühnen (2008).

43. Plut. *Alex.* 3 dates Alexander's birth to the sixth of the month Hekatombaion. Converted, this day in 356 BC coincided with 19 July: Badian (1982), p.48, n.34, or 20 July: Miller (1975), p.229f.; Koch (2000), p.331, n.13. Both days corresponded with the rising of Sirius on the latitudes of the cities of Alexandria and Memphis: Olympiodorus 1.4 (Stüve, p.113). The date is to be regarded as unhistorical, as well as the competing dating to 6 Thargelion (Ael. *Hist.* 25), which need not concern us here. Alexander was to be associated with the rising Sirius and the concomitant constellation of Leo. In a legend dating back to Aristarchus, Philip II dreamed before the birth of his son that he had pressed a signet ring in which the image of a lion was engraved onto the body of his wife. This characterized Alexander as a hero inspired by lion-like courage: Plut. *Alex.* 2; *Vita Alexandri* 1.8.4 and 7. Baldus (1987), pp.408–16, related this to Alexander's signet ring, adopted from the Achaemenids, which later would have been worn by his Roman imitators Pompey and Antonius. On an aureus of Antonius, a lion with a star over the back was depicted. This is neither a mere reference to the stellar character of the lion, so Michel (1967), pp.120–24, nor a solar symbol, so Baldus (1987), pp.414–16. Envisaged is most probably Sirius, rising synchronously with the lion (schol. Arat. *Phaen.* 150). Curt. 9.6.8 designates Alexander as *columen ac sidus Macedoniae*. *Sidus* is not a constellation, but a single star. The anti-Greek Egyptian oracle literature seems to have responded to this stellar propaganda: the demotic Lamb Oracle refers to the Greek invaders as dogs and mentions among them a 'big dog' (vi.19–21). This cannot be other than their leader, that is, Alexander. Cf. Meyer (1997), p.184.
44. Sources at Ameling (1988).
45. Hom. *Il.* 22.25–32.
46. Hom. *Il.* 5.1–8.
47. Hom. *Il.* 11.56–66.
48. Richer (1999–2000) attempts to discover a broader Sirius Achilles typology in a comparative way.
49. Plut. *Is.* 77 (*Mor.* 270a). Avesta: Yasna 8.44 (Panaino).
50. Avesta: Yasna 8.20–33 (Panaino). Merkelbach (1963), pp.70–76, plausibly dates the origin of this myth, because of its Egyptian symbolism, to the time when Egypt was conquered by the Persians. Panaino, who edited the text and interpreted it comprehensively (1990–95), rejects Merkelbach's theory – (1995), ii.55–58 – and sees the myth as already anchored in the Indo-European tradition.
51. Avesta: Yasna 19.31–89 (Panaino).
52. Documentation by Kyrieleis (1986); see Bechtold (2011), pp.77–127. Possible Sirius references, however, are not envisaged here, as in other scholarship.
53. Cic. *Div.* 1.100; Livy 4.15; 16.8–11; Dion. Hal. *Rom. Ant.* 12.10–13.
54. Dion. Hal. *Rom. Ant.* 12.1 dates the event to the time of the rising of the Dog Star and refers to Egypt, where now the Nile was in flood.
55. Livy 5.18.9: *Romane, aquam Albanam cave lacu contineri, cave in mare manare suo flumine sinas; emissam per agros rigabis dissipatam rivis extingues.* See Puhvel (1973), pp.381–85; Puhvel (1988), pp.277–83.
56. Such as Niebuhr (1873), pp.407–20; and Schwegler (1858), p.217. The Troy-typology of the war against Veii has since been treated many times; see, for example, Kraus (1994).
57. Paus. 1.12.1. Both Achilles (Plut. *Pyrrh.* 1.13) and Alexander the Great (Plut. *Pyrrh.* 8.11) were models for Pyrrhos. Perret (1942) presented an unlikely thesis that the Trojan origin of the Romans was then invented by the Greeks. Rather, Pyrrhos seems to have used an already existing myth for his purposes. See Weber (1972), pp.213–15. Erskine (2001), pp.157–60, is sceptical.
58. Livy 40.6.1–40.22.8.
59. Livy 40.22.7.
60. It is an exaggeration that from the summit of Haimos there is a broad view as far as the Adriatic: Polyb. 34.12; Livy 40.22.5.

61. The closest analogy is the ritual observation of the rising of Sirius on a mountain peak on the island of Keos. This practice too belonged to a sacrificial feast with two addressees. Instead of Zeus and Helios, here Zeus and Sirius were recipients of the victim. According to the aetiological myth, the great shepherd Aristaeus once brought the Etesia to life for the first time and thus ended a drought catastrophe or a pernicious and human disease: Callim. *Aet.* 3 F75, 32ff. (Pfeiffer); Apoll. *Argon.* 2.516–27, with schol.; Diod. 4.82.2–3; Nigidius Figulus *Sphaerae Graec.* p.125f. (Swoboda); Hyg. *Astr.* 2.4; Serv. 1.14; Nonn. *Dion.* 5.269–79, 15.278–85. According to Herakl. Pont. F141 (Cic. *Div.* 1.130; Wehrli), the inhabitants of the island made predictions using the meteorological circumstances of the heliacal rising of Sirius, *salubrisne an pestilens annus futurus sit*. The similarity between the hill festivals celebrated at Keos and in Thrace has apparently created the myth that Aristaeus had wandered to Haimos at the end of his life and mysteriously disappeared there (Diod. 4.82.6). Analogous dog-star rites existed in the Cilician Taurus Mountains (Manil. *Astr.* 1.396–401), as well as in Egypt, where they were traced back to a certain Jachim (Aelian F105 [Hercher]). According to the astrological literature, revolts and changes of power were foretold here at the rising of Sirius: Nechepso and Petosiris F12 (Ries); Pseudo-Zoroaster in *Geoponica* 1.8 (Beckh). For the prognostic function of the Sirius rise, cf. Gundel (1927), pp.346–50.
62. *Mundum vultuque gubernat*, is said about Sirius at Manil. *Astr.* 1.407.
63. Apollod. *Bibl.* 1.6.3.
64. Cic. *Div.* 1.103; Val. Max. 1.5.3; Plut. *Aem.* 10. Vaahtera (2001), p.45, sees as the background of this omen only the similarity of the names Perseus and Persa, but does not recognize the stellar symbolism of the 'doggy'.
65. Plut. *Caes.* 60; Suet. *Jul.* 79; without attribution already mentioned in Cic. *Div.* 2.110. For Caesar's war plans, see Malitz (1984).
66. Plut. *Caes.* 61.2.
67. So also Koortbojan (2013), p.121f.
68. Extensively documented by Weinstock (1971). See Bechtold (2011), pp.161–225.
69. E.g., Plin. *Nat. Hist.* 2.93f. For further references and discussion, see Baudy (2001), pp.30–48.
70. Plut. *Ant.* 33.
71. Plut. *Ant.* 34.4, 37.5; Dio 48.39, 49.19. See Martin (1993), p.49.
72. Aug. *Res Gest.* 16.29; Just. 16.29, 42.3. On denarii of 19 BC, a kneeling Parthian (Phraates IV) is pictured, who surrenders the standards. See Hackl, Jacobs & Weber (2010), 2.590–93.
73. Baudy (2001), pp.44–47.
74. See the sources in Hackl, Jacobs & Weber (2010), 1.32.
75. Significantly, Calpurnius Siculus *Eclogae* 1.82f regarded the *sidus Iulium* as an omen for the coming civil wars. See, similarly, Obsequens 68. In the literature on the propaganda wars between Octavian and Antony, the *sidus Iulium* strangely goes unnoticed: Jeanmaire (1921); Scott (1933); Becher (1966); Fadinger (1969); Martin (1993); Clauss (1995). An exception is Pandey (2013) with the problematic thesis that Antony used the *sidus Iulium* ideologically earlier than Augustus.
76. Plin. *Nat. Hist.* 2.94: *interiore gaudio sibi illum (sc. sidus) natum seque in eo nasci interpretatus est.*
77. Dio 50.4; Plut. *Ant.* 54.9. See e.g., Becher (1966), p.24; Clauss (1995), p.45f.
78. Virg. *Aen.* 8.675-81.
79. Virg. *Aen.* 10.270–75.
80. Hor. *Od.* 1.37.21 calls Cleopatra a fatal monstrosity.
81. Serv. *Ecl.* 8.46 speaks of a star (*stella*), *quam quidam ad gloriam Caesaris iuvenis pertinere existimabant.*
82. App. *Civ.* 2.102.
83. Macrob. *Sat.* 1.14; Pliny *Nat. Hist.* 18.211; Plut. *Caes.* 59. See Malitz (1987); Bayer (2002). The model was the *Decree of Canopus* of Ptolemy III in 238 BC. From that time onwards, the day of the Sirius morning rise always should fall on the same calendar day.
84. See Baudy (2001), p.42.

85. Caesar reformed the late Republican calendar, which had 355 days (with months of twenty-eight to thirty-one days). Every second year, twenty-two or twenty-three days were inserted. Caesar in 46 BC interpolated two additional months between November and December. If the alleged sixty-seven intercalation days (Solin. *Coll. Mem.* 1.45; Dio 43.26.1) is supplemented by the leap month, which fell on 45 BC, one arrives at the ninety days claimed by Cens. *Die Nat.* 20.8.
86. For example, Ramsey & Licht (1997); Terio (2006), p.208, n.664.
87. 25 July as the day of the Sirius' heliacal rising: *Calendarium Gemini* p.212f. (Manitius). Serv. *Aen.* 3.141 erroneously names 24 June; the surviving *VIII. K. Iulias* is to be replaced by *VIII. K. Augustas* (= 25 July).
88. *InscrIt* xiii.78.
89. Dio 43.26.2 reports that others have claimed that Caesar had inserted an even greater number of days. This is an important indication of my thesis that the sixty-seven days Dio mentions are not based on tradition but on calculation. Therefore, we have to do an anachronistic calculation ourselves in reconstructing the fixed date, as I did – (2001), pp.38–42. To reproach this anachronism – Ramsey (2006), p.106f., n.136; Terio (2006), p.208, n.664 – is pointless. Even if the Venus festival fell on 25 July in 46 BC, this would not change much in my theory, since Caesar would only have replaced the Egyptian day of the Sirius early rising with the Roman date.
90. Plin. *Nat. Hist.* 2.94; Suet. *Caes.* 8.8; Dio 45.6–7.1; Serv. *Ecl.* 9.46. Like Gurval (1997); Matijević (2005), p.63; and Matijević (2006), p.146 – against the *opinio communis* – I do not consider the miraculous star a real comet, but an imaginary sign. According to Serv. *Aen.* 8.681 it was the persuasive work of Augustus that led the people to see in the star the soul of the deified Caesar. Rather, he invented the apotheosis together with the star.
91. Schmid (2005), p.53, n.195, objects to my theory: 'Above all, the argument that Augustus was able to invent a comet within the framework of an "*image campaign*", is skewed, for whose sighting a good 25 years later many of the eyewitnesses still lived.'
92. So Ramsey & Light (1997).
93. Serv. *Ecl.* 9.46 refers to Baebius Macer and the memoirs of Augustus as sources.
94. Just. 37.2. Again, Ramsey (1999) in my opinion has tried in vain to prove the reality of the two comets by Chinese annals.
95. Just. 38.7.
96. Just. 38.4.
97. In detail Hubaux (1958).
98. The Camillus–Augustus typology has often been dealt with in the research literature, e.g., Stübler (1941), p.71f.; Hellegouarc'h (1970); Haas (2015), pp.201–27.
99. Virg. *Ecl.* 9.46–50.
100. Virg. *Georg.* 4.281–559. Aristaeus receives the revelation of Proteus at the rising of Sirius: Virg. *Georg.* 4.425.
101. Virg. *Aen.* 10.270–75.
102. Virg. *Aen.* 3.73–171; the rising of Sirius: Virg. *Aen.* 3.140f.
103. Varro at *Virg. Aen.* 1.382. See Suerbaum (1985).
104. For the multivalence of the Vergilian star prodigies, cf. Engelhardt (1970); Borzsák (1983); Görler (1986); Botha (1991); West (1993); Williams (2004).
105. Bergmann (1998), p.151f.
106. Calp. *Ecl.* 1.77–88. Sen. *Nat. Quaest.* 7.17.2 proves that Nero's comet was identified with the *sidus Iulium*. A comet was considered a sign of Claudius' death: Plin. *Nat. Hist.* 2.92; Suet. *Claud.* 46. The dating of the Calpurnius poem is controversial. It can be left open as to whether it originated as early as AD 54 – Scheda (1969), p.60; Fugmann (1992), p.204; Merfeld (1999), pp.72–79; Vinchesi (2002), pp.141, 145 – or was later written, be it for the Neronia in AD 60 – so Toynbee (1942), p.90; Rogers (1953), p.241 – or that of AD 65 – so Korzeniewski (1971), p.4; Verdière (1985), p.1911f.; Bergmann (1998), p.14. In any case, the author would then mentally return to the year 54; see Schmitzer (2003), p.215.

107. The comets observed during Nero's reign are not literary inventions: see Rogers (1953); Grzynek (1999). They were regarded by the emperor's enemies as negative omens and transformed by Nero's propaganda into positive omens, as in AD 64 (Tac. *Ann.* 15.47; Suet. *Ner.* 36), when Nero's Egyptian astrologer Balbillus supported the emperor against the Piso conspiracy: Suet. *Ner.* 36. To him or to Nero's educator, Chairemon of Alexandria, who published a book on comets and explained that comets can also be positive signs (*FGrH* 618 F8; by Barzano (1985), p.1997 n.88, related to the comets of AD 60 or 64), the myth may originate in a story that a terrible comet had once appeared in Egypt and been named after the then ruling Typhon (Plin. *Nat. Hist.* 2.91). In Ps. Sen. *Oct.* 227–51, a hostile comet reflects Nero's tyranny, in which the un-godlike rule of Typhon is repeated: 237–44.
108. Tac. *Ann.* 15.44.1.
109. Suet. *Ner.* 38; Dio 62.16.
110. With contradictory locations: Suet. *Ner.* 38; Dio 62.18.
111. Tac. *Ann.* 15.44.2–5.
112. Tac. *Ann.* 15.38.1.
113. For further evidence, see Baudy (1991), pp.13–15. Many researchers attribute the charge of arson against Nero to his Troy poetry without taking into account the date of the fire.
114. Nero imitated Augustus, who wanted to be like Camillus, a second Romulus, and new founder of Rome (Suet. *Aug.* 7.2; Tac. *Ann.* 15.40.2). See Huss (1978), p.138.
115. Only a few examples from the extensive literature are mentioned here: Kienast (1994), pp.425–37; Holland (2000), pp.174–92; Krüger (2012), pp.219–40; Waldherr (2005), pp.210–17; Clauss (2015), pp.78–82; Sonnabend (2016), pp.110–29. Disagreeing with this, however, Champlin (2003), p.185, argues that Nero could have set the fire, but he was out of control. For the popular image of Nero, cf. the reception-historical contributions in Walde (2013).
116. Dio Chrys. *Or.* 21.10. Long after Nero's death, flowers lay on his grave: Suet. *Ner.* 57.
117. Such pseudo-Nerones are attested for AD 69 (Tac. *Hist.* 1.2, 2.8f.; Dio 63.9.3), AD 80 (Dio 66.9.3b) and AD 88–89 (Suet. *Ner.* 57). This influenced Jewish and Christian apocalyptic. See Lawrence (1978); Bodinger (1989); Tuplin (1989); Jakob-Sonnabend (1990), pp.133–51; Klauck (2003).
118. Baudy (1991). This position is agreed with by Bedenbender (2013), p.300f.; and Clauss (2015), pp.78–82. On the whole it is rejected on the grounds that the Christian fire apocalyptic would not be sufficient proof: Lafer (2001), p.33; Sonnabend (2016), p.122f. That is correct, but it is more about older research – Baudy (1991), p.46, n.10 – than my calendrical argument. Harwood (1992), p.306, also considers the Christians as arsonists. Grant (1978), p.138; Fini (1994), p.162f.; Kolb (2002), p.629; and Cross (2006), p.125, n.16, acknowledge the possibility of a Christian attack.
119. Tac. *Ann.* 15.44.5.
120. Representatives of this interpretation claim that Tacitus relieves the Christians of the charge of arson. But this is explained, as has been noted, solely by his anti-Neronian viewpoint. That Christians were condemned only for their *odium humani generis* is a thesis recently proposed by Lund (2008) and Schmitt (2011). Schmitt even denies that they were accused of arson, and Lund rejects that the *Chrestiani* mentioned by Tacitus were Christians at all.
121. Suet. *Claud.* 25.4. See Botermann (1996), pp.57–71; Cineira (1999), pp.2f., 201–24; Baudy (2006), p.44f.; Engberg (2007), pp.99–102.
122. Krauter (2009), p.133f., uses the apparent anachronism as an argument for the thesis that Suetonius' *Chrestus* could not have been Christ.
123. For example, Keresztes (1984), p.409; Keresztes (1989), pp.75–79.
124. For example, Henderson (1905), p.251; Weigall (1943), p.273; Bishop (1964), pp.82–88; Robichon (1986), p.254; Kienast (1994), pp.435–37; Holland (2000), p.183; Waldherr (2005), p.216; Incigneri (2003), p.215f.
125. Rom 13.1–7. That Paul's epistles nevertheless show an anti-Roman tendency is the thesis of an anti-imperial interpretation of Paul: Horsley (1997), pp.1–8, 140–47; Elliott (2008); Lopez (2008); Ehrensperger & Tucker (2010). Krauter (2009) and Kim (2008) are opposed to this.

126. 1 Cor 3.13–15: fire testing on the Day of the Lord. 1 Cor 2.6.2 prophesies the disempowerment of the rulers of this world. The gospel is the odour of death for some, the scent of life for others (2.16). God will soon crush Satan and put him under the feet of Christians (Rom 8.19–23). Similarly, in the pseudepigraphic Letter 2 Thess: Jesus reveals himself in the sky in blazing fire (1.7f.); he kills his adversary with the breath of his mouth and the lustre of his appearance (2.8).
127. 1 Cor 6.3.
128. Apoc 18.6.
129. Apoc 19.11–16.
130. Apoc 11.5.
131. Acts 2.
132. See Baudy (2015).
133. *Passio sancti Pauli apostoli* 23–44, 6–8 (Lipsius).
134. Cf. Rordorf (1982).
135. 2 Cor 10.4; 1 Thess 5.8; Rom 13.12. See also Eph 6.10–17.
136. For example, Macky (1998).
137. 1 Thess 5.1; Mt 24.43f.; Lk 12.39f.; Apoc 3.3; 16.15; 2 Peter 3.10.
138. Gospel of Thomas, Logion 98. Lüdemann & Janßen (1997), p.130, trace the parable back to the historical Jesus.
139. Rom 13.12.
140. Schelkle (1981), p.139, conversely, believes that Christian metaphors have demilitarized Jewish apocalypticism: anyone who claims this has to bear the burden of proof.
141. Tac. *Hist*. 4.54.1–3; see Baudy (1991), p.26.
142. Jos. *Bell. Jud*. 2.14.6 (293).
143. See Kippenberg (1983).
144. Jos. *Bell. Jud*. 6.5.4 (312f.); Tac. *Hist*. 5.13; Suet. *Vesp*. 4.5.
145. This happened through the Jewish defector Flavius Josephus: Jos. *Bell. Jud*. 3.8.9 (399–404). Rabbinic Judaism sought favour with the Romans using a legend, which attributed a corresponding prophecy to Johanan b. Zakkai (Goldschmidt).
146. Jos. *Bell. Jud*. 6.5.3 (288f.).
147. Jos. *Bell. Jud*. 7.5.4 (123f.).
148. Tac. *Hist*. 4.81f.; Suet. *Vesp*. 7.1.
149. Philostr. *Apoll*. 5.20. See Zimmermann (2003).
150. Dio 65.8.
151. Coin pictures show Isis-Sothis riding a dog in the tympanum of the temple: Merkelbach (1995), p.587, fig. 111. 'I'm the one who rises in the dog's star,' says the goddess of herself in the Isis aretalogies: Merkelbach (1995), p.116.
152. Jos. *Bell. Jud*. 4.10.6 (616). According to Jos. *Bell. Jud*. 4.11.5 (654), in return Vespasian received in Alexandria congratulations from Rome, which were also called 'good news'.
153. Thus, in the inscribed calendar decree issued in the province of Asia, which ordered that the year should henceforth begin on the day on which the world saviour Augustus was born: Leipoldt & Grundmann (1982), pp.205–07.
154. Mk 1.14f. Recent research considers Mark to be the author of a 'counter-gospel' who projected back to the time of Jesus experiences from the time of Vespasian: Theißen (1999); Ebner (2003); Heininger (2009); Bedenbender (2013).
155. Hippol. *Ref*. 4.48.12. See Baudy (1991), p.29.
156. Palladius *Opus Agriculturae* 7.9; see Baudy (1986), pp.13–22.
157. According to Aratus *Phaen*. 332–34, the rising Sirius rages also in tree plantations: only the vital plants survive the test. Trees were planted or transplanted in the Near East at this time (Theophr. *Hist. Plant*. 2.6.4; Plin. *Nat. Hist*. 13.37). Theophrastus calls the trees that were destroyed by Sirius *astróbleta*, 'slain by the star' (*Caus. Plant*. 5.9.1). For this he forms the nouns *astrobolía* (5.9.2) and *astrobolesía* (5.9.4). Sirius was considered a dog spitting fire:

Germ. *Aratus* 334; Manil. *Astr.* 5.207 (*latratque Canicula flammas*); compare Manil. *Astr.* 5.17 (*portans incendia*). See Ricoux (1996), pp.140, 142.
158. Tac. *Ann.* 15.44.4.
159. To ward off the damaging effect of the dog star, the Romans sacrificed reddish dogs at the Robigalia in April (Festus, p.358, 27L); cf. p.39, 13L; Ovid *Fasti* 4.905–42; Plin. *Nat. Hist.* 18.14). Of course, this did not happen, as Ovid falsely asserts (*Fasti* 4.904), because the dog star had risen on 25 April, but rather because its periodically manifesting power during the summer ascent extended over the whole year. Cf. Serv. *Georg.* 4.424. The Robigalia were held at the time of the heliacal setting of Sirius.
160. Plin. *Nat. Hist.* 29.56f; Plut. *Fort. Rom.* 12 (*Mor.* 324d–326a); Ael. *Nat. An.* 12.33; Lyd. *Mens.* 4.114; Serv. *Georg.* 8.650. August. *Civ.* 2.22 mentions only the ritual worship of the goose.
161. So Ungern-Sternberg (2000), p.217.
162. See Pliny *Nat. Hist.* 2.152.
163. Lyd. *Mens.* 4.114.
164. See e.g., Theißen (1983); Döring (2006), pp.101–07.
166. See especially Croissan (1994).
166. Lang (2010).
167. Suet. *Vesp.* 13; cf. Dio 65.13; Suet. *Dom.* 10.1.
168. Plut. *Alex.* 14.2. According to Diog. Laert. 6.60, he said to Alexander, who introduced himself as 'the great king', confidently, 'And I am Diogenes, the dog.'
169. Kerkidas of Megalopolis F1 (Powell *CA*); *Anth. Pal.* 7.64; Antipater of Thessalonica (*Anth. Pal.* 11.158). For this epigram poetry, cf. Häusle (1989).
170. I cannot understand the thesis of Navia (1998), p.125f., that Diogenes' cosmopolitanism (Diog. Laert. 6.63, 6.72) would have inspired Alexander to found a universal empire.
171. Based on other observations, Ricoux (2001) also concluded that Jesus was seen as Sirius by his followers. But she does not recognize the subversive message of this assignment, and also overlooks the meaning of 19 July, as she relates all the testimonies to 25 July, the Roman date of the heliacal rising of Sirius.
172. Lucian *De morte Peregrini*. The often-asked question as to whether Lucian's work reflects the historical reality or should be regarded as a literary fiction cannot be discussed here. Even if Lucian invented many things, his portrayal would be revealing of the opinion formed about Christians and Cynics in second-century AD antiquity.
173. Drerichs (1951); Kloft (1994); Hartwich (1994); Huttner (1997); Talbert (1978).
174. Dio Chrys. *Or.* 1.84.
175. Diog. Laert. 9.12–14 quotes an exchange of letters between Dareios and Herakleitos, in which the latter rejects an invitation to come to the royal court. So also Ps.-Herakl. *Ep.* 4. On the transference of Cynic features to Herakleitos: Du Toit (1997), pp.140–47.
176. Ps. Hes. *Scut.* 393–401.
177. Ps. Hes. *Scut.* 153.
178. Plin. *Nat. Hist.* 18.271 (according to Caesar) dates the appearance of the Regulus to 30 July, the rising of Sirius to 17 July, when the sun entered the lion's first degree (*Nat. Hist.* 18.269). The choice of 17 instead of 19 July is explained by the calculation as seen from a more southern latitude. The indication of 21 (Solin. *Coll. Mem.* 32.12) or 22 July (schol. Arat. *Phaen.* 150) presupposes still another place of observation for the synchronous entry of the sun into the lion and the Sirius rising, although the latter has been traditionally placed on 19 July.
179. 1 Peter 5.8.
180. Apoc 5.5. The opposing symbolism of the lion manifests itself in a puzzle of the apocryphal Gospel of Thomas (Logion 7).
181. *Oracula Sibyllina* 5.29, 8.157.
182. In addition, see Pfister (1937). Controversial in later research: Rose (1948); Simon (1955); Aune (1990); Hartwich (1994).
183. This was already seen before Pfister: Ackermann (1912), p.442.

184. See Baudy (2001), pp.48–69.
185. Mt 2.
186. *Opus imperfectum in Matthaeum* (*PG* 56, 637f.). For scholarship on the dating, see Baudy (2001), p.51, n.57; on the Iranian background, see Baudy (2001), pp.54–57, with n.84.
187. For references, see above, n.61.
188. Such as Baudy (1991), p.32; and Ricoux (1995), p.151; Ricoux (2001).
189. Cf. Bidez & Cumont (1938), 1.45f.; Baudy (1991), pp.23f., 32f.
190. Pseudo-Zoroaster in *Geoponica* 1.8, 2.15.
191. Cassel (1886), pp.15–23.
192. Lk 2.8f.
193. Lk 1.78. See Schreiber (2009), p.66.
194. Luke names Bethlehem the city of David: Lk 2.4. Here young David once guarded the sheep (1 Sam 16:11), and Matthew quotes the prophecy that a leader will come forth from Bethlehem to feed the people of Israel (Mt 2.6: Micah 5). See 2 Sam 5.2; Ez 34.23; Psalm 78.70f.; Kollmann (2009), p.35. Wolter (2000), p.507f., rejects a Davidic typology and sees Jesus' natal story standing alone in the bucolic tradition of paganism. Conversely, Schürmann (1969), pp.104–09, and Fitzmyer (2006), p.395, argue for a purely inner-Jewish background. Both positions are not sustainable. The bucolic motifs counteract the Roman power propaganda – see Schreiber (2009), pp.28–54, 65, 67; (2011), p.92 – and are quite compatible with a Davidian messianism: see Schmithals (1973).
195. Lk 2.1.
196. Jos. *Jud. Ant.* 18.1.1 (1–8).
197. See Baudy (2001), p.50f.; Baudy (2002), p.61f. This is attributed to a particular anti-Roman source of Luke by Braunert (1957). Against this, see Schreckenberg (1980), p.105. I do not wish to explore the attempts to prove that the journey of Joseph and Mary to Bethlehem is historically credible, e.g., Rubel (2011).
198. E.g., Moehring (1972); Klein (2000), p.207f.
199. Mk 12.13–17; Mt 22.15–22; Lk 20.20–26.
200. See Bünker (1986); Horsley (1987), pp.306–17; Horsley (2003), p.99; Schreiber (2004), p.94f.; Herzog (2005), pp.182–92; Baudy (2002), p.42f.
201. John 18.36.
202. Mt 26.52.
203. Lk 22.36.
204. See for example, Theißen (2002), p.118. For a counter-argument, see Baudy (2002a), pp.48–50.
205. Jos. *Jud. Ant.* 20.8.18 (185–88).
206. Jos. *Bell. Jud.* 2.17.9 (441).
207. Lk 12.49–52.
208. Lk 12.49–52 (division); Mt 10.34 (sword).
209. Lk 12.52f.; Mt 10.35–37.
210. Jos. *Bell. Jud.* 4.3.2 (131–33). See Baudy (2015), p.49.
211. Just. 41.1.1: world domination shared between Romans and Parthians.
212. Such hopes could correspond to the mistrust of the Romans against the Parthians, despite existing contacts, see Russell (2015), p.258f.
213. Is 44.24–48.22; 2 Chron. 36.22f.
214. Apoc 19.11–16. The Mule Rider is to be identified in my opinion with the first apocalyptic rider in Apoc 6.3. He is armed with a Parthian-style bow which implies the crossing of the Euphrates' border.
215. Dio 65.4.3. In his speech to the insurgents, Agrippa II met wider expectations: Jos. *Bell. Jud.* 2.16.5 (388f.). See Baudy (2001), p.57.
216. Just. 1.4.10. Herodotus knows the myth, but humanizes the female dog as the wife of a shepherd; she was called Kyno (Spako in Persian), 'bitch': Hdt. 1.110.
217. Ricoux (1999), p.224; Ricoux (2000), p.73.
218. Ziegler (1964), pp.67–75; Heil (1997); Ehrhardt (1998).

219. Tac. *Ann.* 15.29.1.
220. Pliny *Nat. Hist.* 30.16; Suet. *Nero* 13; Dio 63.1.1–5.2. The historicity of Tiridates' speech as quoted by Dio is doubted by Müller (2014), p.304f.
221. Jos. *Bell. Jud.* 1.20.1–3 (386–93), *Jud. Ant.* 6.6.6 (187).
222. Mt 4.8–10; Lk 4.5–8.
223. So Theißen (1989), pp.215–32, who opposes an apolitical understanding of Jesus' attitude. See Baudy (2002), p.45.
224. Mk 5.1–13; see Mt 8.28–32; Lk 8.26–33.
225. Reinach (1903); Theißen (1974), p.253; Theißen (1989), p.119; Baudy (2002), p.43f.; Guijarro (2002), pp.48–62; Strecker (2002), pp.48–62; Horsley (2003), p.67f; Klinghardt (2007); Lau (2007); Bedenbender (2013), pp.266–77.
226. Dieterich (1911); Cumont (1933); Gagé (1968), pp.96–113.
227. On the other hand, van Kooten (2015), pp.570–78, 588, unilaterally advocates the Augustan period as a reference point.
228. Baudy (1991), p.31f; Baudy (2001), pp.56–64.
229. Tac. *Hist.* 1.2.2. He was a slave from the Pontus, or a freedman from Italy, who recruited deserters in the East: Tac. *Hist.* 2.8.
230. Dio 66.19.3.
231. Suet. *Nero* 57. Nero's alleged plan to flee to the Parthians (Suet. *Nero* 47) is a legend inspired by the pseudo-Nerones.
232. Sen. *Clem.* 1.3.3.

Bibliography

Ackermann, E., 'Der leidende Hercules des Seneca', *RhM* 67 (1912), pp.425–71.
Ameling, W., 'Alexander und Achilleus. Eine Bestandsaufnahme', in Will, W. (ed.), *Zu Alexander d. Gr. Festschrift Gerhard Wirth zum 60. Geburtstag* (Amsterdam, 1988), pp.657–92.
Aslan, R., *Zelot. Jesus von Nazareth und seine Zeit* (Reinbek bei Hamburg, 2013).
Assmann, J., *Moses der Ägypter. Entzifferung einer Gedächtnisspur*, 6th edn (München, 1998).
Aune, D.E., 'Heracles and Christ: Heracles Imagery in the Christology of Early Christianity', in Balch, D.L., Ferguson, E. & Meeks, W.A. (eds), *Greeks, Romans, and Christians* (Minneapolis, 1990), pp.3–19.
Badian, E., 'Greeks and Macedonians', in Barr-Sharrar, B. & Borza, E.N. (eds), *Macedonia and Greece in Late Antiquity and Early Hellenistic Times* (Washington, 1982), pp.33–51.
Baldus, H.R., 'Die Siegel Alexanders des Großen. Versuch einer Rekonstruktion auf literarischer und numismatischer Grundlage', *Chiron* 17 (1987), pp.395–449.
Bammel, E., 'The Revolution Theory from Reimarus to Brandon', in Bammel, E. & Moule, C.F.D. (eds), *Jesus and the Politics of his Day* (Cambridge, 1984), pp.11–68.
Barzano, A., 'Cheremone di Alessandria', *ANRW* 2.32.2 (1985), pp.1981–2001.
Baudy, G., *Adonisgärten. Studien zur antiken Samensymbolik* (Frankfurt, 1986).
Baudy, G., *Die Brände Roms. Ein apokalyptisches Motiv in der antiken Historiographie* (Hildesheim, 1991).
Baudy, G., 'Das Evangelium des Thamus und der Tod des "großen Pan". Ein Zeugnis romfeindlicher Apokalyptik aus der Zeit des Kaisers Tiberius?', *ZAC* 4 (2000), pp.13–48.
Baudy, G., 'Der messianische Stern (Mt 2) und das sidus Iulium. Zum interkulturellen Zeichengehalt antiker Herrschaftslegitimation', in Beltz, W. & Tubach, J. (eds), *Religiöser Text und soziale Struktur* (Halle, 2001), pp.23–69.
Baudy, G., 'Evangelium und Sohngottmythos. Zur Entstehung einer subversiven Textgruppe in der frühen Kaiserzeit', in Nischik, R.M. & Rosenthal, C. (eds), *Schwellentexte der Weltliteratur* (Konstanz, 2002), pp.33–69.
Baudy, G., '"Auferstehung". Codierung nationaler Wiedergeburt im transkulturellen Dialog der Antike', in Pietruschka, U. (ed.), *Gemeinsame kulturelle Codes in koexistierenden Religionsgemeinschaften* (Halle, 2005a), pp.33–74.

Baudy, G., 'Heiliges Fleisch und sozialer Leib. Ritualfiktionen in antiker Opferpraxis und christlicher Eucharistie', in Gottwald, F.-T. & Kolmer, L. (eds), *Speiserituale. Essen, Trinken, Sakralität* (Stuttgart, 2005b), pp.45–68.

Baudy, G., 'Seuchenmetaphorik im ersten Jahrhundert n. Chr. Die Ausbreitung der Christusbewegung, ihre Bewertung durch das romloyale Judentum und die römische Religionspolitik', in Beltz, W. & Tubach, J. (eds), *Expansion und Destruktion in lokalen und regionalen Systemen koexistierender Religionsgemeinschaften* (Wittenberg, 2006a), pp.25–55.

Baudy, G., 'Heiliger Krieg und Messianismus. Historische Hintergründe des Josuamythos und dessen typologische Funktion im eschatologischen Aktionsprogramm der jüdisch-christlichen Gottesstaatsbewegung', in Feichtinger, B. & Seng, H. (eds), *Krieg und Kultur* (Konstanz, 2006b), pp.21–61.

Baudy, G., 'Biblische Feuermetaphorik. Die Feuertaufe der Auserwählten und die erntezeitlichen Determinanten von Weltenbrand und Höllenfeuer', in Tubach, J., Drost-Abgarjan, A. & Vashalomidze, S.G. (eds), *Sehnsucht nach der Hölle? Höllen- und Unterweltsvorstellungen in Orient und Okzident* (Wiesbaden, 2012), pp.101–25.

Baudy, G., '"Feuerzungen" Zu den politischen Implikationen einer narrativen Trance-Metapher im Gründungsmythos der christlichen Kirche', in Schüttpelz, E. & Zillinger, M. (eds), *Begeisterung und Blasphemie* (Bielefeld, 2015), pp.45–55.

Baumbach, G., 'Die antirömischen Aufstandsgruppen', in Maier, J. (ed.), *Literatur und Religion des Frühjudentums* (Würzburg, 1973), pp.273–83.

Bayer, K., 'Antike Zeitmessung. Die Kalenderreform des Gaius Iulius Caesar', in Herzog, M. (ed.), *Der Streit um die Zeit. Zeitmessung – Kalenderreform – Gegenzeit – Endzeit* (Stuttgart), pp.35–64.

Becher, I., *Das Bild der Kleopatra in der griechischen und lateinischen Literatur* (Berlin, 1966).

Bechtold, C., *Gott und Gestirn als Präsenzformen des toten Kaisers* (Göttingen, 2011).

Bedenbender, A., *Frohe Botschaft am Abgrund. Das Markusevangelium und der jüdische Krieg* (Leipzig, 2013).

Bergmann, M., *Die Strahlen der Herrscher. Theomorphes Herrscherbild und politische Symbolik im Hellenismus und in der römischen Kaiserzeit* (Mainz, 1998).

Bidez, J. & Cumont, F., *Les mages hellénisés*, 2 vols (Paris, 1938).

Bishop, J., *Nero. The Man and the Legend* (London, 1964).

Bodinger, M., 'Le mythe de Néron et l'Apocalypse de Saint Jean au Talmud de Babylon', *RHR* 206 (1989), pp.21–40.

Borzsák, I., 'Innoxia flamma', *Listy filologicke* 106 (1983), pp.33–37.

Botermann, H., *Das Judenedikt des Kaisers Claudius* (Stuttgart, 1996).

Botha, A.D., 'The Stars as a Theme in the Aeneid', *Akroterion* 36 (1991), pp.11–24.

Brandon, S.G.F., *Jesus and the Zealots. A Study of the Political Factor in Primitive Christianity* (Manchester, 1967).

Braunert, H., 'Der römische Provinzialzensus und der Schätzungsbericht des Lukas-Evangeliums', in Braunert, H., *Politik, Recht und Gesellschaft in der griechisch-römischen Antike* (Stuttgart, 1957/1980), pp.213–54.

Bünker, M., '"Gebt dem Kaiser, was des Kaisers ist!" – aber: Was ist des Kaisers?', *Kairos* 28 (1986), pp.85–98.

Busch, P., *Der gefallene Drache. Mythenexegese am Beispiel von Apokalypse 12* (Tübingen, 1996).

Cassel, P., *Zoroaster, sein Name und seine Zeit* (Berlin, 1886).

Champlin, E., *Nero* (Cambridge MA, 2003).

Cineira, D.A., *Die Religionspolitik des Kaisers Claudius und die paulinische Mission* (Freiburg, 1999).

Clauss, M., *Kleopatra* (München, 1995).

Clauss, M., *Ein neuer Gott für die alte Welt. Die Geschichte des frühen Christentums* (Berlin, 2015).

Croissan, J.D., *Der historische Jesus* (München, 1994).

Cumont, F., 'L'iniziazione di Nerone da parte di Tiridate d'Armenia', *Rivista di Filologia d'istruzione classica* NS 11 (1933), pp.145–54.

Dieterich, A., 'Die Weisen aus dem Morgenland', in Dieterich, A., *Kleine Schriften* (Leipzig, 1902/1911), pp.271–86.

Döring, K., *Die Kyniker* (Bamberg, 2006).
Drerichs, W., *Herakles, Vorbild des Herrschers in der Antike*, Diss. (Köln, 1951).
Du Toit, D.S., *THEIOS ANTHROPOS. Die Verwendung von theios anthropos und sinnverwandten Ausdrücken in der Literatur der Kaiserzeit* (Tübingen, 1997).
Ebertz, M.N., *Das Charisma des Gekreuzigten: Zur Soziologie der Jesusbewegung* (Tübingen, 1987).
Ebner, M., 'Evangelium contra Evangelium. Das Markusevangelium und der Aufstieg der Flavier', *BN* 116 (2003), pp.28–42.
Ehrensperger, K. & Tucker, J.B. (eds), *Reading Paul in Context: Explorations in Identity Formation* (London, 2010).
Ehrhardt, N., 'Parther und parthische Geschichte bei Tacitus', in Wiesehöfer, J. (ed.), *Das Partherreich und seine Zeugnisse* (Stuttgart, 1998), pp.295–307.
Eisler, R., *ΙΗΣΟΥΣ ΒΑΣΙΛΕΥΣ ΟΥ ΒΑΣΙΛΕΥΣΑΣ. Die messianische Unabhängigkeitsbewegung vom Auftreten Johannes des Täufers bis zum Untergang Jakobs des Gerechten nach der neuerschlossenen Eroberung von Jerusalem des Flavius Josephus und den christlichen Quellen*, 2 vols (Heidelberg, 1929/30).
Elliott, N., *The Arrogance of Nations. Reading Romans in the Shadow of Empire* (Minneapolis, 2008).
Engberg, J., *Impulsore Chresto. Opposition to Christianity in the Roman Empire c. 50–250* AD (Frankfurt, 2007).
Engelhardt, W. von, 'Der vom Himmel gefallene Stern. Zu Vergil, Aeneis II 692–700', in Gaiser, K. (ed.), *Das Altertum und jedes neue Gute* (Stuttgart, 1970), pp.459–75.
Erskine, A., *Troy Between Greece and Rome. Local Tradition and Imperial Power* (Oxford, 2001).
Fadinger, V., *Die Begründung des Prinzipats. Quellenkritische und staatsrechtliche Untersuchungen zu Cassius Dio und der Parallelüberlieferung* (Berlin, 1969).
Fini, M., *Nero. Zweitausend Jahre Verleumdung. Eine andere Biographie* (München, 1994).
Fitzmyer, J.A., *The Gospel According to Luke (I–IX). Introduction, Translation, and Notes* (New Haven, 2006).
Fuchs, H., *Der geistige Widerstand gegen Rom in der antiken Welt* (Berlin, 1938).
Fugmann, J., 'Nero oder Severus Alexander? Zur Datierung der Eklogen des Calpurnius Siculus', *Philologus* 36 (1992), pp.202–07.
Gagé, J., *'Basileia'. Les Césars, les rois d'Orient et les 'Mages'* (Paris, 1968).
Gelardini, G., *Christus Militans. Studien zur politisch-militärischen Semantik im Markusevangelium vor dem Hintergrund des ersten jüdisch-römischen Krieges* (Leiden, 2016).
Görler, W., 'Kontrastierende Szenenpaare: Indirekte Präsenz des Autors in Vergils Aeneis', *RhM* 129 (1986), pp.285–305.
Grant, M., *Nero. Despot – Tyrann – Künstler* (München, 1978).
Grzynek, E., 'L'astrologie et son exploitation politique: Néron et les comètes', in Croisille, J.-M., Martin, R. & Perrin, Y. (eds), *Neronia V. Néron, histoire et légende* (Clermont-Ferrand, 1999), pp.113–24.
Guijarro, S., 'Die politische Wirkung der Exorzismen Jesu. Gesellschaftliche Reaktionen und Verteidigungsstrategien in der Beelzebul-Kontroverse', in Stegemann, W., Malina, B.J. & Theißen, G. (eds), *Jesus in neuen Kontexten* (Stuttgart, 2002), pp.4–74.
Gundel, W., 'Sirius' *RE* 5 (1927), pp.314–51.
Gurval, R.A., 'Caesar's Comet: The Politics and Poetics of an Augustan Myth', *MAAR* 42 (1997), pp.39–71.
Guyot, P. & Klein, R., *Das frühe Christentum bis zum Ende der Verfolgungen. Vol 2. Die Christen in der heidnischen Gesellschaft* (Darmstadt, 1994).
Haas, P., *Livius, Dionysios, Augustus, Machiavelli. Ein diskursanalytischer Vergleich der römischen Frühgeschichte bei Livius und Dionysios von Halikarnassos und die Rezeption ihrer livianischen Darstellung im Werk des Niccolò Machiavelli* (Wiesbaden, 2015).
Hackl, U., Jacobs, B. & Weber, D. (eds), *Quellen zur Geschichte des Partherreiches. Textsammlung mit Übersetzungen und Kommentaren*, vols 1–3 (Göttingen, 2010).
Häusle, H., *Sag mir, o Hund – wo der Hund begraben liegt* (Hildesheim, 1989).

Ham, C.A., *The Coming King and the Rejected Shepherd. Matthew's Reading of Zechariah's Messianic Hope* (Sheffield, 2005).
Hartwich, W.D., 'Herakles und Jesus Christus als Märtyrer und Imperatoren. Die Gründungsmythen Roms und seiner Feinde', in Rudolph, E. (ed.), *Mythos zwischen Philosophie und Theologie* (Darmstadt, 1994), pp.5–29, 201–03.
Harwood, W., *Mythology's Last Gods: Yahweh and Jesus* (Buffalo, 1992).
Heil, M., *Die orientalische Außenpolitik des Kaisers Nero* (München, 1997).
Heininger, B., '"Politische Theologie" im Markusevangelium. Der Aufstieg Vespasians zum Kaiser und der Abstieg Jesu ans Kreuz', in Mayer, C. (ed.), *Augustinus – Ethik und Politik. Zwei Würzburger Augustinus-Studientage* (Würzburg, 2009), pp.171–201.
Hellegouarc'h, J., 'Le principat de Camille', *REL* 48 (1970), pp.112–32.
Henderson, B.W., *The Life and Principate of the Emperor Nero* (Rome, 1968; 1st edn London, 1905).
Hengel, M., *Die Zeloten. Untersuchungen zur jüdischen Freiheitsbewegung in der Zeit des Herodes I. bis 70 n. Chr.* (Tübingen, 3rd revised and augmented ed., 2011).
Herzog, W.R., *Prophet and Teacher. An Introduction to the Historical Jesus* (Louisville, 2005).
Holland, R., *Nero. The Man Behind the Myth* (Stroud, 2000).
Horsley, R.A. & Hanson, J.S., *Bandits, Prophets and Messiahs. Popular Movements at the Time of Jesus* (San Francisco, 1985).
Horsley, R.A., *Jesus and the Spiral of Violence: Popular Jewish Resistance in Roman Palestine* (San Francisco, 1987).
Horsley, R.A., *Paul and the Empire. Religion and Power in Roman Imperial Society* (Harrisburg, 1997).
Horsley, R.A., *Jesus and Empire: The Kingdom of God and the New World Disorder* (Minneapolis, 2003).
Horsley, R.A., 'By the Finger of God: Jesus and Imperial Violence', in Matthews, S. & Gibson, E.L. (eds), *Violence in the New Testament* (New York, 2005), pp.51–80.
Hubaux, J., *Rome et Véies. Recherches sur la chronologie légendaire du moyen âge romain* (Paris, 1958).
Huss, W., 'Die Propaganda Neros', *AC* 47 (1978), pp.129–48.
Huttner, U., *Die politische Rolle der Heraklesgestalt im griechischen Herrschertum* (Stuttgart, 1997).
Incigneri, B.J., *The Gospel to the Romans. The Setting and Rhetoric of Mark's Gospel* (Leiden, 2003).
Jakob-Sonnabend, W., *Untersuchungen zum Nero-Bild der Spätantike* (Hildesheim, 1990).
Jeanmaire, H., 'La politique religieuse d'Antoine et de Cléopatre', *RA* 19 (1921), pp.241–61.
Keresztes, P., 'Nero, the Christians and the Jews in Tacitus and Clement of Rome', *Latomus* 43 (1984), pp.404–13.
Keresztes, P., *Imperial Rome and the Christians from Herod the Great to about 200 AD*, vol. 1 (Lanham, 1989).
Kienast, D., 'Der Brand Roms und die Christen', in Kienast, D., *Kleine Schriften* (Aalen, 1994), pp.425–41.
Kim, S., *Christ and Caesar. The Gospel and the Roman Empire in the Writings of Paul and Luke* (Grand Rapids, 2008).
Kippenberg, H.G., '"Dann wird der Orient herrschen und der Okzident dienen." Zur Begründung eines gesamtorientalischen Standpunktes im Kampf gegen Rom', in Bolz, N.W. & Hübener, W. (eds), *Spiegel und Gleichnis* (Würzburg, 1983), pp.40–48.
Klauck, H.-J., 'So They Never Come Back? Nero Redivivus and the Apocalypse of John', in Klauck, H.-J., *Religion und Gesellschaft im frühen Christentum. Neutestamentliche Studien* (Tübingen, 2003), pp.268–89.
Klein, R., 'Das Bild des Augustus in der frühchristlichen Literatur', in von Haehling, R. (ed.), *Rom und das himmlische Jerusalem. Die frühen Christen zwischen Anpassung und Ablehnung* (Darmstadt, 2000), pp.205–36.
Klinghardt, M., 'Legionsschweine in Gerasa. Lokalkolorit und historischer Hintergrund von Mk 5,1–10', *ZNW* 98 (2007), pp.8–48.
Kloft, H., 'Herakles als Vorbild. Zur Funktion eines griechischen Mythos in Rom', in Kray, R. & Oettermann, S. (eds), *Herakles/Herkules 1. Metamorphosen des Heros in ihrer medialen Vielfalt* (Basel, 1994), pp.25–46.

Koch, H., 'Todesmonat oder Lebensdauer Alexanders des Grossen? Textkritische Bemerkungen zu Iust. 12,16,1', *RhM* 143 (2000), pp.328–37.
Kolb, F., *Rom. Die Geschichte der Stadt in der Antike* (München, 1995; 2nd revised ed., 2002).
Kollmann, B., *Die Jesus-Mythen. Sensationen und Legenden* (Freiburg, 2009).
Koortbojan, M., *The Divinization of Caesar and Augustus. Precedents, Consequences, Implications* (New York, 2013).
Korzeniewski, D., *Hirtengedichte aus Neronischer Zeit* (Darmstadt, 1971).
Korzeniewski, D., 'Néron et la Sibylle', *Latomus* 33 (1974), pp.921–25.
Kraus, C.S., '"No Second Troy": Topoi and Refoundation in Livy, Book V', *TAPhA* 124 (1994), pp.267–89.
Krauter, S., *Studien zu Röm 13,1–7. Paulus und der politische Diskurs der neronischen Zeit* (Tübingen, 2009).
Kreuz, G.E., 'Gab es in der Antike Terrorismus? Vorschläge zu einer Annäherung an das Problem', in Styka, J. (ed.), *Violence and Aggression in the Ancient World* (Kraków, 2006), pp.117–25.
Krieger, K.-S., 'Die Zeichenpropheten – eine Hilfe zum Verständnis des Wirkens Jesu?', in Hoppe, R. & Busse, U. (eds), *Von Jesus zu Christus. Christologische Studien* (Berlin, 1998), pp.63–76.
Krüger, J., *Nero. Der römische Kaiser und seine Zeit* (Köln, 2012).
Kühnen, A., *Die Imitatio Alexandri in der römischen Politik (1. Jh. v. Chr. – 3. Jh. n. Chr.)* (Münster, 2008).
Kyrieleis, H.,'Theoi horatoi. Zur Sternsymbolik hellenistischer Herrscherbildnisse', in Braun, K. (ed.), *Studien zur klassischen Archäologie* (Saarbrücken, 1986), pp.55–72.
Lafer, R., *Omnes collegiati, <concurrite>. Brandbekämpfung im Imperium Romanum* (Frankfurt, 2001).
Lang, B., *Jesus der Hund. Leben und Lehre eines jüdischen Kynikers* (München, 2010).
Lau, M., 'Die *Legio X Fretensis* und der Besessene von Gerasa. Anmerkungen zur Zahlenangabe "ungefähr Zweitausend" (Mk 5.13)', *Biblica* 88 (2007), pp.351–64.
Lawrence, J.M., 'Nero redivivus', *Fides et Historia* 11 (1978), pp.54–66.
Leipoldt, J. & Grundmann, W. (eds.), *Umwelt des Urchristentums II. Texte zum neutestamentlichen Zeitalter* (Berlin, 1982; 1st edn, 1967).
Lopez, D.C., *Apostle of the Conquered. Reimagining Paul's Mission* (Minneapolis, 2008).
Lüdemann, G. & Janßen, M., *Bibel der Häretiker. Die gnostischen Schriften aus Nag Hammadi. Eingeleitet, übersetzt und kommentiert* (Stuttgart, 1997).
Lund, A.A., 'Zur Verbrennung der sogenannten Chrestiani (Tac. Ann. 14,44)', *ZRGG* 60 (2008), pp.253–61.
Macky, P.W., *St. Paul's Cosmic War Myth. A Military Version of the Gospel* (New York, 1998).
Malitz, J., 'Caesars Partherkrieg', *Historia* 23 (1984), pp.21–59.
Malitz, J., 'Die Kalenderreform Caesars. Ein Beitrag zur Geschichte seiner Spätzeit', *AncSoc* 18 (1987), pp.103–31.
Martin, P.M., 'L'autre héritier de César', in Cizek, E. (ed.), *Marc Antoine, son idéologie et sa descendance* (Lyon, 1993), pp.7–54.
Matijević, K., 'Marcus Antonius und die Vergottung Caesars', in Spickermann, W. *et al.* (eds), *Rom, Germanien und das Reich* (St Katharinen, 2005), pp.46–79.
Matijević, K., *Marcus Antonius. Consul – Proconsul – Staatsfeind. Die Politik der Jahre 44 und 43 v. Chr.* (Rahden, 2006).
Merfeld, B., *Panegyrik – Paränese – Parodie? Die Einsiedler Gedichte und Herrscherlob in neronischer Zeit* (Trier, 1999).
Merkelbach, R., *Isisfeste in griechisch-römischer Zeit. Daten und Riten* (Meisenheim, 1963).
Merkelbach, R., *Isis regina – Zeus Sarapis. Die ägyptische Religion nach den Quellen dargestellt* (Stuttgart, 1995).
Meyer, R., 'Die eschatologische Wende des politischen Messianismus im Ägypten der Spätzeit. Historisch-kritische Bemerkungen zu einer spätägyptischen Prophetie', *Saeculum* 48 (1997), pp.177–212.
Michel, D., *Alexander als Vorbild für Pompeius, Caesar und Markus Antonius. Archäologische Untersuchungen* (Brüssel, 1967).

Miller, S.G., 'The Date of the Olympic Festivals', *MDAI(A)* 90 (1975), pp.215–31.
Moehring, H.R., 'The Census in Luke as an Apologetic Device', in Moehring, H.R. (ed.), *Studies in New Testament and Early Christian Literature* (Leiden, 1972), pp.144–60.
Müller, S., 'Nero und Domitian im Licht östlicher Monarchien', in Bönisch-Meyer, S. *et al.* (eds), *Nero und Domitian. Mediale Diskurse der Herrscherpräsentation im Vergleich* (Tübingen, 2014), pp.293–315.
Navia, L.E., *Diogenes of Sinope. The Man in the Tub* (Westport, 1998).
Niebuhr, B.G., *Römische Geschichte*, vol. 2 (Berlin, 1873; 1st edn, 1830).
Pandey, N.B., 'Caesar's Comet, the Julian Star, and the Invention of Augustus', *TAPhA* 143 (2013), pp.405–49.
Patsch, H., Der Einzug Jesu in Jerusalem', *Zeitschrift für Theologie und Kirche* 68 (1971), pp.1–26.
Perret, J., *Les origines de la légende Troyenne de Rome* (Paris, 1942).
Pfister, F., 'Herakles und Christus', *Archiv für Religionswissenschaft* 34 (1937), pp.42–60.
Puhvel, J., 'Aquam extinguere', *Journal of Indo-European Studies* 1 (1973), pp.379–86.
Puhvel, J., *Comparative Mythology* (Baltimore, 1988; 1st edn, 1987).
Ramsey, J.T., 'Mithridates, the Banner of Ch'ih-Yu, and the Comet Coins', *HSCPh* 99 (1999), pp.197–253.
Ramsey, J.T., *A Descriptive Catalogue of Greco-Roman Comets from 500 BC to AD 400* (University of Iowa, 2006).
Ramsey, J.T. & Licht, A.L., *The Comet of 44 BC and the Comet Coins* (Atlanta, 1997).
Reimarus, H.S., *Von dem Zwecke Jesu und seiner Jünger. Noch ein Fragment des Wolfenbüttelschen Ungenannten* (Berlin, 1778; *The Goal of Jesus and his Disciples*, introduction and translation by George Wesley Buchanan, Leiden, 1970).
Reimarus, H.S., *Apologie oder Schutzschrift für die vernünftigen Verehrer Gottes*, 2 vols (Frankfurt am Main, posthumously published 1972).
Reinach, T., 'Mon nom est Légion', *REJ* 47 (1903), pp.172–78.
Richer, N., 'Achille et Sirius', *Ollodagos* 13 (1999–2000), pp.245–308.
Ricoux, O., 'Sirius ou l'étoile des Mages', in Bakhouche, B., Moreau, A. & Turpin, J.-C. (eds), *Les astres*, vol. 1 (Montpellier, 1996), pp.131–54.
Ricoux, O., 'Les mages à l'aube du chien', in Gyselen, R. *et al.* (eds), *La science des cieux. Sages, mages, astrologues* (Bures-sur-Yvette, 1999), pp.219–32.
Ricoux, O., *Christ caniculaire: la nativité le 25 juillet* (Valenciennes, 2001).
Robichon, J., *Nero. Kaiser, Poet, Tyrann* (München, 1998; *Néron ou la comédie du pouvoir*, Paris, 1985).
Rogers, R.S., 'The Neronian Comets', *TAPhA* 84 (1953), pp.237–49.
Rordorf, W., 'Die neronische Christenverfolgung im Spiegel der apokryphen Paulusakten', *NTS* 28 (1982), pp.365–74 (= *The S. Lex Orandi Lex Credendi* [Paradosis 36], Freiburg, 1993, pp.368–77).
Rose, H.J., 'Herakles and the Gospels', *HThR* 31 (1948), pp.113–42.
Rubel, A., '"Es begab sich aber zu der Zeit…" Neue Überlegungen zur Geburt Christi und zur Glaubwürdigkeit der Weihnachtsgeschichte nach Lukas', *Gymnasium* 118 (2011), pp.563–84.
Russell, F., 'Roman Counterinsurgency Policy and Practice in Judaea', in Howe, T. & Brice, L.L. (eds), *Brill's Companion to Insurgency and Terrorism in the Ancient Mediterranean* (Leiden, 2015), pp.258–81.
Scheda, G., *Studien zur bukolischen Dichtung der Neronischen Epoche* (Bonn, 1969).
Schelkle, K., *Paulus* (Darmstadt, 1981).
Schmid, A., *Augustus und die Macht der Sterne. Antike Astrologie und die Etablierung der Monarchie in Rom* (Köln, 2005).
Schmidt, K.M., *Wege des Heils. Erzählstrukturen und Rezeptionskontexte des Markusevangeliums* (Göttingen, 2010).
Schmithals, W., 'Die Weihnachtsgeschichte Lukas 2,1–20', in Ebeling, G. (ed.), *Festschrift Ernst Fuchs* (Tübingen, 1973), pp.281–97.

Schmitt, T., 'Die Christenverfolgung unter Nero', in Heid, S. (ed.), *Petrus und Paulus in Rom. Eine interdisziplinäre Debatte* (Freiburg, 2011), pp.517–37.

Schmitzer, U., 'Dichtung und Propaganda im 1. Jahrhundert n. Chr.', in Weber, G. & Zimmermann, M. (eds), *Propaganda – Selbstdarstellung – Repräsentation im römischen Kaiserreich des 1. Jhs. n. Chr.* (Stuttgart, 2003).

Schreckenberg, H., 'Flavius Josephus und die lukanischen Schriften', in Haubeck, W. & Bachmann, M. (eds), *Wort in der Zeit. Neutestamentliche Studien* (Leiden, 1980), pp.179–209.

Schreiber, S., 'Caesar oder Gott (Mk 12,17)? Zur Theoriebildung im Umgang mit politischen Texten des Neuen Testaments', *Biblische Zeitschrift, Neue Folge* 48 (2004), pp.65–85.

Schreiber, S., *Weihnachtspolitik. Lukas 1–2 und das Goldene Zeitalter* (Göttingen, 2009).

Schreiber, S., 'Goldene Zeiten? Politische Perspektiven der lukanischen Geburtsgeschichte', in Reinmuth, E. (ed.), *Neues Testament und politische Theorie. Interdisziplinäre Beiträge zur Zukunft des Politischen* (Stuttgart, 2011), pp.83–97.

Schürmann, H., *Das Lukasevangelium I. Kommentar zu Kap. 1.1–9.50* (Freiburg, 1969).

Schwegler, A., *Römische Geschichte*, vol. 3 (Tübingen, 1858).

Scott, K., 'The Political Propaganda of 44–30 BC', *MAAR* 11 (1933), pp.7–49.

Simon, M., *Hercule et le christianisme* (Paris, 1955).

Sonnabend, H., *Nero. Inszenierung der Macht* (Darmstadt, 2016).

Strecker, C., 'Jesus und die Besessenen. Zum Umgang mit Alterität im Neuen Testament am Beispiel der Exorzismen Jesu', in Stegemann, W., Malina, B.J. & Gerd Theißen, G. (eds), *Jesus in neuen Kontexten* (Stuttgart, 2002), pp.53–63.

Strobel, A., 'Die Ausrufung des Jobeljahres in der Nazarethpredigt Jesu', in Gräßer, E., Strobel, A. & Tabbehill, C. (eds), *Jesus in Nazareth* (Berlin, 1972), pp.38–50.

Stübler, G., *Die Religiosität des Livius* (Stuttgart, 1941).

Suerbaum, W., '"Und der Stern zog ihnen voraus." Zum Motiv der göttlichen Leitung der Fahrt des Aeneas bei Vergil und in der vorvergilischen Tradition', in Maier, F. & Suerbaum, W. (eds), *Et scholae et vitae* (München, 1985), pp.22–32.

Talbert, C.H., 'Biographies of Philosophers and Rulers as Instruments of Religious Propaganda in Mediterranean Antiquity', *ANRW* 2.16.2 (1978), pp.1619–51.

Terio, S., *Der Steinbock als Herrschaftszeichen des Augustus* (Münster, 2006).

Theißen, G., *Urchristliche Wundergeschichten* (Gütersloh, 1974).

Theißen, G., 'Wanderradikalismus. Literatursoziologische Aspekte der Überlieferung von Worten Jesu im Urchristentum (1973)', in Theißen, G., *Studien zur Soziologie des Urchristentums* (Tübingen, 1983), pp.79–105.

Theißen, G., '"Wir haben alles verlassen" (Mc X.28). Nachfolge und soziale Entwurzelung in der jüdisch-palästinensischen Gesellschaft des 1. Jahrhunderts n. Chr.', in Theißen, G., *Studien zur Soziologie des Urchristentums*, 3rd edn (Tübingen, 1989), pp.160–97.

Theißen, G., 'Jesus und die symbolpolitischen Konflikte seiner Zeit. Sozialgeschichtliche Aspekte der Jesusforschung', *Evangelische Theologie* 57 (1997), pp.378–400.

Theißen, G., 'Evangelienschreibung und Gemeindeleitung. Pragmatische Motive bei der Abfassung des Markusevangeliums', in Kollmann, B., Reinbold, W. & Streuden, A. (eds), *Antikes Judentum und frühes Christentum* (Berlin, 1999), pp.289–414.

Theißen, G., 'Die politische Dimension des Wirkens Jesu', in Stegemann, W., Malina, B.J. & Theißen, G. (eds), *Jesus in neuen Kontexten* (Stuttgart, 2002), pp.112–22.

Theißen, G., 'Urchristentum als Bewegung. Von innerjüdischen Oppositions- und Erneuerungsbewegungen zur Entstehung einer neuen Religion im Römischen Reich', *CrSt* 24 (2003), pp.489–515.

Theißen, G., *Die Jesusbewegung. Sozialgeschichte einer Revolution der Werte* (Gütersloh, 2004).

Toynbee, J.M.C., 'Nero Artifex. The Apocolocyntosis Reconsidered', *CQ* 26 (1942), pp.83–93.

Tuplin, C.J., 'The False Neros of the First Century AD', in Deroux, C. (ed.), *Studies in Latin History and Roman History V* (Bruxelles, 1989), pp.364–404.

Ungern-Sternberg, J. von, 'Eine Katastrophe wird verarbeitet: Die Gallier in Rom', in Bruun, C. (ed.), *The Roman Middle Republic. Politics, Religion, and Historiography c. 400–133 BC* (Roma, 2000), pp.207–22.
Vaahtera, J., *Roman Augural Lore in Greek Historiography. A Study of the Theory and Terminology* (Stuttgart, 2001).
Van Kooten, G., 'Matthew, the Parthians, and the Magi: A Contextualization of Matthew's Gospel. Roman-Parthian Relations of the First Centuries BCE and CE', in Barthel, P. & van Kooten, G. (eds), *The Star of Bethlehem and the Magi. Interdisciplinary Perspectives from Experts on the Ancient Near East, the Greco-Roman World, and Modern Astronomy* (Leiden, 2015), pp.496–646.
Verdière, R., 'Le genre bucolique à l'époque de Néron: Les "Bucolica" de T. Calpurnius Siculus et les "Carmina Einsidlensia". État de la question et prospectives', *ANRW* 2.32.2 (1985), pp.1845–1924.
Vinchesi, M.A., 'Calpurnio Siculo e i nuovi percorsi della poesia bucolica', in Castagna, L. & Vogt-Spira, G. (eds), *Pervertere: Ästhetik der Verkehrung. Literatur und Kultur neronischer Zeit und ihre Rezeption* (München, 2002), pp.139–51.
Vittinghoff, F., '"Christianus sum" – Das "Verbrechen" von Außenseitern der römischen Gesellschaft', *Historia* 33 (1984), pp.331–57.
Walde, C. (ed.), *Neros Wirklichkeiten. Zur Rezeption einer umstrittenen Gestalt* (Rahden, 2013).
Waldherr, G.H., *Nero. Eine Biographie* (Regensburg, 2005).
Weber, E., 'Die trojanische Abstammung der Römer als politisches Argument', *WS* 6 (1972), pp.213–25.
Weigall, A., *Nero, Kaiser von Rom*, 2nd edn (Wien, 1943).
Weinstock, S., *Divus Julius* (Oxford, 1971).
West, D., 'On Serial Narration and on the Julian Star', *Proceedings of the Virgil Society* 21 (1993), pp.1–16.
Williams, G., 'Nero, Seneca and Stoicism in the Octavia', in Elsner, J. & Masters, J. (eds), *Reflections of Nero. Culture, History & Representation* (London, 1994).
Williams, M.F., 'The Sidus Iulium, the Divinity of Men, and the Golden Age in Virgil's Aeneid', *Leeds International Classical Studies* 2 (2004), pp.1–29.
Wolter, M., 'Die Hirten in der Weihnachtsgeschichte (Lk 2,8–20)', in von Dobbeler, A., Erlemann, K. & Heiligenthal, R. (eds), *Religionsgeschichte des Neuen Testaments* (Tübingen, 2000), pp.507–17.
Yoyotte, J., 'Héra d'Héliopolis et le sacrifice humain', *EPHE, V. section, sciences religieuses* 89 (1980–81), pp.31–102.
Ziegler, K.-H., *Die Beziehungen zwischen Rom und dem Partherreich. Ein Beitrag zur Geschichte des Völkerrechts* (Wiesbaden, 1964), pp.67–75.
Zimmermann, M., 'Der Kaiser als Nil. Zur Kontinuität und Diskontinuität von Repräsentation im frühen Prinzipat', in Weber, G. & Zimmermann, M. (eds), *Propaganda – Selbstdarstellung – Repräsentation im römischen Kaiserreich des 1. Jhs. n. Chr.* (Stuttgart, 2003), pp.317–48.

Chapter 8

The Cult of Mithras and the Roman Imperial Army

Oliver Stoll

Mithras – A 'Military God'?

Mithras has been viewed as a 'god for soldiers' since at least the pioneering research of F. Cumont,[1] but Cumont's assertion did not rely on a meticulous analysis of documented cult members. Rather, it is based on his view that the Roman Army was a principal factor in the spreading of Mithras: in his view, the consistent westward 'flow of recruits' of 'Asiatics' (he assigns particular relevance to the region of Commagene, but also to Syria, Cappadocia, Pontus and Cilicia) and a high degree of mobility, especially of officers and the centurions among them, were constitutive of the Army's influence in the spreading of the cult:[2] the Mithraic religion had been predominantly a 'religion for soldiers,' a 'military religion'. According to Cumont, it was the Oriental soldiers in particular who had maintained pious faith in their national gods (namely, the gods of their home regions) so as not to lose their protection in the tough daily life of the military. These 'fraternities', he asserts, were open to fellow soldiers of all origins and presented a welcome complement to the 'official army religion' (see Figure 8.1).

With each new deployment, the 'convert' thus became a 'missionary' – in this way, the mysteries of the deity from the Commagene region[3] or Cappadocia had spread to Europe with great rapidity – and the cult's presence became evident from the Black Sea to the mountains of Scotland and the Saharan region, extending along the entire former Roman border.[4] More recent studies of the Jupiter Dolichenus cult, comparable in many respects, which similarly spread during the second and third century across large parts of the Empire and which was very popular among the soldiers, in fact attribute the rapid expansion of the cult to the 'military networks' and to the frequent exchange or redeployment of troops within the Empire.[5] Incidentally, this cult in many ways was much more 'adapted' to the military than Mithras. Firstly, there was the deity's iconography: the god dons the Roman officer's accoutrements, and the cultic standards of the Dolichenus cult were modelled on Roman military standards, the *signa*. Secondly, one has to consider the prominent role allocated to commanding officers in this cult, and the relatively high frequency with which military collectives (even entire regiments) were benefactors of the god's temples or altars. Lastly, offerings relied on the imitation of established phrases which were limited to the official Roman Army religion but here extended to the 'private deity'.[6]

Figure 8.1: Mithras-relief, red sandstone, second century AD, from the military *vicus* at Heidelberg-Neuenheim (*CIMRM* 1283, Badisches Landesmuseum Karlsruhe). The central scene with the bull-slaying Mithras (the 'Tauroctony') is framed by subsidiary panels with episodes of the Mithras myth. (*Courtesy of Wikimedia*)

Due to its seemingly straightforward plausibility, the above interpretation of Mithras and his cult as a 'god for soldiers', and of the expansion of the worship of the deity, has had an enormous appeal: the Mithras cult is still considered a 'religion for soldiers' by many scholars, and the god continues to be labelled a 'military deity'.[7] This (errant) view doggedly persists,[8] even though studies and analyses, especially those of R. Gordon and primarily of M. Clauss,[9] have clearly shown that the proportion of military personnel of any kind and from all the different military branches in any of the provinces (the naval branch is the exception, as it still does not appear in the record at all), even in so-called military provinces – with the exception of Britannia (75 per cent) – at best seems to have been between 10 and 20 per cent. In the case of Dolichenus, incidentally, the rate of affiliated or benefactors who unequivocally identified themselves as soldiers and veterans was 40 per cent.[10]

A 'religion for soldiers' cannot be defined by the fact that soldiers were among the affiliated members or benefactors of a cult: if that were the case, virtually any Roman god, given a detailed analysis of cult members and a certain proportion of military among them (the likelihood of this is high, since the erection of stone monuments was a costly affair but which officers, NCOs, soldiers and veterans were able to afford), could be shown to be a 'deity for soldiers'! From a methodological point of view, the issue of classification must follow a different logic: an official army religion exists which is determined by the calendric events of the state's cult deities, the emperor's cult, and the imperial dynasty's cult which is the same for all regiments irrespective of their geographic location. Furthermore, there are cults and religions worshipped by soldiers when not on duty, in private, out of a deeply felt need for protection. Here exists a rather wide range of possibilities and points of contact with the respective civilian population: namely, gods from the soldiers' home region, gods endemic to the deployment location whose individual protection was sought.[11] Oriental religions,[12] such as Mithras, count among these. Should one choose to do so, one could label some 'semi-official', specific military cults as 'deities for soldiers': those deities, that is to say, whose functions are concerned with the day-to-day activities of military duty, deities who grant protection in that sphere and are worshipped by military or tactical and administrative subdivisions of a regiment and who advance group identity, discipline, morality and cohesion.[13]

Belonging to this group are deities such as 'Disciplina' (*RIB* 2092; *ILS* 3810), in other words the divine personification of military discipline, or the 'Campestres' (*RIB* 2417; *RIB* 2135; *CIL* 13.6449), the deities protecting the parade ground, but especially the diverse *genii*, such as the extremely popular *Genius centuriae*, the *genius*, the protective spirit of a *centuria* which was often worshipped near the barracks of the respective division (*CIL* 3.6576; *CIL* 13.7494a–d). In this case, the composition of the cult membership and of the deity itself would be determined by a military context to such an extent that one could legitimately speak of a 'cult for soldiers' and 'deities for soldiers' – the situation in the case of Mithras, however, as in the case of Jupiter Dolichenus,[14] is different. What should be unarguable is the fact that the Mithras cult appealed to soldiers as a private cult[15] – they did not dominate the cult, and they were part of (normally rather small) male communities which were often, but not always, located along the *Limes* in the civilian settlements (*vici*) attached to the *castella*.

It should be mentioned that in the case of Dolichenus and Mithras, the location of sanctuaries – as a rule outside of the *castella* and in the civilian settlements – has its own distinct relevance. There are a few exceptions, some of which can be accounted for rather well, as at Aquincum[16] and Dura-Europos,[17] and some of which cannot, as at Vindolanda.[18] The Mithras sanctuary of Aquincum is located in a tribune's house and therefore has a rather 'private character'; the Dura-Europos *Mithraeum* and the Dolichenus sanctuary, too, are located within the not strictly and hermetically sealed-off 'military precinct' of a narrow and cramped fortress town.[19] The *Dolichenum* of the third and fourth century in Vindolanda was possibly 'integrated' (due to the political and military location and situation) into the periphery of the fort's enclosure out of 'sheer necessity'.

Mithras, a Research Survey: An Extraordinary Cult from the East?

Evidence for the Persian light-god Mithra dates back to the fourteenth century BC, but there are few common elements between the original form of worship and the Roman Mithras cult found between the late first and the fourth century AD during the *Imperium Romanum*. For a considerable time now, scholarship has sought to elucidate the true origin of the Roman Mithraic mysteries and the transformational processes involved; the search for the origin of the cult is the central issue of the study of Mithras.[20] While one group of historians regards the Roman Mithras cult as a new creation and recognizes few connections with the Persian cult,[21] another group stresses the derivations from the Persian cult which, it is argued, had undergone significant changes. A new historiographic approach in recent years indicates that the origins of the Roman Mithras cult are to be found in Italy,[22] and not at all in the East.[23] Early discoveries support this, as does the concentration of evidence in Rome and Ostia, from where the cult, 'made up of component parts', as an innovative cult, spread across the entire Roman Empire. The worship of Mithras and the development and expansion of the cult can subsequently be understood and studied as an integral, constituent part of the Roman deities, and as an element of local and regional religious history. In addition, the reciprocal exchanges between the cult and its worshippers – as well as their social origin and activities – and other cults and religious communities of the Empire equally merit further investigation.

Chronological and Spatial Expansion of the Cult

The cult of Mithras began to expand from Rome and Italy across large parts of the Roman Empire at the end of the first century AD, reaching its peak during the second and third century AD.[24] What are presumably the earliest findings in the provinces are dated between 90 and 110/120 AD from *Germania Superior*, from Nida-Heddernheim near Frankfurt with its four *Mithraea*: the two donors of the altars in the so-called Mithraeum I (*CIMRM* 1092, 1098),[25] a cavalryman of the *ala I Flavia* by the name of Tacitus and a centurion of the *cohors XXXII Voluntariorum* by the name of C. Lollius Crispus, were soldiers of these regiments stationed in this area. The fact that evidence of early offerings and of the cult has been found in the vicinity of the *castella* along the *limites* has led to the frequently heard hypothesis that the Mithraic cult in certain provinces had arrived with the Roman Army.[26] Certainly, military personnel were among the most mobile population groups of the *Imperium Romanum*, be that as individuals or in groups, and, in the context of religions and cults, too, thus belong to the group of potential 'culture-bearers'. Yet, as indicated earlier, the number of the military among the epigraphically attested cult members was substantially lower than that of civilians and other 'occupational groups'.

The geographic epicentres of recorded examples of the cult are located particularly on the northern boundary of the Empire, for instance along the military borders on the Rhine,[27] on the middle and lower sections of the Danube, but also in Britannia along Hadrian's Wall or in Rome and surrounding areas, especially Ostia,[28] as well as Campania (see Figure 8.2 below). As a consequence of the fact that in the nineteenth century, in the course of an emerging research area of '*Limesforschung*' ('Frontier Studies'),[29] the issue of military borders became particularly well researched and documented, the focus of study became somewhat distorted in favour of military sites, as it was turned away from the 'frontier zones' into the 'hinterland'. This contributed to the view that the cult of Mithras was a 'religion for soldiers' which, as shown earlier, is not entirely correct. A considerable number of discoveries and evidence from non-military sites in recent years has begun to shift the assessment of the cult (for example, the *Mithraea* in Wiesloch, Güglingen and Gellep).[30] Here, civilian populations definitely count among the worshippers – even following the

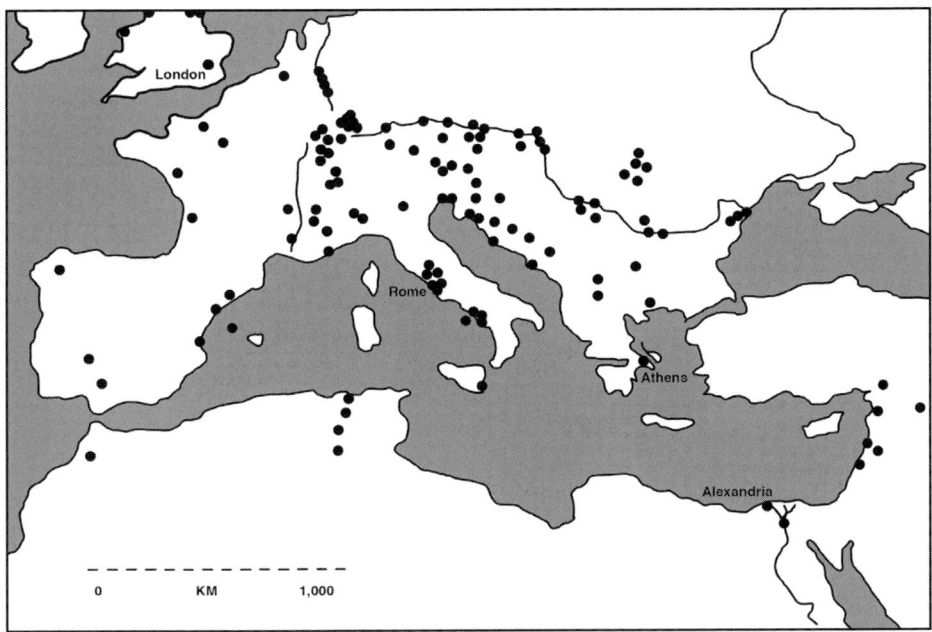

Figure 8.2: Distribution-map of Mithraea throughout the Roman provinces. Clearly visible, there are knots of evidence for the temples and cult-activity of Mithraism in Rome itself, in *Germania Superior* (the 'Obergermanisch-Rätischer Limes'), on the frontiers of the Middle and Lower Danube area and their hinterland, and also on Hadrian's Wall.

withdrawal of the military where that was the case – that is to say, local residents from the more diverse occupational and communal groups who can be identified as worshippers in other concurrent local cults: Mithras was thus integrated into locally existing religious systems.[31]

At present, approximately 140 Mithraic temples over the entire area of the *Imperium Romanum* have been archeologically verified, and evidence for the cult itself – with its normally rather small cult communities – exists in more than 500 locations. Evidence can be found from almost all provinces: about 700 relief representations of the bull-slaying Mithras are known, plus a further 500 reliefs in connection with the cult. To date, more than 1,000 inscriptions provide information concerning the cult, its members, distinct rituals, cult buildings and foundations. These form the basis of an at least rudimentary analysis of the social composition of almost 500 small cult communities.[32] Needless to say, beside the above-mentioned concentration of findings, there are provinces and regions where evidence of the cult has so far proven scarce, for instance in Roman Spain, in the north of Africa, and both in Egypt and the Middle East. Considering the size of the armed forces in Egypt and the Middle East, which were similar to those in lower Germania (i.e., *Germania Superior*), the lack of military evidence of the Mithraic cult is rather astonishing – after all, these too are 'limes zones'.[33] Why is there an almost complete absence of the ostensible 'religion for soldiers'? Nevertheless, the number of findings as evidence of Mithras worship in the Roman orient has grown in recent times, including the two *Mithraea* of Doliche,³⁴ as well as the unusually colourfully painted Mithraeum at Hawarte in Syria.³⁵ Evidence for the cult ends in the fourth century AD; given the protection and support offered by Roman emperors, Christ ultimately prevailed over Mithras. Further consideration will be given to this point below.

The Social Strata of Devotees — Once Again: a 'Cult of the Military'?

Some may wish to maintain the hypothesis that soldiers and the military population were of particular significance in spreading the cult, but the fact is that, according to the analysis of the epigraphic evidence undertaken by Clauss, the deity's following was composed of a much broader segment of imperial society. Other mobile groups which formed a further part might equally be assigned a more significant role in the spreading of the cult, namely, officials of the Roman administration, artisans and merchants. Among the followers of the cult are senators, men of the equestrian rank, *decuriones* (members of the local city-council, *ordo decurionum*), soldiers of all types, full Roman citizens, freedmen and slaves.³⁶ It is possible that, to a large extent, the cult of Mithras was transported by soldiers into its area of expansion, but from there began a wide and rapid spread among the civilian population; as stated earlier,³⁷ the proportion of active soldiers amounted at best to no more than between 10 and 20 per cent. Former soldiers – that is to say, veterans – may here be given a kind of potential 'role as multipliers' (cf. Aurelius Marcellus from Ulcisia Castra [*AE* 1926, 72] who, being a veteran, donated a shrine in AD 297 which he had pledged while in the service, '*quod miles vovit, veteranus solvit*'). As will be discussed below, neither the significance of the former soldiers' 'role as multipliers', nor that of the veterans overall, can be discerned clearly. The number of ex-soldiers among the Mithras devotees in the conclusively documented epigraphy is relatively low, amounting to far less than 1 per cent of documents fitting the classification.³⁸ But attention once more should be given to the role that active soldiers played in the cult.

Firstly, it must be noted that the Mithras cult was a cult for men, as women seem to have been excluded. Women appear in the epigraphic documentation merely as 'accessories' in the inscriptions of male benefactors, their husbands. The contrast to the Jupiter Dolichenus cult once again deserves attention: almost half (approximately 430) of the recorded dedications have a military connection via the dedicant or the context,³⁹ in which, as discussed earlier, there were closer connections to the 'official army religion' (the deity, however, was not a part of the official religious sphere of military life and the 'official army religion' itself). Further, of these, nearly half of the recorded dedications of those undertaken by 'military collectives' (that is from tactical and administrative subdivisions, rank groups and *collegia* up to whole regiments with commanding officers), and especially those by officers and commanding officers, were of remarkable significance. Among those 120 offerings of the Dolichenus cult for which explicit detail is available, twenty-four instances reveal the involvement of centurions. There are fourteen *praefecti*, five *tribuni*, three *legati pro praetore* and the *dux ripae* of Dura-Europos, two *primipili*. Particularly noticeable, therefore, is the group of centurions and commanding cavalry officers (*praefecti* and *tribuni*); less frequent are the 'non-commissioned officers' (twenty in total – *optiones*, *signiferi, custodes armorum* and *beneficiarii*). The rank and file (*gregales*) and veterans appear rarely (six soldiers, five veterans).⁴⁰

What is striking in the Mithras cult is the 'majority' of centurions and NCOs – more than 90 per cent; ordinary soldiers are rare,⁴¹ and the instances overall are mostly from the legions⁴² (see Figure 8.3). This raises some questions. Is the typical cult devotee to be found among the relatively privileged 'career soldiers' and non-commissioned administrative officers, in relatively small and exclusive communities? Does the intimate size of the group account for the adhesion of believers and for the attraction of the cult? Did it represent a kind of 'exclusive circle'? Was discipleship in the Mithras cult regarded as a milieu conducive to ambitious social climbers who sought to build networks of like-minded devotees? This comparison between the function of the Mithras temple as a communal space for festivities and the club houses organized by associations, the *collegia*, has occasionally been drawn in earlier studies.⁴³ The data concerning the military dedications and the donors should be examined more closely, but it must be said that since the printing of *CIMRM*, not much new relevant material has been added – but of course the latter will be included in our considerations.

Figure 8.3: Red sandstone altar, height 64cm, second to third century AD, from Sumelocenna (Rottenburg). *CIMRM* 1308; Landesmuseum Württemberg inv. RL163, Stuttgart: dedication to '*Invicto Mithrae*', to the 'Invincible Mithras', by a certain Publius Aelius Vocco, a soldier of Legio XXII Primigenia pia fidelis stationed in Mogontiacum/Mainz. (*Courtesy of bpk Bildagentur*)

Given the eighty-two relevant inscriptions, there are high numbers of military members of the legions represented, whereas the *alae* (seven), *numeri* (one), *cohortes* (eighteen) and *vexillationes* (three) fall far behind. The prominence of the role given to the centurions is particularly distinct (*CIMRM* 53, 135, 153, 160/161, 379 [praetorians], 840, 1005, 1098, 1295, 1671, 1718, 2273, 2286, 2311, 2312; *AE* 1971: 418; *AE* 2004: 1133; *AE* 2011: 517). Other officers, especially from the equestrian rank or senators, occur rarely: tribunes and prefects of auxiliary cohorts (*CIMRM* 845, 876, 1297; *CIL* 8.21523; *RIB* 1545 – auxiliary troop commandants), senatorial tribunes of a legion (*CIMRM* 1790; *AE* 1990: 814, 818–19; see also *CIMRM* 139), a camp prefect (*CIMRM* 2271), a *praefectus legionis* (*CIMRM* 134), a *praepositus legionum* (*CIMRM* 1594, 1596), a *dux* (*CIMRM* 804) and commanders of a legion (*legati legionis*: *CIMRM* 1968/69, 1952 – an utter anomaly in the latter case, where the *legatus* of Legion XIII Gemina made offerings together with his wife and son).⁴⁴

Rarer instances are 'collective dedications' in the cult of Mithras – such as in Ptuj in the time of the emperor Gallienus (AD 260–268) – undertaken by functional groups, in one instance by an entire group of non-commissioned officers and military clerks (*CIMRM* 1590: *canaliclarii, actarii, codicarii, librarii*; *CIMRM* 1592: *tesserarii, custodes armorum*; *CIMRM* 1594: *officiales*) from two legions, firstly Legion V Macedonia and secondly Legion XIII Gemina. These were all under the command of a certain equestrian officer by the name of Flavius Aper (his rank is given as *praepositus*), who had himself dedicated two altars to the 'Deus Sol Invictus Mithras' (*CIMRM* 1584, 1596). Regrettably, in the case of the latter altar, the reference to the two legions or legion divisions under his command has been lost. Clauss plausibly surmises that the commandant influenced the men in their endowment activities.[45]

Offerings by complete regiments including the commandant, such as are in evidence in the case of the Dolichenus cult, cannot be found.[46] The closest match would be *CIMRM* 149: an offering during late antiquity undertaken by two cohorts (from the same legion, cohorts VII and X of Legion II Herculia). Some instances, arguably only rather distantly relevant, might also be *CIMRM* 866, a 'group dedication' by the *milites legionis II Augustae agentes in praesidio* from Housesteads, and especially *CIMRM* 870 (a vexillation of Legion VI Victrix from Corbridge). *CIMRM* 1223, too, at least concerns a group from Mainz, a *turma* belonging to the *cohors Biturigium* seeking protection, but the benefactor is not named. To the list of offerings made by military clerks from Ptuj can be added *CIMRM* 2177, an offering by *librarii* and by an *actarius* of a *numerus Surorum* in Romula. Where the 'collective dedications by non-commissioned officers' are concerned, *CIMRM* 153, 742 and 1008 can be listed, too: in *CIMRM* 153, a legion *centurio*, an *ala decurio* and a *beneficiarius* act together in their donation; in *CIMRM* 742, several *signiferi*, standard-bearers, act together; in *CIMRM* 1008, *candidati* of Legion XXX Ulpia Victrix, together with an *imaginifer* ('bearer of the *imago* of the emperor'), make this dedication on behalf of the 'soldiers of the legion'.

Offerings by NCOs occur with some frequency (*CIMRM* 743, 1677: *optio*; *CIMRM* 793: *frumentarius*; *CIMRM* 1151: *immunis*; *CIMRM* 1434, 1971: *speculator*; *CIMRM* 1485: *beneficiarius*; *CIMRM* 1638, 1639: two offerings by a *custos armorum* of Legion XIV Gemina from Scarabantia; *CIMRM* 745, 1717, 1962: *signifer*; *CIMRM* 1781: *actarius*; CIMRM 1805: *armorum custos*; *CIMRM* 2375: *strator consularis*; *CIMRM* 1729, *AE* 1979, 425: *cornicularius praefecti legionis*; *CIMRM* 1955: *imaginifer*; NCOs of auxiliary troops: *CIMRM* 1015: *duplarius alae*; *CIMRM* 1153: *medicus*; *CIMRM* 1803: *custos armorum cohortis*). Equally frequent, unlike in the case of the Dolichenus cult, are offerings by the 'rank and file' soldiers (*CIMRM* 1793: two soldiers of Legion II Adiutrix; *CIMRM* 62, 70, 867, 916, 1308 [see Figure 8.3], 1513, 1649, 1711, 1739, 1742, 1921, 1925, 1929; *CIL* 13.8641: soldiers of auxiliary troops; *CIMRM* 1092: *eques alae*; *CIMRM* 1889: *miles cohortis*; *CIMRM* 562: praetorians). In the overall assessment, then, in the epigraphic record we can note differences between the Dolichenus and Mithras cults. In the case of the Mithras cult, there is a higher proportion of centurions and NCOs, but also of rank and file soldiers, while the proportion of equestrian and senatorial military is lower,[47] there are few 'group connections' and no genuine overlap with the 'official army religion'.

In some places – in spite of the rather low proportion of active soldiers in the cult communities which we have repeatedly stressed – there were close connections between local garrisons and the local Mithras community: until about AD 160, the *ala Noricorum* was stationed at the auxiliary fort in Dormagen in lower Germania. It is thought that at that time this regiment became an auxiliary troop of the Bonn-based Legion I Minervia in Lucius Verus' Parthian campaign and never returned to Dormagen. According to the numismatic evidence, after AD 160, the painted Mithraeum with its vaulted ceiling and stone cult relief (*CIMRM* 1011–1015) fell into disuse. Two inscriptions (*CIMRM* 1013, 1015) preserved on the relief mention cavalry soldiers, a *bucinator* and a *duplicarius*, indicating that it was members of the *ala Noricorum* who founded and 'maintained' the Mithraeum between AD 90 and 160, which was then 'closed'[48] following the regiment's departure. Yet, a similar hypothetical account would require detailed examination: from time to time, the question is raised as to why the quantity of inscriptions offered to the deity declines in the third century AD.[49] A possible answer would have been a consideration of the consequences for the Mithras cult of the so-called era of the 'soldier emperors' – did the abandonment of the *Limes* east of the Rhine around AD 260 lead to this drop in numbers because the relevant Mithraea and their communities were consequently abandoned? Or did battle casualties, or redeployment to other front lines, result in depletion of membership in communities? It is clear that the correlation between the military and the prosperity of Mithras communities is greatly overstated.

The question seems to raise its head again as to why the two cults, of Jupiter Dolichenus and Mithras, do not seem to reveal a clear overlap given their military clientele and the frequent neighbouring location in the *vici* of the legionary camps, garrisons and *castella* (for example, Brigetio, Dura-Europos and Stockstadt)? Should an overlap of members and benefactors documented in both cults perhaps be expected? That would be likely, considering the not insignificant amount of epigraphic evidence for both cults. It is therefore astonishing that a congruence, or cross-section between the cults, is hardly reflected at all in the extant record. Moreover, in several cases where it is the case, the reliability or value of the record is in doubt. In Stockstadt, where the Dolichenum and Mithraeum lay in the vicinity of the auxiliary fort, an offering to Jupiter Dolichenus was found in the Mithraeum during excavations in 1908 (*CIMRM* 1208);[50] in Egeta, in the province of Moesia Superior, only a section of a Mithras relief was found in the local Dolichenum.[51] It is not certain whether *CIMRM* 348.2 from San Clemente in Rome, a dedication by a priest to 'Jupiter Dolichenus Augustus', stems from the local Mithraeum, because the fragment was reused as part of the church floor (together with *CIMRM* 348.1, an offering to Mithras).

Pertaining more closely to the initial line of investigation is *CIMRM* 373, a relief (including a representation of Sol) with an inscription: M. Ulpius Chresimus, who refers to himself as *sacerdos Iovis Dolicheni* – a priest in the service of the god Dolichenus – fulfils his sacred vow for the protection of the emperors in his offering to Sol Invictus and the *genius* of the *equites singulares Augusti*, the mounted escort troops of the Roman emperors in which he himself was a member. This inscription was also found in the supposed area of the *equites singulares* camp on the Caelian Hill in Rome, together with, it should be noted, a further inscription to Jupiter Dolichenus.[52] Strictly speaking, however, it is not Mithras who is referred to but 'Sol Invictus', and we cannot be certain that this inscription from the second century AD in fact refers to

Mithras.[53] The ensemble or union of 'Sol', 'Deus Helios Mithras' and Dolichenus is known from the Dolichenum on the Aventine Hill in Rome (*CIMRM* 467–75), but here military personnel were not involved as benefactors. A consecration to 'Deus Sol Invictus Mithras' by C. Valerius Marinianus, a *cornicularius* of the *legatus legionis*, the commander of Legion I Adiutrix, is found in the Dolichenum at the gates of the legionary camp in Brigetio – the military clerk therein fulfilled a sacred vow. A dedication in the Greek language, dating from the early third century AD, to Zeus Helios Mithras and the god Turmasgades, by a soldier of Legion XVI Flavia Firma Antoniniana by the name of Iulianos, is definitely from the Dolichenum in Dura-Europos (*CIMRM* 70).[54]

This almost gives the impression that there were 'two systems' that cannot be made congruent. What differences existed between the dedicants of the two cults? As noted above, the epigraphic evidence records at least some differences – the involvement of military collectives and regiments,[55] the proportion of senatorial and equestrian regimental commanders, and overall of officers, and the proportion of individuals of the rank of non-commissioned officer or rank and file. Apart from the gradual differences of acceptance and 'integration' or assimilation in military life (*viz.* closer proximity of the Dolichenus cult to the 'official army religion'), can we plausibly discern a level of 'class distinction' among the worshippers and different 'spheres' of religious entitlement? There is scope for further research in this regard. But two inscriptions from Dura-Europos must be considered. In *CIMRM* 53, mention is made of the restitution of the temple of 'Deus Sol Invictus Mithras' by Antonius Valentinus, *centurio princeps* and commandant of a vexillation of Legions IV Scythica and XVI Flavia Firma, that is to say a building inscription of the Mithras temple (AD 209/211). The same officer is named at the Dolichenum of Dura, but on an altar of a man freed by him by the name of Agathocles, who consecrated the altar to Dolichenus 'for the protection' of his *patronus*, the officer who otherwise is nowhere present among the findings of the Dolichenus cult in Dura.[56] Would this mean that there were two systems?

The Mithras cult was never officially integrated into the Roman pantheon, but it cannot be denied that its members, be they soldiers, freedmen or slaves employed in the administration, evidently felt a sense of loyal obligation to their superior and to the emperor. A large number of inscriptions attest to the community's expressions of loyalty *pro salute*, 'for the welfare' of the emperor or a superior (for example, *CIMRM* 1008, 1777); or the community consecrates the donation or endowed object *in honorem domus divinae*, 'in honour of the imperial house' (for example, *CIMRM* 1243; for both, *CIMRM* 1438). However, both formulae are conventional and widely used by other cults. Compared with the Dolichenus cult, here there are far fewer members of senatorial or equestrian rank. During the cult's peak time in the second and third century AD, Mithras did not greatly resonate with the Empire's ruling elites.[57]

'Temples' and Sanctuaries

Apart from cave Mithraea (such as those in Schwarzerden-Reichweiler or in Doliche),[58] the floor plans, such as those excavated in Roman Germany, reveal an essentially identical basic scheme that is repeated everywhere. Based on the long rectangular floor plan, the sanctuary space is lowered into the ground, a central aisle is flanked by two raised podiums for the worshippers, and access to the sanctuary space leads through one or two vestibules via downward steps. On the front wall of the cavern was located the central cult image with its representation of Mithras' slaying of the bull (the 'Tauroctony'). Mithras is invariably depicted wearing long oriental trousers, belted tunic, billowing coat and a Phrygian cap on his head, just as he is pushing down the bull's back with his left knee; with his right hand he is thrusting a dagger into the bull's lower neck area (the left hand controls the animal's mouth while pulling back its head).[59] Subsidiary altars and sculptures (such as those of 'Cautes' and 'Cautopates', the torch bearers) supplemented the furnishings of these small sanctuaries. In many cases, the design of the sanctuary ceiling and roof cannot be discerned: in Rome and in Ostia, at least, there were vaulted ceilings featuring open holes to the sky.[60] The walls were often colourfully painted with frescoes, such as in Rome and Dura-Europos, and it is safe to assume that everywhere else, the walls served as the space on which the mystai painted graffiti (see Figure 8.4).

Mithras' temples and sanctuaries are frequently rather modest in size – as a rule of thumb, the dimensions were 6 metres in width and 12 metres in length, at least in Roman Germany. The walls were generally a combination of wood or a timber-framed structure on a bedding of stone. It is likely that as a rule, a *temenos*, a sacred precinct, was part of the general plan of free-standing temples. Mithraea exist in all 'settings of human habitation', in cities, *vici*, near military camps and on the periphery of farming estates.[61] Building materials, however, were combined in many

Figure 8.4: The third- to fourth-century AD Mithraeum under the Basilica St Clemente in Rome. The original 'cave-like space' of the subterranean temple interior (*spelaeum* or *crypta*) is almost intact: there is an altar, *triclinia* ('benches for dining', for the communal meals) and vaulted roof. (*Courtesy of Alamy*)

variations: in Wiesloch, for instance, even grass sods, clay, wooden and wattle lattices and timber-framed structures were combined in the initial construction phase.[62] It should be assumed that some temples were made entirely out of timber, even though archaeological evidence is obviously (more) difficult to ascertain: one example is the case of the cohort fort in Künzing along the *Limes* in Raetia.[63] In spite of its status as a military province, Raetia has thus far provided only very little evidence of the cult's worship.

The sanctuary in Künzing was located in the so-called east *vicus*, some 220 metres from the principate-era auxiliary *castellum*, and was destroyed in the second half of the third century AD. A small community gathered here in two periods (second century AD, a post construction with lattice work walls housing a maximum of eighteen persons; third century AD, a foundation beam construction with timber-framed walls for approximately twenty-five persons). At least during the second phase, the cult image seems to have been painted on plaster and did not consist of a sculptural relief; but here, too, a wide variety of options can be imagined.[64] Oil lamps, sacrificial knives, a bone pit containing animal bones, drinking cups and cult vessels provide evidence for and connect the gatherings to cult practices and cult feasts (in Riegel am Kaiserstuhl, an assortment of cult crockery was found – cups, jugs, plates, cult vessels and censers).[65] The benches (for reclining) would have been laid out with cushions to guarantee comfort for members participating in the feast.[66]

Inscriptions are almost entirely lacking in Künzing, but a small altar records an honourably discharged veteran ('*missus honesta missione*'), Valerius Magio, as a worshipper of the 'Undefeated Mithras' (Mithras Invictus).[67] Veterans, that is to say soldiers who had been discharged honourably with all attendant privileges and financial settlements, can occasionally be found as dedicants in the record (for example, *CIMRM* 153, 630, 1235, 1361–62, 1417, 1543, 1635, 1720, 1724–25, 1776, 1959, 1960, 2222, 2250). However, these instances mostly refer to legionary veterans and in few instances to *alae* or Roman city troop veterans. Occasionally, as in Künzing, the honourable discharge – *honesta missio* – is mentioned (for example, *CIMRM* 630), but that practice was widespread and not unique to this cult.

After all, the veterans generally represent 'prosperous' members of provincial society who can frequently be found in the vicinity of their old garrison, and who were inclined to make a dedication in a cult in order to document their status and their integration into the local community. Some of these veteran inscriptions therefore 'unite' active soldiers and veterans of a regiment or a specific 'army group', namely, the 'old comrades' (for example, *CIMRM* 153 from El-Gahara), or they refer exclusively to veterans belonging to the same regiment, such as *CIMRM* 1235 referring to three veterans of Legion XXII Primigenia from Mainz. C. Iulius Valens, the veteran referred to in *CIMRM* 2222, an *ex-beneficiarius* of Legion VI Claudia, arguably offers his inscription because he became '*nunc decurio*', a 'town councillor', of the *colonia Viminacium* and therefore indubitably advanced into the local ruling elite. The veteran T. Tettius Plotus, a former soldier of Legion IIII Flavia in Oescus, apparently advanced into the cult's priesthood and reached the grade of *pater*. What is known about the internal structure of these small cult communities which gathered in the temples and sanctuaries discussed above? It is generally assumed that the membership of each community lay between twenty and forty individuals, but a bronze tablet from Virunum (*AE* 1994, 1334) is a building inscription that identifies ninety-eight members of a Mithras community at the beginning of the third century AD, a quarter of which, incidentally, consisted of freedmen.[68] Due to the increase in membership numbers between AD 184 and 201, it was then decided to found a new temple.

Needless to say, given a sufficient number of devotees, several Mithras sanctuaries could co-exist 'side by side' near a single *castellum*. An example of this is found in Frankfurt/Nida-Heddernheim with its (at least) four Mithraea during the late first to third centuries AD, only two of which were already in existence when Heddernheim was a simple *castellum* (before AD 110, after which the *ala I Flavia Gemina*, a cavalry regiment and a cohort also stationed there, presumably the *cohors XXXII Voluntariorum c.R.*, were redeployed to the *Limes*). Here, too, there is proof for the key argument: namely, that the cult was not exclusively sustained by the military, but by the citizens of the settlement, which in the meantime had become a *civitas* capital. Assuming a number of twenty to forty members per community, during the turbulent third century AD there were approximately 120–240 worshippers of the 'invincible' god[69] in the civic settlement of Nida.

Priests and 'Service of Worship', Belief and Ritual

As was the case in other cults, solemn admission to the Mithras community was necessary: a ritual initiation required the 'novice' to prepare and study. Following the identification of a fourth-century AD Egyptian papyrus as a kind of 'catechism' of the cult,[70] and in spite of its fragmentary state of preservation, it seems clear that the initiation was a dialogue-based ceremony, involving a series of ritualized questions and answers. The test gave proof that the new mystes had learned the cult's key elements. Among other things, the 'catechism' also recapitulates the grades of initiation and the hierarchy of the cult. As stated earlier, admission was exclusive to men who had to complete different initiation ceremonies, thereby 'ascending' a ladder of grades of initiation (a ladder with symbolic emblems of the seven grades is depicted in the well-known floor mosaic at the Mithraeum of Ostia/the Mithraeum of Felicissimus, third century AD: *CIMRM* 299).[71] It has occasionally been argued that, due to its apparent familiarity, this hierarchical system would have been particularly attractive to the military.[72] One of the grades is even called 'soldier' (*miles*) (for example, *CIMRM* 1232, 1234, from Wiesbaden) and might thus have promoted the soldiers' sense of identification with the cult. In this regard, perhaps one of the epicleses (epithets) of the god might also have been attractive: 'Invictus',[73] the invincible (for example, *CIMRM* 1025, 1232, 1774, 1844).

Seven grades of initiation are recorded: 'Corax' (raven), 'Nymphus' (bee chrysalis), 'Miles' (soldier), 'Leo' (lion), 'Perses' (Persian), 'Heliodromus' (sun-runner) and the highest rank 'Pater' (father). These are also occasionally named in the inscriptions of the mystai (*CIMRM* 473: 'raven'; *CIMRM* 401: 'Persian') or in the graffiti preserved in some sanctuaries (for example, *CIMRM* 498 from the Mithraeum under the Santa Prisca in Rome, and at Dura-Europos).[74] Each grade and its symbol are connected to a planetary deity; for example, the 'raven' is connected to Mercury or 'Pater' to Saturn. The basic idea might have been that the initiate could ascend[75] to the celestial sphere via the seven planetary spheres. A search for answers concerning practice and liturgy, belief and ritual predominantly has to rely on archaeological findings (temples, monuments, mosaics, paintings and small finds such as crockery and cult utensils), as well as on the epigraphic record, and much more rarely on references found in other source types (such as in the above instance of the 'Mithras catechism'). While there are some (if few) literary references, these all originate 'exterior to the cult' (for example, the works of the philosophers Porphyry and Celsus; the so-called 'Mithras Liturgy', which was developed in the field of Egyptian religion and under the influence of Hellenistic philosophy, employs aspects of the cult for magical purposes; strictly speaking it cannot serve as evidence for the cult itself, or should be considered with caution).

The majority of literary references were penned by 'Christian rivals' (Justin, Tertullian, Firmicus Maternus),[76] whose depictions of the cult were unfavourable and lack clarity. After all, the cult was the 'main rival' of incipient Christianity and required denunciation. The degree of verisimilitude pertaining to the Christian depictions of the cult therefore remains uncertain. Matters are complicated further by the fact that the cult was a so-called mystery religion[77] – in simple terms this means that initiates and cult members were bound to secrecy concerning the cult and its rituals.

A reconstruction of the cult's legends and myths therefore has to rely predominantly on the iconic scenes represented in the cult's imagery, but a definitive interpretation cannot be reached. The cult's iconic centrepiece, either a relief or painting generally affixed to the wall at the end of the temple's central aisle, always represents the 'bull-slaying god', since the killing of the bull is the legend's central element,[78] while smaller subsidiary scenes on the relief frequently illustrate events in the Mithras narrative, such as the hunt for the bull. Cautes and Cautopates are placed on either side of the depiction, and dog, snake, scorpion, raven, sun and moon are also represented in fixed constellations. More complex representations offer a further series of 'standard scenes', such as Mithras being born from a rock, the 'water miracle', the hunting of the bull and the relationship to Sol, the sun god, in a depiction of the shared meal consisting of the bull's meat and blood (or of bread and wine, respectively), as well as of Mithras ascending to the heavens in a chariot.[79]

The killing of the bull might be understood as a parable for human destiny: the killing does not signify the destruction of life by Mithras. On the contrary, death is part of a larger transformation – grain sprouts from the animal's spinal cord, the dog and a snake drink the bull's blood, the scorpion pierces the bull's testicles, the blood becomes a grapevine and from the semen emerges the animal kingdom. The killing of the bull is therefore the central, redemptive event giving expression to the cosmic order and to the becoming and passing of the natural world. Many interpretations of the cult's beliefs and imagery, many explanatory accounts for the 'collection of zodiac signs in the Tauroctony' ('bull killing'), refer to the astrological knowledge of that era and equate the grades of initiation with the planets/zodiacs.

The cult's enigmatic iconography is occasionally even argued to represent an 'astronomic code':[80] it is argued, for instance, that the Mithraic legend of the killing of the bull reflects the discovery of the so-called axial precession. The rotation of the earth's axis was discovered in the first century AD, and attendant to the precession, observable events such as the apparent movement of the celestial horizon and the gradual disappearance of stars in the evening sky. One such example was the gradual disappearance of the Taurus constellation, which was replaced by the Perseus constellation during the second century AD: this event, it is argued, is reflected in the myth of Mithras. Such an interpretation relies on a whole series of prior assumptions and will not be examined here in greater detail. In short, though, it is based on the iconographic design of the figure of Mithras discussed above, which is seen as closely related to representations of Perseus in Greco-Roman art. In this view, Mithras is considered as an almighty god, a cosmocrat, who directly influenced celestial events.

During the third century AD in particular, the connection between Mithras and Helios or Sol, the sun-god, grew closer – some inscriptions contain the phrase *Deo Soli Invicto Mithrae*, 'uniting' the deities (for example, *CIMRM* 1425, 1659, 1915).[81] The equation of the invincible sun-god and Mithras also conferred upon Mithras a notable role as protector of the Roman Empire and its emperors. At the very latest by the time of Aurelian, the emperors preferred the sun-god; in AD 307, Diocletian and his co-emperors considered the *Deus Sol Invictus Mithras* a 'benefactor of their rule' (*fautor imperii sui*: *CIMRM* 1698). Emperor Julian the Apostate, often referred to as 'the last pagan' – who evidently was a Mithras worshipper – on 25 December AD 360 composed a panegyric hymn dedicated to the 'birthday of the sun-god', *dies natalis Solis invictis*, Helios (or to the 'sun-god Mithras'). Julian considered this god the ruler over all the gods, as creator of all beings and as guarantor of protection and prosperity. Evidently, the piquancy of the hymn and of its function as a 'birthday greeting' to the highest god Helios/Mithras lies in the fact that in Rome, since the beginning of the fourth century AD, 25 December was of course reserved for the celebration of the birth of Jesus Christ – in the same manner as Christian theology had absorbed into itself elements of pagan sun symbolism.[82]

Myths become alive when they are 'performed' in ceremonial celebrations[83] and when a member himself is able to play the role of a mythic figure. Rituals also served this purpose: perhaps the Mithras sanctuaries provided spaces ideally suited to this purpose, given their cavernous design and the images that could be mysteriously illuminated, veiled or unveiled, some of which were mounted for rotation (for example, in Nida, *CIMRM* 1083; Dieburg, *CIMRM* 1247; and Rome, *CIMRM* 397).[84] In addition, there were the ceiling paintings (starry heavens). A double-sided rotating relief from Konjic representing a 'normal bull killing' on its front, features on its rear side a depiction of a cult feast including Sol and Mithras (or perhaps priests representing them?).[85] At least two worshippers are shown wearing masks that presumably reflect their grade of initiation, namely the raven on the left and the lion on the right – are the worshippers here shown as performers, as 'actors'? A number of passages from a text by an anonymous Christian author reveal that for certain rituals, the mystai were expected to flap wings, to crow (like ravens) and to roar (like lions). In a sense, the sanctuary's atmosphere and furnishings represented the cosmos. The gathering community, reclining on the benches along the sanctuary side walls, through the cult rituals and communal meals and drinking, the cult feast,[86] was bound and fused into a community of worship. Rituals gave expression to the cult's 'mythology' in various ways, such as prayers or hymns, but also in 'role play' or masked performance, in the transposition of 'mythic events' into enactment by humans – namely, the 'priests, 'initiated' and 'novices'.

The Mithraic Mysteries During the Third and Fourth Century AD: Decline and Rivalry with Christianity

Mithraism is considered one of the main rivals of Christianity in the Roman Empire, developing during the same era and spread across comparable geographic regions. Justin, in the second century AD, considered it a diabolical imitation of Christianity, while Renan commented that, 'if the growth of Christianity had been arrested by some mortal malady, the world would have been Mithraic'.[87] Justin was particularly surprised by the similarity of Christian feasts and those of the Mithras cult, and the Church father Tertullian was of the view that the devil was mimicking the practices of the Christian sacraments. From Firmicus Maternus to the Church father Tertullian, the Christians viewed Mithras as a 'god of darkness', since the ceremonies took place under cover of darkness; the cult's temples were 'veritable camps of darkness', opined Tertullian.[88]

At the start of the fourth century AD, the cult enjoyed a kind of renaissance. A number of pieces of evidence from the age of the tetrarchy indicate that highly ranked state officials (all the way to the top of the hierarchy) were favourably disposed toward the cult (*CIMRM* 1698, 2278).[89] In AD 311 in Klagenfurt, in the province of *Noricum Mediterraneum*, the proconsul had the dilapidated Mithras sanctuary rebuilt (*CIMRM* 1431), and in Gimmeldingen/Rhineland-Palatinate, a new Mithras sanctuary was built as late as AD 325: this is the most recent establishment of a Mithras community on record (the exact date of the dedication is 22 January AD 325: *CIMRM* 1315). In the pagan restoration during the second half of the fourth century, Mithras played a part, even in Rome and within leading senatorial circles (for example, *CIMRM* 522, AD 377).[90]

But at the end of the fourth century, Mithras was defeated by Christ and by Christianity, which in the meantime had become the powerful official state religion – supported by the Roman emperors. The Christian faith had already established itself in Rome by the time of Paul the apostle (his journey to Rome in AD 60/61 indicates an already established community), and was possibly earlier than the Mithras cult, which does not emerge in Rome before the late first century.[91] In contrast to other types of cult in the *Imperium Romanum*, the Mithras cult shared the fate of other mystery cults in that it never became a public cult supported by the state, and it was never recognized in the official festival calendar of state or Army[92] – in spite of the fact that, as seen above, it had occasionally been accepted by emperors and the imperial periphery. Inscriptions and findings give evidence of the cult's demise: although Christianity since Constantine (AD 324–337) was well on the way to becoming the state religion – fully realized only in AD 391/392 with the ban of all pagan cults by the emperor Theodosius – the old cults retained worshippers for decades.

The emperors of the fourth century oscillated between tolerance and persecution of pagan cults. The destruction of many pagan temples (of Mithraea, for example, in Königshofen/Strasbourg and Saarburg) during the last decade of the fourth century is often understood in connection with the triumph of Christianity. But religious violence always had a limited local character and occurred infrequently.[93] Mithras inscriptions in the fourth century were already scarce, and we have no record of any activities taking place in Mithras temples in the fifth century. For instance, the find of coins in the Mithraeum in Pons Aeni (Pfaffenhofen am Inn) shows activity throughout the entire fourth century, but at the turn of the fifth century, the numismatic evidence there comes to a complete halt. The conclusion of the fourth century ushered in the demise of Mithras, and memory of the cult was expunged more thoroughly than was the case with other cults.[94]

Notes

1. Cumont (1911), pp.36–40.
2. Cumont (1911), pp.38–39; Cumont (1959), pp.102–03, 136–37. On Cumont's influence on this point, cf. Gordon (2009), pp.380–81. On the development of studies on this topic, see also Gordon (2013b), pp.237–42. On the ostensible role of centurions and 'national regiments' in the spreading of oriental cults, cf. also von Domaszewski (1895), pp.138–39; however, at pp.146–47 he specifically understands Mithras as a 'private god', not as an '(official) army god'.
3. The Commagene region rightly continues to be considered a 'zone of contact' and a nexus concerning the genesis of the Mithras cult: Winter (2012), pp.162–63; see also Schütte-Maischatz & Winter (2004) on Mithras and Dolichenus in the Commagene region; specifically on Doliche as the 'starting point of religious ideas', see pp.189–201.
4. Daniels (1975), pp.249–74, laid particular stress on the role of soldiers in spreading the cult; see also Martin (2015), pp.121, 126. By contrast, cf. Clauss (1992), pp.267–70; Clauss (2012), pp.37–40.
5. Collar (2011), pp.217–46; Collar (2013), pp.79–145. The Dolichenus cult as a 'military religion' is discussed by Speidel (1978), pp.38–45.
6. On the iconography, see, for example, Speidel (1980a), p.11; Stoll (2013), pp.84–85; on the *signa* in particular, see Speidel (1978), pp.55–63. Established phrases for collective dedications of the official army religion later adapted by the Dolichenus cult: Stoll (2007), pp.461–62, e.g. *AE* 1998, 1156; *CIL* 13.11780, 11782. On the role of officers, entire regiments, and divisions: Speidel (1978), pp.4–11, further examples at pp.64–71. The new inscriptions of the Dolichenum in Vindolanda also represent these types of collective dedications undertaken by regiments and officers: see, for example, Birley & Birley (2010), pp.35–39. Further, Collar (2013), pp.79, 113–17, stresses the role of officers and their networks; cf. also Stoll (2001), pp.197–99. Most recently on Dolichenus and the Roman Army, but with few new findings, Haensch (2012), pp.111–33. On the dedications undertaken by 'closed formations' (e.g., regiments), see Haensch (2012), p.125.
7. See, for example, Speidel (1980b), pp.1–2, 47: the Mithras cult as 'a religion of the Roman army' and its spread a result of the army (and its administrative personnel). The same view is essentially maintained in Herz (2015), p.824; similarly in Rives (2007), pp.81, 139, 141. On the 'transportation' of cults by the army and on its role as a bearer of culture or mediator, cf. Stoll (2001), pp.176–209; Stoll (2007), pp.468–71; Stoll (2013), pp.83–84, 94–102.
8. See, for example, Martin (2015), p.6: The membership of the Mithras cult is argued to have been 'largely drawn from the ranks of the military': see also pp.121, 126.

9. Gordon (2009), pp.379–450, esp. 414–15; see also Gordon (2012), p.974; Clauss (1992), pp.267–69; Clauss (2012), p.39.
10. Speidel (1978), pp.38–39; Stoll (2007), p.469; Stoll (2013), pp.96–97. Of course, non-military members of these cults might have been 'influenced' by the military, since the social composition of the garrisons consisted of veterans, soldiers' families and otherwise variously networked communities – Birley & Birley (2012), p.244 n.29 are absolutely correct; cf. also Collar (2013), pp.94–95 – they lived together in the sense of '*nota et familiaria castra*' (Tac. *Hist.* 2.80.3). Nevertheless, as a basis for statistical proof, only the unambiguous evidence can be considered, where the inscription itself identifies the acting individual as soldier or veteran.
11. On this 'system', see, for example, Stoll (2001), pp.126–32, 133–209; Stoll (2007), pp.451–76, esp. 452; see also Stoll (2013), pp.79–110; and Herz (2015), pp.822–28.
12. On the concept of 'oriental religions' and its implications, interpretations and new scholarly perspectives, compare Witschel (2012), pp.13–38.
13. Stoll (2007), pp.453–54, 462; Ankersdorfer (1973), pp.136–39, 140, 206–13.
14. On the Jupiter-Dolichenus cult as a 'religion for soldiers' or on the 'alliance of the cult with Roman state power', although never having become an 'official god of the army', cf. Speidel (1978); Speidel (1980a), pp.7, 10–11 (but with also the important reservation that it was not only soldiers who were worshippers: women are named as benefactors, and sanctuaries existed in the civilian hinterlands; other members consisted of slaves, merchants, officials), 18; Schütte-Maischatz & Winter (2004), pp.68, 195.
15. Cf. Speidel (1978), pp.5, 34: 'Mithras … was worshipped by select groups of initiates in secret rites underground' (34); he emphasizes the 'private nature' of the cult and its difference to the Dolichenus cult.
16. Kocsis (1989), pp.81–93; Kocsis (1991), pp.117–97. See also Gordon (2009), pp.407–08, who on the basis of Kocsis' interpretation – (1989), pp.83–85 – presents in even more detail the private character of the Mithraeum; the actual benefactor of the Mithraeum had been a slave or freedman, therefore a member of the officer's *familia*.
17. Cumont (1975), pp.152–214; Francis (1975), pp.424–45; see also Clauss (2012), pp.42–45.
18. Birley & Birley (2010), pp.25–51; Birley & Birley (2012), pp.231–57.
19. On the religious communities in Dura and the location of the two temples, cf. Dirven (2011), pp.201–20; see also Stoll (2001), pp.350–60.
20. Witschel (2013), pp.201–10.
21. On the 'Persian prehistory of the god', and on Mithras in Hellenistic Asia Minor, principally in the Commagene region, and among the Parthians and Sassanids, see the many references in Gordon (2012), pp.968–72; also Clauss (2012), pp.14–17; Witschel (2013), pp.201–05; Hensen (2013), pp.21–24.
22. For a summary of the history of the Roman cult, see, for example, Gordon (2012), pp.972–75; Witschel (2013), pp.205–09.
23. Witschel (2013), pp.208–09, summarizes the different scholarly approaches; see also Hensen (2013), p.86.
24. Gordon (2007), p.395. On the overall temporal and spatial spreading of the cult, cf. also Clauss (1992), pp.11–13, 253–60; Clauss (2012), pp.27–35.
25. Cf. also Spickermann (2003), pp.203–04. On the inscription by Lollius Crispus, cf. also Gordon (2009), pp.392–93.
26. See, for example, Spickermann (2003), p.313.
27. Compare, for example, the list in Spickermann (2003), pp.293–314 for *Germania Superior* only.
28. On the large number of Mithraea especially in Rome and Ostia, compare the estimates by Martin (2015), pp.10–11.
29. Gordon (2009), pp.386–89, rightly establishes the connection to the 'Limesforschungen' (German *Limes* scholarship, starting in the nineteenth century) in the interpretation of the cult.
30. Gordon (2007), p.396.
31. Spickermann (2003), p.314.

32. Clauss (2012), p.11; Martin (2015), pp.7, 90, 91.
33. On the lack of evidence in Egypt, see Martin (2015), pp.119–27; on the lack of evidence in the Middle East and the Near East, as well as the inconsistent spreading of the cult, see Daniels (1975), pp.272–73.
34. Winter (2012), pp.162–63; Schütte-Maischatz & Winter (2004), pp.79–187.
35. Hawarte near Apameia: Gawlikowski (2007), pp.337–61.
36. Clauss (1992), pp.261–79; Clauss (2012), pp.36–47; see also Gordon (2012), pp.973–74. For examples, see also Hensen (2013), p.27, e.g., *CIMRM* 1247: Schuster, Steinmetz; see also *CIMRM* 703; *AE* 1997, 1187: traders/merchants (*negotiatores*).
37. Here cf. Gordon (2009), p.395, who stresses the view that in some provinces the military did not play a very relevant role (Dalmatia, Noricum, Raetia, Moesia Superior and the two Pannonian provinces in the Danube hinterland, as well as the majority of Hispania, Gaul and Belgica – and of course Italy itself).
38. Clauss (1992), pp.263, 268–69, 270.
39. Collar (2013), p.93.
40. Collar (2013), pp.113–14. Cf. also Haensch (2012), pp.117–21, with a slight variation in the figures and tables at 125–33, with concrete epigraphic proof in each case.
41. Gordon (2009), p.417; Clauss (2012), p.39.
42. Gordon (2009), pp.423–30, offers a corresponding epigraphic list of 'military evidence' of the cult.
43. Gordon (2012), p.975. See also Hensen (2013), pp.32, 47, where the comparison is to cult and burial associations.
44. But this is in fact an offering devoted to 'Sol': according to *CIMRM* 1952 there is uncertainty – and rightly so – whether Mithras was the god in question.
45. Clauss (2012), p.37.
46. Speidel had already rightly noted this – (1978), pp.5, 34 n.110.
47. Hensen (2013), p.27, shares this observation concerning the higher officer ranks.
48. Huld-Zetsche (2001), pp.350–51.
49. Fleck (2006), p.299.
50. Concerning the altar discovery in the so-called Mithraeum I, the commentary and references in *CIMRM* 1208 point out that the altar was possibly 'abducted' (transferred later) from the neighbouring Dolichenum. On the Mithraeum, cf. also Clauss (1992), pp.119–21.
51. Clauss (1992), p.212.
52. Speidel (1978), pp.12–18, on the inscriptions, and 19–20 on the temple.
53. Doubts also in *CIMRM* 373, p.164; compare also Speidel (1978), pp.29–30, who also does not see Mithras in this instance.
54. Concerning this dedication, see also Stoll (2001), p.462 n.65; Clauss (1978), p.241: soldiers from the unit of Julian also made offerings at the Dura Mithraeum; Clauss argues therefore that the membership was 'spread' across the two communities; on other cross connections, see Stoll (2001), pp.353, 354.
55. Concerning the previously noted regimental dedications or those undertaken by officers and entire regiments – for example, Speidel (1978), pp.5–11, see also 68–70 – in the Dolichenus cult, it is important to consider those dedications in which the benefactor or dedicant professes his connection to the corps and to his group and regimental identity – by undertaking his dedication *pro salute*, 'for the welfare', of his regiment; see, for example, Speidel (1978), p.14, n.15 and 16 (both for the *equites singulares Augusti*, 'imperial cavalry' in Rome); 50, n.28 (Legion XII Gemina).
56. Stoll (2001), pp.353–54, 458–59 n.58, 460–61 n.61.
57. Fleck (2006), pp.297–98; Clauss (2012), p.36, notes an exception: the pagan restoration during the fourth century in Rome when some senators are in evidence as 'cult fellows'.
58. Huld-Zetsche (2001), pp.340–51; cf. also Gordon (2013a), pp.213–17; Clauss (2012), pp.48–56; Hensen (2013), pp.32–47. The term 'Mithraeum' is a neologism; *spelaeum*, literally 'cave',

246 *Religion & Classical Warfare*

or simply *templum* and *crypta* are the terms used in the inscriptions to designate the building (e.g., *CIMRM* 1397, 1431, 1673, 1846): Gordon (2007), p.394.

59. On the iconography, see Heyner (2013), pp.219–29, with further references. In particular, see Clauss (2012), pp.56–60; see also Hensen (2013), pp.48–51.
60. Huld-Zetsche (2001), p.341.
61. Spickermann (2003), p.309.
62. Huld-Zetsche (2001), p.342; Spickermann (2003), pp.308–09.
63. Schmotz (2007), pp.135–43.
64. Huld-Zetsche (2001), p.343, considers wood or painting on wood, stucco, bronze relief or bronze sculpture.
65. Huld-Zetsche (2001), p.343. Note also the wide spectrum of pottery-types from the Mithraeum in Mainz: Huld-Zetsche (2008), pp.27–76. For Mithraic vessels with figurative ornamentation, compare the notable example from Mainz with its depiction of seven ranks of initiation: Huld-Zetsche (2008), pp.77–79, 99–108. For further important 'crockery deposits' in connection with the cult, for example in the area of the Mithraea in Riegel or Tienen, see Gordon (2007), p.397; Gordon (2009), pp.401–02.
66. Compare, for example, Clauss (2012), p.52. On the temple as the venue of the cult feast, see also Hensen (2013), pp.36–38, on the design of the *podia* or *triclinia*; see also Hensen (2013), p.42.
67. The inscription is in *AE* 1998, 1007; *AE* 2000, 1140.
68. Compare Gordon (2007), pp.396, 400. On the size of the communities, see also Gordon (2009), p.397; Gordon (2012), pp.979–80. Cf. Clauss (2012), pp.62–64; Hensen (2013) on the role of the Mithras cult in Romanizing and integrating regions within the *Imperium Romanum* and the associated processes.
69. Huld-Zetsche (1986), pp.43–46; Clauss (1992), pp.115–17; see also Spickermann (2003), pp.203–05.
70. Brashear (1992); cf. Kloft (2010), p.76; but see Martin (2015), p.120; a critical view: Gordon (2012), p.997.
71. Beard, North & Price (2011), pp.305–06.
72. Rives (2007), p.139; Beard, North & Price (2010), p.300; Herz (2015), p.824.
73. See also Clauss (2012), pp.29–32, 39.
74. Beard, North & Price (2011), pp.316–19: names, ranks of initiation, 'hymns', and 'prayers' (?) from Santa Prisca; Dura-Europos: Francis (1975), pp.424–45. In general, see also Clauss (2012), pp.124–33; Frackowiak (2013), pp.230–36; Hensen (2013), pp.29–32.
75. Huld-Zetsche (1986), pp.8–11.
76. Beard, North & Price (2011), p.305, and for select passages with further references, 311–16; see also Gordon (2012), pp.991–93, 999–1002. On the 'Mithras liturgy', compare Betz (2003); Gordon (2012), pp.995–97; Martin (2015), p.120. On the status of extant sources on ritual practice, cf. also Martin (2015), pp.32–34, 41–56. On the 'theology of the cult', cf. Hensen's remarks (2013), pp.79–80.
77. Already in the third century AD, Porphyry refers to the cult as a mystery cult: Gordon (2007), p.394; see also Gordon (2012), pp.980–84. On Mithras as a mystery cult, cf. Kloft (2010), pp.69–81; and 82–110 on the characteristics and shared attributes of mystery cults. Cf. esp. Clauss (2012), pp.23–26; but see Gordon (2012), p.965.
78. Clauss (2012), pp.65–97; Hensen (2013), pp.48–52.
79. Gordon (2007), p.398. On the subsidiary imagery and its themes, see also Gordon (2012), pp.976–78; Hensen (2013), pp.52–60.
80. An influential view: Ulansey (1989); compare also Huld-Zetsche (2001), pp.346–50. Beck (2006) also discusses the astral symbolism in depth.
81. Compare the findings from the tribune's house in Aquincum: Kocsis (1989), pp.83–91 (*AE* 1990, 814, 817–20; *ILS* 4250); Gordon (2007), p.401. Here the god is given a succession of names: Sol Invictus, Invictus Mithras, Deus Sol Invictus Mithras, Sol Invictus Mithras

and Invictus Mythras (*sic*). On the emperors and Mithras, see Clauss (1992), pp.257–60. For Mithras and Sol, see Clauss (2012), pp.139–47; see also Hensen (2013), pp.72–73.
82. Kloft (2010), pp.80–81. But note the critical view of Gordon (2012), pp.994–95, 1003–04.
83. In general, see Clauss (2012), pp.98–109. For an overview, see also Hensen (2013), pp.61–72.
84. Huld-Zetsche (2001), p.352 with n.50, 51. On the 'special effects' of the cult and its sanctuaries, see also Gordon (2012), pp.978–79, including many references.
85. Frackowiak (2013), pp.233–34; Clauss (2012), pp.105–06; Clauss (2013), pp.243–44.
86. On the cult feast, compare Clauss (2012), pp.104–09; for 'Kultgeschirr' (that is 'dishes for the communal meals in the cult'), pp.111–16.
87. Justin *Apology* 1.66. The quotation is from Renan, E., *Marc-Aurele et la fin du monde antique* (Paris, 1882), p.579: '*On peut dire que, si le christianisme eût été arrêté dans sa croissance par quelque maladie mortelle, le monde eût été mithriaste.*' See Ulansey (1989), p.8; cf. Martin (2015), p.10.
88. Tert. *Cor. Mil.* 15; Clauss (2013), pp.243–49. More generally, see also Clauss (2012), pp.159–67.
89. Clauss (2012), pp.32–35.
90. Clauss (2012), pp.33–34. On Gimmeldingen, cf. Hensen (2013), p.83.
91. Huld-Zetsche (1986), pp.5–6. On the emerging power of the Christian Church, compare Beard, North & Price (2010), pp.364–88.
92. Cf. also Clauss (1992), pp.256–57.
93. Cf. Gordon (2012), pp.1005–06; but see also Clauss (2013), p.249, on Letter 107.7 of Hieronymus (Jerome), which makes reference to a city prefect in Rome (a certain Gracchus) who in AD 376/377 is reported to have 'destroyed, chopped up and burned … all the unnatural likenesses in the cave of Mithras'.
94. Clauss (2013), p.249.

Bibliography

Ankersdorfer, H., *Studien zur Religion des römischen Heeres von Augustus bis Diokletian*, Phil. Diss. (Konstanz, 1973).
Beard, M., North, J. & Price, S. (eds), *Religions of Rome I. A History* (Cambridge, 2010).
Beard, M., North, J. & Price, S. (eds), *Religions of Rome II. A Sourcebook* (Cambridge, 2011).
Beck, R., 'Mithraism since Franz Cumont', *ANRW* 2.17.4 (1984), pp.2002–15.
Beck, R., *The Religion of the Mithras Cult in the Roman Empire. Mysteries of the Unconquered Sun* (Oxford, 2006).
Betz, H.D., *The 'Mithras Liturgy'. Text, Translation, and Commentary* (Tübingen, 2003).
Birley, A. & Birley, A., 'A Dolichenum at Vindolanda', *Archaeologia Aeliana*, 5th series, 39 (2010), pp.25–51.
Birley, A. & Birley, A., 'A New Dolichenum, Inside the Third-Century Fort at Vindolanda', in Blömer, M. & Winter, E. (eds), *Iuppiter Dolichenus. Vom Lokalkult zur Reichsreligion* (Tübingen, 2012), pp.231–57.
Brashear, W.M., *A Mithraic Catechism from Egypt (P. Berol. 21196)*. *Tyche Suppl. 1* (Wien, 1992).
CIMRM: see Vermaseren (1963).
Clauss, M., 'Heerwesen/Heeresreligion', in *Reallexikon für Antike und Christentum 13* (Stuttgart, 1986), pp.1073–1114.
Clauss, M., *Cultores Mithrae. Die Anhängerschaft des Mithras-Kultes* (Stuttgart, 1992).
Clauss, M., *Mithras: Kult und Mysterium* (Darmstadt & Mainz, 2012).
Clauss, M., 'Mithras und Christus. Der Streit um das wahre Brot', in *Imperium der Götter. Isis – Mithras – Christus. Kulte und Religionen im Römischen Reich* (Darmstadt, 2013), pp.243–49.
Collar, A., 'Military Networks and the Cult of Jupiter Dolichenus', in Winter, E. (ed.), *Von Kummuh nach Telouch. Historische und archäologische Untersuchungen in Kommagene. Dolichener und Kommagenische Forschungen IV* (Bonn, 2011), pp.217–46.
Collar, A., *Religious Networks in the Roman Empire. The Spread of New Ideas* (Cambridge, 2013).
Cumont, F., *Textes et monuments figures relatives aux mystères de Mithra*, vols i–ii (Brüssel, 1896–99).

Cumont, F., *Die Mysterien des Mithra. Ein Beitrag der Religionsgeschichte der Römischen Kaiserzeit* (Leipzig, 1911).
Cumont, F., *Die orientalischen Religionen im römischen Heidentum* (Darmstadt, 1959).
Cumont, F., 'The Dura Mithraeum', in Hinnells, J.R. (ed.), *Mithraic Studies I: Proceedings of the First International Congress of Mithraic Studies* (Manchester, 1975), pp.151–214.
Daniels, C.M., 'The Role of the Roman Army in the Spread and Practise of Mithraism', in Hinnells, J.R. (ed.), *Mithraic Studies I: Proceedings of the First International Congress of Mithraic Studies* (Manchester, 1975), pp.249–74.
Dirven, L., 'Strangers and Sojourners: The Religious Behavior of Palmyrenes and Other Foreigners in Dura Europos', in Brody, L.R. & Hoffman, G.L. (eds), *Dura Europos. Crossroads of Antiquity* (Chestnut Hill MA, 2011), pp.201–20.
Domaszewski, A.V., 'Die Religion des römischen Heeres', *Westdeutsche Zeitschrift für Geschichte und Kunst* 14 (1895), pp.1–124.
Fleck, Th., 'Isis, Sarapis, Mithras und die Ausbreitung des Christentums im 3. Jahrhundert', in Johne, K.P., Gerhardt, Th. & Hartmann, U. (eds), *Deleto paene imperio Romano. Transformationsprozesse des Römischen Reiches im 3. Jahrhundert und ihre Rezeption in der Neuzeit* (Stuttgart, 2006), pp.289–314.
Frackowiak, D., '"Mithras ist mein Kranz". Weihegrade und Initiationsrituale im Mithras-Kult', in *Imperium der Götter. Isis – Mithras – Christus. Kulte und Religionen im Römischen Reich* (Darmstadt, 2013), pp.230–36.
Francis, E.D., 'Mithraic Graffiti from Dura Europos', in Hinnels, J.R. (ed.), *Mithraic Studies II* (Manchester, 1975), pp.424–45.
Gawlikowski, M., 'The Mithraeum at Hawarte and its Paintings', *JRS* 20 (2007), pp.337–61.
Gordon, R.L., 'Institutionalized Religious Options: Mithraism', in Rüpke, J. (ed.), *A Companion to Roman Religion* (Oxford, 2007), pp.392–405.
Gordon, R.L., 'The Roman Army and the Cult of Mithras: A Critical View', in Wolff, C. (ed.), *L'armée romaine et la religion sous le Haut-Empire romain* (Paris, 2009), pp.379–450.
Gordon, R.L., 'Mithras (Mithraskult)', in *Reallexikon für Antike und Christentum* 24 (Stuttgart, 2012), pp.964–1009.
Gordon, R.L., '"Glücklich ist dieser Ort…" Mithras-Heiligtümer und Kultgeschehen', in *Imperium der Götter. Isis – Mithras – Christus. Kulte und Religionen im Römischen Reich* (Darmstadt, 2013a), pp.211–18.
Gordon, R.L., 'Von Cumont bis Clauss. Ein Jahrhundert Mithras-Forschung', in *Imperium der Götter. Isis – Mithras – Christus. Kulte und Religionen im Römischen Reich* (Darmstadt, 2013b), pp.237–42.
Haensch, R., 'Die Angehörigen des römischen Heeres und der Kult des Iuppiter Dolichenus', in Blömer, M. & Winter, E. (eds), *Iuppiter Dolichenus. Vom Lokalkult zur Reichsreligion* (Tübingen, 2012), pp.111–33.
Hensen, A., *Mithras. Der Mysterienkult an Limes, Rhein und Donau* (Darmstadt, 2013).
Herz, P., 'Religions: Principate', in Le Bohec, Y. (ed.), *The Encyclopedia of the Roman Army III* (Oxford, 2015), pp.822–28.
Heyner, R., 'Aus dem Felsen geboren … Die Ikonographie des Mithras-Kultes', in *Imperium der Götter. Isis – Mithras – Christus. Kulte und Religionen im Römischen Reich* (Darmstadt, 2013), pp.219–29.
Huld-Zetsche, I., *Mithras in Nida-Heddernheim. Gesamtkatalog. Museum für Vor- und Frühgeschichte Frankfurt am Main. Archäologische Reihe 6* (Frankfurt, 1986).
Huld-Zetsche, I., 'Der Mithraskult im römischen Germanien', in Spickermann, W. (ed.), *Religion in der germanischen Provinzen Roms* (Tübingen, 2001), pp.339–59.
Huld-Zetsche, I., *Der Mithraskult in Mainz und das Mithräum am Ballplatz* (Mainz, 2008).
Kemkes, M., *Der Soldat und die Götter. Römische Religion am Limes* (Esslingen am Neckar, 2004).
Klöckner, A., 'Mithras und das Mahl der Männer. Götterbild, Ritual und sakraler Raum in einem römischen "Mysterienkult"', in Egelhaaf-Gaiser, U., Pausch, D. & Rühl, M. (eds), *Kultur der Antike. Transdisziplinäres Arbeiten in den Altertumswissenschaften* (Berlin, 2011), pp.200–25.
Kloft, H., *Mysterienkult der Antike. Götter – Menschen – Rituale. Vierte Auflage* (München, 2010).

Kocsis, L., 'Inschriften aus dem Mithras-Heiligtum des Hauses des tribunus laticlavius im Legionslager von Aquincum aus dem 2.-3. Jahrhundert', *Acta Archaeologica Academiae Scientiarum Hungaricae* 41 (1989), pp.81–93.
Kocsis, L., 'Das Haus der tribuni laticlavii aus dem Legionslager in Aquincum', *Budapest Régiségei* 28 (1991), pp.117–97.
Martin, L.H., *The Mind of Mithraists. Historical and Cognitive Studies in the Roman Cult of Mithras* (London, 2015).
Quack, J.F. & Witschel, C. (eds), *Entangled Worlds. Religious Confluences between East and West in the Roman Empire. The Cult of Isis, Mithras and Jupiter Dolichenus* (Tübingen, 2014).
Rives, J.B., *Religion in the Roman Empire* (Oxford, 2007).
Schmotz, K., 'Der Ostvicus von Künzing: Lage, Ausdehnung und "Sondereinrichtungen"', in Thiel, A. (ed.), *Forschungen zur Funktion des Limes. Beiträge zum Welterbe Limes 2* (Stuttgart, 2007), pp.133–49.
Schütte-Maischatz, A. & Winter, E., *Doliche – Eine kommagenische Stadt und ihre Götter. Mithras und Iupiter Dolichenus* (Bonn, 2004).
Schwertheim, E., *Die Denkmäler orientalischer Gottheiten im römischen Deutschland – mit Ausnahme der ägyptischen Gottheiten* (Leiden, 1974).
Speidel, M.P., *The Religion of Iuppiter Dolichenus in the Roman Army* (Leiden, 1978).
Speidel, M.P., *Jupiter Dolichenus. Der Himmelsgott auf dem Stier* (Stuttgart, 1980a).
Speidel, M.P., *Mithras-Orion. Greek Hero and Roman Army God* (Leiden, 1980b).
Spickermann, W., *Germania Superior. Religionsgeschichte des römischen Germanien I* (Tübingen, 2003).
Spickermann, W., 'Mysteriengemeinde und Öffentlichkeit', in Rüpke, J. (ed.), *Gruppenreligionen im Römischen Reich* (Tübingen, 2007), pp.127–60.
Stoll, O., *Zwischen Integration und Abgrenzung: Die Religion des Römischen Heeres im nahen Osten. Studien zum Verhältnis von Armee und Zivilbevölkerung im römischen Syrien und den Nachbargebieten* (St Katharinen, 2001).
Stoll, O., 'The Religions of the Armies', in Erdkamp, P. (ed.), *A Companion to the Roman Army* (Oxford, 2007), pp.451–76.
Stoll, O., 'Einheit und Vielfalt. Religionen und Kulte der römischen Armeen der Kaiserzeit (1.-3. Jh. n. Chr.)', in Bertholet, F. & Schmidt, Chr. (eds), *Entre archéologie et épigraphie. Nouvelles perspectives sur l'armée romaine* (Bern, 2013), pp.79–110.
Ulansey, D., *Die Ursprünge des Mithraskultes* (Stuttgart, 1989).
Vermaseren, M.J., *Corpus Inscriptionum et Monumentorum Religionis Mithriacae*, vols i–ii (Den Haag, 1956–60) (= *CIMRM*).
Vermaseren, M.J., *Mithras: The Secret God* (New York, 1963).
Vollkommer, R., 'Mithras', in *LIMC* 6.1 (Text), 6.2 (Plates) (Zürich, 1992), pp.325–68, 583–626.
Winter, E., 'Doliche. Eine kommagenische Stadt und ihre Heiligtümer', in Wagner, J. (ed.), *Gottkönige am Euphrat. Neue Ausgrabungen und Forschungen in Kommagene* (Mainz, 2012), pp.161–66.
Witschel, C., '"Orientalische Kulte" im römischen Reich – neue Perspektiven der altertumswissenschaftlichen Forschung', in Blömer, M. & Winter, E. (eds), *Iuppiter Dolichenus. Vom Lokalkult zur Reichsreligion* (Tübingen, 2012), pp.13–38.
Witschel, C., 'Die Ursprünge des Mithras-Kults. Orientalischer Gott oder westliche Neuschöpfung?', in *Imperium der Götter. Isis – Mithras – Christus. Kulte und Religionen im Römischen Reich* (Darmstadt, 2013), pp.201–10.

Chapter 9

Constantine and Christianity in the Roman Imperial Army

Christopher W. Malone

The religious world of the Roman Army changed significantly in late antiquity. In the early third century, the legions marched behind Jupiter's eagles, and the emperor would offer sacrifices ahead of battle to ensure success. At the end of the fourth century, an emperor might spend the night before battle fasting in a chapel and take advice from hermits in the Egyptian desert, while the army marched to victory behind Christian banners and crosses.[1] The pivotal figure in this transformation was the emperor Constantine I. Constantine was the first Christian emperor, and he established the paradigm which all but one of his successors would follow. It is difficult to overstate his influence. In the Roman Army, and indeed in the Empire at large, Constantine began a process of Christianization with far-reaching consequences. Although many Christian thinkers opposed army service, he came to the faith as a result of his military victories. To honour his new patron God properly, Christian symbols patterned after his visions were emblazoned on shields and standards, soldiers were instructed in new ways to pray, and Christians who enlisted were granted privileges. It would be left to his successors to formalize and finalize this process, but Constantine's imprint on Roman Army religion would remain.

Constantine was also instrumental in combining Christianity with imperial ideology, causing old Roman ideas to be reinterpreted in new Christian forms and leading Church thinkers to reconsider the place of warfare and violence in their worldview. This chapter will thus focus primarily on Constantine himself, his experience of battlefield Christianity, the changes he wrought in the appearance and practices of the Roman Army and what effect all this had. To truly understand him, however, we cannot operate in a vacuum, and so before turning to the emperor himself we begin by considering the problematic relationship between Christianity and the Roman Army in the period before Constantine.

Milites Christi before Constantine

Scholars generally agree that Christian participation in the Roman Army before Constantine was a limited affair, but the earliest indications of Christian soldiers actually centre around the turn of the third century. At this point we not only find Christians in the Roman Army, but an ongoing debate over their role and whether they should be there at all.[2] Christians in general were a minority in early imperial society, and were mostly found in cities, whereas many army recruits came from a more rural background. It is therefore difficult to imagine large-scale recruitment, particularly combined with the disapproval of many of the Church fathers, but there were Christians in the legions all the same.[3]

Discussion of the Army and early Christianity is very often tightly and even contentiously linked to debates about the place of violence and pacifism in both ancient and modern Christianity.[4] In 1979, Helgeland took this tradition to task, deconstructing scholarly views on Christianity and the Army based on individual scholars' own religious and cultural backgrounds.[5] Shean has since called this 'confessional' approach into question,[6] but it highlights the importance of separating modern and ancient points of view, and of recognizing that Christianity has always been a religion incorporating multiple differing traditions.

That said, the majority of Christian authors in the period before Constantine did disapprove of Christians serving in the Roman Army. The objection was twofold – violence and bloodshed were moral and ethical issues, but there was also the problem of the Army's traditional cultic practices, understood as idolatry, particularly the cult of the standards. The Church fathers were not unanimous, however, and questions may be raised as to how representative our written sources were of 'ordinary' Christians' views.[7] Patristic sources barely even mention the Army before the end of the second century, and when discussion does appear, there is already debate. Even non-Christians were aware of it: Celsus, who published a long attack on Christianity in the late AD 170s, argued that Christians were disloyal, as they refused to serve in public office or in the Army, and he urged them to do so.[8] Origen's refutation was that Christians did help the Empire – as priests, praying for victory, doing more good than soldiers.[9] Origen is very much part of the anti-military tradition, though praying for victory implicitly accepts the emperor's use of violence and warfare as righteous.[10]

Tertullian is the best example of the anti-military viewpoint, and is the early Christian author with the most interest in the Army. He certainly seems well-informed about military life, and his father was likely a centurion.[11] Over time, Tertullian moved from disapproving acceptance of Christian soldiers to outright opposition.[12] The problem with the Army, in his view, was primarily an issue of idolatry, both in traditional Army religion and the presence of Mithraism and other cults which were encountered serving in the legions.[13] To follow Christ, he argues, one cannot serve the emperor – the *sacramentum* of one conflicts with the other.[14]

His major work on the topic, *de Corona* (*On the Crown*), bans military service outright. This work was inspired by an unnamed Christian legionary, who rejected the military decoration of a laurel crown at a military parade around AD 201, at which the troops were receiving a donative. He was martyred for it. Tertullian praises this legionary, and censures the other Christians who were part of the unit, and who apparently saw no conflict between their service (and laurels) and their faith.[15] Tertullian also argues at length in *On Idolatry* that military service is unacceptable. In the course of his discussion there, he cites and refutes a number of objections to his position, which not only confirms there was disagreement within Christian communities, but also demonstrates that each side was arguing from both ethics and scripture.[16]

Tertullian's contemporaries and co-religionists therefore held diverse opinions. Origen, we saw, would agree with his stance, and while Hippolytus also wanted to ban Christians from enlisting, the wording of his canons allows a Christian soldier to stay in the Army if he can avoid shedding blood and reciting the oath.[17] Clement of Alexandria, by contrast, saw soldiering as just another profession – God is God of everything, after all.[18] Thus, although the majority took an anti-military stance, there were shades of difference among Christian commentators.

Some patristic authors could even celebrate Christian participation in the Roman Army, and Tertullian, in his earlier career, was among them. His *Apology*, from AD 197/198, talks about Christians praying for the emperor and his armies, and points to Christians everywhere in the Empire, including forts and army camps (*castella* and *castra ipsa*).[19] He also celebrates Christian legionaries in the famous story of Legion XII Fulminata, the 'Thundering Legion'.[20] Around AD 174, Roman troops campaigning under Marcus Aurelius against the Marcomanni found themselves cut off in the forests, out of food and water and blockaded by the enemy. Suddenly, and miraculously, the heavens opened, rain fell to refresh the Romans, and hail and lightning crashed into the barbarian camp, driving them off. Then, apparently, everyone fell to arguing about whose god had intervened. Our sources show a religious debate lasting at least into the fifth century: was it Jupiter, another rain god, an Egyptian mage conjuring Hermes Trismegistos, Julian the Chaldaean or even Marcus himself who brought the lightning?[21] Or was it the God of the Christians? Already at the time, Bishop Apolinarius of Hierapolis claimed this was so, and that Legion XII Fulminata was in fact full of Christians.[22]

Tertullian himself was aware of this story and mentions it approvingly – Christians being present in Legion XII Fulminata suited his apologetic purposes, especially since the legion was among the loyalists who helped put down the revolt of Avidius Cassius.[23] It is worth stressing that the Christian versions do not have the legionaries fighting, only invoking the miracle. Nevertheless, the idea of an entire unit being made up of Christians was apparently credible for a Christian audience in the early third century. The legion's apparent recruiting grounds, Melitene and Cappadocia, were in a region that shows signs of Christianization fairly early, especially compared to the Western provinces, and this may have added to the credibility of the tale.

Our literary sources thus indicate a noticeable level of Christian involvement with the Roman Army – indeed debate over the validity of such service assumes it. Our earliest non-literary evidence for Christians in the Army is in fact contemporary with Tertullian's *de Corona*: an epitaph dated to AD 201 for a soldier of Legion II Parthica in the catacombs of Domitilla.[24] It is therefore clear that there were Christians serving in the Roman Army by the start of the third century, and some of them obviously did not agree with the view of thinkers like Tertullian and Origen that there was conflict between Christianity and armed service. Although the coincidence in timing is not definitive, the sudden appearance of this issue in our sources may well be tied to increased enlistment under the better service conditions offered by Septimius Severus.[25]

Christian participation in the Army increased during the third century, particularly in its later half, the so-called 'peace of the church' initiated by Gallienus' cessation of official persecution around AD 260. According to Digeser, Christians of the later third century 'quietly commingled with their fellow citizens in the classroom, in the army, in the government, and even in the palace'.[26] Soldiers from the garrison at Dura-Europos, for example, seem to have participated in the town's Christian community, as graffiti from the house church shows soldiers' names we also find in the military district.[27]

Several hundred epitaphs of ancient Christian soldiers are known, but very few can be convincingly dated before AD 324.[28] Their existence indicates that some Christian communities – and the soldiery – accepted and commemorated Christian troops,[29] and a wide variety of ranks are attested, even in the pre-Constantinian examples: centurion, *evocatus*, *beneficiarius*, *lanciarius* and praetorian guards all appear.[30] Christian phrases are often the giveaway for these inscriptions, especially (*requiescat*) *in pace*, which is found alongside traditional religious phrases like *D(is) M(anibus)*.[31] Two Christian soldiers, the brothers Florentius and Herodius, may in fact have fought *against* Constantine at the siege of Verona in AD 312.[32] In other cases, thoroughly traditional material may appear with Christian symbols. Mercurelli identified a sarcophagus belonging to a praetorian guardsman who served under Gallienus, which shows several Christian symbols,[33] while on a more humble scale, the epitaph of Valerius Thiumpus has *panes decussati*, loaves of bread with crosses on them, alongside traditional wording.[34] For other inscriptions, context rather than content is key – especially for soldiers' epitaphs found in the catacombs.[35]

Military Martyrs and Constantine's Context

It therefore seems there was a significant Christian presence in the Army of the early fourth century, although certainly still only a minority. This was the period of Constantine's rise to power, during the breakdown of the Tetrarchy. The religious ideology of the regime was based on an aggressive focus on old Roman ways and imperial divinity, and so alternative religions like the Manicheans and Christians were targeted as social and political problems. This came to a head in the last great persecution of the Christians, which began in AD 303. Importantly, it actually began with the military, both in terms of the initial purge and the supposed incident which incited it. Lactantius relates the story of Christian palace guards attending a sacrifice and disrupting the omens by crossing themselves as an apotropaic gesture – something which gives us an example of how Christians in the military may have dealt with Roman Army rituals. Diocletian subsequently ordered that all soldiers had to sacrifice or be dishonourably discharged, and the scope of persecution expanded in the following years.[36]

Two examples of soldiers who served the Tetrarchy and appear to have lost their posts in this way are worth noting. Most well-known is the cavalry officer Aurelius Gaius, who recounts his decorated career and exotic travels on his wife's epitaph, finishing with an obviously Christian reference to the Resurrection.[37] The other is Julius Eugenius, who had served the Tetrarchy – with distinction, his epitaph tells us – until he too left during persecution in the reign of Maximinus Daia. This tells us Eugenius had actually stayed in the service for some years after the initial decree. He nevertheless went on to become Bishop of Laodicea around AD 315, so Christians not only could and did serve in the Army, but a military background was no impediment to entering Church office at this point, and moreover a bishop in AD 340 apparently need feel no embarrassment about being an ex-soldier.[38]

Not everyone simply left the Army, of course, and the great persecution also produced a number of accounts of soldier martyrs.[39] These are important not only as further evidence for Christian soldiers, but also for the variety of possible Christian responses to how armed service fitted with their faith.[40] The most celebrated case of hard opposition is the young martyr Maximilian, who in AD 295 refused conscription on religious grounds, arguing that as a Christian he could not serve.[41] Tertullian would have been pleased, but the magistrate Dion tried to talk him into it, pointing out there were other Christians in the Roman Army, even in the imperial *comitatus*![42] Maximilian replied that what others do is on their own consciences: 'They know what is best for them. I however am Christian, and cannot do wrong.'[43] While some Christians – and apparently the pagan Roman governor – saw no problem with Christians serving in the legions, Maximilian and his hagiographer did.[44]

Other military martyrs seem to have reached some kind of crisis point and decided to quit their service. Tertullian's martyr in *de Corona* is an example; we also have the centurion Marcellus. We do not know how long he had been serving, but as an officer it must have been for some time. The text does not make clear whether he enlisted as a Christian or converted while in the Army, but at the festivities for the imperial birthdays in AD 298, Marcellus threw down his belt, sword and centurion's switch, rejecting the imperial cult and announcing himself a Christian.[45] He was put on trial and executed, as the judge in the text declares, for breaching his discipline and oath.[46]

A similar example is Julius the veteran, again a long-time soldier. He had in fact re-enlisted, but refused Diocletian's order that soldiers had to offer sacrifice. At his trial he defended himself on the grounds of his twenty-seven years' loyal service, during which he went on seven campaigns and was the inferior of no man in the battle line – and was a Christian all the while.[47] Again the judge, the prefect Maximus, encouraged him to just go along with it, even offering a bribe. Maximus clearly did not care if there were Christians in the Army – he cared that his men followed orders, even just to burn incense. Julius had apparently served for decades without encountering any religious problems. It is unclear how common this would have been, and it would certainly have depended on the individual commander, but Eusebius implies that for many soldiers Diocletian's order to sacrifice or face dismissal was the first time they had really been forced to choose.[48]

All these soldier-martyrs essentially called attention to their resistance, and we read of several others who came forward during persecutions to reveal themselves.[49] There were others who, it seems, would have kept on serving had they not been called out. Eusebius discusses two examples. A certain Basilides was asked by his comrades to swear an oath for some reason, but he refused, as a Christian – they laughed it off, but felt forced to present him to the authorities when Basilides' steadfastness (or obstinacy, depending on your perspective) continued.[50] The other was Marinus, a good soldier of good family, who around AD 260 had worked his way up to the rank of *optio* and was about to be promoted to centurion when a rival snitched to the commander that Marinus was a Christian. It was only at this point that the bishop came to him and demanded he choose between his service and his faith: Marinus chose martyrdom, but he had seen no ethical conflict prior to this, and presumably would have accepted the promotion.[51]

Lee wonders whether Marinus had managed to get out of imperial cult rites, or if he just went through the motions.[52] The point of view of the Army in these texts is essentially that soldiers could believe what they liked, so long as they did their duty – including their duty to the imperial cult.[53] Soldiers of Jewish or Mithraic faith seem to have been given some leeway in their observance of traditional military cult rites – initiates of Mithras apparently also rejected their military crowns – and it is plausible that some Christians in the Roman Army were given the same latitude.[54] We should be careful not to blindly assume that all worshippers of Christ were necessarily strict in their monotheism. Severus Alexander, for one, supposedly had Christ and Abraham among his *lares*, and Constantine himself was hardly exclusive in his religious adherence for several years after his conversion.[55]

Diocletian's attempt to purge the Army of Christians in AD 303 leads MacMullen to think there must have been few if any left by AD 312,[56] but estimating numbers like this is difficult, especially since the policies of persecution were unevenly employed and questionably effective, not to mention largely ignored in the West. We know, too, that once persecution had ended, soldiers were offered their old posts back, and this was the case both for those persecuted under the Tetrarchy and those Christians briefly targeted by Licinius in AD 324.[57] The Nicaea canons likewise make clear that some Christians, having left the Army, re-enlisted even during periods of persecution.[58] So, even if the initial purge was effective, there is no reason to think its effects were long-lasting, as at least some men came back under the policy of toleration. Given that Constantine had bishops in his retinue even before AD 312, Christians in the Western armies may never have been as strongly pressured to leave the ranks.

The Milvian Miracle of AD 312

The tale of Constantine at the Milvian Bridge is well known, but is worth considering at some length because of its importance for understanding not only Constantine himself, but also military religion under his reign – and therefore the rise to prominence of Christianity in the later Roman Army.[59] On 28 October AD 312, after a rapid but hard-fought campaign down through Italy, Constantine faced off with his rival Maxentius near the Milvian Bridge, just north of Rome. Like Constantine, Maxentius had forced his way into power during the breakdown of the Tetrarchy, and was the last obstacle to Constantine's control of the western half of the Empire. In Constantinian propaganda, of course, he was a cruel tyrant oppressing the people of Rome.[60] Maxentius initially planned to withstand a siege, so the Milvian Bridge itself had been destroyed, but he had been goaded out either by omens or by popular unrest in the city. The battle seems to have been straightforward – Constantine's veteran force broke their enemy and sent them fleeing back towards the river, where the weight of the rout collapsed the temporary pontoon crossing which had replaced the bridge. Maxentius was one of the many who drowned.

The victory left Constantine as master of the capital and the western provinces, but the real importance of the battle is his claim that he owed his victory to the Christian God. Before the battle, Constantine had apparently experienced some kind of divine epiphany in a vision or dream, and afterwards caused his men to march under a new sacred sign in recognition of his new divine patron. The Christian narrative was, unsurprisingly, first promoted by his Christian supporters, and although imperial sources were initially vague about what had happened, the emperor came to back it as the official explanation. As such, each of our sources differs in detail on the issue of divine intervention, but all maintain the line that Constantine had some supernatural help. Even Zosimus, hostile as he is to Constantine, records omens and portents surrounding the battle.[61]

Christians saw Constantine's victory as their God's doing, and it was most likely the Christians in Constantine's retinue who convinced the emperor this was the case.[62] The earliest narrative account comes from one of them – Lactantius, once professor of Latin at Nicomedia, and tutor to Constantine's eldest son, Crispus.[63] On Barnes' dating, Lactantius was already with Constantine in Gaul by AD 310, making him a source close to events, though he may not have been present at the battle himself.[64] In his book *On the Deaths of the Persecutors*, published around AD 315, Lactantius narrates the emperor's dream on the eve of battle, in which Constantine was instructed to draw the heavenly sign – a cypher for the name of Christ – on his men's shields.[65]

Lactantius' description of the symbol is a little ambiguous:[66] he describes a bisected X with a looped top, which can be read as describing the *chi-rho* monogram or christogram (☧), made up of the first two letters of Christ (Χριστός) in Greek. Though rarely used at the time, this was later employed extensively by Constantine and his Christian successors as both an imperial and a religious symbol. Alternatives have been proposed, like the staurogram (⳨), which appears in Christian literary and funerary contexts from the early third century.[67] Other, more dubious interpretations, minimizing Constantine's conversion, have ranged from an ankh to a six-pointed star, or even a spoked solar wheel. Whatever the case, Lactantius is specifically describing a Christian symbol, and asserts an entirely Christian version of events. The year that Lactantius published, Constantine was already taking tentative steps to publicly associate himself with the *chi-rho*: the symbol appears on two milestones from AD 312/313, and a medallion from Ticinum minted in AD 315 depicts the emperor's frontal portrait with the symbol on his helmet (see Figure 9.1).[68]

The other contemporary Christian source is Eusebius – probably Constantine's biggest

Figure 9.1: Ticinum Medallion (obverse), showing Constantine wearing the *chi-rho* on his helmet, AD 315 (*RIC* 7 Ticinum 36). (© The Trustees of the British Museum)

fan – who offers two accounts. The earlier, in his *Ecclesiastical History*, does not specifically mention a vision, perhaps having been published before that part of the story was well known in the East, and focuses instead on depicting Constantine as a new Moses.[69] In the panegyrical *Life of Constantine*, written in the AD 330s, Eusebius gives us a more developed narrative, which he tells us he heard from Constantine himself.[70] Here the vision occurs simply some time before the battle, not on its eve.[71] Constantine was looking for a powerful god to help him, and followed his father's example of seeking out the supreme deity.[72] This god then responded with a midday vision, a cruciform trophy in the sky over the sun, and the words 'by this conquer' in Greek (ἐν τούτῳ νίκα) visible to all. Later, he had a dream instructing him to build a copy of the sign from the vision. Constantine consulted his episcopal advisors, who explained and interpreted his visions as sent by Christ, and so he had the new banner built, a cross-shaped *vexillum* topped with the christogram, which would become the late Roman battle standard, the *labarum*.[73]

Eusebius portrays an already openly Christian Constantine entering Rome in triumph after the battle, displaying Christian symbols on placards, and also describes a victory statue holding either a standard or a cross – or maybe both, if the *labarum* was intended – with an inscription making reference to the 'saving sign', in language largely reminiscent of the surviving inscription on his arch.[74] It is possible that this was the colossal statue whose pieces are now outside the Capitoline museums, but scholars have been tentative about this identification. While it is not impossible that Constantine displayed Christian symbols already, the description perhaps belongs to a subsequent visit, like his *decennalia* in AD 315.

Divine visions on momentous occasions were hardly new. Roman culture was overflowing with signs and portents from the gods, both genuinely believed and cynically manipulated.[75] The interpretation put on the victory in AD 312 was essentially traditionally Roman, in that divine favour had won the day, even though the god involved was not part of the traditional pantheon. The drama of the tale grew in the telling: when Rufinus came to adapt Eusebius's *History* into Latin, for example, he inserted a new more spectacular vision, so that Constantine, anxiously praying for guidance, sees a fiery cross in the eastern sky accompanied by angels proclaiming 'in this sign you will conquer' (*in hoc signo vinces*).[76]

There are also surviving non-Christian versions of the events of AD 312, some of which have a claim to reflecting the contemporary 'official' line. Constantine's arch in Rome – dating, again, to AD 315 – refers simply to the vague *instinctu divinitatis*. The battle scenes on the frieze do not show any obvious divine assistance, though Victory and Tiber are both depicted.[77] We can connect this to the description of the battle in the panegyric of AD 313. Here there is no vision, and Christianity makes no appearance, but the orator seems to have understood the need to sell a religious angle to the battle, and does so in carefully ambiguous language.[78] A 'supreme deity' is mentioned in several places as the emperor's guiding inspiration, and the only named traditional god is the River Tiber. This ambiguity stands in stark contrast to the very traditional and overt theology of the earlier tetrarchic panegyrics, which allude frequently to Jupiter and Hercules in particular.[79] It therefore seems to indicate a changing religious mood at court.

By AD 321, the battle had accrued diverse supernatural elements. Nazarius' panegyric of that year still does not name the supreme deity, referring to 'that divinity' who habitually helped Constantine,[80] but does describe the appearance of a celestial army to support Constantine at the Milvian Bridge, led by none other than his divine father, Constantius I.[81] Alföldi suggested this was a pagan attempt to replace the now-widely publicized Christian vision.[82] Rodgers instead wonders whether it was aimed more at Constantine's last competitor and one-time ally Licinius, who, it was believed, had also been granted a vision and divine help in battle.[83]

Licinius had once been a hero for the Christians too, jointly enacting the AD 313 Edict of Milan with Constantine, which granted legal recognition to Christianity and established a policy of religious toleration.[84] According to Lactantius, he had also defeated the last persecutor, Maximinus Daia, with the help of the Christian God, and had been granted a vision in which an angel taught him an ambiguous but monotheistic prayer for his men to recite before battle.[85] Indeed, it is Licinius, not Constantine, who appears at the climax of Lactantius' narrative, and there were most likely more Christians in Licinius' army than in Constantine's, since there were many more in the East in general.[86]

When Constantine finally decided to get rid of his erstwhile ally and marched against him in AD 324, Licinius needed to be rewritten as a tyrant and an enemy, not just of Constantine, but of the Church and of God.[87] In AD 325, Eusebius added an extra book to his *History*, and revised earlier material to depict Licinius as a persecutor, describing Constantine's decision to overthrow him as motivated by the plight of the Eastern Church.[88] Eusebius casts Licinius as emulating Diocletian in going after Christians in military commands, suggesting incidentally that they were once again somewhat common.[89] Both emperors had collaborated on the Edict of Milan, but Licinius seems to have been less interested in Christianity than his colleague. While Constantine had become convinced his *summus deus* was the Christian God, Licinius had not, favouring Jupiter as his patron. He may have originally accepted some Christianizing measures on Constantine's recommendation, but he did not adopt the *labarum*.[90] He nonetheless maintained the policy of toleration until relations with Constantine (now the darling of the Christians) broke down, and he came to recognize the Church as a potential danger.[91] The conflict was presented by Christian authors as a clash of religions, and while clergy and even Constantine himself may have seen it that way, it seems unlikely that the ordinary troops would have.[92]

After the defeat of Licinius in AD 324, Constantine was able to project a more confident and clear Christian image. The last remaining pagan god, Sol Invictus, disappeared from his coinage, the title *victor* replacing the traditional pagan *invictus*,[93] and he presided over the ecumenical Council of Nicaea. The emperor's own *Oration to the Saints* announces his Christianity around this time, literally preaching to the choir[94] and even connecting the vague language of his early reign to Christ.[95] His new faith is made clear in his AD 325 letter to the provincials of Palestine, and around the same time was announced abroad in his letter to the Persian king Shapur II.[96] This letter contains what appears to be a statement of faith, as well as a recommendation of the Persian Christians to the king's protection. The implicit threat that Constantine might otherwise have to intervene to protect their interests may point to early preparations for a war with Persia.

One of the greatest points of controversy in the study of Constantine has been the sincerity of his Christianity. Exactly when and whether he 'really' converted (whatever that means) is a perennial and ultimately unanswerable question, but that has not stopped historians ever since his own day.[97] Constantine initially favoured the patronage of Sol Invictus, the unconquered sun god, a very common religious trend at the time, one to which his father may have adhered. His coin issues from AD 310–323 often feature Sol, which has been seen as a religious statement, but the real importance of the Sol issues is not that they were still being minted after AD 312, but the fact that they stopped for good in AD 324.[98] At the time, however, the panegyric of AD 310 related another, solar, visionary experience.[99] According to the panegyrist, Constantine was shown a vision in that year which he associated with Gallic Apollo, a local stand-in for Sol.[100] He saw Apollo and Victory offering him laurel wreaths, vouchsafing thirty years of rule each.[101] This panegyric in particular contains a number of attempts to redefine Constantine as a ruler in his own right, rather than as part of the tetrarchic system, emphasizing his supposed descent from Claudius II, and focusing on his father and his divine support as sources of legitimacy.[102]

This too-early vision has exercised scholarship. It is plausible that the Milvian vision itself was not a separate event, but rather a reinterpretation two years later of the earlier vision, after Constantine had mulled it over and discussed it with the Christian clergy who were already part of his retinue. This would very much fit the pattern of a slower religious conversion which was centred around AD 312, rather than happening all at once; it likewise meshes with Eusebius' claim that Constantine was actively searching for the right patron god.[103] An alternative is that Constantine was (or wanted to present himself as) a man prone to visions, to which Eusebius does also allude.[104] Attempts have been made to locate the 'real' vision in a natural phenomenon, such as the solar halo effect, but what exactly Constantine saw is of less importance than what he did afterwards, and how he used this idea of his visionary experience.[105] This can be pushed further, to suggest that the initial use of the *chi-rho* symbol in AD 312, whether on shields or made into a banner, was actually ambiguous, like much of the religious rhetoric of Constantine's early reign: while it appeared obviously Christian to a Christian audience, it could have been interpreted as solar by pagans.[106] The Christian version eventually won out, and there were, after all, already solar associations that were acceptable within Christianity.[107] In the end, we should not expect an all-or-nothing conversion in AD 312; as Nock demonstrated, religious conversion was and is a slow process, even though it is very often remembered later as a moment of sudden revelation in the manner of the road to Damascus – or the Milvian Bridge.[108]

The emperor's public behaviour and self-portrayal are much more important than speculation about his private beliefs – and are actually accessible to us. He acted as a major patron to the Church and raised his sons as Christians, and after he gained sole control of the entire Empire, he increasingly portrayed himself as Christian to the Empire at large.[109] He was also quickly willing to get involved in Church disputes 'like a universal bishop appointed by God', and even quipped that he was himself 'bishop of those outside'.[110]

Constantine was no theologian, and his Christianity was predicated on military victory, so he honoured his new God, who had gained him Rome in AD 312 and then won him sole rule in AD 324.[111] Maintaining his new powerful patron and sustaining unity among his subjects were his main interest, rather than the specifics of doctrine. Constantine's reaction to the Arian controversy shows this clearly.[112] Arian doctrine placed Christ as subordinate to the Father, rather than equal or the same being, and most of our Christian authors see it as one of the most vital and defining religious disputes of the fourth and fifth centuries. Constantine dismissed it as a silly bit of semantics, before trying to solve it by introducing a compromise formula at the Council of Nicaea.[113]

As part of his response to his heavenly patron, he carried through several general measures on behalf of the Church – whose political usefulness he clearly recognized, even beside his personal beliefs. First, he and Licinius collaborated on religious toleration, but then we find him giving grants of money, privileges and immunities,[114] bankrolling the Bishop of Carthage as early as AD 313,[115] inviting Christian priests to court,[116] banning crucifixion in AD 316[117] and appointing Christian governors, courtiers and officials because he knew – Eusebius explains – that they would be well-disposed to him and loyal.[118] Judicial powers were granted to bishops as early as AD 318,[119] marriage laws changed in AD 320 to remove sanctions on celibacy,[120] and numerous churches and Christian buildings were erected in Rome, Palestine and across the Empire, demonstrating considerable interest in sponsoring the faith (including, perhaps programmatically, erecting the Lateran basilica over the demolished camp of Maxentius' 'horse guard', the *equites singulares*).[121] For Harries, the new churches and benefits were more than just patronage for a favoured cult, 'they were a statement of Constantine's confidence in divine support for his rule'.[122]

In AD 321, the *dies Solis* (that is, Sunday) was made a festal day, on which legal and public business was banned.[123] Eusebius characterized life in the palace by the AD 330s as pious and almost church-like, the emperor himself occasionally giving philosophy lectures which touched on theological, moral and ethical topics.[124] Christian symbols also began to be seen in the palace, and Eusebius even mentions a painting of Constantine trampling a dragon.[125] Brown comments that Constantine took from Christianity 'a grass-roots certainty that the Christian God "stood close by" to grant "victory" to his worshippers', an ideal that had evolved out of the experience of martyrdom but seemed confirmed through Constantine's victories.[126] Whatever we might think of Constantine as a visionary, the Christian version of AD 312 quickly came to dominate his path, and the first connection between Christianity and imperial power had therefore come about through the military; more particularly, the first of the Christian emperors came to the new faith with an understanding of Christ as a patron god who would win him battles.

Christianizing the Roman Army

The Army of the late Empire differed in several respects to its earlier form, largely due to reforms carried out under the direction of Diocletian and Constantine.[127] The size of the Army was significantly increased, both in terms of manpower and number of individual units, though these were smaller than early imperial legions. The old distinction between legionary and auxiliary was removed, and instead the Army was divided into two broad categories – the field armies (*comitatenses*), centralized, mobile forces with better conditions of service, and the troops on the borders (often called *limitanei*). The Praetorian Guard was dissolved, replaced by new imperial guards, particularly the elite cavalry of the *scholae palatinae*. The *comitatenses* were initially commanded by the emperor himself, and later the new high generals, the *magistri*, took over running the central field armies, while the border units were under the command of regional military *duces*, severing military command from civilian provincial government. Greater use was made of heavily armoured cavalry, and barbarian troops were employed extensively. New equipment also appeared, like the fearsome dragon banners (*dracones*). We can be confident that Constantine's reign saw the final division of troops into *comitatenses* and *limitanei*, the creation of the new *magistri* and the final dissolution of the praetorians – and of course the introduction of new Christian elements.

Establishing an exact timeline for these military reforms is difficult, as our narrative sources are not that interested – though Lactantius complained about Diocletian's reforms, and Zosimus about Constantine's.[128] Nevertheless, major reorganization was only really feasible with the entire Empire in Constantine's hands, and so post-AD 324 is the most likely period for him to have introduced changes in Roman Army religious practices too.[129] Jones, however, would backdate them slightly, arguing that the more obviously Christian elements were initially put into place as a kind of religious propaganda aimed at the more Christianized Eastern provinces during his conflict with Licinius.[130]

The most visible change was the introduction of the *labarum*, a new battle standard, directly linked to the Milvian vision.[131] Eusebius gives us our fullest description of its form, apparently from eyewitnesses in the AD 320s or 330s. It was a golden pole with a cross bar, topped by a wreath containing the *chi-rho* monogram, made of gold and gems. From the bar hung a tapestry banner, covered in gold thread and precious stones, along with portraits of the emperor and his sons.[132] Eusebius understands the entire object as a Christian symbol, and for him its cruciform shape was its most important feature.[133] Originally there was just the one – it may have been first built in AD 312 (though not in the spectacular form Eusebius saw it), but the *labarum* was certainly in use by the AD 320s, when Constantine's forces marched under it to take control of the East.[134] Later, it seems each army may have been given its own *labarum*.[135] In the 360s, Gregory Nazianzen described it as the primary imperial standard, above and leading the other banners, portraits and dragons.[136] Adopting a Christian sigil like this, and tying it to imperial military power, helped build Constantine's self-portrayal as the champion of Christianity.[137]

Constantine attached a guard of fifty or so elite troops to carry and defend the *labarum*,[138] and it quickly became more than just a symbol – it was believed to have a mysterious protective power for the Romans, and its sheer force could rout enemies both mortal and spiritual.[139] Eusebius heard from the emperor that on one occasion one of the bannermen panicked and handed the *labarum* off to a comrade in order to flee (so presumably its aura of courage did not work on everyone), and was immediately killed by a javelin, while the soldier now holding the standard found the *labarum* blocked all incoming projectiles.[140]

Constantine himself mentions the *labarum* in his letter to the Eastern provincials in AD 325, declaring it led him to victory and protected him.[141] This became the standard understanding: Prudentius credited the banner with making Constantine unconquerable,[142] while the Church historian Socrates insists Constantine's army, marching under its power, defeated the northern barbarians so completely that they converted.[143]

Changing the legionary standards was a major step. The cult of the standards, especially the golden eagle-topped *aquilae*, was as old as the Empire and central to military religion – the reverence shown them was a major reason patristic authors opposed Christians serving in the Army. The Roman obsession with the standards can be glimpsed by the effort spent when they had been lost, like those regained from Parthia by Augustus. The traditional military cult attributed a certain amount of totemic or numinous power to the standards, which seem to have been genuine objects of devotion.[144] Associating the new *labarum* with these revered objects allowed Christian troops to participate in the cult in a way they could not before, and helped elevate the status of Christianity in the Army. Redirecting the cult to include a Christian military icon would also come to influence military opinions, perhaps even to win converts – Sozomen thought this was Constantine's aim.[145] Outside of the Army, the adoption of a Christian symbol perhaps offered a rapprochement between patristic disdain for idolatrous practices in the legions and the desire of lay Christians to serve as soldiers.[146]

The first depiction of the *labarum* on coins dates to the aftermath of the war against Licinius. On the less-than-subtle *SPES PVBLICA* issues of AD 327–328, the *labarum* – depicted, as in Eusebius, as a *vexillum* topped by the *chi-rho* with three dots on the banner, perhaps the imperial portraits – pierces a serpent, generally agreed to be a stand-in for Licinius, but perhaps also for evil in general – a Judeo-Christian association that pagans would not make (see Figure 9.2).[147] This was not

Figure 9.2: *SPES PVBLICA* ('Public Hope') issue, showing the *labarum* piercing a serpent, AD 327 (*RIC* 7 Constantinople 19). (Courtesy of Classical Numismatic Group)

the first time the *chi-rho* itself was depicted in an 'official' way: we already see it on two milestones dating to late AD 312/early AD 313 in North Africa.[148] The vision and symbol were well-enough known to Christians in Rome that graffiti on a wall under St Peter's, dated to AD 315 by Guarducci, depicts several epitaphs with the *chi-rho*, in one case paired with the Constantinian tag *hoc vin(ces)*.[149]

It had also appeared on coinage in AD 315, on the Ticinum medallion for Constantine's *decennalia* (see figure 9.1).[150] Stars and crosses of similar form are found frequently as mintmarks or decorations in field on Constantinian coins; from the Arles mint, some of them are clearly *chi-rhos*, while at Antioch, the staurogram appears. This was elaborated in the AD 330s: the *GLORIA EXERCITVS* ('Glory of the Army') reverse shows soldiers with standards and the *chi-rho* floating between them; some *ROMA* types show the *chi-rho* above the she-wolf.[151] In the last years of Constantine's reign, the *labarum* began to become more prominent on coins. The *GLORIA EXERCITVS* type was revised to have two soldiers flanking one large standard with a banner, on which the christogram appears on issues from several Western mints (see Figure 9.3).[152]

Figure 9.3: *GLORIA EXERCITVS* ('Glory of the Army'), showing soldiers flanking the *labarum*, AD 336 (*RIC* 7 Arles 394). (Courtesy of Classical Numismatic Group)

After Constantine, this form of the *labarum* became a fixture on Roman coinage, along with the motif of the emperor as standard bearer, an innovation of Constantinian iconography.[153] It is very tempting to associate this motif entirely with the *labarum*, though the earliest versions show the banner empty or with abstract dots or crosses; later emperors are much more clearly holding the Christian banner (see Figures 9.4, 9.6).

While Constantine's own coins may not have put the christogram front and centre, his successors took up Christian military symbols with gusto, and the conflict to secure his inheritance shows a fight over the iconography.[154] His sons all feature the *labarum* on their coins, usually held by the emperor himself, whether alone, being crowned by Victory, dominating captives or standing on the prow of a ship (see Figure 9.4).[155] The attempted usurpers Magnentius and Vetranio also both issued coins featuring

Figure 9.4: *FEL TEMP REPARATIO* (*Fel[icium] Temp[orum] Reparatio*: 'Re-establishment of Fortunate Times'). Constantius II on galley with phoenix, Victory and *labarum*, AD 350–355 (*RIC* 8 Thessalonica 174). (*Courtesy of Classical Numismatic Group*)

the *labarum*,[156] and both tried to co-opt Constantine's vision: Magnentius devoted issues to the christogram itself (see Figure 9.5), while Vetranio went as far as using the slogan *hoc signo victor eris* ('by this sign you will be victorious').[157]

The *labarum* and the standard bearer motif became a regular feature on imperial coins throughout the fourth century and into the fifth, even coming to dominate Western gold issues of the early fifth century (see Figure 9.6).[158] The *labarum*, the first Christian symbol used by the Empire, thus shifted from a commemoration of one of Constantine's victories to a general symbol of Christian imperial triumph.[159] It does eventually disappear from the coinage, around the time of Theodosius II and Valentinian III – it was replaced by the cross, which became a vital element in imperial iconography. However, variations of the Christian standards do reappear later, often being carried by Victory herself (see Figure 9.7).[160]

Figure 9.5: Magnentius adopts the *chi-rho*, AD 353 (*RIC* 8 Amiens 34). (*Courtesy of Classical Numismatic Group*)

Figure 9.6: *RESTITVTOR REI PVBLICAE* ('Restorer of the State'). Reverse: Valentinian I with *labarum*, AD 364–367 (*RIC* 9 Lyon 1b). (*Courtesy of Classical Numismatic Group*)

Although it was superseded on coinage, the *labarum* continued to hold its vital place in the Roman Army. Ambrose describes the troops as led by the name and worship of Christ, not by eagles or the flights of birds,[161] while Jerome refers to crosses on the banners.[162] The record of the accession of Leo I in AD 457 refers to multiple *labara* in attendance, along with other military standards, which were all lowered until the emperor was crowned, then raised aloft with acclamations.[163] As late as the ninth century, the imperial throne in Constantinople was still flanked by the Christian military standards Constantine had introduced.[164]

Figure 9.7: *VICTORIA AVGGG* ('Victory of the Augusti'). Obverse: Anastasius I. Reverse shows Victory holding a reversed variation of the old *labarum*, AD 507 (Hahn & Metlich, 2013, 6a). (*Courtesy of Classical Numismatic Group*)

Christian symbols also appeared elsewhere in the Roman Army. In Lactantius' account of AD 312, the christogram had been displayed not on a banner, but painted on the shields of Constantine's men, and Eusebius does confirm that Constantine had Christian symbols marked on his soldiers' shields later in his reign.[165] No complete shields survive from the fourth century to check, but there are examples in late Roman art.¹⁶⁶ Constantine's first son, Crispus, is depicted on coins carrying a shield, which in some variations bears the *chi-rho*.¹⁶⁷ On a silver dish from the time of Constantius II, the emperor is shown flanked by a guard who carries a *chi-rho* shield (see Figure 9.8);¹⁶⁸ other tableware depicts similar soldiers, including a niello cup now in St Petersburg and a glass beaker from Cologne.¹⁶⁹

Sketches of the lost decorations from the columns of Theodosius and Arcadius show soldiers carrying shields with the monogram, and christograms on shields and armour continue to appear on fifth-century coins even after the *labarum*

Figure 9.8: Gilt silver plate showing Constantius II in triumph: note the soldier's shield. Photograph © The State Hermitage Museum. (*Photo by Vladimir Terebenin*)

ceased being depicted.¹⁷⁰ The most famous depiction is probably the mosaic of Justinian in the church of San Vitale in Ravenna (dedicated in AD 547), which likewise shows an imperial guard with a christogram on his shield standing alongside the emperor (see Figure 9.9). Strangely, the illustrated *Notitia Dignitatum* does not show many Christian shield-symbols, despite a copious catalogue of designs, though a few do seem to bear crosses. Blame for this is often put on the Carolingian copyists.¹⁷¹ It is also possible that only select troops used the *chi-rho* shield, perhaps those closest to the emperor.¹⁷²

Figure 9.9: Mosaic of Justinian from San Vitale, Ravenna, AD c.547. (*Photo by the author*)

Helmets and other parts of military kit were also emblazoned with Christian iconography. Constantine himself had the christogram on his helmet on the abovementioned Ticinum medallion (see figure 9.1), and Eusebius refers to his habit of wearing it.[173] Coins with the emperor in the same style of helmet were issued in subsequent years, particularly AD 319. The *chi-rho* recurs on one variant, though more common is a six-pointed star, which, it has been suggested, may mimic it.[174] In later Church historians, the symbol on his helmet becomes instead a relic: it was believed that Constantine had the nails from the crucifixion – brought back after his mother Helena's visit to the Holy Land – worked into his helmet and his horse's bridle as protective measures.[175]

There have been some finds of pieces of ordinary military equipment that have Christian symbols on them, perhaps in emulation of the stories about Constantine. Bishop and Coulston discuss a number of helmet badges and what seem to be crest pieces with gilded and copper alloy christograms. Belt fastenings have also been found with the *chi-rho*. Most elaborate are gilded silver helmet sheathings, found in the walls of the Roman fort at Alsóhetény in Hungary, dating most likely to the AD 370s, which have an embossed *chi-rho* symbol on the nose ridge, near the eyeline.[176]

The adoption of the new Christian iconography was joined by alterations in the religious pattern of army life. We know from Vegetius that the military oath (*sacramentum*) had become Christian by the early fifth century at the latest. Soldiers, of whatever religious stripe, now all swore by God, Christ and the Holy Spirit, and by the majesty of the emperor, to serve emperor and Empire.[177] Lee stresses the importance of the ritual of oath-taking – not just its religious nature, but its potential use in inculcating loyalty and values, especially as a repeated part of what has always been a very ritualistic profession.[178] Vegetius also records explicitly Christian watchwords like *deus nobiscum* among more traditional ones such as *virtus* or *triumphus imperatoris*.[179] Other changes were slower to take hold. In Vegetius' day, the war-cry was still the rolling *barritus*, which had been adopted from Germanic troops;[180] it is not clear when this shifted, but by the sixth century at least, Christian slogans had replaced it, with '(*deus*) *nobiscum!*' (God with us!) being customary. Maurice, however, recommends chanting the phrase with psalms and the *kyrie eleison* before leaving camp, rather than shouting it at the charge.[181]

Constantine gave the troops time off on Sundays to attend church, so Christians under arms were no longer sidelined by the Army cult. Non-Christian soldiers were issued a usefully ambiguous monotheistic prayer to recite together. This seems to point to an effort to replace some parts, at least, of existing Army rites. The prayer would read easily as a Christian prayer to a Christian, but the theology is primarily about military victory.[182] Barnes suggests it may have been introduced as early as AD 313, connecting it to Licinius' prayer reported by Lactantius, though the text is different.[183] It is not entirely clear whether the prayer and Sunday leave were the general practice for the whole military, or just troops in the capitals and imperial *comitatus*. It is, however, in line with Constantine's other more general measures about the *dies Solis*, with the banning of public business noted above.[184] Exactly when the pagan associations of sun-day were drowned out by Christian ones is unclear, but already in AD 386 the emperors refer to the *dies Solis* as being called *dominicus* (the Lord's Day) by their predecessors, so Constantine had clearly had an effect.[185]

Troops heading to mass presumably needed priests. Sozomen claims Constantine provided some kind of military chaplains attached to units, but there is general agreement that he is projecting his own fifth-century situation backwards.[186] Theodoret, in a letter from the AD 440s, specifically mentions someone we would recognize as an army chaplain: a deacon, Agapetus from Hierapolis, appointed to a Roman Army unit in Thrace to guide them in religious matters. It appears from context that this was now a widespread practice.[187] The sources are silent for something like this in the fourth century; such priests *may* have existed earlier, but it is very unlikely any formal or organized version was established by Constantine.[188] We know other cults had priests in military units, some of whom were serving or ex-soldiers, but not in any centrally organized way, and they were cultic officials who served in the unit, not priests of the unit.[189] Priests had in fact long travelled with the legions – Roman generals had always had priestly personnel, primarily to take the auspices, and of course the emperor could perform rites as *pontifex maximus*, as Trajan does in several scenes on his column.[190] Christian clergy travelling with an army in this manner, attached to the emperor, do appear in the fourth century. Constantine brought some on campaign against Licinius,[191] and intended to do so when he was planning to invade Persia – the bishops said at the war council that they would come and fight alongside him through prayer.[192]

There is some limited evidence from the fourth century for chapels or churches being built within forts along the northern frontiers. About a dozen are known – fewer than we might expect, but urban billeting was common in this period, which would give the troops access to regular churches.[193] Constantine is also reported as having a portable church-tent, like Moses in the desert.[194] There, according to Eusebius, he would attend the rites and also receive occasional revelations from on high, upon which he would rush immediately to attack the foe (and, of course, win).[195] Sozomen claims Constantine also had church-tents distributed to the legions, but other emperors are reported as going to actual churches before battles, which suggests tabernacle tents may have been a quirk of Constantine's.[196] In a letter dating to AD 403, Jerome does mention the Goths marching with church-tents, but these more migratory Arian armies perhaps needed to create their own spaces for worship in the officially Catholic Roman Empire of the fifth century.[197]

The Roman Army thus, fairly rapidly, became 'symbolically Christian' in its practices and symbols, and the majority of this was put in place by Constantine.[198] His measures facilitated Christians in the Army, but group conversion is a slow process. Theodoret held that the soldiers had been taught their catechism by Constantine and his sons, and that Constantius II even encouraged his men to be baptized before battle.[199] But not even Constantine could create immediate cognitive change in a culturally and religiously diverse group like the late Roman Army.[200] The changes in symbols and practices would exert a top-down pressure, and begin the process of Christianization, but for the time being the Army was not made religiously exclusive.

An ongoing and significant pagan presence during the fourth century is most likely.[201] In a preamble to a law, probably from AD 326, Constantine's men acclaim him with a pagan salutation: 'Augustus Constantine, the gods [plural] preserve you for us' (*dei te nobis servent*). The veterans then seek their special privileges, which Constantine of course grants. The non-Christian opening was altered when the law was carried over into Justinian's Code, becoming the singular *deus te nobis servet*, and making the text (and the troops) properly orthodox.[202] Theodosius II's editors had not been so precious about the salutation, suggesting there was still some way to go in terms of Christianization in the mid-fifth century.[203] Even if the emperor was already on his way to becoming Christian, some (perhaps most) of Constantine's veterans were not Christians, but still followed him. Despite promotion and encouragement of Christianity, no choice needed to be made outside of one's own ethics until the end of the fourth century, and soldiers could largely carry on with their own religious traditions.[204]

Assessing the impact of Constantine's measures is therefore tricky. They were not empty gestures: the cult of the standards was an old practice, and the *labarum* is a significant introduction to it; the new oath, made upon enlistment and repeated annually, mattered.[205] Christians are found as commanders and officers as early as the AD 320s – they may have received preferential promotion – and their presence only increased under Constantine's sons. Exact numbers are elusive; both the ranks and the command structure were a mix of pagans and Christians.[206] It is difficult to gain an accurate picture of religious adherence in the Army, since at any point we only know the details of some prominent individuals. Salzman's study of Christianity in the Western upper classes found a limited increase of Christians among high military officers in the fourth century, though the effect becomes much more prominent in its last decades.[207] Christians only began to predominate in the fifth century.[208] The existence of Christian officers would play a role in influencing the religious make-up of the Roman Army generally, but perhaps more influential is the fact that after Constantine, all but one of the emperors were Christian.

'Soldiers who Know Only How to Pray'

The reign of Julian offers something of a test case for how quickly the Army changed under Constantine's new order. When Julian took power in AD 361, there had been a bit more than a generation for new ways to take root. Constantine's sons had all been Christians, and after Julian the emperors were all Christian, though of differing confessions; the apparent ease with which fourth-century soldiers served these rulers with diverse doctrines has led some scholars to consider the Army as a whole to be largely uninterested in religious questions, in stark contrast to the noisy public religious discourse of the cities.[209]

Julian had been raised Christian, but once he became sole emperor he openly promoted a kind of organized paganism he termed 'hellenism'. As Caesar he had performed his public Christianity, like attending mass for Epiphany ahead of the Battle of Vienne. He did so, in Ammianus' words, 'to win the favour of all and opposition of none', which strongly suggests a level of Christianization among both populace and troops.[210] Even if this was somewhat surface-level, participating in Christian rites had already become the expected and right thing for an emperor to do. However, as Julian later crows in a letter to the philosopher Maximus, once he was openly pagan, his troops came to his sacrifices anyway; something Ammianus remembers with some distaste for the excesses at Antioch.[211]

Julian attempted to restore the old religion in the military just as he did in the civilian sphere. The *labarum* was put aside in favour of the eagles and pagan images, which had been partly removed either by Constantine or, more likely, his sons.[212] In a more subtle move, Julian required soldiers to offer incense when receiving their donatives, reintroducing an imperial cult rite. Libanius says this worked a charm, but in so doing indicates an awareness that different army groups had already developed prominent religious differences. Julian led an army made up partly of his own Western loyalists, and partly of Eastern troops who had belonged to the Arian Constantius II. Libanius tells us Julian's Gallic forces were largely pagan, though there were at least some Christians in the Western ranks: men like the less-than-willing Martin of Tours, for example,[213] and an escort of 350 Christian troops that Constantius had provided for Julian when he was appointed Caesar.[214] Constantius' troops, according to Libanius, lacked reverence for the gods – that is, they were primarily, perhaps entirely, Christian. Julian therefore needed to spend months training them, improving morale and gaining the help of the gods, including his donatives-for-incense scheme.[215]

This prompted outrage among Christian authors, aimed at the soldiers as much as at Julian. There was so little apparent resistance among the troops to the reintroduction of pagan rites that Ephraim Syrus derided the soldiers in a hymn, saying they had turned back to paganism or were even crypto-pagans, rejecting the cross and Christian banners and thereby ensuring military failure against Persia.[216] Gregory Nazianzen instead fell back on stereotypes of soldiers as simple and greedy, but by default obedient.[217] Both, interestingly, seem to assume that the troops were all meant to be Christian. Augustine claimed Julian's Christian troops obeyed him only on the field, not in religious rites, but Sozomen is explicit: very few soldiers refused to participate in cult activity, but likewise very few actually converted to hellenism. Instead, 'through ignorance or simplicity', they just did as they were told.[218] There are stories that some of those tricked gave their donatives back when they realized, and some even tried to get themselves martyred, going into exile when they found Julian was not fool enough to cooperate with that.[219]

In outlining the strategies Julian used to try and win over the troops, both Gregory and Sozomen refer to a combination of his personal efforts and charisma, the use of officers, rewards like the donative, and removing and replacing Christian army symbols.[220] All of these are strategies Constantine himself had used to introduce a level of Christianization in the first place. Apparently they worked. Julian was nonetheless pragmatic, and kept on skilled Christian commanders who had served Constantius, even taking them into Persia; they were ultimately the ones who would elect Jovian afterwards.[221] We may also detect some remaining ambiguities of the kind Constantine encouraged in his early reign. Linguistically, Ammianus recalls the use of the singular *deus* by the troops under Constantius and Julian in both his Christian and pagan periods.[222] It was not unusual in polytheism to refer to 'the god' singular, of course, but the religious context of the mid-fourth century and the rote nature of shouted slogans make this stand out. The troops may have expected it by now.

It is difficult to perceive what ordinary soldiers thought at any point in history. It may be as simple as that they followed the emperor like they were trained to do; if he ordered them to offer incense, most of them would do so.[223] Julian was a successful commander and had won an incipient civil war without striking a blow, and this was a powerful argument that reflected a belief as old as Rome, that divinities favoured successful commanders. If the emperor's god (or gods) helped him to victory, then why not honour them? Constantine's own religious experience had essentially this basis. Tomlin suggests soldiers were convinced by charisma and victory, not by doctrines, and so religious considerations did not really affect army loyalty.[224] Liebeschuetz similarly sees soldiers' religious adherence as determined by their loyalty to their emperor.[225] Our sources are aware that some people did indeed simply follow the current emperor's lead. Socrates felt Julian's enticements to sacrifice helped show the real Christians from those in name only, and notes individuals who changed what they professed depending on the emperor's beliefs.[226] This had been an issue under Constantine as well, as some conversions were made in the hope of honours and rewards.[227] Later, Libanius would warn Theodosius of the dangers of false conversions made out of force or fear.[228]

We might see the troops' apparent disinterest in religious change as a sign of the slow progress of Christianization,[229] but we must remember that Christian soldiers before Constantine also often went along with non-Christian rites, and this did not make them any less Christian, except to the moralists. Even if we read it as simply a religious veneer over the Roman Army, that veneer certainly worked both ways. Despite Christian authors' horror at the troops following Julian's rites, his religious 'seduction' of the troops barely outlived him. Jovian had one last pagan sacrifice performed, to read the omens, but reinstated a Christian regime for the rest of his tenure.[230] According to Theodoret, Jovian originally resisted election as emperor because he did not think he could lead a pagan army – apparently he thought Julian had done a thorough job – but his troops replied that not only were they Christians, but the older men had been instructed in the faith by Constantine himself.[231]

Was this just a willingness to go along with the emperor's views? There are signs that some soldiers at least were active members of their faith communities. When Jovian was met outside Antioch by Arians from Egypt, seeking to replace their strict Nicene bishop Athanasius, one of Jovian's soldiers shouted them down – apparently he too was a staunch Nicene, despite having marched behind Julian.[232] Religion mattered to some soldiers, then, and this sort of anecdote can point to individual instances of both pagans and Christians in the Army. Fundamentally, it seems that the Roman Army as a whole did not experience internal divisions around religious issues, at least not in a way that carries through to our sources. It probably goes too far to see the Army as totally indifferent, but trained obedience and discipline surely played a role in following the emperor's lead. Constantine's conversion, then, did not suddenly convert the Army any more than it did the Empire at large. However, his measures clearly had already changed things, since Julian took great pains to try to arrest and reverse the Christianization of his soldiers. Though the troops were still religiously mixed, a large proportion were already Christian. Constantine had begun the process of Christianization, and Julian could do nothing to stop it.

Constantine's Legacy

After Julian, all Roman emperors followed Constantine's lead, and the Empire slowly but surely became a Christian state. Theodosius I made Nicene/Catholic Christianity the official orthodox religion of the Empire in AD 380, pagan rites were outlawed and the Roman Army became officially Christian.[233] The further we go in late antiquity, the greater the impact of Christianization, and, as the initiator, Constantine's mark was indelible. In the diptych of Petronius Probus, for example, the emperor Honorius is shown holding a *labarum* with a tiny *chi-rho* and the inscription 'in the name of Christ may you always conquer'. This is a clear sign of the ongoing force of Constantine's vision a century later, and demonstrates the centrality of victory in warfare to the way Christianity was expressed at the imperial level.[234]

Honorius was the first, in AD 408, to decree that everyone who served in the palace, including court officials and generals, should be Catholic. This level of religious confidence was disrupted, however, as he was forced to rescind the decree in order to keep a skilled pagan general on staff.[235] At the same court, Claudian felt confident enough to satirize the cult of the saints and the belief that they were effective aids in battle – but he also shows how familiar Christianity was becoming to non-Christians.[236] In subsequent years, anti-heretic and anti-pagan laws continued to be passed, but in the unstable situation of the fifth century, emperors were pragmatic about keeping men in their armies. We still find pagan officers as late as the middle of the fifth century,[237] and in AD 428 the emperors grudgingly confirmed that heretics were still permitted to serve, but only as ordinary soldiers.[238] This was not a policy of tolerance, however: Jewish soldiers were banned in AD 418,[239] and paganism was subject to numerous injunctions. Pagans themselves do not seem to have been prevented from serving in the fifth century, though they were excluded from the civil service.[240] Nevertheless, in the sixth century, religious orthodoxy was required of soldiers by law.[241] Thus it seems the religious milieu of the fifth-century Roman Army was the reverse of the pre-Constantinian one. The Army itself was formally Christian, but men of other religious persuasions were still largely permitted.

The tipping point had been reached, however, and in some ways the Army itself became an agent of Christianization. It is widely recognized that the legions had always had a role in the spread of religions across the Empire – the cults of Jupiter Dolichenus and Mithras largely followed the standards, for example – but, by embedding Christianity in military iconography and practices, Constantine had set the Army up as a method of conversion.[242] Although recruits still often came from less-Christianized areas like Illyricum and Isauria, a recruit's background would not prevent them from embracing the official religious traditions of the Army once inside.[243] An individual soldier's ongoing exposure to the *labarum* and Christian symbols, Sunday rites, the annual oath and in the fifth century attendant priests was likely to inculcate Christianity more rapidly than the civilian world could.[244] This was perhaps especially true for barbarian recruits, who became a primary source of Roman manpower. When the Goths crossed the Danube in AD 376, for example, their leader Fritigern offered to convert to Christianity as a sign of good faith and loyalty to the emperor.[245] Prosper of Aquitaine is explicit about this, saying that barbarians serving in the Roman Army would often bring Christianity home with them after discharge.²⁴⁶ There are signs of soldiers engaging with the faith: one of Theodoret's letters is a reply to some soldiers about a point of theology, apparently following an argument with some of their comrades.²⁴⁷ Similarly, when Arcadius wanted to arrest John Chrysostom, he relied on new recruits to do so, worrying that ordinary troops would balk at going after a bishop, which perhaps points to an expectation of conversion in the ranks.²⁴⁸

The Christianization of the Army, of course, went hand-in-hand with the wider Christianization of the Empire. Moving into the sixth century, the religious context of the Army, like that of the whole Empire, is thoroughly Christian. We saw above that Maurice's late sixth-century military handbook assumes Christianity, with Christian chants, prayers and war-cry (*deus nobiscum!*), and priests leading the troops in prayer before battle.²⁴⁹ Icons and relics accompanied the armies to inspire the men.²⁵⁰ One of Justinian's pretexts for his campaign of reconquest was the persecution of Catholics by the Arian Vandals.²⁵¹ At the launching of the first expedition, a recently baptized soldier was specifically added to the commander's ship, as a kind of charm. This does indicate that not every soldier was necessarily baptized, but also suggests how deeply Christianity had become part of the fabric of military and imperial pomp.²⁵²

Narses, Justinian's eunuch general, was believed to receive military advice from the Virgin, and did not engage until she had given her blessing.²⁵³ The Army became so drenched in Christian practice that their enemies could take advantage. Belisarius worried that a period of Lenten fasting before Easter had weakened his men in AD 531 (rightly, as it turned out), indicating the importance of religious rites even for an army on the march.²⁵⁴ Theophylact mentions the Persians attacking the Romans specifically on a Sunday, since they would be unprepared on a day of rest; the Berbers in Africa also took advantage of this, and Corippus depicts priests with the army saying mass, decorating the camp like a chapel and praying for victory and divine help in the battle.²⁵⁵ To be fair, the Romans had also done this at least once before, as Stilicho had sent one of his pagan generals, Saul, to attack the Arian Goths at Pollentia during their Easter celebrations in AD 402.²⁵⁶

The Roman Army thus became Christian as a long-term result of Constantine's actions. But, just as with the pre-Constantinian Army, the Christians in the ranks are not the whole story, and it is important to briefly consider Constantine's influence on the way Christian authors thought about the Army and warfare. The emergence of Constantine very much changed the terms of the earlier debate, and his adoption of Christianity meant a scramble for Church thinkers to catch up – a conquering Christian emperor challenged the anti-military line of moralists held since Tertullian.²⁵⁷ Lactantius, notably, had rejected all killing in his *Divine Institutes*, even in warfare, saying that a just man may not be a soldier; faced with Constantine's successes, his anti-military stance had to shift.²⁵⁸ He praises the young Constantine for his military skill, among other qualities, and of course celebrates the victorious battles of Constantine and Licnius in AD 312–313.²⁵⁹ Eusebius' view, by contrast, was essentially informed by the experience of the persecutions and of Constantine's victory and favour for the Church, and so for him war was acceptable, and he mentions no issues with idolatry in the Army, probably because Constantine's changes meant it was no longer forced on Christian recruits.[260]

Church councils adapted quickly. At Arles in AD 314, far from banning Christians from the Army as Hippolytus had, it was resolved that soldiers who threw down their arms *in pace* were to be excommunicated. There is debate over the exact implications of this laconic phrase, particularly whether 'in peace' means in peacetime, that is, when the soldier is not on campaign, or whether it refers to the new peace between the Church and the Empire.[261] On either reading, however, it points clearly to ecclesiastical recognition and acceptance of Christians in the Army, of the kind Tertullian would never have agreed to. We might, with Helgeland, even see it as Church leaders in the West trying to find a rapprochement between Constantine's maintenance of old military rites and his new openness and favour for Christians.[262] Later canons accepted Christian soldiers by necessity, since they became the majority, but restrictions were established on ex-soldiers' participation in Church offices as a way of keeping armed service distinct from the service of the Church.[263]

Many Christian authors thus came to accept warfare as potentially positive, when carried out by a Christian emperor for the right reasons. Already in the AD 350s, Athanasius allowed that killing in wartime was a distinct category, which could be praiseworthy.[264] Later martyrs and saints with no connection to the Army were given invented military connections,[265] and generals found that their roles could be elevated on a par with clerics. Maximus of Turin for example commends a military count who had built a church in northern Italy – he does good work in slaying the emperor's enemies, and now in building a new church to help fight demons.[266]

The best example of this is Boniface. While military governor of Africa in AD 421, he was on the verge of quitting the military and joining a monastery after the death of his wife. Augustine took it upon himself to talk Boniface out of it, sending letters and even crossing North Africa for a personal visit. Augustine argued that Boniface could serve God as a soldier almost as well as any monk. The soldier fought barbarians, the corporeal equivalent of monastic spiritual warfare against demons; Boniface's strength and skill at arms were a gift from God, and warfare anyway, Augustine declared, was aimed at peace, stemming from love of God and one's neighbour.[267] This was a sentiment almost unthinkable for Christian moralists of earlier periods, especially the counsel to stay a soldier, rather than commit himself to the religious life. Boniface stayed in the Army, rising eventually to the rank of count, though his conflict with the rising star of Aetius put an end to his further advancement.[268]

Ultimately, 'imperial Christianity's potential to wage war was not really constrained by clerical Christianity's adherence to the idea that war was a great evil and peace reflected God's will'.[269] But even under Christian emperors, some Christians continued to oppose military service. Violence and bloodshed were the key problems now, since army idolatry was replaced by Christian rites.[270] Sulpicius Severus, for example, glosses Martin of Tours' military career to depict him as having an anti-war stance, while Paulinus of Nola took the opposite view to Augustine and encouraged a friend to leave his military career.[271] Basil of Caesarea's measured approach nicely reflects the rethinking of the military issue that was going on. He sees military service as acceptable, recognizing that violence needed to be understood as legitimate in some contexts, and that Christians under arms were still Christians, but he still lays down a three-year excommunication for those who killed, even in open battle.[272]

In the Christian Roman Empire then, warfare was still contentious, but on the whole, armed service was seen as legitimate. For fifth-century thinkers, the question was not *whether* a Christian should fight but *when* it was right for a Christian army to go to war.[273] It is in this context that we find the emergence of a Christian theory of just war. Ambrose had a hand in developing this, but the central figure is Augustine, who developed the model which would be taken up in the Middle Ages. Augustine's theory distinguishes between the sinful conqueror, who is nonetheless used by God to chastise, and the pious and moderate Christian soldier, who serves God and only fights for peace.[274]

In developing his theory, Augustine leans heavily on Cicero, but updates and reworks him for the Christian context. This actually points to one of the major knock-on effects that Constantine had, which was to bind together Roman imperial and Christian ideologies. Traditional Roman ideas came to be expressed in Christian modes. Constantine's conversion story centred around divine favour bringing him victory on the battlefield; other than the specific divinity in question, this was how the Romans had always thought the world worked. When Justinian attributed his successful reconquest campaign to God's help, he too was acting in this traditional manner.[275] Warfare and victory were still caught up in faith and piety,[276] and defeat in battle came therefore to imply sin or even heresy, especially during civil wars.[277] For example, even though the attempted usurper Eugenius was a practising Christian, his defeat by the orthodox Theodosius led to his being depicted by Christian historians as a champion of paganism.[278] Ambrose closely aligns military victory and Christianity, and tells Gratian it was lack of faith that led to loss of territory to the Goths.[279] Theodosius II and especially Heraclius cast their Persian conflicts in religious terms, essentially as holy wars,[280] and the new Christian ideology of military victory would be taken up by Rome's successors too – according to Gregory of Tours, the Frankish king Clovis justified his conquest of Gaul as reclaiming it from heretics.[281]

Conclusion

So what difference did Constantine make? In the long view, he began the Christianization of the Empire and its armies. While things may not have changed as quickly as someone like Eusebius would have liked, Julian's attempt to turn back the tide of religious change demonstrates a significant shift occurring within a generation. Constantine's Christianity was not really about personal salvation, but was predicated on military victory, and therefore was connected deeply to his role as emperor, in a fundamentally very Roman way of thinking. He was extremely influential in the melding of ideologies that had once been opposed: traditional Roman ideas like the importance of piety to military success or the concept of a just war became Christianized.

Constantine's introduction of a layer of Christianity to the Roman Army would change it irrevocably. Constantine had come to Christianity in an entirely military context, and for him the Army was intrinsically connected to the faith. He established measures to facilitate the presence of Christian soldiers, legitimizing the religion and placing a new, powerful Christian banner alongside the traditionally venerated standards, ultimately supplanting the traditional Army cult. The introduction of Christian measures like Sunday leave, semi-Christian prayers and the constant focus on divine help would pave the way for army chaplains and for the military oath to become Christianized. In so doing, Constantine set up the fundamental paradigm that would produce the religious framework for the Byzantine army. When Tertullian complained that Christian faith was incompatible with the military oath, he could never have anticipated that the solution would be to combine the two, but doing just that was at the heart of Constantine's influence on Roman Army religion.

Notes

1. All reported for Theodosius at the Frigidus in AD 393: Rufinus *Hist. Eccl.* 11.32–33; Sozom. 7.22–24.
2. The New Testament largely overlooks the topic, though the Gospels generally disapprove of violence (e.g. Mt. 26.52) and Jesus was given the title Prince of Peace. However, Paul's insistence on the imminent Second Coming led him to recommend that everyone stay in their jobs, presumably soldiers included (I Cor. 7.17–24), and the convert centurion Cornelius did not resign his post (Acts 10).
3. Lee (2007), p.178.
4. Scholarly opinion has ranged from acceptance of mainstream Christian pacifism, for example Hornus (1980), to categorical rejection, like Helgeland (1974), p.156: 'there was no such thing as early church pacifism' – and indeed to tendentious moralizing, as with Hall (1913) calling his study of the partnership of the Church with Constantine 'the fatal compromise'. For a variety of perspectives, see Bainton (1946); Gero (1970); Swift (1979); von Harnack (1981); Helgeland *et al.* (1985); Daly (1986); Shean (2010), pp.71–103; and Gaddis (2005), who rightly points out (pp.15–16) that it is important not to look for some single, monolithic, 'authentic' Christian tradition on violence.
5. Helgeland (1979), pp.725–33. Bainton (1946), pp.189–90, writing at the end of the Second World War, had already considered this, stating that 'objectivity is difficult for Christian scholars dealing with this question, because the problem is still acute'.
6. Shean (2010), pp.10–11, arguing it oversimplifies.
7. Lee (2007), pp.178–85; Hornus (1980), p.68; Shean (2010), p.11.
8. Origen *Cels.* 8.73; Helgeland (1979), p.750. Bainton (1946), p.192, comments that while Celsus is clear in what he thought, he was mistaken.
9. Origen *Cels.* 8.69–70, 73.
10. As Helgeland *et al.* (1985), p.42, rightly point out.
11. So Jer. *Vir. Ill.* 53.1. Tertullian seems to imply it himself in *Apol.* 9.2, though there are MS variants. See O'Malley (1967), p.107; cf. Helgeland *et al.* (1985), p.24.
12. Helgeland (1979), p.733.
13. Tert. *Idol.* 19, *Cor. Mil.* 1.11; Helgeland (1979), pp.738–41; Helgeland *et al.* (1985), pp.21–30; Swift (1983), pp.42–46.
14. E.g., Tert. *Cor. Mil.* 1.11. A related side issue is the adoption of military metaphors by Christian authors, even those who reject the actual military. Paul (II Tim. 2.3–4) already uses the phrase 'soldiers of Christ', and from Tertullian onwards, the idea of the *militia Christi* (as opposed to *militia Caesaris*) becomes a prominent way of understanding Christian life, particularly during the hard times of persecution. Although showing its age, von Harnack (1981) is still a useful introduction to this concept.
15. Tert. *Cor. Mil.* 1.

16. Tert. *Idol.* 17.2–3, 19.1–3; *Cor. Mil.* 1.6, *et passim*.
17. A rather difficult prospect, it must be admitted. Hippol. *Apostolic Tradition* 17–18; cf. comments in Lee (2007), p.179; Swift (1983), p.47; Helgeland *et al.* (1985), pp.35–37; Helgeland (1974), pp.160–61.
18. Clem. Al. *Protr.* 10.80P; cf. Helgeland (1979), pp.744–45; Lee (2007), p.179.
19. Tert. *Apol.* 30.4–5, also 37, 42.2–3. Cf. Origen *Cels.* 8.69; Bainton (1946), pp.191–94; Helgeland (1974), pp.156–60.
20. For general discussion, see Helgeland (1979), pp.766–73; Fowden (1987); and now especially Kovács (2008).
21. Jupiter: see Kovács (2008), pp.107–12, 169–80; Hermes Trismegistos: Dio 72.8–10; Julian the Chaldaean: Claud. *VI Cons. Hon.* 339–55, *Suida* I 334; Marcus himself: *SHA Marc.* 24.4. See generally, Kovács (2008), pp.23–94.
22. Euseb. *Hist. Eccl.* 5.5.1–6; Gregory of Nyssa *Homily on the Forty Martyrs*, 1 – trans. in Kovács (2008), n.8.
23. Tert. *Scap.* 4, *Apol.* 5.6; Helgeland (1979), pp.772–73.
24. Leclercq (1932), n.29 (= *CIL* 6.32877).
25. Gero (1970), pp.285–91. Shean (2010), pp.11–12, suggests that the breakdown of the *pax Romana* also played a role; cf. Swift (1979), p.845; Harnack (1981), p.82, who see it as a brand-new controversy.
26. Digeser (2000), p.2.
27. Lee (2007), p.178.
28. Helgeland (1979), pp.791–93; Tomlin (1998), p.24; Lee (2007), p.178.
29. Bainton (1946), pp.192–93. Some were instead set up by soldiers for their loved ones: Hornus (1980), p.121; *CIL* 13.5383, 3.8752, 3.8754, 6.32691.
30. See Helgeland (1979), p.792; cf. Hornus (1980), pp.118–22; Shean (2010), pp.182–88.
31. Leclercq (1932), n.30, 31 (*CIL* 6.32977); *CIL* 6.32943, 6.32691; Madgearu (2001), p.112.
32. *ILS* 9075; Madgearu (2001), p.111.
33. Mercurelli (1939), pp.73–99, though the overall argument that there were many Christians in the Praetorian Guard may go too far. Cf. Madgearu (2001), p.112; Hornus (1980), pp.280–81. *AE* 1935, 155 belongs to another Praetorian centurion found in a Christian cemetery, but Hornus dismisses the find site as insufficient evidence.
34. See on this Madgearu (2001).
35. Leclercq (1932), no.25, 32, 33 (a centurion from Philip's Praetorian Guard); *AE* 1939, 171; *CIL* 6.37273 (probably Severan in date).
36. Lactant. *Mort. Pers.* 10; Euseb. *Hist. Eccl.* 8.4.3.
37. Originally published in Drew-Bear (1981); a useful English translation can be found in Campbell (1994), n.391. Drew-Bear (1981), pp.140–41, argued Aurelius was forced out during the great persecution, which has found general acceptance. From the inscription, his career continues after AD 297, but when he retired is unclear. Perhaps in AD 299 – so Barnes (1996), pp.542–43 – though Colombo (2010), pp.121–26, has offered an alternative reconstruction that has him still serving as late as AD 304, arguing that some Christians remained in the *comitatus*, facing growing hostility.
38. Text and translation in Calder (1920), pp.44–45; see discussion in Hornus (1980), pp.120–21, who admits it runs counter to his thesis.
39. See in general, Musurillo (1972); and also comments in Swift (1983), pp.71–79; Helgeland *et al.* (1985), pp.56–66; and, in more detail, Helgeland (1979), pp.774–90. The martyrdoms discussed in this section are among those considered more reliable.
40. Despite the claims of Hornus (1980) and Demacopoulos (2017), pp.116–17.
41. *Acta Maximiliani* (Musurillo, n.17) 1–2.
42. Perhaps the palace guard, though Jones (1964), pp.52–54, suggests *comitatus* here means the field army; Campbell (1994), pp.237–38, follows him. Cf. Helgeland (1979), pp.777–78.
43. *Acta Maximiliani* (Musurillo, n.17) 2.9: *ipsi sciunt quod ipsis expediat. Ego tamen Christianus sum, et non possum mala facere.*

44. Helgeland (1979), p.779.
45. *Acta Marcelli* (Musurillo, n.18) 1–2. Helgeland (1978), p.1495, notes rejection of the uniform is part of the martyr's behaviour in both cases; cf. Tert. *Cor. Mil.* 1.
46. *Acta Marcelli* (N recension; Musurillo, n.18) 5; Helgeland (1979), p.782.
47. *Passio Iuli Veterani* (Musurillo, n.19) 2.1–3.
48. Euseb. *Hist. Eccl.* 8.4.2–4; Tomlin (1998), pp.24–25.
49. E.g., Euseb. *Hist. Eccl.* 6.41.22–23, 7.11.20.
50. Euseb. *Hist. Eccl.* 6.5.5–6.
51. Euseb. *Hist. Eccl.* 7.15. Not seeking out Christians but punishing any who came to light or caused problems was exactly the policy Trajan outlined in Pliny. *Ep.* 10.97, presumably still in force. Nock (1952), p.226, suggests such denunciations were rare.
52. Lee (2007), p.180.
53. Helgeland (1978), pp.1496–97.
54. For Mithraic crowns, see Tert. *Cor. Mil.* 15; on Jewish troops in general, see Roth (2007). Shean (2010), p.253, points to the Dura-Europos church in particular as an example of leeway being offered to Christian legionaries.
55. Helgeland *et al.* (1985), p.55, suggest a pattern of this sort: 'Mars for victory, spring nymphs for fresh water, Jupiter Dolichenus for weapons that do not break in combat, and Christ for when your weapon does break and you die.' For Severus Alexander: *SHA Alex. Sev.* 29.1–3.
56. MacMullen (1984), pp.44–47.
57. Euseb. *Vit. Const.* 2.20.4, 2.33. See Swift (1983), pp.90–92; Cameron & Hall (1999), pp.24–42.
58. Nicaea *Canon* 12, censuring those who did this in Licinius' army: Helgeland (1979), p.807.
59. See van Dam (2011) in general for the way the events of AD 312 were explored and retold.
60. E.g., Euseb. *Vit. Const.* 1.26.
61. Zos. 2.16.1–2 includes no vision, but a perplexing number of owls were an omen of divine presence.
62. Lenski (2016), p.69, lists among them Ossius of Cordoba, Reticus of Autun, Marinus of Arles, Maternus of Cologne and Lactantius.
63. The two had perhaps met in Nicomedia in the early AD 300s: Roldanus (2006), pp.34–35. Digeser (2000) stresses his influence on Constantine's views.
64. Barnes (2014), pp.176–78.
65. Lactant. *Mort. Pers.* 44.
66. Lactant. *Mort. Pers.* 44.5–6: *transversa X littera summo capite circumflexo Christum in scutis notat*. Bardill (2011), pp.161–62 discusses the history of translating and emending the MS, including the possibility an *I* has fallen out of the text.
67. E.g., *P. Bodmer* 2 and 14, with John's Gospel; see Bardill (2011), pp.161–67; Hurtado (2006),. pp.207–11. Alföldi (1959) discusses a statuette of Constantine with this symbol on his shield.
68. Milestones: *AE* 2000, 1799, 1801; coin: *RIC* 7 Ticinum 36.
69. Euseb. *Hist. Eccl.* 9.9.2–13. On the dates of Eusebius' versions, see Barnes (1980), who suggests Book 9 of Eusebius' *History* was put together *c*. AD 313. Cameron & Hall (1999), p.204, hold he had limited information about the West before AD 325.
70. Euseb. *Vit. Const.* 1.28; Cameron & Hall (1999), pp.2–3, note he was probably still working on the *Life* when he died in AD 339.
71. This detail convinces Jones (1949), p.96, that Eusebius has the genuine story; cf. Holloway (2004), pp.3–4, who agrees he is more accurate than Lactantius.
72. Euseb. *Vit. Const.* 1.27, cf. 36.
73. Euseb. *Vit. Const.* 1.28–32; the *labarum* is discussed in more detail below.
74. *Soterion semeion*: Euseb. *Vit. Const.* 1.40.1–2; Euseb. *Hist. Eccl.* 9.9.11; Cameron & Hall (1999), pp.216–18.
75. Potter (2013), pp.150–56. Holloway (2004), pp.3–4, traces the tendency back to Sulla and the Anatolian Bellona.
76. Rufinus *Hist. Eccl.* 9.9. For a recent sympathetic view of what Rufinus was trying to do with Eusebius' work, see Humphries (2008).

77. Speidel (1986), p.258.
78. *Pan. Lat.* 12.2.4–5, 12.4.1, 12.11.4, 12.13.1–2: called variously *divina mens* and *deus ille*. Van Dam (2011), p.105, argues that this language is too vague for any real interpretation, in contrast to Barnes (2014), p.99, who sees a deliberately Christian tinge. Digeser (2000), pp.68–70, points out that such language was unusual in Christian texts, but not entirely unknown, as Lactantius himself uses *summus deus* for God. For the poetical address to Tiber: *Pan. Lat.* 12.17–18.
79. E.g., *Pan. Lat.* 9.8.1, 10.2.1, 10.11.6. Potter (2013), pp.135–36, 142, points out that already in AD 311, the vague and ambiguous *mens divina* is the power that aids Constantine, perhaps indicating the emperor's already changing beliefs.
80. *Pan. Lat.* 4.13.5; Liebeschuetz (1979), pp.289–90, detects Christian philosophical and moral ideas.
81. *Pan. Lat.* 4.14, 4.29.1.
82. Alföldi (1969), p.72.
83. Rodgers (1989), p.245; cf. Nixon & Rodgers (1994), p.358.
84. Lactant. *Mort. Pers.* 48.
85. Lactant. *Mort. Pers.* 46: 'Supreme God, we beseech thee; Holy God, we beseech thee; unto thee we commend all right; unto thee we commend our safety; unto thee we commend our empire. By thee we live, by thee we are victorious and happy. Supreme Holy God, hear our prayers; to thee we stretch forth our arms. Hear, Holy Supreme God' (*Ante-Nicene Fathers'* trans.); Long (2009), p.233.
86. Helgeland (1979), pp.807–08; Swift (1983), pp.92–93.
87. See on the construction of this new policy, Barnes (2014), pp.105–06.
88. Euseb. *Hist. Eccl.* 9.9.1, 12, 10.8; cf. Euseb. *Vit. Const.* 2.3.1–2. On the date, see Barnes (1980), pp.198–201.
89. Euseb. *Vit. Const.* 1.49–54.
90. Jones (1949), pp.88–89, 129–30; Odahl (2004), pp.145–50; Harries (2012), pp.110–13.
91. Odahl (2004), pp.149–52; Harries (2012), pp.110–13.
92. Eusebius puts the idea into Licinius' mouth at Euseb. *Vit. Const.* 2.5.2–4, cf. 2.16.2; Whitby (1998), p.192; Shepherd (1967), p.68; Potter (2013), p.210.
93. McCormick (1986), pp.103–04, sees the replacement of the pagan term in connection with the adoption of the diadem and a general refocusing of imperial ceremony and image.
94. Drake (2006), p.126; Harries (2012), pp.167–68. The date is uncertain, but probably soon after the defeat of Licinius.
95. So Heid (2007), p.413. See *Oration to the Saints* 26.1, cf. 15.4. Barnes (2014), pp.11–13, still sees ambiguous language, perhaps to reassure pagans at court.
96. Letter to the provincials: Euseb. *Vit. Const.* 2.24–42; cf. Cameron & Hall (1999), pp.44–45; Barnes (2014), pp.107–08; letter to Shapur: Euseb. *Vit. Const.* 4.8–14; Brown (2013), pp.60–61; see in general, Smith (2016), pp.17–64.
97. Drake (2017), p.50, has recently called it our 'traditional parlour game'. The conversion has dominated studies of Constantine since late antiquity – where Lactantius and Eusebius linked the conversion to the Milvian Bridge, Zos. 2.29.1–4 ascribes it to his guilty conscience over the deaths of Crispus and Fausta fourteen years later (cf. Sozom. 1.5, who refuted this). Viewpoints traditionally swing between Constantine the cynical manipulator and Constantine the earnest believer; recent understandings of the emperor's religiosity tend to view Constantine as a genuine Christian, but one who was not exclusionary nor a hardliner. Lenski (2016), pp.4–6, has compiled a recent brief review of the debates, but in general on the issue see (*inter multa alia*): Jones (1949); Setton (1967), pp.47–48; Shepherd (1967); Alföldi (1969); Liebeschuetz (1979), pp.279–81; Barnes (1981), pp.15–16 *et passim*; Kee (1982), pp.17–22; Elliott (1987); Humphries (1997), p.463; Weiss & Birley (2003), pp.252–53; Odahl (2004); Lenski (2006), p.72; Drake (1976) and (2009); Potter (2013).
98. Barnes (1981), p.48, dismissed the Sol coins as 'the dead weight of iconographic tradition', but they do fit with Constantine's deliberate ambiguity about his religious leanings in his

early reign, aimed at consensus-building, which was less necessary after AD 324. Cf. *RIC* 7 p.61; Barnes (2014), p.18.
99. See Roldanus (2006), p.35.
100. Weiss (2003), pp.238, 249–50, corrects the common reporting of this as a vision of Apollo: it was a vision of the *praesens deus*, and he made for the nearest appropriate temple, Apollo of Autun.
101. *Pan. Lat.* 6.21; Nixon & Rodgers (1994), pp.249–51, offer useful bibliography concerning this vision.
102. *Pan. Lat.* 6.2–4; cf. Euseb. *Vit. Const.* 1.13–17 for Constantius I's religion. Rodgers (1989) and Harries (2012), pp.156–59, discuss Constantine's mastery of image manipulation.
103. Euseb. *Vit. Const.* 1.27.
104. Euseb. *Vit. Const.* 2.12.1–2; see Drake (2017), p.66.
105. Ice in the upper atmosphere can give the sun a halo or radiating arms like a cross. The model is often associated with Weiss (1993) – recently revised and published in English by Weiss & Birley (2003). Barnes (2014), pp.74–76, discusses the often negative reception of Weiss' model, though it has found some recent acceptance. Note that Jones (1949), pp.96–97, had also suggested the solar halo. One major flaw (which Weiss acknowledges) is that the Romans were already aware of the solar halo as a phenomenon (and an omen) in its own right. Other scholars, for example, Bardill (2011), pp.159–60, Drake (2009) and Drake (2017), pp.63–64, see no need for a literal naturalistic vision in a world where divine signs were really quite commonplace, and view Weiss' model as reductionist. To paraphrase Drake, if Constantine had never seen his vision, does anyone really think he would have just gone home quietly and given up?
106. As a cross-section of interpretations of the new symbol: Jones (1949), pp.97–98; Drake (1976), pp.72–74; Liebeschuetz (1979), pp.282–85; Singor (2003), pp.490–96; Weiss (2003), pp.254–55; Long (2009), p.232; de Haan & Hekster (2016), pp.18–19.
107. E.g., Tert. *Nat.* 1.13; Jones (1949), p.131; Nicholson (2000), pp.312–16.
108. Nock (1933); MacMullen (1984), p.44; and Potter (2013), pp.158–59, may well be right in suggesting both gods were simply acceptable to Constantine during his early reign.
109. Barnes (2014), pp.108–09.
110. Euseb. *Vit. Const.* 1.44, 4.24.
111. Alföldi (1969), pp.19–23 (very condescending about it). MacMullen (1997), pp.81–82, similarly says the emperors of the late third and early fourth century were more or less 'ordinary' men, and their religiosity that of the soldier.
112. Euseb. *Vit. Const.* 2.64–72, 3.21.
113. Dismissive comments in his letter at Euseb. *Vit. Const.* 2.69.2, 2.70.6; see 3.10–14 for the council.
114. Euseb. *Hist. Eccl.* 10.6–7, *Vit. Const.* 1.41–2; *C.Th.* 1.27.1, 16.2.2, 16.2.4; see summary in Cameron (2005), p.108; Jones (1949), pp.80–82. Digeser (2000) argues that this was not initially favouritism, but trying to bring the new legal religion up to pace with the rest, though after AD 324 she sees his favouritism as more open.
115. Euseb. *Hist. Eccl.* 10.6, 10.7.2; Barnes (1981), p.49.
116. Euseb. *Vit. Const.* 1.42.
117. Sozom. 1.8.13; Aur. Vict. *Caes.* 41.4.
118. Euseb. *Vit. Const.* 2.44, 3.1.6.
119. *C.Th.* 1.27.1, 4.7.1; *Sirmondian Constitutions* 1 (Pharr).
120. *C.Th.* 8.16.1.
121. Speidel (1986), pp.255–57; Lenski (2006), pp.71–72; Barnes (1981), pp.49–51.
122. Harries (2012), p.120.
123. *Cod. Just.* 3.12.2, modified later that year to permit manumissions: *C.Th.* 2.8.1; cf. Euseb. *Vit. Const.* 4.18.1–3, who interprets it as a day of prayer as well. Constantine *may* also have promoted 25 December as Christmas, aiming to reorientate the religious year, and perhaps syncretise Sol and Christ further: Barnes (2014), p.85; Heid (2007), pp.416–17.

124. Euseb. *Vit. Const.* 4.17, 4.22, 4.29; Constantine's *Oration to the Saints* is perhaps an example. Van Dam (2011), p.66, comments that he 'obviously liked to talk'.
125. Euseb. *Vit. Const.* 3.2–3, 49.
126. Brown (2013), p.67. Cf. Constantine's own assertion of this in his letters: Euseb. *Vit. Const.* 2.28–9, 55.
127. On the nature of the late Roman Army in general, see Lee (1998); Elton (2006); Southern & Dixon (1996), esp. pp.17–37; Whitby (2004), pp.156–67.
128. Lactant. *Mort. Pers.* 7.2; Zos. 2.34.
129. Lee (2007), p.182.
130. Jones (1949), pp.132–34.
131. The term *labarum*, it is worth noting, appears not in the text of Eusebius but in the chapter headings, perhaps added by a copyist or editor to Euseb. *Vit. Const.* 1.31. The term was certainly in use by the AD 360s, when Gregory Nazianzen *Or.* 4.66 gives the current folk etymology from Latin *labor*. The word probably had a Gallic root – which may argue for its early adoption while Constantine was in the Western provinces.
132. Euseb. *Vit. Const.* 1.30–31.
133. Cameron & Hall (1999), pp.207–08; van Dam (2011), p.63. Christian commentary had recognized that the *vexillum* had a cross shape for some time, e.g., Tert. *Nat.* 1.12, who mocks the Romans for it.
134. Euseb. *Vit. Const.* 2.4–7, 16. Barnes (1981), p.48, opts for AD 312; van Dam (2011), pp.63–64, holds that AD 324 is the earliest possible date.
135. Euseb. *Vit. Const.* 1.31.3.
136. Greg. Naz. *Or.* 4.66.
137. Lenski (2016), p.70.
138. Euseb. *Vit. Const.* 2.8.
139. Euseb. *Laus Const.* 2, 6.21, 9.8–12; cf. Euseb. *Vit. Const.* 4.5.2–6.1.
140. Euseb. *Vit. Const.* 2.9.1–3; Sozom. 1.4.
141. Euseb. *Vit. Const.* 2.55.1.
142. Prudent. *Symm.* 1.464–69.
143. Socrates *Hist. Eccl.* 1.18, but cf. Sozom. 2.26, who agrees they converted but not as a result of defeat.
144. Tac. *Ann.* 2.17.2 refers to the eagles as the *numina* of the legions; Helgeland (1978), pp.1476–78; Campbell (2002), pp.37–38; Shean (2010), pp.6–7. Christians recognized this, e.g., Tert. *Apol.* 16.8; *Nat.* 1.12.
145. Sozom. 1.4; cf. Lee (2007), pp.182–83.
146. So Shean (2010), p.205.
147. *RIC* 7 Constantinople 19, 26.
148. *AE* 2000, 1799, 1801; see Lenski (2016), pp.8–9, with sketches.
149. On the site, see Guarducci (1960), pp.111–31. Bruun (1997), p.43, instead holds that the earliest epitaph with a christogram dates to AD 331.
150. *RIC* 7 Ticinum 36.
151. *RIC* 7 Arles 381–6, 400, Antioch 98–101. See Alföldi (1932), pp.14–15; cf. *RIC* 7 p.62; and Odahl (2004), pp.148–49, 222–23, possibly overstating the importance of cruciform mintmarks.
152. For detail, see Bruun (1997), pp.46–48, pointing out some variations and details missed in the *RIC*. For types: *RIC* 7 Arles 394–99; Trier 586–88, 590–95; Lyons 276–78, 280–88; Aquileia 139–47; Siscia 252–56. Variant forms were the christogram, upright cross, X and O (a wreath?).
153. *IC* 7 Trier 27–31, 572–76, 578; Ticinum 33; Siscia 135; Heaclea 100; Nicomedia 81–83; Constantinople 65–66. Trier 549, Rome 399 and Siscia 207 all show, it has been suggested, not just a *vexillum* but the *labarum* itself, with the *chi-rho*. The editors are sceptical, but suggest Siscia 207 might be the prototype for later emperors' *labarum* issues.

154. See Bruun (1997), pp.45–54; van Dam (2011), pp.48–50.
155. As representative examples (of over 200 types): *RIC* 8: Trier 30–32; Rome 107–35; Thessalonica 107–13, 119–22; Alexandria 50–53. The Constantinian type of a *labarum* flanked by soldiers also reappears: Siscia 85–104.
156. Magnentius: *RIC* 8 Trier 260–8, Lyon 108–14; Aquileia 124, 130–31, 141, 148; Vetranio: *RIC* 8 Siscia 260, 293–94; Thessalonica 125–27, 131–32, 135, 138; and with a *labarum* in each hand: Siscia 270–71, 273–74, 276–77, 280–81, 284–85, 289–90.
157. Magnentius' *chi-rho*, alpha and omega: *RIC* 8 Amiens 34–45; Trier 318–27, 332–37; Arles 188–202; Vetranio with *labarum* and the slogan HOC SIGNO VICTOR ERIS: *RIC* 8 Siscia 272, 275, 278–79, 282–83, 286–88, 291–92.
158. This was Honorius' so-called *signifer* type, named for Claud. *VI Cons. Hon.* 22; see discussion in *RIC* 10 56, 124–25. Examples of the type: *RIC* 10 1216, 1260–61, 1292. Cf. Bruun (1997), pp.55–56; Kent & Painter (1977), n.493.
159. Lenski (2016), p.10; de Haan & Hekster (2016); Singor (2003), pp.484–85.
160. E.g., *RIC* 10 950 (Zeno); Hahn (1973), pp.6a, 34 (Anastasius; Justin I). Instead of a banner, there is a pole topped by the *chi-rho* or staurogram. These were also depicted in the early fifth century, e.g., *RIC* 10 1310. Victory, alone of the old gods, remained in iconography. She may have looked enough like an angel to be acceptable.
161. Amb. *Fide* 2.16.142: *non hic aquilae militares, neque volatus avium exercitum ducunt: sed tuum, domine Iesu, nomen et cultus*. Helgeland (1979), p.806, seems to read this as a recommendation, rather than the description implied by the verb tense.
162. Jer. *Ep.* 107.1–2: *vexilla militum crucis insignia sunt*.
163. Const. Porph. *Cer.* 1.91. The acclamations are entirely Christian, even referring to the *Christianon basileion*, the Christian Empire.
164. de Haan & Hekster (2016), p.19.
165. Euseb. *Vit. Const.* 4.20–21; cf. Sozom. 1.8.
166. Some fragments of shields survive: see Bishop & Coulston (2006), pp.216–17; Coulston (2013), pp.475–76.
167. *RIC* 7 Trier 372.
168. Kent & Painter (1977), n.11.
169. See Singor (2003), p.490; Tomlin (1998), p.25.
170. E.g., *RIC* 10 12–15, 1902, 2013 (Victory holding shield); 37–44 (on Arcadius' armour); 2605–08, 2612–14, 2623–39 (on Majorian's shield). The *chi-rho* also appears on its own as a monogram, e.g., 2051–57, 2525–27.
171. *Not. Dig.* 5.7–9.22, 7.8.21 could be read as having crosses or even some stylized *chi-rho*s: Coulston (2013), pp.476–77; Bishop & Coulston (2006), p.218. Christianity itself is largely absent from the document: Brennan (1996), p.158; Tomlin (1998), p.36.
172. Suggested by Elton (2006), p.336, cf. Singor (2003), pp.484–85.
173. Euseb. *Vit. Const.* 1.31.1.
174. Alföldi (1932), pp.10–11; the *RIC* 7 editors disagree (pp.62–63). The issues are Siscia 61, 74, 82, 84, all from AD 319/320. Lenski (2016), p.38, stresses the importance of these coins since the emperor was in residence there.
175. Theodoret *Hist. Eccl.* 1.17 has this done on Helena's orders; cf. Socrates *Hist. Eccl.* 1.17; Sozom. 2.1.
176. Helmets: Bishop & Coulston (2006), p.214; Coulston (2013), p.472; belt fitting: Entwistle (2010), p.25.
177. Veg. *Mil.* 2.5: *iurant autem per deum et Christum et sanctum spiritum et per maiestatem imperatoris*. The oath probably changed under Theodosius rather than Constantine: Lee (2007), p.184.
178. Lee (2007), pp.52–53. Tertullian stressed the old *sacramentum* as one of the great barriers to Christian participation in the Army in the early third century.
179. Veg. *Mil.* 3.5.
180. Veg. *Mil.* 3.18.
181. Maurice *Strategikon* 2.18.

182. Euseb. *Vit. Const.* 4.18–20. Like Eusebius, Odahl (2004), pp.152–53, sees this as a thoroughly and explicitly Christian move. The prayer is at 4.20.1: 'You alone we know as God, you are the King we acknowledge, you are the help we summon. By you we have won our victories, through you we have overcome our enemies. To you we render thanks for the good things past, you also we hope for as giver of those to come. To you we all come to supplicate for our Emperor Constantine and for his Godbeloved sons: That he may be kept safe and victorious for us in long, long life, we plead' – trans. Cameron & Hall (1999).
183. Barnes (1981), p.48; Lactant. *Mort. Pers.* 46.
184. *C.Th.* 2.8.1; *Cod. Just.* 3.12.2(3).
185. *C.Th.* 2.8.2: *solis die, quem dominicum rite dixere maiores.*
186. Sozom. 1.8.
187. Theodoret *Ep.* 2; Jones (1953), pp.239–40; Lee (2007), pp.191–92.
188. Brennan (1987), p.120.
189. Brennan (1987), pp.118–20.
190. Campbell (2002), p.42; Shean (2010), p.5.
191. Euseb. *Vit. Const.* 1.42.1, 2.4.1; cf. 1.52 for priests and bishops attending court.
192. Euseb. *Vit. Const.* 4.56.2–3; cf. Amm. Marc. 25.4.23. On the problems with the text and MS, see Fowden (1994), p.147; Smith (2016), pp.47–48.
193. Lee (2007), p.185, also indicating several dedications at the (civilian) church at Anemurium made by soldiers.
194. Euseb. *Vit. Const.* 2.12.1; Sozom. 1.8; Smith (2016), pp.48–62.
195. Euseb. *Vit. Const.* 2.12–14; cf. Sozom. 1.8, where the emperor is granted vision and divine guidance against the Goths and Sarmatians.
196. E.g., Sozom. 7.24.
197. Jer. *Ep.* 107.2.
198. Whitby (1998), p.192.
199. Theodoret *Hist. Eccl.* 3.1; cf. Euseb. *Vit. Const.* 4.20.
200. Shean (2010), pp.7–13.
201. Zos. 2.29.5 reports Constantine engaging in pagan rites so as not to upset the soldiers.
202. *Cod. Just.* 12.46.1.
203. *C.Th.* 7.20.2. Possible dates are AD 307, 320, 326: see Pharr (1952), pp.179–80; Campbell (1994), pp.245–46; Lee (2007), pp.182–83. Shean (2010), p.180, speculates that it may be important that pagan soldiers were being discharged.
204. Whitby (1998), pp.192–93.
205. Lee (1998), p.227; cf. Shean (2010).
206. Euseb. *Vit. Const.* 2.44; Shean (2010), pp.284–85; Barnes (1995), p.142; MacMullen (1984), pp.56–57.
207. Salzman (2002), pp.128–32. The situation may have been different in the East: Lee (2007), pp.185–86; cf. Barnes (1995), pp.135–47; Shean (2010), pp.409–13.
208. Salzman (2002), pp.130–31; Barnes (1995), p.145.
209. E.g., Nock (1952), pp.226–27; Liebeschuetz (1979), p.253; Lee (1998), p.228.
210. Amm. Marc. 21.2.4–5: *utque omnes nullo impediente ad sui favorem illiceret.*
211. Julian *Ep.* 8.415B-C; Amm. Marc. 22.12.6.
212. Euseb. *Vit. Const.* 4.21; Sozom. 5.17; Greg. Naz. *Or.* 4.66; Woods (1995), pp.61–63.
213. Sulpicius Severus *Vita Martini* 2–4.
214. Zos. 3.3.2, quoting a lost work of Julian's saying they 'knew only how to pray'; cf. Julian *Ep. Ath.* 277d; Liban. *Or.* 18.37, 94.
215. Liban. *Or.* 18.166–70.
216. Ephraim Syrus *Hymni contra Iulianum* 3.8–11; in Dodgeon & Lieu (1991), pp.209–13.
217. Greg. Naz. *Or.* 4.64–65; cf. Tomlin (1998), pp.31–32.
218. August. *Enn. in Ps.* 124(125).7; Sozom. 5.17.
219. Sozom. 5.17; Theodoret *Hist. Eccl.* 3.12–13; Greg. Naz. *Or.* 4.82–4; see Woods (1995), p.63.
220. Sozom. 5.17; Greg. Naz. *Or.* 4.64–6.

221. MacMullen (1984), p.47; Tomlin (1998), p.35, noting also Jovinus, left in charge of the Gallic troops, who went on to fund a church in Rheims.
222. Amm. Marc. 17.13.33, 24.1.1. Julian spoke like this before outing himself as pagan too: 15.8.10: *deus caelestis*; 16.12.18: *superum numen*; 24.3.6: *deo meque*.
223. Tomlin (1998), pp.33–34.
224. Tomlin (1998), p.29.
225. Liebeschuetz (1979), p.253 n.4.
226. Socrates *Hist. Eccl.* 3.13.
227. Euseb. *Vit. Const.* 4.54.2–3; Sozom. 2.5.
228. Liban. *Or.* 30.27–99.
229. Lee (2007), p.183; and earlier Lee (1998), p.228, suggesting 'acquiescence or indifference'. Tomlin (1998), pp.31–34, sees them as time-servers; Shean (2010), pp.180–81, however, argues for a majority of genuine Christians who eagerly accepted the return to orthodoxy under Jovian.
230. Amm. Marc. 25.6.1; Tomlin (1998), pp.33–35.
231. Theodoret *Hist. Eccl.* 4.1. Tomlin (1998), p.35, argues this is a literary double of 3.1, where Julian fears he cannot lead a Christian force, but the story was already known to Rufinus: *Hist. Eccl.* 11.1.
232. Athanasius *Ep.* 56 app. 1 (*PG* 26.820). Tomlin (1998), p.35, calls him 'a survivor who had kept his head down'.
233. *C.Th.* 16.1.2. Numerous laws targeted pagan rites, such as Theodosius' final ban of sacrifice in AD 391: *C.Th.* 16.10.10; see Lee (2007), pp.185–86.
234. *In nomine XPI vincas semper*; see Cameron (2007), pp.191–94.
235. Zos. 5.46.3–4. The law in question is *C.Th.* 16.5.42. The text uses the phrase *intra palatium militare*, which, given it is addressed to both the *Magister Officiorum* (head of the bureaucracy) and the *Comes Domesticorum* (head of the palace guard), clearly refers to all branches of service in the palace. Shean (2010), p.326, is wrong to claim the law was a final ban on all pagans in the Army; cf. Lee (2007), pp.188–91, on the progress of Christianization.
236. Claud. *Carm. Min.* 50, cf. 32. The Christian *Magister Equitum* Jacobus, at whom it was aimed, had apparently criticized Claudian's poetry. On the poem, see Vanderspoel (1986).
237. E.g., *PLRE* 2 Apollonius 3, Litorius; see Lee (2007), p.190.
238. *C.Th.* 16.5.65.3.
239. *C.Th.* 16.8.24.
240. *C.Th.* 16.10.21 in AD 415/416, and again in AD 425: *Sirmondian Constitutions* 6 (Pharr). There is perhaps some ambiguity on this point, as the term *militia* (sometimes qualified by *armata*, *palatina*, etc.) in this period was used for bureaucrats as well as soldiers, and even officials at court, but the context of the relevant laws seems to concern the administration rather than the Army.
241. *Cod. Just.* 1.4.20 seems to be aimed at the soldiery; cf. the comments of Lee (2007), pp.190–91.
242. A central claim of Shean (2010); cf. Tomlin (1998), p.23, who thinks Christian pacifism would impede this.
243. Shean (2010), pp.177–78, 284.
244. Shean (2010), pp.284–85.
245. Sozom. 6.37; Socrates *Hist. Eccl.* 4.33. Amm. Marc. 31.12.8–9 records that the Goths used a Christian priest as envoy before the Battle of Adrianople. See on this Heather (1986).
246. Prosper of Aquitaine *de vocatione omnium gentium* 2.33 (*PL* 51.717–8).
247. Theodoret *Ep.* 145; Lee (2007), pp.188–89.
248. Shean (2010), p.179.
249. Maurice *Strategikon* pr., 2.18, 8.2.1.
250. E.g., Theophylact Simocatta 2.3.4–6; cf. 5.16.11 for the wood of the Cross built into a war banner, perhaps a *labarum*. See Whitby (1998), pp.196–200.
251. Whitby (1998), pp.194–95; Procop. *Vand.* 3.10.18–21, having been berated by a visionary bishop.

252. Procop. *Vand.* 3.12.2.
253. Evagrius 4.24.
254. Procop. *Pers.* 1.18.14–23, 37, explicitly saying they have all been observing the fast.
255. Theophylact Simocatta 2.2.7; Corippus *Iohannis* 8.213–77, 318–50; see discussion in Lee (2007), pp.188–94.
256. Vandespoel (1986), pp.253–54.
257. Helgeland (1979), pp.757–59; Grant (1983), pp.175–76.
258. Lactant. *Div. Inst.* 6.20.16, cf. 1.18.8; see Helgeland (1979), pp.757–59. Swift (1983), pp.61–68, considers him a transitional figure, reflecting the change in attitude of the Christian community at large.
259. Lactant. *Mort. Pers.* 18.10, 52.4; see Swift (1983), pp.65–66.
260. Helgeland (1979), pp.760–62; see Demacopoulos (2017) for an assessment of how Eusebius reframes violence in a Christian context.
261. Arles (314) canon 3: see Lee (2007), p.187, for a brief discussion of the debates this canon has provoked; cf. Swift (1983), pp.90–92; Elton (2006), p.335; Harnack (1981), p.102. Hornus (1980), pp.172–75, argues that the mention of peacetime meant they could refuse to fight in wartime; Helgeland *et al.* (1985), pp.71–72, suggest it was aimed at people like Marcellus who left the army in protest of idolatry.
262. Helgeland (1974), pp.163, 200.
263. Rome (386) canon 3, and Toledo (400) canon 8: see Lee (2007), pp.187–88.
264. Athanasius *Ep.* 48 (*To Amun*: *PG* 26.1173b) in Swift (1983), p.95; cf. Grant (1983), p.176.
265. See on this Brennan (1990), pp.331–40.
266. Maximus of Turin *Sermons* 87.2.
267. August. *Ep.* 189.4–6. Euseb. *Laus Const.* 1.6–2.3, wrote similar things about Constantine.
268. Augustine blamed Boniface's lust and sins: August. *Ep.* 220.5–7.
269. Koder & Stouraitis (2012), p.10.
270. Whitby (2004), p.176; Hornus (1980), pp.143–57; Swift (1983), pp.149–57.
271. Sulpicius Severus *Vita Martini* 4; Paulinus of Nola *Ep.* 25.1–3.
272. Basil *Ep.* 188.13; cf. 155, and 106 where he counsels that men should be known by their souls, not their uniforms; Grant (1983), p.176; Swift (1983), pp.93–95.
273. Helgeland *et al.* (1985), pp.3–4; Swift (1970), pp.536–40.
274. For Ambrose, see Swift (1970); Swift (1983), pp.97–110. For Augustine, see e.g., August. *Civ.* 4.15, 19.12, *Faust.* 22, *Ep.* 189.6; and commentary in Swift (1983), pp.110–49.
275. Justinian *Novellae* 30.11.2.
276. McCormick (1986), pp.102–11, discusses the increasingly Christian overtones of imperial victory celebrations.
277. August. *Civ.* 19.15.
278. August. *Civ.* 5.26; Sozom. 7.22; Rufinus *Hist. Eccl.* 11.31–3; Theodoret *Hist. Eccl.* 5.24.
279. Amb. *de Fide* 2.16; Cf. Jer. *Ep.* 107.2, who wondered if the Goths' Christianity was why they often beat the Romans.
280. Humphries (2007), p.264; Whitby (1998), p.195.
281. Gregory of Tours *Hist. Franc.* 2.37.

Bibliography

Alföldi, A., 'The Helmet of Constantine with the Christian Monogram', *JRS* 22 (1932), pp.9–23.
Alföldi, A., '*Cornuti*: A Teutonic Contingent in the Service of Constantine the Great and its Decisive Role in the Battle at the Milvian Bridge', *DOP* 13 (1959), pp.169, 171–83.
Alföldi, A., *The Conversion of Constantine and Pagan Rome*, trans. Mattingly, H. (Oxford, 1969).
Bainton, R.H., 'The Early Church and War', *HThR* 39 (1946), pp.189–212.
Bardill, J., *Constantine, Divine Emperor of the Christian Golden Age* (Cambridge, 2011).
Barnes, T.D., 'The Editions of Eusebius' *Ecclesiastical History*', *GRBS* 21 (1980), pp.191–201.

Barnes, T.D., *Constantine and Eusebius* (Cambridge MA, 1981).
Barnes, T.D., 'Statistics and the Conversion of the Roman Aristocracy', *JRS* 85 (1995), pp.135–47.
Barnes, T.D., 'Emperors, Panegyrics, Prefects, Provinces and Palaces (284–317)', *JRA* 9 (1996), pp.532–52.
Barnes, T.D., *Constantine: Dynasty, Religion and Power in the Later Roman Empire* (Chichester, 2014).
Bishop, M.C. & Coulston, J.C.N., *Roman Military Equipment. From the Punic Wars to the Fall of Rome*, 2nd edn (Oxford, 2006).
Brennan, P., 'Jupiter Dolichenus and Religious Life in the Roman Army', in Horsely, G. (ed.), *New Documents Illustrating Early Christianity*, vol. 4 (Sydney, 1987), pp.118–26.
Brennan, P., 'Military Images in Hagiography', in Clarke, G. (ed.), *Reading the Past in Late Antiquity* (Sydney, 1990), pp.323–45.
Brennan, P., 'The *Notitia Dignitatum*', in Nicolet, C. (ed.), *Les Littératures Techniques dans l'Antiquité Romaine* (Geneva, 1996), pp.147–78.
Brown, P., *The Rise of Western Christendom. Triumph and Diversity* AD *200–1000*, rev. edn (Chichester, 2013).
Bruun, P.M., *The Roman Imperial Coinage VII: Constantine and Licinius* AD *313–337* (London, 1966).
Bruun, P., 'The Victorious Signs of Constantine: A Reappraisal', *NC* 157 (1997), pp.41–59.
Calder, W.M., 'Studies in Early Christian Epigraphy', *JRS* 10 (1920), pp.42–59.
Cameron, Al., 'The Probus Diptych and Christian Apologetic', in Amirav, H. & Romeny, B.H. (eds), *From Rome to Constantinople. Studies in Honour of Averil Cameron* (Leiden, 2007), pp.191–202.
Cameron, Av., 'The Reign of Constantine, AD 306–337', in Bowman, A.K., Garnsey, P. & Cameron, Av. (eds), *The Cambridge Ancient History*, vol. 12 (Cambridge, 2005), pp.90–109.
Cameron, Av. & Hall, S.G. (ed. & trans.), *Eusebius: Life of Constantine* (Oxford, 1999).
Campbell, B., *The Roman Army, 31* BC–AD *337. A Sourcebook* (London, 1994).
Campbell, B., *War and Society in Imperial Rome 31* BC–AD *284* (London, 2002).
Colombo, M., 'Correzioni testuali ed esegetiche all'epigrafe di Aurelius Gaius (regione di Kotiaeum in "Phrygia")', *ZPE* 174 (2010), pp.118–26.
Coulston, J.C.N., 'Late Roman Military Equipment Culture', in Sarantis, A. & Christie, N. (eds), *War and Warfare in Late Antiquity*, vol. 8 (2013), pp.461–92.
Daly, R.J., 'Military Service and Early Christianity: A Methodological Approach', *StudPat* 18 (1986), pp.1–8.
de Haan, N. & Hekster, O., '"*In Hoc Signo Vinces*": The Various Victories Commemorated through the *Labarum*', in Verhoeven, M., Bosman, L. & van Asperen, H. (eds), *Monuments and Memory: Christian Cult Buildings and Constructions of the Past. Essays in Honour of Sible de Blaauw* (Turnhout, 2016), pp.17–30.
Demacopoulos, G.E., 'The Eusebian Valorization of Violence and Constantine's Wars for God', in Siecienski, A.E. (ed.), *Constantine: Religious Faith and Imperial Policy* (London, 2017), pp.115–28.
Digeser, E.D., *The Making of a Christian Empire. Lactantius and Rome* (Ithaca NY, 2000).
Dodgeon, M.H. & Lieu, S.N.C., *The Roman Eastern Frontier and the Persian Wars* AD *226–363. A Documentary History* (London, 1994).
Drake, H.A., *In Praise of Constantine: A Historical Study and New Translation of Eusebius' Tricennial Orations* (Berkeley, 1976).
Drake, H.A., 'The Impact of Constantine on Christianity', in Lenski, N. (ed.), *The Cambridge Companion to the Age of Constantine* (Cambridge, 2006), pp.111–36.
Drake, H.A., 'Solar Power in Late Antiquity', in Cain, A. & Lenski, N. (eds), *The Power of Religion in Late Antiquity* (Farnham, 2009), pp.215–26.
Drake, H.A., *A Century of Miracles. Christians, Pagans, Jews, and the Supernatural, 312–410* (Oxford, 2017).

Drew-Bear, T., 'Les voyages d'Aurélius Gaius, soldat de Dioclétien', in Fahd, T. (ed.), *La géographie administrative et politique d'Alexandre à Mahomet* (Leiden, 1981), pp.93–141.
Elliott, T.G., 'Constantine's Conversion: Do we Really Need it?', *Phoenix* 41 (1987), pp.420–38.
Elton, H., 'Warfare and the Military', in Lenski, N. (ed.), *The Cambridge Companion to the Age of Constantine* (Cambridge, 2006), pp.325–46.
Entwistle, C., 'Notes on Selected Recent Acquisitions of Byzantine Jewellery at the British Museum', *British Museum Research Publications* 178 (2010), pp.20–32.
Fowden, G., 'Pagan Versions of the Rain Miracle of AD 172', *Historia* 36 (1987), pp.83–95.
Fowden, G., 'The Last Days of Constantine: Oppositional Versions and their Influence', *JRS* 84 (1994), pp.146–70.
Gaddis, M., *There is No Crime for Those who have Christ. Religious Violence in the Christian Roman Empire* (Berkeley, 2005).
Gero, S., '"Miles Gloriosus": The Christian and Military Service According to Tertullian', *ChHist* 39 (1970), pp.285–98.
Grant, R.M., 'War – Just, Holy, Unjust – in Hellenistic and Early Christian Thought', in Grant, R.M. (ed.), *Christian Beginnings: Apocalypse to History* (London, 1983), pp.173–89.
Guarducci, M., *The Tomb of St. Peter*, trans. McLellan, J. (London, 1960).
Hahn, W., *Moneta Imperii Byzantini: Rekonstruktion des Prägeaufbaudes auf Synoptisch-Tabellarischer Grundlage*, vol. 1 (Wien, 1973).
Hahn, W. & Metlich, M.A., *Money of the Incipient Byzantine Empire*, 2nd edn (Wien, 2013).
Hall, T.C., 'Christianity and Politics: II. The Fatal Compromise', *The Biblical World* 41 (1913), pp.86–91.
Harries, J., *Imperial Rome* AD *284 to 363. The New Empire* (Edinburgh, 2012).
Heather, P., 'The Crossing of the Danube and the Gothic Conversion', *GRBS* 27 (1986), pp.289–318.
Heid, S., 'The Romanness of Roman Christianity', in Rüpke, J. (ed.), *Blackwell Companion to Roman Religion* (Oxford, 2007), pp.406–26.
Helgeland, J., 'Christians and the Roman Army AD 173–337', *ChHist* 43 (1974), pp.149–63, 200.
Helgeland, J., 'Roman Army Religion', *ANRW* 2.16.2 (1978), pp.1470–1505.
Helgeland, J., 'Christians and the Roman Army from Marcus Aurelius to Constantine', *ANRW* 2.23.1 (1979), pp.724–834.
Helgeland, J., Daly, R.J. & Burns, J.P., *Christians and the Military, The Early Experience* (Philadelphia, 1985).
Holloway, R.R., *Constantine and Rome* (New Haven, 2004).
Hornus, J.-M., *It is Not Lawful for Me to Fight. Early Christian Attitudes Toward War, Violence, and the State*, rev. edn, trans. Kreider, A. & Coburn, O. (Scottdale Penn, 1980).
Humphries, M., '*In nomine Patris*: Constantine the Great and Constantius II in Christological Polemic', *Historia* 46 (1997), pp.448–64.
Humphries, M., 'International Relations', in Sabin, P., van Wees, H. & Whitby, M. (eds), *The Cambridge History of Greek and Roman Warfare*, vol. 2 (Cambridge, 2007), pp.235–69.
Humphries, M., 'Rufinus' Eusebius: Translation, Continuation, and Edition in the Latin *Ecclesiastical History*', *JECS* 16 (2008), pp.143–64.
Hurtado, L.W., 'The Staurogram in Early Christian Manuscripts: The Earliest Visual Reference to the Crucified Jesus?', in Kraus, T.J. & Nicklas, T. (eds), *New Testament Manuscripts: Their Texts and their World* (Leiden, 2006), pp.207–26.
Jones, A.H.M., *Constantine and the Conversion of Europe* (London, 1949).
Jones, A.H.M., 'Military Chaplains in the Roman Army', *HThR* 46 (1953), pp.239–40.
Jones, A.H.M., *The Later Roman Empire 284–602. A Social Economic and Administrative Survey*, vol. 1 (Oxford, 1964).
Kee, A., *Constantine versus Christ. The Triumph of Ideology* (London, 1982).
Kent, J.P.C., *The Roman Imperial Coinage VIII: The Family of Constantine I*, AD *337–364* (London, 1981).

Kent, J.P.C., *The Roman Imperial Coinage X: The Divided Empire and the Fall of the Western Parts* AD *395–491* (London, 1994).
Kent, J.P.C. & Painter, K.S. (eds), *Wealth of the Roman World* AD *300–700* (London, 1977).
Koder, J. & Stouraitis, I., 'Byzantine Approaches to Warfare (6th–12th Centuries): An Introduction', in Koder, J. & Stouraitis, I. (eds), *Byzantine War Ideology between Roman Imperial Concept and Christian Religion. Akten des Internationalen Symposiums (Vienna 19–21 Mai 2011)* (Vienna, 2012), pp.9–16.
Kovács, P., *Marcus Aurelius' Rain Miracle and the Marcomannic Wars* (Leiden, 2008).
Leclercq, H., 'Militarisme', in Cabrol, F. & Leclercq, H. (eds), *Dictionnaire d'archéologie chrétienne, et de liturgie* 11.1 (Paris, 1932), pp.1108–82.
Lee, A.D., 'The Army', in Cameron, A. & Garnsey, P. (eds), *The Cambridge Ancient History*, vol. 13 (Cambridge, 1998), pp.213–37.
Lee, A.D., *War in Late Antiquity: A Social History* (Malden MA, 2007).
Lenski, N., 'The Reign of Constantine', in Lenski, N. (ed.), *The Cambridge Companion to the Age of Constantine* (Cambridge, 2006), pp.59–90.
Lenski, N., *Constantine and the Cities. Imperial Authority and Civic Politics* (Philadelphia, 2016).
Liebeschuetz, J.H.W.G., *Continuity and Change in Roman Religion* (Oxford, 1979).
Long, J., 'How to Read a Halo: Three (or more) Versions of Constantine's Vision', in Cain, A. & Lenski, N. (eds), *The Power of Religion in Late Antiquity* (Farnham, 2009), pp.227–36.
MacMullen, R., *Christianizing the Roman Empire (*AD *100–400)* (New Haven, 1984).
MacMullen, R., *Christianity and Paganism in the Fourth to Eighth Centuries* (New Haven, 1997).
Madgearu, A., 'A Note on the Christians' Presence in the Sacer Comitatus before 313 AD', *Aevum* 75 (2001), pp.111–17.
Martindale, J.R. (ed.), *The Prosopography of the Later Roman Empire*, vol. 2 (Cambridge, 1980).
McCormick, M., *Eternal Victory. Triumphal Rulership in Late Antiquity, Byzantium, and the Early Medieval West* (Cambridge, 1986).
Mercurelli, C., 'Il sarcofago di un centurione pretoriano cristiano', *RAC* 16 (1939), pp.73–99.
Musurillo, H. (ed. & trans.), *The Acts of the Christian Martyrs* (Oxford, 1972).
Nicholson, O., 'Constantine's Vision of the Cross', *VChr* 54 (2000), pp.309–23.
Nixon, C.E.V. & Rodgers, B.S. (ed. & trans.), *In Praise of Later Roman Emperors. The Panegyrici Latini* (Berkeley, 1994).
Nock, A.D., *Conversion. The Old and the New in Religion from Alexander the Great to Augustine of Hippo* (Oxford, 1933).
Nock, A.D., 'The Roman Army and the Roman Religious Year', *HThR* 45 (1952), pp.187–252.
Odahl, C.M., *Constantine and the Christian Empire* (London, 2004).
O'Malley, T.P., *Tertullian and the Bible: Language-Heresy-Exegesis* (Utrecht, 1967).
Pharr, C. (ed.), *The Theodosian Code and Novels and the Sirmondian Constitutions* (New York, 1952).
Potter, D., *Constantine the Emperor* (Oxford, 2013).
Roberts, A. & Donaldson, J., *The Ante-Nicene Fathers VII. Fathers of the Third and Fourth Centuries* (Grand Rapids, 1956–62).
Rodgers, B.S., 'The Metamorphosis of Constantine', *CQ* 39 (1989), pp.233–46.
Roldanus, J., *The Church in the Age of Constantine. The Theological Challenges* (London, 2006).
Roth, J.P., 'Jews in the Roman Army: Perceptions and Realities', in de Blois, L. & lo Cascio, E. (eds), *The Impact of the Roman Army (200 BC–AD 476): Economic, Social, Political, Religious and Cultural Aspects* (Leiden, 2007), pp.409–20.
Salzman, M.R., *The Making of a Christian Aristocracy. Social and Religious Change in the Western Roman Empire* (Cambridge MA, 2002).
Setton, K.M., *The Christian Attitude towards the Emperor in the Fourth Century, Especially as Shown in Addresses to the Emperor* (New York, 1967).
Shean, J.F., *Soldiering for God. Christianity and the Roman Army* (Leiden, 2010).
Shepherd, M.H., 'Liturgical Expressions of the Constantinian Triumph', *DOP* 21 (1967), pp.57–78.

Singor, H., 'The Labarum, Shield Blazons, and Constantine's *Caeleste Signum*', in de Blois, L., Erdkamp, P., Hekster, O., de Kleijn, G. & Mols, S. (eds), *The Representation and Perception of Roman Imperial Power* (Amsterdam, 2003), pp.481–500.

Smith, K., *Constantine and the Captive Christians of Persia. Martyrdom and Religious Identity in Late Antiquity* (Oakland CA, 2016).

Southern, P. & Dixon, K.R., *The Late Roman Army* (London, 1996).

Speidel, M.P., 'Maxentius and his "Equites Singulares" in the Battle at the Milvian Bridge', *ClAnt* 5.2 (1986), pp.253–62.

Swift, L.J., 'St. Ambrose on Violence and War', *TAPhA* 101 (1970), pp.533–43.

Swift, L.J., 'War and the Christian Conscience I. The Early Years', *ANRW* 2.23.1 (1979), pp.835–68.

Swift, L.J., *The Early Fathers on War and Military Service* (Wilmington, 1983).

Tomlin, R., 'Christianity and the Late Roman Army', in Lieu, S.N.C. & Montserrat, D. (eds), *Constantine. History, Historiography and Legend* (London, 1998), pp.21–51.

van Dam, R., *Remembering Constantine at the Milvian Bridge* (Cambridge, 2011).

Vanderspoel, J., 'Claudian, Christ and the Cult of the Saints', *CQ* 36 (1986), pp.244–55.

von Harnack, A., *Militia Christi: The Christian Religion and the Military in the First Three Centuries*, trans. McInnes, D. (Philadelphia, 1981).

Weiss, P., 'Die Vision Constantins', in Bleicken, J. (ed.), *Colloquium aus Anlaß des 80. Gerburtstages von Alfred Heuß* (Kallmünz, 1993), pp.143–69.

Weiss, P. & Birley, A.R., 'The Vision of Constantine', *JRA* 16 (2003), pp.237–61.

Whitby, M., '*Deus Nobiscum*: Christianity, Warfare and Morale in Late Antiquity', *BICS* 71 (1998), pp.191–208.

Whitby, M., 'Emperors and Armies, AD 235–395', in Swain, S. & Edwards M. (eds), *Approaching Late Antiquity: The Transformation from Early to Late Empire* (Oxford, 2004), pp.156–86.

Woods, D., 'Julian, Abrogastes, and the *signa* of the *Ioviani* and *Herculiani*', *JRMES* 6 (1995), pp.61–68.

Chapter 10

'Anointed with your Blood and Holy Oil': Byzantines, Crusaders and Warrior Saints in the Eastern Mediterranean (324–1099)

Lynda Garland

From the conversion of Constantine the Great in AD 312 and the consequent endorsement of Christianity as an officially acceptable religion in the Roman Empire, sainthood became an immediate and noteworthy phenomenon across the Mediterranean. One group of saints quickly became particularly prominent, the important cadre of 'military' or 'warrior' saints (the 'stratelatai'), whose popularity was a reaction to the persecutions of Christians in the previous two decades. The terms 'military' or 'warrior' are in fact misleading, as these saints were not necessarily soldiers (though some had had a career in the army), but were so termed as they were martyrs for the faith who had fought for the cause of Christianity by willingly suffering persecution under the pagan emperors of Rome, especially Diocletian (AD 284–305) and his colleagues Galerius (AD 293–311), Maximinus Daia (AD 305–313) and Maximian (AD 286–305): there had also been regional third-century persecutions in AD 249 under Decius (AD 249–251) and in AD 257–258 under Valerian (AD 253–260).[1] The veneration of these 'warrior' saints was widespread across the Empire, and the long-standing popularity of their cults is shown by the existence of texts of their martyrdom narratives and miracle collections in a multiplicity of languages, including Greek, Syriac, Latin, Armenian, Ethiopian and Coptic.[2]

These warrior saints, with regional variations, attained phenomenal popularity among worshippers and were reverenced by all Christians in the East. The most notable of them, who were known as the 'Great Martyrs' (Delehaye's 'état-major' or officer corps), were St Theodore Teron ('the Recruit'),[3] St Theodore Stratelates ('the General'),[4] St George of Lydda,[5] St Merkourios of Caesarea,[6] St Prokopios (the earliest Palestinian martyr)[7] and St Demetrios of Thessaloniki.[8] There were others whose veneration was more localized, of whom the most important were Sts Sergios and Bacchos of Syria,[9] St Menas of Egypt,[10] St Eustratios and the Holy Martyrs of Sebaste in Armenia,[11] St Artemios of Egypt[12] and St Eugenios of Trebizond.[13]

Persecutions and the Martyrs

During the persecutions under Diocletian and his colleagues between AD 303 and 313, Christians who were put to death were generally not proactively targeted because of their faith, but suffered execution because they refused to engage in emperor-worship. These martyrs who died during the persecutions were later seen as attaining the ultimate crown as champions of the faith; with the official acceptance of Christianity, those saints who were prepared to die to proclaim their faith came to be seen as warriors against the pagan forces of evil, with the emperors engaged in the persecutions depicted as malevolent fiends inspired by demons and diabolic priests. The martyrs' dogged resistance to pagan duress, including tortures of every description as described and illustrated with relish in the sources (see Figure 10.1), meant that they could be portrayed in militaristic terms, with their deaths seen as victories against paganism and won under the standard of the Cross (the *vexillum regis*, 'standard of the King'): St George, for example, the 'great martyr' ('*megalomartyras*'), was said to have been miraculously revived after various attempts to execute him, and to have been finally beheaded after surviving being chopped into pieces, buried alive and burnt.[14] The 'warrior saint' was, therefore, so described because he was a '*miles Christi*' or '*miles Dei*' (soldier of Christ or soldier of God) and a member of the '*militia Christi*' (the army of Christ).

As early as AD 323 or 324, in his *Martyrs of Palestine*, Eusebius, Bishop of Caesarea, recorded the names of 135 Palestinian martyrs: 120 men and fifteen women.[15] The term martyr ('*martys*'), originally meaning 'witness', was used for these men and women because they gave witness to their faith through their sufferings and death, but by the fourth century it had come to refer to those who were willing to die for their Christian beliefs;[16] the first unambiguous use of the term refers to St Polycarp of Smyrna c. AD 160.[17] At a very early date, their shrines – such as that of Thekla,

Figure 10.1: The martyrdom of St Blaise of Sebaste (Armenia), a healer, from the *Menologion* of Basil II (MS Vat. Gr. 1613). Blaise was supposedly beheaded under Licinius in AD 316, after being flogged and torn with iron combs. (© *ART Collection/Alamy Stock Photo*)

the ever-popular if fictitious follower of St Paul[18] – became important centres of worship and attracted immense numbers of pilgrims,[19] and their relics were seen as having a particular potency in attaining favours and miracles for their venerators.[20] The supposed tomb of Thekla at Meriamlik near Seleucia was visited, for example, by both St Gregory, Bishop of Nazianzus (and later Patriarch of Constantinople), in AD 374 and the western pilgrim Egeria in AD 384.[21]

Warrior Saints and the Army

The persecution of Christians at the end of the third century and beginning of the fourth was the historical context for the narratives of most of these martyrs: this is even the case for Theodore Stratelates ('the General'), the account of whose martyrdom can be dated no earlier than the ninth century. The early lives and passions of the military saints focus on their steadfastness in the face of torture and death, and they are not distinguished from other martyrs: their miracles seldom had any link with defence of the Empire and are most frequently connected with healing. By the sixth and seventh centuries, however, perceptions of these saints had begun to shift and they are seen more frequently as members of the army of God and called on for aid in battle, although depictions of them still tend to portray them in court dress rather than as soldiers. In a late sixth-century icon in the monastery of St Catherine on Mt Sinai, for example, Saints Theodore Teron and George are portrayed flanking the Mother of God (the Theotokos) and Child (see Figure 10.2) dressed in ceremonial court costume and carrying the crosses of martyrs.

The Diocletianic persecution of AD 303 had specifically targeted professional soldiers in the Roman Army who were Christians, while Licinius, as emperor of the East (AD 313–324), had forced Christians to resign from his forces as part of his anti-Christian measures: his edict was reversed by Constantine, who allowed Christian soldiers, if they chose, to resume their former military rank.[22] Realistically, there must have been tensions for Christians in the pre-Constantinian Roman Army, for example when

Figure 10.2: A sixth-century icon from the Monastery of St Catherine, Mount Sinai, depicting Saints Theodore (left) and George in court dress flanking the enthroned Virgin and Child with archangels behind. (*Photo © Evgeny Ardaev via Wikimedia Commons*)

taking the oath of allegiance to the emperor, and hence membership of the armed forces was a useful plot device leading to a saint's persecution and martyrdom. But, despite the fact that warrior saints came increasingly to be seen as having been soldiers prior to their martyrdom, this had not been the case for a number of them in the earliest sources, and, prior to the tenth century, warrior saints were not seen as a homogenous 'type', except for the fact that they had all suffered martyrdom for their faith.

The backgrounds and careers described in their passion narratives varied greatly: while some, like Menas and Theodore Teron, were said to have been soldiers and George, Merkourios and Theodore Stratelates army officers, Demetrios and Nestor were civilians, Artemios was governor of Egypt and Prokopios a member of the clergy. It was, however, later thought appropriate that the 'histories' of those saints, who had not seen armed service or been associated with the armed forces, be revisited. St Demetrios (a proconsul) and St Prokopios (a bishop), for example, were reimagined as soldiers. Another development in the hagiography was the belief that a major role of these 'warrior' saints was to use their military skills in interventions to protect Christians on the field of battle, assassinate leaders of the enemy and defend cities against barbarians and pagan marauders. This perception of their duties and responsibilities as saints exponentially expanded until, by the tenth and eleventh centuries, they are seen riding alongside Byzantine and crusader armies in defence of the forces of good against rebels, invaders and infidels.

The Warrior Saint Cult

When, in the tenth-century, the warrior saints came to be seen as a homogenous group – a spiritual military elite – a new iconography emerged, in which they were often depicted on horseback rescuing captives from pagan enemies and combating mythical beasts such as dragons (see below). Furthermore, these saints became a clearly defined corps under the Macedonian emperors, with the first extant reference to the '*martyroi hoi stratelatoi*' ('warrior martyrs') apparently by Constantine VII Porphyrogennetos (AD 913–959) in his *De ceremoniis*, where they are named alongside Christ, the Theotokos (Mother of God) and the 'arch-general' Michael as the protectors of Constantinople.[23] Constantine's son Leo VI (AD 886–912) was personally responsible for the increased popularity of these saints: both he and his wife (St) Theophano experienced a vision of St Demetrios, as a young man in military dress, after Leo had been imprisoned by his father Basil I, and the emperor himself wrote three homilies on the subject of this saint (*BHG* 536–38), as well as a hymn, and dedicated a church to him in the Great Palace.[24]

From the reign of Leo, Byzantium saw the production of new lives of these saints, with hymns written and churches built in their honour; in addition, art began to depict them together as a group, although the saints chosen for illustration were not always consistent. An ivory triptych of Constantine Porphyrogennetos, now at the Palazzo Venezia in Rome, depicts Theodore Teron, Eustathios, Prokopios and Arethas, and George, Theodore Stratelates, Demetrios and Eustratios in two divisions of four, on either side of a central panel with a 'Deesis' scene (Christ, flanked by the Virgin and John the Baptist) and five apostles. This is apparently the earliest depiction of a group of more than two military saints. An inscription on each side reads: 'An emperor had the four martyrs sculpted, with them he puts to flight the enemies by authority' and 'here is the foursome of the martyrs, who decorate the crown with the four virtues'.²⁵ Despite the army background of several of these saints, they are all depicted on this triptych in formal court regalia, although one of each group – Eustathios and Theodore Stratelates – carry swords. Elsewhere, at this period, they are depicted in military garb: the ivory triptych in the Hermitage depicts in the central panel the death of the forty martyrs of Sebaste (who died in a frozen lake), while fully armed warrior saints, again four on each side, occupy the two wings (see also Figure 10.7 for St Demetrios).²⁶ The mosaic cycle of the Boeotian monastery of Hosios Leukas, completed in the 1020s, also depicts Merkourios, Prokopios, Teron, Stratelates, Demetrios and George as soldiers, while the medallion portraits of six of these saints (Stratelates, Demetrios, George, Prokopios, Merkourios and perhaps Teron) in the *Psalter* of Basil II (976–1025), which flank Basil in parade armour on the frontispiece, show them equipped with shields and lances above cowering figures, identified as Bulgarian prisoners or Basil's reverential subjects, with the legend 'The martyrs are his allies, for he is their friend. They smite those who are lying at his feet' (see Figure 10.3).²⁷

Figure 10.3: A replica of a miniature of Basil II in triumphal garb as a Roman general, from his early eleventh-century *Psalter* (BNM, MS. Gr. 17, fol. 3r). The archangels Michael and Gabriel are handing Basil his lance and crown, and he is flanked by medallions of the warrior saints, also armed with lances: Theodore Stratelates and Demetrios (left), George, Prokopios and Merkourios (right) and perhaps Theodore Teron (bottom left). (© *The Picture Art Collection/Alamy Stock Photo*)

The popular epic-romance *Digenis Akritas*, compiled in the eleventh and twelfth centuries based on earlier oral tales from the Eastern frontier, describes its hero (Basil the 'two-blood border lord') as assisted against the Arabs and other enemies by St George, the Theodores and St Demetrios, as well as by Christ, the Virgin and archangels:

> 'Having as his help the grace of God, the unconquerable Mother of God, the angels and archangels too, and the victorious great martyrs, both the all-glorious Theodores, the General and the Recruit, and much-labouring noble George, the miracle-worker and martyr of martyrs, and glorious Demetrios, the patron of Basil [Digenis] and the boast and pride of the one who vanquished all his foes, the Hagarenes and Ishmaelites and barbarous Scyths who rage like dogs.'²⁸

Precedents for Divine and Angelic Epiphanies

The Classical World

The topos of the gods or heroes intervening in battle and assisting one or other of the opposing sides is a frequent plot device in the *Iliad*. Generally in these cases the gods are invisible to the mortal combatants. Only on one occasion are the heroes able to see deities on the battlefield, when Athena gives Diomedes the power to discern the gods in combat, removing the mist which veils men's sight (at which he spears Aphrodite, wounding her in the arm, and attacks Apollo three times before being warned not to match himself against immortals).[29] Pritchett lists forty-nine instances of battlefield apparitions in ancient Greek history,[30] with a variety of epiphanies occurring during the Persian Wars, including, at Marathon, Theseus, Echetlos, Pan and a giant hoplite, and, at Salamis, the phasma of a woman and the Aeacidae.[31] In 279 BC, according to an inscription from Kos,[32] Apollo appeared to help drive off the Celtic attack on Delphi; a thanks-offerings was made to the god 'for manifesting himself during the perils which confronted the sanctuary'. The Greek gods' concern for their cities lasted into Christian times. Zosimos' *New History*, written perhaps *c*.AD 500, covers Roman history down to AD 410. He is one of the last pagan historians, fiercely opposed to Christianity. He records that, when Alaric attacked Athens in AD 395, he saw Athena walking along the city walls, dressed just like her statue: this was presumably the Athena Promachos, which stood on the acropolis between the Erechtheion and the Propylaia, rather than the Athena Parthenos, the cult statue from the Parthenon. The 7-metre high Athena Promachos was garbed in an aegis decorated with the Gorgon's head and a helmet with a horsehair crest, while the Athena Parthenos stood 12.7 metres tall and was armed with an aegis, shield, spear and helmet.[33] Not only was Athena in full armour ready to defend her city, but Alaric also had a further vision of Achilles 'raging' in front of the walls, as described by Homer when he was engaging the Trojans in revenge for the death of Patroklos. He was so struck with these epiphanies that he sent heralds with proposals for peace, and Athens and Attica were left unharmed, preserved by their presiding deity and a great hero of legend.[34]

The Romans also believed that the gods manifested themselves to mortals and protected them in battle, as well as actually participating in action on the battlefield alongside human combatants. In early Roman history, it was believed that the Dioscuri, Castor and Pollux, in the guise of two young horsemen, assisted the Romans against the Latins at the Battle of Lake Regillus *c*.496 BC,[35] and a temple was built in the Roman forum in their honour, in the place where they were said to have watered their horses. Two hundred years later, it was rumoured that the god Mars had come to the help of the consul Luscinus (cos. 282, 278 BC): when the Romans attacked the Lucanians' camp near Thurii, an armed warrior of formidable size was seen carrying scaling-ladders, who could not be found the next day. Valerius Maximus reports that the finding of a helmet with two feathers was seen as evidence of divine intervention having taken place, and that a thanksgiving was consequently held in honour of Mars.[36] It was usually, however, the Dioscuri who were thought to intervene in battle, and Cicero's *de natura deorum* also records an incident in which Castor and Pollux were thought to have delivered the news of the defeat of Perseus at Pydna in 168 BC. When P. Vatinius was returning to Rome from Reate, two young warriors on white horses told him that on that very day, Perseus had been taken prisoner. He reported the news to the Senate, who threw him into prison for spreading an unfounded report, but was released when a dispatch arrived from the general L. Aemilius Paullus which confirmed the account, and was recompensed with a grant of land and exemption from military service. Castor and Pollux also purportedly announced the victory at Pharsalus in 48 BC, while the noise of clanging armour and a sounding trumpet in the sky during the wars with the Cimbri suggested their involvement.[37]

The Biblical Tradition
Numerous works in the Bible also provided evidence of divine intervention in warfare by angels and saints. In the Old Testament, Yahweh himself was frequently portrayed as smiting the Israelites' enemies, such as the Egyptians' first-born children and the Egyptian army at the Red Sea, as well as the Philistines and Moabites.[38] Divine assistance was actually provided for Judas Maccabaeus on the battlefield, when angels intervened in two engagements against the Seleucid ruler Antiochos IV Epiphanes (175–164 BC): in one, five resplendent men on horses with golden bridles protected Judas, showering arrows and thunderbolts on the enemy, while in the other a celestial horseman, clad in white and equipped with weapons of gold, instilled courage in the Jewish troops.[39] The Maccabees, who died at the hands of Seleucid oppressors because they refused to abandon the Torah, were seen by fourth-century bishops as proto-martyrs, and venerated alongside Christian martyrs and saints (see below). Judas was also handed a golden sword by the prophet Jeremiah in a dream prior to the Battle of Adasa in 161 BC, and told to use 'this holy sword, the gift of God' to crush his enemies, which he successfully accomplished.[40]

A similar epiphany had occurred earlier, when Seleukos IV (187–175 BC), Antiochos' brother, instructed his minister Heliodoros to appropriate the riches of the temple in Jerusalem: the spectators saw 'a horse, splendidly caparisoned, with a rider of fearsome aspect, which rushed fiercely at Heliodoros, and reared up, attacking him with its hooves'. The rider was wearing golden armour, while 'there also appeared to Heliodoros two young men of exceptional strength and outstanding beauty, splendidly dressed, who stood on either side of him and scourged him, ceaselessly raining blows upon him.' The apparition quite naturally terrified all those who accompanied Heliodoros and impressed the bystanders.[41]

There are also references in books of the Bible to a heavenly army, and it was actually the 'multitude of the army of heaven' (πλῆθος στρατιᾶς οὐρανίου: generally, but somewhat misleadingly, translated as the 'heavenly host') which celebrated the birth of Christ and the angel's announcement to the shepherds.[42] This army appears to have had an archistrategos (commander), an unnamed warrior who appeared to Joshua outside of Jericho, standing in front of him with a drawn sword to encourage him to claim the Promised Land, while in the Book of Daniel the archangel, Michael the 'Prince', features as Israel's guardian angel or commander, who opposed the guardian angel of the Persians.[43] The conflict between the forces of heaven and those of darkness are portrayed in the Book of Revelation as a war between two heavenly armies, in which Michael leads his angels against the dragon and the dragon and his angels are hurled to the earth, losing their place in heaven. Elsewhere in the same book, the 'armies in heaven' (τὰ στρατεύματα τὰ ἐν τῷ οὐρανῷ), riding on white horses and wearing clean, white linen, follow the 'rider on the white horse, whose name is Faithful and True', who judges with justice and wages holy war. These capture the beast and the false prophet and cast them into the fiery lake of burning sulphur.[44]

As a result, the dragon, or flying serpent, became the embodiment of evil in early Christian iconography, and Constantine the Great had a picture set up in the portico of his Constantinopolitan palace of a dragon, 'that hateful and savage adversary of mankind', depicted under his feet and that of his children, stricken through with a dart and cast headlong into the depths of the sea. According to Eusebius, the dragon represented 'the secret adversary of the human race', illustrating the prophecy that 'God would bring his great, strong and terrible sword against the dragon, the flying serpent, and destroy the dragon that was in the sea.'[45] The serpent also appeared on Constantine's coinage representing his defeat of Licinius and paganism in general: coins minted at Constantinople from AD 327 depict on the reverse a *labarum*, crowned by the *chi-rho* symbol, spearing a serpent-dragon, symbolizing Constantine's victory over his pagan rivals (see Figure 9.2). The legend reads *SPES PUBLICA*: 'Public Hope', or 'Hope of the State'.[46] The iconographic type is linked to the amulets depicting Solomon, or a Holy Rider (St Sisinnios of Antioch, for example), spearing a prostrate demon, such as the female demon Obyzouth or Gillo, who strangled new-born babies: amulets of this type date from the fourth century or earlier.[47] The idea of a 'divine army' supporting Constantine was articulated by the pagan Nazarius in an oration in AD 321, who claimed that at the battle against Maxentius in AD 312 his soldiers had seen a host in the sky marching in battle array to his assistance, with flashing shields and armour. According to Nazarius, Constantine's father, the deified Constantius Chlorus, led this army of heaven (the force appears to have been pagan rather than Christian), and he compares the apparition of the Castor and Pollux duo who intervened at Lake Regillus with the celestial army that supported Constantine.[48]

St Merkourios and the Death of Julian the Apostate

It is with Julian 'the Apostate' that warrior saints were believed to have seriously taken up arms against enemies of the faith. From as early as the fourth century, the saints were believed to have been involved in the assassination of pagan or heretic emperors, and this intervention later expands into action on the battlefield against enemies of the Empire. Initially, these episodes are reported at second hand, and the dramatic action takes place in visions or dreams, which are then confirmed by accounts of the emperor's death. The fourth-century emperors Julian (AD 361–363) and the Arian Valens (AD 364–378), both of whom were antagonistic to Orthodoxy, died in battle in unknown circumstances. In each case there were competing explanations for their deaths, which gradually evolved into the belief that their deaths had been caused by the intervention of a warrior saint. In both cases the involvement of the saint was revealed in a dream.

The death of the pagan emperor Julian in June AD 363 was ascribed to St Merkourios, and the legend predates the first attestation of Merkourios' cult in Cappadocia in the early sixth century. While a popular saint, Merkourios possessed no church in the capital. According to the tenth-century martyrdom narratives, he was a young and handsome valiant warrior, appointed stratopedarches (a senior military commander) by the emperor Decius. When the emperor asked him to sacrifice to Artemis, he refused, and so was tortured and put in prison, despite his previous victories over the barbarians, and was executed by beheading at Caesarea.[49]

Julian, nephew of Constantine the Great, had left Antioch in March AD 363, intending to attack the Persian capital Ctesiphon. He was persuaded by his generals not to attempt a siege of the city, and during a withdrawal on 26 June was wounded by a spear to the abdomen in a raid on his troops by the Sassanid army.[50] In the accounts of his death outside Ctesiphon, the responsibility for the killing evolves exponentially from the action of a Persian or Saracen or Christian soldier until it comes to be attributed directly to the hand of God. Libanios (c.AD 314–392), in his funeral oration, was the first to suggest that the person responsible for his death might have been a Christian in Julian's own army, while Philostorgios (c.AD 368–439) stated that the spear had been hurled by one of the Arab horsemen in service with the Persians, though he admitted that some thought the blow had been struck by Julian's own friends.[51] Similarly, Socrates Scholastikos (c.AD 380–after 439) listed several current theories for the death of Julian: a Persian who hurled his javelin and fled; one of his own men (the preferred explanation); and – an account recorded by one of Julian's bodyguards, Kallistos – a demon, though Socrates adds that 'this is possibly a mere poetical fiction, or perhaps it really was true, for vengeful furies have undoubtedly destroyed many people'.[52]

By the mid-fifth century, the vengeance of God through the agency of an angel or warrior saint was being openly scouted as a possibility: Theodoret (c.AD 393–466) comments that 'whether it were a man or angel who plied the steel, without doubt the doer of the deed was the minister of the will of God'. His citation of Julian's exclamation, 'Thou hast won, O Galilaean', as he flung a handful of his blood into the air in his last moments, is the first evidence for these famous last words.[53] Sozomen (c.AD 400–450) suggested three possibilities: that Julian's death was the work of a Persian or Arab ('Saracen'); or a soldier, possibly a Christian, angry that Julian had imperilled the army; or that supernatural agency had been responsible – but heavenly, not demonic as suggested by Socrates. In this proposed scenario, two saints had been dispatched to slay the emperor as agents of divine wrath. Like the gods of the *Iliad*, they were invisible to the combatants on the battlefield, but were seen by two people in dreams – one a friend of Julian and the other a philosopher from Alexandria. In this account, Julian's friend had fallen asleep in a church where he had taken shelter while on a journey to join Julian in Persia, and saw 'either in a dream or a vision' all the apostles and prophets assembled, deliberating on how to take vengeance on Julian for his persecution of Christians. Two of the assembly stood up and volunteered to take action, leaving in haste 'as if to deprive Julian of the imperial power'. In suspense, the dreamer did not continue his journey, but awaited a further revelation, and the next night saw the sequel to his original dream, when the two saints returned to the same assembly and announced that Julian's death had been accomplished.[54]

The second vision was sent to Didymos at Alexandria (c.AD 313–398), who had continually fasted and prayed for the cessation of Julian's persecution of the Church. From worry and hunger on this occasion he had fallen asleep in his chair, and dreamt that he saw white horses riding through the air and heard a voice saying to them, 'Go and tell Didymos that Julian has been killed exactly at this time; let him communicate this news to Athanasius, the bishop, and let him get up and eat.' Athanasius was intermittently the Orthodox Bishop of Alexandria (he was exiled five times) between AD 328 and 373. Sozomen, the author, states that he had been 'credibly informed' that Didymos and Julian's friend had actually seen these visions, and that these were not far from the truth.[55]

Sozomen does not identity these bellicose saints by name, but Nikephoros Kallistos Xanthopoulos in his *Church History* states that they were Merkourios and Artemios:[56] Artemios, governor of Egypt, was an Arian, who had suffered martyrdom at Antioch under Julian in AD 362, and hence an appropriate choice for the role. While a warrior saint, Artemios' main claim to fame was his specialization in cures for men suffering from hernias and diseases of the genitalia: the petitioners incubated overnight in his church in Constantinople in hope of a cure.[57] It is probable that Sozomen, as an Orthodox Church historian, did not name the two saints because Artemios was an Arian, and hence it was inappropriate that he be given the credit for successfully eliminating the pagan emperor.

By the sixth century, it was taken as a matter of faith that a warrior saint had been the agent of divine vengeance against Julian, and the deed was ascribed to Merkourios. In an anonymous Syriac source, Jovian (Julian's Orthodox successor, AD 363–364) is said to have experienced a dream in which Merkourios appeared to him, armed with a bow and three arrows, and informed him that he was going to kill Julian in three weeks' time, warning Jovian in effect of his future imperial status.[58] Byzantine chroniclers in the sixth century also recorded that St Merkourios had been the agent (see Figure 10.4), and validate their accounts by having the revelatory dream experienced by no less a churchman than St Basil 'the Great' of Cappadocia (AD 330–379).

Figure 10.4: An icon from the Church of St Merkourios, Old Cairo, depicting St Merkourios killing Julian the Apostate, with St Basil (who saw the assassination in a dream) watching from the right. (*Photo via Wikimedia Commons*)

The first source to incorporate St Basil in the storyline is Malalas' *Chronicle*, written under Justinian in the mid-sixth century (it ends at AD 563), the first universal Byzantine chronicle written for a popular audience. In this account, Christ instructs Merkourios to kill Julian, and the *Chronicle* records a series of dreams sent to Julian and others to further the plot.[59] While still at Antioch before setting out on his Persian expedition, Julian had a dream of a blond youth – presumably St Merkourios himself – who told him he would die in Asia, and then outside Ctesiphon had a further dream of a man in a light cloak who entered his tent and stabbed him with a spear; when his attendants, eunuchs and guards rushed in and saw his spear-wound, Julian asked them the name of the village where they had set up camp, and when they replied 'Asia', he cried out 'Sun, slay Julian', and immediately passed away. In a dream that same night, Basil, later the Bishop of Cappadocia, saw the heavens open and Christ sitting on his throne. Christ summoned Merkourios, telling him to go and kill the Emperor Julian, who had risen up against the Christians. Merkourios, wearing a shining iron breastplate, disappeared, and later appeared and reported: 'Emperor Julian has been stabbed and died, as the Lord had ordered.' Basil, who was a student friend and frequent correspondent of Julian, woke in shock and reported this dream the next day to his clergy, but they all implored him to be silent on the issue until it was confirmed by outside reports – as, of course, it soon was. The *Chronikon Paschale* closely follows this account, as does John of Nikiu.[60] Unfortunately, Basil only became bishop in AD 370, seven years after Julian's death, but the story is delightfully anecdotal.

In the *History of the Patriarchs of the Coptic Church of Alexandria*, the date of which is uncertain, the dying Julian himself realized that his death had been accomplished by a saint, and Basil's dream of the assassination is corroborated by two others, who experienced the dream while in prison with him:

> 'He [Julian] saw in the night an army which came upon him from the air, and one of the soldiers struck him with a lance on the head so that it pierced him through the body. Then, realising it was one of the martyrs, he filled his hand with his blood and threw it upwards saying, "Take that Jesus, for you have conquered the whole world." And Basil, the holy man, three days before the death of Julian, who was in prison, woke from his sleep and said to the two who were with him, "I have seen tonight the martyr St Merkourios entering into his church and taking his lance saying, 'In truth, I will not allow this unbeliever to blaspheme against my God.' When he had said this he disappeared and I did not see him again." Then both his companions said to him, "I also saw the same thing." So they said to one another, "We believe without doubt that this has taken place." And they sent to the church of the martyr St Merkourios to look for his lance, which was kept there, to see whether it was still there or not. And as they could not find the lance they were convinced of the truth of the dream. And three days later the letters with the news of Julian's death arrived at Antioch.'[61]

According to tradition, Julian had had Basil incarcerated prior to his departure to the Persian front. It is not made clear where the church and lance of St Merkourios were located, but the disappearance of the saint's weapon from the church is seen as evidence for the belief that a spiritual being could make use of a physical weapon.[62]

Sergios, Theodore and the Emperor Valens

Warrior saints also – allegedly – encompassed the death of the Arian emperor Valens (AD 364–378), who died at Adrianople fighting against the Visigoths in August AD 378. This was the worst defeat suffered by the Empire since the Battle of Cannae: Valens' body was never found and his fate not known. Ammianus gives two different accounts of his death: that he was mortally wounded by an arrow, and that he was wounded and carried to a wooden hut, which was torched by the Goths.[63] Socrates Scholastikos likewise gives alternative versions: that he was burnt to death, or that he removed his imperial garb and ran into the ranks of the infantry, where he was cut down.[64] However, the account of Faustus of Byzantium, an Armenian historian whose work covers the period from c.AD 330–387, but which was probably written in the 470s, records that St Theodore Teron ('the Recruit') and St Sergios were the agents responsible for Valens' death. Sergios, an army officer, had supposedly been executed by Maximian, together with his companion Bacchos (Justinian and Theodora built a church to the saints in Constantinople, often called the 'little Hagia Sophia').

Sergios was martyred at Resafa, and his cult acquired more prominence than that of his comrade Bacchos.[65] In this narrative, which closely resembles that of Merkourios and Julian, a sophist (perhaps Libanios of Antioch), travelling to Byzantium at Valens' request to write a refutation of Christianity (Valens was actually an Arian, not a pagan), spent the night in the martyr-chapel (martyrium) of Thekla outside Antioch. There, while still awake, he saw a gathering of many martyrs, including Thekla, all adorned with great brilliance. When they were seated, the martyrs bemoaned the fact that 'the saints of the Lord who have not yet departed from the earth' were suffering persecution, imprisonment and exile, and that they had therefore assembled to avenge the faithful of the Lord by removing Valens, who was hindering Christ's labourers, including the diligent labourer Barsilios (St Basil). 'Come then', they said to each other, 'let us send two of our number to go and remove the evil-doer Valens from life'. One of these saints was called Sargis (Sergios), the other Theodoros (Theodore).

The sophist who had experienced the dream refused to continue his journey the next day with his escort, and on the following night he again had a vision of the assembly of the martyrs, to which Sargis and Theodoros returned, reporting that they had killed Valens, enemy of the truth. The whole assembly arose, praised Christ and departed. Upon revealing what he had seen, the sophist risked execution for treason, but was given three days' grace, during which Valens' death was confirmed.[66]

While there has been some debate about whether this story is simply an imitation of the better-known Merkourios and Julian anecdote, in this case there was no reason for the identity of the saints to have been changed, and it is now generally agreed to be a 'stand-alone' episode, which deliberately promoted the cults of two Eastern warrior saints.[67] St Sergios, together with his companion and fellow-martyr Bacchos, was particularly popular in Syria and Christian Arabia, with his major shrine at Resafa (Rusafa) in Syria, at the extreme eastern end of the Empire.[68] The city was an important pilgrimage site from the fourth century and was renamed Sergiopolis after its major saint from c.AD 425, the date of the earliest known shrine to Sergios. He was a logical choice for an Armenian source, as he was venerated in the Armenian Church as a military saint, as was his namesake Sarkis the General, who was martyred under Shapur II with his son Martyros.[69] Euchaita (modern Avkat) in Pontos in northern Asia Minor was the main cult centre of Theodore, who was already by AD 380 venerated as a military saint for intervention in battles (see below) and famous in Syria, Palestine and Asia Minor.[70]

The Appearance of Saints on the Battlefield

The first Christian saints actually believed to have engaged the enemy on the battlefield were not warrior saints but the apostles John and Philip, and they were again seen not by the actual participants in the conflict, but in a dream. The occasion was the battle between Theodosius I and the usurper Eugenios in AD 394. Even though Eugenios was a practising Christian, his defeat by the orthodox Theodosius led to his being depicted by Christian historians as a champion of paganism.[71] The incident is recorded by Bishop Theodoret of Cyrrhus, writing between AD 444 and 450, who is therefore hardly a contemporary source.

The opposing sides met at the River Frigidus (to the east of Aquileia in Italy), and while asleep, Theodosius was said to have had a vision of 'two men clothed in white on white horses', who urged him to be of good cheer, and arm and marshal his men for battle at dawn, 'for we are sent to fight for you. I am John the evangelist and I am Philip the apostle.' A soldier in the ranks who also saw the vision reported it to his centurion, and the story thus reached the emperor, confirming his own dream.[72] Other 'miracles' are recorded for the battle: Theodosius prayed for a storm, and a fierce tempest blew in the faces of the Western troops, even sweeping their own arrows back into their faces, while a great dust storm blinded them. Theodoret may have been drawing on narratives of Castor and Pollux, with perhaps hints of the Book of Revelation where the army of heaven battled the forces of darkness and the dragon. The authenticity of the dream, as with the Coptic account of Merkourios' slaying of Julian, is confirmed by its also being experienced by a third party.

There was also a legend that St Peter (and perhaps St Paul too) had intervened to prevent Attila marching on Rome. In AD 452, at a meeting between Attila and Pope Leo, two huge men appeared (or in the version of the eighth-century source Paul the Deacon, only one), dressed in priestly robes with swords, and threatened Attila and his army with death if they attacked Rome: these saints, whose apparition helped convince Attila of the inadvisability of proceeding on to Rome, were said to have been Saints Peter and Paul.[73]

Patron Saints of Cities

One of the main duties of a warrior saint was the protection of their city against invaders, of which St Demetrios' concern for Thessaloniki is the prime example (see below). Where the capital itself was concerned, the Theotokos was always its main defender, and from the late sixth century the city had been seen as under her direct protection. She personally intervened to defend it when under siege, and, when the

Avars besieged Constantinople in AD 626, their khagan saw 'a woman in stately dress rushing about on the walls all alone'. According to Theodore Synkellos, 'she was present everywhere, winning uncontested victory and inflicting fear and horror on her enemies. She gave strength to her servants, protected her subjects from harm, and destroyed the enemy hordes.'[74] However, from the sixth century on, warrior saints also began to take a prominent part in the defence of their cities or the Empire as a whole, either of their own volition or sometimes as generals under her command and carrying out her instructions. The Theotokos, however, remained a preeminent defender of her city and Byzantine troops in the field, and was credited with military successes: after his victory in Bulgaria in AD 971, John I Tzimiskes (AD 969–976) had an icon of the Theotokos carried in his triumphal chariot while he processed into the capital on foot; and in his civil wars in AD 989, Basil II (AD 976–1025) was said to have personally carried an icon of the Theotokos into battle.[75] It was also customary for icons of saints to be taken into battle, with John I Tzimiskes considering the icons of the Saints Theodore as his 'allies and protectors against the foe' (see below).

Demetrios was not the only saint recorded as intervening successfully when his city was under attack. St Sergios was renowned for having prevented Khusrau (Chosroes) I in AD 543 from successfully storming Resafa (now renamed Sergiopolis).[76] The Persian ruler sent 6,000 men to besiege the city to loot its treasures, but an Arab Christian in his army warned the town in time. Only 200 Roman soldiers were there to defend the city, but the spy informed them that the besiegers would only have water for two days. According to the historian Procopius in the sixth century, it was faith in Sergios and the citizens' prayers that saved the city. In Evagrius' account, written at the end of the century, the saint took a more direct role. The Persians had been informed that the city was only manned by women, children and invalids, but as they approached they perceived an immense army on the battlements and as a result Khusrau's army retreated the next day:

> 'Khusrau advanced his whole army against the city. Suddenly along the circuit of the walls, in defence of the place, innumerable shields appeared, and when they saw these the people sent by Khusrau returned, describing, with wonder, the number and type of the weapons. And when, on further enquiry, he learned that very few persons remained in the city, and that these consisted of the elderly and children due to the absence of the men of fighting age, he realised that the miracle was the work of the martyr [Sergios], and, influenced by fear and wonder at the faith of the Christians, he withdrew back to his own country.'[77]

In this case, while the inhabitants realized that their survival was due to the intervention of St Sergios, the vision was actually vouchsafed to the enemy army, and Khusrau retreated because he understood that the city was under the protection of its warrior saint and was therefore impregnable.

Constantine VII Porphyrogennetos himself, in the *de administrando imperio*, recorded that Patras in the northern Peloponnese was saved in AD 805 by St Andrew (the apostle), its patron saint, when the town was attacked by the Slavs. Andrew was not a warrior saint, but he took on the mantle of one in defence of his city.[78] A scout had been instructed to give a signal (the lowering of his standard) to announce the arrival of the military governor to the city's aid. When, however, he found that the governor was not coming, he began to return to the city, holding his standard erect. Owing to the intercession of the apostle Andrew, his horse slipped and he dipped the standard. The inhabitants of the city, seeing the signal and believing that the military governor was on his way, opened the gates of the city and sallied out. There they saw Andrew on horseback charging upon the barbarians, who were totally routed. He was also seen by the Slavs, who in their terror fled to his church for refuge:

> 'And the barbarians saw him, and were amazed and confounded at the violent assault upon them of the invincible and unconquerable warrior and captain and marshal, the triumphant and victorious first-summoned apostle Andrew. They were thrown into disarray and disconcerted, fear possessed them, and they fled for refuge into his most sacred church.'[79]

In both these cases, the enemy had received visual proof that the saint was protecting his city, one by conjuring up a miraculous army of defenders and the other by participating personally in the engagement and terrifying the attackers. Interestingly, on this occasion, the saint was seen not just by the enemy, but by both sides in the conflict.

St George and his Dragon

The archetypal and still today the most popular military saint in Greece and Europe generally, the 'Great Martyr' (*megalomartyras*), was St George of Lydda (known in Greek as Diospolis, the 'city of Zeus'), a town in Palestine, south-east of Jaffa. This was an early centre of Christianity and supposedly the site of his burial, even though his martyrdom narratives describe him as a young aristocratic military officer from Cappadocia, who was allegedly executed by Diocletian at Nikomedeia in Bithynia in AD 303. There is no actual evidence that George was an historical figure (unlike many of the other military saints), and he is not mentioned by the fourth-century sources Eusebius or Jerome.[80] Church authorities themselves in the early sixth century considered his *Life* to be fictitious, and it was listed in the *Decretum Gelasianum*, a work supposedly composed by Pope Gelasius (AD 492–496) but probably dating to the early sixth century, which listed apocryphal writings such as accounts of saints and martyrs compiled or recognized by heretics and schismatics and which were not accepted by the Church.[81] At this point, therefore, George's *acta* were seen as apocryphal, or at least ahistorical. His burial place at Lydda was, however, a pilgrimage site from the early sixth century; while the sanctuary there may have been built at the end of the fourth century, the earliest pilgrimage account is the sixth-century pilgrimage travel guide, the *de situ terrae sanctae*, of the archdeacon Theodosius (written between AD 518 and 530).[82] The earliest church of George in Constantinople was mentioned in AD 518; there were nine churches in total dedicated to him in the capital.[83]

While St George was one of the warrior saints who was actually said to have been a soldier, none of the miracles in his miracle collections involve combat or army service, and his martial ethos is relatively late in developing: he is often shown as healing children or saving them from captivity among his other feats, as in the mosaic from the Church of St Demetrios in Thessaloniki (see Figure 10.5).[84] He generally appears, however, as a soldier on horseback (he was depicted as a warrior in a sixth-century wall-painting from Bawit in Egypt),[85] and some of his miracles portray a pugnacious quality, particularly towards non-Byzantines, such as Arabs. His portrait in military garb was sufficient to repel a band of 'Saracens', who intended to destroy the mosaic decorating the façade of his church where he was depicted dressed in armour and carrying a lance, while on another occasion some Saracens camping in Lydda went to sleep and gamble in George's church. Though they were warned that St George would punish them, one of the Saracens threw his spear at the saint's icon, which returned upon him straight through the heart. His companions were killed as they ran away. A miracle collection of Adamnan of Iona, *On the Holy Places*, recording the Frankish pilgrim Arculf's account of his travels in the late seventh century, also shows the icon punishing disrespect towards the saint: an unbeliever threw his lance at a column on which the image of St George was depicted, but the lance passed through the column, his horse died, and when he tried to retrieve his lance his hand got stuck inside the column until he repented.

Figure 10.5: A seventh-century mosaic from the Church of St Demetrios in Thessaloniki, depicting St George in court dress as the patron of two young children: his hand is on the shoulder of one child, and he is blessing the other. (© *Art Collection 2/Alamy Stock Photo*)

In another anecdote that St Arculf claimed to have heard in Constantinople, a large force was assembling for an expedition. One of the cavalry entered the city and addressed the depiction of George, commending himself and his horse to George's protection, and asking that by virtue of his prayers they would both return safe and well. Many thousands perished in the campaign, but this man returned to Diospolis on the same beloved horse because he had requested George's protection for them both. When the cavalryman attempted to give George increasing amounts of gold in exchange for the horse, the animal remained rooted to the spot and refused to move. Finally, the soldier realized that he had consecrated his horse to the saint and 'assigned him as a gift to the holy confessor', together with the sixty gold coins with which he had tried to ransom him.[86] Accounts portray George as an expert at protecting his shrine: according to the *Khuzistan Chronicle*, written in the mid-seventh century, following the Persian conquest of Jerusalem in AD 614 a Persian commander attempted to despoil George's church. His soldiers were unable to enter the building, and when he himself attempted ingress, the hooves of his horse stuck to the ground and he was immobilized. To release himself, he had to vow a silver dedication in the shape of the church, an object which from that day was pointed out to pilgrims as proof of the saint's powers.[87]

Arkadios, Archbishop of Cyprus in the seventh century, praised George's role in earthly and heavenly armies, describing him as 'the unconquerable shield of the soldiers of Christ, ally of the emperor, fortification of fighting men'.[88] However, in early accounts where George's intervention made a difference to history, his involvement tended to be 'hands-off' rather than as a participant in violent conflict. In one miracle in an Ethiopian account, George, together with the archangel Michael, was responsible for violently deposing Diocletian himself from the throne (the reader will no doubt remember that George was said to have been martyred under Diocletian). One of Diocletian's generals, Euchios, who had been sent to destroy George's shrine at Lydda, broke the lamp of the shrine. The flying glass from the lamp impaled itself in his head and he developed leprosy where the oil had splashed on him, dying horribly on the third day. Diocletian prepared to take revenge for this by destroying the shrine, but before his fleet could embark at Constantinople, George descended from heaven along with St Michael and overturned Diocletian's throne, the golden pomegranates of which crushed his eyeballs. Diocletian was not killed, but Constantine assumed the throne in his place.[89]

Another occasion on which George ensured victory for the right side is mentioned in the *Life of Theodore of Sykeon* in Galatia (*c.* AD 540–613), written by a contemporary author, one of Theodore's disciples.[90] The popularity of George's cult is apparent in this *Life*, in which George plays a prominent role protecting Theodore from demons and temptations. However, for all George's martial qualities, when Domnitziolos, nephew of the emperor Phokas (AD 602–610), was sent as general against the Persians and requested divine assistance, it was his prayers to George that ensured his success, rather than actual intervention from the saint: Domnitziolos asked Theodore's advice prior to the campaign, and Theodore commended him to God and St George. When the general fell into an ambush, he prayed to George and thus escaped from danger.[91]

The heroic deeds for which George was primarily celebrated from the eleventh or twelfth century onwards related to the killing of dragons, a legend which may date to as early as the seventh century. In a seventh-century painting in Cappadocia, he is shown with St Theodore Teron attacking two serpents around a tree, but George is mostly shown in combat with a man prior to the eleventh century, and Theodore Teron's association with dragons goes back much earlier than that of George (see below). George and Theodore are frequently represented together on horseback killing a dragon, which is either serpent-like or lizard-like, and sometimes with two heads.[92] George's rescue of a princess was first attested in an eleventh-century Georgian manuscript, and the legend was made famous by Caxton's *Golden Legend*, a fifteenth-century English translation of Jacobus da Voragine's thirteenth-century work *Legenda Sanctorum*, which records how a fierce dragon which was ravaging the city of Silene in Libya was placated daily by two sheep. When these ran out, they had to resort to humans, but George saved the king's daughter when she was about to be sacrificed, refused the offered treasure and converted the entire city to Christianity.[93]

His cult, like that of the other warrior saints, grew exponentially in the second half of the tenth and first quarter of the eleventh centuries, under the military emperors Nikephoros II Phokas (AD 963–969), John I Tzimiskes (AD 969–976) and Basil II (AD 976–1025), when emperors were celebrated for their courage and victories on the battlefield against Bulgar, Rus and Arab foes. George, like other warrior saints, was frequently invoked on campaign. In AD 971, after a defeat of the Kievan Rus in Bulgaria, John I Tzimiskes made offerings for victory to George, 'the gloriously triumphant martyr', as the Byzantines had charged the enemy on George's feast day, 23 April. In the final encounter, however, at Dorostolon (Drista), it was St Theodore Stratelates that intervened to assist the Byzantines to victory (see below). As the warrior saint best known in the West, the Crusaders in the Holy Land were particularly attracted to George's cult, and he was seen to intervene in their interests during the Crusades in battle against the Moslems on several occasions (see below). As a result of the crusades, Edward III (1312–1377) made George patron saint of England instead of Saints Peter and Paul, and he was invoked at Agincourt in 1415 against the French. More than any other warrior saint, George's career went from strength to strength across Europe: in Russia, he intervened on behalf of Alexander Nevsky against the Swedes in 1240 and the Teutonic Knights in 1242, and fought alongside other saints against the Mongols at the Battle of Kulikovo in 1440.[94] Even in the First World War, the British Parliamentary Recruiting Committee in its posters presented St George as symbolizing the uprightness and morality of Britain's challenge to the Germanic dragon (see Figure 10.9). Unfortunately, the value of St George as a symbol of righteous victory was appreciated by others than the English, and in the same war Germany put illustrations of St George on its war-loan posters, on one of which George's banner bears the German double-headed eagle, while George is shown as triumphing over the wicked dragon – the Allies – with the legend 'Thanks be to God / Givest thou a mite / Be it never so small / Thou shalt be blessed by God'.[95]

Theodore 'the Recruit' and Theodore 'the General'

Theodore 'the Recruit'

Theodore Teron (Latin, *tiro*; Greek, *teron*), an ordinary soldier from Euchaita (Avhat) in Pontos, was one of the earliest and most venerated of the warrior saints.[96] He is mentioned *c.*AD 380 in a late fourth-century encomium by Gregory, Bishop of Nyssa, as a recruit in the infantry, who refused to sacrifice to the pagan gods and who set light to the temple of 'the Mother of the gods' in Amaseia. He was therefore condemned to be burnt in a fiery oven. In his miracles as described by Gregory, Theodore is shown as warding off demons, curing illnesses, providing protection on journeys and assisting the poor. Gregory also mentions his recent defence of Euchaita against Scythians ('for in the past year, as we believe, he calmed the barbarian storm and stopped the horrible war of the wild Scythians'), and Gregory begs Theodore as saint to 'fight for us as a soldier':[97] an early example of the way in which the role of the warrior saints was overwhelmingly to develop into that of protection against external enemies. As

Euchaita was on the eastern frontiers, it was a pivotal location in Arab–Byzantine conflict, which doubtless encouraged accounts of Theodore's intervention on the battlefield.[98] In the late tenth or early eleventh century, during the reign of Basil II, the general Nikephoros Ouranos reworked Theodore's life and miracles.[99] In this account, Theodore's role as protector of his city, Euchaita, against external enemies – even in the face of divine plans for its destruction – had come to full fruition: the saint warded off a barbarian attack after initially being instructed by angels to stand aside to allow the barbarian invaders to succeed. Unwilling to let his city suffer, he prayed for the divine order to be rescinded and with his help Euchaita was saved.

In other miracles, a woman had a vision of Theodore, armed and on horseback, warding off a barbarian attack, while the Arabs were unable to destroy his sanctuary, with their leader being made to roll around on the ground, biting his tongue.[100] Already by the seventh century, a legend had arisen in which Theodore killed a dragon near Euchaita – it was Theodore, not George, who was the original dragon-slayer.[101] In a version of his life dating to AD 890, he dealt with a dragon who was blocking a road by making the sign of the Cross and cutting off its head, assisted by a princess named Eudokia, while in Ouranos' later account, he rescued his mother from a dragon when she was drawing water from a spring. Iconographically, he was associated with a dragon from the sixth century (see, for example, Figure 10.6), and three seals dated from the mid-sixth to the early eighth centuries (one belonging to a Bishop Peter of Euchaita) feature a bearded figure, who is probably Theodore, spearing a snake-like dragon.[102]

Figure 10.6: An engraved agate seal ring (intaglio) depicting St Theodore Teron slaying a many-headed dragon, dating to c.1300. An inscription on the reverse reads: 'Jesus Christ, Lord, help your servant, whom you, Holy One, know.' (*Photo courtesy of the Metropolitan Museum of Art, New York, Accession number 1999.325.227: Gift of Nanette B. Kelekian, in memory of Charles Dikran and Beatrice Kelekian, 1999*)

Theodore 'the General'

While there is evidence from at least the fifth or sixth centuries for the cults of the other members of the elite corps of warrior saints, Theodore Stratelates (the 'General') is an exception: the term 'stratelates' can signify a high army rank or be a more generic term for a high-ranking officer.[103] This Theodore first appears in the literary record in the ninth century in the *laudatio* written for him by Niketas of Paphlagonia, and Niketas is the first writer to explicitly refer to two saints, not one, named Theodore.[104] Stratelates' execution was placed in the reign of Licinius (martyrdom by flagellation), and his biography appears to closely parallel that of Teron. He was associated with Euchaneia (not far from Euchaita) as the site of his cult, and does not appear to have had any churches in Constantinople. A contemporary, his servant Augaros or Abgar, was said to have written his earliest vita (preserved in an eleventh-century manuscript). There appear to have been specific class-based reasons behind the spread of his cult, so that with the increased militarization of Byzantine society and the rise to power of aristocratic generals the veneration of the more lowly Theodore Teron ('the Recruit'), a soldier of no rank, was balanced by that of a high-ranking officer. This Theodore was often paired iconographically with Theodore Teron, and from the eleventh century, Stratelates is shown with a forked beard to distinguish him from Teron, whose beard is shown as pointed.[105] His first extant portrayal appears to have been that in the *Menologion* of Basil II (a compilation of saints' lives: see below), in which he alone of the warrior saints is depicted as an army officer, with a lance, sword and shield: the others are depicted in the act of being martyred.

The cult of this saintly 'officer and gentleman' became particularly prominent during the reigns of the more militaristic emperors of the later tenth and early eleventh centuries: Nikephoros II Phokas, John I Tzimiskes and Basil II. Both Theodores are prominent in the epic-romance *Digenis Akritas*, which glorifies aristocratic independence and warfare as a fine art, and Digenis built a church in honour of one of them on his estate (presumably Stratelates); he swears on their names, and received two gilded icons of them as wedding presents, as well as – taking Theodore Teron as a model – fighting off a dragon who attempted to seduce his wife.[106]

Stratelates' cult quickly became popular with the military, particularly the Eastern armies,[107] and certainly by the third quarter of the tenth century, emperors were invoking him in battle. His pre-eminence as an imperial warrior saint was assured after he assisted John I Tzimiskes against the Rus in 971 on his feast-day. Even earlier, St Basil the Younger (died AD 944), in his *Life* written by a contemporary,[108] had predicted that the Rus would attack the capital in AD 941 and that Theodore 'the most holy general who has the surname Spongarios [perhaps Sphorakios, the designation of a church dedicated to Theodore in Constantinople] will lead the defence, with the Mother of God and all the saints'.[109] It is not impossible that John I deliberately chose to attack the Rus on Theodore's feast-day as a result of this prophecy.

Theodore Stratelates and the Battle of Dorostolon
In AD 971, John I Tzimiskes faced a problem resulting from the presence of Sviatoslav and the Kievan Rus in eastern Bulgaria.[110] Tzimiskes' predecessor, Nikephoros II Phokas, had employed the Rus against the rebellious Bulgarians, and Sviatoslav invaded the region, probably in the summer of AD 968. He had to return home to deal with a Pecheneg attack, but was in Bulgaria again the following year, when he deposed Boris II and captured the major city of Preslav. Unfortunately for the Byzantines, however, he was so impressed by the region that he planned to stay permanently: Bulgaria compared so favourably to the Ukraine that he decided to transfer his capital from Kiev to Little Preslav (Preslavets or Presthlavitza), near the mouth of the Danube. According to the *Russian Primary Chronicle*, he explained to his court that it was a far better site for a capital than Kiev, and that 'all the riches would flow there:

gold, silks, wine, and various fruits from Greece, silver and horses from Hungary and Bohemia, and from Ruthenia furs, wax, honey, and ancient laws'.[111] Finally, in AD 971, Tzimiskes captured Preslav and restored Boris to his throne, and Sviatoslav was besieged in Dorostolon (Dristra), near the mouth of the Danube, where he surrendered in July. The Byzantine victory was attributed in no little measure to the intervention of Theodore Stratelates, and the Rus were soundly defeated, with most of them killed (15,500) or wounded, as opposed to only 350 Byzantine casualties.

There are two accounts of Theodore's role in events. Both agree that when the encounter took place at Dorostolon, on the feast day of Theodore Stratelates (8 June), a storm arose and blew strongly into the Rus faces, impeding their advance. Leo the Deacon, in an account written not long after the battle, described as pivotal the appearance of an unknown figure on the battlefield:

> 'It is said that a man on a white horse appeared who went ahead of the Romans [Byzantines] and encouraged them to advance against the Scythians [Rus]; he broke through the enemy regiments in a miraculous fashion and threw them into disarray.'

No one in the camp had previously seen this warrior, and even though the emperor had him looked for afterwards so that he could present him with suitable rewards, he could not be found. 'Therefore a definite suspicion came about that it was the great martyr Theodore, whom the emperor used to pray to in battle to protect and preserve him together with all the army.' This suspicion was corroborated by the fact that, on the evening before the battle, a nun had dreamt that she saw the Mother of God, escorted by men 'in the form of flames' (i.e., angels), and that she instructed them to summon the martyr Theodore. When the saint, a brave young man in armour, appeared, the Theotokos said to him, 'Lord Theodore, your John, who is fighting the Scythians at Dorystolon, is now in great difficulty. Make haste to help him. For if you are too late, he will be in danger.' The saint replied that he would obey her commands, and departed to assist the emperor: the nun then woke up.[112]

This slightly hesitant account (Leo is reporting a third-hand account, and only after the battle was it realized that the warrior was St Theodore) was updated by Skylitzes in the second half of the eleventh century, with a more elaborate narrative, in which he records that Theodore had been seen by the entire army:[113]

> 'A man appeared to the entire Roman army, riding on a white horse, pressing forward, routing the ranks of the enemy and throwing them into disarray, a man previously and subsequently unknown to anyone. They say he was one of the gloriously victorious martyrs named Theodore, for the emperor always used [the icons of] these martyrs as allies and protectors against the enemy.'

Again, a dream by a third person is used to confirm the authenticity of the account. At Byzantium, a woman confirmed that the apparition was true:

> 'for she had a dream before the engagement in which she seemed to be in the presence of the Theotokos and heard her saying to a soldier, "Lord Theodore, John my friend and yours is in trouble. Go swiftly to help him." She reported this to her neighbours at sunrise.'

To honour the martyr and repay him for his timely aid, Skylitzes states that John Tzimiskes built Stratelates a splendid and well-endowed shrine for his relics and renamed Euchaneia as Theodoroupolis ('city of Theodore'); this city, the main centre of the cult of Theodore Stratelates, was situated not far from Euchaita, the cult centre of Theodore Teron. Leo the Deacon, however, reports more probably that it was the city of Dorostolon itself, the site of the encounter, that was renamed Theodoropolis, and a seal belonging to a 'katepan [commander] of Theodoroupolis' has been found nearby at Preslav.[114]

This episode is remarkable as the only occasion in Skylitzes' history in which a saint makes a personal appearance, and the first time in which a military saint is shown as a comrade-in-arms of the emperor, coming to assist him personally on the battlefield and being rewarded for his intervention by a new shrine and the renaming of a city. While the plot device of a dream is used as corroboration of the narrative, the Byzantine troops as a whole are said to have experienced the apparition of the saint, thus transforming a vision of an unknown combatant into a divine intervention witnessed by all participants – at least those on the winning side. Both the Saint Theodores also worked together in the thirteenth century to help Theodore II Laskaris (1254–1258) retake the fortress of Melnik in Bulgaria in 1256. According to Theodore Pediasimos, the emperor invoked their help while in Serres, and he later saw two handsome young men who routed the enemy.[115]

Basil II 'the Bulgarslayer' and the Warrior Saints

John's successor, Basil II (John was in effect regent for the young emperor, having married his aunt), who spent nearly forty-nine years on campaign against Bulgars and Arabs, was particularly devoted to the warrior saints. On one occasion, when en route to Bulgaria in AD 991 after the end of lengthy civil wars against pretenders and rebels, he made a particular point of stopping at Thessaloniki to make a thanks-offering to St Demetrios for his assistance.[116] His *Psalter* and *Menologion* (a compilation of 430 brief saints' lives, each with an illustration) both show his devotion to military saints and the degree to which he relied on them, particularly for their patronage and protection during his campaigns. The *Menologion* (Vat. gr. 1613), now in the Vatican library, was commissioned by or made for him sometime after AD 979. This volume actually comprises a synaxarion, a list of saints and their feast days, with a short life for every saint, each a summary of exactly sixteen lines, taking half a page, with the other half for the illustration. This is the most lavishly illustrated of all Byzantine liturgical manuscripts. The volume only covers the feast days between September and February, so there may have been a second volume which is now lost.

The illustrations are given particular prominence, and it would have been a suitable volume for a hard-working but pious emperor to take on campaign. While a number of different types of saints are featured, three-quarters of the subjects are martyrs, and the warrior saints are almost invariably shown in the act of engaging with their martyrdom, with their sufferings and torture portrayed in some graphic detail (see Figure 10.1 for Blaise of Sebaste). The only one depicted in full armour is Theodore Stratelates, now one of the most pre-eminent of the warrior saints after his victory at Dorostolon, who is shown with lance, sword and shield.[117] The emphasis on the warrior saints and their martyrdoms no doubt reflected Basil's choice of heavenly protectors.

The dedicatory poem addresses Basil as 'sun of the purple, reared in the purple robes, excelling both in victories and in learning', and describes how the work will assist and support him in his role as emperor:

> 'This book contains beautiful images like stars, wise prophets, martyrs and apostles, of all the righteous, of angels and archangels … may he [Basil] find as his active helpers during his reign all [saints] whom he has had portrayed with colours, to be allies in his battles, deliverers from hardships, curers of illnesses, and in the Last Judgement fervent intercessors with the Lord.'[118]

Basil's dedication begs the saints and angels portrayed in this volume to assist him in his campaigns and intercede for him on Judgement Day. The illustrations appear to have been intended to function as icons, with the emperor being able to call upon the help and divine protection of as many holy persons as possible, whatever the crisis, and to provide a brief biography of the saint appropriate for each day throughout the year. The format suggests that Basil was not a reading man, and that his spiritual exercise would focus primarily on the icon itself, which was briefly elucidated by the text.

We are also fortunate enough to have Basil's *Psalter* (a book of devotional material, such as the Book of Psalms), which shows his devotion to the warrior saints. In the frontispiece, a miniature of Basil himself, portrayed as a triumphant Roman general (see Figure 10.3), he is flanked by roundels of six of the most prominent warrior saints, all armed with lances. The accompanying poem describes the scene, highlighting the award of the crown and lance to Basil by the archangels, and describes the warrior saints as his fellow-soldiers, fighting by his side in battle and casting down his enemies.[119]

St Demetrios of Thessaloniki

Thessaloniki, from at least the middle of the fifth century, was devoted to its patron saint Demetrios, who had supposedly been martyred under Maximian,[120] and his primary role from the earliest period had been to defend Thessaloniki from the threats of attacks and sieges by the Avars and Slavs from the north. Demetrios, at least in this early period, was not thought to have had a military background, but is described as of senatorial family and proconsul of Greece, rather than a career soldier.[121] He was also known as '*myroblytos*', the myrrh-giver, as a sweet-smelling oil (*myron*) flowed from his relics in the church at Thessaloniki. This was believed to have therapeutic qualities and was taken away in special flasks (*enkolpia*) by pilgrims from at least the eleventh century.[122] It was also believed to give protection in battle, and amulets with the oil were carried into combat (see Figure 10.8). Despite a Latin version of Demetrios' passion being written by Anastasius Bibliothecarius in the ninth century, he did not enjoy the same popularity in the West as in the East until the time of the Crusades (see below).

There are two seventh-century collections of his miracles, the earliest of which was composed by 'John the archbishop' in the first decade of the century, and which comprises fifteen stories dating to c.AD 582–615. Many of these are concerned with healing miracles at the ciborium (the structure thought to mark the site of the saint's tomb and the focus of the cult which contained a silver image of the saint) and relate to his miraculous myron: according to John (Miracle 10), the ciborium stood on the left-hand side of the church, had a hexagonal base, eight columns and carved silver partitions with a cross on a silver globe on the top. The saint cured Marianos, the governor of Thessaloniki, of paralysis, as well as a prefect who suffered from a discharge of blood: he appeared to both in dreams and they were cured after being taken to his shrine. Miracles 13–15, however, present Demetrios conclusively as saviour of his city, warding off the sixth- and seventh-century attacks by Avars and Slavs.[123] In Miracle 13 in John's collection, he is portrayed, probably in reference to the siege of the city in AD 586, as involved in the actual fighting at the walls, 'not just in our imagination, but before our very eyes, on the wall dressed as a hoplite, and the first to ascend the ladder'.

After attacking the convent of St Matrona, the Slavs tried to scale the walls, but Demetrios appeared in military dress and struck the first of the enemy with his lance, making him fall backward onto those behind him on the ladder and killing him.[124] In Miracle 14, he brought about the apparition of a large army which scared off the city's besiegers. One of the barbarians saw him in person as 'a ruddy and radiant man, seated on a white horse and wearing a white cape'. In Miracle 15, a man who took refuge to pray in the cathedral during a siege had a vision in which Demetrios was summoned to heaven by two angels as the city was going to be surrendered to its enemies. In the vision, Demetrios refused to abandon his people, and the man left the cathedral and ran along the walls shouting, 'Take courage brothers, the victorious one is with us.' The city was saved.[125]

The second collection was written seventy years later, and includes six further miracles which happened in the time of the anonymous author.

Figure 10.7: An ivory icon of St Demetrios with spear and shield, dating to 950–1000. The cleft in the frame's base may have supported a standard for carrying the icon in processions or into battle. (*Photo courtesy of the Metropolitan Museum of Art, New York, Accession number 1970.324.3: The Cloisters Collection, 1970*)

The writer summarizes them as 'release of prisoners, healing of the sick, help in wars, guiding sailors', while Demetrios' involvement in healing illness and demoniac possession was so well known that it was not worth writing about. In Miracle 2, he causes a projectile inscribed 'in the name of God and Saint Demetrios' to collide with one launched by the enemy, both missiles landing in the enemy camp; in another, he comes to the relief of the city on foot, his chlamys (cloak) thrown up and carrying a rod in his hand. In Miracle 1, he is seen in his chlamys marching along the walls of the city and on the sea.[126]

In the miracles described in the Latin version of Demetrios' *Life* by Anastasius the Librarian (Bibliothecarius), the saint also helped to provision the city when a famine accompanied the siege. When the city sent ambassadors to the emperor for help, Demetrios, 'just as he is depicted in paintings' (his icons were obviously well known), appeared on the island of Chios to a shipmaster named Stephen who was taking 200 bushels of corn to Constantinople, and instructed him to sail instead to Thessaloniki. The man, terrified at the apparition, replied that he had heard it was on the point of falling to the barbarians. The saint, however, told him to proceed there and tell any ships he might meet that Thessaloniki had been saved by the mercy of God. The saint began to walk in the direction of Thessaloniki on the sea; Stephen sailed there and found that the enemy had recently abandoned their siege due to divinely inspired fear. Similarly, in Miracle 6, Demetrios provisioned the city by sending grain-carrying ships at Chios to Thessaloniki. But Demetrios was still renowned generally for his healing skills: when Cyprian, an African bishop, was enslaved by Slavs while en route to Constantinople, Demetrios ('a soldier of the great emperor') liberated him and led him to the gates of Thessaloniki. Realizing that his rescuer was the saint, Cyprian returned home to Africa and built there a church and ciborium like that at Thessaloniki, using porphyry which miraculously arrived by sea. This shrine too was a healing one: 'if any sick person goes to this temple in prayer, and if he is anointed with oil from his [Demetrios'] lamp, he will be cured.'[127]

Demetrios, like other warrior saints, was initially depicted as a youthful martyr in tunic and chlamys as in the early seventh-century mosaic on the façade of his church. But by the tenth century, his portrayals were becoming more militarized, and in the Middle Byzantine period, like other warrior saints, it was quite normal for him to be portrayed in military dress (see Figure 10.7). When Demetrios appeared to Leo VI and his wife Theophano in prison, according to her *Life* (composed c. AD 895), it was as a young man in military dress with a spear and shield.[128] From this point he was often paired with St George as a warrior, both iconographically and in literary accounts.[129] The gold and enamel pendant St Demetrios reliquary in the British Museum dating to the eleventh century depicts both George and Demetrios and was intended to hold holy oil (myron) from Demetrios' shrine and blood-soaked earth from the site of his martyrdom, both of which had healing and apotropaic powers, as well as other relics: this reliquary was clearly intended to be taken on campaign (see Figure 10.8). Encircling the picture of St George, the inscription in Greek reads, '[The wearer] prays to have you as his fervent protector in battle.' Around the side, there is another inscription in Greek, 'Anointed with your blood and holy oil'. Inside the amulet, an eighteenth-century inscription in Georgian states that it is the 'Queen's relic' and contains a fragment of the True Cross.[130] Demetrios' myron was valued at all levels of society: an octagonal silver-gilt reliquary in Moscow (in the State Historical and Cultural Museum), with portraits of Constantine X (1059–1067) and Eudokia Makrembolitissa, was commissioned by the mystographos (notary) John Autoreianos. The dedication reads:

> 'I am a true image of the ciborium of the lance-pierced martyr Demetrios. On the outside I have Christ inscribed, who with his hands crowns the fair [imperial] couple. He who made me anew is John of the family of the Autoreianoi, by profession mystographos.'[131]

The saints Nestor and Loupos, two companions of Demetrios associated with his martyrdom, are also depicted.

In any crisis faced by the inhabitants of Thessaloniki, their immediate response was to turn to Demetrios. Of course, there had to be some explanation for those occasions when he failed to save the city from attackers. After Thessaloniki was sacked by the Arabs in AD 904, the patriarch Nicholas Mystikos preached a sermon in Constantinople explaining that the saint had been so distracted by Christ's anguish at mortals' sins that he was too preoccupied to become involved. Alternatively, according to John Kaminiates – who describes himself as a contemporary eyewitness of events in the city – Demetrios did try to intercede but was refused divine permission to become involved.[132]

The belief in the protection of Demetrios and the apotropaic and salvific nature of his miraculous myron was displayed in 1041 during a Bulgarian siege of the city by the general Alousianos with 40,000 troops. After six days, the citizens kept an all-night vigil at Demetrios' tomb, and then smeared themselves with the myron which flowed from his tomb before marching into battle on the following morning, throwing the Bulgars into disorder by their unexpected sortie. Skylitzes commented that 'the Bulgarians were not in the least willing to offer a sustained or courageous resistance, for the martyr was leading the Roman army and smoothing a path for it', while Bulgarians captured in the battle reported on oath that they saw a youth on horseback leading the army and exuding a fire which burnt up their troops. Fifteen thousand Bulgarians were killed and a similar number taken prisoner. It is only fair, however, to state that the account of the battle by the Byzantine moralist Kekaumenos was critical of Alousianos for not establishing a camp or resting his men.[133]

Emperors campaigning in Thessaly requested Demetrios' aid as a matter of course. Just as Basil II, when en route to Bulgaria in AD 991 after the end of the lengthy civil wars, had made a particular point of stopping at Thessaloniki to make a thanks-offering to St Demetrios for his assistance,[134] Alexios I Komnenos nearly 100 years later relied on the saint for help against the encroachments of the Normans in northern Greece, according at least to his daughter Anna Komnene, who presents a picture of her father as the epitome of imperial piety. When Bohemond and the Normans were besieging Larisa, south of Thessaloniki, in 1082–1083, Alexios had a dream the night before he met them in battle. He dreamt he was in the sanctuary of Demetrios and heard a voice say, 'Cease tormenting yourself and do not worry: tomorrow you will win.' The voice seemed to come from an icon of the saint, and Alexios prayed to the martyr and promised that if he won he would travel to Thessaloniki and formally process through the town on foot in his honour. On the next day he was victorious.¹³⁵ Alexios was the first emperor to put Demetrios on coins, during his Norman campaign against Guiscard (the issue was struck at Thessaloniki). The saint was portrayed as a soldier, in short tunic, breastplate, sagion (a military cloak) and sword, handing a *labarum* to the emperor.¹³⁶

In the thirteenth century, Demetrios was said to have assassinated Kalojan (Johanitsa), the Bulgarian voivode (military leader), when he was besieging Thessaloniki in 1207 episode. In this, Demetrios was being ascribed the tyrant-killer role played by earlier saints such as Merkourios. In fact, Kalojan was known to have been assassinated by another voivode, Manastras. Nevertheless, the chance to ascribe a further miracle to Demetrios was too good to pass by, especially as the city was currently under Latin control following the ill-fated Fourth Crusade which captured Constantinople. Robert of Clari, who served with the crusade, recorded:

> 'John "the Vlach" and the Cumans [allies of the Bulgarians] went and besieged Thessaloniki and set their engines up to attack the city … Now in this city there was the body of my lord St Demetrios, who would never permit his city to be taken by force. And there flowed from his holy body such great quantities of oil that it was a great wonder. And it happened, as John the Vlach was lying one morning in his tent, that my lord St Demetrios came and struck him with a lance through the body and killed him. When his own people and the Cumans knew that he was dead, they broke camp and went away to their land.'¹³⁷

The 'Latins' were only too anxious to appropriate Demetrios as their own saviour and protector, and hoped that he would desert the Byzantines and transfer to them his services towards the city of Thessaloniki and its inhabitants – a sanguine state of mind which they had demonstrated throughout the Crusades in the Eastern Mediterranean from even before their capture of Antioch, not un-akin to the 'godnapping' of the ancients, who appropriated the local gods whenever they took possession of enemy cities or territories.¹³⁸

Warrior Saints and the First Crusade

Following the military engagements of the First Crusade in Asia Minor and the Crusaders' experiences during the long trek south, the cult of the warrior saints became especially popular in the West, and their veneration an integral element of knightly piety. A particular catalyst for the popularity of these saints was the Crusaders' victory at Antioch over the besieging army of Kerbogha in 1098.¹³⁹ Warrior saints had not been unknown, however, in the West prior to this period: Orderic Vitalis, writing *c.*1130, stated that Gerold d'Avranches at the court of Hugh of Chester in the 1070s had exhorted knights by tales of the saints Demetrios, George, Theodore, Sebastian, Maurice and the Theban Legion, and Eustace. All of these were martyred saints, some of whom were particular to the West, though Eastern saints like Demetrios were also included.¹⁴⁰ Orderic may, however, have included the Eastern saints Demetrios and Theodore because of their prominence

Figure 10.8: A gold and enamel pendant reliquary, 37mm in diameter, with the enamelled half-figure of St George carrying a sword, and (inside) a hinged enamel panel featuring St Demetrios in the tomb and four compartments for relics. Dating to the eleventh century, the amulet originated at Thessaloniki and contained Demetrios' holy oil and blood-soaked earth from the site of his martyrdom. (*Courtesy of the British Museum, accession number 1926.0409.1*)

in Outremer (the Frankish conquests in the Holy Land) after the First Crusade. Sebastian, Maurice and Eustace were military officers who had suffered martyrdom in the western empire, where their major cult sites were located. In England, the Anglo-Norman *Laudes regiae*, of which the earliest example was composed between 1084 and 1095, also invoke the intercession of Saints Maurice, George and Sebastian (all of whom were popular in the West) on behalf of English princes and warriors.[141]

It was, however, during the First Crusade that warrior saints came to be seen both as intercessors for the crusading forces and as their supporters on the actual battlefield. On their way to Constantinople, Crusade contingents had passed through Thessaloniki, where Adhémar of Le Puy, the papal legate, spent time recovering from a Pecheneg attack. While there, Crusaders would have visited the church of St Demetrios and witnessed the miraculous myron produced by Demetrios' relics. They would also have heard how Demetrios had spectacularly saved the city from the Bulgarian siege in 1041. Likewise, during their sightseeing in Constantinople, they would have become acquainted with the major churches of Eastern warrior saints in the capital, such as the magnificent construction of St George of Mangana by Constantine IX Monomachos (1042–1055) and the churches of St Theodore Teron, of which there were fifteen in the capital, with one particularly singled out for mention by Anna Komnene.[142] The leaders would also have been given the chance to venerate the holy relics of the crucifixion housed in the Great Palace, in the Church of the Theotokos of the Pharos, which would have whetted their appetite for the acquisition of Eastern relics. This palace chapel held many of the items from the life and crucifixion of Christ, including fragments of the True Cross, the Crown of Thorns, Sponge and Sacred Lance, the Holy Nails and the Virgin's girdle.[143]

At their departure from Constantinople for the long journey south through the mountains and passes of Asia Minor, the Crusaders were accompanied by Greek bishops who would have helped them to engage with the centres of worship through which they passed. They thus became acquainted on their journey with some of the local cult centres of Eastern saints, such as that of St George at Lydda near Jerusalem, whom they believed would help them in battle.[144] As their trek towards Jerusalem took them ever further from home, with the soldiers often suffering unbelievable hardships in alien conditions and beset by dangers and enemy forces almost beyond their comprehension, it was only to be expected that they called on the help not only of those saints they venerated at home, but also of those whose cults they encountered in these terrifying and unfamiliar conditions, to aid them in their penitential journey of faith.

It was logical that the Crusaders should invoke the warrior saints for assistance, as they related their own personal sufferings to those of the saints themselves, and saw their own trials and the deaths of their comrades on God's service as an act of martyrdom which they had willingly embraced, as the saints had done. Since they also believed that during their lifetime the saints had been soldiers, this gave them an even closer emotional and pietistic bond with them. In his account of the successful siege of Nicaea in 1097, the author of the *Gesta* commented: 'Many of our men suffered martyrdom there, and gave up their blessed souls with joy and gladness … All of them entered heaven in triumph, wearing the robe of martyrdom they had won.'[145] As well as seeing themselves as successors and imitators of the warrior saints, the Crusaders also viewed the Maccabees as exemplars for their struggles: they were well aware of the angelic help given to Judas Maccabeus, and saw him as a forerunner of the Christian tradition and a proto-martyr.[146] The Crusaders actually considered that their own struggles and commitment both surpassed the military exploits of the Maccabees and equalled their spiritual victories.[147] Consequently, they too expected to be granted angelic help in their engagements with the enemies of Christ.

That the clerics on crusade knew of a number of Eastern warrior saints, and hoped for their assistance, is clear from a letter written in January 1098 during the siege of Antioch by the Latin and Greek bishops with the crusade. In this communication, they called on Western leaders to supply them with additional troops and specifically ascribed the victories to date that they had gained against the Muslims (five battles won, and forty cities and 200 castles captured) to the protection of saints George, Theodore, Demetrios and Blaise, their 'fellow-travellers' on crusade. In the missive, the bishops asserted that 'we do not trust in any multitude, nor in power nor in presumption, but in the shield of Christ and justice, under the protection of George and Theodore and Demetrios and Blaise, soldiers of Christ truly accompanying us'.[148] The choice of saints is an interesting one. George, Theodore and Demetrios were, of course, traditional warrior saints, not unknown in the West (Demetrios less so than the other two, although many of the Crusaders would have been made aware of his feats on behalf of his city as they passed through Thessaloniki).[149] Blaise (Blasios), however, is an intriguing addition here, since the saint was an Armenian healer, martyred under Licinius (see Figure 10.1), and well-known for his healing miracles, particularly his aid in treating objects such as fish-bones stuck in the throat. The sixth-century doctor Aetios of Amida in northern Mesopotamia recommended the following exhortation in such cases:

> 'If a patient has a bone stuck in the throat, the doctor should sit opposite him and say the following: "Come up bone, whether bone or stalk or whatever else, as Jesus Christ drew Lazarus from his tomb, and Jonah out of the whale, thus Blasios, the martyr and servant of God, commands 'Bone come up or go down'".'[150]

Blasios' main shrine was at Sebaste (modern Sivas) in far eastern Asia Minor, and it seems unlikely that the Crusaders would have had any contact with his cult. The Blaise referred to in the letter may in fact not be St Blaise of Sebaste, but the lesser Blaise, a martyred shepherd whose cult was based at Caesarea in Cappadocia, an area through which the Crusaders passed after the Battle of Heraclea in September 1097, and to whom they may have prayed for assistance after coming across a church dedicated to him during their journeying.[151] This St Blaise is not known for any particular deeds of military intervention, but this reference to him by the bishops suggests that the Crusaders were in the habit of calling on the aid of local saints as they encountered their churches on their journey and of ascribing their victories to their intervention. As they drew ever further from home in Turkish-occupied territory, it must have seemed increasingly natural to attribute their survival to date to supernatural assistance and the fact that the saints of the region were on their side.

That warrior saints had actually intervened in a specific engagement in favour of the Crusaders was first mentioned by Raymond d'Aguilers, a chaplain serving with Raymond of Saint-Gilles, Count of Toulouse. Raymond's history was written soon after the event and completed before 1105, and of all the chroniclers of the First Crusade, he is perhaps the most open to suggestions of miraculous apparitions and supernatural assistance. This episode took place during the engagement against the Seljuq leader Kilij Arslan on 1 July 1097, while the Crusaders were proceeding south through Asia Minor after the siege of Nicaea. They had split up to make provisioning of the large army less challenging, and the force in advance of the others – that under the leadership of Bohemond – encountered Kilij Arslan's army at Dorylaion and was surrounded by the Seljuqs. Upon the arrival of the Provençal troops under Saint-Gilles, Kilij decided to retreat. Raymond, however, records that, according to some witnesses, two handsome knights in flashing armour – unnamed, but presumably to be identified as George and Demetrios – came to the Crusaders' assistance, causing the Turks to flee in panic. Raymond admits that these reports only came from Turkish deserters and that he was not an eyewitness himself:

> 'Although we did not see it, some related a remarkable miracle in which two handsome knights in flashing armour, riding before our soldiers and apparently invulnerable to the thrusts of Turkish lances, terrified the enemy so that they could not fight. Although we learnt this from apostate Turks who have now joined us, we can cite as evidence that for two days on the march we saw dead riders and dead horses.'[152]

The only evidence given for this miracle, therefore, were the corpses of riders and horses met with on the following two days of their march, and the Crusaders themselves, according to his account, did not experience the vision. If Raymond is correct that some of the renegade Turks reported that they had seen this supernatural intervention, these may have been influenced by episodes in the *Quran* where it is foretold that angels would assist Muhammed's army at the Battle of Bedr if the Muslims kept faith: 'if you are patient and godfearing, and the foe presses upon you, your Lord will reinforce you with 5,000 swooping angels.' The eighth-century *Life of Muhammed* by Muhammed ibn Ishaq also mentions that in this battle, Gabriel was heard spurring on his horse ('Forward, Hayzum!') and that some Meccans reported that they saw horsemen clad in white between heaven and earth, whom no one could withstand.[153] It would be intriguing, to say the least, if Turkish deserters played a part in encouraging the Crusaders' expectation of supernatural assistance as they fought to gain control of the Holy Land.

From this point, warrior saints make a number of appearances in Raymond's chronicle, as aids in battle and signs of divine favour, as well as guides and guardians of the army, and he clearly believed in their efficacy, as he did in that of the Holy Lance miraculously discovered at Antioch on 15 June under the church of St Peter, which the Crusaders took as a sign of their divinely foretold success and which encouraged them to attempt to break Kerbogha's siege of the city.[154]

The Battle for Antioch, June 1098

The apparition of warrior saints who rode alongside the Crusaders when they marched out of Antioch to face Kerbogha's besieging army in 1098 is one of the best-known episodes of the First Crusade. The city had finally been taken by the Crusaders on 3 June that year after a prolonged siege lasting from 21 October 1097 (although the citadel still remained under Moslem control). It was then besieged on 7 June by Kerbogha of Mosul, with a large force. The Turkish army was numerically superior to that of the Crusaders, but as these were facing starvation they decided to make a sortie and meet their besiegers in battle. Guibert of Nogent, in the *Dei gesta per francos* (*Deeds of God Done by the Franks*), describes the famine in Antioch (he was not an eyewitness): the suffering of the men was so great that they were compelled to eat the foulest food, the flesh of horses and donkeys, while they were weakened by long hunger, suffering from steady, destructive starvation.[155]

The sortie was attempted on 28 June, the troops hoping for divine assistance from the Holy Lance, which was carried in the line of battle by the Pope's legate, Adhémar, Bishop of Le Puy. As they engaged with the Turks and were on the point of being surrounded, according to the *Gesta Francorum*, the earliest eyewitness account of events written c.1100–1101, there was a miraculous intervention when Saints George, Merkourios and Demetrios rode to the Crusaders' assistance at the head of a divine host of cavalry, routing the Turks:

> 'There appeared from the mountains an innumerable host of men on white horses, whose standards were all white. When our leaders saw this army, they

were completely ignorant as to what it was, and who they might be, until they realised that this was the help sent by Christ, and that the leaders were Saint George, Merkourios, and Demetrios. This is quite true, for many of our men saw it.'[156]

The chronicler, probably a cleric from southern Italy serving with the Norman Bohemond, and who would therefore have been acquainted with Greek saints,[157] obviously felt that he had to defend the truth of his account. He understood that it might be viewed with scepticism: he does not explicitly say that he saw the apparition himself, only that 'many of our men' did so. Furthermore, the Crusaders as a whole did not immediately make sense of the apparition, and only later realized it was divine help sent from heaven. Presumably, the identity of the riders and spiritual army was confirmed after the battle by the army leaders and bishops, who had already asserted that they were receiving valuable assistance from warrior saints. The Crusaders were in a mind-set to expect supernatural aid against the Turks, and only too willing to be convinced of the authenticity of the experience, while it was in their leaders' interests to encourage the rank-and-file to believe that they could hope for assistance from warrior saints and the 'heavenly host' on the battlefield.

The heavenly host was not the only example of celestial phenomena seen at Antioch prior to the engagement: the Crusaders were obviously not only prepared for, but actually expecting omens and portents from above foretelling their victory whatever the odds. The fact that many of them were half-dead with hunger and exhaustion would also have played a part in encouraging them to believe that they experienced supernatural phenomena. Before they marched out of the city, the *Gesta* describes that they saw a fire in the western sky, which 'approached and fell upon the Turkish army, to the great astonishment of our men and of the Turks also'.[158] Robert the Monk (Robert of Rheims), who was writing *c*.1107, concurs, saying that

> 'a flame appeared in the sky coming from the West and fell onto the Turkish army. This sign deeply impressed everyone, particularly the Turks amongst whose tents it fell. They began to see glimmerings of what would come to pass, that the fire descending from heaven represented the anger of God; because it had come from the West it symbolised the armies of the Franks through whom he would make his anger manifest.'[159]

Earlier, while the Franks were besieging Antioch in December 1097, they had seen 'a remarkable reddish glow in the sky and besides felt a great quake in the earth, which rendered us all fearful. In addition many saw a certain sign in the shape of a cross, whitish in colour, moving in a straight path toward the East.' In this case, the apparition fuelled their guilty belief that they were being warned that they were wasting time at Antioch and had deviated from their primary mission to reach Jerusalem.[160]

Robert the Monk also recorded a comet on the night of 2/3 June 1098, as the Crusaders were about to take Antioch: 'On that night a comet blazed amongst the other stars in the heavens, giving off rays of light and foretelling a change in the kingdom. The sky glowed fiery red from North to East. It was with these portents shining prominently in the heavens and as dawn began to bring light to the earth that the army of God entered Antioch.'[161] At critical points in the campaign, participants thought it quite natural that supernatural phenomena would foretell their path to victory, or some aspect of divine assistance manifest itself. The finding of the Holy Lance is just one case in point, despite certain misgivings about the circumstances of the discovery (not everyone believed Peter Bartholomew's account of events and the details of his vision of St Andrew). Moreover, the leaders at least would certainly have seen the 'genuine' Lance in the palace at Constantinople, one of the relics – like the fragments of the True Cross and the Crown of Thorns – on which they swore the oath that they would hand over any ex-Byzantine possessions (like Antioch) that they conquered.[162] The Lance found at Antioch was, however, genuinely accepted at this point by many of the soldiers as *the* relic from the Crucifixion. They believed that it had been sent to them as a divinely inspired aid in battle, while it was not in the interests of the leaders to diminish their enthusiasm too openly.

Where the vision of the warrior saints riding alongside the army outside Antioch is concerned, it is interesting that the saints that helped the Crusaders to victory were not exactly the same as those mentioned in the letter of the bishops earlier in the year: Theodore is replaced by Merkourios,[163] another, if less well-known, Eastern warrior saint, while Blaise is omitted. Perhaps the Crusaders' views of the most appropriate saints to assist them in battle had evolved during their travels in the Near East. In addition, the letter was written by a council of bishops, whereas, after the heat of battle, it is likely that one of the 'leaders of the army' (who, according to the *Gesta*, interpreted the miracle to their troops) would have identified the saints as those most recognizable by his men. Since the *Gesta* is a Norman source, and the Norman leader Bohemond had been recognized by the other leaders as the incoming Prince of Antioch, it is likely that what we may have here is an identification of this miraculous triad with saints acceptable to the Norman contingent.

Nearly all subsequent accounts of the First Crusade, many of which are based on the *Gesta*, record the appearance of the saints at the battle outside Antioch, or some equivalent form of divine intervention, though frequently the saints are not mentioned by name.[164] Not everyone can have believed in this vision of George, Demetrios and Merkourios, or there were at least a number of different versions as to what had occurred. Fulcher of Chartres (a participant), Albert of Aachen and William of Tyre omit any mention of the intervention, which suggests that there were genuine doubts about what had taken place. Furthermore, a letter asking for support for the Crusade, written in October 1098 by the clergy and people of Lucca, narrates the experience of Bruno, a layman from that town, who had been present at the victory at Antioch. Bruno had reported that the Crusaders were assisted by the miraculous appearance of a large, resplendent host ('*vexillum admirabile excelsum valde et candidum, et cum eo multitude militum innumera*'), but had not mentioned the presence of any warrior saints at the head of this heavenly army – this suggests that Bruno did not believe that he had personally seen them, and perhaps the individual saints were not so well known to the ordinary soldiers as to their leaders, and thus their involvement impressed the rank and file less than the heavenly host in its spectacular entirety.[165]

Similarly, Raymond d'Aguilers, who was also present, does not refer to specific warrior saints participating in this battle, riding forth from the mountains to the Crusaders' assistance, but to a miraculous host that silently joined the army outside the city. He presumably considered that this body of men, which he believed had assisted the Crusaders, consisted of those of their comrades who had died en route: these had been miraculously sent to aid them on this occasion, in continuation of their vow. Raymond may perhaps have been concerned to play down the role of specific saints in the victory, as he attributed it to the miraculous powers of the Holy Lance. Not only was the Lance present on the battlefield, carried by Adhémar of le Puy, the papal legate, but Raymond – who was in the same division – states he had the honour of carrying it at some point. His account of the supernatural intervention records that:

> 'When all our fighting men had exited the city, five other lines appeared among us. Our princes had drawn up only eight, but there were thirteen of our lines outside the city. ... God multiplied our army in such a way that we, who before appeared to be fewer than the enemy, were more numerous than they were in the battle ... The lines of the enemy fell upon those of us in the squadron of the Bishop, and even though their forces were greater than ours, because of the protection of the Holy Lance which was there, they there wounded no one and failed to hit any of us with arrows. I saw these things of which I speak and I carried the Lance of the Lord there.'[166]

Even when the chroniclers follow the account of the *Gesta* and describe the intervention of the saints, they do not always consistently agree on the saints' identity: the Poitevin priest Peter Tudebode – whose account of the First Crusade, written before 1111, is based closely on that of the *Gesta* – considered that the divine riders were George, Demetrios and Theodore, not Merkourios. He describes a vast army riding white horses and flying white banners, which appeared from the mountains:

> 'Our forces were very bewildered by the sight of this army until they realised that it was Christ's assistance, just as the priest Stephen had predicted. The leaders of this heavenly host were Saint George, the Blessed Demetrios and the Blessed Theodore. Now this report can be believed because many Christians saw it.'[167]

He expands on the episode, stating that the saints' intervention had been promised beforehand by Christ, as long as the Crusaders proved their piety and commitment to the faith. In this elaboration of the backstory, prior to the battle, a priest called Stephen had experienced a vision in which Christ promised the Crusaders aid if they repented, gave alms and celebrated masses – 'then they shall begin the battle and I shall give them the help of St George, St Theodore, St Demetrios and all the pilgrims who have died on the way to Jerusalem'.[168] Like the Crusaders in the *Gesta*'s account, Tudebode states that the soldiers, as they marched out to meet Kerbogha's troops, were uncertain of the identity of the army that came to their assistance, only realizing after the event that this had been the fulfilment of Stephen the priest's vision.

Clearly, the appearance of Merkourios, who was not so well known in the West as some of the other warrior saints, was considered something of a difficulty.

Like Tudebode, the account of William of Malmesbury in the 1120s omits him, mentioning only George and Demetrios. In William's account, the Crusaders 'were convinced they saw those ancient martyrs who had been knights in their own day, and who by their deaths had purchased the crown of life, St George and St Demetrios, with flying banners come charging from the hill-country, showering missiles on the enemy and aid upon themselves'.[169] Saints could also be selected for nationalist purposes. According to Robert the Monk, a fourth saint, Maurice, accompanied George, Merkourios and Demetrios at Antioch.[170] St Maurice was a patron saint of the Holy Roman emperors, whose relics had been translated to Magdeburg by Otto I in AD 961. As he was alleged to have been a soldier in the Roman Army, and commander of the Theban Legion – all of whom were martyred by Maximian – he was in the Westerners' view appropriately qualified as a warrior saint, and had been identified as such even before the First Crusade.[171] It may have been felt appropriate to include him in the divine support crew to encourage all the Germans on crusade and to put in a claim for further support from the Holy Roman emperor.

Robert's account engaged with the metaphysical question of how saints and other spiritual beings were able to intervene physically on the battlefield. His narrative includes a (suppositious) conversation between Bohemond and a Turk, Pirrus, who betrayed Antioch to the Crusaders, in which Pirrus asked for an explanation as to how natural laws allowed for the saints' appearance and physical intervention. According to Robert, it was only in Bohemond's conversation with Pirrus that he was alerted to the saints' presence in the battle. Pirrus had asked Bohemond about the identity of 'the white force' whom he had seen come to the Crusaders' assistance, and where they were encamped. Realizing that this must have been a heavenly host, Bohemond explained that they comprised a divine army from the sky that appeared at the command of Christ, and which was led by Saints George, Demetrios, Merkourios and Maurice, who had 'suffered martyrdom for the faith of Christ and fought against unbelievers across the earth'. When Pirrus enquired as to how the saints were equipped with physical horses, armour and banners, and how they were able to take part in a terrestrial battlefield engagement, Bohemond was forced to reply that this was 'beyond his understanding'. He referred the query to his chaplain, who explained that, when God sends spiritual beings into the world, they take on physical forms so that mortals can see them:

> 'When the all-powerful Creator decides to send his angels or the spirits of the righteous to earth, they assume bodies of air so that they can appear to us, because they cannot be seen in their essential spiritual form.'[172]

Some Crusaders must have had concerns about the reality of the apparitions and how the saints were able to manifest themselves corporeally. Most, however, expected supernatural assistance in their quest and would have resisted any attempt to question their memory or perception of saintly interventions, considering the practical help given them more important than the underlying theology.

With regard to the perception that warrior saints assisted Christian armies, there is a clear line of transmission from Byzantine to Crusader sources, with the degree of divine assistance exponentially increasing with time. At Antioch, for example, saints are recorded as actually appearing on the battlefield and intervening in conflicts, as they had been doing in Byzantine sources in the tenth and eleventh centuries. Rather than individual saints, however, like St Demetrios or St Theodore, the Crusaders have them appear en masse, supported by an entire heavenly army. Alternatively, they believed that thousands of dead comrades had been miraculously resurrected to fight alongside them. This willingness to accept the presence of the supernatural presumably reflected the dangers and crises faced by the Crusaders in hostile territory far from home, as well as their belief that they were themselves contemporary martyrs courting suffering and death for their faith.

Warrior Saints in Western Europe

In Byzantine sources, Saints Demetrios, Andrew, Theodore and Merkourios are recorded as having protected their worshippers or fought alongside Byzantine emperors and armies against human but demonically inspired enemies. While many of those from Northern Europe would have known little of Eastern saints, the Normans on the First Crusade were well acquainted with Greeks and Greek culture in Sicily and southern Italy, and many of them had served as mercenaries in the Byzantine army. They were therefore far more *au fait* than other contingents with regard to the identity of Eastern warrior saints and details of their cults. The Normans already viewed George in particular as a potent help in battle, and Geoffrey Malaterra records an apparition of the saint as early as 1063, when the Muslims were defeated near Cerami in Sicily by the future Roger I. It should be noted, however, that Geoffrey was writing long after the event, and that his narrative ceases abruptly with the events of July 1098, contemporaneous with the battle for Antioch, although his account does not seem to have been influenced by events in the East. He records that a certain knight, magnificently armed, was seen by the Normans, mounted on a white horse and carrying a white standard with a splendid cross on it tied to the tip of his lance: 'It were as if this knight were advancing with our battle line and rushing at the enemy where they were the thickest … our men were elated and called out again and again "God and St George".' Struck with the joy of such a vision to the point where they were shedding tears, the troops eagerly followed the horseman into battle. Many also saw a banner containing a cross hanging from the top of the count's lance, a banner 'only God could have placed there'.[173]

In addition, the Normans had not been above an attempt to suborn a Byzantine warrior saint's loyalties – Theodore, in this case. Anna Komnene records an incident when the Norman leader, Robert Guiscard, specifically attempted to gain the favour of this Byzantine military saint and use his assistance against the emperor, her father Alexios, and his army. Prior to the Battle of Dyrrachion in 1081, Robert arrived at the shrine of the martyr Theodore (presumably, but not definitely Theodore Teron), which was located outside its walls. There, according to Anna, the Normans 'throughout the night sought to propitiate the Deity, and also partook of the Immaculate Sacred Mysteries' – in other words, they entreated a Byzantine saint to desert his own side and assist them in their attack on the Byzantine Empire.[174] With much the same mindset, Roger II and his Normans acquired the icon of Theodore

Stratelates when they raided Corinth in 1147. As well as prisoners ('the most comely and deep-bosomed women'), they also appropriated the icon of Theodore, 'the greatest among martyrs, renowned for his miracles'. As justification for the theft, it was argued that Theodore had made the deliberate choice not to protect Corinth, because he wanted his city and icon to be captured: he had abandoned the Byzantines and gone over to the side of the Normans.[175]

Where the capture of Antioch was concerned, it was in the interests of Bohemond, the first prince of Antioch, and his Normans to validate as far as possible his claim to the city and his refusal to return it to the Byzantines. Antioch had only fallen to the Turks in 1084, and, in the agreement made at Constantinople between Alexios I and the First Crusade leaders as they passed through early in 1097, the latter had sworn that, in return for Byzantine assistance and supplies en route, 'whatever towns, countries, or forts that had formerly belonged to the Roman Empire – which of course included Antioch – would be handed over'. Despite this, according to Raymond, all the princes (except for Raymond of St-Gilles) agreed that if Antioch was captured it was to be offered to Bohemond,[176] and he remained there while the other Crusaders continued to Jerusalem. This may give an insight into the context of the warrior saint apparition in the battle against Kerbogha outside Antioch. The *Gesta*, which first reported the saints' battlefield intervention, was a Norman source, and the episode may have been inspired by the Normans' wish to justify their claim to Antioch and refusal to return it to Alexios by proclaiming that Byzantine saints had themselves assisted in the city's defence against the Turks, legitimizing the Crusaders' claim to Antioch and vindicating their decision to renege on their oath to the emperor.

The Crusaders and St George

En route to Jerusalem, the Crusaders stopped at Ramla, which lay near to the famous cult centre of St George at Lydda (Lod). Considering that there was a general belief among the soldiery that St George had aided them in person at Dorylaion and then at Antioch, it was natural that the Crusaders would want to pay him homage at his centre of worship, seeing him as a potent intercessor and fellow-combatant against the Turks. On their travels, they had even acquired, rather underhandedly, the relic of one of his arms, which then accompanied them on the Crusade. It had been found in an unspecified monastery in Asia Minor or Syria by a priest named Gerbod (Gerbault) of Lille, who was in the service of Robert of Flanders. As the relic had been purloined, and worse, because it was not venerated in the proper manner, the priest who acquired it died, as did everyone else who was successively responsible for the care of the arm until Robert intervened, punishing those who neglected it and installing it with reverence in his tent.[177] The sickness and deaths then ceased and the relic began to work miracles.

Raymond d'Aguilers also records a rather implausible anecdote about relics of St George (in addition to the discovery of the Holy Lance) being found at Antioch while the Crusaders were besieged there. This miraculous find followed a dream experienced by a cleric, Peter Desiderius, which led to George's bones being found in the church of St Leontios, along with those of Saints Cyprian, Omechios, Leontios and John Chrysostom. In the dream, St George (without identifying himself) instructed Peter to collect the relics of the four saints and take them with them to Jerusalem. When Peter and his companions, including Raymond himself, found the bones of a fifth saint whom they tenuously identified as Merkourios, they left the relics in the church because they were unsure of the saint's identity. In a second vision, George appeared to Peter and claimed the bones to be his own, describing himself as the standard bearer of the army (and hence of the greatest assistance to the Crusaders), and instructing him to ensure that they took his relics to Jerusalem together with those of the other four saints.[178] Raymond also documents other miracles on the Crusaders' journey: their forces were miraculously increased in the battle against Ridwan of Aleppo on 9 February 1098, and a miraculous rain filled the moat of the fort of La Mahomerie in March, while a shooting star fell near Kerbogha's encampment on 13/14 June.[179]

As the army was so enthusiastic in its veneration of St George, when they reached Ramla in June 1099 on their approach to Jerusalem, the leaders decided to create an episcopal see in George's honour. George was the best known of the saints who had personally aided them, and his cult centre was to date the only one of a major warrior saint they had encountered in Asia Minor. The *Gesta* describes the decision as follows:

> 'Near Ramla is a church worthy of great reverence, for there lies the most precious body of St George, who there suffered blessed martyrdom at the hands of the treacherous pagans for the name of Christ. While we were there, our leaders chose a bishop to protect and build up this church, and they paid him tithes and endowed him with gold and silver, horses and other animals, so that he and his household could live in an appropriate and pious manner.'[180]

The Crusaders must have felt that they were finally approaching their stated objective in the Holy Land. Robert of Rouen was installed as the first bishop in 1099, and virtually every subsequent chronicle of the First Crusade mentions this episode. While it was the leaders who decided on this foundation, George was regarded as a powerful intercessor by both clerics and laymen in the army, and this bishopric acknowledged the help given by the saint to the Crusaders over the last three years. From 1115, Roger of Antioch (regent for Bohemond II) minted coins featuring St George on horseback killing a dragon.[181]

In his account of events at Ramla, Raymond refers to St George as 'our avowed leader', and states that the Crusaders founded the episcopate, so that 'St George would be our intercessor with God and our faithful leader through his dwelling place'.[182] The fact that the Crusaders successfully took Jerusalem a month later, in July 1099, even though George's assistance or intercession there is not made much of in the chronicles, would have strengthened the army's belief in his protection, which only increased with time. The twelfth-century epic poem, the *Chanson de Jérusalem*, actually records that the Crusaders met the Moslems outside Ramla before proceeding to Jerusalem, and that this was the site of a major conflict. During this engagement, Bohemond called on the Holy Sepulchre and St George, at which a heavenly force appeared consisting of Saints George, Barbaros, Demetrios, Denys and Maurice, plus a legion of angels. St George was the leader of the host, killing the emir of Ascalon and unhorsing many others: with his assistance, Ramla was secured.[183] The fictional nature of the episode is shown by the fact that Bohemond had actually remained behind at Antioch and that no battle took place at Ramla, but it reveals how intrinsically the warrior saints had come to be associated with the Crusade's success. St Denys was obviously included because of his connections with the kingdom of France: the chanson was, after all, composed in French for French speakers. St Barbaros was venerated in the East as a (very) minor warrior saint, with whose cult some of the Crusaders must have become acquainted, for him to be included here. Bohemond was said to have publicly offered thanks to George after the battle, and promised to install a bishop at Ramla along with twenty clerics.[184]

While it was at Antioch that supernatural assistance by warrior saints was generally accepted and from this point taken as an almost expected occurrence in the heat of battle, there was also a suggestion that one particular saint – George – aided the Crusaders in their capture of Jerusalem: Raymond d'Aguilers is once again the source. At one point, when the leaders were on the point of withdrawing their siege engines, which had been badly damaged, from the city walls, a knight whose name Raymond did not know 'signalled with his shield from the Mount of Olives to the Count of Toulouse and others to move forward'. This account is repeated in the history of William of Tyre.[185] Neither historian names the knight, but he was later believed to have been George. In the *Golden Legend*, *c*.1275, the Crusaders are described as not daring to mount the scaling ladders in view of the defenders' resistance, until encouraged by the saint:

> 'and when it was so that they had assieged Jerusalem and durst not mount ne go up on the walls for the quarrels and defence of the Saracens, they saw appertly S. George which had white arms with a red cross, that went up tofore them on the walls and they followed him, and so was Jerusalem taken by his help.'[186]

In addition, according to a number of witnesses, the papal legate Adhémar of Le Puy, who had died at Antioch on 1 August 1098, was seen by many leading the final assault on Jerusalem. He had appeared beforehand in a vision to Peter Desiderius, giving instructions for the Crusaders to fast and process around Jerusalem as a penance for their past offences to ensure victory. William of Tyre adds that, when Jerusalem had been captured, many of the Crusaders saw their dead companions, who had 'risen again in spirit', visiting the holy places in Jerusalem – evidence that 'those who had been called from this temporal life to the enjoyment of eternal blessedness were not deprived of their heart's desire, but accomplished to the full that which they had sought with such fervent devotion'.[187] Even those Crusaders who had died en route were restored to life and permitted to reach Jerusalem and the Holy Sepulchre, and so fulfil their vow.

The Afterlife of the Warrior Saints

In the twelfth century, belief in the invincibility of the warrior saints had in no way waned, and the Byzantines certainly believed that Sts George and Theodore were able to give them aid against the encroaching waves of Turks occupying Asia Minor. The catalyst for the permanent loss of Anatolia to the Seljuks was in 1176, when Manuel I Komnenos was seriously defeated at Myriokephalon after the Byzantine army was ambushed by the Turks in south-western Asia Minor – a disastrous end to the final attempt to recover the interior of Anatolia from Turkish control.

As with earlier defeats, the faithful demanded an explanation as to why the warrior saints had failed to come to the emperor's aid, while everyone – up to and including the emperor – had been anxious for advance knowledge of whether the warrior saints would come to their assistance on this occasion. One version explaining why the saints were absent in this battle was given by the historian Niketas Choniates. He recorded that a citizen named Mavropoulos, an interpreter, had approached the emperor to tell him that he had had a dream about the warrior saints. Manuel was clearly anxious to learn of any possible prophecy relating to the campaign. Mavropoulos had dreamt that he had entered a church of St Cyrus, and there he heard a voice proceed from an icon of the Theotokos stating that the emperor was in the greatest danger. 'Who will go out in my name to help him?' the icon asked. Someone unseen said, 'Send George.' 'He is lethargic', came the response, and the other voice then suggested, 'Let Theodore go forth.' He was also rejected, and finally the icon sorrowfully proclaimed that no one could avert the forthcoming evil.[188] The episode suggests that the intervention of one of the saints in battle was eagerly hoped for, but that under these dire circumstances even George's or Theodore's assistance was judged inadequate by the Mother of God. The battle was consequently lost.

While the warrior saints continued to intervene in battle on behalf of the Byzantines after the First Crusade, in the West the idea of saints assisting 'Crusaders' – anyone who was fighting for the Christian faith in battles against pagans and Muslims (as in the account of the Battle of Cerami) – swept across Europe, taking particular root in Spain because of the frontier shared between Muslims and Christians. A great many victories in the past were now attributed to saintly intervention. According to sources that postdate the First Crusade, St James the Greater (the apostle), who became known as St James 'Matamoros' ('the Muslim-killer'), had reputedly aided a Christian army at the Battle of Clavijo against the Moors in Spain in AD 844, when he appeared in full armour at the head of a legion of angels. Later, he was also said to have intervened at Simancas in AD 939 and to have helped Ferdinand I capture Coimbra in 1064. However, all the sources which mention Saint James postdate the First Crusade and his interventions are retrojected into accounts of earlier conflicts. But his legend continued: the saint was later translated to the New World, and in Latin America he became Santiago Mataindios ('Indian-slayer'), and in the nineteenth century, by a further translation by anti-colonialist Indian-Americans, Santiago Mataespañois ('slayer of Spaniards').[189] When fighting the infidel, there was a confident expectation of divine help, and it was a matter of pride for all sides to receive saintly assistance, which legitimized both the cause and the conflict.

The belief in support from warrior saints for the nationalist cause was continued into the twentieth century in Greece itself. When the Greeks recaptured Thessaloniki from the Ottomans on Demetrios' feast day, 26 October 1912, it was taken as a divine sign that the town was intended to be permanently Greek,[190] while during the

First World War in 1917 the church on Tinos (the most important pilgrimage site in Greece) took charge of making the 'sacred banner' of the National Army, which jointly featured St George (the patron saint of Greece) and the icon of the Panayia (Theotokos) of Tinos, the island where a miraculous icon of the Virgin was found in 1823. The local newspaper reported that this banner would render the soldiers as invincible as Achilles.[191] Warrior saints even intervened in the Second World War: it was reported that in December 1940, in the Greek–Italian war, forty unknown soldiers suddenly appeared and started fighting alongside the Greeks. After the victory, they disappeared into the ruins of an old Byzantine church (presumably that near Onchesmos, where a monastery dedicated to the forty Martyrs of Sebaste was founded by Justinian, AD 527–565). It was then believed that this had been an apparition of the Forty Saints (*Agioi Saranta*), the forty martyrs who were the elite of a Roman legion, who were originally venerated in that foundation and had emerged to help their compatriots. The town, now in southern Albania, is now known as Saranta in honour of the forty saints.[192]

Battlefield 'Miracles'

Since ancient times, there have been theories of social manipulation to account for epiphanies and 'miracles' (for example, the deliberate manipulation of ancient omens, both on and off the battlefield), as well as theories that experiences of supernatural phenomena had been triggered by superstitious fancies or overactive imagination, which resulted in the blurring of boundaries between fancy and reality.[193] But this is not to deny that throughout history, 'miracles' have been not only accepted but experienced simultaneously by large bodies of combatants and widely celebrated as proof of divine favour. In antiquity, reports of epiphanies were (generally) met with credulity and taken seriously: the Athenians, for example, do not seem to have doubted Philippides' encounter with Pan after Marathon, and honoured the god with a shrine and festival.[194] Such encounters, and the belief in them, are not confined to pre-modern times. A study by the Israel Defense Forces regarding epiphanies of Rachel the Matriarch in Gaza during Operation *Cast Lead* (2008–2009) concluded that, even in the twenty-first century, soldiers genuinely believe in miracles on the battlefield, and are neither lying nor hallucinating in their reports of such incidents. Rachel the Matriarch was seen by a number of soldiers, deterring them from entering houses that were later found to have been laid with explosives.[195] Such miracles take place within a specific social and cultural context, and soldiers naturally experience visions which align with their religious beliefs (for example, a Christian is more likely than a Jew to experience an intervention by St George), while miracles are more likely to present themselves to soldiers who are already influenced by a religious mindset.

Battlefield miracle stories can range from unexpected (or even expected) weather conditions (like driving rain or wind) to the halting of bullets by some solid object (like a religious text in a pocket) or natural phenomena such as eclipses, comets or fog. They can also simply involve timing, such as a weather event which favours one of the two sides, rather than, for example, a supernatural apparition or epiphany. The appearance of a venerated figure in battle is at the extreme end of a typology of miracles, being a violation of natural laws and involving the intentional intervention of a supernatural force in the natural course of things (for example, walking on water). The divine epiphanies which were a feature of the ancient and medieval world generally comprised miracles of the extreme type; in Rosman's investigation, which proposed a range of categories for military miracles, these are defined as having violated nature, involved the divine, been benevolent in intent and possessing a clear purpose.[196]

The usual scenario in such interventions involved a supernatural entity lending assistance to one side of the combatants at a crucial stage of a battle.[197] There is a degree of consistency in the descriptions of such interventions in the Byzantine and medieval world, with an underlying pattern determined by the preconceptions and expectations of the participants: the warrior saints here are a case in point. Their normal *modus operandi* is to appear unexpectedly on the battlefield, whether recognized or not by the troops, and drive off the opposing side. Sometimes their involvement is only acknowledged after the event, while their actions may simply be perceived in a vision or dream by a single protagonist, although a 'confirmatory' dream might also be received by another party to provide corroboration of the original dream.

The apparitions of warrior saints on the battlefield are akin to experiences which have been termed the 'Third Man Factor' and the 'Sensed Presence' (SP), where more than one person – and sometimes a group – share the same experience of a sense of having been guided by an unseen or otherworldly presence: the terms 'Illusory Shadow Presence' and 'Felt Presence' are also employed.[198] The term 'Third Man Factor' was inspired by the scene in T.S. Eliot's *Waste Land* ('Who is the third who walks always beside you…?').[199] Eliot was himself inspired by Sir Ernest Shackleton's Antarctic expedition of 1914–1915, where three members of the expedition all experienced the sensation of an unseen presence as they trekked across the ice to the whaling station on South Georgia. Numerous examples of such episodes, which occur in a conscious or waking state, suggest a genuine psychological experience, which happens in situations of extreme stress (as experienced by our medieval protagonists in battle),[200] and can consist of a vision of the beneficent intervention of a supernatural entity at an opportune moment, and which appears to its visionaries as a real-life experience.

Visions of this type frequently take place in unusual, high-risk situations, and are often met with on battlefields, in cases where the visionaries have been suffering deprivation, stress and fatigue, with the future outcomes of the conflict unpredictable and uncertain. The hallucinations experienced in SP epiphanies are transient and of non-psychiatric etiology, and occur in the course of the traumatic episode (not after the event); typically, they are experienced in an extreme life-threatening situation by mentally healthy people in a waking state.[201] There is little resemblance to epiphanies during sleep, which result from a different mental condition.[202] On occasions, sometimes dozens or hundreds of combatants experience the SP episode, and the images related to their vision are culture-specific and drawn from the repertoire of images of the visionaries' cultural heritage. When the impressions of the episode are later shared, the stories are adjusted for consistency, and others can convince

Figure 10.9: Parliamentary Recruiting Committee Poster No. 108, Spottiswoode and Co Ltd, 1915. St George is shown in full plate armour on horseback, driving his lance into the body of a winged dragon, symbolizing Germany. (*Imperial War Museums PST 0408.* © *IWM Art*)

themselves by auto-suggestion that they shared the experience. Visions can also be contagious, and transmitted at the time of the episode through body language or verbal communications.[203]

It is only to be expected that surviving descriptions of such events show signs of embellishment and literary embroidery, but few of the battlefield interventions discussed above appear to be entirely fictitious: 'Soldiers, being in intense, life-threatening situations, in need of making order out of the chaos of battle, are good candidates for reporting miraculous stories.'[204] Furthermore, if a war is framed in religious terms, combatants will be more open to observing miracles during the course of the action. The participants in the First Crusade, who saw themselves as voluntarily involved in a penitential, divinely commanded activity, expected such interventions and, being empowered by their religious beliefs, were able to rise above their exhaustion, deprivation and alien environment and use such visions as a coping mechanism. The telling of such miracle stories was also a bonding device between comrades and different contingents. Similarly, soldiers in the Byzantine army, fighting for their emperor or their city, were able to interpret such epiphanies as signs of divine favour. Some interventions were considered so normal that they were confidently expected: it was when St Demetrios *failed* to avert an attack on Thessaloniki that an explanation had to be found for his actions, or lack of them.

Reports of supernatural intervention have been staunchly defended in modern times, and positively encouraged by army leaders, politicians and the media – and even accepted by historians. For example, there is the account of the angelic horsemen riding white horses and clad as medieval knights allegedly sighted by some of the soldiers of the British Expeditionary Force as they retreated from Mons in Belgium between 23 and 26 August 1914. The vision was proclaimed a miracle by patriotic newspapers at home in the UK, and, as late as the 1960s, noted historian A.J.P. Taylor accepted the reality of the Mons apparition.[205] The only problem is that the episode was totally fictional – there is no evidence that soldiers at the time believed that they had witnessed a supernatural intervention – and grew out of a short story 'The Bowmen', inspired by the retreat from Mons, written in 1915 by the journalist Arthur Machen. In this piece, one of the soldiers in the force calls on St George with an invocation that he remembered seeing in a London vegetarian restaurant ('*adsit Anglis, Sanctus Georgius*': 'St George help the English!'); St George then (in the story) appears leading the bowmen of Agincourt to destroy the Germans with invisible arrows.[206]

St George was already a powerful symbol of recruiting propaganda (see Figure 10.9), and the legend satisfied patriotic needs and became a powerful and enduring part of the mythology of the First World War, while the rumours even expanded to include the details that French soldiers had seen a vision of Joan of Arc (Jeanne d'Arc), and Russian soldiers one of General Skobelev.[207] Machen himself over the next thirty years (he died in 1947) was unable to persuade anyone that his story was completely fictional, even though not a single Mons veteran came forward with an unambiguous account of a vision he had personally witnessed. With the bowmen transformed into angels – as more appropriate for a Church of England audience – the episode was showcased as a centrepiece of patriotic sermons, poured over by spiritualists, printed and reprinted in national newspapers, and reproduced in pamphlets sent to the front.[208] The legend became self-perpetuating and an integral part of popular belief and national identity, with its accuracy passionately defended at all levels. In a time of national crisis, rumour and superstition thus created an enduring and powerful legend in which St George in 1914 led an angelic host to protect ordinary English soldiers against their dastardly enemies. This train of narrative causality, in which a story takes shape of its own accord in defiance of any 'facts', leads directly back to the battle for Antioch in 1098 and the earlier interventions of warrior saints to protect Byzantine cities and armies.

Conclusion

For troops in the field – both Byzantines and Westerners – episodes of divine intervention in battle proved that their army was divinely favoured: they were certain that they were fighting on the *right* side. Since they were fighting on the right side, they expected, therefore, to receive supernatural assistance. Robert the Monk asked what of comparable importance to the First Crusade had taken place in more than a millennium, since the mystery of the crucifixion itself, 'than our journey as pilgrims to Jerusalem – a task that itself was not human, but divine?'[209] In such circumstances, the Crusaders were convinced that supernatural assistance would support them in times of crisis – nothing else could be more important than the fulfilment of their quest. Even when warrior saints were not visible on the battlefield itself (as they were at Antioch and, supposedly, Jerusalem), they were thought to be fellow-travellers on crusade, providers of support and assistance to the troops, and exemplars of the willing martyrdom endured by the Crusaders, who were 'under the protection of George and Theodore and Demetrios and Blaise, soldiers of Christ truly accompanying us'.[210]

Similarly, since the fourth century, the Byzantines had believed that, along with the Theotokos, protectress of Constantinople, warrior saints were the defenders of their cities and empire. As a result, it was natural that they must have been involved in the assassination of pagan and heretic emperors, and Merkourios, Sergios and Theodore were therefore portrayed as responsible for the removal of Julian and Valens. When emperors on campaign invoked the saints, had their icons carried into battle and engaged the enemy on a particular feast day, the saints were bound to respond and assist the army: with every victory to which they contributed, their interventions, as reported, become more overt, more decisive, more highly anticipated by the combatants and more publicized by grateful generals.

It would, however, be judgemental to assume that the accounts of these medieval interventions were the result of either cynical manipulation, ignorant superstition or neurological or pathological states: armies in the field throughout history, up to and including the twenty-first century, have believed that they had experienced supernatural interventions in battle, and in a significant number of these cases, however apocryphal, these epiphanies spurred them on to further victories by giving them hope and encouragement amidst the horrors of war.

Notes

1. See Frend (1965), esp. pp.477–535; Delehaye (1933); Walter (2003), pp.19–22.
2. On the cult of the warrior saints, see especially Delehaye (1909); Walter (2003), esp. pp.22–28.
3. Delehaye (1909), pp.11–25; Walter (1999); Walter (2003), pp.44–58; Haldon (2016).
4. Delehaye (1909), pp.26–43; Halkin (1981); Oikonomides (1986); Walter (2003), pp.59–66; Haldon (2016).
5. Budge (1888), (1930); Howell (1969); Riches (2000); Walter (1993); Walter (2003), pp.109–44.
6. Delehaye (1909), pp.234–48; Binon (1937); Binon (1937a); Walter (2003), pp.101–08.
7. The first Palestinian martyr, beheaded in Caesarea during Diocletian's persecution, according to Euseb. *On the Martyrs of Palestine* 1.1–2; Delehaye (1909), pp.228–33; Walter (2003), pp.94–100.
8. Delehaye (1909), pp.103–09; Lemerle (1979); Lemerle (1981); Cormack (1989); Walter (2003), pp.67–94.
9. Peeters (1921); Fowden (1999); Walter (2003), pp.146–62.
10. Delehaye (1910a); Devos (1959); Devos (1960); Grossman (1998); Duffy & Bourbouhakis (2003), pp.65–81; Walter (2003), pp.181–90.
11. Halkin (1970); Weitzmann (1979); Walter (2003), pp.219–22.
12. Crisafulli, Nesbitt & Haldon (1996); Walter (2003), pp.191–94.
13. Rosenqvist (1996).
14. Budge (1888); Brooks (1925); see also Malone, in this volume.
15. Euseb. *On the Martyrs of Palestine* 1–13.
16. Revelation 2:13, cf. 6:9; Euseb. *Hist. Eccl.* 5.2 (AD 177); Amm. Marc. 22.17.
17. *Martyrdom of Polycarp* 9.3.
18. Dagron (1978); Johnson (2012); Festugière (1971), pp.33–82.
19. Euseb. *Vit. Const.* 3.28: μαρτύρια (martyrs' shrines).
20. See Grabar (1946); Walter (1982), esp. pp.144–58.
21. Maraval (1982), pp.226–331; Davis (1998); Walter (2003), p.28.
22. Euseb. *Hist. Eccl.* 8.4, *Vit. Const.* 2.33; see also Malone, in this volume.
23. Const. Porph. *Cer.*1.481.
24. Kurtz (1989), p.10; Janin (1934); Magdalino (1990), pp.198–201; for the hymn, Const. Porph. *Cer.* 2.89.
25. Pentcheva (2006), pp.82–83; Nelson (2011–12), pp.186–87, with fig. 15.
26. Nelson (2011–12), p.188, with fig. 16; Walter (2003), fig. 46.
27. Sevcenko (1962), p.272.
28. *Digenis Akritas* 1.19–25.
29. Hom. *Il.* 5.121–444.
30. Pritchett (1979), p.39; see also Wheeler (2004); Graf (2004).
31. Hdt. 6.105, 117, 8.84; Plut. *Thes.* 35.5, *Them.* 15.1; cf. O'Sullivan (2020).
32. *SIG*³ 398.
33. Lundgreen (1997), pp.190–97; Dinsmoor (1934), pp.93–106. Both statues were taken to Constantinople, the Promachos in AD 465, while the Parthenos (or a copy: the original was badly damaged by fire in 165 BC) was recorded as being there in the tenth century.
34. Zos. 5.6.
35. Livy 2.20; Dion. Hal. *Rom. Ant.* 6.13; Cic. *Nat. Deor.* 2.6; Delehaye (1904), pp.427–32.
36. Val. Max. 1.8.6; Amm. Marc. 24.4.24.
37. Cic. *Nat. Deor.* 2.6; Dio 41.61: Pharsalus; Plin. *Nat. Hist.* 2.148, cf. 7.86: the Cimbri. See Roussel (1931) for Q. Labienus' failure to take Panamara in 40 BC, when he was repelled by Zeus Panamaros.
38. For example, Exodus 12:29, 15:1–21; 1 Samuel 5:6–12; 2 Samuel 8:1–18.
39. 2 Maccabees 10:29–30, 11:8–9.
40. 2 Maccabees 15:11–16.
41. 2 Maccabees 3:24–26.

42. Luke 2:13–14.
43. Joshua 5:15; Daniel 10:13–21.
44. Revelation 12:7–8, 19:14, 20.
45. Euseb. *Vit. Const.* 3.3; cf. Isaiah 27:1.
46. For an example, see a nummus minted in AD 327 at Constantinople: *RIC*, vol. 7, 572.19, cf. 64: at https://www.britishmuseum.org/collection/object/C_1890-0804-11.
47. Bonner (1950), p.221; Walter (2003), pp.33–38, 241–42.
48. *Pan. Lat.* 4.14.1–4, 4.15.4–7, 4.29.1.
49. Delehaye (1909), pp.234–48; Walter (2003), pp.101–08; Binon (1937); Binon (1937a).
50. Amm. Marc. 25.3.3.
51. Liban. *Or.* 18.274; Philostorgios *Hist. Eccl.* 7.15.
52. Socrates *Hist. Eccl.* 3.21.
53. Theodoret *Hist. Eccl.* 3.20, cf. 3.18.
54. Sozom. 6.1.
55. Sozom. 6.2; for Didymos, see Theodoret *Hist. Eccl.* 4.26.
56. Xanth. *Hist. Eccl.* 10.35.
57. Miracles of Artemios: Papadopoulos-Kerameus (1909), pp.1–79; Crisafulli & Nesbitt (1997); Mango (1979); Walter (2003), pp.191–94.
58. Delehaye (1909), pp.92–101.
59. Malalas 13.25. In the account of John Damascene, it is the Theotokos who dispatches Merkourios: Walter (2003), p.105.
60. *Chron. Pasch.* 550–51 (s.a.363); John of Nikiu *Chronicle* 80.19–26.
61. Evetts (1907), pp.419–20 (*History of the Patriarchs* 2.420); Baynes (1937), pp.22–29. For the ninth-century miniature in Paris (gr.510, fol. 409v), which shows Merkourios spearing Julian, who has fallen from his horse, see Brubaker (1999), pp.232–35.
62. Cf. Xen. *Hell.* 6.4.7; Diod. 15.51.2–4; Cic. *Div.* 1.74 for Herakles' weapons disappearing from his shrine in Thebes prior to the Battle of Leuktra in 371 BC, 'evidence' that he had gone to do battle against the Spartans.
63. Amm. Marc. 31.12–13.
64. Socrates *Hist. Eccl.* 6.38.
65. On Sergios, see Peeters (1921); Fowden (1999); Walter (2003), pp.146–62.
66. Baynes (1937).
67. Baynes (1937), who argued that Valens is here a title and refers to Julian; Garsoïan (1989), esp. pp.130–32; Peeters (1921), pp.70–73.
68. Walter (2003), pp.146–62; Fowden (1999). For Sergiopolis: Procop. *Buildings* 2.9.3–9.
69. Woods (1997), pp.335–67; Efthymiadis (2011), pp.310–16.
70. Delehaye (1909), pp.127–35, 183–201; Walter (1999), pp.163–210.
71. Sozom. 7.22; Rufinus *Hist. Eccl.* 11.31–3; Theodoret *Hist. Eccl.* 5.24; see also Malone, in this volume.
72. Theodoret *Hist. Eccl.* 5.24.
73. Paul the Deacon *Historia Romana* 14.12; cf. Prosper of Aquitaine *Epitome chronikon* 1367; cf. Robinson (1905), p.51, for the miraculous tale built on Prosper's contemporary account. Raphael's painting of the encounter between Leo and Attila can be accessed at: http://www.museivaticani.va/content/museivaticani/en/collezioni/musei/stanze-di-raffaello/stanza-di-eliodoro/incontro-di-leone-magno-con-attila.html.
74. *Chron. Pasch.* 180; Theodore Synkellos, *Homily on the Siege of Constantinople in 626*, 19; cf. Av. Cameron (1978), pp.96–102; Pentcheva (2006), pp.37–59. For accounts of the Avar siege, including that of Theodore Synkellos, see Barisic (1954), pp.371–95.
75. Leo Deac. 9.12; Psellos *Chron.* 1.16.
76. See Fowden (1999), p.134.
77. Procop. *Pers.* 20.1–16, *Buildings* 2.9.9; Evagrius *Hist. Eccl.* 4.28.
78. A different St Andrew – Stratelates ('the General') – was one of the corps of warrior saints: Walter (2003), pp.245–46.

79. Const. Porph. *DAI* 1.229–31.
80. Euseb. *Hist. Eccl.* 8.5 mentions a man of distinction martyred at Nikomedeia, but there is no reason to take this to refer to George; see Walter (1993), pp.295–326. For George's passion and miracles: Brooks (1925); Budge (1888); Cumont (1936); Noret (1974). On his cult, see Didi-Huberman, Gabretta & Morgaine (1994); Howell (1969); Riches (2000); Walter (1995).
81. Leclerq (1924).
82. Geyer (1898); Wilkinson (1977), p.65.
83. Janin (1969), pp.69–78.
84. James (2017), figs 104, 105; see Aufhauser (1913); for healing children suffering from leprosy and demonic possession, see Budge (1888); for captivity, see Grotowski (2003), with figs 1–9.
85. Walter (1995), pp.317–18.
86. See Festugière (1971), esp. pp.268, 308–10; Budge (1931); Sahas (1986); Meehan (1983), pp.113–17 (Adamnan 3.4.1–13).
87. Greatrex & Lieu (2002), pp.235–36.
88. Krumbacher (1911), pp.78–81; cf. Noret (1974).
89. Budge (1888), pp.270–74; in another version, Diocletian did reach Lydda, but the archangel Michael struck him blind: Walter (2003), p.120.
90. Festugière (1970); trans. Dawes & Baynes (1948).
91. Festugière (1970), p.97.
92. Walter (2003), figs 27, 28.
93. de Voragine (2012), pp.238–39, trans. Caxton (1483) at: https://sourcebooks.web.fordham.edu/basis/goldenlegend/GL-vol3-george.asp. See also Walter (2003), pp.125, 321; Hengstenberg (1912); Howell (1969); Kuehn (2011), pp.108–09.
94. Walter (2003), pp.132–34.
95. A poster by Fritz Boehle (1873–1916) at: http://www.english.emory.edu/LostPoets/GermanPosters.html; see Darracott & Loftus (1981). In 1999, a candidate for a Greek ecological political party (concerned over NATO's bombing of Serbia) had himself portrayed on posters as St George fighting against a dragon with the head of Bill Clinton: Seraidari (2009), p.144.
96. For Theodore Teron, see Halkin (1962); Halkin (1981); Delehaye (1966); Walter (1999), pp.163–210; Leemans (2003); Haldon (2016).
97. Cavarnos (1990), pp.61–71; Leemans (2003); Zuckerman (1991), pp.479–86.
98. Cavarnos (1990), pp.61–71; cf. Walter (2003), pp.45, 49. For an inscription from Euchaita describing Theodore as 'Christ's athlete who is a citizen of heaven, Theodore the guardian of this city', see Mango & Sevcenko (1972), pp.378–84.
99. Miracles: Delehaye (1909), pp.194–201; Sigalas (1921), pp.50–79; Halkin (1962), pp.308–24; Delehaye (1909), pp.183–201; Haldon (2016), pp.92–111.
100. Delehaye (1909), pp.196–98.
101. Hengstenberg (1912), pp.78–106, 241–80; Walter (2003), p.309.
102. Zacos & Verglery (1972), pp.792–93; Walter (2003), pp.51–56, with figs 23a, 23b, 25; see Kuehn (2011), pp.108–09.
103. For Theodore Stratelates, see Haldon (2016); Oikonomides (1986), pp.327–35; Woodfin (2006), pp.111–143.
104. Walter (2003), pp.59–64.
105. Maguire (1996), pp.20–23, figs 11–15.
106. *Digenis Akritas* 1428, 1861, 2406–10, 3031–34, 3242–43. Trapp (1976) compares episodes in the *Digenis* epic to the lives of the Saints Theodore.
107. Oikonomides (1986), pp.327–35; Walter (2003), pp.44–66.
108. Sullivan, Talbot & McGrath (2014).
109. *BHG* 263–64f; Grégoire (1938), pp.291–300.
110. For warrior saints and the Rus, see esp. White (2004); White (2013).
111. *The Russian Primary Chronicle* 6477.
112. Leo Deac. 9.9.

113. Skylitzes 308–09.
114. Skylitzes 309; Leo Deac. 158; Jordanov (1995), nos 228–31.
115. Walter (2003), p.64; Treu (1899), p.21.
116. Skylitzes 339. For Basil's visit to the tombs of St George and the two Theodores to ask for protection in battle, see Crostini (1996), p.78.
117. Nelson (2011–12), pp.190–91, with fig. 18.
118. Sevcenko (1962), dedicatory poem at p.273.
119. See Cutler (1976–77); Stephenson (2003), pp.54–55. For the lance as the primary weapon of warrior saints, see Grotowski (2010), pp.313–33.
120. For the relative importance of Thessaloniki and Sirmium in the beginnings of the Demetrios cult, see Vickery (1974); Lemerle (1981), p.202.
121. Delehaye (1909), pp.103–09, 259–63; Frendo (1997); Obolensky (1974); Skedros (1999). For the church at Thessaloniki: Cormack (1969); Cormack (1985); Walter (1973); Bakirtzis (2003).
122. See Grabar (1954).
123. Miracles: Lemerle (1979), pp.50–165 (John of Thessaloniki: *BHG* 499–523), 168–241 (anonymous: *BHG* 516z–522).
124. Lemerle (1979), p.135.
125. Lemerle (1979), pp.157, 164; cf. Woods (1999).
126. Lemerle (1979), pp.168–241, esp. 190–94.
127. Woods (1999).
128. Kurtz (1898), p.10; Magdalino (1990), pp.198–99.
129. For depictions of him, see Walter (2003), pp.83–87; Cormack (1989).
130. Further views of the reliquary, including photographs of the hinged St Demetrios panel and the compartments for relics, can be found at: https://www.britishmuseum.org/collection/object/H_1926-0409-1.
131. Moscow, State Historical Museum and Cultural Museum (Moscow Kremlin), Inv. no: Mz 1148; see Grabar (1950), pp.3–28.
132. Westerink (1981), pp.8–17; Böhlig (1973), p.22.
133. Skylitzes 413–14; Walter (2003), p.82; Kekaumenos 160–62.
134. Skylitzes 339; Crostini (1996), p.78.
135. Anna Komnene 5.5.
136. Morrisson (2003), pp.174–76.
137. Robert of Clari 116; cf. Akropolites *History* 26, where Kalojan himself saw an armed man who appeared before him in his sleep and struck his side with his spear. See Walter (2003), pp.87–88; Grotowski (2010), pp.103–04; Lapina (2009); Obolensky (1974), pp.19–20.
138. See Dillon (2020).
139. MacGregor (2004), p.319.
140. Chibnall (1972), 3.214–16; MacGregor (2003), pp.220–22. See also Roach (2016), pp.177–201; for Maurice: O'Reilly (1978); Girgis (1993); Woods (1994).
141. MacGregor (2003), pp..224–25. For a late eleventh-century prayer in which God was asked to protect a knight who defended a church or other ecclesiastical institution from his enemies though the help of Maurice, Sebastian and George, see Flori (1978), pp.274–78, 436–38.
142. Walter (2003), p.50; Janin (1969), pp.148, 152–53; Anna Komnene 8.3.
143. Klein (2006).
144. Riley-Smith (1982), p.57.
145. Hill (1962), pp.16–17.
146. For Gregory Nazianzen's homily 'On the Maccabees', see Vinson (1994), pp.166–92; for John Chrysostom's three homilies on the Maccabees: Mayer (2006); cf. Joslyn-Siemiatkoski (2009).
147. For example, Hill & Hill (1969), p.53 (Raymond d'Aguilers on the battle against Ridwan of Aleppo, 9 February 1098); Fulcher *Hist.* 117; cf. Lapina (2012), pp.1–6.
148. Hagenmayer (1901), pp.69, 147, 271–72; Lapina (2009), p.93.
149. Demetrios became popular in the West after the crusade: see Lapina (2009), pp.93–112; MacGregor (2003), p.233.

150. Garrison (1929), p.123; Hirshberg (2000), pp.131–32; Faraone (2018), p.213 and n.105.
151. MacGregor (2004), pp.322–23 with n.13.
152. Hill & Hill (1969), pp.45–46; see Lapina (2007), pp.117–39.
153. *Quran* 3:125, 8:9; Guillaume (1967), pp.303, 310.
154. See Ashbridge (2007), pp.3–36.
155. Huygens (1996), pp.218, 299, 308.
156. Hill (1962), p.69.
157. Morris (1993), pp.55–71; MacGregor (2004), pp.325–26.
158. Hill (1962), p.62.
159. Bull & Kempf (2013), p.69; see also Bull (2014).
160. Fulcher *Hist.* 224.
161. Bull & Kempf (2013), p.54.
162. Ashbridge (2007); Anna Komnene 10.9–11; Hill & Hill (1969), p.55. The Holy Lance had probably been in Constantinople since AD 629; in the tenth century, it was kept in the palace chapel of the Theotokos of the Pharos and was venerated by the Byzantine court on Good Friday. Robert of Clari was certainly shown it (in the palace of Boukoleon) in 1204: Const. Porph. *Cer.* 1.34; Robert of Clari 68–69; Klein (2006), pp.79, 87 with n.66, 91.
163. Delehaye (1909), pp.91–101; Walter (2003), pp.101–08.
164. Riley-Smith (1982), pp.55–56.
165. MacGregor (2004), p.326 n.19; Hagenmayer (1901), p.167.
166. Hill & Hill (1969), pp.81–83.
167. Hill & Hill (1977), pp.111–12.
168. Hill & Hill (1977), pp.98–100.
169. Mynors, Thomson & Winterbottom (1998), 1.638–39.
170. Bull & Kempf (2013), p.76: Robert also states that Bishop Adhémar himself was the first to see the heavenly army and cried out to the troops that God was fulfilling his promise of assistance.
171. Girgis (1993); O'Reilly (1978); Woods (1994).
172. Bull & Kempf (2013), pp.51–55.
173. Pontieri (1928), p.44.
174. Anna Komnene 4.6.
175. Choniates *Hist.* 76; Lapina (2015), p.71.
176. Anna Komnene 10.9–11; Hill & Hill (1969), p.55.
177. MacGregor (2004), p.336.
178. Hill & Hill (1969), pp.131–34.
179. Hill & Hill (1969), pp.45, 56–57, 62, 74; cf. Ashbridge (2007). For the shooting star, cf. Hill (1962), p.62; Fulcher *Hist.* 243–44.
180. Hill (1962), p.87; for Ramla and other cult sites of St George, see Delehaye (1909), pp.45–50.
181. Kuehn (2011), p.99.
182. Hill & Hill (1969), p.136.
183. Thorp (1992), pp.50–53, lines 690–854.
184. Delehaye (1910), pp.276–301; MacGregor (2004), p.340 and n.55.
185. Hill & Hill (1969), pp.149–50; William of Tyre 8.16.
186. de Voragine (2012), p.242; trans. Caxton (1483) at https://sourcebooks.web.fordham.edu/basis/goldenlegend/GL-vol3-george.asp.
187. William of Tyre 8.22; Brundage (1959).
188. Choniates *Hist.* 190–91.
189. Lapina (2015), p.148; García (2006); Farina (2018), pp.64, 103–12; Erdman (1977), pp.274–75.
190. Mackridge & Yannakakis (1997), p.21 with n.20.
191. Florakis (1990), pp.25–26; Seraidari (2009), p.142.
192. Florakis (1990) p.103; Seraidari (2009), p.154 with n.12.
193. Herman (2011).
194. Hdt. 6.105.

195. Rosman (2018).
196. Rosman (2018).
197. Herman (2011), p.130.
198. See Suedfeld & Geiger (2008); Geiger (2009); Shermer (2010); Herman (2011).
199. T.S. Eliot, *The Waste Land*, 5: 'What the Thunder Said'.
200. Geiger (2009).
201. Herman (2011), pp.147–50.
202. Herman (2011); for dreams in Classical Antiquity, see Harris (2009).
203. Geiger (2009), pp.241-42.
204. Rosman (2018).
205. Taylor (1966), p.29.
206. Machen (1915).
207. Clarke (2002), pp.152–53; Mikhail Dmitriyevich Skobelev (1843–1882) was famous for his heroism and conquests in Central Asia during the Russo-Turkish war of 1877–1878. Dressed in white, and mounted on a white horse, he was known by his soldiers as the 'White General'.
208. Clarke (2002), pp.156–67; Clarke (2004), p.236, calls it 'a classic example of a contemporary "urban" legend'. Cf. the widely promulgated angelic visitation and clairvoyant vision that George Washington was said, during the American Revolution, to have experienced at the Valley Forge encampment in the winter of 1778, the first account of which appeared in the *National Tribune* 4.12, in December 1880.
209. Bull & Kempf (2013), p.4: '*sed post creationem mundi quid mirabilius factum est preter salutifere cruces misterium, quam quod modernis temporibus actum est in hoc itinere nostrorum Iherosolimitarum?*'; Lapina (2015), p.144.
210. Hagenmayer (1901), pp.69, 147, 271–72.

Bibliography

Ashbridge, T., 'The Holy Lance of Antioch: Power, Devotion and Memory on the First Crusade', *Reading Medieval Studies* 33 (2007), pp.3–36.
Aufhauser, J.B., *Miracula S. Georgii* (Leipzig, 1913).
Bakirtzis, C., *The Miracles of St. Demetrius. The Collections of Archbishop John and of Anonymous* (in Greek) (Athens, 1997).
Bakirtzis, C., 'Pilgrimage to Thessaloniki: the Tomb of St Demetrios', *DOP* 56 (2003), pp.175–192.
Barisic, F., 'Le siege de Constantinople par les Avares et les Slaves en 626', *Byz.* 24.2 (1954), pp.371–95.
Baynes, N.H., 'Rome and Armenia in the Fourth Century', *English Historical Review* 25 (1910), pp.625–43.
Baynes, N.H., 'The Death of Julian the Apostate in a Christian Legend', *JRS* 27.1 (1937), pp.22–29.
Binon, S., *Essai sur le cycle de saint Mercure* (Paris,1937).
Binon, S., *Documents grecs inédits relatifs S. Mercure de Césarée* (Leuven, 1937a).
Böhlig, G. (ed.), *Kaminiates, De expugnatione Thessalonicae* (Berlin, 1973).
Bonner, C., *Studies in Magical Amulets, Chiefly Graeco-Egyptian* (Ann Arbor and Oxford, 1950).
Brooks, E.W., 'The Acts of St. George', *Le Muséon* 38 (1925), pp.67–115.
Brubaker, L., *Vision and Meaning in Ninth Century Byzantium* (Cambridge, 1999).
Brundage, J.A., 'Adhemar of Puy: The Bishop and his Critics', *Speculum* (1959), pp.201–12.
Budge, E.A.W., *The Martyrdom and Miracles of St George of Cappadocia* (London, 1888).
Budge, E.A.W., *George of Lydda, the Patron Saint of England. A Study of the Cultus of St George in Ethiopia* (London, 1930).
Bull, M., 'Robert the Monk and his sources', in Bull, M. & Kempf, D. (eds), *Writing the Early Crusades: Text, Transmission and Memory* (Woodbridge, 2014), pp.127–39.
Bull, M. & Kempf, D. (eds.), *The Historia Iherosolimitana of Robert the Monk* (Woodbridge, 2013).

Cameron, A., 'The Theotokos in Sixth-Century Byzantium: A City Finds its Symbol', *Journal of Theological Studies* 29.1 (1978), pp.79–108.
Cavarnos, J.P. (ed.), *Gregory of Nyssa, Sermons*, vol. 2.1 (Leiden and New York, 1990).
Chibnall, M. (ed. & trans.), *The Ecclesiastical History of Orderic Vitalis*, 6 volumes (Oxford, 1969–80).
Clarke, D., 'Rumours of Angels: A Legend of the First World War', *Folklore* 113.2 (2002), pp.151–73.
Clarke, D., *The Angels of Mons* (Chichester, 2004).
Cormack, R., 'The Mosaic Decoration of St Demetrios, Thessalonica: A Re-examination in Light of the Drawings of W.S. George', *Annual of the British School at Athens* 64 (1969), pp.17–52.
Cormack, R., *The Church of Saint Demetrios: The Watercolours and Drawings of W.S. George* (Thessaloniki, 1985).
Cormack, R., 'The Making of a Patron Saint: The Powers of Art and Ritual in Byzantine Thessaloniki', in I. Lavin (ed.), *World Art: Themes of Unity in Diversity*, Volume 3 (Philadelphia, 1989), pp.547–54.
Crisafulli, V.S., Nesbitt, J.W. & Haldon, J. (trans.), *The Miracles of Saint Artemios: A Collection of Miracle Stories by an Anonymous Author of Seventh-Century Byzantium* (Leiden, 1996).
Crostini, B., 'The Emperor Basil II's Cultural Life', *Byz* 66 (1996), pp.55–80.
Cutler, A., 'The Psalter of Basil II', *Arte Veneta* 30 (1976–77), pp.9–19, 31; pp.9–15.
Cumont, F., 'La plus ancienne légende de saint Georges', *Revue d'histoire des religions* 114 (1936), pp.5–51.
Dagron, G., *Vie et miracles de Sainte Thècle. Texte grec, traduction, et commentaire* (Brussels, 1978).
Darracott, J. & Loftus, B., *First World War Posters*, 2nd edn (London, 1981).
Davis, S.J., 'Pilgrimage and the Cult of Saint Thecla in Late Antique Egypt', in Frankfurter, D. (ed.), *Pilgrimage and Holy Space in Late Antique Egypt* (Leiden, 1998), pp.302–39.
Dawes, E. & Baynes, N.H., *Three Byzantine Saints* (London, 1948).
de Voragine, J., *The Golden Legend: Readings on the Saints*, Volume 1, trans. Ryan, W.G., with introduction by Duffy, E. (Princeton, 2012).
Delehaye, H., 'Castor et Pollux dans les legends hagiographique', *AB* 23 (1904), pp.427–32.
Delehaye, H., *Les légendes grecques des saint militaires* (Paris, 1909).
Delehaye, H., 'Les actes de S. Barbarus', *AB* 29 (1910), pp.276–301.
Delehaye, H., 'L'invention des reliques de S. Ménas à Constantinople', *AB* 29 (1910a), pp.117–50.
Delehaye, H., *Les origins du culte des martyrs*, 2nd edn (Brussels, 1933).
Delehaye, H., 'Euchaïta et la légende de Saint Théodore', in Delehaye, H. (ed.), *Mélanges d'Hagiographie Grecque et Latine* (Brussels, 1966), pp.275–80.
Devos, P., 'Un récit des miracles de S. Ménas en copte et éthiopien', *AB* 72 (1959–60), pp.451–63, 78; pp.154–60.
Didi-Huberman, G., Gabretta, R. & Morgaine, M., *Saint Georges et le dragon* (Paris, 1994).
Dillon, M.P.J., 'Evocatio: Taking Gods Away from Enemy States and Peoples', in Dillon, M. & Matthew, C. (eds), *Religion and Classical Warfare: The Roman Republic* (Barnsley, 2020), pp.53–103.
Dinsmoor, W.B., 'The Repair of the Athena Parthenos: A Story of Five Dowels', *AJA* 38.1 (1934), pp.93–106.
Duffy, J.M. & Bourbouhakis, E., 'Five Miracles of St. Menas', in Nesbitt, J.W. (ed.), *Byzantine Authors: Literary Activities and Preoccupations* (Leiden and Boston, 2003), pp.65–81.
Efthymiadis, S. & Déroche, V., 'Greek Hagiography in Late Antiquity (Fourth–Seventh Centuries)', in Efthymiadis, S. (ed.), *Ashgate Research Companion to Byzantine Hagiography: Volume 1* (Farnham, 2011).
Erdmann, C., *The Origin of the Idea of Crusade* (Princeton NJ, 1977).
Evetts, B. (ed. & trans.), 'History of the Patriarchs of the Coptic Church of Alexandria', *Patrologia Orientalis* 1.2 (1907), pp.101–214.
Faraone, C., *The Transformation of Greek Amulets in Roman Imperial Times* (Philadelphia, 2018).
Farina, W., *Saint James the Greater in History, Art and Culture* (Jefferson NC, 2018).

Festugière, A.-J., *Vie de Théodore de Sykeon (BHG 1748)* (Brussels, 1970).
Festugière, A.-J., *Collections grecques de miracles: Sainte Thècle, Saints Côme et Damien, Saints Cyr et Jean (extraits), Saint Georges – traduits et annotés* (Paris, 1971).
Florakis, A.E., *The Panayia of Tinos during the War of 1940* (Tinos, 1940).
Flori, J., 'Chevalerie et liturgie', *Le Moyen Age* 84 (1978), pp.274–78, 411–42.
Fowden, E.K., *The Barbarian Plain. St Sergius between Rome and Iran* (Berkeley and Los Angeles, 1999).
Frend, W.H.C., *Martyrdom and Persecution in the Early Church* (Oxford, 1965).
Frendo, J., 'The Miracles of St Demetrius and the Capture of Thessaloniki', *BS* 58 (1997), pp.205–24.
García, J.D., 'Santiago mataindios: la continuación de un discurso medieval en la Nueva España', *Nueva Revista de Filología Hispánica* 54.1 (2006), pp.33–56.
Garland, L., 'Infant Mortality, Michael Psellos, and the Byzantine Demon Gillo', in Beaumont, L., Dillon, M. & Harrington, N. (eds), *Children in Antiquity* (London and New York, 2021).
Garrison, F.H., *An Introduction to the History of Medicine*, 4th edn (Philadelphia, 1929).
Garsoïan, N.G., *The Epic Histories attributed to Pawstos Buzand* (Cambridge MA, 1989).
Geiger, J., *The Third Man Factor* (Harmondsworth, 2009).
Geyer, P. (ed.), *Itinera Hierosolymitana* (Vienna, 1898).
Girgis, S.F., *Saint Maurice, the Commander of the Theban Legion* (Bülach, 1993).
Grabar, A., *Maryrium. Recherches sur le culte des reliques et l'art antique*, 2 vols (Paris, 1946).
Grabar, A., 'Quelques reliquaires de saint Démétrios et de martyrium du saint à Salonique', *DOP* 5 (1950), pp.3–28.
Grabar, A., 'Un nouveau reliquaire de saint Démétrios', *DOP* 8 (1954), pp.307–13.
Graf, F., 'Trick or Treat? On Collective Epiphanies in Antiquity', in Shanzer, D. (ed.), *Divine Epiphanies in the Ancient World* (Urbana-Champaign, 2004), pp.111–30.
Greatrex, G. & Lieu, S.N.C. (eds), *The Roman Eastern Frontier and the Persian Wars, A Narrative History* (London and New York, 2002).
Grégoire, H., 'St Théodore le Stratilate et les Russes d'Igor', *Byz* 13 (1938), pp.291–300.
Grossman, P., 'The Pilgrimage Center of Abû Mînâ', in Frankfurter, D. (ed.), *Pilgrimage and Holy Space in Late Antique Egypt* (Leiden, 1998), pp.281–302.
Grotowski, P., 'The Legend of St George Saving a Youth from Captivity and its Depiction in Art', *Series Byzantina* 1 (2003), pp.27–77.
Grotowski, P., *Arms and Armour of the Warrior Saints: Tradition and Innovation in Byzantine Iconography (843–1261)* (Leiden, 2010).
Guillaume, A. (trans.), *Ibn Ishaq, the Life of Muhammed* (Oxford, 1967).
Hagenmayer, H., *De Kreuzzugsbriefe aus den Jahren 1088–1100* (Innsbruck, 1901).
Haldon, J. (trans.), *A Tale of Two Saints: the Martyrdoms and Miracles of Saints Theodore 'the Recruit' and 'the General'* (Liverpool, 2016).
Halkin, Fr., 'Un opuscule inconnu du Magister Ouranos (La vie de Théodore le conscript, *BHG* 1762m)', *AB* 80 (1962), pp.308–24.
Halkin, F., L'épilogue d'Eusèbe de Sebastie à la Passion de S. Eustrate et de ses compagnons, *AB* 88 (1970), pp.279–83.
Halkin F., 'L'éloge de saint Théodore le Stratélate par Euthyme Protasecretis', *AB* 99 (1981), pp.221–37.
Harris, W.V., *Dreams and Experience in Classical Antiquity*, (Cambridge MA and London, 2009).
Hengstenberg, W., 'Der Drachenkampf des heiligen Theodor', *Oriens Christianus* 2 (1912), pp.78–106, 241–80.
Herman, G., 'Greek Epiphanies and the Sensed Presence', *Historia* 60.2 (2011), pp.127–57.
Hill, J.H. & Hill, L.L. (eds), *Le 'liber' de Raymond d'Aguilers* (Paris, 1969).
Hill, J.H. & Hill, L.L. (eds), *Petrus Tudebodus, Historia de Hierosolymitano itinere* (Paris, 1977).
Hill, R. (ed.), *Gesta Francorum et aliorum Hierosolymitanorum* (London, 1962).
Hirshberg, J., *The Ophthalmology of Aëtius of Amida*, trans. Waugh, R.L. Jr (Oostende, 2000).
Howell, D., 'St George as Intercessor', *Byz* 39 (1969), pp.121–36.

Huygens, R.B.C. (ed.), *Guibert of Nogent, Dei gesta per Francos* (Turnhout, 1996).
James, L., *Mosaics in the Medieval World from Late Antiquity to the Fifteenth Century* (Cambridge, 2017).
Janin, R., 'Les églises byzantines des saints militaires', *EO* 33 (1934), pp.331–39.
Janin, R., *La géographie ecclésiatique de l'Empire byzantin, Volume 3: Les églises et les monastères*, 2nd edn (Paris, 1969).
Johnson, S.F., 'Miracles of St Thekla', in Talbot, A.-M. & Johnson, S.F. (eds), *Miracle Tales from Byzantium* (Cambridge MA, 2012), pp.3–201, 415–29.
Jordanov, I., *Pecatite ot strategijata v Preslav* (Sofia, 1995).
Joslyn-Siemiatkoski, D., *Christian Memories of the Maccabean Martyrs* (New York, 2009).
Klein, H.A., 'Sacred Relics and Imperial Ceremony at the Great Palace of Constantinople', *Byzas* 5 (2006), pp.79–99.
Krumbacher, K. (ed.), *Der heilige Georg, in der griechischen Überlieferung* (Munich, 1911).
Kuehn, S., *The Dragon in Medieval East Christian and Islamic Art* (Leiden, 2011).
Kurtz, E. (ed.), *Zwei griechische Texte über die Hl. Theophano, die Gemahlin Leo VI* (St Petersburg, 1898).
Lapina, E., '"Nec signis nec testis creditor…": The Problem of Eyewitnesses in the Chronicles of the First Crusade', *Viator* 38 (2007), pp.117–39.
Lapina, E., 'Demetrius of Thessaloniki: Patron Saint of Crusaders', *Viator* 40.2 (2009), pp.93–112.
Lapina, E., 'Maccabees and the Battle of Antioch (1098)', in Signori, G. (ed.), *Dying for the Faith, Killing for the Faith: Old-Testament Faith-Warriors (1 and 2 Maccabees) in Historical Perspective* (Leiden, 2012), pp.147–59.
Lapina, E., *Warfare and the Miraculous in the Chronicles of the First Crusade* (Philadelphia, 2015).
Leclerq, H., 'Gélasien (Décret)', *Dictionnaire d'archéologie chrétienne et de liturgie* 6 (1924), pp.745–73.
Leemans, J., 'Gregory of Nyssa: A Homily on Theodore the Recruit', in Leemans, J., Mayer, W., Allen, P. & Dehandschutter, B. (eds), *Let Us Die That We May Live: Greek Homilies on Christian Martyrs from Asia Minor, Palestine and Syria (c. AD 350–AD 450)* (London and New York, pp.82–91).
Lemerle, P. (ed. & trans.), *Les plus anciens recueils des miracles de Saint Démétrius*, 2 volumes (Paris, 1979/81).
Lundgreen, B., 'A Methodological Enquiry: The Great Bronze Athena by Pheidias', *JHS* 117 (1997), pp.190–97.
MacGregor, J.B., 'The Ministry of Gerold d'Avranches: Warrior-Saints and Knightly Piety on the Eve of the First Crusade', *JMH* 29 (2003), pp.219–37.
MacGregor, J.B., 'Negotiating Knightly Piety: The Cult of the Warrior-Saints in the West, ca. 1070–ca.1200', *American Society of Church History* 73.2 (2004), pp.317–45.
Machen, A., *The Bowmen and Other Legends of the War* (London, 1915).
Mackridge, P. & Yannakakis, E., *Ourselves and Others. The Development of a Greek Macedonian Culture since 1912* (Oxford and New York, 1997).
Magdalino, P., 'Saint Demetrios and Leo VI', *BS* 51 (1990), pp.198–201.
Maguire, H., *The Icons of their Bodies. Saints and their Images in Byzantium* (Princeton, 1996).
Mango, C., 'On the History of the Templon and the Martyrion of St Artemios at Constantinople', *Zograf* 10 (1979), pp.40–43.
Mango, C. & Sevcenko, I., 'Three Inscriptions of the Reign of Anastasius I', *BZ* 65 (1972), pp.378–84.
Maraval, P. (ed & trans.), *Egérie, Journal de voyage* (Paris, 1982).
Mayer, W. (trans.), *John Chrysostom, The Cult of Saints: Select Homilies and Letters* (New York, 2006).
Meehan, D. (ed.), *Adamnan's De Locis Sanctis* (Dublin, 1983).
Morris, C., 'The *Gesta Francorum* as Narrative History', *Reading Medieval Studies* 19 (1993), pp.55–71.

Morrisson, C., 'The Emperor, the Saint, and the City: Coinage and Money in Thessalonike from the Thirteenth to the Fifteenth Century', *DOP* 57 (2003), pp.173–203.
Morton, N., 'The Defence of the Holy Land and the Memory of the Maccabees', *JMH* 36.3 (2012), pp.275–93.
Mynors, R.A.B., Thomson, R.M. & Winterbottom, M. (ed. & trans.), *William of Malmesbury, Gesta Regum Anglorum*, 2 vols (Oxford, 1998/99).
Nelson, R.S., '"And So, With the Help of God": The Byzantine Art of War in the Tenth Century', *DOP* 65/66 (2011–12), pp.169–92.
Noret, J., 'Deux avatars du panégyrique de S. Georges par Arcadius de Chypre', *AB* 92 (1974), pp.165–70.
Obolensky, D., 'The Cult of St Demetrius in the History of Byzantine-Slav Relations', *Balkan Studies* 15 (1974), pp.3–22.
Oikonomides, N., 'Le dédoublement de S. Théodore et les villes d'Euchaïta et d'Euchaneia', *AB* 104 (1986), pp.327–35.
O'Reilly, D.F., 'The Theban Legion of St. Maurice', *Vigiliae Christianae* 3 (1978), pp.195–207.
O'Sullivan, L., 'Epiphanies in Classical and Hellenistic Warfare', in Dillon, M., Matthew, C. & Schmitz, M. (eds), *Religion and Classical Warfare: Ancient Greece* (Barnsley, 2020), pp.243–86.
Papadopoulos-Kerameus, A. (ed.), *Varia graeca sacra* (St Petersburg, 1909).
Peeters, P., 'Un miracle de SS Serge et Théodore dans Faustus de Byzance', *AB* 39 (1921), pp.70–73.
Pentcheva, B.V., *Icons and Power: The Mother of God in Byzantium* (Philadelphia, 2006).
Pontieri, E. (ed.), *Gioffredo Malaterra, De rebus gestis Rogerii Calabriae et Siciliae comitis et Roberti Guisgardi ducis fratris eius* (Bologna, 1928).
Pritchett, W.K., *The Greek State at War*, Volume 3 (Berkeley LA and London, 1979).
Riches, S., *St George: Hero, Martyr, and Myth* (Stroud, 2000).
Riley-Smith, J., 'The First Crusade and Saint Peter', in Kedar, B.Z., Mayer, H.E. & Smail, R.C. (eds), *Outremer: Studies in the History of the Crusading Kingdom of Jerusalem* (Jerusalem, 1982), pp.41–63.
Roach, D., 'Orderic Vitalis and the First Crusade', *JMH* 42.2 (2016), pp.177–201.
Robinson, J.H., *Readings in European History* (Boston, 1905).
Rosenqvist, J.O., *The Hagiographic Dossier of St Eugenios of Trebizond in Codex Athous Dionysiou 154: A Critical Edition with Introduction, Translation, Commentary, and Indexes* (Uppsala, 1996).
Rosman, E., 'Towards a Typology of Battlefield Miracles: The Case of Operation "Cast Lead" in the Israel Defence Forces', *Religions* 9 (2018), p.311.
Roussel, P., 'Un miracle de Zeus Panamaros', *BCH* 55 (1931), pp.70–116.
Russell, E., *Demetrius, the Military Saint of Byzantium: Cult and Worship in the Middle Ages* (London, 2010).
Sahas, D., 'What an Infidel Saw That a Faithful Did Not: Gregory Dekapolites (d. 842) and Islam', *Greek Orthodox Theological Review* 31 (1986), pp.47–67.
Seraidari, K., 'Objects of Cult, Objects of Confrontation: Divine Interventions through Greek History', *History and Anthropology* 20.3 (2009), pp.289–307.
Sevcenko, I., 'The Illuminators of the Menologium of Basil II', *DOP* 16 (1962), pp.243–76.
Sevcenko, N.P., 'The Posthumous Miracles of St Eustratios on a Sinai Templon Beam', in Sullivan, D., Fisher, E. & Papaioannou, S. (eds), *Byzantine Religious Culture. Studies in Honor of Alice-Mary Talbot* (Washington DC, 2012).
Shermer, M., 'The Sensed-Presence Effect', *Scientific American* 302.4 (2010), p.18.
Sigalas, A. (ed.), *Des Chrysippos von Jerusalem Enkomion auf den hl. Theodoros Teron* (Leipzig, 1921).
Skedros, J.C., *Saint Demetrios of Thessaloniki: Civic Patron and Divine Protector 4th-7th Centuries CE* (Harrisburg, 1999).
Stephenson, P., 2003, *The Legend of Basil the Bulgar-Slayer*, Cambridge.
Suedfeld, P. & Geiger, J., 'The Sensed Presence as a Coping Resource in Extreme Environments', in Ellens, J.H. (ed.), *Miracles: God, Science, and Psychology in the Paranormal*, Volume 3 (Westport CT, 2008), pp.1–15.

Sullivan, D.F., Talbot, A.-M. & McGrath, S., (ed. & trans.), *The Life of Saint Basil the Younger* (Washington DC, 2014).
Taylor, A.J.P., *The First World War* (Harmondsworth, 1966).
Thorp, N.R., *La Chanson de Jerusalem* (Tuscaloosa, 1992).
Trapp, E., 'Hagiographische elemente im Digenes-Epos', *AB* 94 (1976), pp.279–86.
Treu, M. (ed.), *Miracula utriusque S Theodori a Theodoro Pediasimo (BHG 1773)* (Potsdam, 1899).
Vickery, M., 'Sirmium or Thessaloniki? A Critical Examination of the St Demetrius Legend', *BZ* 67 (1974), pp.337–50.
Vinson, M.,'Gregory Nazianzen's Homily 15 and the Genesis of the Christian Cult of the Maccabaean Martyrs', *Byz* 94 (1994), pp.166–92.
Walter, C., 'St Demetrius: The Myroblytos of Thessalonika', *Eastern Churches Review* 5 (1973), pp.157–78.
Walter, C., *Art and Ritual of the Byzantine Church* (London, 1982).
Walter, C., 'The Intaglio of Solomon in the Benaki Museum and the Origins of the Iconography of Warrior Saints', *Deltion tes Christianikes Archaiologikes Hetaireias* 15 (1989–90), pp.35–42.
Walter, C., 'The Origins of the Cult of St George', *REB* 53 (1993), pp.295–326.
Walter, C., 'Theodore, Archetype of the Warrior Saint', *REB* 57 (1999), pp.163–210.
Walter, C., *The Warrior Saints in Byzantine Art and Tradition* (Aldershot, 2003).
Weitzmann, K., 'Illustrations to the Lives of the Five Martyrs of Sebaste', *DOP* 33 (1979), pp.95–112.
Westerink, L.G. (ed. & trans.), *Nicholas I Patriarch of Constantinople, Miscellaneous Writings* (Washington DC, 1981).
Wheeler, G., 'Battlefield Epiphanies in Ancient Greece: A Survey', *Digressus* 4 (2004), pp.1–14.
White, M., 'A Byzantine Tradition Transformed: Military Saints under the House of Suzdal', *The Russian Review* 63.3 (2004), pp.493–513.
White, M., *Military Saints in Byzantium and Rus, 900–1200* (Cambridge, 2013).
Wilkinson, J., *Jerusalem Pilgrims before the Crusades* (Warminster, 1977).
Woodfin, W.T., 'An Officer and a Gentleman: Transformations in the Iconography of a Warrior Saint', *DOP* 60 (2006), pp.111–43.
Woods, D., 'The Origin of the Legend of Maurice and the Theban Legion', *Journal of Ecclesiastical History* 45 (1994), pp.385–95.
Woods, D., 'The Emperor Julian and the Passion of Sergius and Bacchus', *Journal of Early Christian Studies* 5 (1997), pp.335–67.
Woods, D. (trans.), 'The Passion (*BHL* 2122) and Miracles (*BHL* 2123) of Anastasius the Librarian' (1999), at https://www.ucc.ie/archive/milmart/BHL2122.html.
Zacos, G. & Verglery, A., *Byzantine Lead Seals*, Volume 1.2 (Basle, 1972).
Zuckerman, C., 'Cappadocian Fathers and the Goths: Gregory of Nyssa's *Enkomion* for St Theodore the Recruit and the Gothic Riots in Asia Minor in 379', *Travaux et Mémoires* 11 (1991), pp.479–86.

Index

Achilles, 7, 190–1, 193, 195, 295, 330; dresses Patroclus' wound, 136, fig. 5.5; woundwort, 150 n.80; *see also* dressings; medicine, military; medics
Adamklissi, 78, 82–3, 159, fig. 3.15
Adhémar of Le Puy, 317, 320, 323, 328
Aemilius Lepidus, M., 29
Aeneas, 102–104, 130, 132, 141, 193, 196, fig. 5.3
Aesculapius, *see* Asclepius
Agrippina the Elder, 130
Alexander III, the Great, of Macedon (336–323 BC), 5, 7, 96–8, 100–102, 104, 106, 112, 115, 117 n.83, 160, 190, 193, 195, 203, 208, 212 nn.43, 57; Alexander sarcophagus, 96–7, 118 n.126, fig. 4.2
Alexios I Komnenos (1081–1118), 315–16, 325, 326
Altars, *see Ara Maxima*; *Ara Pacis Augustae*; Victory, Altar of
Ammianus Marcellinus, 36, 67, 131, 137, 149, 269–70, 301
amulets, 6, 145–7, 155 n.237
Anastasius I (491–518), 265, fig. 9.7
angels, 296–7, 312, 324; announce birth of Christ, 205, 296; avenging, 298, 306, 336 n.89; in battle, 294, 312, 328–9, 333; Constantine, 257; crusaders, 318, 324, 328; and *Digenis Akritas*, 294; epiphanies of, 296, 310, 324, 328–9, 339 n.208; fall of Jerusalem, 60–1; heavenly host and, 296–7; Licinius, 258; the Maccabees, 296, 318; messengers, 308, 310, 313; of Mons, 9, 332–3; Muhammed, 320; Victory, 282 n.160; figs 10.2–3; *see also* St Michael
'angels of Mons', 9, 332–3; *see also* angels; St. George; warrior saints
Antioch, sieges of, 316, 320–3, 326
Antiochos IV Epiphanes (175–164 BC), 296
Antoninus Pius (T. Aelius Hadrianus Antoninus Augustus Pius, 138–161), 2, 47, 54, 91 n.213; and Hercules, 108–109, 116 n.48, 120 n.175
Antony, Mark (M. Antonius), 13, 30, 40 n.95, 60, 62, 67, 102, 103, 117, 192, 193, 196, 213 n.75; descended from Hercules, 102–103; Dionysos-Osiris, 193; *sidus Iulium*, 193; *see also* Cleopatra
Apollo, 102, 105, 112, 118 n.104, 141, 193, 211 n.38, 295; Actium, 80; Apollo Autun, 280 n.100; Apollo Cunomaglus, 127, 154 n.210; Apollo Grannus, 145, fig. 5.8; Apollo Sosianus, 103; Constantine, 259, 280 n.100; healer, 132, 140, 142–3; Hercules, 103–104; hot springs, 144–5; war spoils in temple, 64
Appian, on military indiscipline, 28, 34; military oath, 39 n.81, 40 n.94
aquila, *see* eagle standard
aquilifer, 52–3, 85 n.38, 177; funerary monument, 170–1, fig. 6.8; *see* Bridgeness Slab; *imaginifer*; *vexillarius*

Ara Maxima, 99–101, 107, 115 n.38, 116 n.55, 119 n.142
Ara Pacis Augustae, 2, 65
Arcadius (395–408), 266, 273, 282 n.170
arches, triumphal, *see* triumph
Arianism, 260, 268, 271–3
Armilustrium (army purification), 46; *see also lustratio*
Artemis, 298; Artemis Azzanathkona, 44
Asclepius 'Zimidrenus', 143
Asclepius, Aesculapius, 127, 132, 141–4, 153, 155; Augustan Aesculapius, 143, 153 n.197; incubation, 6, 127, 141–3, 147; and Hygieia dedication, 142, fig 5.7; temples, 127, 142, 144
Astarte-Uni, 115 n.38
Athena, 116 n.42, 191, 295; defends Athens in AD 395, 295; Menrfa (Athena), 98; Minerva/Athena, 98
atomic theory, 146
Attila, 302
Augustine, *see* St Augustine
Augustus (including Octavian), 1, 193, 196–7, 201; *Ara Pacis Augustae*, 2, 65; army medical corps, 137–8; army oath and, 30–1; Augustalia, 46; birthday, 47, 217 n.153; civil war, 30, 193; the corona civica, 76; dedications to, 84; fetials, 61–2, 87 n.93; *Gemma Augustea*, 75–7, fig. 3.10; Hercules, 102–104; Herod, 209; Julius Caesar, 47, 65, 192–6, 214 n.90; Mars Ultor, 4, 10, 43, 61, 64–6, 77, fig. 1.1; Nero imitates, 196–7, 209, 215 n.114; Parthian standards, 65, 192, 262; pax Romana, 15; portents, 54, 57; becomes princeps, 1, 47, 192–3; revival of rites, 61–2; *Res Gestae*, 62, 64, 67; *sidus Iulium*, 192–6, 201, 205, 207–209, 213 n.75, 214 nn.90–91; *spolia opima*, 63–4; statue of Victory, 13, 17 n.34; temple of Janus, 61, 67; his troops, 29–31, 137; *tropaea* of, 61, 80–82, fig. 3.14; victory at Actium, 12–13, 67, 80–1, 193; vows to the gods, 12, 57, 64, 68; vows for his welfare, 45; figs 1.1, 3.10, 3.14
Augustus (as god), 83; on *Gemma Augustea*, 76, fig. 3.10; Augustan Aesculapius, 143; Augustan Heaven, 143, 153 n.197; Augustan Mercury, 140; Augustan Hygieia, 153 n.197; Augustan Mars, 140; venerated at Dura-Europos, 47

Baal, 143
Bacchus, 111
bandages, *see* dressings
Basil II 'the Bulgarslayer' (976–1025), Psalter of, 294, 311–12, fig. 10.3; Menologion of, 309, 311–12, fig. 10.1; and Theotokos icon, 303; and warrior saints, 311–12
Bedr, battle of, 320

Bellona 87, n.91, 90 n.195, 278 n.75; Ma-Bellona, 57; temple of, 62, 84
Bendis, 90 n.175
Bohemond, 321–2, 324, 326, 328
booty, dedicated to the gods, 1, 10, 13, 62, 64; *see also manubiae*
Boscoreale cup, 75, 89 n.172
Bridgeness Slab, 53–5, fig. 3.4
Britain, Britannia (place), 2–3, 11, 53, 131, 171–2; Campestres, 51; Claudius conquers, 78, 135, 138; Discipulina, 51–2; distance slabs, 53–4, fig. 3.4; Hercules, 1, 107, 110, fig. 4.5; Jupiter Dolichenus, 48, 50; Mithras, 228, 230
Britannia (goddess), 53

Caesar, *see* Julius Caesar
Caligula (C. Caesar Augustus Germanicus, 37–41), 33; Hercules, 104, 109; military cult, 47; military oath, 33
Camillus, *see* Furius Camillus
Campestres, the, 229; dedications to, 51; temple, 51, 54
Caracalla (198–217), 47, 179, 181; Hercules, 111, 120 n.182; Jupiter Dolichenus, 140
Carmelus, 60, 87 n.88
Castor, 49, 112, 160, 295–7; *see also* Dioscuri; Pollux
Catiline, 19, 53
Cato the Elder, 25, 55, 127–8, 145
Cato the Younger, 134
Cautopates, Cautes, 237, 240
cavalry, 6, 177; altar, 51; charges, 148 n.13; Christian, 253, 305; dedication by, 49; *decursio,* 91 n.213; elite, 261; Epona, 51; festival, 66; funerary monuments, 166–7, 172, 177–8, 180, fig. 6.4; Jupiter Dolichenus, 140; killing enemy, 54–5, fig. 3.4; medic, 129, 142; Mithras, 230, 232, 235; oath, 21; pay, 167, 172; prayers for health and safety, 140, 142–3, 305; restore temple, 51, 54; St George, 305, 320; Trajan's Column, 69; *tropaea,* 78; *vexillum,* 52, 86 n.47; wounded, 129, 131–2, fig. 5.1
Celsus, 128, 131–2, 134–5, 137–8, 140, 144, 148–9, 150, 152
cemeteries, 6, 161–4, 181; Christian, 277 n.33; finds from, 96; fig. 6.1
Charon, 164
chemical warfare, 134, 150
chi-rho symbol, 53, 256, 259, 261–4, 272; on armour and shields, 256, 265–7, figs 9.1–9; *see also* Christianity; Constantine; *labarum*
Christ, *see* Christianity
Christianity, 7–8, 10, 160–1; apocalypticism, 188–90, 199, 201–202, 205, 208, 211 n.39, 215 nn.117–18; Arian, 260, 268, 270–1, 273; army, 36, 71–3, 160–1, 250–6, 260–76; *chi-rho* symbol, 53, 256–9, 261–7, 272, figs 9.1–9; Christian rites in the Army, 258, 260, 265, 267–8, 272–3, 275–6; column of Marcus Aurelius and, 71–3; Constantine and, 250, 253, 255–60, 261–69, 271, 272–6, fig. 9.1; conversion of soldiers to, 254, 262, 268–73, 275; early, 186–89, 198–99, 203–204, 209–10; fire of AD 64, 186–90, 196–202, 207, 209; Gospels and, 204–209; Herculean symbolism, 113; Jesus of Nazareth, 186–9, 199, 202–207, 209, 216 n.126; Julian, 269–71; military oath, 35–7, 252, 254, 267, 269, 272, 276; Messiah and, 187, 198–200, 208, 210; 'Milvian Bridge', 255–9; Mithraism, 160–1, 240–3, 255; opposition to military service, 251–4, 262, 274; pacifism 251, 274, 276 nn.2, 4; pagan symbolism, 241; persecution, 54, 199, 202–203, 253–5, 258, 290–93, fig. 10.1; presence in the Roman Army before Constantine, 250, 252–8, 271, 277 n.33; 'rain miracle', 71–73, 252; *sidus Iulium,* 202, 204–205, 207–210; standards and, 53, 250, 257–8, 261–4, 269, 270, 272, figs 9.2–7; Trinity, 8; triumph of, 13, 242–43, 258, 272; goddess Victory and, 43, 264, fig. 9.7; *see also chi-rho* symbol; crusades; Holy Lance; *labarum*; martyrdom; Tertullian; warrior saints
Christogram, *see chi-rho* symbol
Cinna, 29
Cirta, 161, 163
Claudius (Ti. Claudius Caesar Augustus Germanicus, 41–54), 33, 47, 88 n.120, 214 n.106; coinage, 78; expels Jews, 198; invades Britain, 78, 135, 138; military arch, 78
Claudius II (M. Aurelius Claudius Gothicus, 268–270), 259
Cleopatra (51–30 BC), 13, 30, 61–2, 67, 102, 193; *see also* Antony
Clovis, 275
cohors, cohort, 52; Cohors XX Palmyrenorum, 45, 47, other named cohorts, 230, 234, 239; *genius* of, 37; Mithras, 234
Commodus (L. Aelius Aurelius Commodus, 180–192), 108–12, 120
Constantine I, the Great (Flavius Valerius Constantinus, 306–337), 7–8, 11, 35, 113, 250, 253, 255, 258, 275–6, 290, 292, 297, 306; coinage, 256, 258–9, 262–3; conversion, 257–60, 275, 279 n.97; dragons, 297; letters, 258, 262; military reforms, 260–1, 267–8, 275; as patron of the church, 259–60; triumphal arch, 71, 108; visions, 11, 256–7, 259–61, 268, 272; fig. 9.1
Constantine VII Porphyrogennetos (945–959), 293–4, 303–304
Constantius I (Constantius Chlorus, 305–306), 113, 258, 297
Constantius II (Flavius Iulius Constantius, 337–361), 13, 36, 67, 259, 263–4, 266, 268–70, figs 9.4, 9.8
conversion of soldiers, 254, 262, 268–73, 275
Cornelius Scipio Aemilianus, P., 99
Cornelius Scipio Africanus, P., 23, 160
crusaders, crusades, 8–9, 316–25; at Antioch, 320–6, 328; St Demetrios, 312, 316–24, 327; First, 316–25, 329; Fourth, 316; St George, 307, 317–24, 326–28; at Jerusalem, 327–8; St Merkourios, 320–3, 327; *see also* Christianity; Holy Lance; warrior saints
cupping, medical, 134
Curio, *see* Scribonius Curio
Cybele, 160
Cyrus, 195, 208

Dacia (goddess), 70
Dacia (place), Dacians, 68, 80, 84, 107, 130, 140, 142–4, 154 n.204, 159, 162, 180; Danuvius (Danube) attacks,

69; embassy, 46, 52, fig. 3.2; genius, 143, 153 n.197; Hercules, 107; Jupiter Tonans smites, 43–4, 68, fig. 3.1; poisoned arrows, 134; *tropaea*, 78, 79, fig. 3.13; Tropaeum Traiani, 82; *see also* Trajan, column of

Danuvius (Danube, river god), supports Roman army, 68–70, fig. 3.6

Decius, 290, 298

decursio, 83, 91 n.213

Diana, on *Gemma Augustea*, 76–7, fig. 3.10; Diana Regina, 140; healer 140, 143–4

diet, 128, 135, 141–2, 147

Digenis Akritas, 294, 309, 337 n.106

Diocletian (C. Aurelius Valerius Diocletianus, 284–305), 8, 54, 112, 261; Mithras, 241; persecutes Christians, 36, 161, 253–5, 258, 290, 292, 304, 306

Diogenes the Cynic, 203–204

Dionysius of Halicarnassus, 23, 27

Dionysus, 96, 102, 104, 111, 144; Antony as Dionysos-Osiris, 193

Dioscorides of Anazarbus, 134, 138, 149, 150

Dioscuri, 24, 49, 160, 295–6, fig. 2.1; *see also* Castor; Pollux

discipline, military, 19–20, 22, 26, 28–30, 34, 51, 138, 148 n.14, 160, 254, 271; *see also Disciplina*, cult of

Disciplina, Discipline, cult of, 51–2, 81, 85 n.22, 229

dislocated limbs, 144, 146; *see also* medical instruments; surgery

divination, *see* dreams; omens; visions

doctors, *see* medicine, military; medics

dogs, 202–203, 212 n.43, 217 n.159, 294; as healers, 144; rabid, 149 n.71, 202

Dolichenus, *see* Jupiter Dolichenus

Domitian (81–96), 180; and Adamklissi, 82, 159; dream, 90 n.176; as Hercules, 105–106, 109, fig. 4.4; Minerva, 90 n.176, 105; river god, 89 n.143; statue, 106, fig. 4.4; *tropaea*, 77, 82, 99 n.208, fig. 3.11; Vestal Virgins, 12

Dragons, on army banners, 261–2; Cleopatra as, 193; on Constantine's coinage, 297; *Digenis Akritas*, 309; St George, 8, 306–308, 327, 336 n.95; Nero, 189, 211 n.39; painting of, 260, 297; Pompey as, 211 n.39; Satan as, 297, 302; St Theodore Teron, 8, 306, 308–309, fig. 10.6; Typhon, 192; warrior saints, 293; World War I, 307, fig. 10.9

dreams, of Caesar, 101; Constantine, 256–7; Domitian, 90 n.76; Galba, 58; Germanicus, 56–7; healing, 141–5; Judas Maccabaeus, 296; Julian's assassins, 297; Nero, 60; Otho, 58; Philip II, 212 n.43; pre-battle, 56–8; prognostication, and interpretation, 141–2, 145; saints intervene through, 8, 297–301

dressings, ointments, and plasters, 129–30, 134–8, 147, fig. 5.5; *see also* Achilles; hospitals; medicine, military; medics

Drusus (Drusus Julius Caesar, son of Tiberius), honoured with *decursio* and marble arch, 83

Drusus (Nero Claudius Drusus, younger brother of Tiberius), defeats Marcomanni, 82; *spolia opima*, 64; triumphal arch with *tropaeum*, 78, fig. 3.12

Dura-Europos, 32, 165, 229, 235–7, 239; shrine of Jupiter Dolichenus, 50; military calendar of 44–7; *see also* Mithraea

eagle (bird), 48, 97; Jupiter Dolichenus, 49; omen sent by Jupiter, 4, 57–9, 61, cf. 265; on *Gemma Augustea*, 76, fig. 3.10; of Germany, 307

eagle standard (*aquila*), 4, 43–4, 46, 54, 65, 69, 71, 82, 84, 250, 270, figs 3.2, 3.6; cult of, 45, 51–4, 170, 262; as chief *signum*, 52; criticised by Tertullian, 53; description, 52; as divine statues, 52; gold, 52; as *numina*, 54; Varus loses three, 12; *see also aquilifer*

Eliot, T.S., 331

emperors, 1, 3, 9–10; Altar of Victory, and, 13–15; imperial women venerated by army, 67; military oath: *see sacramentum militiae*; *see also* individual emperors: Alexios I Komnenos; Anastasius I; Antoninus Pius; Arcadius; Augustus; Basil II 'the Bulgarslayer'; Caligula; Caracalla; Claudius; Claudius II; Commodus; Constantine; Constantius I; Constantius II; Constantine VII Porphyrogennetos; Decius; Diocletian, Domitian; Eugenius; Galba; Galerius; Geta; Gordian III; Gratian; Hadrian; Heraclius; Honorius; John I Tzimiskes; Julian; Julius Caesar; Justinian I; Leo VI; Licinius; Lucius Verus; Magnentius; Manuel I Komnenos; Marcus Aurelius; Maurice; Maximian; Maximinus Daia; Maximinus Thrax; Nero; Nerva; Nikephoros II Phokas; Octavian; Otho; Pertinax; Phokas; Pupienus (Maximus); Septimius Severus; Severus Alexander; Theodore II Laskaris; Theodosius I; Theodosius II; Tiberius; Titus; Trajan; Valens; Valentinian I; Valentinian II; Valentinian III; Valerian; Vespasian; Vitellius; *see also* Drusus; Germanicus

epiphanies in the Classical world, 295–98; in the Bible, 296–97; of Theodosios I, 302; *see also* miracles, battlefield; omens; visions; warrior saints, interventions of

Epona, 51, 140, 152 n.163

Eugenius (392–394), 15, 275

Eusebius of Caesarea, 254–61, 265, 267, 273, 291, 297

evocatio, 12, 316

eyes, diseases of, 129, 138–9, 142, 144, 148

feriale Duranum, *see* Dura-Europos, military calendar of

Fides, 112; temple of 78

Fimbria, *see* Flavius Fimbria

Flavius Fimbria, C., 29

Fontes Sequanae, 144–5

food poisoning, 139, 152

Fortuna, 190; Fortuna Redux, 143

Forum Boarium, 98–100, 103, 107–109, 115 n.38, 116 n.49, 118 n.108, 119 n.140; *see also Ara Maxima*

funerary monuments, of soldiers, 6–7, 165–9, 171, 173, figs 6.2-9; imagery, 168–73; inscriptions, 174–81; motifs in funerary inscriptions, 174, fig. 6.10; *see also* Adamklissi; cemeteries

funerary rites, 82, 161–65, 167; *see also* cemeteries, Manes

Furius Camillus, M., 195, 197

Furius Camillus Scribonianus, M., 33

Gades, 96, 99, 101, 103, 108, 115, 118–19

Galba (Ser. Sulpicius Galba, 68–69), military oath, 31–3; omens, 58, 87 n.79; Mars Ultor coinage, 66

Galen, 130, 134–5, 138, 140, 142, 145–6, 148
Galerius (C. Galerius Valerius Maximianus, 305–311), 54, 290
Gallienus (P. Licinius Egnatius Gallienus, 260–268), 111–12, 121
Gemma Augustea, *see* Augustus
genius, 143; of the army, 54, 86 n.56, 229, 235; of *centuria* (century), 229; cohorts, 37; Carthage, 143; cavalry, 51, 54; Dacia, 143; emperor, 43, 47, 54, 144, 150 n.101; escort troops, 235; imperial family, 47, 144, 150 n.101; legions, 54; military camps, 86 n.56; military oath, 37; Mogontiacum (Mainz), 140; *genius sacramenti*, 37; standards, 37
Germanicus (Germanicus Julius Caesar), 117 n.65; translation by, xii, battle omens, 56–7; buries war-dead, 91 n.212, 162; Gemma Augustea, 75; gods support, 83; Rhine, 69; tends wounded, 130, cf. 138; *tropaea*, 78, 82–3, cf. 80; venerated by army, 47, cf. 110
Geta (209–211), 111
ghosts, *see Manes*
gods, *see* Asclepius, Aesculapius; Aphrodite-Isis; Apollo; Artemis; Artemis Azzanathkona; Astarte-Uni; Athena; Augustus; Baal; Bacchus; Bellona; Bendis; Britannia; Campestres; Carmelus; Castor; Christ; Cybele; Dacia (goddess); Danuvius; Diana; Dionysus; Dioscuri; *Discipulina* / Discipline; Dolichenus, *see* Jupiter Dolichenus; Epona; Fides; Fortuna; *Genius*; Helios; Heliopolitanus; Hermes; Hermes Trismegistos; Hercules; Hygieia; Isis; Isis-Sothis; Janus; Jove, *see* Jupiter; Juno; Jupiter; Jupiter Dolichenus; Lares; Liber; Lucina; Luna (Lucifera); Ma-Bellona; Magna Mater; Magusanus; Manes; Mars; Augustan Mars; Mars Nodens; Mars Pater; Mars Ultor; Mars Victor; Master of Animals; Matres; Melqart; Menrfa; Mercury; Mercury Augustus; Minerva; Sulis Minerva; Mithras; Mother of God (Theotokos); Mother of the Gods; Muses; Neptune; Nikai; *numina*; Oceanus; Ogmios; Oikoumene; Palmyrene Gods; Penates; Pluto and Proserpina; Pollux; Quirinus; rain-miracle god; Rhine river-god; river gods; Roma; Salus; Saturn; Serapis; Seth; Shadrapa; Silvanus; Sol; Sol Invictus; Sulis Minerva; Tellus; Turmasgades; Tyche of Dura and Tyche of Palmyra; Venus; Vesta; Victory / Victoria; Virtus Augusta; Vulcan; Zeus; Zeus Helios Mithras; Zeus Panamaros; *see also* Cautopates, Cautes; Christianity
Gordian III (M. Antonius Gordianus, 238–244), 111, 145
gout, 144, 146
Gratian (367–383), 14, 17 n.41, 275

Hadrian (P. Aelius Traianus Hadrianus Augustus, 117–138), 7, 47, 50, 108–109, 119–20, 135, 137, 144, 148 n.13, 151, 230; *Discipulina*, 51; as Hercules, 108–109, fig. 4.7
Hadrian's Wall, 7, 135, 230, 231
Haidra (Ammaedara), 163, 166
Hannibal, 22, 53, 56, 100–101, 130, 162, 195
headache, 138, 144–5
healing spas, 144–5, 154 n.220

health, *see* Aesculapius/Asclepius; cupping; dislocated limbs; dressings; eyes, diseases of; food poisoning; gout; headache; healing spas; hospitals; humoral theory; Hygieia; medical instruments; medicine, military; medics; pharmaka; post-traumatic stress disorder; prosthetics; scurvy; surgery; temple healing (incubation); war-wounded
Heliopolitanus, as Jupiter, 141
Helios, 116 n.48, 191, 213 n.61, 241; Deus Helios Mithras, 236; Julian, 231; *see also* Sol; Sol Invictus
Heraclius (610–641), 275
Hercules, 5, 10, 11, 94–126, 204, 257; *Ara Maxima*, 99–100; Alexander in Hercules' lion skin cap, 97, fig. 4.2; bust of Commodus as, 110, fig. 4.8; coins of Trajan, 107, figs 4.5-4.6; of Hadrian, 109, fig. 4.7; of Postumus, 111, fig. 4.9, of Maximian, 113, fig. 4.10; dedication to, 51; healing god, 141, 143–4; Hercules Epitrapezios, 116 n.48; Hercules Magusanus, 100; identified with Phoenician gods, 111; Hercules Romanus, 109; statue of, 98, fig. 4.3; temples, 99, 107–108, 116 n.49; *see also* Invictus, Hercules
Hermes, 72; Hermes Trismegistos, 252, 277 n.21
Herodian, 34–5
Hippocratic corpus, 128, 141–2
Holy Lance, the, 320, 322–3
Honorius (395–423), 15, 282 n.158, 272
Horus, 188, 193
hospitals, 135, 137–9, 145, 147, 151; *valetudinarium* (legionary hospital), 138–9, fig. 5.6; *see also* dressings; medical instruments; medicine, military; medical training; medics; pharmaka; surgery; war-wounded
humoral theory, 142, 147
Hygieia, 140, 142–4, fig. 5.7; Hygieia Augusta, 153 n.197
Hyginus Gromaticus, 139, 151

imaginifer, 52, 85 n.38, 234
incantations, 127, 145–7
instruments, medical, *see* medical instruments
Invictus, Hercules, 99–103, 108–110, 112–13, 117 n.62, 119 n.145, 121 n.192; Scipio 99; Pompey 99, 101–102; Caesar 99, 101; Trajan 106; Commodus 120 n.175; *see also* Sol Invictus
Isis, 160; Cleopatra as Aphrodite-Isis, 193; the 'Isis' medical dressing, 136, 153; Isis-Sothis, 188, 200–201
ius iurandum, 4, 20–22
iustum bellum, 62, *see also* fetials

Janus, 55; Janus Quirinus, 62; temple doors closed, 61, 65, 66–8, 81, fig. 3.5; witnesses declaration of war, 62
Jerusalem, 186, 205, 306, 318, 327–28, 333; sack of, 12, 52, 60, 64, 67, 200; temple, 61, 64, 94, 189, 296
Jews, defeated, 200; expelled from Egypt, 186, 188; expelled from Rome, 198; loyal to Rome, 198, cf. 207; Messiah, 187, 198, 200, 208, 210; Persian Empire, 208
John I Tzimiskes (969–976), 9, 303, 307, 309–11
Josephus, 206–207; on the Roman eagle, 52; prediction of, 60
Joshua, 186–7

Jove, *see* Jupiter
Jove Optimus Maximus Dolichenus, 48–9; dedication to, fig. 3.3; *see also* Jupiter, Jupiter Optimus Maximus
Julian 'the Apostate' (Flavius Claudius Iulianus, 361–363), 8, 36, 269–71, 298; assassination of, 297–302, 333–4, fig. 10.4
Julius Caesar, C., 176; and Alexander the Great, 160; assassination of, 30, 65, 192; calendar, 193–4, 214 n.85; civil war, 29–30, 60; *corona civica*, 76; as divus Iulius, 47, 101, 192–5, 214 n.90; Hercules, 94, 99–101; honours voted to, 63, 76, 192; *ludi victoriae Caesaris*, 194; Octavian, 47, 65, 192–5, 214 n.90; Parthia, 192, 207; reforms of, 193–4; *sidus Iulium*, 192–6, 201, 205, 207, 213 n.75; statues of, 58, 60, 101, 194; temple, 64; treatment of wounded, 130–1, 137–8, 146; troops, 25, 28–30, 130–1, 137–8, 146; victories of, 94, 99, 101–102, 160
Juno, 47, 74, 159; Juno Mamaea Augusta, 47; Juno Regina, 48–9
Jupiter, 1, 10–12, 43, 48–9, 52–3, 55, 57–9, 61, 67, 76, 80, 83–4, 111–12, 120 n.175, 140–1, 144, 159–60, 189, 252, 257–8, 260, 270; Adamklissi, 83; Beneventum arch, 79; Capitoline, 73, 75; columns, 80; Domitian as son, 106; healing, 140, 142, 144; *ius fetiale*, 62; promises 'empire without end', 13, 16, cf. 103; *see also* eagle
Jupiter Custos, 74
Jupiter Dolichenus, 1, 7, 140, 143–4, 229; bronze dedication to, cover image, 49. fig.3.3; bronze plaques, 48–9; Doliche temple destroyed, 50–1; *Dolichenum*, 229; eagle, 49; eastern origin, 48; Jove Optimus Maximus Dolichenus, 48–9, fig. 3.3; soldiers' cult, 50; temples pillaged, 50
Jupiter Feretrius, receives *spolia opima*, 63-4; temple, 87 n.98
Jupiter Optimus Maximus, 4–5, 12, 43–5, 47, 74, 75, 140, 142; Augustus' vow to, 12; oath to, 23; temple, 74–5, fig. 3.9
Jupiter Tonans, 10, 43–4, 68, 71, fig. 3.1; Jupiter Valens, 140; Jupiter Victor, 45, 47
Justinian I (Flavius Petrus Sabbatius Iustinianus, 527–565) lawcode, 269; 'little Hagia Sophia', 301; Martyrs of Sebaste, 330; reconquests, 273, 275; San Vitale, 266, fig. 9.9

Khusrau I (531–579), 303

labarum, 11, 14–15, 257–8, 261–6, 269–70, 272, 276, figs 1.2, 9.2–4, 9.6–7; *see chi-rho* symbol, *signa*, *vexillum*
Lactantius, 54, 253, 256, 258, 261, 265, 267, 273
Lake Trasimene, 22, 130, 162
Lambèse, 163, 167, 176, fig. 6.1
Lares, military, 143, 255
legions, Legion I Adiutrix, 177, 180; Legion I Germania, 169; Legion II Augusta, 51, 53; Legion II Italica, 162; Legion II Parthica, 252; Legion II Traiana Fortis, 106; Legion III Augusta, 162, 167, 176–8, 181; Legion III Gallica, 180–1; Legion VI Victrix, 55; Legion VIII Augusta, 170; Legion XI (Claudia), 55; Legion XII Fulminata, 161, 252; Legion XIV Gemina, 150 n.102, 171; Legion XX Valeria Victrix, 171; Theban, 161; Thundering Legion, 72; remains of a legionary *valetudinarium*, 139, fig. 5.6; *see also* cohors, eagle, *signa*
Leo VI (886–912), 293, 314
Lepidus, *see also* Aemilius Lepidus 29
Liber, 101, 141; Liber Pater/Dionysus/Bacchus, 111
Licinius (Valerius Licinianus Licinius, 308–324), 255, 258, 260, 262, 267–8, 273, 292
linen legion (*legio linteata*), 21, 25–6
Livy, 52, 191; Cincinnatus, 148 n.12; on Hercules, 99; *ius fetiale*, 62; on omens, 56, 87 n.70; *sacramentum militiae*, 19–22, 25–6; *spolia opima*, 63; war-wounded, 151 nn.135–6, 152 n.141
Lucan, 130, 134
Lucina, 153 n.175
Lucius Verus (L. Aurelius Verus, 161–169), 47, 109, 110, 181, 235
Luna (Lucifera), 49, 57, 112
lustratio (purification of the army), 45, 52, 69, 75, 191; on Trajan's column, 69–70; Aurelius' column, 70–1

Ma-Bellona, 57
Maccabees, the, 296, 318
Machen, Arthur, 332–3
Magi, 204, 207–10
Magna Mater, 141
Magnentius (350–353), 41 n.141; adopts *chi-rho* symbol, 263–4, fig.9.5
Magusanus, as Hercules, 100, 111, 112, 117 n.66
Manes, 159, 160, 164–5, 170, 175; *see also* cemeteries; funerary rites
manubiae, 92; Augustus', 64–5; definition, 64; *see also* booty
Manuel I Komnenos (1143–1180), 329
Marcomanni, defeated by Drusus (Tiberius' brother), 82, by Marcus Aurelius, 70–4, 138, figs 3.7, 3.9
Marcus Aurelius (M. Aurelius Antoninus, 161–180), 9, 138, 140, 161–2, 179, 181; column, 4, 10, 43, 61, 69, 78, 84; Danuvius (Danube), 69; dedication for health of, 140; Hercules, 108–109; *ius fetiale*, 62; Marcomanni, defeats, 70–4, 138, figs 3.7, 3.9; rain-miracle, 70–3, 252, fig. 3.7; thanks-giving sacrifice, 74–5, fig. 3.9; triumph, triumphal arch, 74–5, 110, fig. 3.9; *tropaea* 70; venerated, 47
Marius, C., military reforms of, 27
Mark Antony, *see* Antony, Mark (M. Antonius)
Mars, 43, 55, 66, 83, 90 n.195, 102, 112, 117 n.62, 120 n.115, 144, 159, 295; forum Martius, 65; *Gemma Augustea*, 76–7, fig. 3.10; Augustan Mars, 140; Mars Nodens, 127, 144; Mars Pater, 47; Mars Victor, 55
Mars Ultor (the Avenger), 1, 4–5, 10, 43, 47, 55, 77–8, 83, 91 n.212; Actium, 88; Adamklissi, 78, 82, 159; at Beneventum, 79; booty for, 64–5; emperors, 66; temple of, 10–11, 43, 57, 61, 64–6, 84, fig. 1.1; *tropaea*, 79
martyrdom, 161, 251, 253–5, 260, 270, 274, 278 n.45, 290–4, 296, 299, fig. 10.1; *see also* persecution; warrior saints
Master of Animals (Master of Lions), 95–99, 114, fig. 4.1

Matres, the, 51
Maurice (emperor, 582–602; for St, *see* below), 267, 273
Maximian (M. Aurelius Valerius Maximianus, 286–305), 290; executes Christian officer, 301; Hercules, 113, fig. 4.10
Maximinus Daia (Galerius Valerius Maximinus Daia, 308–313), 253, 258, 290
Maximinus Thrax (C. Julius Verus Maximinus Thrax, 235–238), 34–5; pillages temples of Jupiter Dolichenus, 50
medicine, military, 5-6, 127–58, figs 5.1–9; *see also* Achilles; cupping; dressings; eyes, diseases of; food poisoning; gout; hospitals; medical instruments; medics; medicine, military; pharmaka; prosthetics; scurvy; surgery; war-wounded
medics, 127–8, 131, 134, 136–8, 141–2, 144, 147, 151; *see also* hospitals; medical instruments; medical training; medicine, military; surgery
medical instruments, bivalve rectal speculum, 132, fig. 5.2; Dioclean cyathiscus, 132–3, fig. 5.4; forceps, 132, 133, figs 5.2–3; *see also* dressings; hospitals; surgery; war-wounded
medical training, 130–1, 137–8, 147; *see also* medics
medicinal herbs, *see* pharmaka
Melqart, 95–8, 101–103, 108, 111, 114–15, 119; as Hercules 95–8, 101–103, 108, 111, 115 n.6
Menrfa (Athena), 98
Mercury, 72, 145; Augustan Mercury, 140
military monuments, *see* temples; triumph; *tropaea*
military oath, *see sacramentum militiae*
military reforms, 27, 30–1, 40 n.103, 260–61
Milvian Bridge, battle of, 11, 255–60, 261, 279 n.97; *see also* Constantine; visions
Minerva, 45–7, 51, 80, 90 n.195, 144, 159; Domitian, 77, 90 n.176, 105; completes *tropaeum*, 77, fig. 3.11; Hercules, 105; on Marcus Aurelius' chariot, 73–4, fig. 3.8; Minerva *Medica,* 140; statue of, 98, fig. 4.3; Sulis Minerva, 141, 145
miracles, 252, 256–7, 261–2; battlefield, 330–3, 334; *see also* dreams; omens; rain-miracle; visions; warrior saints, interventions of
Mithraea, construction of, 235, 236–38, 241–2, figs 8.3–4; cult feasts at, 238, 240–2, fig. 8.4; decoration, 235–8, 240–42; destruction of, 243; locations of, 229–32, 235, 237–38, 239, 242, fig. 8.2; size of, 237–9; *see also* Mithras
Mithras, 1, 7, 140–1, 152, 160, 255, 272; in Britain, 228–31, 234; bull-slaying by, 228, 237, 240–41, fig. 8.1; centurions, 232–4, 236; Christianity, 232, 240–3; cult members, 227–9, 232–36, 238–9; dedication to, 233, fig. 8.3; Deus Helios Mithras, 235; geographical location, 229–31, 235–8, 242, fig. 8.2; group dedications to, 227, 232–4; iconography of, 227, 231, 237, 240–1; initiation in, 238–42; Julian the Apostate, 241; Jupiter Dolichenus, 227, 229, 232–5; military deity, 227–36, 238–9, 242, fig. 8.3; mystery religion, 240, 242; Oriental cult, 227, 229–30; origins of, 227, 229–30; Ostia, 230, 239; ruling elite, 232–3, 236, 242; social activities, 233, 238, 240, 242; Sol Invictus, 234, 235–6, 241; tauroctony, *see also* bull-slaying; women 232

Mithridates VI Eupator (120–63 BC), 195
Mons, retreat from battle of, 332–3
Moses, 186–7, 189
Mother of God, *see* Theotokos
Mother of the Gods, 307
Muses, 160; Hercules of, 99
mutiny, 29, 33

necropoleis, *see* cemeteries
nefas, 26
Neptune, 46–7, 80; Actium, 81, 90 n.105; healing god, 141, 143; Neptuna Redux, 74; Neptunalia festival, 46
Nero (Nero Claudius Caesar Augustus Germanicus, 54–68), 6, 34, 56, 58, 65–6, 80, 110, 118 n.124; closes temple of Janus, 61, 66–8, fig. 3.5; comet, 196; as Hercules, 104–105, 109; ominous dream, 60; fire in AD 64, 186–226 *passim,* esp. 189–90
Nerva (Nerva Caesar Augustus, 96–98), 47
Nikai, 79; *see also* Victory
Nikephoros II Phokas (963–969), 307, 309
numen, numina, of Aesculapius, 143; legions and legionary eagles, 52, 54, 57, 281 n.144, 284 n.222

oath, military, *see sacramentum militiae*
Oceanus, 76, 108, 119 n.142, fig. 3.10
Octavian, *see* Augustus
Ogmios, Celtic god identified with Hercules, 114, 120 n.175
Oikoumene, goddess of the world, 76, fig. 3.10
omens, 2, 33, 53–4, 56–61, 69, 84, 191–3, 196, 215 n.107, 255, 257, 271, 278 n.61, 280 n.105, 320–3, 326–7; of Carrhae, 53; Christian, 253, 256–7, 321–22; manipulation of, 257, 330; sent by Jupiter, 4, 43, 52, 57, 61; *see also* dreams; miracles, battlefield; Sibylline Books; Sibylline Oracles; *sidus Iulium;* visions; warrior saints, interventions of
Operation Cast Lead, 330–1
Osiris, 188, 193; Antony as Dionysios-Osiris, 193
Otho (M. Otho Caesar Augustus, 69), 40 n.105, 131; military omens, 58

Palmyrene Gods, temple of, 47
pax Romana 15, 77, 277 n.25
Penates, military, 143
persecutions, of Christians, 290–93, 298, 301, 304; *see also* Christianity; Diocletian; martyrdom; warrior saints
Perseus, 191–2
Pertinax (P. Helvius Pertinax, 192–193), 40 nn.105, 123, 66; soldier prays for, 143; venerated by army, 47
Petreius, M., 30
phallic pendants, 146, fig. 5.9; *see also* amulets
pharmaka (drugs), 127, 134–5, 147, 150; *see also* poisons
Phokas (602–610), 306
Pliny the Elder, 82, 128, 131, 150 n.77, 202; and medicine, 135, 141, 144, 146, 148 n.19, 150 nn.81, 85–86, 95, 154 n.216; omens, 60
Pliny the Younger, 12, 31, 33, 106, 176
Plutarch, 29, 34, 102, 151 n.109
Pluto and Proserpina, 141

poisons, 127, 129–30, 132, 134, 150; *see also* pharmaka
Pollux, 49, 160, 295–7
Polybius, 19–20, 191; military oath, 21, 23; on religious conviction, 26
Pompey (Cn. Pompeius), 29, 40 nn.90, 93, 60, 99–102, 117 n.76, 148 n.12
pontifex maximus, 268; Domitian as, 12; Marcus Aurelius, 75; Trajan, 69–70, 268
Pope Damasus (366–384), 14
Pope Gelasius I (492–496), 304
Pope Leo I (440–461), 302
portents, *see* omens
post-traumatic stress disorder, 139, 152
Postumus (M. Cassianius Latinius Postumus, c. 260–269), 111–12, 121 nn.191–95, fig. 4.9
Praetorian Guard, 142, 161
princeps, 1, 47, 60, 65, 67, 103; military oath to, 4, 32; *see also* Augustus; emperors
Probus (M. Aurelius Probus, 276–282), 112, 121
prosthetics, 139, 152 n.147, 331
Prudentius, 262; Altar of Victory, 15; imperium *sine fine*, 16; statue of Victory, 13
Punic War, Second, 3, 23, 24; *sacramentum militiae* in, 21–3
Pupienus (M. Clodius Pupienus Maximus, 238), military oath, 34–5
Pyrrhus of Epirus (297–272 BC), 98, 191, 195

Quinctilius Varus, P., 12, 54, 57, 91 n.212, 162, 171, 173, fig. 6.9
Quirinus, 66, 101, 117 n.73; Janus Quirinus, 62

Rachel the Matriarch, 330
rain-miracle, on column of Marcus Aurelius, 70–3, 252, fig. 3.7
Raymond d'Aguilers, 319–20, 322–3, 326–8
relics, reliquaries, 314–15, 317–18, 322, 326–27, fig. 10.8; *see also* Holy Lance
Republic, Roman, 56–7, 61–2, 64, 66–7, 95–103, 116, 137; differences in religious practices between the Republic and the Empire, 9–13
river gods, in Britain, 55, in Dacia, 70; Domitian, 89 n.142; Rhine, 69; *see also* Danuvius
Roma (goddess), 46–7; Amazonian, 73–4, fig. 3.8; *Gemma Augustea*, 75–6, fig. 3.10
Romulus, 16, 63, 101, 215 n.114

sacramentum militiae (*military oath*), 3–4, 252, 267, 269, 272; bond of loyalty, 25, 27; Christians, 8, 36–7; civil war, 27–30, 33–4; on coins, 24, figs 2.1–2.2; content, 23, 32; effectiveness, 33–4, 37–8; emperors, 25, 29, 31–2; images, 23–4; initiation, 25–6; occasion, 23–4, 31–2; origin, 20–2; in Republic, 20–30; third-century crisis, 34–5; *sacer*, 22; usurpation, 34–6
sacred chickens, 56
Saints, *see* St; warrior saints
Salus (Safety), 46–7
Samnites, 13; military oath, 21, 25–6
Saturn, 74; Saturnalia, 46
scholarship on religion and Roman Imperial warfare, 2–3

Scipio, *see* Cornelius Scipio
Scribonianus, *see* Furius
Scribonius Curio, C., 28–9
Scribonius Largus, 134–5, 138
scurvy, 139
Seleukos IV (187–175 BC), 296
senate, senators, 1, 61, 64–8, 70, 76, 78, 82–3, 197, 296, 312; cult of Mithras, 232, 236, 242, 245; oath to, 30, 32–4; Victory statue and, 13–15
Seneca the Younger, 33
'Sensed Presence', the, 331–2
Septimius Severus (L. Septimius Severus, 193–211), 25, 47, 66, 181, 252; legions' nicknames, 179; Hercules, 111; Jupiter Dolichenus, 140; Mars Ultor, 66; Temple of Peace, 67; venerated by army, 47 (cf. 140); victory arch, 79
Sequana, *see* Fontes Sequanae
Serapis, 60, 200–201
Servius, 23, 29
Seth, 188
Severus Alexander (M. Aurelius Severus Alexander, 222–235), 143, 151 n.137, 160; army sacrifices for, 45, 47; Christ among *lares*, 255; Mars Ultor, 66; oaths to, 35
Shadrapa, 111
Sibylline Books, 12, 60, 118 n.104, 153 n.180, 196
Sibylline Oracles, 73, 89 n.166, 192, 204
sidus Iulium, 192–6, 201, 205, 207–209, 213 n.75, 214 nn.90–1
signa (singular *signum*), 32, 46, 52, 54, 64, 113, 129, 170, 227, figs 3.2, 5.1; Tertullian criticised, 53; venerated, 45, 251, 255, 261–2, 265, 270; *see also* labarum; *vexillum*; Victory
Silius Italicus, 130, 134, 145
Silvanus, 141, 143–4, 154 n.204, 159; Silvanus Pegasianus, 152 n.152
Sirius, 6–7, 188, 190–7, 200–205, 208
Social War, 24
Sol, 49; Sol Invictus, 246–7 n.81, 258-59; Deus Sol Invictus Mithras, 235–6, 241, 246 n.81, 258–9; *see also* Helios; Julian; Mithras
soldiers, on coins, 24, figs 2.1-2.2; on monuments, 43, 46, 69, 72, 79, 83, 129, 167 169, 171, 173, 263, figs 3.1–2, 3.6–7, 3.13, 3.15, 5.1, 6.4, 6.7–9, 9.3; *see also* cohorts; legions; *lustratio*; *sacramentum militiae*; war-wounded
spolia opima, 2, 62–4
St Ambrose, 14–16, 265, 275
St Andrew the Apostle, 303–304
St Arculf, 305
St Arethas, 293
St Artemios, 290, 293, 299
St Augustine, 16, 161, 275; Boniface, 274; Julian, 270
St Basil the Great, 299–300, fig. 10.4
St Blaise of Caesarea, 319
St Blaise of Sebaste, 291, 318–19, fig. 10.1
St Cyprian, 161, 314
St Demetrios, 290, 293, 312–16, 319–21, fig. 10.3; church of, 314–15, fig. 10.5; ciborium of, 313, 315; and the crusaders, 312, 316, 318–24, 327;